Integrated Brand Promotion Management
Text, Cases, and Exercises

John H. Murphy
Isabella C. M. Cunningham
Liza S. de Lewis

The University of Texas at Austin

Kendall Hunt
publishing company

www.kendallhunt.com
Send all inquiries to:
4050 Westmark Drive
Dubuque, IA 52004-1840

Copyright © 2011 by John H. Murphy, Isabella C. M. Cunningham, and Liza S. de Lewis

ISBN 978-0-7575-7791-8

Kendall Hunt Publishing Company has the exclusive rights to reproduce this work,
to prepare derivative works from this work, to publicly distribute this work,
to publicly perform this work and to publicly display this work.

All rights reserved. No part of this publication may be reproduced,
stored in a retrieval system, or transmitted, in any form or by any
means, electronic, mechanical, photocopying, recording, or otherwise,
without the prior written permission of the copyright owner.

Printed in the United States of America
10 9 8 7 6 5 4 3 2 1

Contents

Part I Introduction — 1

Chapter 1 The Case Method — 3

Chapter 2 How to Develop and Deliver Effective Presentations — 11

Chapter 3 The Marketing Context of Advertising and Promotion — 23

Exercises — 30
- Case 3.1 Lady Bird Johnson Wildflower Center (A) — 33
- Case 3.2 Amy's Ice Creams (A) — 45
- Case 3.3 The Home Depot: Eco Options Program — 55

Part II Advertising Management Decision Making — 61

Chapter 4 Advertising Research — 63

Exercises — 72
- Case 4.1 Sports Trading Cards — 75
- Case 4.2 Amplex Consumer Products Super Ultra Bathroom Tissue — 83
- Case 4.3 Diet and Exercise Campaign Extension—North Central Region — 89

Chapter 5 Establishing IBP Objectives — 93

Exercises — 101
- Case 5.1 MacLeod's Furniture Centers — 105
- Case 5.2 Don't Mess with Texas (A) — 117

Chapter 6	**Determining the Advertising Appropriation and Budgeting**		123
	Exercises		136
	Case 6.1	The Happy Dog Company	137
	Case 6.2	BusinesSuites (A)	141
	Case 6.3	The Corner Flower Market	151
	Case 6.4	Ben's Workshop	161
Chapter 7	**Developing Creative Strategies**		167
	Exercises		186
	Case 7.1	Rita's TasteeBurger	187
	Case 7.2	Costa Del Mar Sunglasses	193
	Case 7.3	BusinesSuites (B)	205
Chapter 8	**Developing Media Strategy**		209
	Exercises		216
	Case 8.1	Hospitality Inns	223
	Case 8.2	Healthy Dog Gourmet	239
	Case 8.3	Henigan's Department Stores	245

Part III Integrated Brand Promotion Mix   251

Chapter 9	**Personal Selling**		253
	Exercises		260
	Case 9.1	Mary Kay Cosmetics, Inc.	261
	Case 9.2	The Vino, Vino! Company	275
Chapter 10	**Sales Promotion**		281
	Exercises		287
	Case 10.1	BusinesSuites (C)	289
	Case 10.2	Don't Mess with Texas (B)	299
	Case 10.3	Bath-So-Nice	305
	Case 10.4	New Chase Condominiums	311

Chapter 11	**Direct Marketing**	315
	Exercises	320
	Case 11.1 Lady Bird Johnson Wildflower Center (B)	323
	Case 11.2 Bethany College	333
	Case 11.3 Alloy.com	341
Chapter 12	**Public Relations**	353
	Exercises	358
	Case 12.1 Amy's Ice Creams (B)	361
	Case 12.2 Shawntana Development Corporation	365
	Case 12.3 Whole Foods Markets	369
	Case 12.4 BusinesSuites (D)	377
	Case 12.5 Carlyle Labs, Inc. (A)	381
	Case 12.6 The Coca-Cola Company	387
	Case 12.7 *The Wall Street Journal*'s "Two Brothers" Commercial	395
	Case 12.8 Decker, Villani & Bishop	399
Chapter 13	**Event Sponsorships, Product Placements and Branded Entertainment**	405
	Exercises	410
	Case 13.1 Shiner Beer	413
	Case 13.2 And Now, a Word from Our Sponsor	419
	Case 13.3 Bank of America Sports Sponsorship	429
	Case 13.4 I Lost My Volvo in New Haven	439
Chapter 14	**Internet Marketing, Web Sites, Viral, Social Networking, Experiential, and Guerrilla Marketing**	451
	Exercises	459
	Case 14.1 "Gossip Girl" Viral Promotion	461
	Case 14.2 Amy's Ice Creams (C)	471
	Case 14.3 BusinesSuites (E)	477
	Case 14.4 Imperial Majestic Hotels	487
Chapter 15	**Evaluating the Effectiveness of IBP Strategies**	491
	Exercises	494
	Case 15.1 MedNet.com Confronts "Click-Through" Competition	497
	Case 15.2 Giant Consumer Products	509
	Case 15.3 Reliance Baking Soda	523

Part IV Additional Consideration Affecting IBP Programs — 537

Chapter 16 Client/Agency Relations — 539

Exercises — 548
Case 16.1 Columbia Savings — 549
Case 16.2 Carlyle Labs, Inc. (B) — 553
Case 16.3 Gordon, Wolfberg, Miller & Friends — 557

Chapter 17 Ethical Considerations — 563

Exercises — 572
Case 17.1 The Maryland State Planning Council on Developmental Disabilities — 575
Case 17.2 Abel, Atwater and Combs Advertising and Public Relations — 579
Case 17.3 Tropical Distributing Company — 583

Index — 587

Acknowledgments

This book was developed with the cooperation and support of many individuals beyond the three principal authors. Without these individuals, our book would not be as thorough or complete. In the paragraphs below we would like to acknowledge these individuals.

First, we are indebted to our spouses—Sue, Bill and William—for their continued support throughout our careers.

Second, a number of organizations and individuals employed in those organizations contributed materials for cases and examples used in our book. These individuals are: Saralee Tiede, the Lady Bird Johnson Wildflower Center; Teresa Noll and Amy Simmons, Amy's Ice Creams; Kim Greenia, The Home Depot; Katie Porter, Chris Fedorczak and Stan Richards, The Richards Group; Brenda Flores-Dollar, Texas Department of Transportation; Christina Moss, EnviroMedia; John Jordan and Heather Younger, BusinesSuites; Bill Morey, Ben's Workshop; Amy Hiles-Maynard, Norwegian Cruise Lines; Luke Sullivan, GSD&M Idea City; Jeffery Palmer, Accor Hospitality; Jennifer Layton, MINI; Lynda Richardson and Chris Cardinal, Butler Shine Stern & Partners; Dana Cizmadia, Volkswagen Group; Lilian Ojeda, John Minty and Colleen McGee, Venables Bell & Partners; Al Perkinson, Costa del Mar Sunglasses; Jennifer Costello and Mark McGarrah, McGarrah Jessee; Tricia Hawk, Bethany College; Kevin Casis, The Whitley Company; Roberta Lang and Liz Burkhart at Wholes Foods Market; Les Hinton, *The Wall Street Journal;* Stacey Williams, The Gambrinus Company; Rick Haskins, The CW Network; and, Cathy Raggio, Maryland Department of Disabilities.

Third, thirteen students from The University of Texas at Austin devoted significant time and energy to the project. We would like to thank five UT students who coauthored cases: Erin Cutchen, Lauren Johnson, Jason Sears (who coauthored three cases and contributed a case of his own), Lindsy Signet and Michelle Troutt. Further, we appreciate the excellent work of Andrew Burton, Sarah Bovagnet, Sarah Douglas, Chelsea Pyle, Julia Robinson, Elizabeth A. Williamson and Mackie Wood who conducted background research and helped with exercises and content material used in some of the text chapters. Importantly, we appreciate Amanda Thomas who contributed the cover design.

In addition, we also thank Janie Castillo-Flores at The University of Texas at Austin and Michelle Bahr and William England at Kendall Hunt who provided support and encouragement throughout the development of this project.

Finally, we appreciate the support and encouragement of our family and friends who, at times, had to put up with our work on this book. Also, to all those other people who helped out but we failed to mention above, thank you as well. Happy trails all.

JHM
IMC
LSL

Part I
Introduction

The opening section of this book sets the stage for using the case method to facilitate student learning and establishes the general context for the more specific discussion of integrated brand promotion (IBP) mix strategies and tools to come in later chapters in the book. Chapter 1 introduces the case method and some of the basic ground rules for using this method of learning effectively. The chapter also presents a decision-making framework that is useful in analyzing IBP management problems and opportunities. This framework provides a standard structure for organizing student thinking about and analyses of all the cases presented in the book.

Chapter 2 focuses on the development and delivery of effective presentations. Conducting a brilliant analysis of a case is not enough. The analysis must be presented in a clear, persuasive manner to others whose approval or agreement is sought. The purpose of the chapter is to provide students with guidelines for constructing and delivering their analyses to the class. The valuable experience each student gains in planning, delivering and observing case presentations should be an integral part of each student's course takeaways.

Chapter 3 provides an overview discussion of the general context and environment of IBP management decision making. All decisions regarding the proper combination of IBP mix elements plus the strategic utilization and coordination of mix components must be adjusted in light of the competitive market environment facing the brand.

Chapter 1
The Case Method

"The active intellectual and emotional involvement of the student is a hallmark of case teaching. . . . Case discussion demands total participant involvement in a variety of ways, first and foremost in the give-and-take of class discussion."[1]

This book identifies and provides a preliminary discussion of seventeen areas of integrated brand promotion (IBP) management decision making. The discussion of each of these areas is followed by a set of actual case situations that challenge each student's analytical and decision-making skills. The book was developed to help students acquire decision-making skills through the study of a combination of advertising and marketing theory and conventional wisdom, short practical exercises, and traditional case work. In this introductory section of the text, we explain the general philosophy of the book plus stress the importance and use of case analysis in training managers.

This book does *not* contain elaborate and lengthy theoretical chapters. The text portion of each chapter provides a summary of selected, essential concepts and theoretical principles. These summaries function as a review tool for students preparing to handle the problems and cases that follow. The text material opening each chapter provides a general overview of the materials with which students should be familiar, but is not intended to cover all aspects of the topic in detail. Students are encouraged to be responsible for supplementing the material covered in the chapter openings with additional reading.

This book is designed to reflect contemporary brand marketing practices through use of specific examples. After students have read the chapters on each of the IBP management topics, they should be ready to analyze the exercises that follow. These were developed to encourage an orderly transition from theory and conventional wisdom to practice for those students who have not previously had a case-based course. As students become familiar with the general problem-solving procedures recommended, they will be able to progress from the simpler to the more complex analyses of the cases under each topic. The following section explains the philosophy and purpose of case teaching. It also provides some simple guidelines for case analysis and discussion.

---

[1]"Teaching with Cases at the Harvard Business School," in *Teaching and the Case Method,* ed. Louis B. Barnes, C. Roland Christensen, and Abby J. Hansen (Boston: Harvard Business School Press, 1994), p. 48.

THE CASE DISCUSSION METHOD OF LEARNING

The management of IBP campaigns or programs is an art and science that requires both basic knowledge and—above all—decision-making skills. Cases are designed to train students to develop those skills. Skills are best learned through practice, and cases that stimulate decision-making situations allow students to role-play and attempt to solve actual management problems as they occur.

Typically, cases do *not* afford simple solutions. Further, in most management situations, there really is no single right or wrong answer. The heart of decision making is the ability to analyze the variables critical to the issue. By sharing this task in a group situation, students benefit from the group's insights as well as their own knowledge and experience.

There is no perfect formula or set of procedures for approaching a case analysis. Some general questions can, however, be asked in any decision-making situation: What is the problem we need to solve? What is the situation at this time? What factors are critical to a solution? What variables can be manipulated when devising a course of action?

A case study is simply a written description of a management problem. Analyzing a case study in administration can be thought of as the equivalent of providing a medical second opinion, with the student being the person asked to provide a medical second opinion. Like a consulting physician, the student must review the relevant facts described in the case, analyze them, reach some conclusion about the problem and its cause, and recommend some treatment or appropriate action.

Unlike medical cases, however, administrative cases are analyzed in a class of 20 or more students. Each student will have invested time outside class working individually on the case before the class discusses it. The discussion will allow each student to benefit from all the other students' insights and to work toward a final decision or recommendation, which may differ from the one he or she reached individually.

The purpose of the case experience is to develop each student's ability to consider hard evidence, personal experience, and other factors in arriving at a sound decision and shaping a convincing recommendation. This process duplicates real-life situations in the best possible manner.

For both instructor and student, case-based learning requires sailing a narrow channel between overcontrol and ambiguity. The promise of the case method, for those who successfully thread this course, is not that it will produce an excellent decision maker. Rather, with the instructor's aid, the student will be transformed into a more skilled decision maker through the experience. Therefore, *to have a meaningful experience, students must have carefully studied each and every case used in the course, even though they may not be required to turn in a written assignment on most of the cases discussed.* If they have not prepared carefully, the class discussion will be of much reduced benefit to them.

Because management cases are dissected through discussion in a community of learners, each student should be an active participant, dynamically questioning the validity of his or her individual analysis continually as the group discussion unfolds. Thus, unlike in many classroom settings, the student spends much time *thinking* about his or her own point of view, which is constantly challenged by the other participants, who will have developed different views based on the same facts presented in the case. Therefore, the ability to present ideas and persuade others is also critically important to case discussion.

In addition, case analysis teaches future managers to keep all options open and to listen carefully to information presented during the discussion. Because there are no right or wrong solutions to a case, information and discussion allow participants to develop an informed and logical way of making a decision.

The practical nature of the problems and opportunities presented in an advertising and marketing communication management case means that students must be able to deal with such quantifiable concepts as costs, efficiency of messages as measured by exposures, expected results, Web site analytics, profits, and sales. Students are expected to be able to handle calculations with skill and acumen. Although personalities and human relations are important aspects of management, the bottom line is always a major consideration. Therefore, it is important to be able to handle appropriate mathematical calculations.

Many advertising and marketing communication management problems require the development of creative ideas and concepts. Others demand the ability to plan media schedules, and budgets, plus viral and guerrilla marketing efforts. Cases allow students to focus their energies and resources on one discrete issue at a time. More comprehensive issues dealing with the development of complete campaigns can also be examined using the cases in this book. Our overriding goal is to develop students' ability to deal with the issues involved in managing a firm's communications functions by projecting themselves into the role of company brand manager, advertising or PR agency account executive, or any other role pertaining to the management of IBP efforts.

Several frameworks can be used in conducting a case analysis. The following section presents some suggestions and recommendations designed to aid students in analyzing cases.

CASE ANALYSIS FRAMEWORK AND OTHER GUIDELINES

A time-tested framework for organizing the analysis of a case is presented in Exhibit 1. This procedure can also be used as an outline for developing a concise written analysis of a case.

Exhibit 2 presents a decision tree, or flowchart, of the same case analysis process. This exhibit clearly indicates that a case analysis is a developmental process. For example, students may redefine the problem statement after evaluating alternatives. Students can glean many useful insights into conducting a case analysis by studying these two exhibits. In addition, several other general steps to analyzing a case and approaching its class discussion should be followed.

First, the students will enhance their understanding of the situation at hand by actively playing the role of the decision maker described in the case. This encourages them to commit themselves to a position and then actively defend it. Because management decisions consist substantially of analysis, choice, and persuasion, role playing realistically involves students in defending their positions.

Second, in preparing a case, students should begin by reading the case quickly to grasp the general problem, understand the position of the main character(s) in the case, and develop an initial appraisal of the situation. After this first reading, it is imperative that students reread the case in detail, retracing their steps as many times as they feel necessary to absorb all the important details.

After the second reading is completed, students will be ready to begin isolating the main decision issues in the case. What is the best target for the promotional message? Is the salient issue scheduling media or developing and allocating a media budget? Such questions are at the center of the secondary phase in case analysis.

These decision issues may lead logically to questions about the specific case. At this point, students should go back to the case and single out the facts and numbers that they can analyze to answer their questions. Identifying costs and assessing their relative importance, ranking media vehicles according to their ability to reach specific target markets, and establishing the relative values of different target audiences are some of the many analysis questions that can be used to fully understand the problems at hand. Whenever complete information is not found in the case, research should be done or reasonable assumptions made. Logic, experience, and similar cases and situations can all be used to develop acceptable assumptions.

Exhibit 1 ■ Framework for Case Analysis

The following framework is a logical and practical procedure to follow when analyzing decision-making situations. The approach is recommended for use in organizing your thinking and developing a recommended course of action.

1. *Statement of the Problem.* Clearly define the central problem (or opportunity) posed in the case. The statement may mention symptoms and minor problems.

    In analyzing a case with no stated emphasis, it is easy to identify symptoms as the problem. In other words, what may at first appear to be the problem may, in fact, be a mere symptom or manifestation of a more central issue. For example, an advertising strategy may be identified by management as "ineffective" simply due to the misguided decision to advertise under unfavorable conditions.

2. *List of Critical Factors.* Identify and list the critical factors related to the **solution of the identified problem,** as opposed to factors documenting that there is a problem. These should be listed in order of importance in developing a solution to the problem. Do *not* evaluate these factors or relate them to the problem or possible solutions at this point in your analysis. Simply list them in order of importance.

3. *Definition of Alternatives.* In this section, state several alternative courses of action for coping with the identified problem and evaluate them using the critical factors. Some alternatives may be obvious from the material supplied in the case; others will require much analysis to formulate.

    After each alternative has been concisely stated, a discussion of its pros and cons should be presented. **This balanced discussion is the heart of the analysis framework.** The critical factors are introduced into this discussion as appropriate. These are keyed as they are discussed, using the rank-order numbers assigned in the Critical Factors section.

    The most critical aspect of the analysis is the evaluation of alternatives. To engage in analysis is to separate parts of the situation to discover the nature, proportion, and function of and underlying relationships among a set of variables. Thus, to analyze is to dig into and work with the facts to uncover associations that may be used to evaluate possible courses of action. Also, *changes in the ordering and additions/deletions to the list of critical factors should occur during the analysis of alternatives.* At this point, it should become clear that the framework is a dynamic tool for analysis.

4. *Conclusion.* Indicate the alternative(s) most appropriate for dealing with the problem. Briefly justify the recommended alternative(s) based on the previous discussion. Identify the recommended alternative(s) by number.

5. *Additional Comments.* This section of the analysis is optional. Included here are observations, recommendations, and so on, which are not necessarily directly related to the central problem. For example, students might indicate future problems that are likely to develop, areas that warrant future research, or suggested operational improvements. This section is particularly useful in demonstrating a grasp of the total situation.

Note: Unless otherwise noted, the cases in this text are listed under the major area of IBP management to be emphasized in their analysis. Thus, the problem statement should clearly reflect this emphasis.

Exhibit 2 ■ Case Analysis Process

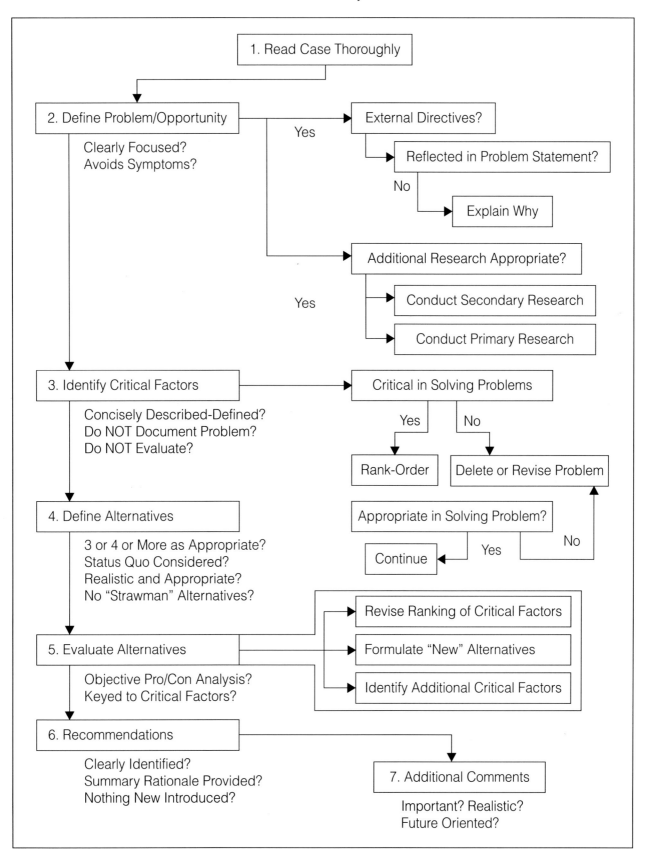

Once these tasks have been completed, students should be ready to identify the best course of action. This is perhaps the hardest step in the process of case analysis. Most of us dislike taking risks, and students tend to shy away from taking a specific stand, given the uncertainty surrounding a decision situation. Two of the most common objectives raised by students faced with case analysis are that there is not enough time to gather needed information or that the case contains too little information. Yet such pressure is typical of almost all decision-making situations: They are characterized by inadequate time and information.

It is helpful for students to try out their solutions in a group discussion prior to class discussion of the case. This allows them to justify their position, prepare for objections, or perhaps even reconsider their solution.

Finally, students should always be encouraged to culminate their analysis by recommending a specific course of action. In most case situations, it is helpful for students to develop two or three feasible solutions to the case, analyze each alternative in depth, and finally, choose the best solution. Whether the instructor prefers to have students discern alternative solutions or immediately opt for one course of action, it is important that a student's case analysis result in a single decision.

THE ORGANIZATION OF THIS BOOK

This chapter has explored the purpose and usefulness of case analysis and has suggested a method for conducting the analysis. Case analysis is the heart of the book and its major teaching tool.

To further develop students' managerial skills and to generate thoughtful class discussion, the instructor may require that students make individual or group presentations to the class or to an audience of classmates and professionals. Such presentations typically involve analyzing and solving a case or an exercise taken from this book. As an example, a student or a group of students might be asked to play the role of a consultant for Amy's Ice Creams and to suggest a strategy for generating more visitors to the firm's Web site.

IBP professionals frequently make such presentations. These presentations involve important presentation and other skills, including the ability to approach an issue in a thorough, analytical manner. Such skills can be achieved and sharpened by role playing, as well as by observing fellow students' presentations.

Presentation skills are as important to managers as effective speaking skills, interpersonal skills, and organizational ability. Managers are required to argue for budget allocations, defend competitive positions, and develop positive client relations. Presentations are a useful strategic tool in all these situations. Because guidelines for effective presentations are so important, we dedicated a full chapter to their discussion.

This book is organized to help teach future IBP professionals the skills needed to make them effective. The text preceding each set of exercises and cases summarizes important background knowledge required to handle the decision-making challenge involved. The exercises are provided to present students with clearly defined problems, whereas the cases duplicate the real-life situations they will encounter when in a position to make strategic and tactical marketing communications decisions. Here the issues are not always as clearly defined.

The first section of the book (Introduction) identifies some guidelines for tackling the casework and presentation tasks they will be asked to undertake. The second section of the book (Advertising Management Decision Making) examines the main components of advertising decision making. This section is divided into six chapters dealing with the contextual relationship of advertising and other IBP tools to the other marketing tasks, research, establishing advertising objectives, determining the advertising appropriation and budgeting, developing creative strategy, and developing media strategy.

The third section of the book (Integrated Brand Promotion Mix) focuses on other elements in the IBP mix. Each of these activities was chosen for inclusion because of its timely importance in the overall spectrum of marketing communication in our economy. Students are asked, therefore, to concentrate on the factors that make personal selling, sales promotion, direct marketing, and public relations especially effective communication activities. In addition, separate chapters are devoted to crisis management, event marketing/branded entertainment, Internet marketing/Web sites, experiential/viral/social networking/guerrilla marketing, and evaluating the effectiveness of IBP strategies.

Last, the fourth section of the book (Additional Considerations Affecting IBP Programs) includes separate chapters on client/agency relations and ethical considerations. Such considerations are an integral part of the managerial decision-making process. This section poses questions about the type of relationship agencies and clients should have, the fairness of compensation practices, and the ethical responsibility of agencies in representing products that are considered harmful or unsafe to all or certain segments of society. Further, although management's primary obligation is to produce a positive bottom line for their firm, they must do so while acting in an honest, equitable, and fair manner, compatible with the basic values of our society.

This book has been designed to touch broadly on vital areas of management decision making involving advertising and IBP issues. A list of suggested readings is presented at the end of each chapter to aid students in gathering supplemental information. The book also allows instructors adequate flexibility to tailor their course to a diverse audience of students by choosing those chapters, cases, and exercises that best fit their needs.

The next chapter provides detailed suggestions for making presentations. This chapter concludes the introductory section of this text.

Chapter 2
How to Develop and Deliver Effective Presentations

A successful presentation engages the audience emotionally as well as rationally. The successful presenter is liked and trusted.[1]—Jon Steel

One of the hallmarks of a successful marketing person is the ability to communicate effectively and persuasively through the vehicle of a presentation. The presentation is widely recognized as an extremely important part of business communication. For example, it is not enough for the vice president of marketing communication and the firm's agency partner to develop an excellent campaign plan. The VP must also secure authorization to implement the plan by selling the plan to others via a presentation. Brilliant ideas for a new communication program will never reach consumers unless the ideas are first persuasively sold to, and receive the approval of, top management.

In fact, most important promotional recommendations are delivered in the form of a presentation to upper-level marketing or top management. Further, it is rare in a new business competitive pitch for an agency to be awarded an account before several presentations have been made and evaluated by the prospective client.

Nothing happens until someone sells something.

Further, the bigger the stakes and the more important the decision, the more likely the selling job will be in the form of a formal presentation. The implications are clear:

To be effective, an IBP person needs to know how to put together and deliver a persuasive presentation.

The purpose of this chapter is to outline a set of basic considerations useful in developing effective presentations. These suggestions have passed the test of time. Reviewing and following the suggestions and conventional wisdom presented in this chapter will greatly improve one's chances of developing and delivering effective and successful presentations.

---

[1] Jon Steel, *Perfect Pitch: The Art of Selling Ideas and Winning New Business* (New York: John Wiley & Sons, Inc., 2007), p. XX.

The chapter is divided into five major sections. The first section examines common shortcoming of presentations, presentation strategy and structure, and audience focus. The second section highlights strategies for opening and closing presentations. The third section focuses on stage management, including the use of props, PowerPoint slides, presentation boards, equipment, and so on. Section four stresses the importance of advance preparation. Finally, the chapter concludes with a summary checklist for evaluating presentations and some advice.

INITIAL CONSIDERATIONS

This section briefly identifies important background considerations that provide a foundation on which clear, concise, persuasive presentations can be built. The first part of this section identifies common presentation problems to be avoided. The second part identifies the strategy and a standard structure that works for many presentations. Part three quickly identifies a key consideration in all persuasive presentations—the need to focus the presentation from the audience's perspective.

Common Shortcomings

In examining the issues involved in developing effective presentations, Ron Hoff has suggested that a logical starting point is to identify common mistakes of presenters and presentations.[2] To accomplish this, Hoff interviewed top people in the advertising business in New York and Chicago and identified the following seven common complaints about presentations and presenters:

1. The failure to precisely state the problem and relevant factors
2. The failure to stay within time allotments
3. The failure to properly use props
4. The failure to put oneself in the other guy's shoes
5. The failure to inspire confidence
6. The failure to properly prepare and rehearse
7. The failure to have a sense of the theater; that is, this is a boring delivery.

To make these common shortcomings more memorable, Hoff condensed the seven failures into three cardinal sins. The most common and devastating failures to be avoided by presenters are being (1) imprecise, (2) unorganized, and, (3) deadly dull.

Presentation Strategy and Structure

A presentation is designed to accomplish one purpose: to persuade. The strategy behind every presentation is to persuade the audience of the reasonableness and appropriateness of the presenter's recommended plan or program.

---

[2]Ron Hoff, "FCB Presentation Course" (Chicago: Foote, Cone & Belding, 1976), p. 3–11.

Presenting is *not* just an exercise in which, for example, the presenter shows a mock-up of a new online landing page for a contest offer and then describes the illustration, reads the text copy, and suggests how the target audience is likely to respond. *Presenting should be an exercise in logic*—like a lawyer pleading his/her case by laying a foundation, presenting evidence, marshalling arguments, and guiding the jury to a decision in his/her client's favor.[3]

The presentation should build a case by providing a logical explanation (rationale) of why the recommendations make sense. Therefore, the presentation should unfold in a natural and logical sequence that leads the audience to agree with the recommendation. The strategy should be to get the audience in the habit of agreeing with the points made in the presentation. Ideally, the audience should be mentally nodding, "Yes!" to what the presenter says, "Yes!" to the way the presenter thinks, "Yes!" to the way the presenter understands the client's business and problems, and then, "Yes!" to the presenter's recommendations. To accomplish this, the presenter must move carefully.

Experience indicates that a standard sequence is most effective in building a logical case and leading the audience to the recommended position. The five segments of a standard new business presentation are:

1. *Introduction.* The opening segment should engage the audience and provide an overview of the entire presentation.
2. *Background or situation analysis.* This segment should present an insightful analysis of such relevant considerations as the competitive environment, consumer trends, and past and future sales trends. This analysis sets the stage for the following segments of the presentation.
3. *Problems and opportunities.* Growing out of the background analysis, this section concisely identifies the problems the recommendations are designed to solve and/or the opportunities to be capitalized on.
4. *Recommendations.* This segment presents the recommended solutions, along with supporting rationale.
5. *Summary.* This section includes a quick recap of key points and ends with a clear directive to the audience to act.

Audience Focus

All presentations should focus on the audience's needs and problems and show how the proposed program(s) can help to meet these needs. Ultimately, the audience's perceptions, concerns, and priorities are most relevant to obtaining approval of a recommendation.

Mayer and Greenberg, in their classic *Harvard Business Review* article, "What Makes a Good Salesman," underscored the importance of the prospect's perspective in any selling situation. They stressed that one of two basic characteristics of successful salespeople is empathy—the ability to understand the selling situation from the prospect's perspective and to relate the sales pitch to that perspective.[4]

---

[3]Ibid., p. 15.

[4]David Mayer and Herbert Greenberg, "What Makes a Good Salesman," in *Business Classics: Fifteen Key Concepts for Managerial Success* (Boston: *Harvard Business Review,* 1975), pp. 51–57. Note that their second characteristic was "ego drive," which they defined as a burning desire to make the sale that goes beyond just the money involved.

The marketing concept suggests that to be most successful, one must see the world from the buyer's point of view. To be most effective, one must structure all marketing activities around the consumer or audience.

Clearly, a presentation is a marketing activity. Therefore, considerable attention should be devoted to focusing the presentation on the audience's concerns. A presenter can work wonders if he/she relates everything in the presentation to the audience's problems and opportunities.

Sullivan offered revealing insights in terms of selling advertising creative work to an agency's clients.[5] Perhaps his most important suggestions are (1) learn the client's corporate culture, and (2) base your defense on strategy. Getting to know brand managers and marketing staff people is important because the more they know you, the more they trust you. By knowing key players and the tone of the company, it will be easier to size up what they may be likely to accept or reject. Defending creative work with relevant product/market/consumer data rather than on emotional grounds is speaking the language of client management and, hence, more likely to succeed.

Finally, as part of audience focus, it is important to find out as much as possible and practical about the key decision makers in the audience. What are their business and personal backgrounds and biases? The presentation should be designed to focus on the key individual(s) who will have the most important say in making the decision advocated. The more one knows about the key decision maker(s) and their business background, the easier it is to build tidbits into the presentation that will appeal to them. In the absence of such intelligence, a presenter may be swimming upstream and not know it.

THE OPENING AND THE CLOSING

The opening and closing of a presentation are the most important parts of a presentation. These two critical segments are discussed in this section.

The Opening

The opening of a presentation is critical because most members of the audience decide during the first 90 seconds whether or not it is going to be worthwhile to listen. The opening should arouse your audience's interest, relate to their situation, and create credibility and rapport.[6] Therefore, the presentation must get off to a good start. The most effective openings are (1) memorable, and (2) provide an overview of the entire presentation.

Be Memorable
Kershaw suggested that a presentation is a serious business occasion to be treated with decorum and seriousness. The presenters should be polite and pleasant, but businesslike. Kershaw recommended that the presenter avoid opening with a funny story or with profuse thanks for the privilege of having been invited to compete for the account. Ideally, the opening should be memorable.[7]

---

[5]Luke Sullivan, *Hey Whipple, Squeeze This. A Guide to Creating Great Advertising,* 3rd ed. (New York: AdWeek Media/John Wiley & Sons, 2008), pp. 237–247.

[6]Mary Munter, *Guide to Managerial Communications,* 4th ed. (Upper Saddle River, NJ: Prentice Hall, 1997), p. 86.

[7]Andrew Kershaw, "How to Make Agency Presentations" (New York: Ogilvy & Mather, 1976).

As an example, Kershaw cited David Ogilvy's "Shell is strong!" opening that focused on the underlying proposition for an entire campaign and effectively captured the audience's attention. This opening initially puzzled the audience of Shell Oil executives but boldly engaged their curiosity and attention. As the presentation unfolded, Ogilvy explained how the recommended campaign capitalized on Shell's strengths.[8]

Munter suggested four general possibilities for developing a memorable or "grabber" presentation opening by referring to something unusual. These were a relevant: (1) vivid image, (2) statistic, (3) rhetorical question, and, (4) startling example or story.[9]

A key criterion for evaluating a possible memorable opening is its relevance to the entire presentation. Further, it is useful if the memorable opening can be referenced later during the presentation, especially in the closing.

An excellent example of a memorable and relevant opening was provided in a presentation to the marketing and general management of Chili's restaurants. Chili's had requested recommendations for an introductory advertising campaign to announce the opening of its first store in the Austin, Texas, market. After the audience was seated and attentive, the agency presenter, Brent Ladd, opened with what at first seemed to be a strange set of questions:

"Who is Chili's? (pause)
"What does Chili's serve? (pause)
"Where is Chili's located? (pause)

After a pause to let the suspense build, the presenter continued, "You and I know the answers to these questions. But *your prospective customers* out there (gesture) in the Austin market don't know the answers to these simple questions! (pause) That is why we are here this afternoon . . ."

The entire presentation to Chili's was focused on the most effective and efficient way to communicate the answers to these three basic questions to the target customers. In the conclusion, the opening presenter emphasized how the recommended campaign would convey this information to the target in a meaningful way.

Although ideally the opening of a presentation should be memorable, such openings are often risky. If an appropriate grabber opening cannot be developed, the presenters would be well advised to use a less dramatic opening. It is essential to have a relevant opening and one that is in good taste—if not, scrap it.

Provide an Overview

In addition to being memorable, the introduction should provide an overview of the entire presentation geared to stimulate interest and establish confidence. Note that an overview will help reduce some of the tensions inherent in any presentation situation.

Schultz and Barnes stressed that there is an inherent adversarial relationship between presenters and their prospects. The presenters are challenging the audience's marketing knowledge and putting pressure on the audience to approve a recommendation. Also, the prospects do not know what to expect next, as the presenters are in control. This open-ended, challenged, and uncertain position is unsettling to the audience.[10]

These audience tensions need to be reduced in the introduction. The presenters can accomplish this by telling the audience what to expect and by establishing themselves as

---

[8]Ibid.

[9]Munter, *Guide to Managerial Communications,* p. 87.

[10]Don Schultz and Beth Barnes, "Selling Management on the IBC Plan," in *Strategic Brand Communication Campaigns* (Chicago: NTC Books, 1999), pp. 360–368.

friendly, problem-solving partners of the prospects. Hence, the first presenter should outline the presentation agenda. This should make it clear how the presentation will unfold and what decision the prospects will be asked to make and when. Essentially, the presenter says, "This is where we are going in our presentation, this is how we'll get there, and this is what we'll ask you to do." This outline helps to put the audience at ease by alerting them to what to expect.

The Closing

In closing or summarizing, the presenter needs to accomplish three objectives: (1) to provide a summary recap of key points, (2) to end forcefully, and (3) to ask for the order. In providing a summary recap, the closing presenter hits key aspects of the situation facing the prospect, the recommended course of action, and the rationale for the recommendation. This summary recap will serve to reinforce the overall selling message. The Greek rhetorical axiom definitely applies to a presentation:

> *Tell them what you are going to tell them (introduction), tell them (situation analysis, problem/opportunities definition, recommendations), and tell them what you've told them (closing).*

Repetition is important because people remember little of what they hear only once. The recap will help to more firmly establish the key points of differentiation in the prospects' minds.

The strongest presenter on the team should wrap up with a strong ending. Never allow the presentation to taper off or end with a whimper. Finally, be sure to clearly ask the key prospect for action. Make the desired action as easy as possible. For example, present the prospective client with a contract appointing the agency or an authorization to proceed with a project, closing with, "All we need is your okay (or signature), authorizing us to begin implementing the exciting ideas we've outlined this afternoon." Depending on the situation, this may be qualified by indicating that you expect the prospective client to sign, but only after they have reviewed the work of other agencies. Exhibit 1 presents an example of such a contract.

STAGE MANAGEMENT

Kershaw points out that if the stage management of a presentation is handled well, the presentation will at least look professional. In addition, a strong stage management job may disguise some shortcomings in content. On the other hand, if the staging is badly bungled, the audience will forget the content and recall most clearly that the slides were upside down and backward, or the chart fell on someone's head, or someone forgot to bring the crucial DVD. Above all else, the audience will remember the disaster![11]

Basic Considerations

Following are some basic suggestions for stage management:

1. When appropriate and possible, *make the presentation in your own office.* There is a home field advantage—it's easier and more comfortable to make a presentation in a familiar

[11]Kershaw, "How to Make Agency Presentations." p. 12.

Exhibit 1 ■ Example of a Contract Used in a Competitive Agency Pitch[1]

Letter of Agreement Between ABC, Inc. and the XYZ Group

The XYZ Group (agency) will provide advertising and PR agency services for ABC, Inc. (client) until this agreement is cancelled by either party with 90-days notice. The agency's services include strategic recommendations that focus on developing and implementing a targeted and impactful integrated marketing communication plan designed to support and build the client's brand.

Compensation to the agency will be derived from a fee system coupled with a bonus or incentive fee system. Both aspects of this plan are explained below.

Fee System

(1) The agency will be paid based on billable hours for the work it does, not by how much the client spends; (2) The agency does not mark-up outside costs incurred on the client's behalf. All expenses, such as production charges, travel, copies, etc. will be billed at net to the client; and, (3) The agency's hourly billing rate is the employee's base salary multiplied by a factor to cover overhead costs (120%). A profit percentage (20%) is then added and the sum of these three items represents the costs billed to the client.

Base salaries for the agency's employees are set yearly using regional industry averages, which are compiled by the AAAA. The agency uses the average regional salary for each job title by department for agencies with gross income between $3.75 million and $7.5 million.

Bonus System

The bonus system has two distinct benefits to the client: (1) The bonus will be used to reward the agency based on their contribution to achieving the client's brand health and incidence of sales objectives; and, (2) allocation of the bonus will be solely at the client's discretion, based on the client's evaluation of the agency's performance against the measurable objectives specified in the marketing objectives section of the agency's plans book. The total amount of the bonus fund equals one-half the agency's anticipated profit or ten percent (10%) of the total salary plus overhead costs that the agency will contribute to the fund. In addition, the client will match the agency's allocation and that total will comprise the bonus fund. After an annual review of performance, the client determines what portion, if any, of the fund will be paid to the agency as a bonus.

Note that the agency trusts the client to grade our efforts fairly and award an equitable bonus. The agency believes in accountability and welcomes the challenge of leaving a portion of our compensation tied to performance. The agency team assigned to the client's account is aware of this arrangement and both welcome the challenge and expects to share in the rewards. This arrangement helps to build team focus and commitment.

_____   _____
On behalf of the client   On behalf of the agency

Date: _____

[1]Note: This document is modeled on a fee/bonus contract developed and successfully used by Carmichael Lynch, an advertising agency headquartered in Minneapolis, Minnesota.

setting. The most advantageous time for a presentation is after 10:00 a.m. and before 3:00 p.m. on a Tuesday, Wednesday, or Thursday.[12] Never exceed an assigned or requested time limit.

2. *The arrangement of the room and positioning of the presenters in relation to the audience is critical.* Ideally, presenters should be physically close to the prospects when they are talking and off to the side, out of the sight line of prospects when not speaking.

3. *The presentation team should look for ways to convey that they are a team and that they like each other,* for example, by having a team member hold a presentation board while another member describes the content or by using two presenters and a back-and-forth format for presenting pros and cons or referring to each other by first name works (e.g., "In just a moment Karen will describe how we recommend you use social networks to generate buzz for this program.")

4. Do *not* distribute handouts before or during the presentation. This results in divided attention. If a handout or outline is distributed, the presenter should read aloud the entire handout to the audience before proceeding.

5. *Use props*—for example, the physical product, competitive ads, a mock up of a Web site, or a $100 bill.

6. *Control the situation.* Make it your show, and do not let the audience take over. Discourage premature questions. To avoid interruptions, in the introduction the lead presenter could point out, "We would be happy to entertain your questions, but at the end of presentation."

7. *Encourage questions after the presentation.* Anticipate questions and have replies ready. Listen to each question carefully before answering. Never bluff an answer. The questioners may know the answer and the fact that you do not and may be just checking your honesty. There is nothing wrong with responding, "That's a good question. I don't know the answer. I'll check and get back to you tomorrow."

8. Make sure *one person* is clearly in charge of all props and equipment, such as computers, projectors, easels, and presentation boards. Do not make bringing the props and equipment to the presentation a group effort. Murphy's Law states, "Anything that can go wrong will go wrong," and it does for disorganized presenters and presentation teams.

9. *Dress is an important presentation variable.* Molloy pointed out a truism, "The way we dress has a remarkable impact on the people we meet professionally or socially and greatly affects how they treat us."[13] Do not let costume or the way presenters are dressed get in the way of communication. If an error in dress is made, it is better to be too formal rather than too informal. As an advertising wag observed, "If you can't put clothes together, why should they believe you can put a coordinated IBP campaign together?" One must look the part.

Visual Aids

Although visual aids are a must for most formal presentations, their use, particularly the use of PowerPoint slides, is a controversial issue. Used appropriately, visual aids support the

---

[12]Sandra Moriarty and Tom Duncan, *Creating & Delivering Winning Advertising & Marketing Presentations* (Lincolnwood, IL: NTC Business Books, 1995), p. 23.

[13]John Molloy, *Dress for Success* (New York: Warner Books, 1975).

presentation and rivet attention to key points, in addition to making the presentation easier to follow. Most important, visual aids increase audience attention, comprehension, and retention.[14]

Choose a medium to fit the situation. For informal communication of a few simple facts to one or two individuals, a single 8.5x11 sheet may be appropriate. For small groups, presentation boards or flip charts work best. For large groups, PowerPoint slides are generally regarded as most appropriate.

However, Steel argued against the use of any PowerPoint slides and points out the detrimental affect PowerPoint slides can have on making human connections. He stressed that the use of PowerPoint with clip art, complex slides jammed with words and numbers, and presenters who read slides to the audience undermine the effectiveness of a presentation.[15] Jensen suggested, "PowerPoint and similar tools are clogging our companies with more clutter and crap than illumination." He suggested that if PowerPoint slides are used, the presenter follow a 3:1 ratio rule. That is, if the slides are text heavy or contain tables, no more than one slide should be presented every three minutes. Hence, for a 30-minute presentation this means 10 slides for a 20-minute show; seven slides are recommended. This forces the presenter to take time to explain, connect, and illuminate the gist of each slide.[16]

Experience indicates that the majority of presenters do *not* use PowerPoint effectively. The audience is too often faced with a choice of either listening to the presenter or reading the slides. Presenters too frequently use heavy-word-count slides with multiple points on each slide. Hence, for example, while the presenter is discussing bullet point one of eight points, a member of the audience has read ahead and is stuck on the meaning of point six and is not listening to the speaker. One partial answer is to limit the words on slides to key concepts only and roll out points to track along with the presenter's coverage.

PowerPoint slides also draw attention away from the presenter. This can be detrimental because connecting on a human level is important. For example, eye contact with prospects is critical in terms of such a connection, projecting sincerity, and so on. Further, presenters tend to be more effective when they use physical props, including working off presentation boards. Finally, physical proximity, being close to your audience, is important in connecting with them on a personal level. All these considerations argue in favor of using presentation boards instead of PowerPoint slides.

Finally, Kershaw offered four sage suggestions for using visual aids:

1. Remember that the audience reads visual aids. When the words on the visual do not match the speaker's words, a problem exists. What the eye sees and the speaker says must march together. One of the most common conflicts occurs when "target audience" is on the visual but the speaker uses "target market."
2. The presenter should never turn his or her back on the audience to read a visual.
3. Learn to use a pointer. The audience will be riveted to it, and it enables the presenter to stay out of the audience's line of vision.
4. Inevitably, some charts or visuals will contain a misspelling or a wrong figure. To avoid this, proofread carefully prior to final production. If it's too late to correct a mistake, always point it out in advance. Never let the audience spot a typo or error before the presenter points it out.[17]

---

[14] Munter, *Guide to Managerial Communications,* p. 111.

[15] Steel, *Perfect Pitch,* p. 124.

[16] Bill Jensen, "Chapter 6: Do Less and Still Deliver an Awesome Presentation," *The Simplicity Survival Handbook* (New York: Basic Books, 2003), pp. 44–52.

[17] Kershaw, "How to Make Agency Presentations," p. 25–27.

ADVANCE PREPARATION

Rehearsal and Practice

It is critical that presenters both rehearse and practice their presentation. Rehearsal is fine-tuning, adjusting and rearranging the sections of the presentation. Practice is simply an individual presenter going over their part of a presentation to become more comfortable with it.

It is important to have at least one dress rehearsal with all participants, using all visual aids and props to run through the presentation, just as it will be delivered, in the room where it will be made, if possible. Rehearse everything just as it will be. It is most unprofessional to begin by apologizing for not having the correct connector to show a DVD of the agency's work or to discover that it is difficult to read visual aids because of the lighting.

In addition to rehearsing the presentation, individual presenters should practice their parts alone. The more comfortable the presenters are with their material, the more likely they are to be successful.

Visualization

The day or morning before a major presentation, it is useful to go through a visualization exercise. One member of the team describes what will happen just before, during, and after the presentation. Describing in some detail how the events surrounding and including the presentation will unfold generates a sense of confidence. The following is a fragment from such an exercise,

> "... O.K., after Jane closes with that line, there will probably be some positive comments, maybe even applause. At that point, Jane will ask if there are any questions. Then, Mr. Goldfish will most likely ask about our use of radio in the media plan. We're ready for that! Jack will tackle it by quickly reviewing three or four points as Mr. Goldfish nods in agreement. Next, we'll most likely be asked about the focus on older women ..."

Such an exercise helps to establish a sense of control and mastery of the situation, putting individual presenters more at ease.[18] This exercise is particularly recommended for less-experienced presenters operating in highly charged environments.

Improving Your Delivery

The most efficient way to improve your ability to speak in public is to take lessons from a professional speech coach. The second best way is self-analysis of a film or video of your performance. Third best, you can listen to an audiotape of yourself. These are humbling but useful experiences.

---

[18]Moriarty and Duncan, *Creating & Delivering Winning Advertising & Marketing Presentations*, p. 113.

Should you read or speak from notes? This is a personal decision, but play it safe. Many speakers are most effective if they script every word they want to say but practice to the point that they almost know their script by heart. Then they can read their script, but it will not appear that they are reading.

Some presenters prefer to use 3x5″ index cards with a few key points that can be referenced as they deliver their presentation. These cards can be used unobtrusively and effectively plus they provide a safety blanket if the speaker loses track of what comes next.

Clearly, using no notes is potentially the most effective style. In a group presentation, this should be a team decision. If the decision is that some members need note cards, all should have them, even if they are not referenced during the presentation.

Following are some basic considerations for improving delivery.

1. The most important voice characteristics are energy and enthusiasm.
2. Stand when you present, and make eye contact with the audience.
3. Be especially careful with your first few sentences. It is critical to get off to a good start, and you should know your opening cold.
4. Avoid distracting habits such as leaning on the podium, rattling keys in your pocket, chewing gum, or putting your hands in your pockets while speaking.[19]
5. If you are nervous, do *not* apologize for it. This only draws attention to your nervousness. The best way to overcome nervousness is rehearsal, practice, and visualization. The better you know your material, the less likely nervousness will be debilitating. Arriving early to check out the room and settle in will also allow you to feel in charge and ease your tension about the presentation. Preparation is the key to handling nervousness.

CONCLUSION

In conclusion, the checklist in Exhibit 2 highlights many of the points stressed in this chapter. Number three on the checklist—delivery or the public speaking skills of the presenters—is the single most important element, but to be most effective, the presentation must perform well in all ten areas.

In working on the development of your presentation skills (a lifelong task), learn from your presentation successes and your failures. Become a student of all public presenters from the president of the U.S., the local television sportscasters, speakers at PTA meetings, and so on. It is amazing what one can learn, often from unexpected sources.

In a competitive presentation setting, it is easy to be a gracious winner, much more difficult to be a gracious loser. Always take the high road, congratulate the winner, and move on to the next challenge wiser from the experience.

You should now be ready to tackle the problems and challenges that you will find in this book. As you proceed, you may find it useful to refer back to the first two chapters. Do so as often as you need, and add your personal observations and changes as you see fit. Each of us has a personal management style. Time and careful observation will help you develop your own. Good luck!

---

[19]Kershaw, "How to Make Agency Presentations," p. 44.

Exhibit 2 ■ Checklist for Evaluating Presentations

1. Professional Approach. Were the tone, presenters' dress, preparation, strategy, and style all appropriate? Was the presentation within the time limit?
2. The Opening. Memorable, appropriate, included an overview, and set the tone effectively?
3. Delivery. Smoothness, wording, pace, volume, worked off visuals and props effectively, confidence, and easy to follow? (The most common shortcoming is speaking too rapidly. Remember, this is the first time the audience has heard the information. Slow down and speak clearly.)
4. Innovativeness. Did the presentation team do something that was appropriate and different that set them apart and added audience interest?
5. Visual Aids. Was an appropriate medium used for maximum clarity and impact? Coordinated with the presenters? Summary support of key points, large enough to read easily, and professional level of finish?
6. Audience Focus. Was it clear from the opening that the presenters understood and related to the prospect's perspective? Were the proposed programs focused directly and consistently on the prospect's problems and opportunities?
7. The Closing. Was there a summary recap, forceful ending, and did they clearly ask for the order or indicate the desired action?
8. Enthusiasm. Did the presenters convey that they strongly believe in what they recommended? Would the presentation team be an energetic and fun group with whom to work?
9. Positioning of the Presentation Team and Room Arrangement. Did they use the most effective arrangement of the room? Were the presenters physically close to the prospects? (The most common shortcoming is a technology lock exerted by the position of a projection screen. That is, screen position dictates the arrangement of the room and prevents human connections from being established.)
10. Questions and Answers. Was this critical segment after the formal presentation handled effectively? Did they listen to the questions and have concise responses? Were they willing to admit that they did not know the answer to some questions? Did they convey that they were a team that respects and works well with each other?

SUGGESTED READINGS

Hoff, Ron. *I Can See You Naked.* Kansas City, MO: Andrews and McMeel, 1992.

Jensen, Bill. *The Simplicity Survival Handbook.* New York: Basic Books, 2003.

Moriarty, Sandra, and Tom Duncan. *Creating & Delivering Winning Advertising & Marketing Presentations.* Lincolnwood, IL: NTC Business Books, 1995.

Munter, Mary. *Guide to Managerial Communications,* Upper Saddle River, NJ: Prentice Hall, 4th edition, 1997).

Steel, Jon. *Perfect Pitch: The Art of Selling Ideas and Winning New Business.* New York: John Wiley & Sons, 2007.

Sullivan, Luke. *Hey Whipple, Squeeze This. A Guide to Creating Great Advertising,* 3rd ed. New York: AdWeek Media/John Wiley & Sons, 2008.

Chapter 3
The Marketing Context of Advertising and Promotion

We are no longer in the business of advertising; our business is to help out clients, by whatever means, with the orderly management of change in the marketplace.[1]

—*Carl Spielvogel*
BACKER SPIELVOGEL BATES

THE ROLE OF ADVERTISING

Advertising is a strong marketing force. It pervades our media and is noticed by audiences of all ages, economic profiles, and walks of life. Every consumer in a developed economy today knows about advertising, and, what is more, considers him or herself an advertising expert.

Advertising is important to our economy. Expenditures on advertising and promotion have grown for the past century in steady proportion with out economic growth.

Such an activity, therefore, must be carried on with professionalism and a thorough understanding of its role in the economy and in society. In addition, the interaction of the advertising function with the other marketing functions performed by the firm must also be comprehended fully, so that advertising can be effective and efficient in achieving its purpose.

This chapter is concerned with advertising within the marketing environment. Its role as a marketing tool will be considered, as well as its contribution to the marketing of products and services.

Advertising as a Marketing Function

Advertising is one of many functions performed in the context of an overall marketing program. A marketing program is intended to plan how products or services are taken from the point of production to the point of consumption in such a way as to develop a positive relationship between consumers and the producer that will foster additional or repeat usage. As such, marketing is

---

[1] "The Party's Over," *The Economist,* February 1, 1992, 69.

concerned with both short-term and long-term results. The advertising function, therefore, must fit the marketing objectives set by the firm and cannot be effective if considered in isolation.

A marketing plan should contain a statement of *short-term* and *long-term* objectives. It should then spell out the particular strategies and tactics that will be implements to achieve these objectives. Strategic objectives will be met by the use of marketing tools such as advertising, marketing research, product packaging and design and personal sales. Authors have attempted to group the marketing functions into basic categories. One of the most common summaries groups the marketing functions into (1) product functions, (2) price functions, (3) distribution functions, and (4) communication functions. Advertising is one of the communication functions to be performed within the marketing plan.

Because products and services are very diverse, not all marketing plans use the same mix of marketing functions. As an example, advertising is a major element of the marketing mix for products such as breakfast cereals and soft drinks. On the other hand, the manufacturers of mainframe computers do not rely as heavily on advertising to move their products; instead, they invest considerable time and effort in personal sales functions. For some products or services, the use of advertising could generate negative, rather than positive results. Medical doctors and health-care organizations have found that large investments in advertising can be counterproductive. It is important, therefore, to understand fully just how advertising fits in the overall marketing program before proceeding with the actual planning and implementation of the advertising function.

The Marketing Process and Advertising

The marketing planning process generally starts with a thorough *situation analysis*. This enables a firm to recognize the challenges and opportunities that face it within the marketplace. A situation analysis is also necessary to understand the role to be performed by the advertising function. The situation analysis involves examining all the important factors operating in a particular situation. It invariably involves the use of research. A situation analysis will investigate consumer motivation and behavior with regard to the product or service at hand. In addition, it will consider the economic and competitive environment facing the firm and the changes that might affect market demand.

The second step in the marketing planning process is setting overall *marketing objectives* and goals for the firm. Objectives and goals are general and broad in nature. They may be concerned with obtaining a specific market share, securing repeat purchases, or increasing profits. In any case, it is important to know what the marketing objectives of the firm are because they will determine the marketing strategy and the communication objectives the firm will pursue.

The third step in the marketing planning process is to develop a *marketing strategy*. The marketing strategy deals with the use of all the elements of the marketing mix, of which communication is but one. This is the planning stage, in which the interplay and interdependence of the elements of the marketing mix can best be seen and understood. The marketing executive controls decisions affecting the marketing mix. Price setting, product design and packaging, distribution strategy, promotional objectives, and tactics can all be manipulated internally by the firm. Although market forces may affect the direction(s) in which the firm chooses to act, the manager's actions will still be crucial in this phase of the planning process.

The marketing strategy utilized by the firm will be set with its *target market* in mind. This is the segment of the overall market to which the firm wishes to appeal. The identification of its target market is a very important step in the marketing planning process of the firm.

An example of how the different elements of a marketing mix may affect promotion decisions is the case of national brands versus generic products. The quality of generic products such as paper towels and canned vegetables is class or category. Nationally advertised products, however, command higher prices, have packages designed to attract shoppers' attention, and are featured in nationally advertised campaigns and sales promotions. Brand is an essential element of a nationally advertised product, and most of the communication campaign effort is designed to build brand loyalty and consumer recall and recognition for the product.

Generic products, on the other hand, are developed to compete primarily on the basis of price. They do not feature a brand name. Their package is not designed to call attention to the product, and usually they do not command a lot of shelf space. Generic products are not advertised; it is assumed that buyers will understand and opt for the price economy they represent.

It is clear from this example that advertising and promotion decisions must be developed as an integral part of the overall marketing strategy. The following section will consider the elements of an advertising and promotion strategy.

THE ADVERTISING AND PROMOTION PLAN

The promotion and advertising plan is an essential element of the marketing mix. It can be a small portion of the overall marketing strategy, as with some industrial products, or it can dominate the marketing program, as happens often with such products as cosmetics and soft drinks.

It is important to understand that advertising and promotion together are only one of the marketing tools employed to influence consumer decisions. Advertising by itself cannot close the sale of a product; rather, it should be used as a facilitator of the sale. Advertising decisions, therefore, must involve a clear understanding of the intended effects of advertising for the specific marketing situation at hand.

Any advertising plan will encompass three major decisions: establishing advertising objectives and the necessary budget allocation, determining the contents and structure of the message to be conveyed to the intended audience, and deciding which media to use when conveying the message to the audience. Therefore, budget, message, and media are the three main elements of an advertising and promotion plan.

When making such decisions, the advertising manager must always go back to the information gathered for the situation analysis. The evaluation of alternative courses of action will involve those factors which makes each situation unique. Questions that must be part of the advertising planning process include: What is the competitive approach? How many new products are likely to be brought to the market? How have consumers' buying decisions changed?

The Establishment of Objectives

The central aspect of any management plan is the *development of objectives* that will direct operational decisions. Operational objectives serve as a standard of performance and as a tool to measure results. Advertising budget decisions are dependent on and tied to objective decisions. Only when the manager knows what advertising is supposed to accomplish can he or she allocate the necessary and appropriate budget to carry out the task. The advertising *budget,* therefore, should begin with a detailed specification of what a firm expects to accomplish with advertising. Then the specific amounts required to carry out each task can be determined.

An example of this specific management task is the 1992 change in Perrier's advertising campaign. Perrier, which was America's best-selling brand of sparkling water, suffered serious market share losses in 1990 when Source Perrier ordered a worldwide recall of over

70 million bottles of the product. The recall was caused by the discovery of traces of benzene in some bottles, and consumer confidence in the product was shaken considerably by it.

In 1992 the company engaged in an effort to position its product as an everyday drink. This objective was part of the overall sales and market share. Perrier was perceived as a "country-club drink," according to James Caporimo, creative director at Waring & LaRosa, the company's advertising agency.[2]

To accomplish its objective and promote Perrier as a mass-market product, the advertising agency developed ads with the tagline, "Perrier. Part of the local color." The campaign showed a cross section of real people and real places across America, along with the product. In addition, because the message was designed to reach a much broader segment of consumers, the advertising budget was increased 60 percent over that of 1991. This boost in ad spending was combined with a shift from television to magazine advertising.

The 1992 Perrier advertising strategy shows the interdependence of marketing and advertising budget that allows the achievement of company objectives and goals.

The Development of Advertising Messages

Once the advertising and promotion objectives have been stated, the theme of the communication must be determined. The *message* is a very important component of the advertising and promotion decision. In many instances, the wrong message can jeopardize the whole communication plan.

The first step in developing a message is to decide which of several alternative central themes best serves the communication goals. The theme will then be used to develop specific advertising messages.

The advertising messages are often tested before being implemented in order to assess their relative effectiveness. The advertising manager must therefore, understand both the creative process involved in writing advertising messages and the management goals that advertising must serve.

Sometimes the messages that appear most creative and potentially memorable are not received by all in a positive manner. The "Socially aware" Benetton ads featuring dying AIDS patients, a rainbow of colored condoms, and a nun kissing a priest have met, at best, mixed reviews from consumers. The company and its agency claim that their ads are designed to bring people together and raise awareness of social issues, but a survey conducted by *Advertising Age* showed that only 38.9 percent of respondents perceived the ads as having a positive effect, whereas the other respondents felt they had a negative effect or no effect at all. Some Benetton customers said the ads were in bad taste and would actually keep them away from Benetton stores. An overwhelming majority of the survey respondents (72 percent) felt that the campaign was not an effective marketing strategy.[3]

The company's position concerning its advertising message poses important questions: How effective is the Benetton advertising? How can we measure the effectiveness of the advertising expenditures by Benetton? What criteria should be used for setting the advertising budget? These questions should be answered when establishing advertising objectives and determining and advertising budget. In the case of Benetton, however, management has stated

---

[2] Alison Fahey, "Perrier Ads Sell Common Appeal," *Advertising Age,* April 6, 1992, 38.

[3] Adrienne Ward, "Socially Aware" or "Wasted Money?" *Advertising Age,* February 24, 1992, 4.

its objectives in a vague and general manner. It would be hard to measure whether the campaign has succeeded in raising society's awareness of issues such as AIDS, safe sex, and illegal immigration, among others.

It is understandable, therefore, that such a campaign would meet with mixed reviews. It might even have a negative effect on sales of Benetton products. Management must be careful to develop *specific* and *measurable* advertising objectives and to set a budget that will allow it to accomplish these objectives.

In addition, the firm must test its messages to verify that they are understood by consumers in a positive and productive manner. Although controversial and strong messages may be memorable, they do not always produce the intended effects. The objective of the Benetton campaign—raising social consciousness—might have produced a favorable image for the company if its messages had been different. Research would have been helpful in determining the nature and content of the messages most likely to be received favorably by the intended audiences.

The Establishment of the Media Budget

The last component of the advertising decision process deals with the allocation of budgets to specific *media*. Media allocation is the task of determining which audiences to reach and the nature and effectiveness of specific media vehicles. Because it is such a complex task, mathematical models have been developed to aid managers in making media allocation decisions.

When developing a budget for a campaign, the advertising manager must take into account several factors in additions to the media expenditures themselves. Many companies have started to look at advertising and promotion budgets in a more integrated manner. Companies are increasingly concerned with *all* the marketing variables, which combined may produce a synergistic effect and increase the efficiency of their advertising expenditures.

An example of this integrated approach to advertising management is the successful use of cross-promotional efforts by Kmart. During the 1991 holiday season, Kmart was involved in joint programs with Walt Disney, Eastman Kodak, Chrysler, Coca-Cola, and Burger King. These cross-promotions involved the distribution of game cards, prize giveaways, sweepstakes, and other promotional tools. Because most retail advertising is intended to build increased store traffic, the development and advertising of cross-promotions should be even more effective than retail advertising alone. Kmart's holiday sales were up 10.6 percent over the previous year's sales, and management was happy with that performance.[4]

Marketers often use cross-promotions to maximize their advertising and marketing expenditures. Setting up cross-promotions is not a simple task, however. Managers must find compatible and strong partners who share similar target markets so that the cross-promotions will be beneficial to all. In addition, partners must be willing to commit adequate resources so that the promotions will result in a strong response.

Advertising budgets should also consider nontraditional media channels and technologically innovative ways to reach consumers. In 1992, General Motors sent out 250,000 promotional videocassettes to young, upper-income families featuring its new TransSport minivan. The families were also offered a $500 discount coupon along with the cassettes. The cost of this innovative and targeted type of advertising should also be included in the development of a budget.[5]

---

[4]John Cortez, "Kmart Happy with Holidays," *Advertising Age,* February 3, 1992, 28.

[5]"The Party's Over," p. 69.

It is clear, therefore, that setting the advertising budget is a task that must take into consideration all the other marketing variables. In the General Motors example, pricing and distribution were an integral part of the promotional campaign for the TransSport minivan. Advertising and promotion are not independent functions; they are one of the elements of the marketing strategy of a company.

These three elements—budget, message, and media—combine to form the advertising plan. Not all advertising plans are similar, however, because the external environmental factors facing each advertiser may vary a great deal. In addition, because the task assigned to advertising will depend in part on decisions made concerning other marketing elements, the interdependence of advertising and the other components of the marketing mix must be underscored. The elements in the marketing mix not only influence the task of the advertising manager, but also the amount of money available for advertising. The advertising manager's job, therefore, must be viewed as an important element of a complex team effort designed to achieve the overall marketing objectives of the firm.

DEVELOPMENT OF AN ADVERTISING PLAN WITHIN A FIRM'S MARKETING CONTEXT

The Phenomenon of Tooth Whiteners

This section provides an example of an advertising plan. The example shows that marketing variables must be considered carefully when developing a marketing plan. The data in this example are derived from facts and figures obtained from business data on the health and beauty products industry in the United States. For the purpose of this chapter the data have been disguised.

The development of an advertising plan by a fictitious company. Percare, a personal care products manufacturer, is considered in this section. The company is one of the leading competitors in the personal care products market, which includes 750 companies with combined annual sales of $40 billion.

Demand for personal care products is driven by population growth and consumer preferences. Companies that are capable of maintaining continuous product innovation and development, and invest in effective sales and marketing strategies are more likely to have a higher profitability.

Major products in this industry include cosmetics, hair products, and creams and lotions, which together account for over 79 percent of total sales in this industry. Another very important product segment is that represented by oral care products. This segment includes toothpastes, mouthwashes, and tooth whiteners, among other products. In 2008, total sales of tooth whiteners in the United States was in excess of $500 million. Percare sales of its dental bleaching product was almost $250 million.

Situation Analysis

The first step in the development of an advertising plan is a complete situation analysis. This includes an overview of the industry as a whole, an appraisal of the company's competitive position, and an examination of the firm's long-term and short-term marketing strategies for its products.

The U.S. personal care market is divided among 750 manufacturers, but two companies have almost 70 percent of the total market. Percare has almost a 48 percent share of all U.S. sales of personal care products. Its two other major competitors, the L&H Corporation and the Homeproducts Co., have, respectively 36 percent and 11 percent of the market. The remaining 6 to 7 percent is divided among a number of other small producers.

In 2003, sales of "tooth whiteners" or "tooth polishers" grew substantially in the United States. Although these products sales are a very small part of Percare and its major competitor's sales, by the end of the first quarter of 2003, Americans spent nearly $300 million on home-use whitening products, a 90 percent growth over the same quarter in the previous year. This growth provided an opportunity for the three leaders in the market to establish several brands and to take advantage of all possible marketing opportunities to strengthen their competitive position in this market segment.

Percare's Candid Smile brand, supported by a strong advertising program, achieved a market share of 63 percent in 2003. The L&H Corporation quickly introduced a rival brand. White Smile and gathered 18 percent of the market share. The success of the home whitening strips was such that a line of products followed its introduction. Night whitening products, whitening gels, and other products were introduced by the two major producers as well as by a number of their small competitors.

The major market target for tooth whitening products were high-income women between 25 and 50 years of age. Advertising campaigns were designed to persuade consumers that a pure and white smile was indicative of a younger and more attractive appearance. The night whitening products advertising targeted primarily consumers who smoked and drank coffee but wanted to maintain a white and bright smile.

By 2007, the two major competitors: Percare and L&H Corporation, were engaged in an active marketing battle to maintain and increase their respective market share of the tooth whitening products. During the period between 2003 and 2007, a number of other companies in the personal care products segment introduced their own brands and developed sophisticated marketing strategies to reach and secure small segments of the total market.

As competition increased, the growth in sales of tooth whiteners continued until the end of 2008, when total sales for the United Sates reached over $500 million. It was not until the beginning of 2009, that growth in sales started slowing down. By then, Percare and its competitors were facing major challenges to maintain their brands' market shares. Both Percare and the L&H Corporation had invested considerable resources in advertising and promotion to launch their tooth whitening products and to maintain their market share since 2002. Although some growth in the total market size of these products was expected in future years, as the 55 to 64 age group in the United States continued to grow at a 5 percent rate, the industry leaders believed that sales in 2009 were indicative of the fact that tooth whitening products had reached the mature stage of their product life-cycle. Increases in revenue could only be achieved at the expense of competitors' market share, and innovative marketing strategies would be needed to maintain revenues and profitability in this market segment.

The Problem

The marketing vice president of Percare decided it was important to develop a long-range marketing and advertising strategy for the company's tooth whitening products. Should the company continue to concentrate its advertising and promotion efforts on its two leading products, Candid Smile and its night whitening product, Snow White? Should the company invest in additional R&D expenditures and try to develop other whitening products designed to appeal to other market segments, such as older consumers and middle-aged men, and develop advertising appeals for each specific and discrete segment of potential consumers? How should Percare react to the increasing number of products introduced by the smaller competitors in this market, designed to appeal to very narrow consumer segments?

All these strategies would involve an increase in expenditures in advertising, promotion, and R&D and would decrease the profitability that Percare had enjoyed in this segment. It was important to note, however, that the tooth whitening products provided a healthy return for Percare with a net margin of 25 percent of revenues.

The Solution

The marketing vice president of Percare should weigh all the information gathered in the situation analysis against the strengths and weaknesses of the company and its products. Although tooth whitening products are a small share of the overall Percare sales, they appear to be an important product line and one that has an established share of consumers' interest and expenditures. The fact that this line of products still provides Percare with a healthy return on sales should be a major consideration in developing a long-term marketing communication strategy. A marketing plan should be developed first, based on the market and competitive data available to the company.

The advertising strategy should be developed as a result of the marketing plan. The creative appeals, advertising budget, and media strategy should take into account the market profile and the company's best forecast of demand trends. A process to continuously monitor the company's performance and adjust to market changes should also be in place to avoid future problems.

An integrated marketing approach is essential to allow marketing and advertising executives to develop a sound strategy. The interaction of advertising and marketing decisions will benefit the company's long-term planning and allow for an efficient decision-making process.

REFERENCES

Berner, Robert, Nannette Byrnes, and Wendy Zellner. "P&G Has Rivals in a Winger." *Business Week,* October 4, 2004.

De Lisser, Eleena. "The Cranky Consumer Works on Its Smile." *Wall Street Journal,* January 14, 2003, p. D1.

Ives, Nat. "The Media Business: Advertising; The Giants of Tooth Whitening See Spinoff Products Expanding a Fast-Growing Market." *New York Times,* April 2003.

Neff, Jack. "Future Gets Brighter." *Advertising Age* 60, no. 3 (June 23, 2003): 18.

Exercise One

On Tuesday, January 26, 2010, Toyota Motor Corporation announced that it would halt production and sales in the U.S. of most of its popular selling models. This is an unprecedented move by a company that has built its reputation for solid and reliable cars. The popular eight models include the following:

2009–1010	RAV4, Corolla, Matrix
2005–2010	Avalon
2007–2010	Camrys (Excluding Hybrids) and Tundra
2010	Highlander
2008–2010	Sequoia

Toyota stated that mechanisms in the gas pedal could become worn and makes it harder to depress the accelerator. The worst case scenario would be the pedal getting stuck in a partially depressed position.

In addition, there have been several cases of sudden acceleration that led to fatal car accidents. Sales of the eight affected models represent 57% of Toyota's 2009 sales. The announcement of the recall was made before a solution had been found by Toyota engineers.

The U.S. has been experiencing a major recession with auto sales taking huge losses, and, this recall comes just at a time when many analysts believe the recession to have ended and customers beginning to return to the showrooms for vehicle purchases.

If you were marketing management at Toyota—what kind of marketing plan would you come up with to make sure current Toyota owners and future Toyota owners, still consider Toyota a reliable and solid brand? How could advertising play a role in your marketing plan? What would you want to communicate to current Toyota owners and future owners?

Source: Kate Linebaugh, "Toyota Halts Sales Over Safety Issue," in the Marketplace Section, The Wall Street Journal, January 27, 2010, B1.

Exercise Two

"Green Marketing"—brands claiming to be good for the environment, began appearing more and more in the U.S. in the late '00's and continues in 2010.

Two companies are hoping to profit from the movement for 'green' products. Non-mainstream household cleaners, Seventh Generation and Method Products, are planning their first major marketing campaign towards consumers in 2010.

These companies claim that their cleaning and personal care lines, known as "ethical" household products, are safer for both people and the environment. Industry defines, "ethical," household products as those that are marketed on the basis of meeting an ethical standard.

At a time when U.S. households are spending less on name brand packaged goods, sales for these types of 'green' products have been strong, despite the U.S.' weak economy in 2009 and early 2010—even though they are premium priced.

According to market-research firm, Packaged Facts, sales of ethical household products nearly tripled, reaching an estimated $1.6 billion in 2009.

If you were marketing management at Seventh Generation or Method Products, what would be your marketing strategy to increase sales of these types of products to more consumers? Remember, the U.S. economy is starting to exit a major recession, but, the unemployment rate is still historically high. Explain what type of message you would create for consumers as well as the media choices you would recommend.

Source: Ellen Byron and Suzanne Vranica, "'Green' Products to Get a Push," in the Media and Marketing Section, The Wall Street Journal, January 11, 2010, B5.

Exercise Three

During the major U.S. recession in 2009, retail sales of clothing—especially designer clothing/luxury goods—plummeted. Many experts believe that, although many Americans, were not negatively affected by the recession, they were feeling a lot guiltier about shopping.

Guilt in making purchases has been around for a long time—not just during economic downturns. But, it is so strong during this recession, that, industry experts believe, it is delaying the recovery of the luxury-goods industry.

People were even avoiding going into stores—in order to avoid temptation to buy, according to retail executives. As a result, Internet shopping has increased in order to avoid, "Luxury Shame,"—walking out of luxury store with a large, showy, bag full of merchandise. According to Baine and Company, it is one of the major reasons for a 20% increase in web sales.

You are a marketing executive at a major luxury retailer. How would you help convince consumers (who can afford to shop) that they should not feel so guilty about shopping again?

What would your marketing strategy be? What would marketing communication's role be? How would you help get them back into stores and make shopping fun again – with a purchase at the end of the experience?

Source: Christina Passariello, "Fighting Back Against Shoppers Guilt," October 30, 2009. http://online.wsj.com/article/SB10001424052748704597704574487342734060448.html

Chapter 3 ■ The Marketing Context of Advertising and Promotion 33

Case 3.1

Lady Bird Johnson Wildflower Center (A)[6]

BACKGROUND INFORMATION

In 1982, Lady Bird Johnson, the actress Helen Hayes, and a group of dedicated volunteers founded the National Wildflower Center as a 501(c) (3) nonprofit organization. Twenty-four years later in 2006, the Center became a component of The University of Texas at Austin in what was recognized as a mutually beneficial union.

The Lady Bird Johnson Wildflower Center (WC) became an Organized Research and Outreach Unit of the university integrated into the College of Natural Sciences and the School of Architecture. The merger included the transfer to the university of the Center's 279 acres of landscapes, botanical gardens and buildings in southwest Austin and substantially all of the Center's endowment valued at $8.5 million at the time of the transfer.

The mission of the WC was: "To increase the sustainable use and conservation of native wildflowers, plants and landscapes."

The WC sought to achieve its mission by producing educational and interpretive solutions-oriented programming, complemented by demonstration gardens, research, and information and referral activities. The WC sponsored a number of national and international programs. For example, the WC's efforts included collecting seeds for the Millennium Seed Bank, restoring landscapes for corporate and governmental clients, and research into green roofs and urban ecology.

Key goals of the WC were to: (1) establish the WC as the most recognized and effective voice for native wildflowers, plants and landscapes; (2) build the WC's reputation for research on native wildflowers, plants and land restoration; (3) realize the potential of the WC's site and facilities, increase public and governmental demand for and access to native plant material; and, (4) ensure the WC's long-term stability. The WC's educational and advocacy programs were designed to encourage people to become familiar with their native flora and to understand the role of native plants in their local ecology.

The WC's headquarters was located at 4801 La Crosse Avenue, in southwest Austin, Texas and was opened in 1995. The facility included a native plant botanical garden with natural areas, auditorium and other meeting rooms, research facilities, a Visitors Gallery, café, gift shop, administrative offices, and an observation tower all designed to harmonize with the local ecosystem (see Exhibit 3.1.1 map). A full-time staff of 40 directed the WC's operations supported by a local volunteer force of over 400. The WC had 12,000 members worldwide and approximately 100,000 visitors annually.

As a self-sustaining component of The University of Texas, funding was derived from membership dues, entrance fees, foundation and corporate funding, gift store and café sales plus facility rentals. While a major portion of the WC's budget was supported by revenue from admissions, sales, rentals, consulting, and other services; the WC's operations were also heavily supported by donations and charitable gifts. Additional support for specific program initiatives was secured from foundations, corporations, government agencies, and individuals.

Exhibit 3.1.2 presents data on the number of visitors to the Center by months for the past two years. Note that these data are consistent with the well-established pattern of a heavy concentration of visitors in the spring.

---

[6]This case was written by John H. Murphy, The University of Texas at Austin. The case is designed to serve as the basis for classroom discussion and not to illustrate either the effective or ineffective handling of an administrative situation. The case is used with permission granted by Lady Bird Johnson Wildflower Center.

Exhibit 3.1.1 ■ Map of Wildflower Center

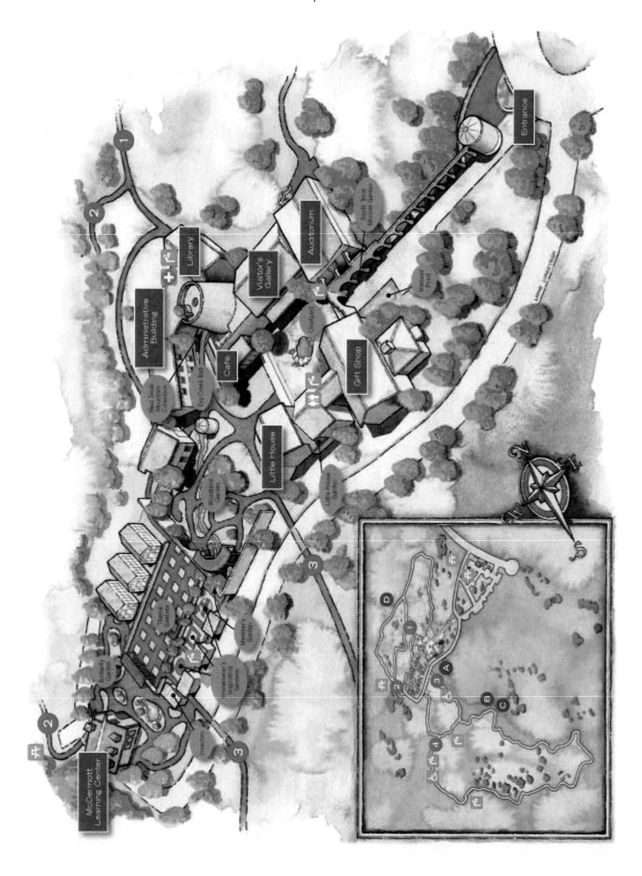

Exhibit 3.1.2 ■ Visitors Monthly Summary Report by Visitor Type (Rate Level)

	Last Year								
Month	Adult Visitors	Senior Visitors	Student Visitors	Child Visitors	Adult Tour Visitors	Youth Tour Visitors	Facility Rental Visitors	Workshop Visitors	Total Visitors
September	2,064	648	142	541	97	226	1,567	467	5,752
October	4,107	1,123	179	1,307	93	322	1,867	220	9,218
November	1,581	440	96	414	68	522	1,836	39	4,996
December	3,353	386	233	1,308	33	40	555		5,908
January	1,240	73	96	302	20	68	677	53	2,529
February	934	411	82	148		132	1,519	205	3,431
March	6,438	2,606	735	1,600	443	1,249	1,072	860	15,003
April	12,294	5,098	678	2,588	1,476	1,593	1,618	145	25,490
May	4,620	1,962	467	677	373	1,835	1,727	86	11,747
June	1,623	585	164	277	44	621	1,091	289	4,694
July	3,401	739	339	1,556		378	1,048		7,461
August	1,138	334	136	304	162	82	1,457		3,613
Grand Total	42,793	14,405	3,347	11,022	2,809	7,068	16,034	2,364	99,842

	Year Before Last								
Month	Adult Visitors	Senior Visitors	Student Visitors	Year Before Last	Adult Tour Visitors	Youth Tour Visitors	Facility Rental Visitors	Workshop Visitors	Total Visitors
September	3,403	580	292	1,606		387	930	143	7,341
October	4,155	914	174	1,457	111	1,373	1,445	167	9,796
November	1,556	395	86	557	20	980	1,044	77	4,715
December	1,501	513	129	491		8	586	41	3,269
January	1,249	70	64	87	42		655	106	2,273
February	602	166	36	107	77	128	1,302	110	2,528
March	5,212	2,040	486	1,361	155	833	275	246	10,608
April	9,552	4,495	833	2,067	812	2,562	1,233	438	21,992
May	6,578	1,704	479	685	677	740	2,347	64	13,274
June	1,787	593	208	351	253	616	1,840	207	5,855
July	3,675	605	300	968	27	219	1,081	33	6,908
August	1,398	574	168	297	25	63	1,614	7	4,146
Grand Total	40,668	12,649	3,255	10,034	2,199	7,909	14,352	1,639	92,705

CURRENT MARKETING INITIATIVES AND PROGRAMS

Recently, the WC took a number of integrated steps to strengthen its brand. A new logo was approved and this was integrated across letterhead stationary, business cards, and news releases. Further, a new color and design palette was adopted. These were chosen to reflect the energy and movement of the WC and the colors were botanically inspired. The new color and design palette were also reflected in new posters, bookmarks and notepads used to promote the WC and programs.

In addition, electronic and print templates were developed to standardize the WC's personality across media. All new collateral and a website redesign were also coordinated to reflect the new look and feel. Navigation was streamlined on the website and the size of the site was reduced from 250 page views to 55. New website features were added, including an interactive map, downloadable pages and a number of new user-friendly features. As a result, the website (www.wildflower.org) had experienced a strong increase in traffic with daily visits averaging 7,800 per day. In the past year over 2.4 million unique users have accessed millions of pages of information.

The WC's public relations efforts paid handsome benefits. For example, print coverage in the first six months of this year exceeded the previous year by 40%. The WC had consistently received wide coverage by newspapers and magazines across the country. Local electronic media were generous in their coverage and promotion of the WC.

Last year, the WC received sponsorship in local media valued at over $100,000. Local media partners included KVUE (ABC TV affiliate), KLBJ (radio), KGSR (radio), Majic 95.5 (radio), the *American-Statesman*, KUT (radio), and *Texas Highways*. In addition, the WC placed paid ads in *Texas Monthly*, as well as the *American-Statesman*, the *Austin Chronicle, Texas Highways* and radio station KUT.

The WC made extensive use of direct mail to recruit and retain members. Exhibit 3.1.3 presents selected panels from a brochure that was used as part of a package in member acquisition direct mail programs. The Center also distributed over 50,000 rack cards each year in hotels, motels and tourist offices in Central and South Texas, San Antonio, and parts of Houston and Dallas. See Exhibit 3.1.4 for an example of one of these rack cards.

Finally, the Center marketed selected facilities as an exclusive location for weddings, meetings and special events. Exhibit 3.1.5 lists the rooms available, their size and seating capacity, and rental fee per day.

LOOKING AHEAD

As she reviewed the WC's current marketing activities and began planning for the next calendar year, Ms. Saralee Tiede, Director of Communications, felt that the first order of business was to prioritize the WC's marketing efforts and establish objectives for key programs during the coming year. Then she could turn her attention to deciding which promotional tools should be applied and what mix to fashion to most effectively accomplish the tasks required.

Ms. Tiede's overall task was to develop a complete integrated marketing communication plan for the WC for the next fiscal year (September 1 through August 31). The overall marketing communication appropriation for next year had already been set at $350,000. This amount was to cover all expenses except staff salaries. Note that cost efficiency was a major concern in operating the WC and Ms. Tiede must be able to illustrate the cost effectiveness of all her recommendations.

Importantly, the overall plan was to be designed to facilitate increases in daily visitors, program attendance, membership dues revenue, donations from both individuals and corporations, sales at the store and café, and facilities rental. Ms. Tiede would need to suggest appropriate targeted increases to be achieved in each of these areas.

Exhibit 3.1.3a ■ Brochure Soliciting New Members

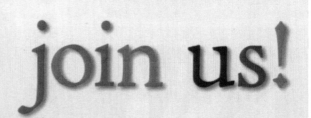

CONTACT US

CALL
512.232.0200, Ext. 163 or 137 Monday – Friday, 8 a.m. until 5 p.m.
If you leave a message after hours, we'll get back to you promptly.

VISIT
Memberships may be purchased on-site during regular Center hours.

MAIL
Please fill out and mail the form on the reverse to:
Lady Bird Johnson Wildflower Center • Membership Department
4801 La Crosse Ave. • Austin, TX 78739

FAX
Please fill out and fax the form on the reverse to 512.232.0156.

ONLINE
Convenient 24-hour ordering at www.wildflower.org

YOUR INVITATION TO MEMBERSHIP

join us!

With your support, we can increase the
sustainable use and conservation of native
wildflowers, plants and landscapes

HOURS TUESDAY – SATURDAY, 9 a.m. TO 5:30 p.m.
SUNDAY, NOON TO 5:30 p.m.
OPEN DAILY EACH SPRING

4801 LA CROSSE AVENUE • AUSTIN, TEXAS 78739
512.232.0200 • WWW.WILDFLOWER.ORG
MEMBER@WILDFLOWER.ORG

Printed on recycled paper. ©2007 Lady Bird Johnson Wildflower Center

AUSTIN, TEXAS • WWW.WILDFLOWER.ORG

Exhibit 3.1.3b

Levels

INDIVIDUAL
For one person, this membership includes
all the Membership Benefits for one Member. — $40
Senior (60 and older) Individual option — $30
Student (with valid ID) Individual option — $30

DUAL
For two people, this membership includes all the
Membership Benefits for a Member, plus a spouse or guest. — $50
Senior (60 and older) Dual option — $38

FAMILY
For families with up to two adults and all children
under 18 living in the same household, or visiting
grandchildren under 18, this membership includes
all the Membership Benefits plus children are eligible
to join our fun and educational EcoExplorers Club at
50 percent off the regular rate. — $65

SUPPORTER
This membership includes all the Membership Benefits
of the Family level, plus free admission for two additional
guests each time you visit the Wildflower Center. You
will also receive invitations to special events and
members-only exhibit openings. — $100

CONTRIBUTOR
This membership includes all the Membership Benefits
listed above plus free admission for two additional guests
each time you visit the Wildflower Center (total of four).
It also includes two free wristbands to the annual
Gardens on Tour event ($50 value). — $250

SUSTAINER
This membership includes all the Membership Benefits
listed above, plus: recognition in *Wildflower* magazine,
free admission for two additional guests each time you
visit the Wildflower Center (total of six) and an invitation
to our Annual Gala. — $500

CHAMPION
This leadership level membership includes all the
Membership Benefits listed above and you will be
recognized at the Champion Level. — $1000

YES! I want to make a difference!

Name to appear on membership card (MR./MRS./MS./MISS/DR.)
_____

2nd name on card (for Dual level and higher) (MR./MRS./MS./MISS/DR.)
_____

Address _____

City/State/Zip _____

Phone (_____) _____

E-Mail _____

If gift membership, please complete the donor information
below and we will notify the recipient of your gift.

Donor name (MR./MRS./MS./MISS/DR.)
_____

Address _____

City/State/Zip _____

Phone (_____) _____

E-Mail _____

ANNUAL MEMBER LEVEL & DUES
○ $40 Individual
○ $30 Student
○ $30 Senior
○ $38 Senior Dual
○ $50 Dual
○ $65 Family
○ $100 Supporter
○ $250 Contributor
○ $500 Sustainer
○ $1,000 Champion

MEMBERSHIP TYPE
○ New Membership
○ Renewal/Rejoin
○ Gift Membership

Membership Dues $ _____

Additional Contribution $ _____

Total Amount Enclosed $ _____

○ Check/Money Order (payable to Wildflower Center)
○ MasterCard ○ Visa ○ Discover ○ American Express

Card Number _____

Expires _____ Name on Card _____

Signature _____

The Wildflower Center occasionally shares its mailing lists with other worthy organizations. Please check here ○ to exclude your name. (The Center does not share phone numbers or e-mail addresses.) Memberships are good for one year from time of purchase. Memberships are non-transferable. Photo ID may be required. Please allow two to three weeks for receipt of your personalized membership card. Tax information will be mailed separately.

We appreciate your support of the Lady Bird Johnson Wildflower Center.
We look forward to welcoming you as a member!

Exhibit 3.1.4 ■ Representative Rack Card

Exhibit 3.1.5 ■ List of Rental Facilities

PREFERRED PROFESSIONALS

The Lady Bird Johnson Wildflower Center strongly encourages utilization of the following professionals for your upcoming event. Superior in their fields, these industry experts have been hand-selected to compliment and enhance your occasion.

Category	Company	Telephone	Website	Page
Cakes	Simon Lee Bakery	512.990.4888	www.simonleebakery.com	11
Catering	Austin Catering	512.467.8776	www.austin-catering.com	12
	Catering by Rosemary	512.443.1111	www.cateringbyrosemary.com/austin	9
	Chez DeWitt Catering	512.441.0111	www.chezdewitt.com	13
	Circle C Cafe & Catering	512.301.7235	www.circleccatering.com	10
	Creative Creations Catering	512.442.3829	www.creativecreationscatering.com	14
	Kurant Events	512.206.0610		14
	Pappasito's Catering	512.459.6438	www.pappas.com	11
	Word of Mouth Catering	512.472.9500	www.wordofmouthcatering.com	15
Event Planning	Kurant Events	512.206.0610		14
Florists	Tana's Terrains	512.301.3299	www.tanasterrains.com	12
Invitations and Stationery	Inviting Affairs	512.331.2133	www.invitingaffairs.com	12
Music • Live & DJs	Austin Wedding Jookbox	512.442.6653	www.austinweddingjookbox.com	14
Photography	aimage*	512.300.2252	www.aimage.com	11
	Brenda Ladd Photography	512.707.0070	www.brendaladdphoto.com	13
	Innovative Phtography	512.371.7778	www.innovativephotography.com	9
Rental Equipment	Austin Party Central	512.292.3900	www.austinpartycentral.com	13

This brochure was produced and published by Hawthorn Publications. No portion may be reproduced or distributed. www.hawthornpublications.com © 2005

There was also the issue of identifying target groups against which to apply promotional efforts. Ms. Tiede suspected that past efforts had too often been focused on more of a mass audience instead of more tightly defined targets. For example, given the older profile of current members, it seemed to make sense to focus some resources on attracting young, environmentally conscious, professionals age 25–34 with families. Further, in terms of increasing both visitors and members, who were the best prospects based on their geographic location and/or other factors? What strategies would be most effective in reaching these prospects?

During the coming year the WC would host a mix of themed programs (see Exhibit 3.1.6). Ms. Tiede believed that four of these programs held strong potential for attracting both new visitors and new members. These four programs were the Fall and Spring Plant Sale & Gardening Festival (October 10-11 and April 11-12); Goblins in the Garden (October 25); the Artists and Artisans Festival (March 21-22); and, the Gardens on Tour (May 9). Which of these events to promote, to whom, and how were all issues to be decided.

Many other issues also presented themselves. For example, what balance should be struck in terms of devoting time and resources to present member retention versus recruiting new members? Retaining memberships was an important priority for the WC. In the past, approximately 70% of members renewed their membership. During the coming year, Ms. Tiede would like to increase the retention rate to 75%. She wondered about what would be the best way to go about affecting this increase?

Given the many issues on her plate regarding next year plus the pressure of managing the present, ongoing programs and her staff, Ms. Tiede realized that time for planning the WC's marketing efforts for next year was in short supply.

Exhibit 3.1.6 ■ Upcoming Program Events, Next Year

Annual Public Events at the Lady Bird Johnson Wildflower Center

These events occur every year at the Wildflower Center. Look for exact dates and times on the Web site under Events a month or so before the event.

Tree Talk/Winter Walk—Learn about trees and select one or more to grow at home during our annual tree celebration and sale usually held the last Saturday in January.

Artists and Artisans Festival—This early spring event features the work of local artists and artisans, all working with a nature theme. You will find watercolors, metalwork, pottery, jewelry, photography, woodwork and more, all lovingly made by hand at our festival, usually held the second Saturday and Sunday in March.

Wildflower Days—from mid-March until April 30, the Wildflower Center is open 9 a.m. to 5:30 p.m. every day so you can see our spring wildflowers. Lots of children's activities and fun for families as they look at the bluebonnets, Indian paintbrush and dozens of other blooms.

Spring and Fall Plant Sale & Gardening Festival—The Wildflower Center has a Spring Plant Sale, usually the second weekend in April, and a Fall Plant Sale, usually the third weekend in October, when experts conduct guided tours with lots of information about native plants. A fantastic selection of thousands of flowers, shrubs and trees are available just at the right time for planting. 9 a.m. to 5 p.m. Saturday and Sunday, with a special preview day beforehand for members.

Gardens on Tour—Join us Mother's Day weekend for an exclusive look into some of Austin's most unique gardens. Gardens on Tour is an annual self-guided tour of carefully selected private landscapes and the celebrated gardens of the Lady Bird Johnson Wildflower Center.

Nature Nights—These interactive family evenings provide fun for kids while they learn about snakes, insects, birds of prey, fossils and other nature lore. Once a month in the spring and the fall and four Thursday nights in July from 6 to 9 p.m. $1 admission and a free treat for each child in the store. **The spring ones are on one Friday a month in March, April, May, and again in September, October, and November.**

Goblins in the Garden—Halloween activities for the children, when our tower is haunted and spooky places abound in our gardens. Kids should put on their costumes for a special evening. 6 to 9 p.m. the Sunday closest to Halloween.

Holiday Shopping Event—Artists and artisans offer their work for sale in the Visitors Gallery while all sorts of special gifts are available at the store. This special event will be **Friday, Saturday and Sunday,**

Luminations—Hundreds of luminarias light our garden paths, and twinkly lights light the trees as we celebrate the holidays with two free nights of music and festivities. Bring some canned goods for the Capital Area Food Bank. 6 to 9 p.m. This event is held the Saturday and Sunday before Christmas each year.

NOTE: Date of members-only events are not listed above, but are the day before the Plant Sales and Luminations dates listed above. This event is held the Saturday and Sunday before Christmas each year.

Name _____ Date _____

QUESTIONS FOR DISCUSSION AND REVIEW

1. What external factors will have the most impact on the success or failure of the programs Ms. Tiede is planning? Why? What internal factors will be most important to success? Why?

ext.- the weather - most of their events are outdoor, accessibility, competitors i.e. Blanton, economy, int.- if Tiede can manage time and budget, membership focus, staffing - full-time v. volunteers, ratio of staffers to attendees, ~~price~~

2. Which of the broad areas the plan is be designed to impact is most important to the long-term success of the WC? What about in the short-term?

long-term - member retention, branding, reputation, sponsors, ~~events~~   events
short-term - direct mail

3. Logically, where should Ms. Tiede begin in making decisions about the direction and specifics of the WC's marketing efforts for next year?

Define target markets and prioritize, ~~they know~~ ~~they who they are and how they~~ Keeping the old and getting the new
↑ social media

4. Is it realistic to attempt to allocate marketing resources without making estimates of the likely effectiveness of specific promotional tools and executions?

No. Use old numbers to project for the future. Nonprofits don't have the money to take risks.

5. What information would be most useful in planning the WC's marketing efforts for next year?

Budget, effectiveness of previous marketing efforts, what competitors are doing

6. How important is the WC's website in accomplishing the objectives for next year? How can the website be integrated most effectively across all programs and efforts?

Really important, if they're trying to target young adults, these are going to be the most web savvy, integrating an e-newsletter, hyping up events on the website

7. How might social media be employed in appealing to selected WC visitor and member prospects? Could social media be substituted for some of the current direct mail efforts?

photo contests; use social media to reach their new target market; FB, Twitter

Case 3.2

Amy's Ice Creams (A)[1]

COMPANY BACKGROUND

Company History

Amy Simmons opened her first retail ice cream store in 1984 on Guadalupe Street in Austin, Texas a few blocks north of the University of Texas campus. Over the years, Amy's expanded to 12 stores in Austin plus one in Houston (established in 1993) and one in San Antonio (established in 1997). In terms of sales, the firm had enjoyed steady growth to approximately $6.1 million in 2008 (see Exhibit 3.2.1 sales by store 2002–2008).

From it inception, Amy's had always been a free-spirited and unconventional company. While sales were an important measure of acceptance by the community, increasing sales was not the primary objective of Amy's.

The Culture of the Company

Amy's culture was central to the company's success. Much of the guiding force behind the culture was expressed in Amy's statement of "Company Philosophy and Objectives" (see Exhibit 3.2.2). As indicated in this statement of philosophy, Amy's sought not only to please customers but also to entertain them by creating an "ice cream theater." Further, see Exhibit 3.2.3, "The Theatrical Aspects of Service," for a flavor of what Amy's customers experienced during a visit.

Playful cartoon cows, used in store signage, flyers, and so on, helped to convey the fun, zany, and maybe even a tad mischievous culture of Amy's (see Exhibit 3.2.4). Further, including vintage 1950s black/white photo booths for customers' use and the practice of maintaining a collection of eclectic hats for sale inside the firm's stores expressed the good natured, off-the-wall culture of Amy's. The irreverent and somewhat chaotic Amy's website also conveyed a clear message about the firm's culture (see www.amysicecreams.com).

The recruitment and retention of individual "Scoops" (Amy's term for ice cream servers) had been one key to the firm's success. To recruit creative, fun-loving Scoops, Amy's used a paper bag job application form. Each prospective employee was given a paper bag and told to be creative. The point was to be creative and "show us what you are made of."

---

[1] This case was written by John H. Murphy, The University of Texas at Austin. The case is designed to serve as the basis for classroom discussion and not to illustrate either the effective or ineffective handling of an administrative situation. The case is used with permission granted by Amy Simmons, Founder and CEO of Amy's Ice Creams.

Exhibit 3.2.1 ■ Annual Sales by Store 2002–2008

Same store sales	2002	2003	2004	2005	2006	2007	2008
3500 Guadalupe	$556,715.44	$555,443.01	$527,335.04	$541,059.32	$470,364.03	$520,645.13	$572,709.64
Arboretum	$545,049.13	$518,711.71	$511,646.98	$507,342.74	$483,773.56	$450,900.76	$473,445.80
6th & Lamar	$457,623.50	$440,308.25	$405,151.96	$433,557.95	$432,484.76	$477,008.65	$524,709.52
Mira Vista	$165,149.65	$169,052.82	$183,036.21	$176,703.70	$187,632.65	$194,364.13	$213,800.54
Farnham Houston	$355,353.76	$409,512.86	$411,549.91	$395,482.53	$386,018.60	$414,630.69	$456,093.76
Catering	$256,795.80	$223,525.63	$237,396.23	$333,694.37	$336,600.52	$399,928.44	$439,921.28
Wholesale	$101,466.79	$154,699.23	$194,471.20	$174,351.40	$196,943.59	$217,035.03	$238,738.53
Houston Wholesale	$76,108.07	$79,493.75	$101,044.59	$112,919.28	$143,962.81	$156,574.00	$172,231.40
Quarry SA	$358,808.01	$347,195.45	$356,524.42	$344,135.84	$315,509.17	$321,355.68	$353,491.25
Westgate	$379,223.40	$378,360.77	$396,336.86	$437,370.03	$444,753.34	$417,963.49	$397,065.32
Austin Airport	$381,154.66	$381,198.14	$402,565.40	$407,694.16	$445,555.51	$480,216.74	$528,238.41
Balou's	$96,596.23						
The Wood	$179,670.76	$199,042.74	$211,162.19	$224,315.00	$210,195.90	$228,230.72	$251,053.79
South Congress	$18,900.83	$211,012.26	$249,052.53	$244,456.80	$234,649.72	$279,809.19	$307,790.11
Woodway			$132,241.15	$130,221.77	$114,216.70	$63,004.29	
Burnet				$76,895.85	$398,145.18	$431,892.84	$475,082.12
Super South				$83,823.32	$179,059.68	$194,644.19	$214,108.61
The Grove						$270,285.69	$367,314.26
Kiosk						$4,122.13	$104,000.00
Total Sales	$3,928,616.03	$4,067,556.62	$4,319,514.67	$4,624,024.06	$5,052,261.68	$5,522,611.79	$6,089,794.35

Exhibit 3.2.2 ■ Company Philosophy and Objectives

In an industry characterized by "me-too" operations, we have successfully built a unique reputation and market presence through our philosophy towards our customers and their experience at Amy's. Our goal is to consistently offer a superior product matched with a standard of service previously unimaginable from a retail ice cream shop. Our faith in the wisdom of emphasizing service can not be overstated. We have repeatedly seen evidence that it is **service first** and product second that brings customers back to our shops. Only a handful of ice cream shops across the country—and none in Texas except Amy's—have chosen to orient themselves so completely towards the customer's experience. While this philosophy may limit the company's growth potential, we believe it is a solid foundation to build our company upon.

From a simple definition to please the customer at any cost and every time, our philosophy and store concept challenges us to do more. We try not only to please people, but also to **entertain them.** We believe that beyond our product and service standards, the best thing we can do to make our shops stand out against others is to **offer the customer something unique and appealing.** A special reason to come to Amy's. This idea is rooted in our understanding of why people come to an ice cream shop in the first place. They come to treat themselves; to get away from the boredom or pressures of the home, office, or school. With this in mind, we try to make a customer's visit an occasion of sorts, with laughter, music, and an intriguing and dramatic presentation of the product. We strive to create an **"ice cream theater"** where individual flair is an important part of a production staged daily to impress and entertain our varied audiences. The dramatic aspect of our shops is never a substitute for the basic courtesies, but a complementary effort to further strengthen Amy's identity and appeal.

The company's objective is to see that our philosophy becomes our trademark. We want Amy's to become distinctly known for our unique brand and level of service. In the long run, we want people to think of Amy's when they think of ice cream, and we want them to think of ice cream more often because of us.

Never Underestimate

The Power of Ice Cream!

Ice cream is about more than just desserts!

It is part of celebrations: birthdays, anniversaries, finishing your finals, winning a game. . . .

It is part of socializing with friends: Out on a date, before you go to a party,
during movie marathons. . . .

It is part of frustration and healing: after you suffer a loss, when you've had a bad day or you just
need cheering up after your tonsils are yanked out. . . .

We are here to give our customers more than just an ice cream dessert. We are here to be a momentary or even lasting part of their lives while they celebrate, mourn, socialize, heal, blow off steam and party.

Remember that every person who walks through our doors has a story. Demand that you and your coworkers provide the highest quality product and service in a truly welcoming atmosphere. Remind your self often of Amy's Mission Statement:

To Make People's Day!!

And remember . . . Never underestimate the Power of Ice Cream!!

Exhibit 3.2.3 ■ Theatrical Aspects of Service

I began working at Amy's in March of 1985 while I was an acting major at The University. I scooped here all through college, quit (Amy's and college) and finally went back (to Amy's as the business manager and college to finish). Some 40 productions later I now have a Master in Fine Arts from Ohio University and I'm a working professional actor (Yipee). One of the most difficult things in the world is to presume to entertain people. There are some short cuts but the most important ingredient is to love what you do. When I had a neurotic bout of stage fright (for about 2 months I couldn't seem to go on stage . . . which was bad since I was doing Summer Stock in Massachusetts and opened 7 different shows in a 12 week period) one of my favorite Actors told me, **"Paige, just do it. It's not brain surgery, Have fun!"**

If you have the gift of gab and the soul of a ham, you'll get great reviews during your run at Amy's. Not everyone is naturally hammy so don't worry. If you're an introvert, be courteous and polite and let the extroverts handle it. Some things to remember if you put on a show:

1. **Work as much of the crown as you can.** In the theater we say "Play to the back of the house. Make whatever you're doing carry to the back row". Don't leave them out. They paid the price of a ticket, they deserve to see the show. The customer shouldn't be waiting for something to happen, their experience starts when they walk in the door. Also: you will save yourself some time if you get them thinking about what they want to taste and what the process is.
2. **Know your audience.** Kids are different from teenagers who are different from college coeds who are different from senior citizens. Be sensitive. The show changes depending on who is out there. Even the same script has different peaks and valleys each time you do it. Remember: Theater is interactive while film is not. Theater is a live, changing, spontaneous, a participatory event; it demands that someone watch it and your performance grows and shifts depending on how they react. A film runs the same each time whether anyone is watching or not. You want the audience to enjoy your work and feel included. You need the audience. If they don't come to the theater, if they don't tell friends, "it was a great show go see it", the show will close and so will the theater. Don't act in a void. Play to them.
3. **Talk and Listen.** Actors must work with and off each other. We say, "Don't drop the ball". Work with each other to keep the show going and moving. LISTEN to each other. LISTEN to the audience. Hold a moment for laughs but don't anticipate them. Just as the laughter peaks and begins to die- come in with your next line.
4. **Always leave them wanting more.** Don't overstay your welcome. Don't drag moments out expecting laughter or applause. Don't push your performance, it should fall out of you easily and naturally. Know when to move on- when to speed up and get 'em out of there.
5. **Don't let them get ahead of you.** Comedy is about timing and speed. If they see the joke coming it's not funny. Stay one step ahead of the game.
6. **Finally:** An interviewer once asked Spencer Tracy what he did to prepare, how did he give such great performances? He said,

"Know your lines and don't bump into the furniture."

Exhibit 3.2.4 ■ Amy's Cartoon Cows

Mission Statement

Amy's overall mission was: "To make people's day!" The company's goals are explained in the following quote:

> *"Our purpose and objective at Amy's Ice Creams is to consistently offer a superior product matched with a standard of service previously unimaginable from a retail ice cream shop.*
>
> - *Objectives:*
>   - *Play a leadership role:*
>   - *In our community*
>   - *In education*
>   - *In support of charitable organizations*
>   - *Have a positive impact on each individual with whom we come into contact, from employees to customers and suppliers to other businesses and job applicants to the mailman.*
>   - *Provide a positive, rewarding and educational work environment for our employees.*
>   - *Support small business as a major force in our economy by forming cooperative alliances with other small businesses and by educating others on issues confronting small businesses.*
> - *Focus on continual growth and improvement while providing a reasonable return to our investors.*
>
> *If you understand the mission statement and these basic objectives that are at the base of everything we do, it will simplify everything else. It is vital to the survival of this company that you have a clear idea of our priorities. When you understand them, it will make problem solving easier, despite busy shifts or other circumstances."*

The Product

The foundation of Amy's success was the product. Amy's produced all of their ice cream in a small plant in north central Austin. Through a long-term agreement with a dairy in north Texas, Amy's had a source of high-quality cream for use in making her ice cream.

Amy's ice cream was available in a wide range of flavors that tasted great and were made with 14% butter-fat. Further, Amy's offered a wide range of "Crush-Ns" (e.g., gingersnaps, M&Ms, etc.) that the Scoops could use to mix custom creations on the spot. Amy's also offered hundreds of flavors. The most popular flavors were Mexican Vanilla, Belgian Chocolate, Just Vanilla, Sweet Cream, Cinnamon, Strawberry, and Oreo.

All of Amy's stores carried seven standards flavors: Sweet Cream, Just Vanilla, Mexican Vanilla, Belgian Chocolate, Dark Chocolate, Coffee, and White Chocolate. Other flavors were offered seasonally and based on demand at the individual store level. Other featured products included malts, shakes, banana splits and fruit smoothies.

AMY'S MARKETING EFFORTS

Amy's marketing philosophy and strategy was to spend no money on advertising. Amy's believed in investing dollars to sponsor and participate in local events and charities rather than using traditional advertising. The company preferred tactics like event sponsorship and guerrilla marketing to conventional marketing because it fit the ethos of the firm and its unconventional style.

Part of Amy's marketing strategy centered on working at the community and neighborhood-level in stimulating customer allegiance. Amy Simmons' view was captured in the quote, "The community is us and we are the community." For example, annually Amy's donated 20% of all sales for one day to the Health Alliance for Austin Musicians (HAAM). The mission of HAAM was to provide access to affordable health care for Austin's low-income, uninsured musicians, focusing on prevention and wellness.

Another example of Amy's grassroots approach to marketing was the firm's support and presence each July 4th in Independence Day parades in the following neighborhoods: Allendale, Travis Heights, and Westlake. The firm sent one of their three SWAT trucks (see Exhibit 3.2.5) to be in each parade and served as the focal point for distributing free ice cream. This participation was reflective of Amy's desire to connect with their customers on a neighborhood level.

Cause marketing and partnering with local nonprofits was a key component in enhancing Amy's reputation as a good member of the community. For example, Amy's partnered with the Central Texas Blood and Tissue Center by offering a free pint of their ice cream to each donor for each pint of blood donated. This offer was promoted in PSA (public service announcements) television commercials produced and run by the Tissue Center. Amy's also recently sponsored a fund-raising event, "Home Fur the Holidays," to benefit Austin's Town Lake Animal Shelter. Amy's supplied ice cream and entertainment at the fund-raising event plus matched all monetary donations.

Amy's philanthropy also supported cancer treatment for kids at Dell Children's Hospital. Amy's donated $25,000 to outfit one of the treatment rooms with medical equipment. Amy's also decorated the room with fun murals featuring their signature cartoon cows. In addition, Amy's committed to supply free ice cream forever at the Dell Children's Hospital.

Publicity via free media coverage had been a staple of Amy's marketing success. Amy's had been featured in numerous articles in the media. The list of newspapers and magazines that have featured the company over the years was most impressive and included the *Wall Street Journal,* the *Dallas Morning News,* the *Austin American-Statesman,* the *New York Times, Texas Monthly, Entrepreneur, Austin Monthly, Inc., Forbes,* the *Austin Business Journal, Southern Living,* and *People.*

FUTURE MARKETING EFFORTS

As Teresa Noll, Amy's Operations Manager and in charge of marketing, began to plan for the upcoming year, she faced some interesting general questions. She wondered what promotional efforts would be most appropriate for marketing Amy's? In continuing and extending past policies, what local events and causes should

Exhibit 3.2.5 ■ Amy's SWAT Van

Amy's choose to support and at what level? What new partnerships and joint marketing efforts would make sense, given Amy's preference for local affiliations? How might social networks, viral marketing, and the firm's website be most effectively incorporated into the firm's marketing efforts?

As Ms. Noll considered these and other related issues, she noted that three specific areas needed special attention during the upcoming fiscal year. These areas were (1) how to increase winter seasonal sales; (2) how to increase on-line merchandise sales; and, (3) the planning of an annual reunion event honoring Amy's Scoops past and present plus celebrating the firm's contributions to the local community.

Winter Seasonal Sales

In devising marketing plans for increasing ice cream sales during the slow winter months of January, February, and March when volume was off about 50%, Amy's had decided not to add hot coffee, hot chocolate or other beverages to the product mix in the winter months. An example of a recently introduced promotion that had been successful in stimulating winter sales was Amy's Valentine's Day promotion. For Valentine's, Amy's offered chocolate covered strawberries. In the first year the promotion generated $67,000 in sales of strawberries. In year three, sales had expanded to $125,000 and the promotion would be continued as long as it proved to be popular.

On-line Merchandise Sales

Regarding on-line merchandise sales, Amy's carried t-shirts, Mexican bags, candles, and gift certificates that were offered for sale on their website. Sales seemed well below potential on these items, and the company was open to adding other merchandise that fit Amy's culture and might be added profitably to the current mix. This, of course, also raised the issue of how to increase the number of visitors to Amy's website.

Reunion Event

In planning for the event and party, Amy Simmons was anxious to design a celebration that focused on all Scoops who had worked at Amy's over the years. It was important that the event and any attendant activities be designed to attract the widest attendance/participation by present and former Scoops. One of the central elements of the celebration was to be a social network page keyed to the event.

Past records indicated that approximately 3,000 individuals had worked as Amy's Scoops for at least three months. Of this group, Amy's had e-mail and mailing addresses for 500. Based on past reunion events, it was anticipated that approximately 500 people would attend the event. Therefore, a venue for this number would need to be selected, a band(s) contracted with to play at the event, invitations and party favors designed, catering plans solidified, and so on.

An integral part of both the promotion of and exposure of the reunion event to the general public would be free media coverage of the event. Ms. Noll wondered how Amy's might most effectively garner maximum media coverage building up to and following this event.

Name _____   Date _____

QUESTIONS FOR DISCUSSION AND REVIEW

1. Given Amy's zany, off-the-wall persona plus the firm's philosophy of marketing and no advertising policy, what elements of the brand's promotion mix should play featured roles in future marketing efforts?

2. Is implementation, or the specifics of how promotional tools are used, more important than which tools are used?

3. What insights can be deduced about the likely demographics and psychographics of Amy's loyal, core customer base?

4. How important has Amy's refusal to use traditional marketing techniques been in defining the firm's image? In developing a loyal, hard-core customer base?

5. What would be the likely impact or effect of Amy's launching a high-profile, traditional advertising campaign on Amy's brand image among members of the local community? Among hard-core loyalists?

Case 3.3

The Home Depot: Eco Options Program[1]

BACKGROUND INFORMATION

The Home Depot's (THD) Eco Options program (EO) was started in their Canadian stores in 2004. The EO program was launched in the United States on Earth Day 2007. EO offered thousands of environmentally preferred products, and it provided information on how to conduct more Earth-friendly projects. Products were included in the program when they meet at least one of the following strict criteria, as certified by an independent third party: support of sustainable forestry practices, reduced energy usage, healthier homes, cleaner air, and cleaner water. Examples of such products included no VOC and low-VOC (volatile organic compound) paints, environmentally preferred cleaners, ENERGY STAR®-qualified products, WaterSense®-labeled bath fixtures, organic plant food, etc. The objectives of the EO program were (1) to empower and inspire customers to make a difference; and, (2) to position THD as an environmental leader and a socially responsible company.

POSITIONING STATEMENT

The Home Depot's Eco Options program is an easy way for people to help the environment and to save money on their monthly energy bills.

ECO OPTIONS TARGET MARKET

Clearly, some people did not place a high priority on either environmentally sustainable products or green home improvements. These people may have believed, for example, that global warming was a nonissue, or they were struggling just to pay their mortgage or medical bills and simply could not make the environment a financial priority. The EO program was irrelevant for this group and would not motivate them to shop at THD.

Other people bought compact fluorescent light bulbs (CFLs), ENERGY STAR appliances, and WaterSense bath products; however, they were concerned primarily with saving money on their energy bills month-after-month. To be sure, they saw reducing their environmental impact as a bonus, but the practical money-saving aspect was the primary reason they bought these products.

In contrast, another group of people were super green. They were genuinely concerned about the environment, and they engaged in a wide variety of ecoconscious activities—from organic composting to using reusable grocery bags to making energy-efficient home improvements. They had demonstrated a willingness to pay more for green products, not because it made sense for their wallet but because it made sense for the future of the planet.

THD EO program was targeted to the mass of customers who are somewhere between those who had no desire to be more green and those who constantly look for ways to reduce their impact on the environment. The EO program target was defined as people who would like to do the right thing for the environment but aren't willing to sacrifice or go out of their way too much to do so.

---

[1]This case was written by Katey Porter-Baumgarten and Chris Fedorczak, The Richards Group. The case is designed to serve as the basis for classroom discussion and not to illustrate either the effective or ineffective handling of an administrative situation. Used by permission of The Home Depot.

MARKETING EFFORTS SUPPORTING THE ECO OPTIONS PROGRAM

THD used a broad range of communication touchpoints to make it easy for the target to learn about the Eco Options program. THD had chosen not to invest in purely green vehicles (e.g., *Living Green* magazine), since that would be too out of reach for the target.

The mix of advertising, promotions, videos, and events on behalf of the EO program used the themeline "Save green. Live green." Included in the mix were the following: TV spots on national television; radio (see Exhibit 3.3.1); branded content developed in a partnership with Ed Begley, Jr. who produced a TV show and four online workshops (for example, "Compost with Ed"); advertising in consumer (see Exhibit 3.3.2) and trade magazines; public relations efforts that resulted in features on the EO program on numerous top news shows; successful Earth Day promotions; plus, online advertising and a microsite devoted to the program (see Exhibit 3.3.3). In addition, the EO program had received considerable support in stores with signage; entrance banners; and, Muzak (in-store) announcements (see Exhibit 3.3.4).

THE CHALLENGE

The EO program had the potential to be a robust, differentiating initiative that helped people easily identify products that have less impact on the environment. However, despite a substantial investment, general awareness and understanding of the program was low. The EO program was unique in the home improvement category, and it was an exclusive to THD, yet research revealed that consumers did not think that THD was any more or less committed to protecting the environment than its competitors. The EO program needed fresh, new approaches to put the spotlight back on the program.

Management believed that the under potential performance of the EO program was, at least in part, a targeting issue. As described above, the EO program had targeted a broad customer base of mainstream consumers who wanted to do the right thing for the environment in their day-to-day lives but are not willing to inconvenience themselves too much. However, this broad audience was expensive to reach with traditional media—and was unlikely to be reached effectively with modest budgets.

Therefore, management felt that what was needed was a new, and most likely tighter, definition of who the best prospects for the EO program were. Once the target audience(s) was identified, a much more efficient and effective communications plan that repositioned the program to the new target(s) could be developed.

The new overall plan should be designed against a new target(s) to: (1) increase awareness of the EO program in a cost-effective manner; (2) raise overall understanding of the EO program; (3) help THD get recognition for its environmental efforts; (4) differentiate THD from other environmental programs; and, (5) fit under the umbrella of the overall "More saving. More doing." tagline.

Exhibit 3.3.1 ■ Radio Commercial "Seed Bogo" (:30) Promoting the Eco Options Program

MUSIC OPEN AND UNDER. ANNOUNCER: "Right now at The Home Depot all seed packets are buy-one-get-one-free. You can grow a bounty of fresh vegetables saving you a bundle at the grocery store. Plus The Home Depot has organic seeds that are part of our Eco Options program. So, you save green and live green. It all starts with seed packets two-for-the-price-of-one. More saving. More doing. That's the power of The Home Depot. Offer valid through April 25 in U.S. only, while supplies last. See stores for details."

Exhibit 3.3.2 ■ Eco Options Consumer Magazine Advertisement

Improve your home. And the environment.

From hundreds of ENERGY STAR®-qualified appliances to compact fluorescent bulbs to environmentally preferred cleaners, the exclusive Eco Options® program at  The Home Depot® has thousands of ideas and products that make it easier for you to do your part for the environment. When it comes to thinking green, go orange.

© 2008 HOMER TLC, Inc. All rights reserved.

homedepot.com/ecooptions

Exhibit 3.3.3 ■ Eco Options Microsite

Exhibit 3.3.4 ■ Muzak In-Store Announcements Promoting the Eco Options Program

ANNOUNCER: "If you are looking for easy ways to improve your home and the environment, check out our Eco Options products. They have less impact than conventional products and can help save money, energy, and water while doing something good for the environment. Ask an Associate for details. The Home Depot. More saving. More doing."

QUESTIONS FOR DISCUSSION AND REVIEW

1. What factors play the most important role in identifying the target audience(s) for a re-energized EO program?

2. How could secondary research profiling two groups: Do-it-Yourself (DIY) consumers and green consumers be combined to provide insights into the most productive ways of segmenting prospects for THD EO program?

3. Realizing that people buy green for different reasons (if at all), what kind of people would find the Eco Options program relevant and compelling? What is their day-to-day routine like? Why are they concerned about the environment? What are the most powerful triggers that might attract them to the THD's EO program?

4. Would examining the purchase cycle for several environmentally friendly product categories potentially be useful in segmenting the market for the EO program? If so, how?

Part II
Advertising Management Decision Making

The emergence of new forms of marketing communication to supplement, and in some cases replace, off-line advertising has reshaped IBP over the past decade. For example, social media, viral and search engine marketing, and other forms of Web-based communications have provided brands with important contact points with consumers. In addition, public relations has emerged as a more effective brand builder in an increasingly rich and fragmented media environment.

Despite these sea changes in the IBP environment, off- and on-line advertising continues to be the single most important component in many consumer and retail brands' communication mixes. The five chapters in this section of the book focus on the development of effective advertising strategies and tactics plus the integration of advertising with other elements in the marketer's IBP mix.

The sequence of chapters in this section of the book follow the order in which these tasks should be addressed by management in planning an IBP campaign. Chapter 4 focuses on advertising and IBP research and briefly examines some of the research approaches that can be useful in building effective strategies. Chapter 5 focuses on establishing objectives for the overall IBP program within which advertising or other mix elements may play the dominant role. In Chapter 6, the task of deciding on the overall IBP investment or appropriation is examined along with budgeting issues. Chapter 7 examines the development of an effective creative strategy brief to guide all IBP efforts, and Chapter 8 introduces the critical task of identifying the most appropriate media strategies for delivering the brand's marketing messages.

Chapter 4
Advertising Research

Advertising people who ignore research are as dangerous as generals who ignore decodes of enemy signals.[1]—*David Ogilvy*

The objective of this chapter is to (1) emphasize the potential value of research in all areas of advertising decision making and identify some of the most widely used research techniques; (2) discuss the use of secondary sources; and (3) briefly examine basic considerations in assessing the validity of focus group research.

This chapter emphasizes the use of secondary and focus group research for three reasons. First, secondary and focus group research are widely used forms of advertising research. Second, as the cost of conducting primary research increases and access to and richness of secondary information also increases, secondary research will grow in importance. Third, a discussion of primary research techniques is beyond the managerial scope of this text.

THE ROLE, SCOPE, AND SIGNIFICANCE OF ADVERTISING RESEARCH

The potential value of research-generated information to decision making in all areas of advertising and marketing communication management is substantial. Information generated through research provides decision makers with the power to make better decisions.

Raymond stresses that research information is useful in making more intelligent decisions in all areas of advertising. He suggests that the six key areas of advertising where research information is useful are as follows:

- What to say?   (Theme, copy platform)
- To whom?   (Target audience)
- How to say it?   (Copy, execution)
- How often?   (Frequency)
- Where?   (Media exposure)
- How much to invest? (Budget)[2]

In addition to these six areas, research should be used to evaluate the effectiveness of the firm's advertising. As discussed in Chapter 5, by specifying specific, measurable objectives, the planner enables an assessment of the impact of an

---

[1] David Ogilvy, *Ogilvy on Advertising* (New York: Crown Publishers, 1983), 158.

[2] Charles Raymond, *Advertising Research: The State of the Art* (New York: Association of National Advertisers, 1976), 3.

advertisement or an advertising campaign. As stressed in that chapter, in most product/market situations, advertising can be more appropriately evaluated by measuring its effectiveness against communication objectives rather than sales objectives.

At the same time, research information should be viewed as an aid to decision making and *not* a substitute for judgment. It is unrealistic to expect research findings to make decisions. The findings of even the best designed and conducted survey, test market, or experiment requires interpretation. Often the data and resulting recommendations do *not* clearly indicate which course of action is most appropriate.

Exhibit 1 identifies a cross section of sources of advertising research information. The exhibit is organized into two sections: secondary data and primary data. The top portion of this exhibit cites several examples of secondary sources. As a rule, primary data collection should be considered only after a thorough search of existing secondary sources has been conducted. Typically, valuable insights into a problem or issue can be developed based on secondary information. Or secondary data can be used to shape the extent and type of primary research ultimately conducted.

Exhibit 1 ■ Examples of Sources of Advertising Research Information

---

Secondary Sources

Examples of secondary research include information obtained from published sources such as the trade and popular press; the firm's internal accounting records; U.S. Bureau of the Census and other U.S. government reports; *Sales & Marketing Management's Survey of Buying Power,* commercial suppliers such as Simmons Market Research Bureau (SMRB) volumes and Mediamark Research, Inc. (MRI); and reports and studies conducted by trade associations.

Primary Sources

Survey Research: measures of target consumers' levels of recall, knowledge, and attitudes and/or other information gathered using a representative sample and structured questionnaire. Conducted by the firm or research suppliers on a project basis.

Qualitative Research

- Focus groups—qualitative data are obtained through informal discussion of the topics of interest led by a moderator. Typically eight to twelve consumers are guided through a discussion outline during an approximately two-hour session.
- Depth interview—one-on-one interview using unstructured probes of underlying motivations.
- Projective techniques—means of tapping underlying feelings through projection situations.

Experimentation: research studies that attempt to demonstrate causation.

- Experimental designs—various plans for controlling conditions related to an experiment.
- Test markets—use of comparable markets to test different levels of exposure to variables of interest.

Laboratory Measures: examination of responses to stimuli under controlled conditions.

- Eye camera—device used to determine what attracts attention, layout impact, etc.
- Tachistoscope—device that varies exposure time of ad to audience and notes what they can identify.

Syndicated Services

- Burke Day-After-Recall—telephone interviews to evaluate TV commercials' impact.
- Starch Readership Studies—in-home interviews to determine impact of print ads.
- Tele-Research, Inc.—service that uses shoppers and forced exposure ads, tracks coupon redemption.
- Gallup-Robinson Impact Test—test that measures ad recall among magazine readers the next day.
- Nielsen Net Ratings—monitors and measures more than 90% of global Internet activity and provides insights about the online universe, including audiences, advertising, video, e-commerce and consumer behavior

Sales Results

- Internal company records.
- Selling Areas Marketing, Inc. (SAMI) warehouse product movement data.
- BehaviorScan—split cable TV exposure to commercials linked to brand sales using UPC data from supermarket data link.

Six major sources of primary data are identified: survey research, qualitative research, experimentation, laboratory measures, syndicated services, and sales results. Exhibit 1 includes a brief description of a wide representative range of advertising research techniques. The sources indicated in this exhibit illustrate the diverse range of research approaches available to the planner.

Although the design, execution, and report writing involved in primary research projects is typically completed by research specialists, the communication manager must exercise sound judgment in applying recommendations based on research. The manager must avoid blindly accepting data or conclusions suggested by research specialists. Healthy skepticism is often a valuable management trait.

In assessing the validity of a primary research project, management should evaluate a number of factors. For example, in reviewing a survey, the size and composition of the survey sample used must be evaluated. Further, the data collection instrument, measurement scaling, and nonsampling error all must be considered. For a thorough discussion of the basic considerations to be used in evaluating primary research projects, see the texts cited in the "Suggested Readings" at the end of this chapter.

The remainder of this chapter examines the importance and application of secondary and focus group research. Advertising and marketing communication managers need to have a solid understanding of these two valuable and widely used sources of advertising planning information. The material presented on each of these techniques is intended to inform and stimulate the reader to learn more about these important information sources.

TRENDS IN ONLINE RESEARCH

With the tremendous growth of the Internet and social networking, it is no surprise that online polls and surveys using volunteer panels have grown as well. This type of online survey/research is very cost-effective and fast. However, there are some limitations that a good researcher should know about before using this methodology.

Research has shown that panelists' main motivation is earning money for doing a survey.[3] Many times there are differences in results using the same research question when compared to a traditional one-on-one interview versus an online panel. In traditional research, respondents have felt that their opinion is very important. When doing an online survey, Sparrow's research finds that with most online surveys, there is no consequence for the respondent to take a very casual attitude to answering questions.

It's evident, by the volume on online research conducted, that this methodology is not going away. In addition, research vendors have "sold" this type of research as inexpensive and faster than traditional research methods. But, it is important to conduct the research with sound methods so the results are valid.

Sparrow suggests the following:

- Make sure respondents spend at least as much time doing the survey as they would in an interview type survey.
- Introduce simple check questions to catch respondents who give contradictory answers.
- Devise on-screen layouts that engage the respondents—not ones that may make the person answer a certain way because of the way the survey is set up.

It is not uncommon today for companies to use social networking sites, like Facebook, to ask their "friends" and "fans" research questions. Just visit your favorite store on Facebook, and you will see a wealth of information that their most loyal customers share—both positive and negative—about the company's products and/or services in the marketplace.

Schillewaert, De Ruyck, and Verhaeghe call this area "connected research." Their definition includes[4]

1. It is an added tool to research that must serve a purpose.
2. The tool set needs to keep up with current *Web x.0 technologies.*
3. Allows learning from social dynamics between participants—instead of "respondents" we have "participants"—it's more *equal, participative,* and *bottom-up* than traditional research methods.

As the authors note, for the first time in history, technology seems to allow everyone to have a voice. As mentioned earlier, it is very low cost and can be done very quickly.

There are both secondary and primary research tools online. Some primary methods include online chat groups, bulletin boards and forums, and research blogs, to name a few. Secondary examples include social networks (like the Facebook example), user forums and chat rooms, mailing lists and e-groups, and natural wikis. This area of research will continue to grow, and it is important that advertising and public relations researchers keep up with the changes and make sure there is a clear understanding of the research validity and limitations.

---

[3]Nick Sparrow, "Quality Issues in Online Research," *Journal of Advertising Research* 47 (June 2007): 179–182.

[4]Niels Schillewaert, Tom De Ruyck, and Annelies Verhaeghe, "'Connect Research': How Market Research Can Get the Most out of Semantic Web Waves," *International Journal of Market Research* 51 (2009): 11–27.

SECONDARY INFORMATION RESEARCH

Secondary information is available and applicable information that has been reported by an organization or individual other than the person using the information. Astute marketing communication planners recognize the tremendous value of secondary information. Therefore, they are constantly reviewing and using available secondary information. (Smart players know how to capitalize on other people's work.)

There are two types of secondary information—internal and external. Internal secondary information may be available from such sources as sales invoices, sales staff reports, distributors' reports, warranty card returns, reports to shareholders, and corporate annual reports. An analysis of potential internal sources may reveal significant useful information and, hence, should be carefully conducted.

Examples of useful external secondary information abound. For example, an advertiser might find the following secondary information useful in developing a statement of creative strategy:

- Estimates of market share reported in the trade press
- A profile of users and nonusers of a product category presented in a report available from a trade association
- Truck registrations reported by a state bureau of motor vehicles
- Vitamin content of ready-to-eat cereals reported by the FDA

In many cases, useful secondary information is readily available at little or no cost. For example, the U.S. Bureau of the Census *Census of Business* reports statistics on business firms classified by SICs by regions and states, and technical information on product performance may be reported by an independent laboratory. Such information can be extremely valuable in developing advertising and marketing communication plans.

McDaniel and Gates provide a 16-page appendix titled "Published Secondary Data" that provides a thumbnail description of widely available secondary information sources. This appendix is an excellent guide to published sources of secondary information available in most libraries.

In locating pertinent secondary information, a reference librarian is a valuable resource. Consulting reference librarians can save time and locate information that might be overlooked or unavailable without their assistance. These specialists' job is to help individuals make the best use of the library's resources, and you should not hesitate to request their assistance. (Smart players know how to enlist appropriate people's assistance to help them find what they need.)

On-line data bases offer the research a quick, thorough, and efficient (though not costly) means of locating potentially useful secondary information. These databases provide information ranging from references to published sources to complete text coverage of topics (based on descriptors such as key words or topics input by the user) to complete raw data from massive survey research projects such as MRI's national study of 20,000 adults' product usage and media exposure patterns.

Individual on-line database vendors provide access to an incredible range of information sources. Such vendors assist researchers by helping determine on-line data bases are most likely to meet their needs. Four of the most popular on-line database vendors are Dow Jones News/Retrieval, Lexis/Nexis, Mintel, and Hoovers, a D&B Company. For information on the contents of the various vendors' databases, your university's library system will often have tremendous resources for you. Often, an initial step in conducting a thorough review of potential secondary information is the preparation of a list of potential sources generated by scanning an appropriate on-line database.

Finally, although there are obvious benefits to the use of secondary information, such information is often limited in several ways. First, many advertising decisions are situation specific and do *not* lend themselves to the application of secondary research. For example, "Which of three specific executions of a creative strategy should be used?" can best be answered only with primary research. Second, secondary information, though useful, often fails to provide all the information the decision maker needs to make a decision. Third, information quickly becomes outdated. Fourth, there is always the danger of obtaining inaccurate information.[5] Therefore, the users of secondary information must beware of its limitations.

FOCUS GROUP RESEARCH

The Nature of Focus Group Research

In an advertising research context, the term *focus group* refers to a group discussion during which a leader or moderator guides a small group of consumers through a consideration of relevant marketing topics. In an informal environment, individual participants are encouraged to spontaneously express their opinions amid the security of a peer group and encouraged by a supportive moderator. A transcript of what was said by participants is later analyzed, and tentative ideas related to the attitudes or behaviors of interest are formulated. This information is used to contribute to the formulation of additional research and/or more appropriate advertising.

Focus groups are used in an attempt to gain insights into "why"-type questions that underlie motivations for behavior and attitudes. The technique is based on group dynamics: individuals are more willing to talk about a subject amid the security of a group of other individuals sharing their thoughts on the same subject. The validity of the technique also stems from the synergy and spontaneity that can be created in an informal group discussion.

Unfortunately, focus groups inherently involve some troubling trade-offs. First, although focus groups are relatively cheap, quick, and easy to set up and conduct, they are difficult to moderate effectively and analyze definitively. Second, because focus groups are qualitative in nature and *not* based on a representative sample, they do *not* support generalizations. Ignoring this fact, users too often generalize their results. Third, focus groups are subject to multiple interpretations, depending on who evaluates the data. Finally, the role of moderator is difficult to perform and exerts a major influence on the validity of the technique. As Calder has pointed out, "there is concern about the subjectivity of the technique, and a feeling that any given result might have been different with different respondents, a different moderator, or even a different setting."[6]

These trade-offs led one advertising wag to refer to focus groups as "hocus groups." Certainly controversy surrounds all aspects of the technique, and there are no accepted guidelines for its use.[7] Critics of focus group research suggest that the findings are simply creative ideas of the analyst and should not even be considered research.[8]

---

[5]Edwin L. Artzt, "Grooming the Next Generation of Management," A.N.A./The Advertiser (Spring 1992):69.

[6]Bobby J. Calder, "Focus Groups and the Nature of Qualitative Marketing Research," Jouranl of Marketing Research 14 (August 1977): 353–364.

[7]Dan Bellenger, Ken Bernhardt, and Jack Goldstucker, Qualitative Research in Marketing, monograph series no. 3 (Chicago: American Marketing Association, 1976), 7.

[8]Harper Boyd, Ralph Wstefall, and Stanley Stasch, Marketing Research—Text and Cases (Homewood, Ill.: Richard D. Irwin, 1985), 46.

Focus groups are subject to two major misapplications. First, focus groups can be used merely as evidence to support preconceived opinions. In evaluating verbal comments, there is always the danger of selectively interpreting what is said and deciding whose opinions to weigh most heavily. Second, definitive conclusions are sometimes drawn from focus group research, even though the technique does not produce projectable data. Unfortunately, this is too often done, as when a product manager concludes, "Listen to what Linda just said—I knew it was a good idea!"

The legitimate application of focus group research is limited. In advertising and marketing research, focus groups may appropriately be used to (1) provide useful background information on consumer attitudes and the language consumers use when they discuss products' performance, (2) generate new ideas for new products, (3) gather consumers' preliminary evaluations of new advertisements and new product concepts, (4) structure a consumer questionnaire, (5) generate hypotheses to test quantitatively, and (6) interpret previously obtained quantitative research findings.[9] The user of focus group research information should beware of applications stretching beyond these areas.

Conducting Focus Group Research

As indicated earlier, one of the dangers of focus groups stems from the fact that they are relatively easy to set up and conduct. Therefore, it is relatively easy for an inexperienced person or firm to abuse the technique.

Exhibit 2 presents an outline of the steps to be followed in conducting a focus group session. The seven steps described represent a typical protocol for such research. Note that the procedure described in each step is simply one approach to conducting the session; other procedures may be equally or more appropriate given the nature of the topic or group. For example, step 6 *(Analyzing the data)* describes only one of many valid means of analyzing the data.

Evaluating Focus Group Research

A focus group that is poorly planned, moderated, or analyzed can result in misleading conclusions. To avoid being misled, the potential user of information based on a focus group session should evaluate the validity of the session. This means that the user needs to understand the basic mechanics of conducting a focus group session.

Exhibit 2 was developed to serve as a guide for evaluating the thoroughness and validity of a focus group research project. Comparing the procedures outlines in Exhibit 2 with those of a specific project may expose major gaps or problems related to careless or inappropriate procedures. This exhibit provides a realistic model against which to compare focus group sessions.

In addition, Exhibit 3 presents 12 specific areas that should be considered prior to accepting and applying the findings drawn from a focus group research project. There are exceptions to the guidelines presented in Exhibit 3 directly related to this individual's background, interpersonal skills, and so on. There is universal agreement that the moderator's role is the crucial factor in determining the validity of a focus group research project.[10]

---

[9]Bellenger, Bernhardt, and Goldstucker, Qualitative Research in Marketing, 18–19.

[10]Ron Hoff, "FCB Presentation Course" (Chicago: Foote, Cone & Belding, 1976), 3–11.

Exhibit 2 ■ Steps in Conducting a Focus Group Session

1. *Establish objectives for the session.*
2. *Construct the discussion outline.* Cover all the topics to be discussed by the group, in sequence. The exact wording must be carefully developed to avoid bias. The moderator should work from the discussion outline, allowing roughly five questions per page with space for notes under each.
3. *Develop screening questionnaire.* Given the objectives of the session, identify a small set of criteria to ensure that the most productive group is formed. The rule of thumb is that the more homogeneous the group, the better. Productive screening criteria are sex, age, household income, education, marital status, and parental status.
4. *Recruit participants.* Ideally, qualified potential participants are contacted via mail and then by telephone. Do not reveal the exact topic of discussion—only the general area. Offer money ($20 to $50) as an incentive for "about two hours of your time to participate in a small-group discussion." If you indicate that the session will begin at 7:00 P.M., realize that it will actually start around 7:20. Recruit a maximum of a week and a half to two weeks in advance. After potential participants agree to attend, send them a thank-you letter that includes a map showing how to find the room. Call the night before the session to remind them. To make sure 8 to 12 attend, recruit 20 who say that they will definitely attend (they won't if anything else comes up). If more than 12 come, pay the extras and send them on their way. Use a flowchart to keep on top of recruitment.
5. *Start and close the session appropriately.*
   a. Use name cards with the participants' first names only.
   b. Have the moderator introduce himself or herself and briefly explain the purpose of the discussion, stressing the importance of obtaining everyone's opinion.
   c. Explain that the purpose of the two tape recorders (in case one doesn't work) is to help the moderator later (he or she can't remember everything).
   d. Tell the subjects that this will be an informal discussion, and they should feel free to get refreshments at any time.
   e. Stress the importance of everyone's opinion.
   f. Have the moderator ask everyone to introduce himself or herself, moving around the table.
   g. The moderator should begin the session with a general question or subject for the group's reaction.
   h. In closing the session, thank the participants for their help and do any appropriate debriefing.
6. *Analyze the data.* Ask the moderator to write up his or her conclusions immediately after the session is over or by the next morning. The moderator can tape impressions if this is easier. The expert doing the analysis should review the moderator's report *after* completing a draft of his or her conclusions. The expert should begin by listening to the tape once to get a general idea of what was said. In drawing qualitative conclusions, one procedure is for the expert to write each idea expressed on a small slip of paper and then arrange the ideas into categories. Multiple groups asked about the same topic can be analyzed at the same time using this procedure. Have the moderator review and discuss the expert's analysis before it is final.
7. *Report the results.* The data are soft and *not* projectable. Do *not* report any numbers. Use language such as "tends to indicate," "impressions," "observations," or "hypotheses for further examination."

Exhibit 3 ■ Checklist for Evaluating Focus Group Research

Evaluation Areas	Guideline Considerations
Moderator's background	Needs formal training is social psychology and group dynamics. Experience is crucial—how many focus groups has moderator handled? In what product categories? With what types of groups?
Moderator's handling of group	How many times does moderator ask why? The more whys, the better. Does moderator really listen to what members are saying? Is questioning directed? Does moderator look members in the eye when they speak? Handle any problems effectively?
Moderator's traits exhibited	Was the moderator kind but firm? Permissive without allowing chaos? Involved? Able to request clarification and expansion where appropriate? Encouraging? Flexible? Sensitive?[a]
Interaction between members	The more group interaction, the better. The less the moderator is involved in the discussion, the better.
Moderator's approach to project	Ideally, the moderator should be involved in planning the session. Does moderator seem to understand the problem and be excited about working on it? Is moderator flexible or rote in conducting multiple sessions?[b]
Homogeneity of group	The more homogenous, the better. Members should be balanced socially and intellectually. Do not mix men and women. Want members who are comparable in terms of age, stage in life cycle, and psychographics. No relatives, friends, or established relationships. No repeat participants.
Moderator's match with group	Same sex, age, and so on encourages more open discussion.
Group size	Eight to twelve is best. Less than eight can be a burden on each member; more than twelve reduces member participation.
Recruitment and compensation	Must be handled professionally and in an unbiased manner.
Length and number of sessions	One and a half to two hours is typically long enough to build rapport without taxing member participation. Depending on the project, three to four sessions are usually sufficient; fewer is suspect.
Physical environment	Informal, relaxed, living room-type setting is best. Serve refreshments to relax atmosphere.
Appropriate conclusions	Remember the qualitative nature of the technique. Data are only directional in nature, not projectable. No statistics on responses should be presented due to the small, unrepresentative sample.

[a]Dan Bellenger, Ken Bernhardt, and Jack Goldstucker, *Qualitative Research in Marketing,* monograph series no. 3 (Chicago: American Marketing Association, 1976), 12–16.
[b]Donald Chase, "The Intensive Group Interview in Marketing," *MRA Viewpoints,* 1973.

SUGGESTED READINGS

Aaker, David, Rajeev Batra, and John Myers. *Advertising Management.* 4th ed. Englewood Cliffs, NJ: Prentice Hall, 1992, 406–438.

Bellenger, Dan, Ken Bernhardt, and Jack Goldstucker. *Qualitative Research in Marketing.* Monograph series no. 3. Chicago: American Marketing Association, 1976.

Calder, Bobby J. "Focus Groups and the Nature of Qualitative Marketing Research." *Journal of Marketing Research* 14 (August 1977): 353–364.

Kinnear, Thomas C., and James R. Taylor. *Marketing Research: An Applied Approach.* 4th ed. New York: McGraw-Hill, 1991.

McDaniel, Carl, and Roger Gates. *Contemporary Marketing Research.* St. Paul, MN: West Publishing, 1991.

Ogilvy, David. *Ogilvy on Advertising.* New York: Crown Publishers, 1983, 158–166.

Ramond, Charles. *Advertising Research: The State of the Art.* New York: Association of National Advertisers, 1976, 3.

Zikmund, William. *Exploring Marketing Research.* New York: The Dryden Press, 1989.

ADVERTISING RESEARCH

Exercises

1. Companies offering environmentally friendly household products are working to boost their marketing presence. "Green" product maker Seventh Generation is hoping to launch their first major marketing campaign, taking advantage of the momentum behind such earth friendly products. The company wishes to prepare itself to compete better against the mainstream brands.

   In the past five years, "ethical" household good sales in the U.S. have been estimated to nearly triple, selling $1.6 billion in 2009. Seventh Generation's products have been positioned as a product for those who believe in the importance of the health and safety of their family. They have traditionally relied on small campaigns, focusing most of their efforts online. Their products include diapers, trash bags, and laundry detergents.

   Seventh Generation wants its first national campaign to coincide with its most recent innovation, disinfectant wipes and spray using a new thyme-based technology. The brand currently holds a very small target market, but would like to extend their products to several more niche groups.

   The sales of Seventh Generation products at mass-market retailers has risen 20% compared to last year. Their 2009 sales came to a total of approximately $150 million. A close competitor of Seventh Generation is spending $10 million developing a new ad campaign.

   You have been asked by Seventh Generation executives to prepare a proposal for an advertising campaign that would target specific groups of potential users of their unique product. You must select two or three niche markets most likely to attract a large number of users. To do so, your agency has decided to conduct a study to gather the necessary information. It is your responsibility to design a study that will best pinpoint the niches with greatest market potential for this product.

   Design a short research proposal to be submitted to your agency's management. Underline the specific goals of the research and the methodology to be used, and develop a budget. Note that the research budget should be kept reasonable, based on the approximate overall advertising expenditures earmarked for the product.

Source: Byron, Ellen, and Suzanne Vranica. "'Green' Products to Get a Push." *Wall Street Journal.* January 11, 2010. Web. February 2, 2010.

2. Proctor & Gamble Co. is concerned with postrecession shopping. During the recession that began in 2009, trends showed consumers switching to store labels and other cheaper options. Consumer product companies are worrying that shoppers won't fully resume their free-spending ways even after the economy improves.

According to a survey conducted by Sanford C. Bernstein of 834 consumers, approximately two-thirds said they had switched to less expensive consumer goods in the past 12 months. More than three-quarters of the consumers said the less expensive products they were using were "as good or better" than the more expensive items.

To lure these shoppers back to their brand-name basics, household product companies have lowered prices. These companies have also relied on heavy advertising, promotional tactics, and new products to tempt shoppers to return to their brand-name basics.

P&G CEO Robert McDonald has stated that he feels the effects of the economy are too general and broadly applied. The company has decided to only make subtle price discounts, keeping their products priced higher, and instead focusing on maintaining the brands' image of superiority.

1. What do you think of P&G's decision?
2. How could the effects of such a decision be tested through the use of research?
3. What type of research study would be most appropriate?

Source: Byron, Ellen. "P&G Meets Frugal Shoppers Halfway." *Wall Street Journal.* January 29, 2010. Web. February 1, 2010.

Case 4.1

Sports Trading Cards[1]

The new business development team of a large advertising agency based in New York City had been charged with the responsibility of identifying attractive potential new clients for the agency to pitch. The team had looked beyond the agency's current client roster for product/service categories with brands whose present marketing efforts were underdeveloped.

The team's objective was to develop a list of prospective categories and specific undermarketed clients in each category whose growth and profit potential were promising. In addition, the team's task was to identify only potential clients that would be an excellent fit with the agency's capabilities and talent.

One of the product categories the team had identified was a somewhat unexpected, yet quite profitable, category: sports trading cards.

Not only was the category seemingly poised to capitalize on the rising interest in the expanding world of professional sports, it also tapped into a potential wave of interest in collecting among a growing base of hardcore enthusiasts. Further, for different reasons, each of the three brands with the largest share in the category seemed to represent an excellent potential client/agency matchup.

With this in mind, Anita Correnti, an account planner and a member of the new business development team, had begun secondary and primary research into the category. As a critical part of this effort, she had planned and helped execute a focus group conducted with a group of eight- and nine-year-old boys who were sports trading card enthusiasts. She was now interested in what information could be gleaned from the session.

The focus group was entirely exploratory in nature. It was conducted as background for a possible speculative new business presentation to one of the three top brands in the category. The primary purpose of the session was to help management and creative personnel at the agency better understand the dynamics of the category. The session was designed to provide insights into the following: (1) trading cards purchase behavior; (2) collecting/trading behavior; (3) determination of the value of a card; (4) motivation for enthusiasm about a card(s); (5) emotional relationships with cards; (6) brand awareness/imagery; and (7) reactions to current marketing efforts of the top three brands.

A marketing research consultant was hired to moderate the group. Potential participants were recruited from New York City, primarily Queens, Manhattan, and the Bronx. To qualify, they had to actively participate in collecting cards. Eight boys participated in the group, which was conducted on a Tuesday evening after school. The group was provided with snacks and soft drinks during the session, which was held in a conference room in the agency's office in lower Manhattan. Microphones, a film camera, and technical people were clearly in view during the session. As compensation for their participation, the boys were each paid $50 and given two packs of trading cards.

Exhibit 4.1.1 presents a discussion guide developed for use by the moderator (Carolyn) in leading the session. Carolyn had five years' experience conducting a wide range of focus groups. Her background included working in three different advertising agencies during the course of the past ten years, conducting qualitative as well as quantitative research.

The lively focus group session lasted approximately one hour and 40 minutes. In addition to a general discussion, participants were asked to complete two written exercises, act out a role-playing exercise, plus view and evaluate current television advertising by sports trading cards companies. Table 4.1 presents the group's evaluation of the three major brands of cards, which were collected using a written exercise. Exhibit 4.1.2

---

[1]This case was written by John H. Murphy, The University of Texas at Austin, to serve as a basis for classroom discussion. The identity of the agency has been disguised, and some of the specifics of the situation have been altered in the case write-up.

Exhibit 4.1.1 ■ Sports Trading Cards Focus Group Discussion Guide

Warm-up

- Hello, my name is Carolyn and I talk to different people about all kinds of different products. Has anyone ever been to a focus group before?
- Do you know that we are going to talk about trading cards—baseball, football, and hockey? You are our experts, and I would like you to tell me everything you can about trading cards. We really need your help, so please don't be afraid to speak up.
- The rules today are that there are no rules. There are no right or wrong answers. And if you disagree with anything said or have a different experience, it is very important that you let me know.
- Before we start, I'd like to go around the room so we can introduce ourselves. I'd like you to tell me your name, age, grade, where you live. What activities are you involved in after school? What other hobbies are you involved in?

Usage/Purchase Patterns

- You all mentioned that you trade baseball cards and other cards. What is so much fun about trading cards? *Probe:* earning money, owning the best players, having better cards than your friends? What is the one best thing about trading cards? What is the one worst thing about trading cards?
- Where do you buy trading cards? Do you usually buy single cards or buy them in packs? How much do packs usually cost? Do you trade one card for another? Do you sometimes trade more than one of your cards for one of someone else's?
- Who do you trade cards with? Do a lot of your friends trade cards? Do you take them around to shows or stores and try to trade them that way? How often do you go to trade shows? Does your father get involved with you and take you to different shows?
- After you have purchased or traded for a card, what do you do with it? *Probe:* Do you put it in an album/box? Does it stay there long or do you try to trade it again?
- In a typical school week, how much time do you think you spend trading your cards or putting them in an album, etc.? Do you spend more time working on your cards than other activities?
- *(Written Exercise)* I would like you to make believe that you are the best baseball card that you own. I would like you to write a story about your life as a baseball card: where you were bought, how much you cost, what your new owner did with you when he bought you, how he felt about owning you, and what he plans to do with you in the future.

Trading and Brand Dynamics

- Do you buy mostly new cards or trade for older cards? How do you know if a card is valuable or not? *Probe:* Do you read magazines? Which ones? Does someone tell you? Who?
- Which cards are more valuable: baseball, football, or hockey? Which of these do you trade most often? Why?
- What makes a card valuable? Are there cards you are not willing to sell for any price? Which ones are they (name specific athletes)? Why is that?
- *(Verbal Exercise)* Since I don't know how to trade for a card, I would like you to help me understand by making believe that (choose respondent) is interested in getting a card owned by (someone else in the group). I would like you to show me how a deal is made. (Try to get at least two pairs of respondents to make a deal in front of the group. Ask about certain language used or try to determine if there is specific terminology used in making the deal.)

- How many cards do you have? Do you have cards made by the same company? Or are they made by different companies? What are the names of the companies that make trading cards?
- Do you like certain cards made by certain companies better than others? Which companies? What is special about them? *Probe:* Do certain companies feature more popular/better ball players than others? Which companies? Does one company show the stats on the back of the card better than another?
- *(Written Exercise only if brand awareness exist)* Rate "Tops," "Score," and "Upper Deck" on a scale of 1–10 on overall rating; featuring popular/good ball players; making a good-quality card (that doesn't tear); featuring clear, interesting stats; and being the best trading card.
- Did you know that bubble gum used to come in the packs? Would you like to buy card packages with bubble gum in them? Why? Why not?

Table 4.1 ■ Focus Group's Rating of Sports Trading Cards Brands[a]

	Tops	**Score**	**Upper Deck**
Overall rating	a—8	a—6	a—10
	b—9	b—7	b—10
	c—8	c—10	c—10
	d—6	d—9	d—10
	e—5	e—7	e—10
	f—9	f—5	f—10
	g—8	g—9	g—10
	h—6	h—7	h—9
Features great players	a—10	a—9	a—10
	b—6	b—2	b—10
	c—5	c—10	c—9
	d—5	d—8	d—9
	e—7	e—7	e—10
	g—7	g—6	g—9
	h—7	h—8	h—10
High-quality card	a—10	a—10	a—10
	b—9	b—3	b—10
	c—7	c—10	c—10
	d—7	d—10	d—7
	e—9	e—9	e—10
	f "waxed"	f "none"	f "none"
	g—6	g—9	g—8
	h—5	h—10	h—7

Continued

Table 4.1 ■ Continued

	Tops	**Score**	**Upper Deck**
Good stats	a—9	a—6	a—7
	b—10	b—6	b—10
	c—3	c—10	c—10
	d—8	d—9	d—2
	e—10	e—9	e—7
	g—8	g—5	g—10
		h—7	h—8
Will become valuable	a—10	a—10	a—10
	b—7	b—1	b—10
	c—9	c—10	c—10
	d—10	d—10	d—10
	e—8	e—9	e—10
	f "yes"	f "yes"	f "no"
	g—9	g—8	g—10
	h—7	h—5	h—8
Best trading card	a—10	a—9	a—10
	b—9	b—1	b—10
	c—10	c—10	c—10
	d—7	d—10	d—8
	e—10	e—8	e—10
	g—7	g—9	g—10
	h—7	h—8	h—10

Verbatim Comments:

Tops—(a) "Best." (b) "Very good." (c) "good." (d) "good excellent good." (e) "good quality." (g) "It's Okay but they're good." (h) A lot of cards to trade, Also, has been around for a long time."

Score—(a) "O.K." (b) "not good." (c) "very great." (e) "good photo." (g) "I don't really like this brand." (h) "Lots of All-Stars and weird names."

Upper Deck—(a) "excellent." (b) "great." (c) "great." (e) "good quality." (g) "Upper Deck, I think is the great." (h) "Has a hologram in every pack. Has a lot of cards in the collection."

[a]Respondents were told to use a scale of 1 to 10 to evaluate the brands, with 1 being the worst and 10 the best. Each respondent is identified by a letter designation. Where no information was provided, no entry is included above.

presents verbatim comments from the "make believe you are your own best trading card" task, which was also a written exercise.

After reviewing the film of the session (available on the text website) and studying the written comments of the participants presented in Table 4.1 and Exhibit 4.1.2, Correnti began to formulate her final report. Her report was to be made the next week in the form of a presentation to the new business team working on the project. As she began, she was concerned about capturing the essence of the bond that clearly existed between the boys and their cards.

Exhibit 4.1.2 ■ "Make Believe You Are Your Best Card" Exercise: Verbatim Comments

8–9-Year-Old Group

- "Baba Ruth by Tops. I brought the baseball card at a Baseball card show. If I was the person who owned it I would sign my singherture on the card."
- "*Score.* My name is Frank Thomas in 1990 I was a good rookie. I am on the White Soxs. I have a good average. I was bought in a card shop. I was sold for $15–$20. My owner put me in the safe and is waiting for the card to go up in value or gets better Home Runs and R.B.I.s"
- "The Card. I have my best card they made of me. I bought myself in a candy store. When I saw myself I ran to my sports value guide and looked up how much I was I was worth. It said I was worth $70.00. I was so happy."
- "The Babe. I was bought in a candy store. I thought no one was going to buy me. I was stuck in between Micky Mantle and Pete Rose. Finally I was bough by myself. I don't"
- Teddy Bergin. I was bought in a comic store he was suprised when he saw me in the future he wants to trade me in because I am worth alot of money."
- "I was bought at a store called Comicmania. I'm worth $3.00. I am a wrestling card hologram. I was born in a card factory. My owner wanted to trade be for a baseball card worth the same. My owner would save me until I went up 20$ in value. The all hologram form of me is worth eight dollars. Adam."
- "Randy Kamintzky I Am the Baseball Card. He was born in Queens New York. I didn't no I'd be a great baseball, but when I new it, I was bout and put in a binder. It was tite but I was all wright. When I took me out I was on top of a guy and saw me worth $85.00/That was the happiest time of my life."
- "Joshua. Roger Clemens, Rockey. I was bought at mint condition. I was put in a plastic case, and in a safe. My owner will keep me for a long time. Now I am worth $20.00."

Name _____ Date _____

QUESTIONS FOR DISCUSSION AND REVIEW
(ANSWER ONLY AFTER VIEWING FILM ON TEXT WEBSITE)

1. Were the mechanics of the session (size of group, physical setting, and so on) handled in a way conductive to generating valid findings? How effective was the moderator's handling of the group?

It would have been nice if they could have based their report on more than one focus group, so that way their conclusions would have been based on more than the opinions of eight.

2. What special procedural and other problems did the age of the participants present for the moderator? How did the moderator handle these problems?

The writing skills of an eit 8-year-old are not very sophisticated, so I would have removed written exercises from the day's activities. Turning in reports verbatim was the right thing to do.

3. Are there any ethical issues related to using children aged eight and nine as participants in focus group interviews? If yes, what are they, and how can they be satisfactorily resolved?

Eight and nine-year-olds are not consenting adults, so you would have to get parents' permission to let them participate. Also, it seems like too much to keep a kid in a focus group for an hour and 40 minutes.

4. How useful were the role-playing exercises in which two members of the group participated in a mock trade? How useful was the "make believe you are your own best trading card" exercise? What about the written exercise in which the group rated each of the top three card companies?

These are all good ideas because it allows you to get into the heads of the consumers who are using the product. However, there are not enough opinions here to make generalizations.

5. What changes would you recommend to make the session more productive?

First of all, I wouldn't let any of the production equipment or crew be visible during any part of the focus group. People behave differently when they know they are being watched.

6. What useful conclusions can be drawn from the session? How might the management and creative teams working on a new business pitch use these conclusions?

Upper Deck seems to be the best received brand of trading cards.

Case 4.2

Amplex Consumer Products Super Ultra Bathroom Tissue[1]

BACKGROUND

The Paper Products Division of Amplex Consumer Products Corporation (ACP) had operated successfully for many years as a major supplier of newsprint. Approximately twenty-five years ago the division began profitably manufacturing a small-volume line of paper napkins and plates. In addition, ACP had established a relationship with several manufacturers of fertilizer and other chemical products to provide them with heavy-duty paper sacks. All of these activities had ensured the profitable operation of the division.

Two years ago, ACP scientists had developed a new bathroom tissue product designed to compete in the premium segment of the category. The tissue had performed well in initial consumer testing in the lab against the major competitors, such as Procter & Gamble's Charmin Ultra and Northern's Ultra.

The ACP ultra tissue had been test marketed under several brand names that were also being evaluated. Backed by heavy price discounting and advertising, the new tissue had performed well in five representative test markets. After studying the test market results, it was concluded that the brand had the potential to garner a significant share of the premium bathroom tissue market in the long-run. Based on the competitive counterattacks the new brand had encountered in the test markets, ACP executives anticipated that a planned regional rollout of the new brand would encounter strong marketing actions from the established brands in the category.

RESEARCH SUBSTANTIATION OF A SOFTNESS CLAIM

To develop a marketing plan for the regional rollout, ACP had hired Nancy Helpert to be the brand manager of the new product. Ms. Helpert had an MBA plus eleven years of experience in consumer product marketing with a package goods manufacturer and a national chain of retail stores. Based on her experience, Ms. Helpert believed that a key to realizing the long-run potential of the brand hinged on the new brand's ability to make a strong comparative advertising claim regarding its superior softness vis-à-vis the major competitors.

Ms. Helpert anticipated that if the new brand made a superior softness claim, one or more competitors would almost certainly challenge the claim by registering a complaint with the Better Business Bureau's National Advertising Division (NAD). The NAD would begin their investigation by requesting ACPs' substantiation data that supported the advertising claim. These data would be made available to the competitor(s) who initiated the complaint for their review in preparation for a hearing on the matter.

In order to investigate the feasibility of such a softness claim, Ms. Helpert suggested that a consumer research project be designed and conducted to examine consumer evaluations of the softness of the new brand versus several leading brands in the premium bathroom tissue category. In designing and conducting the study the utmost care would have to be taken to ensure that the study would stand up under the careful scrutiny of research methodology experts hired by major competitors.

---

[1]This case was written by John H. Murphy, The University of Texas at Austin. The case is designed to serve as the basis for classroom discussion and not to illustrate either the effective or ineffective handling of an administrative situation. The identity of the firms involved and the situation have been disguised.

Four marketing research companies were contacted and asked to submit an initial research proposal for investigating the softness of the leading brands versus the new ACP ultra bathroom tissue. After reviewing the initial proposals, Ms. Helpert selected the two firms with the most appropriate proposals and asked them to develop a more detailed description of their proposed methodology.

The two firms, identified below as A and B, each suggested different approaches to investigating the softness issue. Firm A recommended a longitudinal in-home use test while firm B confidently recommended a central location test. After reviewing the two methodologies (which are briefly described below), Ms. Helpert was faced with making a decision about which firm's approach would yield the most accurate, appropriate, and defensible findings.

TWO ALTERNATIVE RESEARCH METHODOLOGIES

Firm A—In-Home Use Testing

Firm A stressed that their proposed in-home use testing study had been designed in accordance with accepted guidelines and standards established for survey research. These guidelines had been set forth by the Federal Judicial Center in the "Manual for Complex Litigation." These guidelines included such considerations as ensuring that a representative sample had been drawn from the proper universe, and that the data had been accurately analyzed and reported.

Sample Selection. The universe of potential study participants was defined as U.S. residents 13 years of age or older. To allow for regional differences that might exist, the study would be conducted in each of the four U.S. Census Bureau regions—Northeast, South, Midwest, and West. A stratified sampling procedure would be utilized to identify two Metropolitan Statistical Areas (as defined by the U.S. Census Bureau) in each region to be included in the final sample. The two metro areas selected in each region were: Northeast—Boston and Philadelphia; South—Atlanta and Orlando; Midwest—Chicago and Cleveland; and, West—Denver and Los Angeles.

To draw a sample of study participants, shopping malls and testing facilities would be utilized as a means of identifying relevant consumers. To help ensure a representative sample the following age quotas based on data from the Census Bureau's *Statistical Abstract of the U.S.* and adjusted for product usage were established:

Age Group	Females	Males	Total
13–17	4%	4%	8%
18–34	17	17	34
35–49	12	12	24
50+	19	15	34
Total	52%	48%	100%

Screening for eligible respondents would be conducted in high traffic areas of the malls. Once qualified, the potential participant would be escorted into an interviewing facility and their participation in the study solicited by carefully trained and supervised personnel. Potential participants would be offered a $20 monetary incentive to participate in the study and told that their name would also be entered in a drawing to receive one of several attractive prizes to be held after the completion of the study.

Double-Blind Interviewing. The study would be conducted over approximately three weeks under "double-blind" conditions—both the participants and the interviewers would be kept uninformed as to the purpose and the sponsorship of the study. This procedure would help to ensure that participants and interviewers would not bias the study in some way.

In-home Testing Procedures. Participants would each be given two four-packs of bathroom tissue unidentified in terms of brand. One package would be labeled as "Use First," and the other "Use Second." Participants would be carefully instructed to install the first product (that was test brand $\times$ for half, and ACPs' new brand for the other half) in each bathroom they normally used. At the end of the week, participants would be instructed to remove the first product and install the second product via telephone reminders.

At the end of the two weeks, participants would be asked via a telephone interview which of the two products, if either, they found softer. The specific question would be worded as follows:

"Which of the two bathroom tissues did you find softer, the one you tried first or the one you tried second?"

Additional demographic and product use data would also be gathered.

Verification and Data Analysis. An independent validating service would be assigned the task of contacting every participant to confirm that the person existed, s/he met universe requirements, and s/he was actually interviewed for the study. All editing and coding would be conducted following carefully developed written instructions. All data analysis would be checked for accuracy by reviewing the data for logical relationships. A total of 325 completed interviews would be conducted for each comparison. So, for example, if three brands were compared against APCs' brand, a total of 975 interviews would be completed.

Firm B—Central Location, Sensory Comparison Testing

Firm B stressed that the appropriate test would allow for a direct comparison of the two bathroom tissues under examination at the same point in time. Two representative Metropolitan Statistical Areas in each of the four U.S. Census Bureau regions would be selected for inclusion in the study. If two brands were compared against ACPs' bathroom tissue, a total of 1,500 interviews would be conducted—750 paired-comparisons of ACPs' tissue versus each competitor.

Firm B's proposed test involved recruiting potential respondents in high traffic areas of shopping malls and asking them to participate in a brief study in a mall research facility. Qualified potential participants would be offered a $10 monetary incentive to participate in the study and told that their name would also be entered in a drawing to receive one of several attractive prizes to be held after the completion of the study. Approximately 80% of respondents would be female household heads 18 years of age and older and 20% male household heads 18 years of age and older. (This balance, or imbalance, favoring females was justified, firm B explained, since past studies indicate that 78% of usage in the ultra bathroom tissue category is by females and 22% is by males. Further, females made the vast majority of purchases in the category.)

The data collection methodology recommended was as follows: First, participants would be seated in the interviewing facility and the interviewer would follow the script below.

Interviewer: "O.K., I'm going to ask you to feel two different toilet tissues and compare their softness."

{Interviewer places three sheets of tissue labeled "Respondent's left" into the participant's left hand and three sheets labeled "Respondent's right" into their right hand. (A protocol was followed to vary which tissue was placed in the left and right hand.) Interviewers will be instructed to: Place the three sheets flat in the participant's hand so the participant is holding the center parts of the tissue, not the edges.}

Interviewer: "Now, please fold or crumple up these tissues as you normally fold or crumple toilet tissue and feel the softness of each one."

{When the participant finishes, the interviewer would ask the participant to change hands.}

Interviewer: "I'm now going to have you switch hands, and feel each of the tissues in your other hand."

{When the participant has switched hands, the interviewer would ask the participant to fold or crumple up the tissues.}

Interviewer: "Again, please fold or crumple up these tissues as you normally fold or crumple toilet tissue and feel the softness of each one."

{When the participant has finished, the interviewer would ask the softness question.}

Interviewer: "Now, please think of the softness of the two products you are now holding. Which one of these two products, if either, is softer?"

Finally, the interviewer would ask the participant to fill out a self-administered questionnaire. This questionnaire would gather data on all brands of toilet tissue used in the past six months; the one brand used most often in the past three months; household size; employment status of the participant; last grade of school completed by the participant; ethic group membership; and total household income.

After completing the questionnaire, participants would be asked to sign a form acknowledging their receipt of the $10 incentive and required to also print their name and phone number for notification if they had won a prize in the drawing to be held at the completion of the study.

Seven hundred and fifty respondents would be used in comparing each brand versus ACPs' ultra premium bathroom tissue. If two brands were each compared against ACP tissue, 1,500 respondents' answers to the key question would be used to make a softness claim vis-à-vis competitors. Fifteen percent of all of each interviewers completed interviews would be verified.

Name _____ Date _____

QUESTIONS FOR DISCUSSION AND REVIEW

1. How large an influence does the nature of the product category have on the appropriateness of the two research methodologies described in the case?

2. How important a consideration is "realism" or testing under actual use conditions in investigating a softness claim?

3. What problems are likely to be encountered using Firm A's methodology? Firm B's? Which problems are most troubling? Why?

4. In attempting to discredit the research during a NAD review, how might competitors' consumer testing experts be expected to attack the validity of each of the two methodologies?

5. Which of the two methodologies should ACP utilize? Why?

_____

_____

_____

_____

Case 4.3

Diet and Exercise Campaign Extension—North Central Region[1]

FACEBOOK AND FOCUS GROUP RESEARCH PROJECTS

Ms. Joan Bennett was in charge of marketing in the North Central region of a national organization dedicated to promoting healthier lifestyles via improved diets and participation in physical exercise. She was concerned with developing supplements and/or extensions to the organization's national campaign. In leveraging the national campaign in her region, Ms. Bennett felt that targeting a special group of women who were much less concerned about their health than older women should be a priority. This group was young professional women 22–34 who were college graduates and employed outside the home.

Ms. Bennett realized that in targeting this group she needed insights into their attitudes/behavior in order to develop effective programs to supplement the national campaign. To gain such insights Ms. Bennett felt that two research projects might be appropriate: a quantitative Facebook survey and a qualitative focus group session.

The purpose of the studies would be to explore some fundamental issues related to enhancing the effectiveness of the national campaign. These issues included: What health information sources do these women turn to and trust? In general, what are their hesitations or roadblocks to participating in health cause-related campaigns? More specifically, were their hesitations related to the national campaign? What were their general experiences and attitudes toward specific health communication campaigns such as the Susan B. Anthony Race for the Cure, the (Red) campaign to fight AIDS in Africa, the Lance Armstrong Foundation's LiveStrong, and American Heart Association's Go Red for Women campaigns?

The central issue related to planning efforts to influence this target group was what motivates these women to take action related to health issues? How might these women be most effectively encouraged to visit the organization's website, participate in their national outreach programs, donate money to support the campaign, and so on?

Facebook Survey Project. In conducting a survey research project using participants recruited from among friends on Facebook there were many issues that needed to be resolved. These included how to recruit and motivate participants to complete a questionnaire developed for gathering the data. Would it be appropriate to use friends of employees of the organization? What should be included in the questionnaire? How should the questions be worded? In what order should the questions be presented? What sort of trade-off should be struck in terms of open-ended questions versus the use of response category questions?

Should participants be alerted via an initial contact that they will be asked to participate in a survey? What protocol should be followed in following up with non-respondents? Which on-line survey software and questionnaire tool service, such as SurveyMonkey, should be used? How would the data be analyzed, particularly any open-ended questions? What is a reasonable timeline for conducting the project?

---

[1] This case was written by John H. Murphy, The University of Texas at Austin. The case is designed to serve as the basis for classroom discussion and not to illustrate either the effective or ineffective handling of an administrative situation. The identity of the firm involved and the situation have been disguised.

Focus Group Project. In conducting a focus group session, Ms. Bennett wondered about how to efficiently recruit participants to attend the session. Although one of the cardinal rules of a focus group was do not recruit people who already know each other, might this be overlooked given the convenience of recruiting women who fit the profile through a business, religious organization, or special interest group? What topics should be included in the discussion guide? Should a special facility be used or would it be O.K. to use one of the organization's conference rooms? Who would moderate the session? What is a reasonable timeline for planning, conducting, analyzing, and writing the final report? Could a professional research firm or just an experienced moderator be persuaded to conduct the project pro bono?

These and a host of other research issues needed to be resolved if the information generated by the studies was to be valid, timely and useful. Unfortunately, any research needed to be conducted quickly; and, although organization's staff, facilities, and materials could be used, essentially with no budget.

Name _____ Date _____

QUESTIONS FOR DISCUSSION AND REVIEW

1. What should be the relationship between the Facebook and the focus groups studies in terms of planning, collecting, and using the information generated?

   _____
   _____
   _____
   _____

2. Of the issues raised by Ms. Bennett about each study, which is the most important? Why?

   _____
   _____
   _____
   _____

3. What other critical decisions must be made in gearing up to conduct the proposed research?

   _____
   _____
   _____
   _____

4. What other purposes beyond those stated by Ms. Bennett might be productively investigated using each of the two studies?

   _____
   _____
   _____
   _____

5. If only one of the two projects could be conducted, which one is the most likely to generate useful information? Why?

Chapter 5
Establishing IBP Objectives

"Integrated marketing means that your brand messages resonate in complementary ways across marketing channels. . . . Look for opportunities to leverage resources across channels to create maximum synergy and results. . . . You just might find a way to make a blog integrate with your annual report."[1]

THE CONTEXT AND SCOPE OF IBP OBJECTIVES

The first step in the IBP management decision-making process is to conduct a careful situation analysis. A fundamental SWOT analysis (Strengths, Weaknesses, Opportunities, and Threats) is designed to provide information useful in making decisions about how to most effectively communicate with the firm's market(s) and other relevant publics. After the brand/market situation has been evaluated and some initial decisions made about the most appropriate mix of communication tools, the next step is to establish clear, measurable objectives specifying what the IBP mix is to accomplish.

IBP program objectives are simply statements describing what is to be accomplished by the IBP mix to capitalize on opportunities and/or overcome problems facing the brand during the planning period.[2]

Determining appropriate objectives to assign to the firm's IBP efforts is a key part of campaign planning. Objectives set the basic direction for the entire IBP program or campaign. Furthermore, clear, measurable objectives are required for managerial evaluation and control of the firm's communication efforts. Without measurable objectives established prior to the beginning of a campaign or other promotional effort, it is impossible to evaluate whether these efforts succeeded and to plan the most effective use of the IBP mix in future periods.

In specifying what the IBP mix is to accomplish, the planner faces perhaps the most intriguing and frustrating characteristic of marketing communication: the link between the IBP mix and sales. Typically, businesspeople invest money

---

[1]Denise Zimmerman, "A Quick Guide to Integrated Marketing" http://www.imediaconnection.com/content/10031.imc; accessed May 31, 2010.

[2]Note that as described in this chapter, objectives for a multi-tool IBP program focus on the communication variables that are influenced to varying degrees by all the elements in the marketer's IBP mix. In some situations, it may be appropriate to develop separate objectives for individual components that are part of the mix. For example, it may be appropriate to develop separate objectives for the advertising component alone.

in IBP efforts with the belief that stimulating demand for their brand through these efforts will create additional sales, and the revenue generated by these added sales will more than cover the cost of the IBP investment. However, in most situations, two major considerations make the use of sales as a criterion for evaluating the success of an IBP mix inappropriate: (1) the IBP mix is only one of many factors that determine whether or not a sale occurs, and (2) the IBP mix has a carryover, or delayed, effect that extends beyond a quarterly period or a calendar or fiscal year.

Therefore, although overall marketing objectives are stated in terms of sales volume and market share, in most situations it is *not* appropriate to assign such objectives to an IBP mix alone. Rather, IBP objectives should be stated in terms of those variables that the communication mix *can* measurably influence, whether or not sales are consummated.

Only in those product/market situations where these two considerations do *not* apply is it appropriate to use sales as an IBP mix objective. A sales objective may be appropriately assigned in some direct-response situations—those where immediate action is called for in an ad, the merchandise is sold directly to consumers, and advertising alone plays *the* dominant role in the marketing program (this requires the assumption that price and other mix variables are properly aligned). Further, sales objectives apply to some retail advertising that focuses on promoting a limited-time sale or special promotional event. Even in these situations, however, it may be more logical to evaluate advertising based on the number of inquiries received, or the number of prospects who visit a Web site for more information, or a traffic count of the number who attended a sales event.

WHAT SHOULD BE INCLUDED IN A STATEMENT OF IBP OBJECTIVES?

In practice, statements of IBP mix objectives vary widely. Some marketers are content with vague objectives such as "to increase awareness of the brand," "to stimulate trial," or "to enhance the brand's image." Unfortunately, such statements handicap efforts to develop effective and efficient IBP programs and preclude precise evaluation of the firm's marketing communication efforts. In developing statements of IBP objectives, spending the time and effort to develop thorough and specific objectives makes the work that follows easier and the resulting communication efforts more focused and productive.

In his classic 1961 work sponsored by the Association of National Advertisers, Colley suggests that an advertising objective should be defined as "a specific communication task, to be accomplished among a defined audience to a given degree in a given time period."[3] Later in 1969, Britt expanded Colley's definition by suggesting that four components must be clearly covered in a statement of advertising objectives. These are (1) what basic message is to be delivered, (2) to what audience, (3) with what intended effect(s), and (4) what specific criteria will be used to measure the success of the campaign. Britt maintained that unless each of these areas is specified in a statement of advertising objectives, it is impossible for an advertiser to know if advertising efforts succeeded or failed.[4]

Britt's four components, although specifically keyed to advertising, provide a solid foundation on which to build and evaluate an IBP program or mix of communication tools. If these

---

[3] Russell H. Colley, *Defining Advertising Goals for Measured Advertising Results* (New York: Association of National Advertisers, 1961), 6.

[4] Steuart H. Britt, "Are So-called Successful Advertising Campaigns Really Successful?" *Journal of Advertising Research* 9, no. 2 (1969): 3–9.

four areas are clearly specified, the direction of the firm's IBP efforts can be communicated to all the individuals who will be involved in their development, and sound evaluation of their success is possible. Therefore, these areas provide the recommended outline of what should be covered in statements of IBP objectives.

Note that these decisions should be made in sequential order, beginning with a definition of the target audience. Next, the message should be identified, and then intended effects and measurement criteria should be specified. These four components are described and illustrated in the following sections.

Target Audience

The single most important decision the IBP mix planner makes is what group(s) of consumers and/or other relevant publics to target with promotional messages. All other IBP mix decisions flow from this basic decision. Is the budget sufficient? Is the media mix appropriate? Should PR or a sales promotion be used? What about an event sponsorship or marketing partnership with another brand? Is the creative execution appropriate? All such questions are evaluated considering the target audience's size, perspective, concerns, brand preferences, and so on.

A definition of a target audience begins with a concise statement of key demographics. For example, the following target audience was defined for a national chain of day-care centers:

Female household heads aged 25 to 34 employed outside the home who have one or more children under the age of 6 at home and who live in the top 50 U.S. Designated Market Areas (DMAs) as defined by Nielsen.

This target audience definition makes it clear on whom various IBP efforts should be focused by defining the audience in terms of gender, age, employment status, parental status, and geographic location. These factors are critical in identifying women who are attractive prospects for the day-care center's services.

Such a target audience definition is useful in focusing the marketer's IBP efforts; however, it fails to provide insights into consumers' motivations and how the product or service fits into their lives. Lifestyle and psychographic profile data attempt to fill this void by painting a more three-dimensional picture of consumers. Based on its research, Strategic Business Insights suggested an eight-group VALS classification scheme based on consumers' attitudes, needs, and beliefs that has proven useful in segmenting many consumer markets.[5]

Adding mind-set data, such as VALS and other AOI (attitudes, opinions, and interests), information to a demographic definition of the target audience provides everyone involved in the development of the IBP mix with a more realistic and useful understanding of how the selling problem may be best attacked. For example, the following VALS and attitude data gathered through primary research add important additional insights to the demographic profile of working mothers referred to earlier.

The target segment of this demographic group aspires to have both a successful career and family. These women are serious about their child-rearing responsibilities and are avid readers of books and articles on the subject. They are primarily "Achievers" and "Makers" in terms of VALS categories. They are concerned about

---

[5] http://www.strategicbusinessinsights.com/vals/ustypes.shtml, accessed May 31, 2010.

where and with whom they leave their children. Their child's "experience" is of crucial important, while cost of the service is an important, but secondary, concern. They are relatively web-savvy and are heavy users of the Internet. They rely heavily on friends and relatives for information about child-rearing practices.

This description of the target can be supplemented by a hypothetical profile of a typical member of the target group. This profile, which includes a photograph plus a description of important attitudes related to the product category and behaviors of interest, is described and illustrated in Chapter 7, which focuses on the creative strategy brief.

Message Content

The second component of a statement of IBP objectives presents a clear description of the competitive benefit to be conveyed in marketing communication messages. The message content component presents a concise statement of the key benefit the brand promises the consumer if he or she will buy the brand.

Although the consumer benefits are based on product features, a statement keyed on features is not appropriate. The strategist must move beyond features and focus on benefits that are much more powerful motivators of consumers' response.

Wells suggests that the special meaning of the consumer benefit can be appreciated by filling in the blanks of the following statement: "When I _____, I will _____." In this sentence, a typical member of the target audience is the "I," the first blank describes the purpose of the IBP mix—what the marketer wants the consumer to do—and the second, the benefit. Wells provides the following three examples:[6]

- "When I take Amtrak instead of the plane from New York to Washington (purpose), I will be more comfortable, better treated, and more valued (benefit)."
- "When I buy insurance from State Farm instead of from some other insurance company (purpose), I will know that a friendly State Farm agent will be at my side if I need help (benefit)."
- "When I invest in a holiday to Mooréa instead of some other destination (purpose), I will bring romance back into my life (benefit)."

The successful Norwegian Cruise Line (NCL) "Freestyle Cruising" campaign illustrates the difference between features and benefits. The features of "Freestyle Cruising" versus the competition (e.g., Royal Caribbean, Carnival, Princess Cruises) were no schedule to keep or set times or regimentation/rules. The benefits of these features were *freedom from* the type of pressures of the demanding and stressful lives the target lead and the *freedom to* indulge in your own self-interest, cater to your own needs, and control your day. In the context of cruising, the key benefit was summarized as "the freedom to live life (if only for a week) on your own terms."[7]

The NCL "Freestyle Cruising" IBP campaign also provides an excellent example of a concise message statement. NCL's primary target audience for the campaign was adults, 25 to 54,

---

[6]William D. Wells, *Planning for R.O.I: Effective Advertising Strategy* (Englewood Cliffs, NJ: Prentice Hall, 1989), 12.

[7]GSD&M/Idea City, company documents, 2005.

household income of $75,000, professional/managerial, slightly female, and with a free-spirited mind-set. Their favorite TV show was *American Idol,* and they were most likely to shop at The Gap before sailing. The message content to this target was: "NCL's Freestyle Cruising liberates people by providing the ultimate freedom from demanding and stressful experiences and the ultimate freedom to create an experience on their own terms."[8]

Intended Effects

This component of a statement of IBP objectives specifies what the IBP mix is to accomplish—the end result or change stimulated by the target audience being exposed to the messages about the brand.

As pointed out in the opening section of this chapter, in most situations sales is not an appropriate effect to assign to an IBP program. As pointed out earlier, in arguing against the use of increased sales as an objective, Colley stressed that marketing messages should be regarded as communication forces and so assigned only communication tasks. Broadly, a communication force can affect three variables: awareness, knowledge, and attitudes.

The relationship between IBP programs as a communication force and awareness, knowledge, and attitudes, plus their link to sales, was first clearly outlined in Lavidge and Steiner's classic hierarchy-of-effects model of the consumer decision-making process. These authors suggest that a consumer typically proceeds through a standard set of information-processing and reasoning steps or stages in moving from being unaware of a brand's existence to purchasing the brand. These sequential stages are (1) awareness, (2) knowledge, (3) liking, (4) preference, (5) conviction, and (6) purchase.[9]

Briefly, the first step in moving toward a purchase is "awareness"—the consumer is made or becomes aware of the existence of the brand. The second stage is "knowledge"—the consumer learns something about what the brand has to offer. The next three stages—"liking," "preference," and "conviction"—represent the attitude field of the model. Liking represents the assignment of a favorable or unfavorable (+ or −) predisposition to the brand on one or more dimensions. In the preference stage, the consumer's favorable predispositions have developed to the point of preference over other brands in the category. Conviction signals that preference has been coupled with a desire to buy, plus the belief that the purchase would be wise. This final attitude stage of conviction then stimulates the behavioral step in the process—purchase.

Although more elegant models of this process have been suggested, most are patterned on Lavidge and Steiner's basic steps. Further, because of its commonsense qualities, Lavidge and Steiner's model provides the original basis for most marketing managers' view of how the purchase decision-making process works. This model can also be used to provide a sound basis for establishing measurable IBP mix objectives.

In most situations, the marketer's objective in using IBP tools is to facilitate the movement of target consumers up the hierarchy, which will ultimately lead to a purchase of the desired brand. That is, the marketer aims to move consumers from unawareness to awareness, to convey information about the brand and its performance (knowledge), and to favorably affect the consumers' attitudes regarding the brand. Hence, the general intended effects of the

---

[8]Ibid.

[9]Robert J. Lavidge and Gary A. Steiner, "A Model for Preictive Measurement of Advertising Effectiveness," *Journal of Marketing* (October 1961): 59–62.

IBP mix are to *increase* the target audience's levels of awareness, knowledge, and favorable attitudes toward the brand. For example, the intended effects of IBP activities for a hypothetical brand Zippies could be stated in the following form:

- To increase unaided awareness of Zippies from 20 percent to 30 percent (awareness).
- To increase the percentage of the target audience who believe that Zippies contain "the lowest levels of fat" of any brand in the category from 0 percent to 10 percent (knowledge).
- To increase the percentage of the target audience who strongly agree with the statement, "Zippies are environmentally safe" from 15 percent to 30 percent (attitude).

Specific intended effects are required for measurable objectives. Here the strategist must clearly specify how much of an increase is planned—note that this requires establishing a pre-IBP campaign, or benchmark, level against which the postcampaign level will be compared. "To increase unaided awareness among the target audience" is vague; "To increase unaided awareness from 10 percent to 15 percent of the target audience" is specific. In the second objective, 10 percent is the pre-IBP campaign level. Also, note that although the intended effect represents an absolute increase of only 5 percent of the target audience, it represents a 50 percent increase in the precampaign level of unaided awareness ($15 - 10 = 5$; $5 \div 10 = 50\%$).

Determining how large an increase to specify as an intended effect involves considerable uncertainty. This task is made easier when benchmark data are available for more than one year or planning period. For example, the results of three research surveys that included a measure of top-of-mind awareness of hospitals among adults in Austin, Texas, are presented next. With three years' data and experience, the planner for St. David's Hospital is in a much better position to factor in likely changes in competitors' budgets, creative executions, market growth, and so on when developing a realistic and aggressive targeted increase in "first mention" awareness for the coming year.

	"When you think of Austin area hospitals, which ones come to mind?" **Percentage Identifying Each Hospital "First Mention"**			
	St. David's	**Brackenridge**	**Seton**	**Others**
Year 1	38%	33%	18%	11%
Year 2	39	26	25	10
Year 3	47	23	29	1
Year 4	?	?	?	?

Measurement

Sound IBP objectives should specify how the intended effects will be measured after the IBP efforts have been implemented. That is, the measurement component must be described (and a research budget set aside) *before* the IBP mix is executed. This ensures the accountability of the IBP program, and because precampaign or benchmark measures are necessary, it makes research findings an integral part of planning both present and future IBP efforts.

An outline of the purchase process model, along with examples of the types of measurement appropriate at each stage, is presented in Exhibit 1. This exhibit is designed to serve as a practical guide to the data collection techniques that may be used in measuring intended effects.

A wide range of data collection, measurement, and analysis techniques may be utilized in determining if the intended effects were achieved. For example, a pre- and post-campaign survey research project may be conducted using telephone interviews or on-line surveys or mall intercepts with members of the target audience. A series of open- and closed-ended questions, rating scales, adjective checklists, and multiple-choice questions may be used to gather the

Exhibit 1 ■ Hierarchy-of-Effects Model of the Consumer Decision-Making Process
(Measurement at Each Stage)

Stage in the Process	Appropriate Measures	Examples of Measurement
(1) Awareness	■ Unaided recall	"Thinking about toothpastes, which brands come to mind?"
	■ Aided recall	"Have you ever heard of XQB toothpaste?"
(2) Knowledge	■ Direct questions	"Which brand of toothpaste has Z-82 added?"
	■ Playback	"Which brand of toothpaste claims that 'it was invented by the tooth fairy'?"
(3) Liking	■ Ranking	"What are your three favorite brands of toothpaste?"
	■ Rating scales	"On a scale of 1 to 5, with 1 = ineffective and 5 = effective, how does XQB rate on 'cleans my breath'?"
(4) Preference	■ Likert scales	"Please tell me whether you strongly agree, agree, neither agree nor disagree, disagree, or strongly disagree with the following statement: 'I believe XQB is a pleasant-tasting toothpaste.'"
(5) Conviction	■ Semantic differential scales	"Please describe XQB toothpaste using the following adjectives scales: Pleasant to Use 1_ 2_ 3_ 4_ 5_ 6_ 7_ Unpleasant to Use"
	■ Projective techniques	"Tell me about the brands of toothpaste teenagers who just left home to attend a university are likely to use, and why. Which brands would they like to use if money were not a factor? Why?"
(6) Purchase	■ Self-report	"Which brand(s) of toothpaste have you purchased for yourself or your family in the past four weeks?"
		"Which brand of toothpaste do you usually use?"
		"Which brands of toothpaste are presently available in your home?"

necessary data. In addition, Chi-square analysis, T-tests, analysis of variance, and other techniques may be used to determine if differences between the pre-campaign and post-campaign data are statistically significant.

ADDITIONAL SUGGESTIONS FOR DEVELOPING STATEMENTS OF IBP OBJECTIVES

The purpose of this section is to provide some insights into the practicalities and value of developing the type of IBP objectives described in this chapter. The section begins with some basic considerations that apply to most business objectives. It then provides advice for developing useful IBP objectives and discusses the potential value of such objectives.

IBP objectives, like other promotional objectives, must be consistent with marketing and overall corporate objectives. They must be in writing, and they must be understood and subscribed to by the people involved in the development of the IBP mix. The objectives should also specify a time frame.

The objectives should be internally consistent. The message should fit the targeted prospects. The areas or dimensions identified in the message section should be directly related to the intended effects. The measurement method recommended should be appropriate for generating data to evaluate success of the program.

It is important to recognize that IBP objectives are always based on many assumptions. These include, for example, assumptions about how effective the creative execution will be, the adequacy of the IBP appropriation, the effectiveness of the accompanying media plan, the skillfulness of PR specialists in handling media relations, and the actions of competitors. Because some educated guesswork is involved in establishing appropriate increases in the intended effects section, experience is the best teacher.

Further, despite the fact that measurable objectives are set, in the final analysis, judgment and common sense play an important role in evaluating the performance of any IBP program. For example, a major increased investment, plus innovative creative executions, by a competitor may mean it is appropriate for a marketer to conclude that his/her brand's campaign was successful, despite the fact that the campaign did not achieve the levels of awareness and so on specified as intended effects in the IBP objectives established prior to launching the campaign.

Adoption of IBP objectives following the guidelines suggested in this chapter can help other members of the firm's management team understand the proper role of IBP activities within the overall marketing mix. Finally, complete objectives, coupled with a realistic appreciation of IBP's role in the marketing mix, protect marketing communication from becoming a "whipping boy" when sales fall below levels specified in the marketing plan. Too often IBP mixes that effectively deliver their communication messages are blamed when other marketing shortcomings or changes in the competitive environment are the real cause of falling demand for the brand.

SAMPLE STATEMENT OF IBP OBJECTIVES FOR A PROFESSIONAL BASKETBALL TEAM

This section illustrates a complete statement of IBP objectives that covers the four components discussed earlier in the chapter. The data presented in this example have been disguised. The professional basketball franchise city is disguised as Boxworth and the team as the ThunderBolts.

As part of the situation analysis, a research firm was employed to conduct a study of the sports interests and attitudes of male household heads aged 25 to 64 who resided in eight key

ZIP codes in the Boxworth market. Management believed these adults were an attractive target audience for the team's upcoming marketing efforts. One of the purposes of the study was to provide benchmarks against which advertising objectives could be set for the upcoming 201X season.

A statement of IBP objectives based on the research findings is presented in Exhibit 2. Selected data from the study are included in this statement and keyed to the questionnaire. Exhibit 3 presents selected portions of the questionnaire used to collect the information referenced in the effects section.

Note that the planned IBP mix included a broad mix of marketing communication tools. The Thunderbolts' IBP mix included

- Off-line Advertising. An aggressive local broadcast and print media campaign to begin eight weeks prior to the start of the season with flights promoting special nights and events. This campaign was supplemented by outdoor and transit advertising.
- On-line Advertising. A search-engine marketing program was planned to purchase key words and phrases relevant to delivering targeted on-line ads on Google, MSN, and Yahoo!
- Web site Marketing. The team's Web site was redesigned and refreshed to add more involving content and graphics plus to aid easy navigation and to facilitate on-line purchasing of individual game and season tickets.
- Personal Selling. A phone-room team was carefully trained to contact past season and individual game ticket purchasers plus prospects in the targeted ZIP codes with information about new, flexible ticket packages. In addition, three experienced, permanent salespeople called on and met with over meals corporate personnel and individuals who were prospects for boxes and stadium suites.
- Public Relations. The campaign included extensive PR initiatives to garner local media coverage of the team and the work of individual team members involved in local community affairs.
- Marketing Partnerships and Cross-Promotions. The team partnered with a broad spectrum of well-known local businesses, including print and broadcast media, a car dealer, and a regional quick-service restaurant chain with over 40 locations in the Boxworth market. These partnerships produced special promotional games and attendant events throughout the season.

DEVELOPING IBP OBJECTIVES

Exercises

1. Mickey Mouse is an iconic character. For many people, that simple mouse may define their childhood. The Walt Disney Company has protected their beloved "spokesmouse," scared that any changes would tarnish the brand and sales. But concerned that Mickey has become more of a corporate symbol, Disney has decided to take a risky step in re-imagining the mouse for the future, making his look and personality more in tune with new generations of children. In a new video game being developed, Mickey is transformed into "Epic Mickey" who is adventurous, enthusiastic, and curious, but also misbehaves and is a little selfish. His new look will also physically resemble a rat. The new image is meant to induce the new generations of tech-savvy kids to embrace Mickey, while still not alienating older fans.

Exhibit 2 ■ IBP Objectives: Boxworth ThunderBolts' 201X-201Y Campaign[10]

Target Audience. The target audience is male household heads aged 25 to 64 who reside in the eight highest-income ZIP codes in the Boxworth DMA. Many of these men are latent "jocks" who enjoy the vicarious excitement of pro sports. They appreciate the opportunity for camaraderie with other fans, both at the games and in other social encounters. Most are not serious students of the game but enjoy identifying with their team and individual players.

Message. The primary message is that the ThunderBolts players, as individuals, are concerned about the quality of life and general well-being of the local community and, hence, merit fan support. The secondary message is that the ThunderBolts games provide an excellent sports/entertainment value—fans can relax, forget personal troubles, and enjoy active support of their team.

Effects. The effects of the campaign are to increase and strengthen awareness, knowledge, and favorable attitudes toward the team and toward attending games among members of the target audience. Specifically, the effects *among members of the target audience* are as follows:[11]

- To increase *awareness* of the team's name from 85 percent to 90 percent (see Question 3 of the Boxworth Sports Attitudes Study in Exhibit 3).
- To increase correct *knowledge* of the price of individual game tickets from 4 percent to 10 percent (see Question 6a).
- To increase correct *knowledge* of the price of season tickets from 3 percent to 6 percent (see Question 6b).
- To increase the percentage who identify the ThunderBolts as their favorite Boxworth area team from 26 percent to 32 percent (see Question 4) *(attitude change)*.
- To increase the percentage who identify the ThunderBolts as their favorite NBA team from 48 percent to 58 percent (see Question 5) *(attitude change)*.
- To change *attitude* regarding the ThunderBolts' players' concern for the local community from an average of 2.25 to 4.0 (see Question 9).
- To change *attitudes* regarding the relative value of ThunderBolts' games from an average of 1.70 to 3.10 (see Question 10).

Measurement. To evaluate the campaign's success, pre-campaign data were collected from a random sample of the target audience. Selected portions of the questionnaire appear in Exhibit 3. A second set of data will be gathered using the same data collection instrument and a different random sample after the campaign has run. The criteria for success will be achieving the awareness, knowledge, and attitude changes indicated in the "Effects" section above.

Data were collected using telephone interviews with members of the target audience. Two hundred and fifty interviews will be completed in both the pre- and post-campaign phase of the research. A professional research and interviewing service was used to gather and analyze the data.

---

[10]The Thunderbolts' IBP mix campaign was scheduled to run from September 15, 201X, through April 30, 201Y.

[11]In addition, separate targets were established in terms of Web site traffic. These metrics were stated versus last year and included the number of unique visitors, average time on the site, page views, and purchases via the site.

Exhibit 3 ■ Boxworth Sports Attitudes Study

ASK TO SPEAK TO THE MALE HEAD OF THE HOUSEHOLD. Hello, my name is __; I work for Metropolitan Research Services. We're conducting a brief study of the attitudes of men about sports. I'd like to ask you a few questions. I'm not selling anything. First,

1. What is your favorite participation sport?

   __ Baseball __ Basketball __ Tennis __ Football __ Golf __ Bowling
   __ Swimming __ Running __ Other: _____

2. What is your favorite spectator sport?

   __ Baseball __ Basketball __ Tennis __ Football __ Golf __ Bowling
   __ Swimming __ Running __ Other: _____

3. What is the name of Boxwoth's National Basketball Association team? _____

4. What is your favorite sports team in the Boxworth area?

   __ Boxworth Bombers __ Boxworth Rascals __ State University Tigers
   __ Boxworth ThunderBolts __ Other: _____

5. Which team in the National Basketball Association is your favorite?

   __ Boxworth ThunderBolts __ Chicago Bulls __ Detroit Pistons
   __ Boston Celtics __ L.A. Lakers __ Other: _____

6. a. How much do the cheapest single-game tickets cost to attend a Boxworth ThunderBolts basketball game? $_____ per ticket.
   b. What does a season ticket cost? $_____ per ticket.

Next, I'd like for you to indicate the extent to which you agree or disagree with several statements by telling me if you Strongly Agree, Agree, Neither Agree nor Disagree, Disagree, or Strongly Disagree with each. The first statement is, "I regularly engage in strenuous participation sports."
   Would you say that you:
   Strongly Agree, Agree . . . (continue pattern for all statements).

	Strongly Agree	Agree	Neutral	Disagree	Strongly Disagree
7. I regularly engage in strenuous participation sports.					
	5	4	3	2	1
8. I frequently swim for exercise.					
	5	4	3	2	1

Continued

Exhibit 3 ■ Continued

	Strongly Agree	Agree	Neutral	Disagree	Strongly Disagree
9. The Boxworth ThunderBolts players are concerned with the local community.					
	5	4	3	2	1
10. All things considered, Boxworth ThunderBolts basketball games are one of the best sports/entertainment buys in the Boxworth area.					
	5	4	3	2	1
11. The key to a winning basketball team is teamwork.					
	5	4	3	2	1
12. I would enjoy going to more State University Tigers football games.					
	5	4	3	2	1
13. The Boxworth Bombers baseball team has produced more major-league players than any other triple-A franchise.					
	5	4	3	2	1
14. What is your age? _____					
15. What is the ZIP code of your home? _____					
Thank you very much for your help!					

Do you think this is a good idea? What are the implications on Disney's brand loyalty? How does this idea influence advertising and other marketing communication objectives?

Source: Barnes, Brooks. "After Mickey's Makeover, Less Mr. Nice Guy." *The New York Times.* 9 Nov. 2009. Web. 2 Mar. 2010.

2. Wally Amos had a great recipe for chocolate chip cookies and founded Famous Amos in 1975. In the 1990s, he sold the rights to the brand to Kellogg. Sadly, he felt that Kellogg had cheapened the product, and Mr. Amos continued to make his original cookies under the brand name Chip and Cookie. But he has not been able to generate the success of the Famous Amos brand. Even with a crunchier, sweeter cookie, business has been extremely slow.

Do you think Amos can recapture the brand loyalty of customers? What marketing strategies would benefit his brand? How might these strategies be reflected in advertising objectives? That is, define the marketing objectives first, then, create the advertising objectives based on the marketing ones.

Source: York, Emily Bryson. "Famous Amos Can't Capitalize on His Fame." *Advertising Age.* 14 Dec. 2009. Web. 2 Mar. 2010.

Case 5.1

MacLeod's Furniture Centers[1]

Management of MacLeod's, a regional chain of over 50 furniture and appliance stores located in 23 markets in a southwestern state, developed marketing programs tailored to the characteristics of each market in which it operated. In planning an integrated brand promotion program for the coming fiscal year in a large metropolitan market, management was concerned with developing the most effective and efficient efforts to target Mexican-Americans.

Mexican-Americans made up more than 60% of the population of the market and had accounted for a significant portion of MacLeod's business for many years. Although MacLeod's did well in comparison to competitors in selling furniture to Mexican-Americans, management believed that appliance sales to Hispanics were far below potential.

MacLeod's had six locations spread around the metro area and, hence, were at least reasonably accessible to the all furniture and appliance customers in the market. MacLeod's major competitors were Hershall's with five stores, Apex with three, and Simpsons with four stores.

To aid the development of a complete integrated brand promotional campaign for next year, MacLeod's and its advertising/PR agency commissioned a marketing research firm to profile the attitudes of Mexican-Americans toward furniture and appliance stores in the market. A description of the study and findings is presented below.

THE RESEARCH STUDY

The research firm collected data using telephone interviews conducted with a randomly selected sample of female and male household heads with Spanish surnames drawn from the most recent metropolitan telephone directory. In addition, only those potential respondents who described their ethnic background as Mexican-American or Hispanic were included in the final data set.

A questionnaire was developed to collect information from the respondents on their furniture and appliance attitudes and shopping preferences. The questionnaire was carefully pretested prior to final data collection.

Four hundred interviews were completed. Half of the respondents were surveyed regarding their furniture shopping behavior; half were asked about their appliance shopping patterns. Exhibit 1 presents sampling variations associated with a sample size of 200.

The interviews were conducted by a professional interviewing service using bilingual interviewers. The interviewers utilized either a Spanish or an English version of the questionnaire as needed, based on the language preference of the respondent. Following sound research practice, a small sample of each interviewer's work was verified to confirm that an interview had been conducted and that the interviewer had accurately collected the data reported.

---

[1]This case was written by Isabella C. M. Cunningham and John H. Murphy, The University of Texas at Austin. The case is designed to serve as the basis for classroom discussion and not to illustrate either the effective or ineffective handling of an administrative situation. The identities of the firms involved and the situation have been disguised.

Exhibit 1 ■ Probably Deviation (+ or −) of Results Due to Size (n=200) of Sample Only[a]
(safety factor of 20 to 1)

Survey Result Is:	Probable Deviation:
1% or 99%	1.4
2% or 98%	2.0
3% or 97%	2.4
4% or 96%	2.8
5% or 95%	3.1
6% or 94%	3.4
8% or 92%	3.8
10% or 90%	4.3
12% or 88%	4.6
15% or 85%	5.1
20% or 80%	5.7
25% or 75%	6.1
30% or 70%	6.5
35% or 65%	6.8
40% or 60%	7.0
45% or 55%	7.0
50%	7.1

[a]This exhibit presents the range of variation in survey results around the true value in the population being sampled that is due to sample error. For example, with a sample size of 200 and a survey result of 25 percent, you may be reasonably sure (odds 20 to 1) that this result is no more than 6.1 percent off, plus or minus. That is, the true value is between 18.9 percent and 31.1 percent. *Note that other values apply to other sample sizes.* Larger samples reduce the range of sampling error.

THE FINDINGS

The major findings of the study related to planning MacLeod's promotional efforts for the next year are presented in Tables 5.1 to 5.9. Table 5.1 presents the respondents' top-of-mind awareness of furniture and appliance stores; Table 5.2 indicates at which store the respondents shop most often; Table 5.3 indicates whether the respondent had ever shopped at MacLeod's; Table 5.4 lists the reasons why stores were selected. Table 5.5 indicates the sources used to gather information about stores; Table 5.6 presents data on the respondents' perception of how MacLeod's and three major competitors compared on ten selected attributes. Table 5.7 presents data on respondents' overall rating of MacLeod's versus three major competitors; Table 5.8 provides insights into how knowledgeable respondents were regarding MacLeod's local operation. And finally, Table 5.9 provides a demographic profile of respondents.

Table 5.1 ■ Top-of-Mind Awareness: Percentage Citing Each Store

	Furniture Stores		Appliance Stores	
	First Mention	Any Mention	First Mention	Any Mention
David's	8%	22%	11%	30%
MacLeod's	29	46	2	4
Lutz	14	34	a	a
Hershall's	2	11	5	24
Simpsons	14	38	41	78
Apex	9	34	16	64
All others	24	b	25	b
Total	100%		100%	

[a] Less than 1 percent.
[b] Multiple responses by each respondent cause "Any mention" percentages on "All others" to be meaningless.

Table 5.2 ■ Store at Which Respondents "Brought Most" in Past Three Years

	Furniture	Appliances
MacLeod's	17%	2%
Simpsons	12	41
Apex	11	16
Lutz	9	a
National	8	a
David's	3	6
Plaza	2	a
Toudouze	2	a
Hershall's	2	4
All others	34	31
Total	100%	100%

[a] Less than 1 percent.

Table 5.3 ■ Ever Shopped at MacLeod's for Furniture or Appliances?

	Furniture	Appliances
Yes	51%	26%
No	49	74
Total	100%	100%

Table 5.4 ■ Reasons Store Selected

	Furniture Stores		Appliance Stores	
	First Mention	**Any Mention**	**First Mention**	**Any Mention**
Location	10%	34%	11%	33%
Price	32	59	22	54
Store reputation	4	16	3	11
Salespeople	2	11	3	12
Selection	9	27	11	24
Quality	6	28	13	40
Recommended by friend	5	12	2	6
Services offered	6	19	9	26
Type or style	5	8	4	9
Other reasons	21	[a]	22	[a]
Total	100%		100%	

[a]Multiple responses by each respondent cause "Any mention" percentages on "All others" to be meaningless.

Table 5.5 ■ Sources of Information about Stores

	Furniture Stores		Appliance Stores	
	First Mention	**Any Mention**	**First Mention**	**Any Mention**
Television	14%	56%	13%	57%
Magazines	4	18	3	17
Radio	1	18	1	15
Newspapers	40	60	40	63
Circulars or catalogues	4	23	4	22
Websites/Internet	17	36	23	40
Friends	10	27	5	29
Shopping	8	14	8	18
Salespeople	1	5	1	4
Other sources	1	[a]	2	[a]

[a]Multiple responses by each respondent cause "Any mention" percentages on "All others" to be meaningless.

Table 5.6a ■ Respondents' Perception of MacLeod's versus Major Competitors

	Appliances				
	MacLeod's	**Lutz**	**Simpsons**	**Apex**	**Don't Know**
Highest quality	10%	6%	53%	21%	10%
Friendliest personnel	7	4	40	24	25
Most services	2	1	61	28	8
Most convenient locations	5	2	54	28	11
Widest selection	5	2	51	24	18
Most brands	11	8	37	20	24
Best-known brands	7	5	45	21	22
Lowest prices	4	7	36	23	30
Most modern stores	8	13%	36	22	21
Most formal stores	13	8	33	22	24

Table 5.6b ■ Respondents' Perception of MacLeod's versus Major Competitors

	Furniture				
	MacLeod's	**Lutz**	**Simpsons**	**Apex**	**Don't Know**
Highest quality	30%	21%	25%	12%	12%
Friendliest personnel	16	8	31	25	20
Most services	14	8	42	20	16
Most convenient locations	16	5	48	24	7
Widest selection	30	29	20	12	9
Most brands	28	28	16	9	19
Best-known brands	28	24	20	10	18
Lowest prices	23	13	19	16	29
Most modern stores	22	24	18	13	23
Most formal stores	25	14	26	12	23

Table 5.7 ■ Overall Best Place to Shop

	MacLeod's	**Lutz**	**Simpsons**	**Apex**	**All**	**Don't Know**
Furniture	27%	23%	23%	15%	4%	8%
Appliances	6	3	58	27	2	4

Table 5.8 ■ Knowledge of MacLeod's Operations

	Correct	Incorrect	Don't Know/Unsure
Do you know the number of MacLeod's locations in market?			
Furniture stores	15%	15%	70%
Appliance stores	12	16	72
Do you know the number of years MacLeod's has operated in market?			
Furniture stores	8	12	80
Appliance stores	9	10	81
Do you know any brand names of furniture (appliances) available at MacLeod's?			
Furniture[a]	54	11	35
Appliances[b]	15	3	82

[a] In response to the question, "Do you know any brand names of furniture carried by MacLeod's" 65 percent responded "yes" and 45 percent "no." Those who responded "yes" were then asked to specify brands available at MacLeod's. If any were correct, the response was counted as "correct."

[b] In response to the question, "Do you know any brand names of appliances carried by MacLeod's" 18 percent responded "yes" and 82 percent "no." Those who responded "yes" were then asked to specify brands available at MacLeod's. If any were correct, the response was counted as "correct."

Table 5.9 ■ Demographic Profile of Respondents

	Furniture Sample	Appliances Sample
Age		
18–24	15%	14%
25–34	28	25
35–49	26	32
50–64	19	19
65 and over	12	10
Total	100%	100%
Marital Status		
Married	76%	82%
Single	10	8
Divorced, widowed, separated	14	10
Total	100%	100%

Continued

Table 5.9 ■ Continued

	Furniture Sample	Appliances Sample
Household Size		
1–2	27%	20%
3	20	25
4	26	29
5 or more	27	26
Total	100%	100%
Education		
Elementary or less	21%	22%
Some high school	25	21
High school graduate	22	24
Some college	20	19
College graduate	12	14
Total	100%	100%
Total Household Income		
Under $15,000	16%	10%
$15,000–$24,999	19	21
$25,000–$49,999	20	21
$50,000 and over	18	17
Don't know	23	24
Refused	4	7
Total	100%	100%
Sex		
Female	62%	60%
Male	38	40
Total	100%	100%

After an initial examination of the data, three variables appeared to hold the most potential as segmentation criteria for further analysis. These variables were age, household income, and whether or not the respondent had shopped at MacLeod's. Cross-tabulations using these variables revealed that only age provided a clear and useful division of the sample. The significant findings using age (18–34 and 35+) as a segmentation variable for each of the two samples will be discussed next.

Furniture Sample

Cross-tabulations of age against top-of-mind awareness of furniture stores revealed that a much larger percentage of the younger group than the older group (41 percent versus 19 percent) identified MacLeod's. Hershall's was also identified more strongly by the younger than the older group (22 percent versus 8 percent). Simpsons, on the other hand, was much more frequently mentioned by the older group (23 percent, versus 1 percent for the younger group).

Variations between the two age groups on the reasons mentioned for store selection were significant. Price was considerably more important to the younger group. Younger Hispanics appeared to be much more price oriented than older Hispanics when making furniture store selection decisions.

Cross-tabulation of age against the series of comparisons of the four stores across ten dimensions revealed several significant differences. It is important to note that, in each case, a larger proportion of the older group fell into the Don't "Know" category. On the "highest quality" furniture dimension, a larger percentage of the younger than the older group choose MacLeod's (40 percent versus 20 percent). On the "widest selection" variable, MacLeod's and Hershall's were much stronger among the younger group, while Simpsons was identified by a significantly larger percentage of the older group. Finally, a significantly larger proportion of the under-35 group chose MacLeod's on the "most brands" and "best known brands" dimensions. These last two general findings also apply to Hershall's.

On the important "overall best place to shop for furniture" question, MacLeod's was stronger among the younger than the older group (31 percent versus 24 percent), as was Hershall's (31 percent versus 18 percent for the older group). Further, Simpsons was significantly more frequently identified by the older group (27 percent, versus 16 percent for the younger group).

Appliance Sample

Cross-tabulation of age against top-of-mind awareness of appliance stores revealed that a much larger percentage of the under-35 group identified a store classified as "Other" when compared to the older group (37 percent versus 18 percent). The older group, on the other hand, had a much stronger awareness of Simpsons and David's than the under-35 group.

On the "overall best place to shop for appliances" measure, Simpsons was identified by a majority of both age groups. However, Hershall's was identified by a significantly larger proportion of the younger respondents (37 percent versus 21 percent). Cross tabulations on other variables revealed no significant differences.

PLANNING THE IBP PROGRAM

In developing a complete promotional effort for MacLeod's in this market for the next fiscal year, management turned to the research findings for insights and guidance. In using the findings, the first step was to clearly define promotional objectives for next year. Key issues to be resolved included the identification of the most appropriate target audience(s) within the Mexican-American market and the relative amount of attention/resources to devote to promoting furniture versus appliances.

The levels of awareness, knowledge, attitudes, and preferences presented in the tables would be used as pre-campaign benchmarks that the upcoming promotional campaign would be designed to impact. At the end of the one-year effort, the same study would be repeated, using another randomly selected sample of Mexican-Americans. Changes in the post-campaign percentages of responses to key questions would be used to evaluate the campaign's effectiveness against pre-campaign objectives that were to be developed.

Name _____ Date _____

QUESTIONS FOR DISCUSSION AND REVIEW

1. What are the most important findings presented in the tables? Why are they the most important?

   _____

   _____

   _____

   _____

2. What are the major contrasts between MacLeod's relative positions among furniture shoppers versus among appliance shoppers? Between younger and older shoppers?

   _____

   _____

   _____

   _____

3. Given MacLeod's stronger position in the furniture market, what *risks* is the firm likely to run by shifting a larger proportion of its promotional mix to support appliances? What *opportunity costs* might MacLeod's incur by not expanding its promotional support of appliances?

   _____

   _____

   _____

   _____

4. Should MacLeod's promotional appeals be directed to younger or older shoppers? Why? How would the attractiveness of a comparative ad format be affected by which age group was targeted?

   _____

   _____

   _____

   _____

5. What is a realistic statement of promotional objectives for MacLeod's? How would your objectives vary depending on whether you focused on younger or older Hispanics as the target audience? How would your objectives vary depending on whether you focused more heavily on appliances or furniture?

Case 5.2

Don't Mess with Texas (A)[1]

Background Information

The Texas Department of Transportation (TxDOT) launched the "Don't Mess with Texas"® (DMWT) campaign in 1986 to help combat rising litter pickup costs. Since its inception, the campaign has been about litter prevention although the public has stretched the slogan to represent much more. In 2006, DMWT was named America's favorite slogan during Advertising Week and is featured on the Madison Avenue Advertising Walk of Fame. DMWT beat out 25 other well-known slogans including "Just Do It" by Nike, "Got Milk?" by the California Milk Processors Board, and "Have it your way" by Burger King. TxDOT's slogan won with more than 400,000 votes—the most ever recorded by Advertising Week.

EnviroMedia Social Marketing (TxDOT's agency of record for the campaign) has managed the public awareness and education campaign since 1998. DMWT has been a comprehensive campaign that relies on traditional advertising, public relations, social marketing and outreach to communicate with all Texans in ways most likely to reach them. The campaign was based on studies that identified key target audiences, the most common types of litter, and the littering behavior and attitudes of Texans.

Historically, the campaign has showcased the talents of famous Texas musicians, athletes and actors dating to its debut in 1986 when Stevie Ray Vaughan said the words "Don't Mess with Texas." From Willie Nelson to Chuck Norris, these celebrities donated their time to help spread the litter prevention message.

Since 1998, the DMWT campaign has focused on the worst litterers in the state—Texans ages 16–24 who were dubbed "Generation Litterer" or "Gen L." Web banners were strategically placed on popular Gen L Web sites, in addition to advertising being placed on popular cable and TV programs. This was to help drive awareness and traffic to the DMWT Web site, which was an integral part of the campaign and was constantly updated with current information.

To reach these individuals in a more personal setting, the campaign has relied on experiential marketing using a "go where they go" strategy by establishing a presence at concerts, amusement parks, festivals and other popular events. In addition, a social media presence on Facebook and Twitter helped reach them through personal networks. Facebook and Twitter fans are updated regularly with current programs, trivia, contests and events.

Research Studies: Visible Litter and Attitudes & Behaviors Study

Research has played a key role in shaping the DMWT campaign. Over the years, EnviroMedia and TxDOT conducted a number of studies to track the attitudes and behaviors of litterers, as well as to determine the composition of roadside litter.

<u>Visible Litter Study</u>. Every four years since 1995, TxDOT has commissioned the Visible Litter Study to learn about the litter on Texas roadways. In the most recent Visible Litter Study, litter was collected from 136 sites along a representative sample of TxDOT-maintained rights of way and categorized by the most common type of litter. The amount of litter that accumulates on these sites during the study period is also used to project the total number of littered items on Texas roads each year. Top littered items included: cigarette butts, fast food trash and non-alcoholic beverage containers (see Table 5.10).

---

[1] This case was written by John H. Murphy, The University of Texas at Austin, and Christina Moss, EnviroMedia Social Marketing, in coordination with the Texas Department of Transportation. The case is designed to serve as the basis for classroom discussion and not to illustrate either the effective or ineffective handling of an administrative situation. Don't Mess with Texas is a registered trademark of the Texas Department of Transportation.

Major conclusions of the researchers who conducted the most recent Visible Litter Study were: (1) cigarette butts were the most commonly found litter item; (2) overall litter had decreased on the Texas-maintained highway system by 33% from the previous study findings; (3) tobacco products, food-related and non-alcoholic related items comprised 75% of all litter; and (4) most litter (61%) is identifiable by brand name. The most common potential litter sources were convenience stores, shopping malls, and fast-food restaurants.

<u>Attitudes & Behaviors Study.</u> Every two years, a statewide telephone survey is conducted to learn Texans' attitudes and behaviors regarding littering. The most recent survey showed a continuation of extremely high

Table 5.10 ■ Most Common Items within Litter Use Categories

Categories	Percentage of Total Litter	Item Name	Percentage within each Category
Tobacco	33%	Cigarette butt	84%
		Cigarette pack	11
Food	29	Tissue/towel/napkin	18
		Snack wrap	17
		Beverage cup	11
		Food wrap	8
		Cup lid	7
Non-Alcoholic Beverage	11	Beverage can	34
		Beverage bottle	29
		Beverage cup	12
Construction/Industrial	8	Rag	14
		Corrugated box	13
Printed	8	Lottery ticket	22
		Receipt	15
		Label	14
		Instructions	10
Alcoholic Beverage	6	Beer can	71
		Beer bottle	22
Household/Personal	4	Envelope	7
		Carton	5
		Medicine container	5
Automotive	1	Shop rag	37
		Oil container	7
Other	0	Misc. items	12
Total	100%		

Source: Visible Litter Study; Conducted by NuStats International for the Texas Department of Transportation.

awareness of the DMWT campaign slogan (96%) and great support for the campaign (93%). This research also revealed that only 68% of Texas adults recognize that DMWT means don't litter and that 52% of respondents admitted littering. This study also confirmed Texans under age 25 were most likely to litter. Based on this finding, the 16- to 24 year-old demographic was identified by the TxDOT and EnviroMedia team working on the campaign as Gen L.

Further, based on the findings of these studies, the researchers who conducted the study suggested that a single message might be most successful to discourage littering and increase the likelihood of proper litter disposal. For example, one theme was "It may be a small piece of litter, but it is still a big problem in Texas." Additional selected findings from this study are presented in Table 5.11.

Table 5.11 ■ Texans' Attitudes & Behaviors Toward Litter

"In the past three months, have you seen, read, or heard any ads or public service messages related to litter or littering?" Yes 35%, No 62%, Unsure 3%	
"What was the main slogan used in the ads or public service messages?" 37% unprompted and 59% prompted recall of DMWT	
"Please tell me in your own words, what the slogan Don't Mess with Texas means to you?"	
Anti-litter/correct response	68%
Positive message, not exactly correct	15
Incorrect meaning	8
Unsure/refused	9
"Overall, do you support the Don't Mess with Texas litter prevention campaign?" Yes 93%, No 4%, Unsure 3%	
"What types of materials do you think are a serious litter problem?"	
Beer cans and bottles	38%
Soda cans and bottles	37
Plastic bags and other plastic	29
Small pieces of paper (receipts, Lotto tickets, gum wrappers)	20
Cigarette butts	21
Fast food wrappers	14
Construction	10
Litter that falls out of pickup trucks accidently	13
Other food wrappers	6
Food/organic material	3
Cardboard	4
Other	60
Source: Attitudes & Behaviors Study; Conducted by Baselice & Associates, Inc. for the Texas Department of Transportation.	

Establishing IBP Objectives for the Upcoming Campaign

As a point of departure in developing an IBP campaign for next year, the DMWT team had decided initially to focus on conveying the "It may be a small piece of litter, but it is still a big problem in Texas." message. Next, based on a host of assumptions about the appropriation, the direction, and the effectiveness of the campaign targeting Gen L for the next fiscal year (September 1 through August 31); appropriate communication objectives were considered to convey the "It may be a small piece of litter, but it is still a problem in Texas," message.

Using available secondary data plus the data in the two tables to define the target audience for the upcoming campaign, the team wanted to construct a revealing profile of the Gen L group in terms of their typical lifestyles, attitudes, and behaviors. This seemed to be a key to developing a more focused and effective campaign.

An important part of the objectives should address awareness of the DMWT campaign and its connection to litter prevention. In developing these and other objectives, the data in Table 5.11 would serve as a pre-campaign measure of relevant attitudes. (These data may be assumed to be representative of Gen L.)

[Handwritten notes:]

1) litter as a prop?
2) social media
3) What do 16-24 years like to do that contribute to this litter?

1) Don't Mess with Texas has taken on a life of its own.
2) Use a up and coming Texas celebrity as a spokesperson.
3) Maybe get into global warming since it's a hot button issue

Problem — Connecting don't mess w/ TX w/ littering reaching 16-24 year olds

Critical Factors — non descriptive campaign — what coup
— noninformational — facts about littering
— disconnect across mediums as far as using the word "litter"
— perception of litter v. what is actually being littered are not the same.
— their brand name is very strong
— Gen L is not properly defined or well researched
— under utilized social media. Needs to be more effective.

Name _____ Date _____

QUESTIONS FOR DISCUSSION AND REVIEW

1. What external factors and assumptions would play the most important role in influencing the establishment of appropriate DMWT IBP objectives for the upcoming campaign?

2. At this point in the planning process, how might the DMWT team most realistically set objectives for the campaign?

3. What secondary sources might be most useful in more precisely defining the Gen L target?

4. What additional pre-campaign awareness, knowledge, and attitudinal measures would be useful in framing objectives for next year?

5. What mediums best reach the Gen L target, and how could the campaign best utilize those mediums on a limited budget?

_____

_____

_____

_____

6. What would be the most effective way to teach Gen L that Don't Mess with Texas means don't litter?

_____

_____

_____

_____

Chapter 6
Determining the Advertising Appropriation and Budgeting

No company that markets products or services to the consumer can remain a leader in its field without a deep-seated commitment to advertising.[1]
—Edwin L. Artzt, Chairman and CEO, Procter & Gamble

INTRODUCTION

The ultimate objective of most advertising is to sell products or services. When a company or an institution engages in communication with its various publics, it may have some different immediate goal, such as clarifying information about the use of a product, attracting potential investors by sharing corporate goals, or using public relations communication to solidify the company's public image. It is important to recognize, however, that ultimately a company's success is a function of its growth in sales and profits, and most of that growth will be fueled by advertising and marketing communications.

Companies cannot base their budgeting decisions on recent successes and assume that continued investment in advertising is not necessary. An example of this is the decision Pepsi had to make in 2008 to increase overall demand in the carbonated soft-drink market and to solidify its brands' market share. The successful campaign by BBDO that had made Pepsi the "choice of a new generation" was not enough to stop the overall sales declines for carbonated soft-drinks in 2008; the loss of 3% to 4% of the market was affecting the Pepsi brand and the company believed it was necessary to stem that decline while at the same time, fortifying their brands. For that reason, in a bold move, Pepsi decided to invest $1.2 billion over three years in a complete packaging, merchandising, and marketing overhaul of its soft drinks.[2]

Determining an advertising budget is an old challenge. But, as media choices have become more numerous and the "noise" in the marketplace has increased, the budgeting decision has grown increasingly difficult. This chapter explores some traditionally popular advertising budgeting techniques as well as the new challenges facing advertising managers when dealing with the allocation of budgets for advertising efforts.

---

[1] Edwin L. Artzt, "Grooming the Next Generation of Management," *A.N.A The Advertiser* (Spring 1992): 69.

[2] Natalie Zmuda and Rupal Pareh. "Pepsi Upends Brands with $1.2 Billion Shakeup," *Advertising Age,* October 20, 2008—http://adage.com/article?article_id=131846

The relationship between advertising objectives and budget decisions is a vital one. The size of the advertising budget, the selection of media, and the media strategy to be used as well as the creative content of the advertising message are all determined by the objectives that the company is pursuing.

This chapter will consider long-term and short-term advertising objectives as major criteria for budget decisions. The effectiveness of advertising expenditures will also be examined, as budgeting should be considered a control tool as well as a planning ingredient. In fact, one of the most important changes facing advertising agencies and professionals is the increasing demand of accountability for advertising and promotional expenditures by their clients—the advertisers. Approvals to spend money in advertising are a function of how well an agency can demonstrate an economic return. Whether that return is translated into additional sales, or in an increase in the number of potential customers visiting an advertiser's Web site, it is clear that agencies must be able to provide their clients with much more precise tools to measure the effectiveness of their advertising dollars.

TRADITIONAL METHODS OF SETTING ADVERTISING BUDGETS

The advertising budgeting decision can be divided into two major components: (1) how much money should be spent on advertising and promotion within a specific time period, and (2) how the total advertising and promotion budget should be earmarked for different media, different products/services, and different geographic areas or target markets.

Determining the size of the advertising budget is a very important decision because it will affect the future impact of all of the firm's marketing efforts and be instrumental in determining the firm's future marketing strategy. In addition, an advertising and promotion budget is generally a major financial commitment of the firm and will be closely scrutinized by top management. It is crucial, therefore, that such a decision be made with a careful and thorough consideration of its potential effects, along with its constraints and limitations.

Some budgeting methods have been popular among advertising managers for many years. Although all such methods have some shortcomings, they have allowed managers to plan and control the performance of the advertising and promotion functions by comparing against results within their industry or against the performance of major competitors. Such methods will be discussed next.

The Percentage-of-Sales Method

There are two ways of establishing an advertising budget according to the percentage-of-sales method. The first is to calculate advertising allocations as a fixed percentage of *past sales*. This calculation is done by applying a specific percentage number to the previous year's total sales revenue for a product, a line of products, or the whole company. The formula for this calculation is

$$A_2 = f(S_1)$$

where: A_2 is the total advertising budget for next year (or period 2)
f is a percentage figure
S_1 is sales for period 1 (or last year's sales).

Advertising-to-sales ratios are computed by industry every year by professional advertising organizations. An example of such calculations can be seen in Table 6.1.

Table 6.1 ■ Advertising-to-Sales Ratios for Selected Products, Retail Sales and Services

Commodity of Class of Business	% of Annual Sales Spent on Advertising
Air Courier Services	0.9%
Amusement & Recreation Services	5.05
Apparel & Accessory Stores	5.2%
Appliance & Electronics	
Appliance Dealers	3.2%
Electronics Dealers	3.8%
Appliance & Electronics Dealers	3.4%
Auto Dealers, Gas Stations	0.8%
Auto & Home Supply Stores	1.9%
Bakery Products	0.7%
Beverages	6.7%
Bicycle Dealers	3.1%
Books, Publishing & Printing	3.8%
Building Materials, Hardware, Garden (Retail)	2.1%
Cable & Other Pay TV Services	7.3%
Carpets & Rugs	0.8%
Catalog, Mail-Order Houses	3.5%
Child Day Care Services	0.9%
Computer & Office Equipment	0.6%
Convenience Stores	0.1%
Department Stores	5.1%
Direct Mail Advertising Services	1.7%
Drug & Proprietary Stores	0.7%
Educational Service	12.8%
Engineering, Accounting, Research, Management & Related Services	0.2%
Family Clothing Stores	1.9%
Furniture Stores	8.7%
Grocery Stores	0.8%
Hardware, Plumbing, Heating Equipment (Wholesale)	0.1%

Continued

Table 6.1 ■ Continued

Commodity of Class of Business	% of Annual Sales Spent on Advertising
Hardware Stores	
<$500,000	2.4%
$500,000–$1,000,000	2.7%
$1,000,000–$2,000,000	2.5%
>$2,000,000	2.2%
Hobby, Toy & Game Shops	2.9%
Home Centers	
<$2,000,000	1.3%
$2,000,000–$3,000,000	1.0%
$3,000,000–$6,000,000	1.1%
>$6,000,000	0.8%
Home Health Care Services	1.1%
Hospitals	0.6%
Hotels & Motels	1.4%
Household Appliances	1.9%
Household Audio & Video Equipment	6.5%
Household Furniture	6.1%
Insurance Agents, Brokers & Service	0.4%
Investment Advice	1.36%
Jewelry Stores	5.4%
Leather & Leather Products	2.1%
Lumber & Other Building Materials (Retail)	1.7%
Malt Beverages	10.0%
Mortgage Bankers & Loan Correspondents	1.3%
Motion Picture Theaters	1.0%
Musical Instruments	2.2%
Office Furniture (excluding wood)	0.6%
Office of Physicians	1.2%
Ophthalmic Goods	3.5%
Paints, Varnishes, Lacquers	2.1%
Perfume, Cosmetic, Toilet Preparations	19.2%
Photographic Equipment & Supplies	1.4%

Table 6.1 ■ Continued

Commodity of Class of Business	% of Annual Sales Spent on Advertising
Racing, including Track Operations	3.3%
Radio, TV & Consumer Electronic Stores	2.4%
Real Estate Agents & Managers	2.7%
Restaurants	
Full Service, < $15.00	2.0%
Full Service, $15.00–$24.99	1.8%
Full Service, > $25.00	2.2%
Limited Service	1.6%
Security Brokers & Dealers	0.5%
Shoe Stores	2.3%
Skilled Nursing Care Facilities	0.4%
Sporting Goods Stores	
Full Line, < $2,000,000	2.0%
Full Line, $2,000,000–$5,000,000	1.6%
Full Line, > $5,000,000	2.6%
Specialty, < $5,000,000	3.3%
Specialty, $500,000–$999,999	2.7%
Specialty, $1,000,000–$2,000,000	2.6%
Specialty, > $2,000,000	3.0%
Television Broadcast Stations	8.3%
Tires & Inner Tubes	2.2%
Tobacco Products	4.0%
Variety Stores	4.5%
Video Tape Rental	4.7%
Women's Clothing Stores	3.7%

Sources: (as stated in the 2010 NAA Planbook)
Schonfeld & Associates Inc., Advertising Ratios & Budgets, June 2008
North American Retail Dealers Association, Cost of Doing Business Survey Report, 2007
National Bicycle Dealers Association, The Cost of Doing Business, 2006–07
National Retail Hardware Association, Cost of Doing Business Study, 2007
National Restaurant Association, Restaurant Industry Operations Report, 2007–08
National Sporting Goods Association, Cost of Doing Business Survey, 2006–07
Schonfeld & Associates Inc., Advertising Ratios & Budgets, June 2007

The reason for this practice is to provide a general overview of whether total advertising expenditures change over time by industry in response to market or competitive conditions. Year-to-year comparisons are also reported to provide another measure of relative growth for specific industries. For example, an article interpreting the advertising-to-sales figures of Table 6.1 stated that 11 of the business sectors reported had shown an increase in their advertising-to-sales ratio. The relative increase or decrease in advertising expenditures is also considered in light of economic conditions because it indicates the private-sector reaction to projected increases or decreases in sales.

This first budgeting model of advertising-to-sales ratio has some shortcomings. First, the use of past sales to determine future advertising allocation does not seem logical. Advertising is assumed to influence a firm's sales performance, yet the use of past sales to determine future advertising allocations will not take that interdependence into consideration. In addition, such a method would not allow the advertising manager to adjust the budget to meet emerging changes in the marketplace because the only criterion used in the past sales performance of the firm.

The second advertising-to-sales method attempts to eliminate these drawbacks. Instead of basing advertising expenditures on past sales, a forecast of *future (next year) sales* is made, and the advertising budget is calculated as a fixed percentage of that amount. The formula for this model is

$$A_2 = f(S_2)$$

where: A_2 is the total advertising budget for next year (or period 2)
f is a fixed percentage
S_2 is the total sales forecasted for next year (or period 2).

This second model is an improvement over the previous one because it bases its budget calculation on the sales period that will theoretically be affected by the advertising expenditures to be budgeted. However, the model still reflects only one of the possible effects of advertising—its relationship to sales. It ignores all other possible variables that may be influenced by advertising, mainly some of its long-term effects.

The advertising-to-sales ratio is as good a method of budgeting advertising expenditures as a firm makes it. If used to develop a base allocation, which can be modified as the market or firm objectives change, then it is a very good initial yardstick for budget considerations.

Different authors cite 2% to 5% as the usual range of advertising-to-sales ratio. As Table 6.1 indicates, that ratio may vary considerably for specific industries or retail categories. As an example, automobile manufacturers in the United States traditionally spend 1%, or less of sales on advertising, whereas retailers and mail-order houses have had higher spending levels at 4% to 7% of sales.

As more advertisers shift their advertising dollars from traditional media to interactive and mobile media, the advertising-to-sales ratio might change considerably.

One approach to using advertising to sales ratio was developed by James O. Peckham and is known as Peckham's Formula. Below is a short description of that approach.

Peckham's Formula

James O. Peckham developed a formula that establishes a relationship between sales and advertising expenditures by analyzing the Nielsen's store-audit data for grocery, toilet, and drug products, between 1960 and 1978. Peckham's formula is applicable only in product categories where there is a demonstrable correlation between "share of voice" and "share of market." Share of voice is the brand advertising expenditures as a percentage, or share, of the total advertising expenditures for the product category, whereas share of market is the brand's total sales units as a percentage of the total sales for the product category.

Peckham recommends setting a new brand share of voice at one and a half times the target share of market desired at the end of the brand's first 2 years. Peckham's formula was based on existing sales and advertising data collected over an eighteen-year period. Although the formula provides an interesting insight in allocation of advertising dollars for the introduction of a new product, the results of adopting this strategy cannot be generalized. Rossiter and Percy indicate that the "order of entry" of a brand in a market can affect the potential expected market share for that brand. As such, it should also be a major consideration when using Peckham's formula as a guideline for the allocation of advertising dollars.[3]

Leo Bogart indicates that Peckham did not report whether advertising expenditures were distributed equally over the 24-months period. In fact, in one specific case, a substantial portion of the expenditures took place during the initial introductory month.[4] It is important to also underscore that, although Peckham's formula was based on actual sales and advertising data, the environment of advertising and changes in the economy and distribution factors may affect sales results as well. Therefore, although Peckham's formula is an interesting application of the advertising-to-sales ratio model, it must be taken into consideration with prudence and only as an indication that the ratio between sales and advertising for new products entering a market is likely to be higher than that of established products with an existing market share.

The Competitive-Parity Method

Another popular method for setting advertising budgets is the competitive-parity method. This method establishes an advertising budget as a proportion or share of the product or service's market share. The expenditure on advertising for the product is expressed as a share of the total advertising expenditures for all products in that category. As an example, if the total advertising expenditure for athletic shoes is $100 million, and the expenditure for Nike is $30 million, Nike would have a 30 percent share of advertising, or a 30 percent *share of voice*.

The formula for the calculation of the "share of voice" for a specific product/service is as follows:

$$A_{SV} = \frac{A_F}{A_C + A_F}$$

where: A_{SV} is the firm's advertising share of voice
A_F is the firm's advertising expenditures for the period in question
A_C is all competitors' advertising expenditures for the period in question.

The reason for using share of voice as a method for setting advertising budgets is the belief that, in a stable market, a firm's share of voice should ideally be the same as its share of

---

[3](John R. Rossiter and Larry Percy, Advertising Communication and Promotion Management, 2nd ed, New York: McGraw-Hill, 1997). 39–40.

[4]Leo Bogart, Strategy in Advertising, 2nd ed. (Chicago: NTC Business Books, Crain Publication, 1986), 45–46.

market. If a firm were attempting to gain market share over its competition, its share of voice should be greater than its share of market. This would commonly be the case for new products entering a competitive marketplace.

The competitive-parity method also focuses on only one of the many variables affecting advertising. The fact that competitors' actions should be one of the variables considered when establishing advertising expenditures is undeniable. However, this method ignores other important factors that may affect advertising allocation. Changes in consumer habits, economic conditions, and the strategic objectives of a firm are some of the forces that should be taken into account.

This method does have some advantages. It provides a yardstick for comparing results whenever a product faces a very stable market and enjoys a mature competitive position. As such, it is a useful planning and control tool.

The competitive-parity method is used frequently when the total market potential is known and there are well-established competitors with relatively stable shares of the total market. For example, assume we are considering developing an advertising budget for one of the six dry cleaning companies operating in Concord, a community with a population of 350,000 people. The total market for dry cleaning services in Concord is divided among the six companies as follows:

Company	Total Concord Market Share
The Adams Family Company	30%
The Best Look Co.	15%
The Clean and Iron Co.	17%
The Dominion	14%
Excellent Cleaners	8%
Fresh and Ready	16%

Total advertising and promotion expenditures for dry cleaning businesses in Concord is approximately $300,000 per year (as of last year's reported data). Assuming all competitors in this industry in Concord are happy with their current market share and their overall goal for next year is to maintain their respective market positions, it is likely that their relative advertising and promotion budgets for the following year will be consistent with their relative market share.

It is also reasonable to assume that companies with relatively larger market shares and stable sales performance, will normally invest proportionally less in advertising and promotion, whereas less established companies and those with a smaller market share might invest relatively more to defend their market position. Therefore, share of voice for the six dry cleaning businesses in Concord will not reflect exactly their share of market. In other words, The Adams Family Company may decide that it does not need to invest an amount equivalent to 30% of the total advertising and promotion expenditures for the industry, because it can count on its business having greater consumer awareness and on the loyalty of its core customers, as a result of having operated in Concord for a longer period of time than any of its competitors.

Therefore, the dry cleaning businesses in Concord might budget their advertising and promotion expenditures for next year as follows:

Company	Market Share	Share of Voice	Total A/P Budget
The Adams Family	30%	25%	$ 75,000
The Best Look Co.	15%	15%	45,000
The Clean and Iron Co.	17%	16.6%	50,000
The Dominion	14%	15%	45,000
Excellent Cleaners	8%	10%	30,000
Fresh and Ready	16%	18.3%	55,000

It is apparent from the preceding table that, although the dry cleaning businesses in Concord use a competitive-parity method to allocate their advertising and promotion budgets, each business allocation does not reflect the exact share of market of that business. Differences in budget allocation may reflect the desire by some of the businesses to achieve a larger market share. Another possible explanation for these differences is that some of the companies fear more aggressive moves by competitors and are taking a defensive position when deciding on their budget for the following year. Also, the Adams Family Company projected budget may reflect its confidence in continuing to secure the same relative market share without having to increase advertising and promotion spending.

The relationship between share of market and share of voice may not apply to all product categories and industries. Research conducted by J. O. Peckham for the A. C. Nielsen Company showed a demonstrable correlation between these two variables (J. O. Peckham, *The Wheel of Marketing,* Scarsdale, N.Y., Self-published, 1981). Peckham's research was conducted mainly for consumer products sold through retailers such as supermarkets and drugstores, and therefore might apply to most national brands of packaged goods, but not necessarily to other types of products. Therefore, a careful examination of the industry's advertising and promotional expenditures and of the relative share of market and share of voice of the companies that are responsible for the great majority of sales in that industry is necessary before deciding to adopt this budgeting method.

Another important consideration is that the competitive-parity method assumes a relatively stable demand and, therefore, a mature market as well as marketing communication strategies that are comparable across competitors.

The competitive-parity method also takes into consideration the long-term effects of advertising. To establish a stable market share, the competitive-parity method suggests that a firm should maintain a share of voice over a certain period of time. Many leaders in industry believe likewise. Edwin Artzt, chairman and CEO of Proctor & Gamble, stated that "advertising is a longer-term investment, and it shouldn't be intruded upon by short-term needs." This statement supports continued expenditures in advertising despite changes in profits and sales. The expenditures should continue to reflect a firm's competitive position as opposed to a concentration on immediate results.

The Objective-and-Task Method

The objective-and-task method of setting advertising budgets is used by the majority of the largest advertisers in the United States.[5] According to this method, a firm will first set objectives for its advertising task. These objectives may include reaching a certain percentage of the population or of prospective customers, creating awareness of the product among a percentage of the individuals within a specific market or geographical area, and so on. After these objectives have been set, the firm calculates which media to purchase and at what cost. That cost may be arrived at by deciding what percentage of the total population should be reached by the advertisement and how many times each individual in that population should be exposed to the advertising message. The cost of obtaining this advertising reach and frequency will then be translated into an advertising budget.

This approach is more logical than the previous two approaches because it relates specific tasks of advertising to the amount of money being spent to accomplish those tasks. It also relates the theory of advertising effect to the budget decisions. For example, if the main goal of advertising is to develop awareness among the public, then fewer exposures per person will be needed than if the objective is to achieve customer preference for the product.

The major problem with this approach is that it doesn't fully consider the relationship between short-term and long-term effects of advertising or translate them immediately into a budgeting decision. In addition, although a certain number of exposures may produce a specific effect on the audience, that relationship is not always constant or measurable. Nevertheless, the objective-and-task method is an improvement over the percentage-of-sales method and the competitive-parity method. This method has been refined using different mathematical models. Large advertising firms have developed their own internal models which they use to formulate budgets in specific product and service categories. This practice illustrates the belief that the memorability and efficiency of advertising will differ by product categories or according to geographic or demographic factors.

The appreciation of the task-and-objective budgeting method requires clearly stated objectives and fairly reliable estimations of the audience's response to different advertising or promotional messages—as, for example, assume a company's objective is to achieve an increase of 3% in its sales for the following years. The company's total sales are 400MM units; therefore the company's sales goal will be 412MM units.

Based on previous experiences, the company knows that if 100 people will buy its product, two will buy it once a month only and one will buy it an average of three times a month. Therefore if the people try the product, this will result in average sales of five products per month or 60 products per year. To increase total sales of the product by 12,000 units, the company needs to ensure that at least 20,000 new customers will try its product.

The company's advertising program and industry data show that for every 1,000 people that become aware of the product, 250 are likely to try it. Therefore, at least 160,000 consumers must become aware of the product to achieve the company's desired increased sales goal. The company plans to advertise its new product on the cable Food Channel *Family Food* to reach its key potential buyers.

Research provided by the Food Channel to its advertisers indicates that a 20% level of awareness is reached if subscribers are exposed to at least four commercials per month. Because the total audience of the Food Channel is over 1,000,000 people during average

---

[5]Charles H. Patti and Vincent Blasko, "Budgeting Practices of Big Advertisers," *Journal of Advertising Research* 21 (December 1981): 23–29.

viewing times, the company will potentially reach at least 200,000 people if it buys five 30-second commercials every month.

The average cost of a 30-second commercial on the Food Channel is $10,000: therefore, the total media costs for the company would amount to $480,000 per year. In addition, the advertising agency creative fees and production costs are forecasted to be $45,000. Therefore, the total estimated budget for advertising and production is $525,000.

Although there are many other ways to establish an advertising budget, the three methods discussed in this portion of the chapter are the ones most commonly used by advertising firms and agencies. Another method frequently mentioned is the "all-you-can-afford" method, meaning a firm will decide to spend as much money as it can on advertising without regard to specific objectives, to competitive parity, or even to the level of sales. In addition, economic models are used to try to achieve a level of expenditure that will bring a positive marginal gain to the company. Examples of such methods abound in specific studies made for classes or even brands of products over the years. As marketing factors change drastically and as the number of variables affecting marketing decisions increase, economic models to develop advertising budgets and to assess advertising effectiveness are becoming increasingly complicated. Nevertheless, in the future it is expected that more and more firms and advertising agencies alike will resort to such models because advertising expenditures are increasing and the accountability of advertising is becoming more of an issue, at least among U.S. advertisers. The next section will consider recent changes in advertising budgeting methods.

RECENT TRENDS IN ADVERTISING BUDGETING DECISIONS

The late 1980s and the early 1990s witnessed a major change in consumer response to advertising in the United States. Following a period of economic growth caused by massive defense spending by the federal government, U.S. producers found themselves trying to reach a market faced with slowed income growth and higher unemployment. The American recession and the increase in foreign and domestic competition produced a market situation that advertisers had not faced before. One of its immediate effects was an increase in the number of appeals that proposed immediate results for the consumer. Coupons, price-cuttings, discounts, and special promotions became more common in the marketplace, with varying market reactions. One such reaction was the perception that brand advertising no longer worked. Brands are insubstantial things that signal differences between products. Good brands are supported by large amounts of advertising expenditures. Despite the evidence of the value of brands, in the early 1990s, creating and sustaining brands became increasingly difficult. Manufacturers were under pressure to make big short-run gains in sales, and a lot of brand managers gave up long-term advertising expenditures on behalf of short-term promotional tools such as sweepstakes, price-cutting, and price promotions.

The perceived problem of declining importance of brands and the emphasis on promotion to achieve short-term sales gains caused advertisers to seek alternative ways to allocate their budgets. Manufacturers tried to steer consumers' attention away from promotion by developing a stronger image for some of their specific products rather than developing an image for a product class. Campbell's Soup, for example, emphasized in its advertising soups with less salt or soups developed for consumption by children. This strategy of steering away from the umbrella strategy of brand advertising by focusing on specific brand attributes benefitting narrowly targeted audiences has been one of many attempts to reestablish the long-term importance of brand image in the marketplace.

Another trend of the early 1990s was the focus on environmental, political, or controversial issues. Some corporations have developed campaigns dealing with such issues; an example is the Benetton campaign mentioned in Chapter 3. When the topic was so controversial that a specific corporate sponsor might not want to be identified with it, a nonprofit organization of sorts established by interested corporations was used as the campaign spokesperson.

Corporate critics have argued that it is unfair for companies to campaign in their own interest while hiding behind fictitious foundations. An example is the campaign against the animal rights movement by Americans for Medical Progress, an "educational foundation" largely funded by U.S. Surgical Corp. U.S. Surgical is a medical company with annual sales of more than $800 million that kills thousands of dogs each year so that its customers—physicians—can practice surgery using U.S. Surgical products. The campaign features print advertisements with a picture of a white rat and the caption, "Some People Just See a Rat. We See a Cure for Cancer."

Several organizations of this kind provide a public relations front for corporations to campaign for causes that benefit them. The American Council on Science and Health, which counts among its contributors Anheuser-Busch, Philip Morris, and Dow Chemical, is another example of this type of entity.[6]

The twenty-first century has seen major changes in the media and in social communication patterns. The extraordinary growth of digital media,: the emergence and almost universal popularity of search engines such as Google, Yahoo!, and Bling: and the powerful influence of social networks have caused advertising agencies and advertisers alike to develop new communication strategies to reach their customers and their audiences. Advertising budgets in the past ten years have steadily shifted their expenditures from traditional media such as newspapers, magazines, television, and radio to the new channels provided by digital technology. A recent report by TSN Media Intelligence shows that from 2007 to 2008, advertising expenditures in network TV, spot TV, magazines, newspapers, and radio declined, whereas Internet advertising increased by 4.6%.

Some traditional media channels with very targeted audiences, also showed an increase in advertising expenditures. That was true for cable television, Spanish language TV, TV/national syndication, Spanish language magazines, and free-standing inserts.

In an effort to better understand changes in consumer behavior and in their use of all the new communication technology available to them, advertising professionals are attempting to measure more closely the effect advertising expenditures may have on brand equity and the overall sales of their clients.

The Internet's share of total media ad spending has been rising at least 1 percentage point each year since 2000. Online ad spending may exceed $25 billion in 2010.

There are many reasons for this growth: Internet ads are seen as more measurable by advertisers; and Internet ads can be targeted more specifically than traditional media ads. In addition, younger consumers spend less time on traditional media and an increasing amount of time using digital media through their computer and a host of emerging mobile devices.

Although most advertising professionals agree that there will continue to be growth in Internet advertising spending, there are/is still many differing opinions on what types of majors will be most effective on the Web. Continuing research on advertising banners, click-through ads, web videos, product placement, and in-game advertising will hopefully produce the answers advertisers need to allocate their budgets in the most efficient and effective manner.

---

[6]Laura Bird, "Corporate Critics Complain Companies Hide Behind 'Grass-Roots' Campaigns," *The Wall Street Journal,* July 8, 1992, B-1, B-6.

Table 6.2 ■ Percent Change in Measured Ad Spending[1]

MEDIA SECTOR ■ Media Type (Sectors & types listed in rank order of spending)	Full Year 2008 vs. 2007	4th Quarter 2008 vs. 2007
TELEVISION MEDIA	**0.1%**	**−5.1%**
■ Network TV	−0.8%	−10.6%
■ Cable TV	2.1%	−2.3%
■ Spot TV[2]	−2.8%	−3.6%
■ Spanish Language TV	0.1%	−0.1%
■ Syndication–National	6.5%	0.0%
MAGAZINE MEDIA[3]	**−7.5%**	**−13.9%**
■ Consumer Magazines	−7.5%	−13.6%
■ B-to-B Magazines	−10.5%	−18.3%
■ Sunday Magazines	−4.8%	−12.0%
■ Local Magazines	−4.6%	−13.0%
■ Spanish Language Magazines	4.9%	3.4%
NEWSPAPER MEDIA	**−11.8%**	**−16.5%**
■ Local Newspapers	−11.8%	−16.3%
■ National Newspapers	−11.5%	−17.9%
■ Spanish Language Newspapers	−14.2%	−18.3%
INTERNET[4]	**4.6%**	**7.0%**
RADIO MEDIA	**−10.3%**	**−14.8%**
■ Local Radio[5]	−11.1%	−17.7%
■ National Spot Radio	−11.2%	−11.6%
■ Network Radio	−2.7%	−3.2%
OUTDOOR	**−1.7%**	**−11.2%**
FSIs[6]	**1.8%**	**5.0%**
TOTAL	**−4.1%**	**−9.2%**

Source: TNS Media Intelligence
1. Figures are based on the TNS Media Intelligence Stradegy™ multimedia ad expenditure database across all TNS MI measured media, including: Network TV, Spot TV (101 DMAs); Cable TV (52 networks); Syndication TV; Hispanic Network TV (4 networks); Consumer Magazines (241 publications); Sunday Magazines (8 publications); Local Magazines (18 publications); Hispanic Magazines (24 publications); Business-to-Business Magazines (264 publications); Local Newspapers (144 publications); National Newspapers (3 publications); Hispanic Newspapers (49 publications); Network Radio (5 networks); Spot Radio; Local Radio (32 markets); Internet; and Outdoor. Figures do not include public service announcement (PSA) data.
2. Spot TV figures do not include Hispanic Spot TV data.
3. Magazine media includes Publishers Information Bureau (PIB) data.
4. Internet figures are based on display advertising only.
5. Local Radio includes expenditures for 32 markets in the United States.
6. FSI data represents distribution costs only.

CONCLUSION

Advertising budgeting is a very important management function. The advertising budget is a planning tool in that it allows the advertiser to develop both short-term and long-term objectives and to allocate a specific allowance of money to accomplish them. At the same time, budgeting is a control tool in that it allows the advertiser to verify which advertising techniques best serve their intended purposes.

In recent years, advertising budget decision makers in the United States have faced a changing environment. In an effort to adapt to that environment, advertisers and advertising agencies alike have come up with different techniques yet to be proven effective. This experimentation has led to the view that advertising expenditures should be integrated more directly with all other marketing functions of the firm, thereby strengthening their interdependence.

As our markets become more global, the clutter of advertising messages increases, and consumers become more educated and more discriminating, advertising budgets will have to adapt to these changing conditions. More innovative ways of spending advertising allocations will have to be devised by advertising agencies and by manufacturers. In addition, new and innovative media channels are continuing to appear, allowing advertisers to experiment with different ways of conveying their messages to the public. Interactive media and sales channels are but a few that are changing the world of advertising today. An advertising manger should keep in mind that adapting to change is essential to survival, and the ability to adapt and to devise effective advertising methods is crucial to the long-term survival both of the firm and of advertising as we know it today.

EXERCISES

1. The Excellent Company sells (gift) products to retailers in Blanco County. Blanco County covers 711.24 miles, contains 3 cities/towns, and has 9,082 inhabitants. The median income per family of Blanco County is $49,320.

    The Excellent Company products are sold through 15 different stores in the area and retail prices range from $20 for small gift items, such as picture frames, to $200 for larger gift items. Average retail markup is 40% over manufacturers' prices. Total sales of The Excellent Company products in 2007 for all of Blanco County were $6,500,000 (at retail prices).

    In 2006, total sales of The Excellent Company were $2,800,000 (at manufacturer's prices). The Marketing Director decided to increase the annual marketing budget from its customary 15% of past sales to 20% of past sales for 2007. Resulting sales were considerably increased from 2006 to 2007, as shown in the previous paragraph.

    Excited by the 2007 sales results, the Marketing Director decided to increase the marketing budget of The Excellent Company for 2008 to 25% of sales. Total retail sales for 2008 for Excellent Company products were $8,000,000 at retail prices.

    Disappointed by the 2008 results, the Marketing Director decided to cut the overall advertising budget for The Excellent Company for 2009 back to 20% of sales. Total sales for 2009 for the Excellent Company dropped 20% compared to 2008 sales.
    a. Plot the four points on the sales-response-to-advertising curve and estimate from them the shape of the curve.
    b. What do the results indicate about the appropriateness of the current level of advertising?

Case 6.1

The Happy Dog Company

Maryanne Lupus and George Ration started a successful small company manufacturing dog biscuits from only natural organic ingredients. The company struggled during its first two years, but through word of mouth and referrals from dog lovers and other (non-) nonprofit associations, the Happy Dog Company was able to break even the third year of its operations.

During 2002, at the beginning of their fourth year of operations, Maryanne and George made a first modest investment in marketing. Most of their marketing budget was spent in advertising in specialty magazines targeting dog owners concerned with their animals' well-being and health. The demographic profile of the Happy Dog Company's customers was as follows:

Household size:	1 adult	50%
	2 adults	35%
	2 adults and 1–2 children under 18	15%

The age distribution of the heads of the households was:	25–35	60%
	36–45	25%
	46–65	15%

There appeared to be an overall ratio of 60% male and 40% female customers (excluding children under 18) The average household income of Happy Dog customers was $ 85,000.

Most Happy Dog customers described themselves as concerned with health and physically active. Most owned at least one dog, and the average household owned 2.5 dogs. Happy Dog's customers bought their dog food at specialty stores or at their veterinarian practice. After trying the product for two months, they frequently became repeat buyers. In fact, over the three years of operations, the company had only lost 10% of all the customers it had acquired during that period.

Therefore, Happy Dog Company customers were very loyal and appeared to be very valuable ambassadors for its products through their interaction with friends and other dog owners.

At the end of 2001, their second year of operations, the Happy Dog Company had total gross sales of $550,000, and an increase of 50% over the total gross sales of their first year of operations. At the end of 2002, after their first marketing investment, the company owners were anxious to see the results of their advertising campaign. Table 6.1.1 is the Profit and Loss statement of the Happy Dog Company at the end of 2002.

Total gross sales for the Happy Dog Company had grown almost 33% from 2001 to 2002. The owners assumed that although some natural growth could have occurred just as a result of continued word of mouth and perhaps some increase in per capita consumption of their products, it would be reasonable to assume that the expenditures made in advertising in 2002 had been mostly responsible for the company's overall sales results. They just were not sure of what should be the optimal amount of advertising expenditures to ensure the projected gross sales growth and to attain their desired market share goal.

Maryanne and George were hoping to be able to continue to have a growth in gross sales ranging from 20% to 25% a year, until the company had established a market share of 50% in its niche market. The organic dog food and dog biscuits were still a small percentage of the total pet food market.

Table 6.1.1 ■ Profit and Loss Statement, 2002

Gross Sales				730,500
	Less Returns	15,200		
	Less Allowances	7,800		
	Total		23,000	
Net Sales				707,500
	Less Cost of Goods Sold		340,000	
Gross Margin				367,500
	Less Operating Expenses			
	Marketing Expenses	53,000		
	Sales Salaries	89,000		
	Delivery	18,000		
	Total		160,000	
	Administrative Expenses			
	Office Salaries	102,000		
	Office Supplies	9,600		
	Miscellaneous	4,500		
	Total		116,100	
	General Expenses			
	Rent	43,000		
	Miscellaneous	6,400		
	Total		49,400	
	Total Operating Expenses		325,500	
	Net Profit Before Taxes			42,000

In 2003 it was forecasted that total U.S. pet food sales would exceed $13 billion. Dog treats, which included dog biscuits were a small portion of total sales and in 2003 it was forecasted that dog treats would account for $1.8 billion in sales. However, the organic pet food category was growing at a much faster rate than overall sales growth of pet food. Leading manufacturers were just starting to consider entering this new market, and it was very important for new companies, like the Happy Dog Company, to establish their market share and their brand as soon as possible in this growing market.

The Happy Dog Company competed directly with two other manufacturers of organic dog treats. These other companies were much smaller than Happy Dog, but directed their sales efforts to the same customer target sought by the Happy Dog Company. Together the two competitors had gross sales of approximately $100,000 in 2002, but they were planning to expand their sales as their production capacity might allow.

Advertising expenditures as a percentage of sales for the specialty pet food products ranged from 3% of sales to about 8% of sales. No figures were available for the large manufacturers such as Purina, because their advertising and market expenditures were reported as a whole for all the products they manufactured.

Maryanne and George were comparing two possible strategies to set the advertising budget for 2003. Maryanne argued that they should set the budget as a percentage of future sales. She felt that if Happy Dog were to invest at least 7% of future sales in advertising for 2003, the company would be able to increase sales by at least 13%, which was the overall industry growth of sales for dog biscuits for 2003. She also felt that, if they were to allocate around 11% of future sales to advertising in 2003, the company might be able to reach its goal of overall sales increase of 20%.

George was more optimistic. He believed that the 32% growth in sales the company experienced from 2001 to 2002, had been a direct result of their advertising investment of $53,000 during that year. He, therefore, estimated that an investment of a little over 7% of forecasted sales would yield an increase in total gross sales of over 30% for 2003.

If the Happy Dog Company owners were to opt for using a competitive-parity method to develop their company's advertising budget for 2003, their overall advertising expenditures should not exceed an average of 5% of sales every year.

Some additional factors also had to be considered. The variable costs of manufacturing the organic Happy Dog biscuits was also forecasted to increase by 5% in 2003, due to increasing demand of the ingredients needed and due to rising utility costs. In addition, it was very important for the Happy Dog Company to continue to generate a net profit before taxes each year, as it would be its major source of capital for financing future expansion of its market and operations. An average of $40,000 to $50,000 a year in net profit was needed to continue to grow and to take advantage of its expanding niche market.

Consider the data in Table 6.1.1, and assume that all fixed costs for the company would remain the same for 2003. Also, assume that returns and allowances would continue to be the same percentage of overall gross sales. Based on the information Maryanne and George had, and on the data in the case, what would you recommend as the overall 2003 Happy Dog Company's advertising budget, if it were to attain the goals stated by its founders? Please explain your recommendation in detail and provide a pro-forma profit and loss statement for 2003.

Case 6.2

BusinesSuites (A)[7]

THE COMPANY AND CURRENT OPERATIONS

Background

Established in 1989, BusinesSuites' (BSS) core business was to provide office space and infrastructure support to businesses and individuals that were their clients. The company was in the "office business center industry" and offered a one-stop office solution with immediate access to full-service, furnished offices on terms ranging from one week to twelve months.

Based in Austin, Texas, BSS operated 14 centers in four states. BSS had four centers in Maryland (Baltimore, Columbia (2), and Owings Mills); seven in Texas (Austin (3), Houston (2), and Houston suburbs Sugar Land, and The Woodlands); two in Virginia (Newport News, and Richmond); and one in Las Vegas, Nevada. In total, BSS had 829 individual offices available (see www.businessuites.com for a virtual tour of the centers).

The company's mission was to provide their clients "the freedom to succeed by understanding our clients' businesses, anticipating their needs, and personalizing our service." In addition to office space at prestigious addresses, BSS offered their clients a wide range of services. For example, these services included: call screening and patching, data/word processing, copies and scanning, office supplies, and catering.

BSS had 1,188 clients (589 regular office leased and 599 virtual office (VO)). Note that since many regular office clients leased multiple offices, the number of regular office client companies is less than the number of offices leased. VO clients were individuals and businesses that did *not* have a permanent office at BSS but had their telephone calls, mail and delivery services received at a BSS center. VO clients also could arrange to use the BSS conference meeting room or a guest office on an hourly basis. Table 6.2.1 presents a breakdown of the number of VO clients, regular offices leased, square footage, and the number of offices in each of the 14 centers.

During the present year, BSS was projected to have total revenue of approximately $14,500,000. Regular office rentals accounted for 78% of total revenue and services[8] 22%. Classified as service revenue, VO clients accounted for approximately 10.2% of BSS's total revenue.

Led by BSS President John Jordan and his executive team of Nancy Brown, Ronnie Bulanek, and Connie Shortes, BSS had a total of approximately 50 team members. Most of the team members worked at the center level. Each center had a Manager who ran the business by serving as the primary contact on all sales, management, and operations issues. A back office Client Service Coordinator served as the "second in command" to the center manager, providing support and backup on sales, billing, and client support. In addition, each center had a front desk Client Service Coordinator in charge of taking care of the reception desk and meeting and greeting clients in person and on the phone. This coordinator was a critical client service position because this person represented the face and voice of the company to clients.

---

[7]This case was written by John Murphy, the University of Texas at Austin and John Jordan, BusinesSuites. The case is designed to serve as the basis for classroom discussion and not to illustrate either the effective or ineffective handling of an administrative situation. The case is used with permission granted by BusinesSuites.

[8]Services revenue included virtual office revenue (49%), conference room charges (7%), office setup fees (3%), telephone extra services (3%), long distance (8%), parking (5%), postage/currier services (8%), administrative assistance (1%), copies and faxes (13%), other services (2%), and late fees (1%).

Table 6.2.1 ■ Client Categories, Sq. Feet, # Office, Occupancy % by Center

Center	Clients VO	Full S.	Total	Sq. F	# Offices	Occupancy
Austin, TX						
Arboretum	39	40	79	17,499	62	64.5%
Barton Springs	28	47	75	20,174	66	71.2%
Westlake	51	45	96	16,600	55	81.8%
Houston, TX						
Chasewood	28	50	78	18,198	62	80.6%
Sugar Creek	49	50	99	16,371	58	86.2%
Uptown	81	49	130	19,630	59	83.1%
Waterway	44	42	86	14,688	50	84.0%
Las Vegas, NV						
Hughes	78	48	126	20,269	82	58.5%
Southwest Total	398	371	769	143,429	494	75.1%
Baltimore, MD						
Harborplace	68	52	122	16,890	54	96.3%
Owings Mills	37	30	67	12,922	47	63.8%
Park View/T. Center	70	90	160	35,784	121	74.4%
Newport News, VA						
Oyster Point	10	29	39	17,544	65	44.6%
Richmond, VA						
West End	16	17	33	13,017	48	35.3%
Northeast Total	201	218	419	96,157	384	60.9%
Grand Total	599	589	1,188	239,586	829	71.0%

Note: The Park View and Town Center locations in Columbia, Maryland are combined in this table. The two Virginia centers were relatively new and working to become established.

Source: BSS Confidential

Regular Office Clients

BSS offered companies and individuals the option of immediate access to a furnished office with telephone, wireless Internet access, copy and other services in a prestigious location. Note that pricing on the offices varied by center plus the size and location of the space within a center. For example, at the Barton Springs BSS Center a small (130 sq. ft.) interior office leased for $1,150; a slightly larger interior (180 sq. ft.) office for $1,375; a small (160 sq. ft.) exterior office for $1,725; and a large (252 sq. ft.) exterior, corner office for $2,450. Exhibit 6.2.1 presents a floor plan of the Barton Springs Center.

Chapter 6 ■ Determining the Advertising Appropriation and Budgeting 143

Exhibit 6.2.1 ■ Floor Plan Barton Spring Center

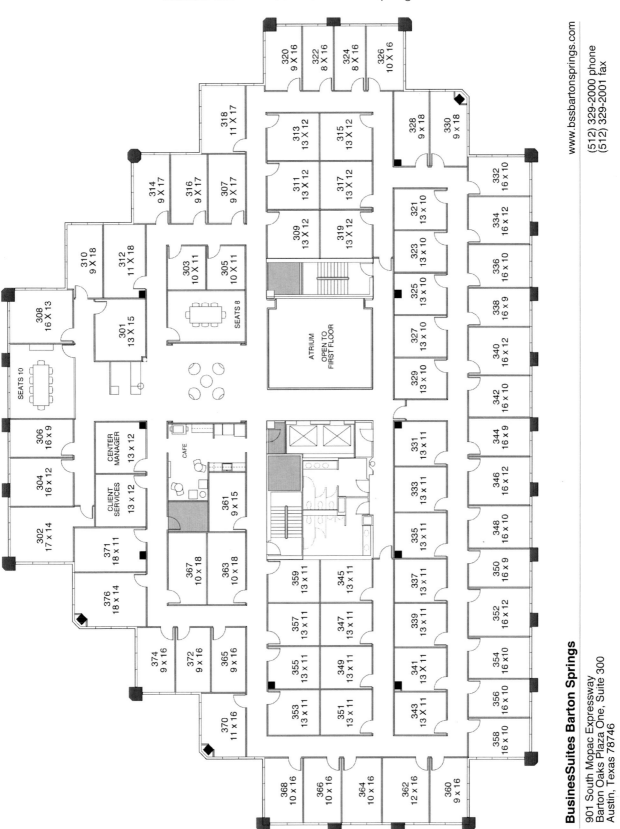

Virtual Office Clients

VO clients were offered a flexible option that allows a company or individual to have access to BSS services and present a professional appearance at a relatively low monthly cost vis-à-vis full-time (regular) office clients. The VO program requires that an individual sign a service agreement with a minimum term of three months. A VO client may receive mail only or mail and telephone service at any one of BSS's centers. Sixteen hours of conference room/day office time per month could also be included in regular VO contract. The use of administrative and other services plus technical support could be negotiated for inclusion in a VO package. Prices for the VO packages ranged from $125 (discounted to $79 at some times) to $350 per month. Table 6.2.2 presents a breakdown of VO clients by categories of service plus service billings for a typical month all by individual centers.

The Competition

BSS competed in the office business center industry that had grown to be a multi-billion dollar market with more than 4,000 locations in North America. Key competitors included Regus and a number of independent operators in a highly fragmented industry. Typically, local competitors tended to target a price point that was about 25% less than BSS in terms of revenue per occupied office. Regus promoted its "network" of thousands of locations worldwide as a primary basis for leasing one of their offices. More information on the industry was available from the Office Business Center Association International (www.obcai.com), which was the industry trade association.

Several national firms who specialize in VOs provided aggressive competition for BSS. These firms included Intelligent Office, Davinci Virtual, and easyvirtualoffices.com.

Current Marketing Activities

Total marketing expenses for the current year were projected to be $432,541. This appropriation was 2% less than the previous year. This total was divided into three broad categories: (1) broker commissions/referrals $82,847; (2) client goodwill and promotions $61,685; and, (3) advertising and marketing $288,009.

Broker commissions/referrals related to direct commissions were paid to traditional commercial brokers and online brokers/referral services as well as promotional programs targeted at commercial brokers. Generally, BSS paid commercial brokers $1,000 when a referred prospect was converted to a client. For online brokers, BSS paid 10% of the value of the office portion of the transaction.

Client goodwill and promotions related to breakfasts, snacks, and luncheons provided regularly to clients. Advertising and marketing expenses consisted of pay-per-click advertising (60%) and direct mail (15%) with the remainder for sales collateral; search engine optimization; collateral and other direct selling supplies; print advertising and print directories; and other advertising and selling expenses.

Table 6.2.2 ■ VO Client by Categories and Monthly Services Billings by Center

Center	Clients[1]					Services[3]
	Conf. R[2]	Mail	M/Phone	Full VO	Total	
Austin, TX						
Arboretum	0	15	10	14	39	$2,214
Barton Springs	0	8	5	15	28	$1,067
Westlake	0	25	15	11	51	$819
Houston, TX						
Chasewood	3	6	5	14	28	$191
Sugar Creek	2	20	11	16	49	$2,491
Uptown	0	43	21	17	81	$823
Waterway	0	16	6	22	44	$734
Las Vegas, NV						
Hughes	0	52	13	13	78	$111
Southwest Total	5	185	86	122	398	$8,450
Baltimore, MD						
Harborplace	3	34	14	17	68	$1,914
Owings Mills	1	20	4	12	37	$870
Park View/T. Center	0	30	23	17	70	$1,381
Newport News, VA						
Oyster Point	0	4	1	5	10	$206
Richmond, VA						
West End	1	6	2	7	16	$273
Northeast Total	5	94	44	58	201	$4,644
Grand Total	10	279	130	180	599	$13,094

Note: Park View and Town Center locations in Columbia, Maryland are combined in this table.

Source: BSS Confidential

[1] Monthly charges for the categories of VO clients were: mail service only at prestigious address $125 (some discounted to $79); mail/phone that included telephone answering $250; full virtual office that included telephone answering plus 16 hours of meeting room time $350.

[2] Conference room VO clients only use the conference rooms (no mail or phone services). Some of these clients paid a fixed amount every month for a block of conference room time (use it or lose it) at a discount and others paid for time as they use it at the "client" rate.

[3] For the most recent one month only.

The company generated new business from the following sources:

Source of New Business	% of Total Value of New Business
Client Referrals & Expansions	31.4%
Pay-Per-Click Advertising and Search Engine Optimization	31.4%
Commercial Real Estate Brokers	18.8%
Online Brokers and Referral Services	8.0%
Direct Mail to New Businesses	4.9%
Signage on and in front of Buildings	4.5%
Other Marketing Efforts	0.8%
Print Advertising and Print Directories	0.2%
Total	100.0%

Based on client feedback, the reasons for selecting an office center, in the order of importance were: (1) location; (2) people; (3) price; and (4) amenities. Jordan noted, however, that BSS's experience was that while everyone cites location as most important, in many cases when it comes down to BSS or a competitor down the road, BSS people and the prospect's interaction with the team during the sales process made the difference in getting the deal closed. Further, in the long-run, BSS has found that their people also made the difference in retaining clients.

Past experience clearly indicates that one of the best sources of new clients is a recommendation from existing clients. Therefore, BSS offered cash incentives to clients for referrals who sign a contract.

Individual center managers were responsible for direct sales to prospects. BSS's broad strategy was that corporate should be responsible for generating leads while center managers are responsible for closing the sales. All managers received formal training in managing the sales process, dealing with objections, and so on. In closing sales, BSS recognized the importance of the first impression of both the center and the manager. Further, BSS relied on their website plus high quality collateral pieces to convey the desired image to prospects during the sales process.

LOOKING AHEAD TO THE NEXT FISCAL YEAR

Marketing Strategy for Next Year

BSS President Jordan established an overall marketing objective for next year's integrated brand promotion plan to be to increase overall revenue by 8%. The fiscal year was from July 1 through June 30. This 8% target was based on a projection of significant VO revenue growth and contributions from regular office leases (improving both pricing and occupancy) and other client service charges.

In achieving this overall objective Jordan anticipated that a significant proportion of this growth would be achieved by (1) increasing occupancy while maintaining and/or selectively slightly increasing prices for regular office clients, especially in low performing centers; (2) significantly increasing the number of VO clients in all 14 locations; and (3) by increasing the services utilized by regular office plus new and existing VO clients.

VO clients were to be a primary focus of BSS's marketing efforts during the coming fiscal year. Further, Jordan believed that any proposed marketing programs would need to be simple, rely on repetition, be focused, easy to execute, and inexpensive.

Consistent with this strategy, the three centers that had occupancy rates below 60% needed special attention. These centers were: Hughes, Oyster Point, and West End. Therefore, each of these centers needed to be individually addressed so that client occupancy rates could be increased to a target of 70% for Hughes and 60% for Oyster Point and West End by the end of the upcoming fiscal year. Oyster Point and West End were both opened in the past two years. This special focus on these three centers was not to suggest that continuing efforts were to be ignored at other centers where constant work and changes were required to maintain their occupancy rates.

An important component of Mr. Jordan's overall marketing strategy was to increase the type and volume of services utilized by regular office and VO clients. A program(s) that specifically increased BSSs' revenue stream via telephone, Internet, day use of offices and conference rooms, and administrative support services provided was an important strategic issue that needed to be addressed. Achievements in this area were to be measured by revenue per occupied office (RevPOO).

One of the possibilities management had considered in the past to stimulate both regular office and VO clients was forming a strategic alliance or partnership with a firm(s) that was important to their clients and prospective clients. Candidates for these alliances included Office Max, The Office Depot, FedExOffice, and UPS. Such a partnership seemed to hold potential for helping both BSS's clients' and the firm's bottom-line.

The IBP Appropriation for Next Year

With BSS's past marketing budgets and the strategy described above in mind, Jordan felt that the first step in planning the firm's IBP efforts for next year was to establish the total appropriation. Once the appropriation was set he could break this down into the three major categories followed by specifying amounts for specific programs.

In approaching this task Jordan felt that it would be prudent to begin by identifying three levels of investment—low, medium, and high. Then, by examining the trade-offs created by funding requirements at these different levels of investment, he felt that a more rational appropriation could be identified.

The final appropriation and budget must include all SEM expenses, production, mailing, media, and other costs. Note that the compensation of center personnel who would be involved in implementing any programs would not be charged against this budget. Finally, cost efficiency and return-on-investment were important criteria in evaluating each level of investment.

Name _____ Date _____

QUESTIONS FOR DISCUSSION AND REVIEW

1. Of the major strategic areas of to be emphasized in the coming fiscal year, which holds the most promise in terms of increasing revenue? Why?

   _____
   _____
   _____
   _____

2. How appropriate is the BSS marketing strategy of corporate being responsible for generating leads and the local center manager closing the sale?

   _____
   _____
   _____
   _____

3. How important is the present year's appropriation level in identifying next year's?

   _____
   _____
   _____
   _____

4. In the coming year, would you recommend that BSS focus more resources on (a) new or underperforming sources of new business or (b) attempting to grow its top sources of new business? Why?

   _____
   _____
   _____
   _____

5. Based on the information provided, how would you rank the return-on-investment for the various sources of new business?

_____

_____

_____

_____

6. Has the company over-invested or under-invested in its marketing efforts or is investment appropriate at the current levels? Why?

_____

_____

_____

_____

Case 6.3

The Corner Flower Market

The Corner Flower Market was a full-service florist shop located in an upscale residential area in a medium-sized city in central Texas. Marion Berry, the owner of the shop had been doing business for over 10 years and had a regular clientele, which was responsible for about 30% of his normal revenue. The store sold primarily cut flowers, flower arrangements, and plants.

The store was a member of wire services, including the FTD national network of florists. Berry believed that service was a most important component of his product offerings; therefore, he did not charge for home deliveries. He also maintained a very diverse stock of items to be used in the preparation of the flower gifts ordered by clients. These items ranged from special baskets or containers, exotic ribbons, elaborate and humorous cards, as well as balloons and other specialty items.

Mr. Berry had a staff of two trained florists, a stock maintenance and storage specialist, and two customer service/order taking persons. The store maintained a sophisticated database on their regular customers, and they were able to identify special dates, as well as the types and sizes of arrangements that were customarily ordered for occasions such as formal dinners and family/friends parties.

Mr. Berry was able to handle also large orders, such as weddings, religious ceremonies, funerals and anniversary parties. A very small percentage of his sales were orders from businesses and corporations, and these were usually businesses owned by his regular residential customers.

Like all other florists, most of the fresh-cut flowers in the store were imported domestically from California or internationally from South America. Mr. Berry believed that his customers were also very price sensitive and was able to establish his prices below those of his competition. Therefore, with a high level of service and competitively lower process, the Corner Flower Market had to achieve a pretty stable level of sales to provide adequate profits.

The U.S. Florists Industry

In 2009, the U.S. Department of Commerce's Bureau of Economic Analysis estimated the size of the floriculture industry at retail in 2008 total revenue was about $35.6 billion. This industry typically includes cut flowers, potted flowers, foliage plants, and bedding and garden plants. There were 1,759 retail florist shops in the United States, and the estimated annual sales per florist were $320,000. Most consumers buy flowers from florist shops, supermarkets, garden centers and discount chain stores. Internet sales of fresh flower arrangements have expanded in the past few years. Sales to businesses make up from 15% to 20% of a retail florist in business.

Most florists nationwide are small businesses, and as an industry, florists have experienced steady growth for the past 20 years at least, despite changing economic conditions. Excluding sales of outdoor bedding and garden plants (46% of total retail sales), fresh flowers account for 36% of total sales and flowering/green houseplants account for the remaining 20% of retail sales.

The consumers market is dominated by women (79%), and this is also true for sales of fresh-cut flowers (65% are purchased by women). The largest segment of consumers for this industry is represented by affluent empty nesters (18%), followed by lower-income empty nesters (13%). Other significant segments are married active elderly, affluent traditional families, and singles.

Sixty-three percent of those who buy florists' products buy for themselves and 37% buy the products as gifts. However, fresh flowers are bought primarily as gifts (67%).

An industry report published in 2010 (1) indicates that calendar events account for only 15% of overall floral sales. Of the remaining 85%, Mother's Day sales are 23% and Valentine's Day sales are 16%. It is also interesting to note that consumers indicated that 21% of all cut flower sales are purchased for

Table 6.3.1 ■ Precentage of Retail Sales by Month

	All Retail Sales	Florists
January	7.0%	6.7%
February	6.9	8.2
March	8.2	7.5
April	8.0	10.0
May	8.4	13.7
June	8.5	6.3
July	8.2	6.2
August	8.8	5.8
September	8.2	6.4
October	8.6	6.7
November	8.9	7.0
December	10.3	15.5

Sources: U.S. Department of Commerce and Florists' Transworld Delivery Association

home decoration. (2) A threat of some concern to the florist industry's growth was the entrance of supermarkets, nurseries, and discount stores into the fresh-cut flowers market. These new entries had in the past concentrated on selling green plants and had met with relatively little success because of the overall weakness of this market. However, many of the larger retailers had begun carrying fresh-cut flowers at lower prices than those of florist shops. The new entries introduced some long-run uncertainties in the market.

Historically, florists had higher sales in the months of April, May and December (see Table 6.3.1). Flowers and plants are generally considered a "safe" gift because they are emotionally appealing and the vast majority of people appreciate receiving them, hence the fact that 67% of fresh-cut flowers are purchased as gifts. The reasons for purchasing flowers as gifts are get-well wishes (20%), funerals (14%), anniversaries (13%), surprise (10%), birthdays (9%), and other occasions (31%).

An important institution in the florist industry is the FTD organization. The number of wire orders for flowers continues to increase since the establishment of the FTD. FTD is a cooperative of over 20,000 florists in the United States and over 52,000 florists in 142 countries. FTD is the only member-owned floral cooperative of its kind. Recently, some other businesses have started to offer floral wire services as well. However, these are still a very small portion of the total market.

TARGET MARKET

In organizing the firm's marketing efforts, Mr. Berry identified its target market. The market consisted of businesses in a ten- to fifteen-block radius of the store. This geographic market area included the downtown area, its immediate upscale residential area, student neighborhoods, and some other affluent residential areas west of downtown. Mr. Berry believed that obtaining business accounts first would lead to a great chance of procuring personal accounts. Not only would the store get the new business account, but also there would be the potential of developing a personal account with every individual who worked in the business.

COMPETITION

The Corner Flower Market competed in a market that was highly fragmented, with no truly dominant florist competitor. Most of the 97 local firms listed in the Yellow Pages under "Florists—Retail" could be classified as reasonably small businesses grossing under $100,000 per year. Eighty-nine percent of the city's florists had only one location. The Rose Shop had the most locations (five), and another large florist had three locations. The bulk of the other multiple-outlet florists had two locations.

Like all other businesses, the Corner Flower Market has developed its own Web site. The Web site provided general information about the store and its location and included instructions for ordering flowers over the telephone and some examples of the baskets and arrangements that were commonly available. The Web site did not allow prospective customers to order online, but Mr. Berry was seriously considering adding more functionality to the Web site to give its customers and prospective customers more flexibility and better service. He felt that online orders would be very attractive to businesses in particular and had been consulting with an advertising agency in town on the possibility of developing a more functional and attractive Web site for his store.

Several of Mr. Berry's competitors made greater use of the Web by advertising their stores on different sites. For example, the local Chamber of Commerce had a Web site that illustrated all the amenities available in the city and around it, and it also allowed local businesses to advertise. The Chamber of Commerce Web site charged different rates for banner ads and for click-through ads, but it did not allow the placement of animated commercials.

CURRENT SALES AND ADVERTISING

The Corner Flower Market was projecting average monthly sales for 2011 of $40,000. It is important to note, however, that the business climate for florists had suffered a decrease in sales because of the economic downturn the country had experienced in 2009, and the projections made for 2011 might not be entirely realistic. Mr. Berry was hopeful, however, that with a smart strategic communication plan and an increase in the annual advertising allocation, the store could achieve total sales for 2011 of at least $450,000.

Traditionally, the Corner Flower Store sales were as follows: 10% sales of cut flowers, 60% sales of flower arrangements; 10% sales of plants, and 20% sales of gift items.

In previous years, the Corner Flower Market advertising consisted of its Web site, a listing in the Yellow Pages directory, two direct mailings to regular customers and potential customers in its geographic area, and one half-page ad in the largest circulation local newspaper in the week prior to Valentine's Day.

NEXT YEAR'S ADVERTISING BUDGET

Mr. Berry wanted to increase awareness in the shop's target market and was considering an increase in advertising for the coming year. As part of this campaign, he had approved a new series of print ads for the coming year. Exhibit 6.3.1 presents three representative ad from the upcoming campaign. He felt these ads were appropriate and would do much to sharpen the store's image. Management's task now was to determine the advertising appropriations for the upcoming year and a supporting rationale. Industrywide, florists used the percentage-of-sales method to set advertising appropriations, and Mr. Berry was willing to invest a percentage of sales in this manner. The average flower shop typically spent between 10% and 15% of sales on advertising. After identifying an appropriate total amount to invest in advertising, management would develop a budget allocation and supporting rationale.

Exhibit 6.3.1

Several questions needed to be answered before the budget could be created. Would the campaign be continuous or seasonal in nature? What media vehicles should be used? Should the target market be divided into business and personal accounts? Should there be a contingency fund to allow for flexibility, and if so, how large should it be? At this point, it became clear that budgeting and media planning decisions were interrelated. Representative media costs are presented in Appendix 6.3.1.

Appendix 6.3.1 ■ Representative Media Costs

THE DAILY Monthly Earned Rate Per-Column Inch		
Inches per Month	**Daily**	**Sunday**
Open-transient rate	$38.98	$47.33
1 to 14	32.21	39.60
15	29.01	35.70
35	26.79	32.96
65	25.90	31.84
350	25.34	31.16
650	25.02	30.80
1,300	24.65	30.31
3,300	24.28	29.87
4,500	23.10	28.38
6,500	22.24	26.87
7,500	21.38	25.34

The Weekly Tabloid					
	1x	**3x**	**6x**	**13x**	**26x**
Full page	$1,150	$1,025	$965	$910	$790
3/4	925	835	785	735	640
2/3, or junior page	850	770	720	680	590
1/2	650	585	550	525	450
3/8	550	485	460	435	375
1/3	485	435	410	385	335
1/4	365	325	310	290	250
1/6	270	250	235	220	190
1/8	220	200	185	170	150
1/12	165	145	140	135	115
1/16	125	115	110	100	90
Color advertising is available upon request. Add $160 per standard color per page to the black-and-white rates.					

Local Business Magazine (Monthly) Display Rates (ROP)

Black & White		1x	4x	7x	13x	26x	39x	52x
Full page		$1,290	$1,225	$1,155	$1,095	$1,030	$970	$900
3/4 page		1,120	1,060	1,015	950	900	840	780
1/2 island		970	920	870	820	775	730	675
1/2 page		885	820	775	730	695	650	605
Magazine 2/3		735	695	655	620	590	550	520
1/4 page		580	545	520	490	465	435	410
Magazine 1/3		485	465	435	415	390	365	340
1/8 page		385	370	350	330	310	290	270
1/16 page		200	190	180	170	160	150	140
Color Rates:								
One process color:	$250							
Full color:	$350							
Two color:	$300							
One PMS color:	$300							

Outdoor Advertising Local Market Only

		Coverage		
		Posters		
Population	GRP/Show	Nonilluminated	Illuminated	Cost per month
850,000	100	12	32	$14,008
	75	9	24	10,626
	50	6	16	7,064
	25	3	8	3,562

| Radio
Cost same for :30 and :60 spots		
KLEB-FM B-93	Time	Cost
AMD	6–10a	$95
MID	10–3p	85
PMD	3–7p	95
NITE	7p-12a	45
TAP	6a-7p	92
KSRU-FM	Time	Cost
AMD	6–10a	$90
MID	10–3p	82
PMD	3–7p	90
NITE	7p-12a	50
TAP	6a-7p	88
KTBJ-AM	Time	Cost
AMD	6–10a	$75
MID	10–3p	45
PMD	3–7p	65
NITE	7p-12a	25
TAP	6a-7p	50

Name _____   Date _____

QUESTIONS FOR DISCUSSION AND REVIEW

1. In planning the advertising appropriation for the coming year, how large a role is the current level of investment likely to play? How might the new advertising campaign (see Exhibit 6.3.1) affect the decision of how much to invest in advertising?

   _____

   _____

   _____

   _____

2. How realistic is the sales increase forecasted for the coming year? How should this forecast be related to the level of advertising investment?

   _____

   _____

   _____

   _____

3. What major considerations should be evaluated in establishing an amount to invest in advertising? What factors are most important in allocating the advertising investment across budget categories, such as target markets and months of the year?

   _____

   _____

   _____

   _____

In addition, if Mr. Berry were to consider spending some of his advertising dollars on improving his Web site or advertising on local and national digital media, the following options were available to him:

1. Development, update and added functionality to the Corner Flower Market Web site:

   Initial production cost: $20,000.00
   Annual maintenance and updating: $10,000/year
   (This was the average bid he had obtained from a local advertising company.)

   _____
   _____
   _____
   _____

2. Advertising on the Chamber of Commerce Web site:

   The cost of a banner ad would be $500/month and the Chamber of Commerce required a minimum of 6-month contracts.

   The "pay-per-click" rate for the same Web site was $3.00 per click, and the Web site data indicated an average of 750 clicks per advertiser per week. "Pay-per-click" ads could be purchased on weekly contracts with a minimum commitment of 4 weeks per year.

   _____
   _____
   _____
   _____

Case 6.4

Ben's Workshop[9]

BACKGROUND

Ben's Workshop (BW) was a first-class automotive repair and maintenance facility committed exclusively to the mechanical repair and servicing of Mercedes-Benz vehicles. Since its establishment by Ben Scholtz in Austin, Texas in 1979, the shop's reputation for professional service and excellent work had propelled its evolution into the largest independent Mercedes-Benz repair facility in the region, and one of the premier facilities in the country.

In 1991, A new, state-of-the-art facility was custom-designed by Scholtz and his father-in-law, an engineer with Brown & Root, an international construction firm. The facility was uniquely tailored to accommodate the repair and maintenance of Mercedes-Benz automobiles. It included an on-site warehouse stocked with Mercedes-Benz parts, sixteen custom service bays, an innovative ventilation system, and a comfortable reception area to welcome clients. But the pride and joy of the shop was its possession of two Star Diagnostic System (SDS) computers introduced by Mercedes-Benz in 1998. All Mercedes-Benz models since 2000 are completely dependent on the SDS, and BW was one of only a few independent service providers in the nation with access to it. This had allowed the shop to build and maintain valuable contacts at Mercedes-Benz, providing insightful benefits that were passed on to its clients.

Such superior facilities attracted not only clients, but talented auto technicians as well. The entire staff at BW averaged 18 years of experience working with Mercedes-Benz automobiles, the majority of which had been accumulated at BW. Each of the technicians viewed their work as a craft, and had genuine concern for the quality of their craftsmanship. The familiar faces under the hood were an important reason for the loyalty of the shop's clients.

In January 2007, Bill and Jennifer Morey purchased BW. Morey's father was an assistant general manager at General Motors, affording Bill ample exposure to all areas of the auto industry. Morey saw an opportunity for BW to expand and grow, while still maintaining the ideals of fairness and quality upon which the shop was founded. All of the shop's employees stayed through the transition, and several new ones were added. Most importantly, clients remained loyal to the shop. This resulted from customers' confidence in BW's quality work and lent stability to the business. One of Morey's first moves was to update the firm's website.

A PROPOSED DIRECT MAIL PROGRAM

The staff at BW defined their job simply: they fix Mercedes-Benz cars. This specificity yielded an equally specific target market of Mercedes-Benz owners, which make up a fractional share of the auto market. The first step in achieving BW's mission was to connect with these Mercedes-Benz owners in the Austin area, and to give them a reason to visit their facility.

To do this in an effective and cost-efficient way was the shop's biggest marketing challenge. BW had approximately 6,000 established customers on file, about half of which were "active customers", or those that had visited the shop within the last 24 months. The shop identified the members of its target market who had not yet visited the shop as "conquest customers". Morey believed that communication with both established

---

[9]This case was written by Erin Cutchen and John H. Murphy, The University of Texas at Austin. The case is designed to serve as the basis for classroom discussion and not to illustrate either the effective or ineffective handling of an administrative situation. The case is used with permission granted by Ben's Workshop.

and conquest customers would be crucial to maintaining and expanding the shop's clientele. Further, he felt that the business's primary method of communication with their present and targeted customers would logically be direct mail.

However, as an advertising medium, direct mail had several disadvantages. First, the effectiveness of direct mail in BW's situation would depend on having a mailer distinctive enough to garner the prospect's attention. Morey felt that, given the volume of mailing piece received by relatively affluent Mercedes owners, designing such a mailer would be challenging. Further, direct mail was relatively costly or incorrect addresses on various mailing rendered some lists inefficient.

On the other hand, Morey felt that since his business's target market was small and specific, direct mail offered several powerful advantages. First, various messages could be tested and refined using samples drawn from mailing lists. Second, these messages could literally be tailored on a consumer-by-consumer basis, allowing for even more precision of communication.

A conversation with a direct mail supplier revealed that BW could have access to all registered automobile owners in the state of Texas, allowing them to identify every Mercedes-Benz owner in Travis County (whose county seat was Austin) and its contiguous counties of Blanco, Burnet, Caldwell, Hayes, and Williamson. The supplier estimated that there would be approximately 14,000 Mercedes-Benz owners in this six county area. For each owner the data base included the owner's name, address, the year, make, and model of their vehicle, and its vehicle identification number.

From this pool of 14,000, the direct mail supplier offered to clean the list and merger it with BM's customer data base, correcting any changes in address and performing a "de-dup", or eliminating duplicate individuals who own more than one Mercedes. The supplier estimated that the cleaned list would contain approximately 9,500 Mercedes-Benz owners of which approximately 7,000 would be classified as conquest customers and 2,500 would be active BW customers.

In planning a direct mail program, Morey felt that potential clients should be contacted at least twice a year. He also felt that every direct mail contact must include a special discount offer of some type to encourage action. Further, if the receiver of the conquest mailer lived in any of the five outlying counties, the card also should include an offer for a free car rental.

For those on the mailing list who were already established BW customers, further divisions could be made, placing the customers into active and inactive categories. Active customers could receive "service reminders", letters alerting the receiver to any services their car may need. Inactive customers could be contacted quarterly, with letters also carrying special offers and a mention of the time elapsed since their last visit. In addition, after any service performed at BW, the customer should receive a thank-you letter asking for feedback, and requesting that the customer recommend the shop to fellow Mercedes owners. This letter would serve to reassure the customer that their money had been well-spent.

PLANNING FOR NEXT YEAR

Further, in planning his new firm's marketing efforts for the coming fiscal year, Morey forecasted total income from repairs, service, sales of parts, and so on of $2.1 million, up 5% from the previous year.

Further, in planning BW's marketing efforts for next year, Morey had decided that while he would consider expanding the total amount of money invested in direct mail, he must definitely sharpen the focus of the firm's direct mail efforts. Perhaps more emphasis should be placed on the "conquest" or the "inactive customers" groups in terms of frequency or the type of mailing piece? In adding more impact to the mailers he wanted to develop new strategies and specific pieces that would enhance the likelihood that the prospects would read, consider, and respond to the offers. Further, he wondered about the use of other vehicles instead of postcards and traditional envelopes to increase the impact of the firm's mail contacts.

As he contemplated these and other possible changes or refinements aimed at improving the effectiveness of the BW's direct marketing efforts, Morey felt that his first decision was to identify the total appropriation or amount to be invested in the direct mail campaign next year. In structuring his thinking he decided to initially establish three levels of investment: high, medium, and low. He reasoned that examining how these levels of spending restricted his direct marketing options should prove useful in deciding on what would be the optimal trade-off in terms of the appropriation for next year.

Exhibit 6.4.1 ■ Floor Plan Barton Spring Center

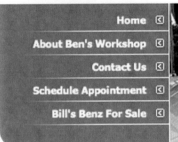

Latest News

$50 OFF YOUR NEXT VISIT

January 15, 2010

Receive $50 off your next visit for mentioning that you visited our new website!

Welcome to Ben's Workshop
Mercedes-Benz Service & Repair, Austin, Texas

For over 30 years Ben's Workshop has developed a reputation as the single source for trusted Mercedes-Benz service and repair. As one of the nations largest independent Mercedes-Benz repair facilities, Ben's Workshop is staffed and equipped in a state of the art facility to serve Mercedes-Benz customers whether they own a classic 60's model or a current year model.

Technicians at Ben's Workshop average over 20 years each of dedicated Mercedes-Benz service and as one of only a handful of repair facilities nationwide, Ben's Workshop subscribes and utilizes the Mercedes-Benz Star Diagnostic System for advanced diagnostic ability.

Centrally located just off 5th Street in downtown Austin, Ben's Workshop offers customer conveniences that include extended service hours, free pick-up and delivery and a dedication on the part of every employee to serve you with the highest level of customer satisfaction.

When I opened Ben's (originally Ben'z) Workshop in 1979 as a one-man shop for the repair and service of Mercedes-Benz automobiles, I had no plans nor vision for it to grow the way it did for the next 28 years. Similarly, in 2007 when I decided to pursue other interests, I had little vision as to what might become of what we had built into the premier independent Mercedes-Benz facility in our part of the country. We were very fortunate, therefore, when Bill Morey took over ownership of the operation and brought with him the skills, desire, and commitment to continue the tradition of high quality service that we had established. I know that because of this, the future portends many more years of satisfied Mercedes-Benz ownership for the thousands of clients both past, present, and future who will enjoy the service they'll find at Ben's.

Name _____ Date _____

QUESTIONS FOR DISCUSSION AND REVIEW

1. What factors play an important role in determining how much money BW should invest in direct mail next year?

   _____
   _____
   _____
   _____

2. What is the relationship between identifying a reasonable appropriation and media costs and planning?

   _____
   _____
   _____
   _____

3. What factors are most important in allocating the direct mail allocation across the three target customer groups?

   _____
   _____
   _____
   _____

4. What other effective yet cost-efficient IBP marketing tools might BW use to further advance their business? How might these tools be used to supplement a direct mail campaign?

   _____
   _____
   _____
   _____

Chapter 7
Developing Creative Strategies

When you write a creative brief, you're not filling out a form. You're crafting the story of your brand and its reason to exist and thrive in the world.[1]

THE PURPOSE AND CONTEXT OF CREATIVE STRATEGY BRIEFS

As stressed earlier in this book, to be most effective, advertising and IBP programs must be based on careful consideration of the environment within which the brand is being marketed. The first step in the IBP management process is a careful situation analysis designed to provide the decision maker with information useful in making IBP management decisions. After the situation has been evaluated, often producing a SWOT analysis (identifying Strengths, Weaknesses, Opportunities, and Threats), the next steps in the process are to establish clear, measurable objectives and then to determine the IBP appropriation.

After these decisions have been at least tentatively made, management focuses on developing a statement of creative strategy that will be used in developing all aspects of IBP programs. Ideally, the development of a statement of creative strategy or brief should be a collaborative team effort involving brand management, account planners, and the creative individuals who will use the statement or brief as a guide in developing specific ads, promotions, and other elements of an IBP program or campaign.

The purpose of developing a statement of creative strategy is to make the advertising and other communications more effective by channeling the efforts of the creative individual(s) in the most productive direction. As Bill Bernbach so aptly pointed out, "a good strategy gives a good creative person something to be creative about."[2]

---

[1] Howard Margulies "What Are You Packing into Your (Creative) Briefs?" *Advertising Age,* May 18, 2009. (http://adage.com/smallagency/post?article_id136711).

[2] "A conversation with Bill Bernbach," film produced by the American Association of Advertising Agencies, 1976.

Bernbach also stressed that management has a responsibility to establish the boundaries or "lay down the tracks" within which the creative specialists should work. This discipline of following an appropriate creative strategy statement sharpens the creative person's work and multiplies its value. In the absence of the discipline and focus provided by a clear statement of creative strategy, there is a danger of misdirected creativity, which can be dysfunctional. In fact, undisciplined creativity can lead to destructive results.[3] For example, prospects that are exposed to unfocused, inappropriate advertising may be less likely to try the brand than those who are *not* exposed!

Four steps are included in the creative process: (1) the development of a clear statement of creative strategy; (2) the creative team, armed with the brief, develops tactical executions; (3) the evaluation of proposed tactical executions to ensure that the executions are "on strategy;" and (4) approval of the executions for dissemination via media and/or other platforms. Once the creative strategy statement or brief has been agreed on and clearly communicated in writing, management should withdraw from step two in the process, leaving the creatives alone to work their magic. Management interference during the ideation process typically will hinder rather than help build the most appropriate executions. Management reenters the process in the evaluation and approval steps after the creative team has developed its ideas. Typically, the creative team will present example executions to management for discussion and approval. These example executions may be roughs or they may be more highly finished.

After the creative team has developed tentative executions, copy-testing research may be used to provide an outside, objective evaluation of the target audience's reaction to the tactical executions. For example, if the creative team has suggested three alternative tactical executions of the creative strategy, ads based on these three executions could then be tested using separate samples of the target audience to measure their reactions. Based on the research findings, a single, best execution would be selected, or modifications and further research might be appropriate.

At the approval level, management's responsibility is to be sure that the executions are consistent with the previously developed creative brief. If the execution or translations of the strategy into advertising or other forms of IBP do *not* conform to the brief, management should be firm in rejecting it. It may be brilliant, innovative advertising, but if it is off-strategy, management should reject it (or consider modifying the strategy).

In evaluating proposed creative executions, management reviews the rationale provided by the creative team explaining how the executions fit the strategy. This rationale is obviously crucial in determining approval of the tactical executions as consistent with the strategy. Hence, the creative team is advised to develop a concise written explanation of how the executions fit each of the strategy points. This rationale can be used to sell the executions to management. Unfortunately, it is not enough to come up with a great campaign idea. The idea must be presented in a way that will enable the idea to clear the hurdle of account management and client approval, as discussed in Chapter 2.

THE ROLE OF ACCOUNT PLANNERS IN DEVELOPING CREATIVE BRIEFS

Account planning emerged as a discipline inside advertising agencies to interject a stronger consumer perspective into the creative process. The account planner is the consumer's advocate in ensuring that first, the most appropriate consumers are targeted and, then, that the tar-

[3] Ibid.

get's needs, perceptions, concerns, and so on are clearly reflected in the creative brief. Ideally, a collaborative team that includes account management, account planning, media, and creative constructs the brief. An account planner often takes the lead role in fashioning the brief.

Having an account planner on the team means that a consumer advocate, who recognizes the complexity of humans and their emotional attachment to brands, will influence the brief during the development process. The planner's role goes well beyond the information supplied by traditional market researchers. Planners must not only study the consumer, but also identify with him or her. A researcher may create a snapshot of the consumer, but a planner should be able to not only tell who the consumers are, but also what they feel.[4]

Planners develop a point of view (POV) in terms of understanding consumers that is shaped by digging out answers to questions such as: How do consumers feel about my brand right now? How many consumers are talking about my brand (volume) on the Internet and who is being affected (reach)? Which issues about my brand and others in the category are consumers discussing, and how is this discussion affecting their perceptions? What past brand messaging and placement influenced consumers in the category? Partial answers to such questions can be inferred from "buzz analysis" of large data sets provided by organizations like Nielsen and from other measures of online word of mouth.[5]

Account planners are the anthropologists and psychologists of human behavior. They have a keen ear for truth and an ability to transform information into creatively digestible insights. Through research and intuition, planners bring clarity and focus to a wide variety of brand development decisions and work to ensure that creative efforts will resonate in the marketplace with consumers. Planners try to understand consumers and how they behave, react, live, and communicate in a cultural context at a particular point in time.[6]

CREATIVE STRATEGY AND TACTICS

In a broad sense, a creative strategy statement is simply a general outline of what is to be communicated in accomplishing advertising objectives and how the message will be conveyed. A tactical execution, on the other hand, is a specific approach, technique, or device employed to effectively convey the message. Strategy comes first and provides a framework within which tactical executions are developed.

In reality, too often this process is reversed. That is, the advertising execution is developed first, and then a strategy statement is fashioned to fit the execution, or no strategy statement is developed at all. An "execution first" approach runs the risk of overlooking substantial opportunities that could be identified through the process of carefully developing the strategy first. The human tendency to jump in and start generating executions first should be avoided.

Note that advertising's impact comes from creativity in advertising execution. The tactical translation of the strategy into advertising provides the spark that stimulates the desired

---

[4] Larry D. Kelley and Donald W. Jugenheimer, *Advertising Account Planning: A Practical Guide* (New York: M. E. Sharpe, 2006).

[5] These illustrative questions were suggested by Neal Burns, Director of the Center for Brand Research, The University of Texas at Austin and former Account Planner at Carmichael Lynch, an advertising agency in Minneapolis, Minnesota.

[6] Account Planning Group. (2001). Account Planners, Strategic Planners, Planners. In *Account Planning*. Retrieved December 28, 2009, from Nation Master database.

response among members of the target audience. It is possible for a brilliant strategy to fail due to a weak execution or for a brilliant execution of a weak strategy to produce acceptable results. On the other hand, a brilliant execution of a solid strategy is the formula for advertising success.

WHAT SHOULD BE INCLUDED IN A STATEMENT OF CREATIVE STRATEGY?

There is considerable variation in what agencies and textbook authors suggest should be included in a statement of creative strategy. Each individual and agency recommends a slightly different list of points that should be included. In recommending one from among the many approaches suggested, Roman, Maas, and Nisenholtz present a solid set of components for guiding the development of advertising and other IBP activities. These authors suggest that statements of creative strategy should include concise coverage of five major components: (1) target audience, (2) objective, (3) key consumer benefit or core idea, (4) support, and (5) personality (Roman, Maas, and Nisenholtz use "tone and manner").

To these five elements it seems appropriate to add an optional "Mandatories"[7] section. That is, to specify elements that must be reflected in executions. For example, a mandatory could be that the brand's logo and package must be prominently featured in the outdoor ads.

Target Audience

Who is your best prospect? This is perhaps the single most important decision IBP management must make. It is imperative that a clear understanding of the target is conveyed in the brief. The creative team must have this to effectively match the message with the audience. If this match does not happen, end of story, not much else matters, and the ad or ad campaign or other IBP communication effort will not achieve its objective.

A multitude of considerations can be relevant to identifying and describing the most appropriate target audience(s). A demographic profile of the key prospects is a basic starting point, but a more in-depth understanding of consumers is necessary to develop the most effective IBP and advertising efforts. Qualitative profiles of consumers that provide insights into their motivations and how products fit into their lives are of great potential value in defining the audience the brand wishes to affect.

An overly simple and sterile description of the target—"women 18 to 34 with one or more children 12–15 years of age who live in the top 20 metro areas"—should be avoided. Such a description does not tell the creative team enough about the people they are selling to—what they are like, how they feel about brands in the category, what values they have that are relevant to advertising the brand, and so on.

AOI (attitudes, opinions, and interests) insights, lifestyle, and psychographic profile data should be included. This type of information paints a more three-dimensional picture of consumers, enabling marketers to develop more effective programs. For example, SRI's VALS (values and lifestyles systems) categories are widely utilized to classify consumers into groups for purposes of designing marketing programs. The VALS groups are based on a composite of attitudes, values, interests, and lifestyle considerations. For example, VALS classifies consumers into group such as "Thinkers," "Experiencers," and "Strivers." These groups provide a much richer understanding of the relationships between consumers and the brands they use.

---

[7]Roman, Kenneth, Jane Maas, and Martin Nisenholtz, *How to Advertise,* 3rd ed. NewYork: St. Martin's Press, 2003.

One of the dangers in defining a target audience is attempting to reach too many consumers with a single strategy. Stretching a benefit or the way the benefit is communicated in an attempt to appeal to a board target audience can be a costly mistake. The purpose of segmentation analysis is to identify *smaller,* more homogeneous subsets of consumers among whom the brand may develop an advantage. Aiming at broad target audiences potentially squanders the advantage or leverage segmentation is designed to create. The planner should consider developing separate statements of creative strategy for secondary or tertiary audiences instead of lumping too many disparate consumers into one target audience.

Objectives

What should the advertising do? In a statement of creative strategy, management is *not* concerned with specificity or measurement. For guiding the creative team, general statements are appropriate. Here are some examples:

"To create awareness of _____."
"To convey the fact that _____."
"To reinforce the fact that _____."
"To generate leads from qualified prospects."
"To stimulate requests for a DVD explaining the product."
"To build distributor or retailer enthusiasm for _____."
"To increase the depth of awareness that Acme Products is a supplier of a wide selection of quality sports and recreation products."
"To drive traffic to XYZ's Web site."

Key Consumer Benefit

Why should the target consumer buy your brand? This is also referred to as the "copy platform" or "purchase proposition." It should be stated in a concise, straightforward fashion. Sound statements of the key consumer benefit should be thoughtfully based on substantial qualitative and quantitative research, experience, projections, and intuition, all boiled down into 25 words or less.

In selecting a key benefit, the emphasis should be on a customer benefit, not a product feature. This distinction is critical. For a commuter train line a service feature is a convenient schedule of departures and arrivals, a stronger consumer benefit is avoiding the hassles, delays, uncertainty, and frustrations of driving to work.

Luke Sullivan provides a vivid example of the difference between product features and tapping into a more fundamental consumer benefit in two ads for FTD Florists. Visualize two full-page print ads each with the same three color photographs of a small, medium, and large bouquet of red roses, left-to-right, against a white background. The only difference between the two ads is the headline under the bouquets. One states, "We're proud of our wide variety of beautiful flower arrangements. One is just right for your budget." The other, "Exactly how mad is she?"[8]

One of the dangers of defining the key consumer benefit is the temptation to include too many key benefits. Cramming too many benefits into a strategy runs the risk of confusing the target consumer and failing to clearly differentiate the brand from the competition. The

[8]Luke Sullivan *Hey Mr. Whipple, Squeeze This!* (New York: AdWeek Books, 2007).

strategist should avoid including a laundry list of benefits in the creative strategy statement. Experience indicates that the most effective, memorable advertising usually consists of *one clear, concise benefit,* directed to a single target audience.

Support

Why should the target consumer believe the benefit? It is important that advertising be based on an underlying foundation of truth. The best long-run interests of everyone involved are then served, regardless of whether or not the support is specifically mentioned in the advertising. In fact, support is typically not mentioned in the advertising.

Support may come from independent laboratory tests of brands in the category, consumer survey data, testimonials from experts, or any of a variety of sources. The American Dental Association's endorsement of Crest's cavity-prevention claim is a classic example. Other examples of support include the following:

- JD Power automobile resale values, used to support a claim that one brand of automobile performs better than another.
- An article in the *New England Journal of Medicine* that evaluates the ingredients in pain relievers.
- A price comparison survey conducted by a supermarket of 25 commonly purchased items at three different chains on the same day.
- A U.S. Department of Agriculture study of the vitamin content of fruits and vegetables.
- A ConsumerDigest.com report on brand performance in the product category.

Personality

What type of person is your brand like? Advertising messages project obvious and subtle information about the character and personality of the brand. These cues are reflected in the mood, tone, manner, and overall atmosphere created by the advertising. Through its tone and manner, advertising can play a key role in forming and maintaining a brand's perceived personality.

In framing a statement of creative strategy, great care must be taken to carefully consider how the brand's personality should be portrayed through advertising. Does the advertiser want an image of the brand to be breezy or businesslike? Simple or complicated? Home-oriented or cosmopolitan? Exacting or forgiving? In developing a description of the brand's personality, the planner uses adjectives that describe the personality of a person. For example, the following adjectives might be appropriate to use in describing a brand's personality: alluring, believable, clever, delicate, exotic, friendly, generous, humble, industrious, jovial, knowledgeable, legendary, maternal, nimble, open-minded, practical, quirky, respected, spontaneous, thoughtful, unassuming, virtuous, witty, xylophonic, youthful, and zany.

Mandatories

What must be included? Mandatory items that must be included in creative executions may be based on a campaign theme such as a tagline. Typically, the rationale for mandatory elements is based on the important of repetition and consistency in long-term brand building communication. Mandatories may include, for example, the brand's logo, package, Web site URL, a 1–800 telephone number, a trade character, an exclusive medium to be used, the use of a background color, or any of a multitude of other considerations. Some categories, such as banking and drug advertising, have extensive and complex mandatory requirements.

SAMPLE STATEMENTS OF CREATIVE STRATEGY BRIEFS AND EXECUTIONS

Four examples of creative briefs and executions are presented in Exhibits 7.1 through 7.4. These briefs are for key clients of four outstanding agencies: The Richards Group (Dallas) and Motel 6; Butler, Shine, Stern & Partners (San Francisco) and Mini; GSD&M Idea City (Austin) and Norwegian Cruise Line; and Venables Bell & Partners (San Francisco) and Audi. These were selected to illustrate the both the similarities and variations in what is covered in briefs. Notice how each of executions fits the target and follows the guidelines specified in the creative brief.

Exhibit 7.1 ■ Motel 6 Creative Strategy Statement and Example Radio Execution[1]

The Richards Group Creative Brief

Why are we advertising?
To convince budget-minded travelers that it's smart to stay at Motel 6.

Whom are we talking to?
Budget-minded travelers with a common sense approach to life who are traveling on their own dime and know the value of a buck.

What do they currently think?
"Motel 6 is inexpensive, but bordering on cheap. Plus the people who stay there are a bit yucky. So people like me don't stay there. I'll pay a few bucks more to stay elsewhere that's newer, cleaner or has better amenities."

What would we like them to think?
"People like me do stay at Motel 6. And it makes sense for me to stay there so I won't waste money—it's cheap chic."

What is the single most persuasive idea we can convey?
Motel 6 is the smart choice because there's no better value for your buck.

Why should they believe it?
Smart travelers choose Motel 6 because you get everything you really need (and nothing you don't) for a clean, comfortable night's stay at the lowest price of any national chain.

Are there any creative guidelines?
Topics: Visiting friends and relatives, leisure travel by auto, blue collar business
Make sure the creative appeals to both users and non-users
TV: Include 1–800–4-MOTEL6 and motel6.com for reservations

[1]Source: The Richards Group and Motel 6, used by permission.

Exhibit 7.1 ■ Continued

> ANN: *Hi. Tom Bodett for Motel 6 with a comparison. You know, in some ways, a Motel 6 reminds me of those big fancy hotels. They've got beds, we've got beds. They've got sinks and showers, by golly we've got 'em too. There are differences, though. You can't get a hot facial mudpack at Motel 6 like at those fancy joints. And you won't find French-milled soap or avocado body balm. You will, however, get a clean, comfortable room, and a good night's sleep for the lowest prices of any national chain. Always a heck of a deal. Motel 6 has over 750 locations from coast to coast. And we operate every darn one of 'em, which means they're always clean and comfortable. Oh sure, it'll be rough to survive one night without avocado body balm or French-milled soap, but maybe the money you save'll help you get over it. It always works for me. Go to motel6.com for reservations. I'm Tom Bodett for Motel 6, and we'll leave the light on for you.*
>
> [2]To reinforce the creative strategy and the long-running campaign, pre-recorded Tom Bodett also delivers wake-up call messages to guests. An example of one of several different messages, "Good morning, Tom Bodett with your wake-up call. Now before you hang up, I want you to think about what I'm about to say: There's free coffee in the lobby. Okay, see you in a few."

THE PERSONAL PROFILE

A statement of creative strategy ideally should be supplemented by a personal profile. A personal profile is a hypothetical description of a typical consumer who is a member of the target audience. Based on statistical data, focus group interviews, and other appropriate information, the typical consumer is given a name, interests, media exposure patterns, and so on that are described in the narrative profile.

The personal profile is similar to the fictitious but representative individual journalists sometimes invent to dramatize the effect of an event on an average person. The purpose of this profile is to provide the creative team with a human being to whom the team can relate to in the spirit of genuine person-to-person communication.

The personal profile is a wonderful device for sharpening the creative team's understanding of the target audience. The person described in the concise, three-dimensional, composite profile could be real because he or she is based on actual demographics, psychographics, and other relevant information. Coverage of activities and experiences relevant to the product category should be included. In addition, an appropriate photograph of the hypothetical consumer should be included along with the profile.

Exhibit 7.5 presents an example of a personal profile for the following demographic target audience: Males, 13–18, who live in the top 20 metro markets and are heavy consumers of carbonated soft drinks.

Exhibit 7.2a ■ Butler Shine Stern & Partners Creative Brief

CREATIVE BRIEF

DATE:	BRAND: **MINI**	ASSIGNMENT: **Clubman US Launch**
CREATIVE: **All Launch Media**	ACCOUNT: **BSSP**	PLANNING: **BSSP**

WHAT ARE WE TRYING TO ACCOMPLISH? (Objectives)
Introduce the MINI Clubman, the newest member of the MINI family, to the US market. Make Clubman part of the MINI family, not a replacement for the iconic Hardtop; *the new MINI*. It is not for everyone, not everybody's darling...and that's OK.

WHO ARE WE TALKING TO? (Insights that make our message relevant)
Post-Modern Trendsetters. They are curious, experimental & experiential.

They pick and choose from music, travel, art, fashion, books—in some ways that might look contradictory, but they believe that "anything goes." They are curators of their own lives.

VALUES	WANTS
Expressive	Personality-Driven Style
	Authenticity
	Sense of humor, Playfulness
Individualistic	Unique Expressions
Design Oriented	Exposure to new things
	Unexpected creativity
Adaptable Wants	Freedom
	Flexibility
Explorer	Discovery
	Personal Narratives

PMTs should never be told how to be, what to think, what to do, where to go, or what to buy. This will lead to instant rejection and disdain. They are cynical when it comes to advertising. PMTs must feel or experience things for themselves.

WHAT EXACTLY DO WE WANT THEM TO THINK & DO? (Desired impact)
   We want them to see the Clubman to be as unique as they are themselves.

WHAT PROPOSITION WILL TRIGGER THIS CHANGE?

The Clubman is a bit odd and enigmatic. It's a unique self-expression.

WHAT SUPPORT CAN MAKE IT COMPELLING? (Proposition ammunition)
We live in constant flux and are seeking enduring substance. But, enduring doesn't mean static or boring--it is meaningful.

Experiences are the modern cultural currency and become our own personal narratives. They are most powerful when shared. Interesting narratives require character and complexity.

The Clubman is asymmetrical, off-balance, has an edge. It is a MINI with the cuteness rubbed out. It's spirited, it speaks for itself, it has its own voice.

WHAT IS THE TONE OF THIS COMMUNICATION? (The right voice)
Nothing rational - don't talk about space, functionality, family use, etc.

WHAT DO WE HAVE TO DELIVER & WHEN? (Deliverables & key dates)
Create stimuli, not ads, that elicit visceral reaction.

Exhibit 7.2b ■ Mini Clubman Launch Creative—Online Banners and Print Ads

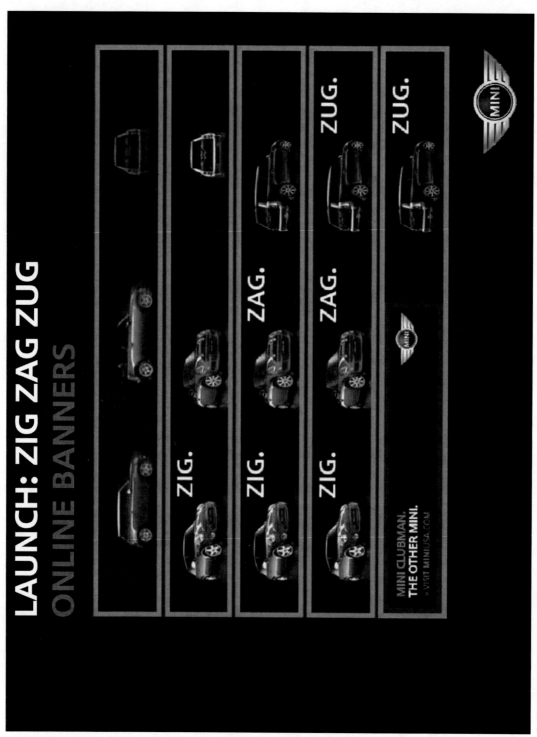

Exhibit 7.2b ■ Continued

Exhibit 7.3a ■ Brand Brief—Norwegian Cruise Line

| Client: NCL | Assignment: NCL brand development |
| Date: 7.29.05 | Job #: NCLCOR5020 |

THE FOUNDATION

What is the task of the assignment?
To develop a unique and ownable brand platform for Norwegian Cruise Line

- Sustainable
- Tone of voice
- Personality/Image
- Competitive differentiation

Describe the people we are talking to.
Americans are famously overworked, overtired, overscheduled, and financially stressed out. Far and away the most frequently mentioned need state voiced by people, was the need to be **free from the pressures and stresses of every day life.** With those pressures lifted on vacation, the opportunity to be "selfish" emerges. "Selfish" in this context means including your own needs in the mix for a change and not catering to others; and creating a day that reflects exactly what you want to do.

*While people seek many things in a vacation, what they need most is the **ability to escape from daily pressures** and be "selfish" for a change. Ultimately, they need some **freedom to follow their own desires** (if only for a week).*

Strategic Target (Current Media Target)
- A25–54,
- HHI $75,000+
- Prof/mgr
- Married
- Slightly female (decision-maker)
- Free-spirited mindset

Core Target
- "Non-conformists"
  - Confident
  - Curious
  - Brand loyal
  - Self-assured
  - Not-easily swayed
  - Go their own way

What are we competing against? How do consumers see our brand?

Competitor #1: Traditional Vacations   > Lots of work/room for error/democratic drawbacks
Traditional vacations can provide a lot of authentic adventures but they can also provide a lot of hassles, work and aggravation.

Competitor #2: Negative Cruise Perceptions > Perceived to be too confining/lack of control (emotionally)
Non-cruisers often feel that the cruise ship experience is too confining, too regimented and too restrictive.

Competitor #3: Direct Competitors   > Claiming a lot of traditional land vacation space
Competitors are well-positioned against benefits more often associated with land vacations. Carnival = the party people/fun ship; Royal Caribbean = thrill seeker/adventure ship. Rarely has there been a category with as powerful an ability to fulfill a driving and fundamental human need, without a category player (usually the leader) claiming the territory for themselves.

Exhibit 7.3a ■ Continued

In a nutshell, our competitors do not deliver the **_freedom from_** hassles and pressure and **_freedom to_** pursue their interests that people are ultimately seeking in a vacation.

NCL: Credit for core attributes, but lack of clear definition

When asked about their opinion of NCL, consumers associate some of the core attributes with the brand: *flexible, low key, no pressure, my way,* but these are all in response to functional product delivery—they don't ladder up to create a distinct brand image, nor does NCL currently promote itself in this way.

What do we want the audience to feel, to think about our product?

NCL provides people with the ultimate **freedom from** demanding and stressful experiences and the ultimate **freedom to** create an experience on their own terms.

What supports this? What is the "reason to believe"?

Freestyle Cruising

Norwegian Cruise Line's Freestyle Cruising provides a unique opportunity to take the category benefit to the extreme and own the most important benefits that people are seeking from a cruise.

Freestyle Cruising has two ultimate values that people are seeking:

1. **Freedom from worry and stress:** being able to decide when and how you want to participate in an activity provides the individual with much greater flexibility and much less stress and pressure.
2. **Freedom to create your ideal vacation:** with regimented schedules lifted and options for every taste or interest laid out before you, the individual is free to follow their heart and construct the perfect day for them. The individual is free to pursue their own self-interests without any pressures to the contrary.

Hawaii
NCL is the clear category leader in Hawaii. More ships, more itineraries and the best way to island hop.

Homeland Ports
NCL sails from more US-based ports than any other cruise line. Provides yet another level of greater flexibility and access.

Exhibit 7.3a ■ Continued

Personality

> Far from being just a compelling feature, Freestyle influences the culture and values of the cruise line.
>
> Norwegian Cruise Line was consistently described as the <u>laid back</u>, <u>relaxed</u>, <u>down-to-earth</u>, respectful, democratic ship; for people who want to <u>go their own way</u> (and see themselves as *"non-conformists"*). **Freestyle shouldn't merely be a "feature"—it should be a way of life aboard NCL ships.**

THE IDEA

Purpose

Defying cruise convention to deliver a liberating experience for all.

Positioning

> **GO YOUR OWN WAY**
> NCL uniquely frees you from the demands of daily life by giving you the opportunity to create the most customizable, flexible experience at sea.

Areas to Explore

- Brand TV
- Consumer magazine
- Trade magazine targeting travel agents
- (Retail) newspaper
- Travel agent collateral
- On-ship materials
- Media-driven concepts
- Website functionality
- Brochures
- Direct mail
- Outdoor
- Radio
- Interactive
- "Stress-centers" (the airport during the holidays, etc.)
- Anything else?

Where appropriate in certain media . . .

- Executions should incorporate a call-to-action: "For more info, call your local travel agent or 1–800 625–5306 or visit www.ncl.com."

Chapter 7 ■ Developing Creative Strategies 181

Exhibit 7.3b

Exhibit 7.4a ■ VB&P and Audi Master Creative Brief

1. What is the business problem we're trying to solve?
Audi is not considered a Tier 1 luxury player in the US luxury category. We needed to change that perception AND launch the all-new Audi A4, (Audi's highest volume model) with approximately 1/3 the media spend of our competitors.
2. Who are we trying to reach? (Demographics, Psychographics, Motivations, Mindset)
These consumers are buying on badge desire that has often been ingrained early in their lives. We need to change this sheep-like buying behavior by disrupting their preconceived notions of luxury badge symbols.
3. What is the category/segment situation?
The Audi A4 competes in the entry-luxury segment, dominated by three entrenched competitors—the BMW 3-series, the Mercedes-Benz C-Class and the Lexus IS. *In the minds of consumers, BMW stands for sporty performance, Mercedes stands for status and Lexus owns quality/reliability. These are all very desirable badge symbols when it comes to a consumers' (usually) first foray in buying a luxury vehicle.*
4. What place does Audi currently hold in the category/segment?
Audi is barely in the conversation. The Audi Brand (and likewise, the A4) don't own a strong position in this segment—more often considered a brand/vehicle of <u>default</u>, not a brand/vehicle of <u>desire</u>. *We need to <u>enter the conversation</u> by putting the A4 in the same ring as the 3-series, C-class and Lexus IS. To do so, we need to challenge our competitors head-on because we know that when doing so, consumers start to see Audi in a different light.* *Once we enter the conversation, we need to <u>change the conversation</u>. To challenge the traditional ideas of luxury and status that these brands have owned. To point out to consumers that all these luxury automotive brands were selling were ubiquity and predictability. An old and tired version of luxury.*
5. What place do we want Audi to hold in the category/segment?
Mercedes Benz (C-class) is your father's luxury car, trapped in the past. *Audi (A4) is a luxury brand that favors progress over protecting the status quo. Audi is about smart sophistication over pomp and circumstance.*
6. What is the real marketing objective?
Launch the all-new A4 in a way that inspires consumers to re-think their preconceived notions of luxury brands.

Exhibit 7.4a ■ VB&P and Audi Master Creative Brief

7.	**What is the big idea?**
	Introducing the all-new Audi A4. The biggest, fastest, most fuel-efficient car in its class.
8.	**What is our ammunition?** (What is head turning? What key product points best support our big idea?)
	<u>*Disrupt Cultural Conventions*</u>—*put the key competitor (Mercedes Benz) in its place in the past. Mercedes Benz is your father's luxury car.*
	<u>*Defy Category Conventions*</u>—*provide the proof that the Audi A4 offers something truly different in the segment. In the automotive world, big usually equals slow and gas guzzling. The juxtaposition of Big + Fast + Fuel-Efficient completely defies category conventions.*
9.	**What is the brand tone?**
	—Challenging the competition, not chasing the competition.
	—Smart, Sophisticated, Progressive

Exhibit 7.4b ■ "Progress is Beautiful"—2009 Audi A4 :60

SFX: Orchestral music

SFX: Orchestral music builds as a continued beat seemingly drives the camera pan forward

SFX: Music continues

SFX: Music continues

SFX: Music continues to build

SFX: Music continues to build

SFX: Full orchestral arrangement climaxes as the old luxury vehicle is replaced on screen with the Audi A4

Exhibit 7.5 ■ Hypothetical Consumer Profile—Soft Drink Beverage Category, Coke Loyalist

Demographic Description: Males, 13–18, who live in the top 20 metro markets and are heavy consumers of carbonated soft drinks.

Below is a Facebook profile of Jacob Fazzio, a 15 year-old high school sophomore. Jacob encapsulates what is cool among urban teenage guys.

Jacob's life is infused with popular teenage trends—his thumbs stay glued to a game controller, he's a texting guru, he's immersed in his AIM convos and constantly updates his Facebook profile plus tweets and follows people on Tweeter.

In the beverage category, Jacob discovered the magic of Coke as a kid and became a life-long Coke loyalist. Whether he's kickin' it with friends or chillin' with family, Coke continuously trickles into Jacob's system. Although many of Jacob's best friends sip on Coke, he still hangs out with a few Mountain Dew and Dr. Pepper fanatics.

Name:	Jacob Fazzio
Sex:	Male
Interested in:	Women
Looking for:	Friendship, Dating, Whatever I can get
Hometown:	Atlanta, Georgia

Image © Jaimie Duplass, Shutterstock, Inc. 2011

Personal Info

Activities	hanging with friends watching movies, video games iming, bball, football
Interests	girls, mustangs, music, second life, xbox, owning josh at halo
Favorite Music	jay-z, nas, ako, paul wall, ti, three 6 mafia Young jeezy
Favorite TV Shows	family guy, Simpsons, adult swim, southpark 106 and park, two a day, real world
Favorite Movies	scarface, jack ass, old school, anchor man, Scary movie, spiderman, fantastic 4, 300!!
About me	my friends already know about me.

Education Info

High School	Murphy High '12

SUGGESTED READINGS

Fortini-Campbell, L., *Hitting the Sweet Spot: How Consumer Insights Can Inspire Better Marketing and Advertising.* Chicago: The Copy Workshop, 2001.

Kelley, Larry D. and Donald W. Jugenheimer, *Advertising Account Planning: A Practical Guide.* New York: M. E. Sharpe, 2006.

Roman, Kenneth, Jane Maas, and Martin Nisenholtz, *How to Advertise,* 3rd ed. New York: St. Martin's Press, 2003.

Steel, Jon, *Truth, Lies and Advertising: The Art of Account Planning.* New York: Wiley, 1998.

Sullivan, Luke. *Hey Mr. Whipple, Squeeze This!* New York: AdWeek Books, 2007.

DEVELOPING CREATIVE STRATEGIES

Exercises

1. Major magazine publishers have teamed up to fund a multimillion-dollar ad campaign to profess print as a still viable advertising method. These ads will attempt to convince that magazines will remain an effective advertising medium, even in the age of the Internet. They argue that web content is fleeting, where as magazines have depth and a lasting quality. The goal of the campaign is to counter the idea that print is a dead medium.
   a. Who is the best prospect for this campaign?
   b. What is the key consumer benefit that the magazine publishers should convey?
   c. What kind of evidence is needed to support the benefit?
   d. How should the "brand's" personality be portrayed?
   e. Come up with some possible taglines for the campaign that will appeal to the target and convey benefits and personality.

Source: Adams, Russell, and Shira Ovide. "Magazines Team Up to Tout 'Power of Print'" *Wall Street Journal.* 1 Mar. 2010. Web. 2 Mar. 2010.

2. Hasbro has plans to launch a digital version of Monopoly. The massive multiplayer online game would let players immerse themselves in the game and culture, using dedication and strategy to succeed in the game.

   Develop a hypothetical personal profile of a consumer who would be included in the primary target audience. Remember to use demographics as well as psychographics in your description.

Source: Parish, Nick. "Hasbro Moves Beyond Uproar to Create a New Web 'Monopoly'" *Advertising Age.* 22 Feb. 2010. Web. 2 Mar. 2010.

3. Buy a current issue of any magazine. Select a full-page advertisement you like.
   a. Briefly describe what you think the brands' advertising objectives are;
   b. Describe the target audience;
   c. What is the brand's personality?
   d. Describe the ad's main message to its intended target.
   e. In your opinion, is the ad effective?

Case 7.1

Rita's TasteeBurger[1]

BACKGROUND

Since the opening of the first Rita's TasteeBurger (RTB) location in March of 1972, the company had grown into a chain of approximately 500 restaurants in 12 states. RTB competed in the crowded Quick Service Restaurant (QSR) category against the standard national chains (McDonald's, Chic-fil-A, Jack-in-the-Box, Wendy's, Taco Bell, et al) plus other regional and local chains and individual restaurants.

RTB had consistently stressed that to ensure the freshness and taste of their hamburgers, all of their burgers were made only after the order was placed and that each burger was made to the customer's exact specifications and served on one of five unique buns. The firm used only 100% USDA "Grade A" beef plus quality ingredients. All of the firm's restaurants were designed in a 1930's art deco style with an aluminum fin roof with giant green-and-red neon "Rita's TasteeBurger" signs on both sides. The neon glow "Rita's TasteeBurger" logo was used throughout the restaurant on napkins, bags, burger wrappers, uniforms and other items. All RTB stores were open 24 hours, seven days a week except Christmas and New Year's Day.

A NEW TARGET MARKET

RTB's advertising and public relations agency was Beaumont, Sims & Jacobs (BSJ). BSJ had a reputation as a creative idea agency that was based significantly on their effective use of insights uncovered by their account planners. Rita's account planner at BSJ was Rebecca Sloan.

After studying Rita's market situation, product offerings, locations, positioning, the competition, their present customer base, and so on; Sloan felt she had located a market segment rich in potential for the agency's client. She had concluded that young adults 18–22 who were full-time college students and resided in one of eight market areas were a segment that offered important potential for expanding RTB's sales.

Survey research among members of this target in the eight markets had revealed that in terms of unaided recall of QSRs only 6% identified Rita's first when asked, "What are the first three quick service restaurants that come to mind?" Further, only 9% identified Rita's among their top three. When asked to name their "favorite hamburger restaurant," only 4% identified Rita's. In addition, 80% reported they had not visited RTB in the past six months.

To gain insights into how this market segment perceived RTB, Sloan designed an innovative research project in which depth interviews were conducted with members of the target members. The purpose of the depth interviews was to help each respondent develop a "mind map" on an 8½ x 11 sheet of paper that captured their attitudes about, experiences with and emotional feelings toward Rita's.

MIND MAPS

Consumers associate meaning, contexts, values, and experiences with brands. Further, the sum of all brand contacts, feelings and so on that are stored in memory represent a brand to an individual. Consumers

---

[1] This case was written by John H. Murphy and Lauren Johnson, The University of Texas at Austin. The case is designed to serve as the basis for classroom discussion and not to illustrate either the effective or ineffective handling of an administrative situation. The identity of the firm involved and the situation have been disguised.

frequently update and modify brand information and add to their brand experiences. To organize this process, consumers create complex networks of brand connections in their brains. A mind map is simply a graphic representation of some of these connections and presents a partial view of an individual consumer's conception of a brand.

The individual's associative network of interrelated meanings attached to a brand can be plotted to reveal a partial explanation of how the individual regards the brand. Physically, a mind map is a two-dimensional network or structural representation of the attributes, associations, comparisons, and other elements through which a consumer creates meaning for an individual brand. Brand information is stored in the human memory in three ways: (1) as the brand relates to attributes; (2) as the brand relates to other objects; and, (3) as the brand relates to events, people, and experiences. Everything we experience is captured in a combination involving the five senses coupled with emotional components.

These maps are potentially powerful tools for understanding the complex, multi-dimensional relationships that exist between consumers and brands. By studying brand mind maps and identifying common linkages and attitudes, account planners can isolate problems and opportunities in terms of how a brand is perceived by consumers.

A NEW RTB CREATIVE BRIEF

Exhibit 7.1.1 presents a composite mind map for RTB. This map was constructed based on an analysis of 40 individual RTB mind maps collected during the research project briefly described above that focused on young adults. After studying this map, Rebecca Sloan began the task of using the information presented in the map to shape a new creative strategy for RTB targeting young adults.

Chapter 7 ■ Developing Creative Strategies

Exhibit 7.1.1

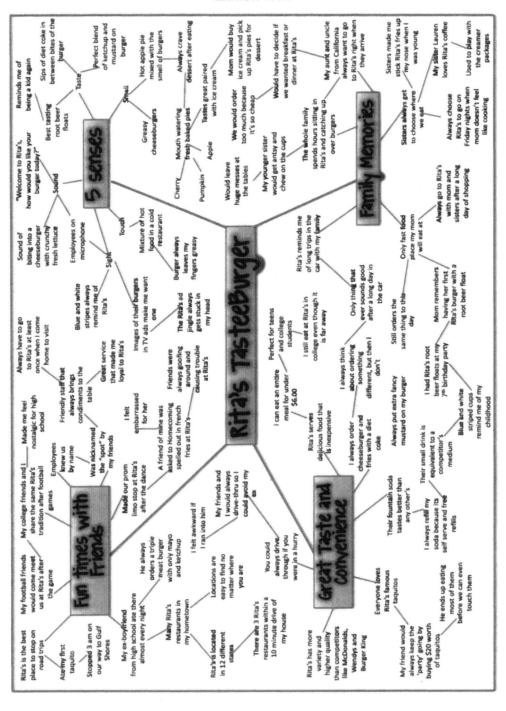

Name _____ Date _____

QUESTIONS FOR DISCUSSION AND REVIEW

1. What are the advantages and disadvantages of using a composite mind map as the basis for formulating a statement of creative strategy?

2. How realistic a portrait of the consumer's conception of a brand is reflected in a mind map?

3. Does the information presented in the Rita's mind map suggest other areas or topics that might be fruitful to explore with additional qualitative or quantitative research?

4. Which elements of the Rita's composite mind map appear to be most useful in formulating a statement of creative strategy?

Case 7.2

Costa Del Mar Sunglasses[1]

BACKGROUND

Costa Del Mar was a premium-priced sport sunglass brand with a cult following among anglers and water enthusiasts. Costa was founded in 1985 by a group of saltwater fishermen that had grown increasingly frustrated with the poor quality of sunglasses. These fishermen set out to create lenses and frames that could withstand the harsh, demanding conditions found on the water.

Costa was a $40 million company with international distribution and a rabid angler fan base. The company's philosophy was based around equipping anglers to pursue epic ocean adventures. As the brand's tagline put it, "See what's out there."

CURRENT TARGET

Costa's core audience was men with an intense love of fishing and adventure. These enthusiasts were segmented into the following five distinct sub-groups: The Hard-Core, Deep-Sea Sport Fishermen, Technical Anglers, Ocean Voyagers and X/Y Bass Anglers from Costa's Brand Development book. See Exhibit 7.2.1 for a profile of each of these distinct target groups.

BRAND DEVELOPMENT AND PRESENCE

Costa sunglasses were hardcore eye gear designed to endure the intense demands of anglers. In terms of communications and marketing, there were three brand tenets used to connect Costa to its adventure angler audience. Hence, these tenets were reflected in all of Costa's marketing communications messages.

1. Adventure Advocate

Costa encouraged people to get outside, off the main road, and into unchartered territories to find great stories. Costas were an essential part of preparation for the unpredictable journey. (See Exhibit 7.2.2 for a poster that reflects and encourages this spirit of adventure.)

2. Unfair Advantage

An unfair technical advantage—that's what Costa's 580 lenses offered. In the simplest terms, 580 lenses reduced the intensity of yellow light. This yellow light, found at 580 nanometers on the light spectrum, tires and

---

[1] This case was written by Jennifer Costello, McGarrah Jessee and John H. Murphy, The University of Texas at Austin. This case is designed to serve as the basis for classroom discussion and not to illustrate either the effective or ineffective handling of an administrative situation. The case is used with permission granted by Costa Del Mar.

Exhibit 7.2.1a

TARGET AUDIENCES

1 2 3 4 5 6 7

We recognize seven distinct groups within the target landscape, ranked in priority for the brand. The first five segments represent the most natural, intuitive targets for Costa based on their need for extreme performance.

1) THE HARD-CORE

Guides, captains, professional saltwater anglers, Coast Guard and others who stake their lives on the water

RELATIONSHIP WITH FISHING: Saltwater fishing and the ocean represent a high-stakes career. Lives, incomes and reputations are constantly on the line - it's a way of life.

SUNGLASS NEEDS: A $250 price tag is reasonable for hard-core protection and exceptional vision in the relentless, inhospitable sun and glare found on the ocean.

ON COSTA: Costas are a piece of safety gear, much like a lifejacket or a GPS.

LOCATED: Near the Gulf, Atlantic and California coasts

PERSONALITY: Sticks to his guns, hearty, unyielding, straightforward

STATS: In 2005, commercial fishing employed between 80,000 and 160,000 fishermen in the U.S. (Source: National Institute for Occupational Safety and Health 2005)

"Customers pay attention to the sunglasses I'm wearing. They think we're professionals - I mean we freaking live out here, in the sun, water, salt, all that. We get it right the first time."

Exhibit 7.2.1b

"It's me versus the fish. I'm in his environment, in his turf. He knows every rock, grass and cranny in that ocean. I have to outsmart him."

2) DEEP-SEA SPORT FISHERMEN

Recreational saltwater anglers seeking the ultimate offshore catch

RELATIONSHIP WITH FISHING: The ocean is a backdrop for thrilling and competitive sport fishing.

SUNGLASS NEEDS: Sunglasses are essential gear, bottom line. They provide a competitive advantage – helping see clusters of baitfish beneath blazing surface glare or diving birds on the horizon.

ON COSTA: Costas were created with saltwater in mind – the hinges won't rust, the glasses fit snugly even when spray is flying and the lenses don't scratch despite repeated shirt swipes.

LOCATED: Near the Gulf, Atlantic and California coasts

PERSONALITY: Challenge-seeker, Competitive, Hemingway-esque, High-energy

STATS: 4% of the U.S. population 18+ owns a fishing license and participates in saltwater fishing and about 887,000 of them go saltwater fishing 2-3 times a month. (Source: U.S. Fish & Wildlife Service; American Sportfishing Association 2001 and U.S. Census; 2007 MRI)

3) TECHNICAL ANGLERS

River, stream and inshore anglers

RELATIONSHIP WITH FISHING: Fishing is a personally issued challenge. It's a great time, but also a test of knowledge and an exercise in preparedness.

SUNGLASS NEEDS: Sunglasses are a piece of technical equipment for sight fishing, especially beneath the surface in murky water and overcast conditions.

ON COSTA: Costas are best suited for extremely bright conditions and mirrored water surfaces, such as what's typically found in offshore saltwater fishing.

LOCATED: Near the Mountains, the Midwest, the Atlantic and Gulf Coasts

PERSONALITY: Patient, tenacious, meticulous, thoughtful

STATS: There are 2.9 million fly fishing enthusiasts in the U.S. (Source: Outdoor Industry Foundation Survey 2005)

"Fly fishing is technical. I love it. It takes a lot of time and patience and practice, like golf."

4) OCEAN VOYAGERS

People who live and love to be on the water - boaters, yachtsmen and sailing enthusiasts

RELATIONSHIP WITH FISHING: The ocean is an open water playground and a leisure travel destination.

SUNGLASS NEEDS: Eye protection is priority number one, especially when at sea for long days in the brutal tropical sunlight.

ON COSTA: Costa is on par with Maui Jim in terms of protection and performance, but the simple styling of Maui Jim is better.

LOCATED: Near the Gulf Coast, Caribbean and the Tropics

PERSONALITY: Lives a comfortable life, prestigious, smart, well-traveled

STATS: In 2005, there were 12,942,414 registered boats in the U.S. About 2.1 million adults go sailing on vacation. (Source: U.S. Department of Homeland Security, United States Coast Guard, Boating Statistics 2005; 2007 MRI)

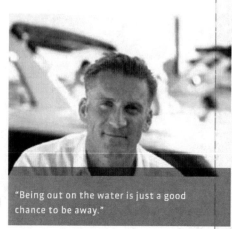

"Being out on the water is just a good chance to be away."

5) GEN X/Y BASS ANGLERS

Typically bass and lake fishermen under the age of 30

RELATIONSHIP WITH FISHING: Bass fishing is an all-consuming pastime and a bond among equally devoted, likeminded friends.

SUNGLASS NEEDS: Unlike older bass anglers, they demand more than polarization and believe in the benefits of technically-advanced lenses.

ON COSTA: Costa represents superior quality and are well worth the price - it's a brand to aspire to own.

LOCATED: In the Southeast, from Texas to the Carolinas

PERSONALITY: Social, dependable, unpretentious, committed

STATS: 13% of the U.S. population 18+ owns a fishing license and participates in freshwater fishing and about 600,000 of them go freshwater fishing once a week. (Source: U.S. Fish & Wildlife Service; American Sportfishing Association 2001 and U.S. Census; 2007 MRI)

"I only go bass fishing, but I'll go 6 or 7 times a month. Mainly with the guys from my bass club."

Exhibit 7.2.2

dries eyes quickly. Costa's 580 lenses killed glare and enhanced contrast, for breathtakingly clear vision. In fact, 580s offered such startlingly clear vision that first time wearers were often overheard muttering to themselves, "holy $@#%." (See Exhibit 7.2.3 that presents a print ad for the 580s.)

3. Higher Calling

An excerpt from Costa Del Mar's website clearly stated the brand's stance on conservation: *"The way we see it, the best equipment in the world won't catch a thing if the waters are empty. Every ocean, river, lake and stream is a resource and a responsibility. If we want future generations to feel the snap of a fish on the line, we have to do our part, and do it now."*

By donating funds and reporting on important issues, Costa helps to educate and empower people to save our world's most important resources. (See Exhibit 7.2.4 for a spread from the Costa catalogue that briefly describes an adventure sponsored by Costa that marries fishing and ecological science.)

MACRO ENVIRONMENT

Stepping back to examine the larger culture, there were a number of macro trends that could potentially influence consumers' perception and interest in Costa.

People think fishing is boring

To those not involved in the sport, fishing wasn't seen as particularly exciting or interesting. To most, the perception was that fishing is staid, fuddy-duddy and boring. This means that it might be difficult for mainstream consumers to associate a fishing sunglass brand with interesting epic adventures.

The culture is experiencing "big fish syndrome"

In recent years, there had been an influx of fish-centric TV shows from mainstream networks like Discovery and the National Geographic Channel. "Shark Week," "Hooked" and "Whale Wars" were among the shows that have taken hold in popular culture and attracted a devoted following outside of anglers. Fish shows with mainstream appeal tend to develop content about especially large, rare, strange looking or dangerous fish and the perilous situations that can occur when unusual fish and curious humans meet.

Adventure travel is accessible

Compared to just 10 years earlier, the larger public had grown interested in the idea of adventure travel. Previously inaccessible places like Cuba and El Salvador had opened their borders. The Internet provided endless access to information about foreign lands. TV shows from Andrew Zimmern, Anthony Bourdain, and The Travel Channel had drawn mass attention and interest in adventure travel. It was a cultural movement that inspired people to collect memories and stories, instead of material possessions.

Chapter 7 ■ Developing Creative Strategies   **199**

Exhibit 7.2.3

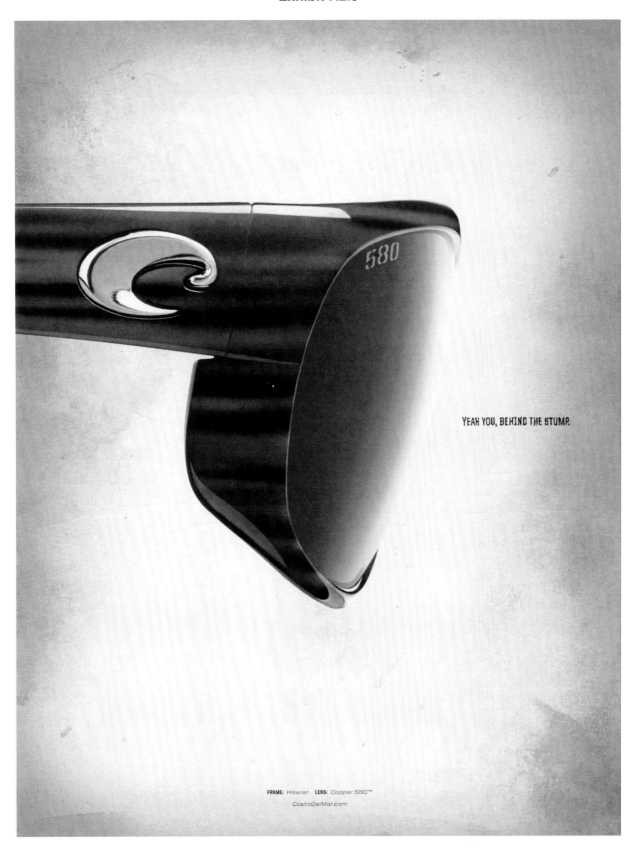

Exhibit 7.2.4

FISHING
WITH A PURPOSE

Fishing is inherently driven by stories. Go to a marina anywhere in the world and tales of fish caught and lost and of sights seen and pondered will be as plentiful as the sea birds that gather about the bait boats. With that in mind, imagine the stories that would be told on a multi-year fishing trip all over the world. A peak into that world is a peak into Chris and Melissa Fischer's pending adventure. It's the sort of adventure that will change with the weather and the tides and ocean currents. There are, after all, many unknowns when it comes to the waters of the world's oceans and the creatures that call them home. It is the pursuit of the unknown that inspired such a task. Are there any great explorers left? What happens when conservation-minded, pro anglers partner with scientists? Is it possible to catch, tag, release and then track the giants of the sea? Chat with Chris Fischer about such things and you'll get some answers.

CURRENT MARKETING

During the present year, Costa had taken a number of integrated steps to strengthen the brand and reinforce authenticity with its four core audiences. The brand's marketing strategy was "block and tackle," devoting resources to establish important marketing basics.

The marketing pieces displayed in Exhibits 7.2.2, 7.2.3, and 7.2.4 encompass the majority of Costa's current marketing efforts and were aimed at Costa's five angler targets. Costa's retailers and sales force received the brand's retail catalog, which detailed an adventure-fishing trip to Belize and Costa's new products (See Exhibit 7.2.5 that presents a spread page for the catalogue that features the Voyager Collection line).

The creative brief that guided the development of these communications was as follows:

Assignment: Develop a campaign idea for Costa that can be applied to multiple media environments, with a focus on non-traditional concepts and executions. Objective: Bring the brand presence to life. Audience: Men, mid-20s to late 50s, that have an intense love of fishing. These five core targets are passionate anglers that live to be on the water. Insight: Uncontrollable conditions are at the heart of fishing and the stuff of great stories. Costas are an essential part of preparation for the unpredictable journey. Idea: Epic adventure ready. Support:

- Founded by serious sport-fishermen with a desire for eye gear that can handle anything nature serves up
- Designed to perform in unpredictably harsh conditions (sun, salt, wind, glare . . .)
- Exceptional vision and clarity that kills glare and allows anglers to see beneath the water's surface
- All polarized and 100% UV A/B protection for eye safety and comfort
- Thoughtful details provide a perfect fit—stainless hinges won't rust or lose shape; temples and nose pads turn tacky when wet

CONNECTION OPPORTUNITIES

Looking ahead to next year, mainstream growth was a key brand objective. There were two distinct groups that were believed to be Costa's best targets for expansion: (1) adventure travel aficionados and (2) college students.

Adventure travel aficionados were men and women that delight in traveling to new and foreign lands. They enjoyed experiencing other cultures, and testing their own limits.

Costa's best college customers are male Greek fraternity members in the eight Southeastern states of Alabama, Georgia, Florida, Louisiana, Mississippi, North Carolina, South Carolina, and Texas. Many of these men appreciated Costa's "preppy cool" look, and had adopted the brand as part of their "uniform."

While there was clearly an opportunity to connect with a broader audience, Costa must establish new ties without alienating its core and sacrificing authenticity. Since adventure travelers are closest to Costa's current audience in terms of sunglass needs and activity drivers, there was a logical reason to consider focusing on this audience first. On the other hand, Southeastern college students represented a well-defined group that was more homogeneous than adventure travel aficionados. Hence, the college target was easier to appeal to and could be reached more efficiently with message and through events.

As Costa's marketing team and their agency developed plans for connecting with the two new targets, they focused on the development of two separate creative briefs. Everyone involved in this process realized that these strategy statements would be critical to the success of marketing communication efforts directed to the two groups.

Exhibit 7.2.5

QUESTIONS FOR DISCUSSION AND REVIEW

1. What additional information would be useful in crafting the two creative briefs?

   What do these two targets like to fish? What kind of fishermen and women are these two targets? Sunglass needs, what they think of Costa, How old are the adventure travel aficionados?

2. How useful is the creative brief provided in the case in guiding the development of the new briefs?

   Not very, the audience is very broad

3. How would the three brand tenants influence the briefs? Which of the three tenants should have the most influence? Why?

   Brand Tenet #1 is good for the adventure travel aficionados. This would probably also be good with the fratties because it plays up the whole cool factor.

4. How important are the three macro cultural trends in shaping the briefs?

   If people think fishing is boring, and Costa is selling itself as fishing sunglasses, that's a problem. However "big fish syndrome" and accessible adventure travel are benefits, so they should use these trends to their advantage.

5. How might Costa management's sensitivity to appealing to these new potential customers without alienating its core and sacrificing authenticity be reflected in the briefs?

Have different objectives for already established targets and new targets, say that you've already had success with these targets and want to branch out and try something new

6. Which of the two briefs is the most difficult to develop? Why?

adventurers - really broad

Case 7.3

BusinesSuites (B)[1]

As the management team at BusinesSuites (BSS) began developing IBP plans for next year, they focused on what they believed was one of the most attractive potential areas for short- and long-term growth: virtual office (VO) clients. Hence, building substantial VO growth during the coming fiscal year was established as a priority. (See BSS (A) case for background on the current situation.)

Although no decisions had been made with respect to how to best reach potential VO clients for BSS's 14 centers, management's past experience suggested that direct mail and pay-per-click on-line advertising would account for a large proportion of their efforts. All VO IBP efforts would focus on driving prospects to the BSS website for information on their VO packages. To sharpen the impact of such advertising and as a next step in the process, the team felt they needed a statement of creative strategy to guide the development of more impactful and efficient advertising.

In developing such a statement, several considerations seemed important. First, an analysis of the BSS's current 599 VO clients (see BSS (A) Table 6.2.2) revealed that a high percentage were small businesses whose owners lived in reasonably close proximity to the BSS location whose office address they used. On average across the 14 centers, 70% of all VO clients lived within five miles of the BSS location they used.

Second, in developing a statement of creative strategy, the team believed that the statement should clearly reflect what differentiates BSS from Regus' VO package and other competitors like the IntelligentOffice.com. Third, the team believed that the BSS tagline, "Providing the Freedom to Succeed," should be included in any creative strategy statement. Finally, the team questioned how knowledgeable some prospects were about the VO concept and how much emphasis should be placed on the range of services available to VO clients.

An interesting twist on selling VO packages was that there were at least three types of prospects. The first type of prospect clearly understood the concept and only wanted a VO. A second type of prospect was a businessperson who really wanted a regular office but upon reflection and consideration of the concept, will settle for a VO. Another category of VO prospects was existing regular office clients. Occasionally, in working with existing tenants, it would be appropriate to suggest that they migrate into a VO client.

[1]This case was written by John Murphy, The University of Texas at Austin, and John Jordan, BusinesSuites. The case is designed to serve as the basis for classroom discussion and not to illustrate either the effective or ineffective handling of an administrative situation. The case is used with permission granted by BusinesSuites.

Name _____   Date _____

QUESTIONS FOR DISCUSSION AND REVIEW

1. What additional information would be useful in developing a statement of creative strategy focused on potential VO clients?

   _____
   _____
   _____
   _____

2. How important an influence on the statement is the VO competition?

   _____
   _____
   _____
   _____

3. What elements or components should be included in a creative strategy statement for BSS's VO efforts?

   _____
   _____
   _____
   _____

4. How might the creative strategy statements differ for regular office versus VO clients?

   _____
   _____
   _____
   _____

5. What are the implications of the three types of VO clients identified at the end of the case?

Chapter 8
Developing Media Strategy

For marketers, however, the mass media are no longer the sole choice. Traditional media retain an important advantage: the "rub-off" credibility that accrues from being part of a broadcast or publication invited into the home. But for many marketers, media advertising is a shotgun. The new technologies provide rifles, which can target prime prospects.[1]
—Stanley E. Cohen

INTRODUCTION

Once a market analysis has been conducted and a total advertising budget established according to the overall objectives set for the advertising efforts, two tasks must be performed: a creative message must be developed and a media plan established that will efficiently and effectively reach the target audience selected for the advertising. This chapter will explore some of the key factors involved in developing that all-important media plan. The last few years have seen a radical transformation in the channels available for advertisers to communicate with their target audiences. A wide variety of choices face the strategic planning of a media program: from the traditional channels such as radio and television, to viral marketing, search engines and social networks. Out-of-home media and mobile media are used to reach audiences where they may be at any time. Advertising within electronic games and product placements are some of the creative ways messages are crafted to achieve awareness and get consumers' attention. Media plans must take into consideration all the possible media tools that will enable advertisers to reach their intended audience in the most effective manner.

The first part of this chapter will deal with the steps needed to select traditional media for an overall advertising plan. The second part of the chapter will focus on nontraditional media sources and their overall importance for future advertisers.

DEVELOPMENT AND SELECTION OF A MEDIA PLAN

The advertising media plan starts with the development of *media objectives*. Media objectives are used to help implement the marketing objectives and strategy. There is no set formula or process to develop or create media objectives. In

---

[1] Stanley E. Cohen, "The Dangers of Today's Media Revolution," *Advertising Age,* September 30, 1991, 18.

many cases the media objectives are stated in terms of reach and frequency—the percentage of the potential audience to be reached and the frequency with which that audience should be exposed to the advertiser's message. In addition, the continuity or consistency of advertising placement in the media could be a consideration in setting media objectives. Using media objectives to develop a media plan involves the following decisions:

1. What target audience should be reached by the media?
2. To which geographic market or markets should the message be directed?
3. How far into the target audience can the advertising reach, given budget constraints?
4. With what frequency should the message reach the target audience during the campaign?
5. At which times should the message reach the intended audience?
6. What type of media and/or specific vehicle provides the best match between the intended market and the actual audience?
7. Which support functions will best ensure the effective performance of the selected media plan?

This portion of the chapter will examine each of these decisions in detail. They are all integral parts of effective media planning.

Identifying the Target Audience

The advertising for a product must be directed to all those audiences that represent prospective or existing customers. Advertising messages are also sometimes intended for a larger audience: the general public, prospective employees, potential investors, other businesses, and many others. The identification of the target audience to be reached by an advertising campaign must therefore be the first step in the overall media planning process. Media planners will look for the similarities between the target market and the media audience.

It is not easy to reach effectively only the intended audience. Advertising campaigns often reach unintended audiences, sometimes with disastrous results. Several years ago a survey of students prepared by BKG Youth, a research and marketing company, suggested that the R. J. Reynolds Tobacco Company's controversial campaign for Camel cigarettes was highly effective at reaching kids under the age of 13. The U.S. Surgeon General and the American Medical Association repeatedly criticized the company for using the Joe Camel cartoon to advertise its cigarettes because they felt that the campaign enticed children to smoke. RFR repeatedly countered this criticism, stating that there was no evidence to substantiate such claims. The research results, however, showed that when asked to recall cigarette brands, 90% of the kids aged 8 to 13 named Camels, and 73% cited Marlboro. This evidence of such an effective reach of the campaign and such high brand awareness among the very young could potentially have a very negative effect on Camel, RJR Tobacco, and ultimately, any kind of advertising.[2]

Wal-Mart also made a strategic mistake in 2000 when it attempted to reach upscale consumers with its Christmas ads. Wal-Mart positioning had always been that of a low-price retailer appealing to lower-income consumers. Placing ads featuring spokespeople with whom its target audience did not identify caused at least confusion and ended up not achieving the goal of attracting a different segment of wealthier and more upscale consumers.[3]

---

[2]Gary Levin, "Poll Shows Camel Ads Are Effective with Kids," *Advertising Age,* April 27, 1992, 12.

[3]"Big Name Brands in 'Hall of Shame,'" by Parija Bhatnagar, CNNMoney.com, March 30, 2006.

Selecting the Geographic Market to Be Reached

As the demand for and sales of products and services vary across areas and markets, it often becomes necessary to use different levels of advertising in different geographic locations. One way to overcome this diversity and plan adequately is to use a system of index figures that portray the relative weight of each geographical submarket. Once the overall objectives of the plan have been stated, they are translated into media goals for each geographic area. This usually corresponds to the distribution of advertising dollars across locations.

The advertising media plan, therefore, can strengthen exposure to advertising in those areas with greater potential or where, for some reason, sales are lagging. Brand management goals will be reflected in media allocations and selections, that complement the overall marketing strategy.

Determining the Desirable Level of Reach, Based on Budget Constraints

Reach is the percentage of the target market that is exposed to the advertising message within a specific time period. The objectives of reach and frequency are usually addressed at the same time because they must be set within the same budgetary constraints.

The advertiser may choose to distribute messages widely, allowing as many prospects as possible to receive at least one message. On the other hand, the advertiser may decide that its objectives would best be served by exposing a small number of prospects to multiple repetitions of the same message.

An example of a shift in reach goals for a campaign is the advertising plan used by Universal Pictures to promote its 1992 film, *Fried Green Tomatoes.* Initially, the campaign was designed to reach an older audience and to feature a greater number of ads directed at such an audience. A few weeks after its release, however, research showed interest in the film among younger audiences. Universal Pictures restructured its advertising strategy, focusing on broader audiences including younger women. Media choices were increased and less emphasis was placed on frequency of messages. The results of this shift were very positive; the movie's revenues increased substantially.[4]

Another example of this problem is the action taken by Ford Motor Company in 2005, when they pulled their ads from *The Advocate* magazine, a publication that caters to the gay community, because of pressure the company received from a conservative Christian group. A few months later, the company reversed its decision, thereby alienating both audience segments.[5]

It should be noted that reach levels are often based on statistical estimates. It is harder to accurately estimate reach for narrowly defined audiences than for broad, general audiences. Also, reach levels should be determined to be compatible with all the other variables in the campaign.

Determining the Frequency with Which the Message Should Reach the Target Audience

The degree of repetition of an advertising message is a very important component of the media plan. As the media environment becomes more cluttered and audiences' attention

---

[4]Thomas R. King, "Little Film Shifts Its Aim to Big Audience," *The Wall Street Journal,* January 31, 1992, B1 and B5.

[5]"Big Name Brands in 'Hall of Shame,'" by Parija Bhatnagar, CNNMoney.com, March 30, 2006.

becomes harder to capture, advertisers are concentrating on increasing the frequency with which their target audiences are exposed to advertising messages. The increase in advertising clutter has resulted in an increase of "zapping," or channel switching, by television audiences, according to a 1992 study by Bozzell, a New York advertising agency. The research points out that an increase of 10% in advertising clutter resulted in a 7% increase in channel switching.[6]

It is easy to understand, therefore, why advertisers would be concerned with increasing the number of times the same audience is *potentially* exposed to an advertising message. There is still little knowledge, however, as to what is a sufficient number of advertising exposures. The answer to this question varies by type of product advertised, level of consumer knowledge of an involvement with the product, and type of appeal used, among other factors. It is, however, a commonly accepted practice to assume that a minimum of four exposures is sufficient to create an acceptable level of awareness among the intended audience. In 1999, John Phillip Jones published the book *When Ads Work: New Proof of How Advertising Triggers Sales* in which he suggests that, in some cases one exposure is sufficient to be effective. This indicates that there are many factors that should be considered when deciding the adequate frequency for an advertising message. It is clear that future research will be needed to refine and perfect these assumptions.

Determining the Timing and Continuity of the Campaign

The nature of the product advertised influences the decision of where and when mass media should be used to reach potential consumers. Some products and services experience an even demand throughout the year. Examples are sugar or financial services. For these products, advertising media selection may be constant throughout the year, and the number of messages at any given period will also be stable.

Many products and services, however, face varied demands at different time periods. For example the demand for toys is highly seasonal, and so is the demand for tourism services. A media plan for products/services with seasonal demand may concentrate advertising expenditures at specific times throughout the year. Also, the number of messages to which the intended audience is exposed may vary in intensity within these periods. As an example, advertisers may choose to concentrate the majority of messages in a specific medium or at the end of each week.

Choosing the Media and Vehicles That Provide the Best Match with the Intended Market

The effect of different media on the impact of a specific advertising message is known as the source effect. It is possible, for example, that exposure to a television commercial will have more impact on the intended audience than exposure to a magazine advertisement. By the same token, a full-page color advertisement may have a greater effect than an identical half-page black-and-white ad. Finally, exposure to an advertisement in one media vehicle might have more impact than exposure to the same advertisement in another vehicle. An advertisement for toothpaste in *Playboy* magazine may cause a very different audience response than exposure to the same ad in *Good Housekeeping*.

Advertising managers, therefore, should carefully consider the media choices at their disposal as they develop a media plan. The media types and vehicles should be compatible with

---

[6] "Clutter Suffers Zap Attacks," *Advertising Age,* March 30, 1992, 38.

the overall objectives of the advertising strategy, and they should provide a positive environment for the product and service advertised. This environment should parallel the image of the brand, product, or service itself rather than provide a contrast that might change its perception by intended audiences.

Some media vehicles have more loyal audiences than others. For example, craft/hobby magazines' circulations revenue accounts for between 65% and 70% of total revenue, indicating that their readers are highly devoted to that medium. Advertisers have taken notice of this, and when the intended market for a product is matched closely by the audience of a craft/hobby magazine, they are quick to secure media purchases from it.

In May 2010, Thomson Reuters Corp. announced that it was launching a financial video service, thereby adding Web-based programming to the media the company traditionally has utilized. Half-million consumers in the financial industry are the intended audience of this new Web service. Users will be able to navigate and organize video and will be able to search for specific stock information. It is clear that Reuters has realized that financial advisors and individual investors rely on more than cable television programs and printed news to gather relevant financial and economic information. This is a clear example of a company choosing an appropriate media vehicle to reach its target audience.[7]

Advertisers should respond positively to the availability of such targeted audiences. Media schedules should attempt to increase the efficiency of ad dollars by targeting closely their intended prospects.

SETTING MEDIA OBJECTIVES

Media plans are built by setting objectives with regard to reach, frequency and timing. The main purpose of a media plan is to deliver the right message to the appropriate target audience as many times as necessary to achieve the goals of an advertising campaign. The timing of the delivery of the message is also an important component of the plan in that it reflects sales goals, or the company's general marketing strategy. An example objective of a media plan would be as follows:

- To reach 60% of males 25 to 35, three or more times each month, during the first six months of the introduction of a new product in the market.

Traditionally, advertising professionals have used some standard measures to evaluate the impact of a media plan in terms of reach and frequency. The most common measures used are: gross impressions and gross rating points (GRPs). Gross impressions are the total number of impressions obtained from a media schedule within a given period. This means counting all exposures and every exposure in a schedule, even multiple exposures to the same person or household. Gross rating points are gross impressions expressed in a percentage form. As an example, a GRP of 20 indicates that 20% of a given population was tuned into that broadcast within which the commercial was placed. If the commercial appeared 3 times during that broadcast, then the GRPs will be $20 \times 3 = 60$.

It is important to underscore that gross impressions and gross rating points are only one of many elements that should be considered when setting objectives for a media plan. Increasingly advertisers are evaluating the effects of media strategies on sales, customer engagement, and increase in customer loyalty.

[7]"Thomson Reuters to Add Financial Video Service," by Russell Adams, *The Wall Street Journal,* May 10, 2010.

Therefore, a media plan is often not complete unless it is monitored and complemented with other functions to ensure it will meet its intended objectives. Sometimes such support functions are provided by direct-response vehicles such as postcards, requests for information, and the like. Such a complement allows the advertiser to monitor differences in responses to advertising in different vehicles, geographic regions, and media types. Other common support functions are provided by toll-free 800 numbers with automated information systems, split copy placements, and free sample redemption promotions.

As technology changes, more support functions will be developed to complement and reinforce advertising messages conveyed in mass media vehicles. Constant control of advertising effects and consequent modifications of media plans are important, as they allow the advertiser to pursue its goals in a flexible and highly efficient manner. The next section will consider some innovative media vehicles and their potential impact on traditional media.

TECHNOLOGY INNOVATIONS AND NEW MEDIA VEHICLES

The media revolution that has taken place during the past two decades had its beginning in the development and subsequent popularity of cable television. The growth in the personal computer market and the increasing sophistication of electronic communication tools such as the videophone, portable phone, and many others opened the door to the development of new media vehicles to serve the needs of advertisers.

Cable and Satellite Television

When the first cable systems were installed in the United States, advertisers and agencies alike were very reluctant to purchase media time on such vehicles. Audience services such as Nielsen did not provide data about cable audiences, and most cable revenue originated from subscribers' fees. Today cable television appeals to many advertisers. According to a report by the New Politics Institute, published in November 2005, the cable TV share of the total U.S. audience increased by 28% from 1986 to 2004. However, cable and satellite television are increasingly challenged by the growing penetration of DVRs (such as TiVo) as well as other innovative technology, such as the pay-per-view services as well as the Internet and videogames.[8]

The pay-per-view network (PPV) allows viewers to choose what they want to watch and to be billed accordingly. The major advantage to PPV is that it delivers very specific audiences, providing advertisers with a very efficient vehicle for penetrating narrow markets.

Shopping channels on cable and satellite television have enjoyed increasing attention and success, allowing direct marketers another choice besides direct selling and magazine advertising. International and multilingual formats and the use of infomercials have all been pioneered by cable, thereby broadening the number and quality of message choices available to advertisers.

Perhaps the most intriguing and least-well-known option available to cable operators is interactive television. A tool that has been introduced experimentally in many formats, initially as Qube, interactive television has not been developed sufficiently to attract advertisers. However, because it would offer consumers the ability to customize programs to their preferences and to responds immediately to polls, surveys, and sales pitches, interactive television might provide an infinite array of options for the future.

---

[8]"Fundamental Shifts in the U.S. Media and Advertising Industries." New Politics Institute, November 2005.

Magazines

Technological innovations have also affected other media. Desktop production facilities have allowed magazines and newspapers a flexibility never known before. Production times have been reduced to hours, and some media firms have customized editions to satisfy geographical and cultural market diversity. Newspapers and magazines of the future will have less text but more variety and graphics. Illustrations and visual aids will replace text and provide consumers with more information. Magazine audiences have also changed over the past 20 years, and there has been a marked increase in per capita magazine readership.

Product Placement

Existing media have also provided additional outlets for advertising. Recently, increased attention has been given to product placement in films and made-for-television programs. After the sales success of Reese's Pieces as a consequence of its placement in the movie *E.T.*, advertisers have paid increasing attention to the benefits of product placement. This new vehicle provides an alternative with less clutter than television and is therefore a sought-after solution for competitive exposures.

The effects of product placements are not yet well known. The widespread distribution of movies has allowed films to reach a much wider audience than that composed of traditional theatergoers. In the future, product placement may be used in an array of audio-visual productions.

CONCLUSION

The media planning function is a vital element of the advertising plan. Traditionally, media planners followed a series of sequential steps to develop an efficient and effective way of conveying advertising messages to intended audiences. The world of media is changing, however. New technology has opened a number of alternatives to traditional media vehicles. These innovative media have not yet been fully tested by advertisers; however, they provide more flexibility in communicating with consumers and, in some cases, the excitement of direct feedback.

Future choices of media will present an exciting challenge for media planners and advertisers. Targeting narrow audiences will be increasingly possible, making the media decision more complex. This specific area of advertising management will be responsible for major changes in the decision-making process of advertisers and agencies.

SUGGESTED READINGS

Banks, Seymour. "Considerations for a New ARF Media Evaluation Model." *Journal of Media Planning* (Fall 1989): 8–10.

Barban, Arnold M., Steven M. Cristol, and Frank J. Kopec. *Essentials of Media Planning: A Marketing Viewpoint.* 2nd ed. Lincolnwood, IL: NTC Business Books, 1989.

"Beam me up, Scottie." *The Economist,* March 28, 1992. 69–70.

Jugenheimer, Donald W., Arnold M. Braban, and Peter B. Turk. *Advertising Media—Strategy and Tactics.* Dubuque, IA: Wm. C. Brown Publishers, 1992.

Landler, Mark. "The Infomercial Inches toward Respectability." *Business Week,* May 4, 1992, 175.

Leckenby, John, and Kuen-Hee Ju. "Advances in Media Decision Models." *Current Issues and Research in Advertising* 12, nos. 1 and 2 (1990): 312–357.

McGann, Anthony F., and Thomas J. Russell. *Advertising Media.* 2nd ed. Homewood, IL: Irwin, 1998.
Spaeth, Jim. "Advertising Effects and Media Planning." *Journal of Media Planning* (Fall 1989): 40–44.
"Special Report: Cable TV." *Advertising Age,* April 6, 1992, S-1 to S-15.
"Special Report: Magazines." *Advertising Age,* March 9, 1992, S-1 to S-18.

DEVELOPING MEDIA STRATEGY

Exercises

1. Tiffany Thompson, the media planner for a large manufacturer of fruit juices that markets to the public in supermarkets and through vending machines, was trying to decide which TV network should receive the bulk of the media's expenditures for 2004. According to a recent report, Nielsen Media Research and ScanAmerica, a new network rating service, differ markedly as to their ranking of the three networks. Table 8.1 shows the differences in the rankings of the two rating services.

   How should Thompson evaluate this information in view of the product she is advertising? Assuming Thompson (had) has $50 million to allocate to network television, should she divide it between two of the three major networks? Why or why not?

2. Creek Road Community Bank in Dripping Springs, Texas was a small community bank that had been founded in 2007 by a group of local investors. The bank had its first moderately profitable year in 2009. The Bank had been successful in responding to the needs of the community and most of its clientele had acquired through personal relationships, word of mouth. The Bank had not allocated any budget to marketing and advertising at all since its establishment.

   George Hammond, president of CRCB, felt that it was time for the bank to start a marketing communication program to keep its present customers, shareholders, and community leaders informed about the company's products and financial performance as well as to reach potential new customers in the bank's geographical area and surrounding communities.

   The bank was located on the main road crossing Dripping Springs, and prominent signage was definitely one of the first items to be considered, because it would provide brand recognition and recall to those driving through that very high traffic road. This would be a one-time expenditure.

   Most community banks relied on personal communication and various types of direct marketing tools to reach their target audiences. Several were also responsive to their local communities' events by co-sponsoring some of them such as rodeos, county festivals and the like.

   A 2007 report by the Direct Marketing Association stated that in that year U.S. banks and credit institutions spent over $13 billion on direct-marketing advertising, and it was the number one American industry spending on direct marketing.

   This report also indicated that ROI per dollar spent on direct marketing for banking and credit institutions was very high at $13.37 per dollar spent.

   The primary channel used by the financial services industry was direct mail. Websites and commercial email and expenditures in that type of direct marketing were expected to continue to grow at a very high compounded annual rate (between 17% and 22%).

Table 8.1

ScanAmerica		
Top 10 Programs	Nielsen Rank	ScanAm. Rating
1. Roseanne	2	21.1
2. 60 Minutes	1	19.8
3. Full House	4	18.8
4. Home Improvement	9	18.7
5. Family Matters	—	18.6
6. A Different World	12	18.4
7. Monday Night Football	11	18.3
8. Cheers	3	17.9
9. The Cosby Show	16	17.8
10. Step by Step	—	17.6
Nielsen		
Top 10 Programs	ScanAm. Rank	Nielsen Rating
1. Roseanne	2	22.6
2. 60 Minutes	1	21.3
3. Full House	8	19.5
4. Home Improvement	3	19.4
5. Family Matters	15	19.1
6. A Different World	11	18
7. Monday Night Football	24	17.2
8. Cheers	29	17.2
9. The Cosby Show	4	17.2
10. Step by Step	14	17.2

Source: Nielsen Media Research, Arbitron Co. Reprinted with permission from the February 24, 1992 issue of *Advertising Age.* Copyright 1992 by Crain Communications, Inc.

Source: Joe Mandese, "Rival Ratings Don't Match Up," *Advertising Age,* February 24, 1992, 1 and 50.

Another direct marketing tool commonly used was telephone marketing, but financial service companies were spending less on all kinds of print advertising.

Mr. Hammond had earmarked a total marketing of $75,000 for 2011. Expenditures for the scheduled outdoor signage were excluded from the marketing budget. Mr. Hammond contacted a local small advertising agency and asked them to submit an advertising plan for CRCB for 2011 based on the $75,000 budget. He wanted to make sure that the bank would effectively reach existing customers to cross-sell to them some of the new products the bank had developed and reinforce the positive image of the bank.

All Markets: Top Ten Industries by DM Advertising Expenditure

(Figures in Billions of Dollars)	2007	2006–2007 % Change
Financial, Banks & Credit Institutions	$13.4	12.5%
Services, Professional, Technical & Management Services	10.9	6.1
Retail Trade, (Non-S) Nonstore, and Other Retailers	9.9	3.2
Information, Communications	9.4	5.2
Wholesale Trade	9.4	5.5
Manufacturing, Motor Vehicles	8.0	−8.7
Retail Trade, Motor Vehicles Dealers & Service Stations	7.3	0.8
Financial, Insurance Carriers, and Agents	6.8	1.9
Retail Trade, General Merchandise Stores	6.7	5.4
Financial, Security & Commodity Brokers, Holding Companies	6.6	14.8

Source: http://www.marketingcharts.com/direct/financial-banks-credit-institutions-top-dm-ad-spenders-3993/dma-top-10-industries-by-dm-advertising-expenditures-2007jpg/

In addition, Mr. Hammond wanted the marketing plan to reach out to potential customers. The bank had over $15,000 customers in 2010 and hoped to increase its total revenue by 20% by the end of 2011.

The agency was considering a wide range of marketing communication options. Among those were: cable television, radio and local newspaper, as well as a number of direct advertising tools such as those used by other community banks.

Based on Mr. Hammond's business goals, how should the agency approach the development of a media allocation strategy for CRCB? What media allocation strategy should be chosen for CRCB? What media choices should be emphasized? Why?

3. The advertising executive for a global investment banking company was considering placing some advertising for the company in international print media. He was given a budget of $15 million, and his goal was to obtain the highest possible audience reach for a minimum of four full-page exposures during each of 10 four-week periods. He did not feel that advertising would be effective during the summer months, as in several European countries business almost stood still during that period. A recent report by *Advertising Age* ranked the highest-circulation dailies, weeklies, and monthlies. (see Table 8.2), and he felt that would give him sufficient information to make a choice.

Develop a media schedule for this investment banking company. Indicate clearly your total expenditures, media vehicles chosen, and number of exposures.

4. An advertiser is selling accounting software and is attempting to decide whether she should include in the media schedule a group of PC users' magazines or a group of business magazines. The PC magazines have a combined circulation of 200,000, and about one-third of their readers are middle- and upper-level managers. Another one-third are

Chapter 8 ■ Developing Media Strategy   219

Table 8.2

100 LEADING MEDIA COMPANIES
Ranked by total net U.S. media revenue in 2007

RANK 2007	RANK 2006	Media Company	Headquarters	TOTAL NET U.S. MEDIA REVENUE 2007	TOTAL NET U.S. MEDIA REVENUE 2006	% CHG	Worldwide Parent Revenue	NET REVENUE FROM U.S. BY MEDIUM IN 2007 Newspaper	Magazine	Out of Home	Digital	Movies & Home Entertainment	TV	Radio	Cable Networks	Cable SYS/SAT	Other	Yellow Pages
1	1	Time Warner®	New York	$35,629	$35,255	1.1	$46,482	$0	$3,600	$0	$3,764	$3,266	$47	$0	$7,197	$14,747	$3,008	$0
2	2	Comcast Corp.®	Philadelphia	26,939	24,719	9.0	30,895	0	0	0	0	0	0	0	1,314	25,625	0	0
3	3	Walt Disney Co.®	Burbank, Calif.	17,489	16,452	6.3	35,510	0	392	0	0	2,761	5,296	157	7,791	0	1,092	0
4	4	News Corp.®	New York	15,695	14,840	5.8	32,996	1,499	0	0	642	2,915	4,911	0	4,182	0	1,546	0
5	5	DirecTV Group	El Segundo, Calif.	15,527	13,744	13.0	17,246	0	0	0	0	0	0	0	0	1,546	0	0
6	6	NBC Universal (General Electric Co.)®	New York	12,161	13,015	-6.6	15,416	0	0	0	0	2,000	4,994	0	3,417	0	1,750	0
7	7	CBS Corp.®	New York	12,051	12,032	0.2	14,073	0	0	1,547	311	162	6,216	1,745	1,145	0	926	0
8	8	Cox Enterprises®	Atlanta	11,899	10,683	11.4	15,000	1,400	0	0	918	0	670	445	166	8,300	0	0
9	9	Dish Network Corp.	Englewood, Colo.	10,728	9,456	13.4	11,090	0	0	0	0	0	0	0	0	10,728	0	0
10	10	Viacom®	New York	9,490	8,474	12.0	13,423	0	50	0	0	2,621	0	0	5,912	0	907	0
11	11	Advance Publications®	New York	8,096	7,736	4.7	0	2,073	3,882	0	0	0	0	0	0	2,141	0	0
12	19	Google	Mountain View, Calif.	6,017	4,085	47.3	16,594	0	0	0	6,017	0	0	0	0	0	0	0
13	13	AT&T®	Dallas	5,851	5,874	-0.4	118,928	0	0	0	0	0	0	0	0	0	0	5,851
14	12	Gannett Co.	McLean, Va.	5,779	6,210	-6.9	7,439	4,618	371	0	0	0	789	0	0	0	0	0
15	14	Cablevision Systems Corp.®	Bethpage, N.Y.	5,733	5,343	7.3	6,484	409	0	0	0	0	0	0	1,138	4,187	0	0
16	15	Charter Communications®	St. Louis	5,630	5,251	7.2	6,002	0	0	0	0	0	0	0	0	5,630	0	0
17	16	Tribune Co.	Chicago	4,838	5,237	-7.6	5,063	3,616	48	0	0	0	1,136	37	0	0	0	0
18	17	Clear Channel Communications®	San Antonio	4,820	4,699	2.6	6,817	0	0	1,381	0	0	0	3,439	0	0	0	0
19	18	Hearst Corp.®	New York	4,641	4,573	1.5	0	1,522	2,341	0	0	0	756	23	0	0	0	0
20	21	Yahoo	Sunnyvale, Calif.	3,839	3,422	12.2	6,969	0	0	0	3,839	0	0	0	0	0	0	0
21	20	Sony Corp.®	New York/Tokyo	3,647	4,061	-10.2	75,230	0	0	0	0	2,773	0	0	0	0	875	0
22	23	Idearc	DFW Airport, Texas	3,189	3,221	-1.0	3,189	0	0	0	285	0	0	0	0	0	4	2,900
23	22	The New York Times Co.	New York	2,954	3,290	-10.2	3,195	2,840	0	0	103	0	0	11	0	0	0	0
24	24	R.H. Donnelley Corp.	Cary, N.C.	2,680	2,685	-0.2	2,680	0	0	0	0	0	0	0	0	0	0	2,680
25	26	•••• Communications®	Livonia, Mich.	2,301	2,331	-1.3	2,242	0	0	0	0	0	0	0	0	0	2,301	0
26	25	McClatchy Co.®	Sacramento, Calif.	2,260	2,455	-7.9	2,260	2,187	0	0	0	0	0	0	0	0	73	0
27	27	The Washington Post Co.	Washington	2,145	2,221	-3.4	4,180	776	288	0	114	0	340	0	0	626	0	0
28	28	Univision Communications	Los Angeles	2,073	2,026	2.3	2,073	0	0	0	46	0	1,532	430	65	0	0	0
29	30	Yellow Book USA (Yell Group)	Uniondale, N.Y./Reading, U.K.	2,004	1,858	7.9	4,441	0	0	0	0	0	0	0	0	0	0	2,004
30	33	Sirius XM Radio®	New York	1,953	1,484	31.6	922	0	0	0	0	0	0	1,953	0	0	0	0
31	32	Microsoft Corp.	Redmond, Wash.	1,920	1,634	17.5	60,420	0	0	0	1,920	0	0	0	0	0	0	0
32	31	Discovery Communications®	Silver Spring, Md.	1,909	1,736	10.0	3,127	0	0	0	0	0	0	0	1,909	0	0	0
33	29	MediaNews Group®	Denver	1,792	1,891	-5.2	1,330	1,787	0	0	0	0	5	0	0	0	0	0
34	34	Scripps Networks Interactive®	Knoxville, Tenn.	1,441	1,334	8.1	0	0	0	0	256	0	0	0	1,185	0	0	0

Source: "Global Media and Marketing." *Advertising Age*, October 28, 1991, S-1 to S-16.
Notes: Dollars in millions. Advertising Age Data Center estimates of U.S. media revenue. Media defined as information and entertainment content distribution systems in which advertising (including branded entertainment) is a key element. Revenue is shown pro forma (*) for 2007 and/or 2006 if acquisitions or divestitures completed in 2008, 2007, or 2006 had significant effect on revenue.
From *Advertising Age*, September 28, 2008. Reprinted with permission of Writer's Media.

Continued

Table 8.2—Continued

100 LEADING MEDIA COMPANIES
Ranked by total net U.S. media revenue in 2007

RANK 2007	RANK 2006	Media Company	Headquarters	TOTAL NET U.S. MEDIA REVENUE 2007	2006	% CHG	Worldwide Parent Revenue	NET REVENUE FROM U.S. BY MEDIUM IN 2007 Newspaper	Magazine	Out of Home	Digital	Movies & Home Entertainment	TV	Radio	Cable Networks	Cable SYS/SAT	Other	Yellow Pages
35	37	Liberty Media Corp.®	Englewood, Colo.	1,335	1,259	6.0	9,423	0	0	0	0	0	15	0	1,066	0	254	0
36	38	Suddenlink Communications®	St. Louis	1,300	1,200	8.3	1,300	0	0	0	0	0	0	0	0	1,300	0	0
37	39	A&E Television Networks	New York	1,299	1,192	9.0	0	0	0	0	0	0	0	0	1,299	0	0	0
38	35	Meredith Corp.	Des Moines, Iowa	1,265	1,318	-4.0	1,587	0	946	0	0	0	318	0	0	0	0	0
39	40	Mediacom Communications Corp.	Middletown, N.Y.	1,237	1,183	4.6	1,293	0	0	0	0	0	0	0	0	1,237	0	0
40	36	EarthLink	Atlanta	1,216	1,301	-6.5	1,216	0	0	0	1,216	0	0	0	0	0	0	0
41	42	Lamar Advertising Co.	Baton Rouge, La.	1,210	1,120	8.0	1,210	0	0	1,210	0	0	0	0	0	0	0	0
42	48	Lions Gate Entertainment Corp.	Santa Monica, Calif.	1,165	861	35.4	1,361	0	0	0	0	898	0	0	0	0	267	0
43	41	Lee Enterprises	Davenport, Iowa	1,128	1,129	-0.1	1,128	1,128	0	0	0	0	0	0	0	0	0	0
44	45	McGraw-Hill Cos.	New York	1,020	985	3.6	6,772	0	916	0	0	0	104	0	0	0	0	0
45	47	Lifetime Entertainment Services	New York	998	924	8.0	0	0	0	0	0	0	0	0	998	0	0	0
46	53	IAC/Inter ActiveCorp®	New York	987	782	26.2	1,333	0	0	0	987	0	0	0	0	0	0	0
47	43	E.W. Scripps Co.	Cincinnati	984	1,080	-8.8	2,517	658	0	0	0	0	326	0	0	0	0	0
48	46	Citadel Broadcasting Corp.®	Las Vegas	945	978	-3.5	720	0	0	0	0	0	0	945	0	0	0	0
49	44	Media General®	Richmond, Va.	932	1,016	-8.2	932	541	0	0	36	0	356	0	0	0	0	0
50	50	Reed Elsevier	New York/London/Amsterdam	841	827	1.7	9,176	0	599	0	0	0	0	0	0	0	243	0
51	52	Monster Worldwide	New York	840	793	5.9	1,351	0	0	0	840	0	0	0	0	0	0	0
52	49	Reader's Digest Association®	Pleasantville, N.Y.	814	828	-1.8	2,517	0	814	0	0	0	0	0	0	0	0	0
53	54	Belo Corp.®	Dallas	777	771	0.8	777	0	0	0	0	0	777	0	0	0	0	0
54	59	Career Builder	Chicago	768	672	14.3	0	0	0	0	768	0	0	0	0	0	0	0
55	60	Insight Communications Co.®	New York	747	658	13.6	747	0	0	0	0	0	0	0	0	747	0	0
56	51	A.H. Belo Corp.®	Dallas	739	818	-9.7	739	739	0	0	0	0	0	0	0	0	0	0
57	56	Landmark Communications	Norfolk, Va.	738	740	-0.3	0	366	0	0	0	0	82	0	291	0	0	0
58	55	Freedom Communications	Irvine, Calif.	718	760	-5.5	0	618	0	0	0	0	100	0	0	0	0	0
59	57	Avista Capital Partners	New York	696	701	-0.6	0	300	0	0	0	0	0	0	0	0	0	0
60	58	Sinclair Broadcast Group	Hunt Valley, Md.	684	682	0.4	718	0	0	0	0	0	684	0	0	0	0	0
61	61	International Data Group	Boston	680	636	7.0	3,020	0	320	0	224	0	0	0	0	0	136	0
62	63	Wenner Media	New York	674	615	9.5	0	0	674	0	0	0	0	0	0	0	0	0
63	128	CW Network	Burbank, Calif.	627	NA	NA	0	0	0	0	0	0	627	0	0	0	0	0
64	64	GateHouse Media®	Fairport, N.Y.	624	606	3.0	589	624	0	0	0	0	0	0	0	0	0	0
65	62	Ravcom Media®	Montgomery, Ala.	597	618	-3.4	0	0	0	0	0	0	597	0	0	0	0	0
66	65	Zuckerman Media Properties	New York	571	591	-3.3	0	315	256	0	0	0	0	0	0	0	0	0
67	67	Cumulus Media®	Atlanta	561	550	2.0	328	0	0	0	0	0	0	561	0	0	0	0
68	77	Metro-Goldwyn-Mayer	Los Angeles	541	480	12.7	1,279	0	0	0	0	353	0	0	0	0	188	0

Source: "Global Media and Marketing," *Advertising Age*, October 28, 1991, S-1 to S-16.
Notes: Dollars in millions. Advertising Age Data Center estimates of U.S. media revenue. Media defined as information and entertainment content distribution systems in which advertising (including branded entertainment) is a key element. Revenue is shown pro forma (*) for 2007 and/or 2006 if acquisitions or divestitures completed in 2006, 2007, or 2006 had significant effect on revenue.
From *Advertising Age*, September 28, 2008. Reprinted with permission of Writer's Media.

Continued

Chapter 8 ■ Developing Media Strategy 221

Table 8.2—Continued

100 LEADING MEDIA COMPANIES
Ranked by total net U.S. media revenue in 2007

RANK			TOTAL NET U.S. MEDIA REVENUE					NET REVENUE FROM U.S. BY MEDIUM IN 2007									
2007	2006	Media Company	Headquarters	2007	2006	% CHG	Worldwide Parent Revenue	News-paper	Magazine	Out of Home	Digital	Movies & Home Entertainment	TV	Radio	Cable Networks	Cable SYS/SAT	Other	Yellow Pages
69	71	Source Interlink Cos.®	Bonita Springs, Fla.	533	524	1.6	2,254	0	533	0	0	0	0	0	0	0	0	0
70	69	Hachette Filipacchi Media U.S. (Lagardere)®	New York	531	541	-1.9	11,729	0	531	0	0	0	0	0	0	0	0	0
71	68	Community Newspaper Holdings	Birmingham, Ala.	517	542	-4.7		498	0	0	0	0	19	0	0	0	0	0
72	70	United Online®	Woodland Hills, Calif.	514	536	-4.1	514	0	0	0	514	0	0	0	0	0	0	0
73	74	LodgeNet Interactive Corp.®	Sioux Falls, S.D.	512	500	2.6	486	0	0	0	0	0	0	0	0	512	0	0
74	73	Morris Communications Co.	Augusta, Ga.	485	511	-5.1	0	375	31	0	0	0	0	18	0	0	0	0
75	66	Journal Communications	Milwaukee	484	567	-14.6	583	266	0	0	0	0	134	84	0	0	0	0
76	75	Entercom Communications Corp.®	Bala Cynwyd, Pa.	479	493	-2.8	468	0	0	0	0	0	0	479	0	0	0	0
77	86	Rodale	Emmaus, Pa.	458	392	17.0	0	0	458	0	0	0	0	0	0	0	0	0
78	80	American Media Operations	Boca Raton, Fla.	453	435	4.1	491	0	453	0	0	0	0	0	0	0	0	0
79	125	National Football League	New York	453	217	109.1	0	0	0	0	0	0	0	0	453	0	0	0
80	72	Westwood One	New York	451	512	-11.9	451	0	0	0	0	0	0	451	0	0	0	0
81	79	•••• Communications	Toledo, Ohio	445	461	-3.5	0	265	0	0	0	0	36	0	0	144	0	0
82	76	Journal Register Co.	Yardley, Pa.	445	487	-8.7	463	445	0	0	0	0	0	0	0	0	0	0
83	81	Nielsen Co.®	New York/Haarlem, Netherlands	441	434	1.7	4,707	0	441	0	0	0	0	0	0	0	0	0
84	78	Harte-Hanks	San Antonio	430	475	-9.4	1,163	430	0	0	0	0	0	0	0	0	0	0
85	123	DreamWorks Animation SKG	Glendale, Calif.	427	222	92.7	767	0	0	0	0	427	0	0	0	0	0	0
86	97	Classified Ventures	Chicago	425	332	28.0	425	0	0	0	425	0	0	0	0	0	0	0
87	89	Bauer Publishing	Englewood Cliffs, N.J.	414	363	14.3	0	0	414	0	0	0	0	0	0	0	0	0
88	88	Catalina Marketing Corp.	St. Petersburg, Fla.	412	377	9.4	508	0	0	0	0	0	0	0	0	0	412	0
89	83	Local TV LLC®	Fort Wright, Ky.	409	420	-2.6	0	0	0	0	0	0	409	0	0	0	0	0
90	87	RCN Corp.	Herndon, Va.	408	379	7.7	636	0	0	0	0	0	0	0	0	408	0	0
91	103	Major League Baseball	New York	400	317	26.2	0	0	0	0	400	0	0	0	0	0	0	0
92	82	LIN TV Corp.	Providence, R.I.	396	420	-5.8	396	0	0	0	15	0	381	0	0	0	0	0
93	85	Philadelphia Media Holdings	Philadelphia	385	400	-3.8	0	385	0	0	0	0	0	0	0	0	0	0
94	84	Sun-Times Media Group	Chicago	370	419	-11.7	372	370	0	0	0	0	0	0	0	0	0	0
95	94	YES Network (Yankee Global Enterprises)	New York	360	340	5.9	0	0	0	0	0	0	0	0	360	0	0	0
96	90	Bonnier Corp.	Winter Park, Fla.	356	350	1.6	0	0	356	0	0	0	0	0	0	0	0	0
97	108	Bresnan Communications	Purchase, N.Y.	354	292	21.2	354	0	0	0	0	0	0	0	0	354	0	0
98	96	American Express Publishing Corp.	New York	347	335	3.6	31,557	0	347	0	0	0	0	0	0	0	0	0
99	91	Macrovision Solutions Corp.	Santa Clara, Calif.	342	348	-1.9	156	0	142	0	13	0	0	0	186	0	0	0
100	93	Radio One	Lanham, Md.	330	341	-3.2	330	0	0	0	0	0	0	330	0	0	0	0

Source: "Global Media and Marketing," *Advertising Age*, October 28, 1991, S-1 to S-16.
Notes: Dollars in millions. Advertising Age Data Center estimates of U.S. media revenue. Media defined as information and entertainment content distribution systems in which advertising (including branded entertainment) is a key element. Revenue is shown pro forma (®) for 2007 and/or 2006 if acquisitions or divestitures completed in 2008, 2007, or 2006 had significant effect on revenue.
From *Advertising Age*, September 28, 2008. Reprinted with permission of Writer's Media.

professionals who may or may not be users of accounting software. The business magazines have a combined circulation of 150,000, and about two-thirds of their readers are middle- and upper-level managers.

The cost of an advertising page in the PC magazines group is $3,000, whereas an advertising page in the business magazines costs $6,000. Which of the two magazine groups would be the better buy for the advertiser of accounting software, assuming the intended target market is middle- and upper-level managers and the secondary target market is professionals?

Case 8.1

Hospitality Inns

Hospitality Inns are a familiar sight to the traveling businessman or family. A lodging chain found in 28 states, Hospitality Inn has more than 200 inns across the Sunbelt, Midwest, and Rocky Mountain areas. Typical Inns are conveniently located near office complexes, universities, medical centers, and regional malls with good airport and highway access. Its customers are frequent travelers on business or vacation who appreciate the reasonably priced, "no-frills" but high-quality lodging found consistently at Hospitality Inns. Guests can expect clean, quiet, and well-maintained rooms with color TVs and AM-FM radios, as well as free local calls, swimming pools, and a quality of management made possible by the smaller size of the Inns.

Hospitality Inns usually contain 106 to 138 guest rooms and have 24-hour front desks and message service, convenient parking, same-day laundry service, a swimming pool, color television with HBO/cable and AM-FM radio, free local telephone calls, wall-to-wall carpeting, and air conditioning. All the Inns are of similar design and architecture and furnishings. Telephone reservations for accommodations can be made free of charge through Hospitality Inns' telephone in the lobbies of all its establishments.

In metropolitan areas, the company effectively penetrates the market by what it calls "clustering"—building several inns to serve separate market areas rather than building a single 1,000-room inn. This reduces financial risk and maximizes chances for high occupancy.

Since the company was founded, it has grown at a steady rate. Expansion plans for the next five years are expected to bring a 15 to 20 percent annual increase in number of rooms. Table 8.1.1 shows some of the Hospitality Inns locations. The organization includes over 4,500 people located at the various inns, over twelve regional offices, and a home office in San Antonio, Texas.

Table 8.1.1 ■ Major Markets in Which Hospitality Inns Are Located

City	Number of Inns
Atlanta	5
Austin	4
Chicago	3
Corpus Christi	3
Dallas/Ft. Worth	15
Denver	5
Houston	10
Indianapolis	2
Jacksonville, Miss.	3
Little Rock, Ark.	4
Memphis	2
Nashville	2
New Orleans	5
Phoenix	2
San Antonio	10
Tampa	2

The hotel and inn business is highly competitive, and the company is in direct competition with other motor inns and hotels in all the areas where it operates. The inn industry is adversely affected by general economic conditions and government regulations that influence or determine wages, prices, construction procedures and costs, interest rates, availability of credit, and the cost of utilities. In addition the demand for accommodations in a particular inn may be affected by changes in travel patterns, relocation of airports, construction or relocation of highways, availability or cost of energy supplies (including gasoline), and other factors.

The demand for inn accommodations for business travel is generally higher Monday through Thursday than on the weekend. Demand also varies by normally recurring seasonal patterns. Room occupancy in most inns is higher in the spring and summer months (March-August) than in the balance of the year. Overall occupancy levels may also be affected by the number of newly opened inns and by the length of time they have been in operation.

Approximately 95% of Hospitality Inns' revenue is derived from room rentals. Other revenue sources include charges to customers for long-distance telephone service and restaurant and fitness club revenues. Table 8.1.2 shows selected financial data for the company from 2001 to 2005, and Table 8.1.3 shows a breakdown of Hospitality Inns' revenue from 2003, 2004, and 2005.

Hospitality Inns is one of the most profitable and well-managed chains of inns in the United States. It has shown continued strength and growth for the past decade. Despite the problems faced by the lodging industry in the United States, Hospitality Inns has continued to show a profit during the past ten years.

THE HOTEL AND MOTEL BUSINESS IN THE UNITED STATES

U.S. Department of Commerce figures show that total receipts for the lodging industry for 2009 totaled $139 billion. These receipts came from 4,476,191 available rooms in 48,062 lodging establishments. In the United States, 41% of the industry's total establishments are franchised, whereas the rest are wholly owned.

Two-thirds of all rooms are filled on an average day in the United States. Occupancy rates vary based on location, region, and the size of the motel. Table 8.1.4 shows a general summary of occupancy rates distribution based on these three factors.

The table shows that occupancy rates are highest in lodgings near airports, followed by those on highways, downtown, and in suburban locations. The Northeast is where occupancy rates are highest, followed by the West, North-central, and South regions. Another factor affecting occupancy is the hotel type; hotels with 600 or more rooms have the highest occupancy rates

In all but resort hotels, single occupancy constitutes the majority of business in the lodging industry. For all hotels, the occupancy rate is more than 60%; double occupancy as a percentage of the total is about 47.2%. Resort hotels, however, have an average occupancy rate of about 66.4%, and 80.3% of their occupancy is double occupancy.

Although 95% of all Hospitality Inns revenues come from room rental, the same is not true of the hotel industry as a whole. Table 8.1.5 summarizes the sources or revenue for the hotel and motel industry in the United States.

Hospitality's percentage of revenues coming from room rentals is higher than the industry average for inns with no restaurant (92.4%). Therefore, Hospitality Inns appears to be a very efficient chain that maximizes room turnaround—a necessary condition for a profitable organization. Nationwide, 12% of hotel and motel guests stay in deluxe or first-class accommodations. Seventy-five percent stay in average, middle-priced accommodations, and only 13% stay in economy/budget-type accommodations. Hospitality Inns competes for the average, middle-priced accommodation with the rest of the industry.

The travel market is divided into three major categories: business, pleasure, and vacation. Because some people travel for both business and pleasure simultaneously, there is more overlap in the different travel segments. 68% of the travel market comes from business travel, 32% from pleasure travel, and 37% from vacation travel. Whereas 43% of the travel market seeks lodging during weekdays, 34% occupies hotels and motels

Table 8.1.2 ■ Selective Financial Data for Hospitality Inns[a]

	2005	2004	2003	2002	2001
Revenues % Change	$136,802 +20.7	$113,378 +10.4	$102,656 +24.0	$82,765 +33.9	$61,825 +28.2
Operating Income % Change	39,305 +7.4	36,590 +5.6	34,646 +26.0	27,498 +34.7	20,415 +31.6
Net Earnings % Change	12,815 −4.8	13,456 +9.5	12,291 +42.7	8,611 +34.3	6,412 +31.6
Earnings per share % Change	.88 −5.4	.93 +3.3	.90 +30.4	.69 +27.8	.54 +28.6
Working capital provided by operations % Change	40,917 +5.4	38,825 +22.9	31,590 +36.2	23,187 +29.5	17,910 +32.7
Additions to property & equipment, and motor inns under development % Change	100,264 +34.1	74,757 −4.5	78,267 +60.0	48,906 −1.1	49,434 +31.1
Total Assets	504,012	404,201	324,370	229,462	178,545
Shareholders' Equity	108,760	93,746	79,324	49,369	29,390
Partners' capital	39,213	26,348	20,030	14,851	10,785
Long-term debt, excluding current installments	296,611	243,451	189,717	139,694	119,054
Return on share-holders' equity[b]	13.7%	17.0%	24.9%	29.3%	28.1%
Effective profit margin[c]	11.7%	14.8%	15.2%	13.2%	13.3%
Combined effective debt-to-equity ratio[d]	2.0	2.0	1.9	2.2	3.0

[a]Dollars in thousands, except per share data.
[b]Net earnings as a percentage of shareholders' equity at the beginning of the year.
[c]Net earnings plus taz-adjusted partners' equity in earnings and losses as a percentage of total revenues.
[d]Ratio of long-term debt excluding current installments to partners' capital plus shareholders' equity at year end.

on weekends. Most of the travel (56%) is through airline trips, whereas 35% of travel involves automobile or truck trips. Almost all hotel guests (88%) arrive with reservations. Forty-one percent of the business and 33% of the pleasure hotel bookings are made by travel agent systems.

Among business travelers, 65% make their own decision about where they want to stay, and 50% place their own reservations. According to research, the most important factors influencing the decision to stay at a

Table 8.1.3 ■ Revenue Distribution for Hospitality Inns

	2003	2004	2005
Motor inn revenue (000)	$131,087.00	$108,281	$98,127
% Increase over prior year	21.1	10.3	24
Number of available room nights (000)	5,339	4,633	3,966
Percentage of occupancy	7,209	71.1	80.0
Occupied room nights (000)	3,889	3,295	3,174
% Increase over prior year	18.0	3.8	12.6
Average daily rate per occupied room	$32.10	$31.09	$29.01
% Increase over prior year	3.2	7.2	10.9

Table 8.1.4 ■ Occupancy Rates for Hospitality Inns[a]

Location		Region		Size (Number of rooms)	
Airport	68.30%	Northeast	69.50%	Under 150	64.90%
Suburban	62.2	North-Central	61.7	150–299	64.9
Highway	66.6	South	59.8	300–600	63.1
Downtown	63.1	West	69	Over 600	68.6

[a]Industry average occupancy rate is 61.6%.

Table 8.1.5 ■ Sources of Revenue

	All Lodgings	Transient Hotels	Resort Hotels	Motels with Restaurant	Motels with No Restaurant
Rooms	60.50%	60.30%	53.50%	63.50%	92.40%
Food	23.5	24	26.7	22.5	
Beverages	8.9	9	9	9.6	
All other	7.1	6.7	10.8	4.4	7.6

specific hotel or motel are as follows: location (25%), recommendation from business associates (24%), image of the hotel (24%), cost (8%), and travel agent's recommendation (7%).

It is clear, therefore, that the lodging industry in the United States is a very diversified one, appealing to different types of customers under different conditions. The characteristics of customers using hotels and motels are important for marketing managers in this industry to understand.

THE HOTEL/MOTEL CUSTOMER

A profile of the hotel/motel customer could reveal that most are male, 35 to 54 years of age (56%), with an income of over $49,000 (67%). Most hotel-motel guests are professionals or middle- and top management (63%). 60% of the guests usually occupy hotels or motels while on business, whereas 34.4% are tourists. Nearly 89% are U.S. residents, and about 40% of hotel/motel occupancy is made up of repeat trade.

92% of people participating in meeting or conventions stay at a hotel or motel. Most of the time, the decision to stay at a motel or hotel for a vacation is made by the male head of the household (51%). Only 30% of the time is the decision made by the female head of the household. The remainder of the time, the decision is made by a travel agent with a credit card (52%), whereas over 22% pay with cash and another 23% pay with other credit, such as corporate accounts or trade.

Research shows that 52% of business travelers avoid high-priced hotels. 31% of the problems guests encounter are room related, such as noisy or dirty rooms, rooms that aren't ready, or early checkout times. 25% of the problems with hotels/motels are service oriented. 26% of the guests complain that there is no restaurant, 25% complain of unfriendly personnel, 26% complain of delays at check-in, and 18% complain of room unavailability or unconfirmed reservations. Service, therefore, is extremely important to hotel/motel customers.

Most Hospitality Inn customers are younger, wealthier males who travel frequently and stay weekday nights at the hotel. Furthermore, a majority of Hospitality guests make their own reservations and arrive by car, and 73% are repeat customers and a source of loyal business. According to the firm's research, Hospitality customers are frequent travelers. Over 60% take more than one trip a month, and 25% take one trip per week. Almost 63% of visitors to Hospitality Inns are for business, and only 22% are for vacation or pleasure. Other reasons for lodging there are personal reasons and conventions. Of people staying at Hospitality Inns, 54.2% use a singly occupancy room, and 38.5% use double occupancy.

The professional profile of Hospitality Inns' customers is very similar to that of the industry as a whole. The average age of the Inns' occupant is 45 years and slightly younger than the average hotel/motel customer. Most Hospitality Inn visitors (55.6%) are married, whereas only 13.7% are single, and their average income is about $47,000 in 1984 dollars.

Most of the business for Hospitality Inns comes from residents of the south-central states. Therefore, Hospitality has unique customers with distinct characteristics, making it easier to segment and reach them through a coordinated advertising program.

THE MARKETING PLAN

A recent five-year plan developed by Hospitality's top management maps out the company's growth strategy. The plan contemplates the addition of new inns at an annual rate of 17%. This rate of growth would increase the number of inns from 125 to 3000 by the end of the five years. The new inns should average 130 rooms—somewhat larger than the current average—and this should result in an annual increase of about 20% in the equivalent number of rooms available.

At the end of the current fiscal year, 60 out of 125 Hospitality Inns were located in Texas, 2 in California, and 5 in Florida. The five-year plan contemplates adding 14 new inns in Texas, 43 in California, and 19 in Florida. If this plan were carried out, the percentage of Inns in Texas would be reduced from 48% to 27%. Texas, California, and Florida together are expected to represent about half of Hospitality Inns' expansion over the next five years. These three states are expected to continue as big population gainers. In addition, the five-year plan emphasizes continued development through the Southeast and Southwest and entry into the east-central region of Virginia, Maryland, and Washington, D.C. Exhibit 8.1.1 shows present and planned locations of Hospitality Inns.

Hospitality presently owns all its properties. This allows management control over operations necessary to ensure a high degree of consistency in both quality and pricing. In a recent survey of hotel/motel customers, Hospitality was rated high in terms of overall quality, chain consistency, and value.

The profile of the business traveler is changing, and although Hospitality seems capable of responding

Exhibit 8.1.1 ■ Present and Planned Locations of La Quinta Motor Inns

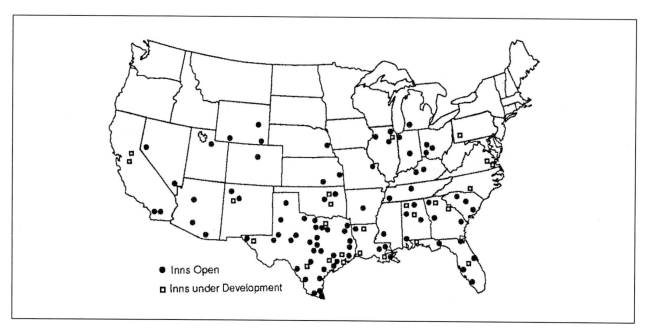

readily to that change, top management is concerned with continuing to lead the industry in innovative marketing policies. More women are entering the business ranks, making women an increasingly larger share of the business. Although these women are also likely to become weekend pleasure travelers, their choice of pleasure or vacation accommodations may not involve the same decision considerations used by their male counterparts. Thus, Hospitality wants to ensure that its services will be as popular among female business travelers as they are among male business travelers.

In addition, the company's management is concerned that the chain appears to be more popular among travelers who reside in Texas than among travelers residing in other states. Although this is not too surprising a finding, because a majority of its inns are located in Texas, the chain hopes to expand nationally and achieve a broad coverage in the future. To do so effectively, the chain will need to increase national awareness of its services and expand its popularity/usage among residents of other states.

At a top management meeting in June of 2008, it was decided that Hospitality Inn would invest in a major advertising campaign in an effort to increase awareness of its brand among business travelers on a national basis and communicate an image that would appeal equally to male and female business travelers without targeting women specifically, because the total advertising budget would not allow such specific targeting. It is important also to underscore that, at the time of this decision, the majority of Hospitality customers were male, and the chain did not want to risk losing its present customer base in an effort to attract women.

The management decided to invest a total of $5 million in national and regional advertising during the 2010 fiscal year. The vice-president of marketing, Martin Tollert, was directed to contact the TLCB advertising agency to request that it submit an advertising plan within that budget. A summary of the advertising plan submitted by the agency follows.

THE ADVERTISING PLAN

The proposed advertising plan recommends the following objectives for Hospitality Inns:

- Increase awareness of the benefits of Hospitality Inns, primarily among adults 25+ (male skew) who are business travelers.
- Provide optimal coverage of key source markets of greatest volume and potential. These markets account for 53% of Hospitality dollars and have high/medium "Bids.". BDI (Brand Development Index) is defined as the individual market's contribution to brand sales. It is calculated as follows.

$$\text{BDI} = \frac{\text{Market X's Share of Total Brand Sales}}{\text{Market X's Share of U.S. Population}} \times 100$$

- Provide emphasis in primary key source markets. These markets account for 37% of Hospitality Inns source dollars and have high "BDIs."
- Schedule advertising to establish presence/maximize continuity throughout the January—May 2011 period.

Table 8.1.6 describes Hospitality Inns key source markets.

Based on these objectives, the advertising agency recommended allocating the advertising budget as shown in Table 8.1.7. The rationale for the spending allocation was based on a study of American Express charges of lodgings by markets, which showed that the primary markets for Hospitality Inns were responsible for 37% of its dollar revenues, whereas its secondary and potential markets were responsible for 16% of the revenue dollars for the chain. The intended media allocations for each market, as stated in the advertising agency plan, are shown in Table 8.1.8.

Tollert was not fully satisfied with the agency's plan. He was not sure that it provided adequate reach and frequency of exposure to ensure the success of the five-year expansion plan. On the other hand, he did not feel qualified to critique the plan or suggest alternative media allocations. Among his considerations were the findings of a recent market survey, which reported the state of residence of Hospitality Inns' customers, along with the percentage of Hospitality Inns' sales by state. Table 8.1.9 and 8.1.10 show the results of the market survey.

Table 8.1.6 ■ Hospitality Inns' Key Source Markets

Primary Markets	Secondary Markets	Potential Markets
Corpus Christi	Oklahoma City, Okla.	Chicago
San Antonio	Shreveport, La.	
Lubbock	Atlanta	
Dallas/Fort Worth	Denver	
Odessa/Midland, Tex.	Kansas City, Mo.	
Austin	New Orleans	
Waco/Temple, Tex.	Phoenix	
Houston	Memphis	
	Tulsa, Okla.	

Table 8.1.7 ■ Recommended Media Allocation for Hospitality Inns' Advertising

Media	Total Period: Adults 25+			
	Reach	Frequency	GRPs[a]	Approximate Number of Weeks
Spot TV	93%	11.1x	1,040	12
Regional Magazines	34%	3.2x	109	20

[a]GRP (Gross Rating Points) is a measure of the total ratings for the individual sponsor programs. A rating point is equal to 1% of the potential audience of a medium, therefore: 150 gross rating points means 1.5 messages per average home.

Source: Jack Z. Sissors and E. Reynold Petray, *Advertising Media Planning,* Chicago, IL: Crain Books, 1976, 311.

Table 8.1.8 ■ Hospitality Inns Recommended Market Area Expenditure Analysis

Hospitality Market Area	Percentage of U.S. TV Households	Percentage of Hospitality Source Dollars	Expenditure by Market (thousands of dollars)	Percentage of Spending by Market
Primary	5%	37%	$1,704.40	73%
Secondary	11	16	625.6	27
Total key source markets	16%	53%	$2330.0	100%
Remainder of U.S.	84	47	—	—
Total U.S.	100%	100%	$2,330.00	100%

Note: The remainder of the advertising budget was spent on production costs, print point-of-purchase displays and leaflets, promotions, and training for Hospitality Inns personnel.

Toller decided it was important to have the agency take a second look at the advertising plan. Most of all, he was concerned with increasing the advertising reach to gain more national coverage. In addition, he had been intrigued recently by the success of some cable stations, particularly the Cable News Network and ESPN. He knew that the majority of his friends and acquaintances were regular viewers of CNN and that a good portion also watched ESPN at least twice a week. Although this group could not be considered heavy television viewers, it certainly mirrored the demographic characteristics of the higher-income Hospitality customers. Should cable TV have been considered in the media plan? The question was a valid one, and he hoped to get some answers.

The agency responded to the questions raised by Toller with a complete report, which can be seen in Appendix 8.1.

Upon receipt of the proposed advertising plan and the subsequent report, Tollert, and the company's CEO, met at length. At the end of the meeting, the CEO stated:

Martin, I am aware that you still feel we should give cable a chance. Why don't you make your own analysis of the agency's recommendations? I trust your instincts and your judgment. I'll recommend to the board the course of action you feel is most appropriate for Hospitality's future. Go ahead, give it a try, and be ready to present your recommendations to the full board next week.

Tollert was flattered by his boss's confidence and intimidated by the task ahead. Nevertheless, he set out to undertake his new mission in an objective and comprehensive manner.

Table 8.1.9 ■ Hospitality Customers by State of Residence

State of Residence	Percentage of All Hospitality Customers
Texas	36.40%
Oklahoma	2.3
Louisiana	2.3
Arkansas	2.5
Georgia	3.8
Illinois	3.3
California	4.8
New York	2.2
Colorado	3.2
Arizona	2.5
Florida	4.3
Kansas/Missouri	2.9
Other	29.5

Table 8.1.10 ■ Percentage of Total Hospitality Inns Dollar Sales by State

State of Residence	Percentage of All Hospitality Customers
Texas	16.60%
Oklahoma	1.83
Louisiana	1.76
Arkansas	1.02[a]
Georgia	2.89
Illinois	6.18
California	5.59
New York	8.5
Colorado	1.89
Arizona	1.1
Florida	1.21
Kansas/Missouri	2.92
Other	48.5

[a]Estimated share

Name _____ Date _____

QUESTIONS FOR DISCUSSION AND REVIEW

1. Should Hospitality Inn approve the advertising agency's proposed media plan?

2. Why do you think Tollert is eager to examine cable television advertising as an alternative to the agency's plan?

3. Do you agree with the CEO's appraisal of Tollert's knowledge? Do you feel the agency would resent Tollert making a separate recommendation to the board? Would this incident cause a strain in the relationship between Hospitality Inn and TLCB?

4. What type of media strategy would be most appropriate for Hospitality? Why?

Appendix 8.1 ■ Report to Hospitality Inns

Question #1: *Would the audience composition of the recommended spot TV buy be as demographically qualitative as that of a cable buy?*

Answer: Yes, by advertising in the dayparts recommended for hospitality in the FY 2010 spot TV buy, the audience composition would be almost as demographically selected as for a cable buy.

	Adults 25+ Audience Composition	
	Business Travelers	**Stayed in Paid Accommodations**
Recommended buy	4%	44%
Cable buy	5	53

For example, in the primary markets, the recommended spot TV buy would provide the following:

- More adult 25+ business traveler impressions/spot
- ESPN spot: 14,530
- ABC Sports spot: 54,488
- Greater cumulative reach potential
- Cable schedule: 44%
- Network schedule: 95%

Question #2: *Would a cable/regional magazine plan or a total cable plan be more effective than the recommended plan in reaching our target audience in the primary markets?*

Answer: No. In the primary markets, the recommended plan would have far more impact than either cable alternative in reaching not only total adults 25+, but also heavy business travelers.

Question #3: *Would either cable plan spend media dollars as effectively as the recommended plan against market areas of greatest potential?*

Answer: Fifty-three percent of Hospitality's source dollars come from key source markets, which comprise only 16% of the U.S. population. Neither cable plan would spend media dollars as effectively as the recommended plan against key source markets, which represent greatest potential for Hospitality Inns.

Question #4: *How would a cable plan affect message delivery against a secondary, nonbusiness traveler audience?*

Answer: Both "cable only" and "cable/regional magazines" plans deliver significantly less reach and total GRPs against the total adult 25+ target audience, thereby reducing overall awareness within key source market areas. Both plans also deliver fewer "heavy business traveler" impressions within key source markets, especially primary markets.

The "cable only" plan delivers 3% more adult 25+ "stayed hotel/motel/other paid accommodations" impressions in key source markets than the recommended plan.

Hospitality Inns Recommended versus Cable Plans:
Target Audience Delivery Analysis for Primary Markets

Plan Alternative	Total Period A25+			A25+ Heavy Business Traveler Impressions (in thousands)	Approximate Number of Advertising Weeks
	Reach	Frequency	GRPs		
Recommended Plan					
Spot TV	93%	11.1x	1,040	3,098	12
Regional magazines	34%	3.2x	109	1,346	20
Total	95%	12.1x	1,149	4,444	20
(Index)	(100)	(100)	(100)	(100)	(100)
Cable/Regional Magazine					
Cable	20%	9.8x	196	783	14
Regional magazines	34%	3.2x	109	1,346	20
Total	47%	6.5x	305	2,129	20
(Index)	(49)	(54)	(27)	(48)	(100)
Cable Only					
Cable	26%	12.5x	325	1,299	23
(Index)	(27)	(103)	(28)	(29)	(115)

Hospitality Inns Market Area Expenditure Analysis:
Recommended versus Cable Plans

Hospitality Market Area	Percentage of U.S. TV Households	Percentage of Hospitality Source Dollars
Primary	5%	37%
Secondary/Potential	11	16
Total Key Source Markets	16%	53%
Remainder of U.S.	84	47
Total U.S.	100%	100%

Hospitality Inns Recommended versus Cable Plans:
Target Audience Delivery Analysis for Primary and Key Source Markets

	Total Period A25+			Total Period Estimated A25+ Impression	
	Reach	Frequency	GRPs	Heavy Business Traveler (in thousands)	Stayed Hotel/Motel/Other Paid Accommodation (in thousands)
Primary Markets					
Recommended plan	95%	12.1x	1,149	4,444	35,850
Cable/Regional magazine plan	52%	7.5x	389	2,129	10,002
Cable-only plan	26%	12.5x	325	1,299	12,514
Key Source Markets					
Recommended plan*	54%	8.2x	442	9,269	44,504
Cable/Regional magazine plan	52%	5.1x	265	9,026	38,777
Cable-only plan	22%	11.8x	259	4,743	45,702

*Includes spot TV weight, which covers primary markets only.

Expenditures/Percentage of Spending by Market

Recommended Plan		Cable/Regional Magazine Plan		Cable-Only Plan	
$852.2	73%	$211.1	18%	$63.5	5%
$1,312.8	27	351.8	30	105.8	9
———	———	———	———	———	———
$1,165.0	100%	$562.9	48%	$169.3	14%
		599.2	52	993.6	86
$1,165.0	100%	$1,162.1	100%	$1,162.9	100%

Hospitality Inns Cable Penetration: Key Source Markets

	Primary Markets			Secondary/Potential Markets	
	Percentage of Cable Penetration	Number of Cable Households (in thousands)		Percentage of Cable Penetration	Number of Cable Households (in thousands)
Corpus Christi	51%	86.1	Oklahoma City	48%	284.4
San Antonio	56	289.2	Shreveport	46	209.1
Lubbock	51	76.8	Atlanta	37	422.2
Dallas	35	532.0	Denver	34	328.5
Odessa-Midland	70	95.3	Kansas City	45	317.5
Austin	53	152.6	New Orleans	46	292.0
Waco-Temple	58	133.6	Phoenix	35	286.1
Houston	42	591.9	Memphis	40	218.7
	———	———	Tulsa	51	232.9
Weighted average	44.4%	1,957.5	Chicago	22	674.0
				———	———
			Weighted average	35.1%	3,265.4
Weighted average key source markets penetration	38%				
National cable penetration	42%				
Index	(90)				

Case 8.2

Healthy Dog Gourmet

John Kirk was finishing his last year as a veterinary school student at A&M University when a friend called him to say that he wanted to discuss a potential joint venture for a product he had been working on for some time. Kirk's friend, Paul Fry had graduated with a master's in biology from the same university and John and Paul had been friends since high school.

John had planned to open his own Veterinary Clinic in Austin, Texas. The capital of the state had a wealthy and diverse population. Young families and young singles were a significant percentage of the overall Austin population. In addition, the city was very friendly to animals and it was a well-known fact that Austin had more pets on a per capita basis of the population than most cities of its size. The market for (V) veterinary services was growing in Austin, and John had been planning to invest a small inheritance he had received from his grandfather to start his clinic.

John and Paul met for lunch to discuss Paul's proposal. Paul had been reading recent articles on the pet food industry in the United States and had become fascinated with the market opportunities for high-end healthy food for dogs and cat owners that were not pleased with the choices offered to them.

Americans love pets. In December 2009, a Humane Society report stated that there were approximately 77.5 million owned dogs in the United States, and that 39% of U.S. households own at least one dog. Therefore, on average, owners have almost two dogs. Dog owners dote on their animals and spend a fair amount of money on them. The same report indicated that on average, dog owners spent $225 annually on veterinary visits.[1] In recent years, some pet owners started being concerned with the ingredients of commercially produced pet food and looked for healthier solutions. A cottage industry of producers of organic pet food emerged, and demand for such products increased on a steady basis. In 2004, organic pet food sales were only 0.09% of total domestic food sales, or a total of $14 million net sales ("Organic Pet Food gets Paws Up,"; USA Today, July 13, 2004, Money, p.1) Despite its small market share, organic pet food was considerably more expensive than regular pet food, and the high margins were starting to attract the attention of major pet food producers. As an example, Newman's Own Organic, a brand of food products regularly sold in supermarkets across the United States, in early 2004 also introduced an organic and pricey line of dog and cat food.

U.S. pet food sales for dogs and cats totaled over $17 billion in 2008, according to the Pet Food Institute. A breakdown of sales by type of food can be seen in Table 8.2.1 on the next page.

The increase in the organic pet food relative share of market was an exciting prospect for Paul. He believed that a growing number of pet owners would be attracted by the quality and the freshness promised by organic pet food producers. Some reports indicated that, among specific demographic groups of pet owners, the rate of adoption of organic pet food was increasing at a rate of about 15% a year. He believed that by 2012, organic and natural dog food sales, as an example, would represent almost 6% of total dog food sales. He estimated that 50% of the growth in organic dog food sales would come at the expense of sales of regular wet dog food, and the other 50% would come from sales of regular dry dog food. So, if total sales of dog food in 2012 were estimated to be $13 billlion (dry and wet dog food combined), total sales of organic dog food that same year could be as high as $780 million.

Paul was not alone in believing in the potential market success of organic and natural dog food. By 2010, over 50 brands of organic dog food, produced by 22 different companies, were already being sold in the United States.

---

[1] "U.S. Pet Ownership Statistics: The Humane Society of the United States,", December 30, 2009, http://www.humanesociety.org/issues/pet_overpopulation/facts/pet_ownership_statistics.html

Table 8.2.1 ■ U.S. Pet Food Sales

	2003	2008
Dog Food—Dry	$5.341	$7.480
Dog Food—Wet	$1.707	$1.838
Dog Treats	$1.417	$1.987
Cat Food—Dry	$2.570	$3.291
Cat Food—Wet	$1.970	$2.147
Cat Treats	$0.177	$0.309
TOTAL	$13.184	$17.055
(in US$ billions) Source: Euromonitor International		

Research showed that pet owners that purchased organic pet food stated that they did so because they did not like the chemicals found in conventional pet food. In addition, pet owners' response to the pet food recalls of 2007 were very indicative of the importance that the safety and well-being of their pets has among pet owners. An article by Pet Food industry[11] reports that a May 2007 Greenfield Online survey found that 93% of pet owners were aware of the pet food recalls. Asked what they did in reaction to the recalls, 62% stated they changed the brand of pet food they used to buy; 28% stated they started making homemade food for their pets; 16% switched to organic pet food; 15% changed the retailer from which they bought their pet food, and the remainder gave other answers.

The research therefore shows that a good percentage of pet owners were aware of and responsive to the option of buying organic pet food as an alternative. Paul believed that, once the pet owner switched to the organic pet food, there was a high probability that they would continue to buy organic products for their pets on an ongoing basis.

Paul believed that a private brand of organic dog food would be a great addition to the products veterinary clinics customarily make available for sale to their clients. He believed that with a relatively modest investment he and John could partner with a small producer of quality organic dog food, develop their own brand, and market it through the veterinary clinic.

Austin was a growing community of over a million people. A large percentage of Austin's households had pets, and a recent survey indicated that of the 300,000 households in Austin, 43% had at least one dog. The demographic profile of Austin's dog owners was very similar to that of the rest of the U.S. population of pet owners. The Table 8.2.2 describes the characteristics of household pet ownership for the United States.

Paul was confident that if they were to sell their own brand of organic dog food in the new veterinary clinic, they would be able to capture at least 25% of the clinic clients over a period of 2 years. Austin had about .09% of the total U.S. households. The average U.S household reportedly spent over $250 a year in dog food, and those households purchasing organic dog food spent an average of 50% more a year on that product.

The new clinic had a great location, in a higher-income area of the city, and only another veterinary clinic was located at a similar driving distance. John was confident that he would be able to attract at least 5 to 7% of all the Austin households of dog owners to his clinic.

Paul and John agreed that it would be an attractive business proposition to market their own brand of organic dog food at the clinic. They needed to develop a plan to reach potential customers, however. They focused on developing a two-year plan because of the limitations on their budget.

Table 8.2.2 ■ Household Pet Ownership: 2006
(Based on a sample survey of 47,000 households in 2006; For definition of mean, see source)

Item	Unit	Dogs	Cats	Birds	Horses
Total companion pet population[a]	Million	72.1	81.7	11.2	7.3
Number of households owning pets	Million	43.0	37.5	4.5	2.1
Percent of households owning companion pets	Percent	37.2	32.4	3.9	10.8
Average number owned per household	Number	1.7	2.2	2.5	3.5
Percent of Household Owning Pets					
Annual household income:					
Under $20,000	Percent	30.7	30.1	4.4	1.5
$20,000 to $34,999	Percent	37.3	33.6	4.2	1.7
$35,000 to $54,999	Percent	39.8	34.1	4.4	2.1
$55,000 to $84,999	Percent	42.8	35.5	3.7	2.3
$85,000 and over	Percent	42.1	33.3	3.7	2.3
Household size:					
One person	Percent	21.9	24.7	2.1	0.8
Two persons	Percent	37.6	33.4	3.9	1.7
Three persons	Percent	47.5	39.1	5.1	2.3
Four persons	Percent	51.9	38.5	5.4	2.7
Five or more persons	Percent	54.3	40.0	6.6	3.6

[a] As of December 31, 2006.

Source: American Veterinary Medical Association, Schuamburg, IL, *U.S. Pet Ownership and Demographic Sourcebook,* 2001 (copyright.) See also http://www.avma.org/

Several alternatives were discussed: the possibility of using mailers to every household in the geographic area of the clinic, the development of a special Website for the dog food, the use of selected radio advertising messages on the local radio stations, and the placement of advertisements in *Austin Monthly,* a monthly publication that highlighted events and businesses in Austin. Because the clinic did not have yet a list of clients, electronic messages to customers were not being considered for the first two years.

The total budget John and Paul had available to develop the initial two-year campaign was $100,000. The costs of the different choices they had outlined were as follows:

Mailers to 10,000 households—$ 2.50 per mailer (including production and distribution)—The partners felt that they would need to send a minimum of three mailers per household over the two-year period.

Web site cost—Development $40,000, maintenance costs $10,000 per year

Radio advertisements—each 30-second commercial would cost $250, but at least four commercials per week were needed for the first six months and after that two commercials per week were recommended by the radio station to maintain awareness for the new product.

Each *Austin Monthly* full-page ad (in color) would cost $3,000. The partners felt that it would be essential to have at least one ad every two months in the first year, and one ad per quarter during the second year.

Paul's wife was a media consultant, and she volunteered to develop a comprehensive media plan for the new product. Paul and John decided to call their new brand of organic dog food *Healthy Gourmet*. The partnership was formed, and the new venture was on its way.

QUESTIONS FOR DISCUSSION AND REVIEW

1. Identify the target market for Healthy Gourmet and develop a strategy for reaching potential customers.

2. You have been recruited by Paul's wife to help develop the media plan within the proposed $100,000 budget. Please write a detailed media plan for Healthy Gourmet.

Case 8.3

Henigan's Department Stores[1]

COMPANY BACKGROUND

John Henigan founded Henigan's Department Stores (HDS) in 1946. Since the first store opened in Springfield, Illinois, the company had grown to 36 stores, in 16 markets, in five Midwestern states: Illinois, Indiana, Michigan, Wisconsin, and Ohio. HDS was one of the few family-owned stores left in the United States and had yearly revenue of approximately $150 million. HDS, which competed most directly with stores like Macy's, JC Penney, and Target, introduced its own credit card in 1994.

The Henigan's card allowed HDS to build a stronger customer base and increase sales. Their cardholders were rewarded with points for each dollar charged and could achieve three levels of membership based on total charges per year. Each level of membership was rewarded one point for every dollar spent in HDS stores. For every 3,000 points earned, the cardholders were sent a $25 gift card to the store. Additional membership level benefits are outlined below.

Level 1: Free standard shipping, up to $100 custom alteration on in-store purchases, and *Early Access* to sales events

Level 2: Free standard shipping, up to $300 custom alterations on in-store purchases, *Early Access* to sales events, and HDS concierge access

Level 3: Free two-day shipping, unlimited custom alterations on in-store purchases, Early access to sales events, and HDS concierge access

CARD MEMBER PROFILE

Table 8.3.1 presents a breakdown of HDS's sales and credit card members by markets. The typical, loyal HDS card member was a middle-aged female with high-school age or older children. She enjoyed shopping at HDS because she was able to shop for the whole family and earn reward points for all purchases. Typically, she saved up her reward gift card points each year and splurged on something special just for herself. She had been a faithful HDS shopper for years and looked forward to moving up the membership levels.

EARLY TICKET SALE PROGRAM

In 2001, HDS launched its Early Ticket Sale program (ETS). This program was designed to increase the attractiveness of the HDS credit card. Consumers with HDS cards were given opportunities to order concert and sporting event tickets 48 hours before they went on sale to the general public. Many of the events included in the ETS Program sold out quickly, so this was a significant advantage presented to HDS cardholders. The idea was to deliver a genuine benefit and, hence, add value to the card.

---

[1] This case was written by Lindsy Signet and John H. Murphy, The University of Texas at Austin. The case is designed to serve as the basis for classroom discussion and not to illustrate either the effective or ineffective handling of an administrative situation. The identities of the firms involved and the situation have been disguised.

Table 8.3.1

Market	Population	Number of Stores	Sales by Market	Percent of Sales	Number of Cardholders
Akron, OH	207,510	2	$9,000,000	6%	594
Ann Arbor, MI	114,024	1	$5,000,000	3%	330
Aurora, IL	174,276	1	$7,000,000	5%	462
Bloomington, IN	72,254	2	$6,000,000	4%	396
Dayton, OH	166,179	3	$10,000,000	7%	668
Evansville, IN	121,582	1	$6,000,000	4%	396
Flint, MI	124,943	1	$5,000,000	3%	330
Fort Wayne, IN	251,591	2	$7,000,000	5%	462
Grand Rapids, MI	197,800	1	$9,000,000	6%	594
Green Bay, WI	100,353	1	$8,000,000	5%	528
Madison, WI	231,916	4	$12,000,000	8%	792
Peoria, IL	372,487	5	$18,000,000	12%	1,188
Racine, WI	81,592	1	$4,000,000	3%	264
South Bend, IN	316,663	4	$17,000,000	11%	1,122
Springfield, IL	116,482	2	$5,000,000	3%	330
Toledo, OH	650,955	5	$22,000,000	15%	1,452
	3,300,607	**36**	**$150,000,000**	**100%**	**9,908**

This in turn boosted the store's image and revenue. This had proven to be a popular program, and management felt it had significantly increased the number of card members over the years.

To promote the ETS program to current cardholders, information about upcoming events was included in small print at the bottom of the monthly bill. In addition, periodically statement stuffers keyed to specific events were inserted in the envelope with monthly bills.

However, management was convinced that the ETS program needed to be more aggressively promoted to the 9,900 HDS credit cardholders. The question was how to do this more efficiently and effectively. One option was to use e-mail to contact cardholders about the program, and a second option was to send separate direct mail pieces to card members. A direct response agency was contacted and asked to provide cost estimates for the direct mail option The direct marketer's estimates that included all printing, labels, preparation, and postage costs using HDS's mailing list for four types of mailing pieces were as follows:

6 × 9 4/C Postcard = $0.34 per piece
#10 Envelope Mailer = $0.47 per piece
Tri-Fold 4/C Self Mailer = $0.59 per piece
Roll Fold 6 × 11 4/C Self Mailer = $0.74 per piece

The direct response firm noted that a 6 × 11″ self-mailer was the largest piece size that qualifies for the letter rate postage. Further, the prices above were based on printing 10,000 pieces and included standard presort postage of $0.23 per piece average and that if HDS wanted to send the pieces presort first class it would be $0.36 postage per piece.

With these estimates in hand, the issue facing management was whether or not to implement the direct mail program and, if so, to decide which of the four options would be most appropriate. Or, if not, what other IBP efforts might be most effective in stimulating card member to participate in the ETS program?

Name _____ Date _____

QUESTIONS FOR DISCUSSION AND REVIEW

1. Considering the direct mail costs presented in the case, would direct mail be an effective way to reach current cardholders? Which of the four mail options would be most effective? Why?

2. What other IBP efforts would work well in coordination with the direct mail campaign?

3. How might the effectiveness of the proposed direct marketing campaign be measured? What would constitute success?

4. On a cost basis, do you think an e-mail campaign would be more or less effective than direct mail? Why?

5. What other options should be considered for stimulating HDS credit cardholders to participate in the ETS program?

___

___

___

___

Part III
Integrated Brand Promotion Mix

In this third major section of the book, the richness and diversity of IBP management decision making is brought into clear focus. In this section, the promotional mix elements beyond more traditional off-line advertising are explored. In total, it is the interaction effect of the thoughtful blending of multiple communication points that adds synergy and impact to the IBP mix. So, for example, it is the careful combining of off- and on-line advertising with PR, viral, and guerrilla programs plus brand entertainment that constitutes an effective IBP program.

Chapters 9 and 10 examine personal selling and sales promotion, respectively, as healthy and essential components to many firms' IBP mixes. Chapter 11 introduces direct marketing, and Chapter 12 focuses on public relations, including crisis management. These IBP tools often play the dominant role in IBP mixes of highly successful brand marketers.

In Chapter 13 the increasingly important IBP tools of event sponsorship, product placements, and branded entertainment are explored. Each of these three broad areas offers unique opportunities to contribute to an individual brand's marketing success. Chapter 14 focuses on the use of the Internet and social networking for IBP purposes. The brand's Web site is examined as often the critical component in the firm's marketing efforts. The chapter also includes coverage of guerilla, viral, and experiential marketing efforts that may or may not be Web based.

The section concludes with Chapter 15 and a brief examination of the evaluation of the overall effectiveness of IBP mixes and strategies. This chapter emphasizes the exercise of management control of the overall IBP planning process by assessing what succeeds and what fails as measured against previously established objectives.

Chapter 9
Personal Selling

I don't know who you are. I don't know your company. I don't know your company's product. I don't know what your company stands for. I don't know your company's customers. I don't know your company's record. I don't know your company's reputation. Now—What was it you wanted to sell me?

—McGraw-Hill Publications

THE IMPORTANCE OF PERSONAL SELLING

Selling is an integral part of the marketing program. Modern-day salespeople are problem solvers, and their activity is customer oriented. Sales personnel are the company's personal link to its customers and clients. They are the company's personification, providing an image with which the firm is often identified. It is crucial, therefore, that they represent the company as efficiently and flawlessly as possible.

To achieve their marketing and sales goals, companies must tailor their marketing communication mix to the needs and wants of their customers. They must also use marketing communication as a tool to distinguish themselves from competitors.

Personal selling is a very effective communication tool. It is particularly powerful when used at certain stages of the buying process; for example, personal selling is most effective when customers are building preference for a product, developing knowledge and conviction about the product, and finally deciding to buy the product.

Selling is the most expensive of all marketing functions. Highly trained professionals engage in a personal interaction with customers; therefore, the unit cost of each call far exceeds the individual costs of advertising and sales promotion. For this reason, selling should be used selectively. Criteria for using personal selling as opposed to, or in addition to, other marketing communication tools must be set and weighed carefully. For example, personal selling should be used for very complex and/or high-ticket items, as opposed to perishable packaged goods.

Competitive position, the types of goods sold, the stage in the life cycle of the product, and several other factors will determine whether an expenditure on personal selling is needed. This chapter will explore the conditions conducive to the use of personal selling.

THE ROLE OF A SALESPERSON

Salespeople perform several vital tasks that contribute to the success of the marketing strategy of a firm.

Salespeople are first of all a very important source of information for a firm's customers. This is especially true for industrial or institutional buyers because they need more complete and detailed information about products. As an information source, salespeople help their customers by explaining the advantages and disadvantages of their products and by fitting their offering to their customers' needs.

This problem-solving ability of salespeople allows them to develop a long-term relationship with their customers. The goodwill of a firm rests on the loyalty of its customers; hence salespeople are a vital element in building such goodwill. Also, because of their problem-solving ability, salespeople are skilled professionals, able to answer sophisticated management questions. The stereotypical image of the salesperson—a good talker who does not offer much—could not be farther from reality. Modern salespeople are important contributors to the firm and to their clients.

Salespeople are the representatives of the whole company, and at the same time they provide the company with vital feedback about its customers. In such a role, salespeople are intelligence gatherers and researchers. They keep management informed about market trends and major changes in the marketplace. In addition, they provide management with information useful in improving the quality of the firm's products and services. Reporting on customers' difficulties in using the products, shipment delays, billing problems, and other causes of customers' discontent is an essential role of salespeople. This type of feedback would not be provided to management by any other source, and without it a company may not be able to maintain its customer base. Salespeople, therefore, provide market research insights and high-quality internal feedback to the firm.

SALES AND THE MARKETING CONCEPT

Firms that practice the marketing concept as their management philosophy believe in integrating all their efforts toward satisfying customers as a means of accomplishing their long-term strategic goals.

The idea that the entire firm focuses on the satisfaction of customer needs implies that the firm will attempt to determine what it can offer its customers that would meet their needs as closely as possible. Because no one company can completely satisfy all its potential customers and markets all the time, companies must strive to satisfy specific markets and specific customer needs.

Salespeople must keep in mind the need to keep the customer satisfied. This means that they will have to integrate their efforts with those of all of the other departments of the firm. Salespeople can adapt the company's marketing mix to the need of each target market; therefore, they have more flexibility in responding to their customers' demands.

The three basic objectives of marketing communication are to inform, persuade, and remind target customers about the company and the products and services it offers. Most firms use a combination of communication tools to reach their intended audiences: advertising, public relations, and personal selling. The appropriate mix of communication is determined by several variables, among them the type of customers to be reached, type of product or service being sold, stage in the product life cycle, and overall competitive strategy adopted by the firm. Some of these variables will be discussed briefly.

Type of Customers to Be Reached

A firm that sells its products and services to industrial or institutional buyers will invest more money in its sales force than a firm that appeals directly to final consumers. Industrial and institutional buyers generally follow stricter directives when placing an order. Sometimes there are very technical questions to be answered and the need for knowledgeable and trained assistance. Final consumers, on the other hand, may respond to the emotional appeals of television advertising. A firm selling to industrial and institutional buyers, therefore, may decide to concentrate its communication efforts in the sales force while spending a smaller portion of the budget on advertising. The reverse would be true for a firm appealing primarily to final consumers.

Type of Products or Service

A firm selling a very complex product or service, or one requiring specific training for usage, will have to concentrate its efforts on personal communication to be able to answer questions and handle specific problems that may arise from the complexity of the product. This would be the case with, for example, personal computers and technologically complex products. Although some advertising could be used to cause awareness of and interest in the product among potential buyers, only in a personal sales situation can information be given that will allow the customer to develop a preference for the product.

On the other hand, in the case of a cake mix, for example, the one-way communication provided through advertising may be sufficient to generate interest and enough preference for a product to motivate its purchase. Although personal interaction with a salesperson might also be helpful, consumers' familiarity with the product and its technological simplicity may cause potential consumers to rely solely on emotional appeals to reach purchase decisions.

Another product characteristic relevant to determine the importance of personal selling is the perceived risk of the purchase decision. The more expensive the product or service, the greater the perceived risk of the purchase. A greater investment in personal selling would be best when selling high-cost items such as automobiles and insurance, whereas more emphasis on advertising might be advisable when selling packaged goods or personal care products.

Stage in the Product Life Cycle

When a product or service is in the early stages of its life cycle, it is important to provide customers with sufficient and relevant information about it. This can best be done through personal interaction with a salesperson. For example, when introducing videophones into the market, AT&T and its competitors would be well advised to spend a significant portion of their marketing communication budget on sales. The same is not the case when selling traditional touch-tone phones, which are now at the maturity stage in their life cycle. Advertising, coupled with product availability and self-service, could provide sufficient information for prospective customers.

Competitive Strategy

The type of marketing communication used could be instrumental in differentiating a product or a service from the offerings of competitors. For example, the heavy investment in personal selling made by Amway has developed a loyal and significant market for that product line. Although Amway detergents and other cleaning products could be considered parity products, the marketing communication and sales techniques used by the firm are unique and give it a differential advantage. By the same token, when Southwest Airlines promoted its automatic ticket-vending machines, it was a major departure from the traditional selling and marketing communication techniques used in the airline business. That alone differentiated Southwest Airlines from its competitors.

It is important to recognize the interaction of personal selling with all the other elements in the marketing mix. The type of product and service sold, the customers targeted, the stage in the product life cycle, and the competitive environment of the firm are all important variables when determining the amount and extent of personal selling efforts required to achieve the firm's long-term goals and objectives. The following section will investigate the major steps in developing a personal selling effort.

Telemarketing and Web Marketing

During the past 20 years, the development and growth of the Web has allowed many companies to reach directly to consumers, as opposed to distributing and selling their products only through wholesales and retailers. Companies utilize at least two types of strategies to reach consumers directly: telemarketing and Web marketing.

Telemarketing is the B to C practice of reaching consumers by randomly dialing phone numbers and employs either an actual salesperson or a computerized message to make a sales pitch. Some of the businesses that employ telemarketing are insurance companies, credit cards, and phone plans; also a number of nonprofit organizations use telemarketing for soliciting donations.

Most companies that utilize Web sites to reach consumers directly do not have salespeople calling on customers or potential customers. The Web sites contain all or most of the information usually required by customers and step-by-step instructions for completing a purchase online.

Whether telemarketing or Web marketing is employed as a strategy to contact potential customers and regular customers, it is still important for a firm to employ people that can answer specific customer questions or provide support before, during, and after the sale. Customer support requires trained salespeople with good knowledge of the product or service, with access to company records and information, and with the training and skills of the traditional salespeople. The lack of customer support causes frustration and produces negative attitudes toward a company and its brands. Such negative attitudes will ultimately affect sales both in the short and in the long run. It is not unusual to hear negative comments from consumers whose questions and complaints were routed to offshore customer service companies and were faced with language difficulties and lack of proper information. It is essential, therefore, that any business contacting customers through automated or electronic means also provide a trained staff of salespeople or customer service specialists to its audiences.

THE MANAGEMENT OF PERSONAL SELLING

Once the decision is made to employ personal selling to communicate effectively with potential customers, a number of steps must be followed to manage the sales efforts. Sales managers must develop a plan, assess the market potential for personal sales, forecast a sales level, and establish a budget for the sales functions. In addition, they must organize and staff the sales force, train and direct it, and finally assess the effectiveness of the sales effort. This portion of the chapter will elaborate on the various management tasks to be accomplished to successfully implement a personal selling program.

Developing a Plan and Assessing Sales Potential

A manager of sales must establish a long-range and short-range plan for the firm that can be realistically achieved through the efforts of the sales force. The first step in planning is that of setting objectives and goals for the firm's sales force. These may vary from firm to firm: in some cases objectives will be translated into dollar sales; in other cases, they will consist of developing awareness and knowledge of a product or service among potential customers.

The objectives and goals stated in a sales plan will be determined by assessing the sales potential of a firm. A survey of market situation and an assessment of the product's relative strengths and weaknesses with regard to competing products are essential inputs for establishing sales levels. Establishing the share of market a firm wishes to obtain, as well as evaluating possible variations in the demand for the product or service of the firm, must be the first steps of the planning process.

Creating a Sales Forecast

A sales forecast may include seasonal or territorial estimates of sales. Because markets are never completely homogeneous, accurate forecasts of sales must be made to efficiently allocate sales personnel.

Quantitative and qualitative forecasting techniques such as trend analysis or focus groups of potential customers may be used to achieve an accurate estimate of future sales. Among some of the models used for sales forecasting are the Delphi technique and the survey of expert opinion. In addition, sophisticated statistical methods may also be used for the same purpose. Whatever method is employed by a firm, it is essential that the results be evaluated in light of logical criteria such as past sales performance and common sense. The resulting estimate will be used to set territorial quotas or other sales goals for the firm.

Budgeting the Sales Effort

A budget expresses a company's goals and operational strategies in specific numerical terms. The sales budget takes into account the anticipated revenues for the period under consideration and the expenditures necessary to achieve such revenues.

Budgets improve and specify the planning goals by describing them in quantities or dollars. They therefore allow a firm to evaluate the sales effort by comparing its performance with budgeted objectives.

Budgets are essential planning and organizational tools. In addition, they allow firms to exercise control and to evaluate the performance of their salespeople.

Organizing, Staffing, and Training the Sales Force

This function must take into account the human resources available to the firm and other variables such as the type of product sold, the type of potential customer targeted, and the overall objectives set for the sales force.

Sales training is a very specialized function. Salespeople are in general independent and entrepreneurial in nature. Sales managers train their employees in several ways, including by providing instruction at the sales office and by assigning trainees to experienced salespeople in the field for several weeks.

Sales managers also perform periodic training services for experienced salespeople. These consist of regular meetings held to discuss mutual sales problems. Also, new products and promotional campaigns are explained in periodic sales training sessions.

Evaluating the Performance

Sales managers are also responsible for evaluating sales personnel. Because sales is such a unique and independent function, evaluating sales efforts is not an easy task. Also, because each salesperson faces unique economic and buying conditions in his or her territory, sales managers must maintain flexibility in applying standards for the evaluation of sales performance.

Sales managers must also keep open lines of communication with managers in all the other departments of a firm. They must provide leadership and stress cooperation among their employees. These tasks must all be accomplished despite environmental factors over which managers have little or no control.

AN EXAMPLE OF THE DEVELOPMENT OF A SALES STRATEGY: THE CASE OF THE LCD PROJECTORS

The following is a hypothetical example of the type of decisions that must be made when a firm is evaluating the appropriateness of using personal sales as one component of is marketing mix. The information in this example is purely fictitious and is used solely for the purpose of illustration.

Tech Pro is a small high-technology company that has developed an LCD screen for use with computers. This product will make presentations a lot easier and more flexible. The projector will allow managers and teachers to develop slides for group presentations and lectures directly on a computer, with the aid of specialized software and the LCD projector.

The potential markets for such a product are many. The firm has decided that because it has a very competitive and technologically advanced product, it must concentrate its efforts on developing a marketing plan that will allow it to cope with the growth of its markets.

Users of the LCD projectors can be found in many groups. One such group is that of public relations agents and/or consultants. Other users are personnel training specialists, corporate audiovisual departments, and educational institutions. This technology allows presentations to be produced economically and, when used with advanced software, is capable of handling multimedia presentations.

The manufacturer of this product competes with two large high-technology firms and a number of other small manufacturers.

The firm is satisfied with the quality of its product. The challenge confronting management now is that of deciding how to best reach potential buyers of the product.

The Marketing Communication Plan

The first step in the development of a marketing communication plan for the LCD projector is the assessment of the market potential for the product. Management must consider all the target segments it wants to reach and decide how many projectors could be purchased by each. Then it must decide what percentage of the total market it wants to secure for itself. In our example, the company felt it could obtain 10% of the total market potential in its region.

After the firm's potential sales revenues have been forecasted, management must determine the appropriate communication mix to achieve these goals. In this case the firm's competitors used mass mailing and catalogs to reach potential users. Advertising in professional and business journals was also very prevalent among high-tech manufacturers.

The management of TechPro felt that an innovative communication campaign would best differentiate the company from its competitors. If a unique method of reaching potential buyers could be implemented, perhaps TechPro could penetrate the market aggressively.

Personal sales was more expensive than mail promotions and catalog selling, but management felt that such a new and complex product would benefit from the personal interaction and immediate feedback that would result from using personal salespeople.

Another important consideration was the financial cost of establishing a sales force for TechPro. The company's managers determined that, over a period of five years, the overall profits of TechPro would be higher if personal sales were used. They felt that customer loyalty and the overall company image would benefit from the positive relationships that could be established between their sales force and their clients.

The final step in the planning process was the hiring and training of the sales force, the determination of sales territories, and the establishment of periodic means of assessing the sales force's performance. TechPro management was able to handle this final step in the process successfully within a six-month period. The results of the marketing communication plan were implemented within the first year.

Conclusion

This example is an attempt to walk students through the important steps in deciding to establish a personal selling plan. Although no figures were discussed or analyzed in this example, such considerations would be an integral part of the final decision. The example provides an overview of the main variable to be considered when establishing a sales plan. Students must attempt to follow such steps when dealing with similar problems.

SUGGESTED READINGS

Clark, William A. "Where to Get Information from Your Competitor." *Marketing Times* 30, no. 2 (March-April 1983): 19–22.

Dubinski, Alan J., Thomas A. Barry, and Roger A Kerin. "The Sales-Advertising Interface in Promotion Planning." *Journal of Advertising* 10, no. 3 (1981): 35–41.

Jackson, Donald W. Jr., William H. Cunningham, and Isabella Cunningham. *Selling—The Personal Force in Marketing.* New York: John Wiley and Sons, 1988.

Kotler, Philip, and Ravi Singh. "Marketing Warfare in the 1980s." *Journal of Business Strategy* 1, no. 3 (Winter 1986): 30–41.

Rogers, Everett M. *Diffusion of Innovations.* 3rd ed. New York: Free Press, 1983.

Stumm, David A. *Advanced Industrial Selling.* New York: Amacom, 1981.

"When Sales Meets Marketing." *Sales and Marketing Management,* May 13, 1985, 59–65.

INTEGRATED BRAND PROMOTION MIX

Exercises

1. Describe the different variables a firm must analyze when it decides to make a major switch from using an intensive and broad-based advertising program to a personal selling program. What marketing factors would be most conducive to using personal selling as opposed to advertising? Explain.

2. The development of Smartphones has revolutionized the ability of people to communicate. Smartphones allow users to talk to each other as they would with a regular cell phone, to receive and send e-mails, to take, collect, and send pictures, and to "surf" the Web at any time. A small technology company has developed additional capabilities for Smartphones. The addition of a flip screen with an imbedded camera allows people talking to each other on the phone to also see each other. If a user does not want to use the screen, it can be disabled easily while maintaining all the other Smartphone functions.

   CMG, one of the largest mobile phone providers in the country has purchased that new technology and will add the screens to the top line of their Smartphones. CMG feels that the new technology will appeal to the "gadget lovers" that want to avail themselves of the emotional "keep in touch" appeal for family and friends. CMG also feels that there may be a demand for Smartphones with the new screen technology by companies and businesses needing "face-to-face" brief meetings between employees or with clients and potential clients. In other words, it would provide mobility to videoconferencing and an alternative to short personal meetings.

   You were hired to train CMG salespeople to reach out to businesses and to service potential high-end customers in their store. Prepare a presentation for each of the appeals described here. Make sure you highlight the key points the salespeople employed by CMG should make when meeting with the two customer targets just described.

3. You are a sales manager for a furniture manufacturer that sells primarily to furniture leasing outlets. About 20 percent of your sales are made to traditional furniture leasing companies or large real estate leasing companies. You are in the process of determining whether you should allocate your sales force by geographic territory or by type of customer. Indicate which of the two methods you would use to allocate your sales personnel. Explain your rationale.

Case 9.1

Mary Kay Cosmetics, Inc.

Most women across the country recognize the name "Mary Kay Cosmetics." What many may not realize is that beyond the pink Cadillac and glitzy award ceremonies is a dynamic company that has experienced phenomenal growth in terms of both sales (Table 9.1.1) and the size of its independent sales force since its inception in 1963.

COMPANY BACKGROUND

Mary Kay Ash started her dream company in 1963 with $5,000 and plenty of determination and perseverance. Since 1953, she had been using a skin care system developed by a hide tanner. He believed that if you could turn a stiff, large-pored hide into soft, small-pored leather, you should be able to achieve the same results on human skin. He began to experiment with his own skin, using a modified form of some of the same principles used in tanning hides. Mary Kay bought the formulas and started her company. She based Mary Kay Cosmetics on the golden rule ("Do unto others as you would have them do unto you") and the idea that women deserved unlimited opportunities for success.

For many years before starting her company, Mary Kay was a sales representative for Stanley Home Products, presenting "home shows" at the residences of customers. Stanley sales were made by "independent contractors" who actually purchased the products from Stanley and then sold them on their own.

That experience was the drive behind Mary Kay's strategy of recruiting women to sell the products of her own company. Her network of "beauty consultants" had to purchase an initial kit and were trained to conduct sales and product demonstrations in private homes. Beauty consultants purchased Mary Kay products at 50 percent below retail and resold them. They were free to recruit salespeople for their territories and received commissions for sales of the salespeople they recruited.

RAPID GROWTH

Mary Kay Cosmetics, Inc., rapidly evolved from a small regional cosmetics firm to a fully integrated manufacturer and distributor of personal care products. Since 1963, the growth of the company has been remarkable. As of 2008, Mary Kay Cosmetics had more than 1.7 million consultants worldwide and excess in wholesales of $2.2 billion.

The company began expanding geographically in 1970 when the first regional distribution center was open in addition to the original one in Dallas. Centers are now located in Costa Mesa, California; Tucker, Georgia; Somerset, New Jersey; Bloomingdale, Illinois; and Dallas, Texas. In 1968 Mary Kay stock was offered over the counter, and in August 1976 it was listed on the New York Stock Exchange. In December 1985, the company was returned to private, family ownership through a repurchase of common stock.

The company formed its first international subsidiary in 1971 in Australia. Subsidiaries were also established in Canada in 1978, Argentina in 1980, West Germany in 1986, and Mexico in 1988. By 2008 Mary Kay cosmetics were sold in over 37 different countries.

This case was prepared by Isabella C. M. Cunningham and John H. Murphy, II. The University of Texas at Austin. The case is intended for class discussion only and not to illustrate either the effective or ineffective handling of an administrative situation. Some figures have been changed to protect confidential information. Used by permission of Mary Kay Cosmetics, Inc.

Table 9.1.1 ■ Mary Kay Beauty Consultant and Customer Profiles

Beauty Consultant Demographics		Customer Demographics	
Marital Status		**Average Age**	
Married	78%	42	
Single	12		
Divorced	8	**Ethnicity**	
Widowed	2	White	88%
		Black	8
Age		Hispanic	4
18–24	10%		
25–34	30	**Employment Status**	
35–44	32	Full time	50%
45–54	20	Part time	25
55 and over	8	Not employed	25
(Average age: 36)			
		Average Household Income	
Education			
College or more	75%	**Average Longevity as a Mary Kay Customer**	
		6 years	
Ethnicity			
White	85%	**Education**	
Black	9	College or more	68%
Hispanic	6		
Area Worked			
Urban/Suburban	75%		
Rural	25		
Average Household Income	$42,000		
Have Other Employment	70%		

Table 9.1.1 ■ Mary Kay Beauty Consultant and Customer Profiles

Beauty Consultant Demographics		Customer Demographics	
Tenure with Mary Kay			
Less than 1 year	35%		
1 to 3 years	27		
3 to 5 years	13		
5 to 10 years	20		
Over 10 years	5		
(Median years: 2.0)			

RECOGNITION

As momentum builders, Mary Kay has structured a sales program that is filled with contests and rewards—in addition to regular income. Outstanding performance at every level in the independent sales force is always acknowledged. There are many forms of recognition, from having one's picture and performance highlighted in the monthly magazine, *Applause,* to incentive gifts, to major luxuries such as vacation trips, diamond jewelry, and cars—VIP cars, pink Buicks and Cadillacs.

The "Ladder of Success" is a recognition program that honors beauty consultants on the basis of quarterly sales achievements. Star consultants receive an attractive ladder pin set with a sapphire, ruby, or diamond. The higher the level of achievement, the more valuable the stone.

Quarterly contests are goal setting tools. Every quarter, Mary Kay offers different prizes. Selecting a specific prize and achieving the corresponding sales and recruiting levels maintains consistency from quarter to quarter. The most well-known awards are luxury cars.

To achieve further growth in sales and in the size of the sales force, new basic skin care and glamour lines were introduced in the late 1980s. Since 1984, 95 percent of the product line has been improved and updated. Marketing strategies were developed to attractive more career women to Mary Kay both as salespeople and as customers.

COMPETITION

The highly competitive cosmetic industry is considered a mature market by most industry analysis. Mary Kay's most direct competitor is Estee Lauder, whose Clinique skin care line is similarly processed and also attempts to project a "scientific" image. In a broad sense, Mary Kay competes against all other mass or prestige cosmetics companies.

A comparison of Mary Kay's products prices with those of companies like Lancôme, Estee Lauder, and Clinique, indicates that competitors' prices for products like concealers, eye colors, eye pencils, lipsticks, powder, cheek color, and so on ranged from 50% to 80% higher than those of Mary Kay.

An online catalog of Mary Kay's products and their prices can be seen at http://www.marykay.com/shopcatalog/layout_02–03.appx.

THE DISTRIBUTION PLAN

Its marketing and distribution plan has played an important role in the success of Mary Kay Cosmetics. The beauty consultant usually begins her association with Mark Kay as a customer. She is introduced to the products and learns about career possibilities at the skin care class. When she investigates the career opportunity, she finds that she will actually be in business for herself, but not by herself, as an independent beauty consultant. Only one "wholesale distributor" exists between the company and the consumer; each beauty consultant runs an individual business.

According to Bartlett, "Each Mary Kay consultant is an independent contractor. She is not an employee of the company. The consultant buys directly from the company on a wholesale basis and sells at retail. The difference between the two is her gross profit—anywhere from 40 to 50 percent for the retail price, sometimes as high as 60 percent during special promotions. Of course, she will have some expenses, but her net profit from retail sales will average over 40 percent. Profitability of the individual consultant selling at retail is one of the reasons for our continuing success and excellent market share in skin care and glamour." The Mary Kay career opportunity has become a serious career choice for thousands of women, from homemakers to new college graduates to seasoned businesswomen.

RECRUITING

Recruiting is an opportunity for the consultant to grow in her career and an opportunity for the recruit to begin a potentially rewarding Mary Kay career of her own. Consultants can earn commissions directly form the company of 4, 8, or 12 percent of each new recruit's production (dependent upon the number of active personal recruits). Just as teaching skin care classes is an important aspect of the business, so is recruiting for those interested in earning leadership positions and building a unit of independent retail salespeople.

Since the program's beginning, more than 100,000 consultants have been qualified for the use of a career car. It is not known how many Directors select the cash options in lieu of the car, but GM estimates that it has built 100,000 pink Cadillacs for Mary Kay.

SEMINAR

Mary Kay Cosmetics' annual seminar in Dallas is designed to be a tribute to the Company and to the women who make it a success. The program consists of four consecutive three-day sessions that welcome over 25,000 beauty consultants and sales directors from across the world. Throughout each seminar, women are encouraged to "dream big"—to do as Mary Kay Ash did in 1963 when she founded the company. The seminar is also an opportunity for consultants to learn about new products, sales techniques, recruiting skills, and business management ideas. It is also an important area for recognition, where those beauty consultants and sales directors with the highest sales and best recruiting performances during the past year receive prizes and applause.

THE MISSION STATEMENT

In 1988, company president Dick Bartlett unveiled the company's mission statement:

> *To be preeminent in the manufacturing, distribution, and marketing of personal care products by providing personalized service, value, and convenience to Mary Kay customers through our independent*

sales force. To provide our sales force an unparalleled opportunity for financial independence, career achievement, and personal fulfillment. To achieve total customer satisfaction worldwide by focusing on quality, value, convenience, innovation, and personal service.

Today, all corporate employees are guided by this statement's vision. Every division, every department, every employee at Mary Kay knows the company's objectives and how their contributions impact company performance and bring them closer to their ultimate goal of preeminence.

PREEMINENCE AT MARY KAY

Preeminence embodies Mary Kay Cosmetics' corporate, manufacturing, and distribution objectives. As defined by Webster's dictionary, preeminence is "outstanding; to have paramount rank, dignity, or importance." At Mary Kay, it means producing the best products, offering the best career opportunity to women, and giving the sales force the best tools and training with which to offer consumers the best value, the most convenience and the best possible personalized service.

A BETTER OPPORTUNITY FOR WOMEN

When Mary Kay Ash started the company in 1963, she did so with the fulfillment of a dream in mind. Today, the company is the outgrowth of Mary Kay's clear vision of a better economic opportunity for women. Mary Kay Cosmetics offers women a flexible, rewarding career opportunity as a beauty consultant and provides them with high-quality products personalized service, and convenience. Market research indicates that today's women consumers demand things that work, buy brand names they know, and want value and quality. They prefer competent, personal service and convenient, enjoyable shopping.

In addition, research shows that the typical Mary Kay consultant looks for financial security, increased time with her family, and feelings of "group membership" that help her gain a sense of identity. She wants to make her own choices. Mary Kay Cosmetics' personal sales structure and marketing plan have never been in a better position to succeed.

THE COMPANY PHILOSOPHY

From the beginning, the company has grown based upon the same philosophy: Every person associated with the company, from the chairman emeritus to the newest recruit, live by the golden rule—"Do unto others as you would have them do unto you"—and by the priorities of God first, family second, and career third. May Kay has proven how successful these principles and priorities can be in the business world.

PRODUCT PROFILE

Mary Kay Cosmetics approaches beauty scientifically. Teams of experts in cosmetic chemistry, dermatology, physiology, biochemistry, toxicology, microbiology, analytical chemistry, process technology, and package engineering are continually testing and improving products.

A staff of trained skin care experts is available to answer questions and solve problems from consultants or customers regarding Mary Kay products. Their opinions and experience, combined with the company's continued emphasis on testing and improving existing products and developing new ones, help to ensure that all Mary Kay products are of the highest quality and packaged for the strongest market appeal.

The company maintains approximately 200 retail products, which not only helps keep the focus on upscale personal care products, but also allows the individual consultant to be competitive with a manageable number of items.

THE SKIN CARE PROFILE

Consultants help each customer complete a skin care profile to determine which products are appropriate for her skin type. This step-by-step guide accurately and easily enables the consultant to recommend personalized formulas for each customer.

BASIC SKIN CARE

Mary Kay's basic skin care program includes five steps: cleanse, retexture, freshen, moisture balance, and protect. For each step there is a specific formula developed to meet the needs of every customer's skin type (dry, normal, combination, oily, or blemish prone). All products, with the exception of Day Radiance cream foundation, are 100 percent fragrance free and clinically tested for skin irritancy, allergy, and comedogenicity. Most of the products are also safe for sensitive skin. Basic skin care products at Mary Kay account for about 30 percent of gross sales and are the most profitable product line for the company. Skin care products are what Mary Kay is known for. In fact, in a nationwide study among women who were regular facial skin care users, Mary Kay Cosmetics was most frequently mentioned as the best brand of skin care products by those who thought there was one best brand.

Following is a description of the five-step Mary Kay basic skin care program:

- Cleanse: Cleansing cream, lotion cleanser, or cleansing bar cleans quickly and gently to remove makeup, surface oil, and impurities without stripping away natural moisture.
- Retexture: Facial mask/scrub improves the texture of skin, removes dead cells, and helps make pores appear smaller.
- Freshen: Skin freshener or toner completes the cleansing process as it conditions and tones facial skin, promoting a finer-textured appearance.
- Moisture Balance: Moisturizer or conditioner helps skin retain its optimum moisture balance, while improving hydration and smoothness.
- Protect: Day Radiance or Oil-Free Foundation provides protection as it covers minor imperfections to give a smooth, even-toned finish.

SKIN SUPPLEMENTS

To meet the special needs of a wide range of skin types and address specific skin care needs, Mary Kay created a line of skin supplements including Nighttime Recovery System, Moisture Renewal treatment cream, Daily Defense Complex, Extra Emollient Night Cream, Extra Emollient Moisturizer, Eye Cream Concentrate, Eye Makeup Remover, and Acne Treatment Gel. The skin care profile helps guide the consultant in recommending skin supplement products to her customers. Skin supplements make up roughly 10 percent of gross sales at Mary Kay.

THE COLORLOGIC GLAMOUR SYSTEM

Mary Kay offers a complete line of lip colors, eye colors, cheek colors, and other products in a wide variety of shades. Each is created to harmonize with a woman's skin tone, hair color, individual wardrobe colors, and personal preference. There's a product and safe for every mood and style, from dramatic to natural. The company's products and shade mix is carefully selected to ensure the line appeals to women of all ethnic backgrounds and age groups. Glamour products account for about 30 percent of gross sales.

PERSONALIZED BEAUTY ANALYSIS

With a combination of technology and glamour, this innovative, computerized beauty tool allows a woman to maximize the power of the Colorlogic Glamour System. The customer and the consultant answer a series of questions together. These questions include the customer's skin type, foundation shade, eye color, hair color, age, wardrobe preference, makeup preference, lip shape, eye shape, and face shape. After the questionnaire is filled out completely, the consultant mails it to the company. Within approximately two weeks, a personalized computer analysis is sent back to the consultant. The analysis recommends colors, products, and application techniques that will enhance the customer's features. The consultant then meets with her customer and reviews her beauty analysis. This tool helps the consultant recommend individualized colors and glamour techniques to bring out the best in each different customer. This is the only personalized analysis available today that recommends colors, plus tells the user how and where to apply them based on her facial features, personal coloring, wardrobe, and makeup preference.

MEN'S PRODUCTS

Mary Kay Cosmetics was one of the first cosmetic companies to focus on men's skin care needs. The Skin Management for Men system is scientifically formulated to meet the needs of a man's skin. The three-step regimen includes a cleansing bar, toner, and conditioner or oil absorber. Specialized products include shave cream and an acne medication.

WOMEN'S FRAGRANCES

The following are examples of how the company describes its "scents for every mood, every occasion, and every personal style":

- ACAPELLA: A spirited floral with "A style all your own."
- GENJI: A fragrant floral Oriental that "Makes the moment linger."
- INTRIGUE: A unique Oriental scent that is "One of the most intriguing things about you."

And, some examples of men's fragrances:

- QUATTRO: A subtle blend of spices and woods that is "A passion you share."
- TAMERISK: A scent of greens, spices, and woods. "It reinforces his style."
- TRIBUTE for MEN: A contemporary blend of fruits, musk, and sandalwood. "In celebration of you."

PERSONALIZED HAIR CARE

Mary Kay Cosmetics has also developed a line of hair care products to meet the needs of most customers. The line features shampoo, conditioner, and styling products to benefit every type and style of hair. These hair care products account for less than 5 percent of gross sales.

BODY CARE

Mary Kay's body care line is a natural extension of the five steps to beautiful skin: a scientifically formulated and uniquely balanced program to care for and beautify body skin. It includes three simple steps: buffing, cleansing, and moisturizing. Body care products account for less than 5 percent of gross sales.

SUN ESSENTIALS

Mary Kay Sun Essential products include six items ranging in sun protection factors from 8 to 30, developed for all ages and all skin tones. These products are specifically formulated to formulated to be compatible with the entire Mary Kay product line. All Sun Essentials sun protection products are safe for everyday use and clinically tested for skin irritancy and allergy by an independent laboratory under a leading dermatologist. They are all PABA free, fragrance free (except for Lip Protector, which has a small amount of products). The consultant has a chance to get to know her customers on a personal basis, allowing her to provide a higher level of customer service.

The guests at the skin care classes are the lifeblood of the consultant's business. These guests provide the consultant with important networking possibilities, leading to new hostesses and customers.

THE IMPORTANCE OF CUSTOMER SERVICE

One of the most important aspects of a consultant's business is customer service. At Mary Kay it is believed that quality is total customer satisfaction. By providing each customer with personal attention and high-quality products, a consultant is able to build strong customer loyalty. Consultants have the unique opportunity to reintroduce personal contact and friendship into the marketplace. The consistent, individualized attention is something customers do not receive when shopping in a department store. Consultants do not forget about their customers after the initial purchase. At a selected point in time, the consultant will telephone the customer to see if she needs any additional products. These additional product sales are much easier than the initial sale. Mary Kay consultants also are able to offer an unconditional "satisfaction or your money back" guarantee on every product they sell. This is Mary Kay's way of helping the consultant and the company retain customer trust and goodwill.

CURRENT MARKETING TOOLS

Mary Kay consultants are supported by a variety of marketing tools. The company utilizes these tools to establish a positive image in the marketplace.

Direct Support

The Direct Support program incorporates the best features of direct mail and Mary Kay's direct-selling approach. Through the Direct Support program, the company supports the consultants by directly contacting their customers with a personalized letter and a beautiful four-color brochure featuring new product launches, limited-edition promotions, and gift—with—purchase offers. There are typically four major programs per year, with each wave going to over three million customers. The consultant pays a small fee for each customer she enrolls in each program. There are four main advantages for the consultant who participates:

1. The consultant saves valuable time and money. By signing up preferred customers for the program, the consultant is liberated from time-consuming and costly mailing that would normally need to be done.
2. The consultant has more time to engage in personal contact activities such as skin care classes, facials, and ColorLogic Glamour System consultations, thereby giving the consultant a greater opportunity for increased sales and a larger customer base.
3. The Direct Support program works directly alongside the consultant while she is actively working at her business. The consultant is reaching customers in entirely new and professional ways—with no additional demands upon busy schedules.
4. Direct Support is an efficient and effective means of an advertising the consultant's products and services.

Although a powerful program in support of a personalized-service sales approach, the Direct Support program also addresses the question of customer retention, which is a major issue facing all forms of retailing in the nineties. In Mary Kay's case, customers tend to be lost when consultants leave the business, as well as for the more traditional reasons, such as moving. There have been over 12 million customers enrolled, and 4 million have been retained by assignment to another consultant. Since it costs five times as much to establish a customer as it does to retain her, this is a very important marketing edge for Mary Kay.

ADVERTISING AT MARY KAY

Mary Kay has advertised only lightly and sporadically for the last decade since the vast majority of promotional dollars is allocated to sales force incentives. Advertising has traditionally attempted to link an interested customer back to a beauty consultant, since the products are only available through this specialized channel. Consultants often use these advertorials in personal presentations to help establish credibility.

Mary Kay ran advertorials in the January 1990 issues of *Essence* and *New Woman* and received 561 inquiries from the former and 516 from the latter. Based on a survey of 294 of those who called, 92 percent obtained the name and number of a beauty consultant. Further, 67 percent contacted a consultant, 23 percent purchased products, and 16 percent became beauty consultants. Finally, it was estimated that every 100 calls generated approximately $1,500 in initial products sales.

The Mary Kay company has a very elaborate and dynamic website that is updated constantly. The website features all of Mary Kay products, contains an online catalog, and also provides detailed support to all its consultants and representatives. The consultants also use their own website and resources from the company's website to keep in contact with their clients and announce new products and promotions.

MARKETING PUBLICITY

Marketing publicity seeks to keep the Mary Kay Cosmetics name and products on the minds of the beauty editors of the top beauty and fashion and women's service magazines in the nation. The editors, in turn, will sometimes include Mary Kay products within their features. The editors are updated on all new product launches through press releases and meeting with corporate staff. Additionally, when appropriate, the press is also briefed on the Mary Kay career opportunity or the company's policies and practices with respect to timely topics such as animal testing or environmental issues.

Mary Kay has also created Skin Wellness, a public service skin cancer awareness and prevention program, in response to the company's growing concern about skin cancer and the public's need for accurate information. This program has not only helped save lives, but has also generated favorable publicity for the company among both the medical community and the general public.

1–800–MARYKAY

Mary Kay's toll-free telephone number, 1–800–MARYKAY, is printed on product packaging, advertisements, and consumer literature. Prospective customers call in to locate a beauty consultant in their area and/or learn more about the career opportunity. Additionally, existing customers who have lost their consultant can call 1–800–MARYKAY to locate another one. Leads are returned to proven performers within the sales force.

WORD-OF-MOUTH ADVERTISING

Word-of-mouth advertising has been a major tool in building Mary Kay's 98 percent aided awareness in the marketplace. Most consultants start as loyal users and are delighted to share with friends, family, and acquaintances the positive experiences they have had with Mary Kay products and services.

CONSUMER BROCHURES

In addition to the consumer brochures distributed through Direct Support, the sales force can purchase a selection of brochures, typically including color photography, which are then distributed by the consultant to her customers to help reinforce her professional image and educate her customers about Mary Kay products, proper skin care, glamour techniques, and other related topics.

CUSTOMER AND SALES FORCE PROFILES

Profiles of Mary Kay's beauty consultants and customers are presented in Table 9.1.1. (Figures have been altered to protect confidential information)

THE FUTURE ROLE OF ADVERTISING

The company has discovered through extensive customer research that many women who have no direct contact with the company have an outdated or negative view of its product and its sales force. Actual customers, however, exhibit great loyalty to the products and to their beauty consultant.

Curran Dandurand, senior vice-president of the marketing group, has wondered about the possibility of developing an advertising program that will not only have immediate impact but also demonstrate that the company's dollars can be profitably allocated to consumer-oriented programs, in addition to the extensive sales force incentives already in place.

She has a total budget of $6 million for next year and, if upper management is convinced of the program's likelihood of success, could look forward to twice that much in the following year. The budget covers production costs and media expenses. Hence, Dandurand has asked her group to recommend how to make the best use of a limited budget relative to that of Mary Kay's competitors in the cosmetic industry. What sort of program should they create? How should the dollars be allocated? Should they recommend mass media and, if so, which specific vehicles? What should be their message to consumer? To what degree, if any, should they address recruiting issues? How will they measure results to convince upper management of the program's success?

Name _____ Date _____

QUESTIONS FOR DISCUSSION AND REVIEW

1. Should advertising be targeted primarily toward recruiting consultants, stimulating demand among present users, encouraging present nonusers to try Mary Kay, or focusing on some other audience? What are the advantages and disadvantages of targeting each of these groups? How viable would it be to target a combination of these or other groups? Why?

2. How are Mary Kay's distribution, pricing, and product mix related to possible advertising strategy recommendations? Which of the other marketing mix elements—product, price, place—is most important in developing an advertising strategy for Mary Kay? Why?

3. How could a new advertising campaign be most effectively integrated into Mary Kay's well-established marketing strategies? More specifically, how might the sales efforts of the consultants be most effectively supported by advertising? Should some sort of responsibilities for advertising be structured around the consultants?

4. Given the $3 million appropriation, would a national or regional test of advertising's ability to contribute to Mary Kay's marketing success be most appropriate? Why?

Case 9.2

The Vino, Vino! Company

The wine industry in the United States was relatively small through the middle of the nineteenth century. Wine production began to increase significantly in this country with the development and expansion of the California industry in the twentieth century.

According to the U.S. Department of Commerce 2006 Annual Survey of Manufacturers,[1] the value of industry shipments of the wine and brandy industry reached an estimated $11.8 billion in that year. The industry employed over 24,000 people. It is estimated that the industry would continue to grow as more and more Americans became acquainted with different kinds of wines. The U.S. winery industry is very fragmented. There are more than 23,000 farms that grow grapes, of which 90% are on plots smaller than 100 acres. According to the Wine Institute, the number of licensed wineries in the United States in 2008 totaled over 6,300. These wineries produced over 600 million gallons of wine in 2008.

The top six wine companies are E&J Gallo Winery, The Wine Group, Constellation Brands, Bronco Wine Company, Foster's Wine Estates, and Trinchero Family Estates. Sales of wine in the United States are segmented as follows: 87% are table wines; 8.5% are dessert wines, and 4.5% are sparkling wines. More consumers are drinking red wines than white and blush; reds account for 43% of all wines sold at retail, whites account for 42%, and blush account for 13%.[2]

The core wine-consuming population in the United States is still relatively small compared to the total U.S. adult population between 21 and 59 years of age (142 million). Only 15.7 million adults are considered core wine consumers, who are defined as individuals who drink wine at least once per week. Adults over 40 years of age make up approximately 63% of the core wine consumer market.

Exhibit 9.2.1 describes the income and spending levels of U.S. households segmented by age. As the population of this country becomes older, wine consumption is expected to continue to increase. In addition, the increase in personal income, the belief that moderate wine consumption is hearth healthy, and the increased amount of advertising by the wine industry also will contribute to a steady and robust growth.

Careful consideration of all these statistics and additional data published by the wine industry was the motivation behind the establishment of the Vino, Vino! Company, a small retail chain dedicated to the exclusive distribution and sale of U.S. wines to middle-upper- and upper-income adults. The chain was the brainchild of Solano Martini, a wine sommelier who had worked for many years in two upscale restaurants in Los Angeles and in New York. Solano had noticed the important role that sommeliers, waiters, retail salespeople and friends' recommendations had in individuals' choices of wine. With funding provided by a venture capital firm, he was able to open his first three specialty wine retail outlets in Texas. Texas was chosen as a first location because the state had a strong economy, and it had a healthy influx of new businesses, especially in the high-tech sector.

Solano believed that he could develop a steady and loyal clientele by providing his potential customers with clear and targeted information, a well-trained sales staff, and establishing Vino, Vino! as the "connoisseur's" choice when purchasing high-quality domestic wines.

According to his research, wine drinkers are confident, savvy adventure seekers and are open to new experiences. In addition, they have their life priorities in order and are not sensitive to brands, but like to believe that they can discern quality.

Women are the majority of wine drinkers, about 53% of all wine consumers. They also account for the majority of wine purchases in most price segments. They enjoy wine in small, intimate gatherings and regularly drink a moderate amount of wine.

---

[1] http://www.census.gov/epcd/naics02/def/NDEF312.HTM#N31213

[2] Ibid.

Exhibit 9.2.1 ■ Income and Spending Levels

All households	
Number of Households	99,627
Average Income	$44,900
Average Discretionary Income	$13,500
Average Spending	$30,300
Under age 45	
Number of Households	47,733
Average Income	$45,300
Average Discretionary Income	$13,400
Average Spending	$30,500
45 to 54	
Number of Households	18,008
Average Income	$59,600
Average Discretionary Income	$16,200
Average Spending	$39,100
55 to 64	
Number of Households	12,401
Average Income	$50,300
Average Discretionary Income	$15,300
Average Spending	$32,100
65 and older	
Number of Households	21,486
Average Income	$28,600
Average Discretionary Income	$9,500
Average Spending	$21,700
Note: Spending data are based on consumer units rather than households, which may understate the actual household total.	
Source: Bureau of Census; *New Strategist*	

Solano's research also confirmed that wine consumers look to personal recommendations as the most prized source of information when choosing a wine. Trusted friends and family, followed by the sommelier or server in a restaurant setting, were mentioned as top information sources. In-store sales people were also mentioned as sources of important information, and nearly 40% of wine consumers reported reading wine information from specialty magazines, lifestyle magazines, and newspapers.

Tasting rooms were also powerful influences in a purchase decision, and Solano had planned his retail stores with a small but well-equipped and staffed room for tasting new products or special promotions.

Consumers drink wine mostly in restaurants and at home, rarely in bars and lounges. They drink wine at meals, especially with dinner. They drink because they like the taste and because it makes their food taste better. Over 9% of regular wine drinkers have a glass of wine before 3 p.m., and most of them wait for the weekend or special occasions to do so.

In an article published by the *International Journal of Wine Business Research,* the authors classified wine drinkers into four different groups: 1. The usual buyer—consumes wine every day, is sensitive to habits, plans his product choice before making the purchase, and does not spend time exploring new alternatives. 2. The rational consumer—consumes wine moderately, searches for products that are consistently displayed on the shelf, and is affected by prices and promotions. 3. The professional of promotion—this individual is sensitive to promotion appeals, has no habit sensitivity or product involvement, lowest in consumption and purchase frequency, and evaluates choices on the basis of the prices displayed on the shelf. 4. The interested buyer—very involved with the product, highest in income, reads and gathers information on the product, price is not a factor, and responds to multiple wine clues. This consumer is more likely to be a male in his forties and with a higher level of income.[3]

Retail sales of wine account for over 80% of total wine sales in the United States. Solano was excited about the opportunity to build and grow a profitable business. He knew that his first task was that of making sure the existence of his retail outlets was known by his prospective customers. In addition, he needed to develop a communication strategy aimed at his desired segment. Those would be consumers more likely to identify with the characteristics of "the interested buyer." He was looking for a consultant to help him develop a two-year communication strategy that would bring prospective wine buyers into his stores. He knew that once they were there, his trained sales force and all the other attractions he had built into his operation would contribute to creating loyalty among his customers.

---

[3]"The Wine Consumer's Behavior in Selected Stores of Italian Major Retailing Chains: by Chiara Seghiere, Leonardo Casini and Francesco Torrisi; International Journal of Wine Business Research," Vol. 19, Number 2, 2007, pp. 130–151.

QUESTIONS FOR DISCUSSION AND REVIEW

1. Develop a strategic communication plan for the Vino, Vino! Company for the next two years.

2. Should Solano advertise on printed media vehicles? If so, what kinds of magazines/newspapers should he select, and why?

3. How important is it for Vino, Vino! to have a well-trained sales force. How could they contribute to the success of the venture?

4. Should Solano recruit his sales force from among people that have received a trade education in the industry?

5. Are there any specific attributes you would require from his sales force?

6. Do you believe Solano will be successful? Why?

Chapter 10
Sales Promotion

A new brand manager comes in and says, "What can I do to make a mark?" He can't fool around with advertising too much because of bureaucracy and because the system is already in place. But he knows if he puts a consumer promotion together, all of a sudden market share will move.[1]

—Lou Houk, Frankel & Co. (sales promotion agency)

Over the past years, many marketers have made significant shifts in their marketing communication investments, reducing traditional media advertising and expanding sales promotion activities. Partially as a result of these shifts, whereas both advertising and sales promotional investments have grown, sales promotion has grown at a faster pace. Evidence of this trend is provided by examining changes in the proportion of total advertising and sales promotional appropriations invested in each of these two forms of promotion. For example, in 1980, 43% of the total was invested in advertising and 57% in sales promotion. According to O'Guinn, Allen, and Semenik, the shift to promotional spending has increased even more during the past decade. The authors state that in 2004 budget allocation on average stood at about 17.5% for advertising, 54% for trade and business promotions, and 28.5% for consumer promotions.[2]

Numerous complex factors underlie this fundamental shift towards sales promotion. These factors include the following:

1. The growing market power and sophistication of retailers have led them to demand marketing dollars from manufacturers.
2. Checkout scanner data has enabled accurate, online sales tracking data to be placed in the hands of retailers.
3. Sales promotion can have a more immediate impact on sales than can advertising.
4. A short-term orientation by marketing managers has created a dependence on sales promotion to achieve monthly or quarterly sales quotas.
5. Sales promotion is more directly accountable than advertising.
6. The fragmentation of traditional mass media advertising vehicles has sapped their power.

---

[1] Aimee Stern, "The Promo Wars," *Business Month* 130, no. 1 (July 1987): 44–46.

[2] Thomas O'Guinn Chris Allen, Richard J. Semenik, "Advertising and Integrated Brand Promotion," 5th Edition, Southwestern, Cengage Learning, (2009): 565–66.

The increasing reliance on sales promotion makes it crucial that marketing communication managers understand this important tool and how to blend it most effectively into the firm's communication mix. In this chapter, sales promotion and its partnership with advertising will be examined.

THE NATURE OF SALES PROMOTION

Consumer sales promotions are marketing offers that provide an additional incentive—beyond inherent product benefits—to purchase a brand by temporarily changing its price/value vis-à-vis the competition's. Trade and sales force promotions, although similar to consumer promotions, are used to stimulate channel member and/or sales force effectiveness. Exhibit 10.1 presents a brief description of ten of the more common sales promotion techniques used

Exhibit 10.1 ■ Common Sales Promotion Activities

Consumer Promotions: Pull Strategy

- *Sampling*—provision of the product at a no or a small charge for purposes of trial use, as when a four-ounce box of ready-to-eat cereal is delivered to all houses in targeted ZIP codes.
- *Coupons*—certificates offering a price reduction, such as 50 cents off suggested retail price.
- *Contests*—the awarding of prizes based on some skill or ability, as when consumers submit a statement of 25 words or less indicating why they use Brand X.
- *Sweepstakes*—the offering of prizes to consumers who submit their names to enter a drawing or chance selection process.
- *Rebates*—offers to return a portion of the purchase price after purchase; for example, $2,000 cash back from the manufacturer on the purchase of a new automobile.
- *Price-off-packages*—price reductions that are indicated on the package, such as "50 cents off."
- *Value packs*—price reductions achieved by including more products at the regular retail price, as when a 12-ounce size is expanded to 16 ounces and sold for the regular 12-ounce price.
- *Premiums*—rewards offered for purchasing a brand, such as a toy in a box of cereal
- *Cross-promotions*—two or more marketers' jointly featuring a special offer; for example, an airline and a camera company offering a free camera as a premium for ticket purchases.
- *Price deals*—temporary price reductions, such as 50% off during a closeout sale.

Trade and Sales Force Promotions: Push Strategy

- *Price deals*—limited-time special discounts or price reductions; for example, "for every two cases purchased prior to June 1, receive a third case at half price."
- *Contests*—the awarding of prizes for achieving a certain level of sales or for outstanding performance, such as a trip for two to Hawaii for all salespersons and retailers who exceed their yearly quotas
- *Push money*—money paid to salespersons to promote specific brands or items
- *Cooperative advertising*—reimbursement of retailers by manufacturers for advertising their brand, such as 50% reimbursement from a co-op fund, based on sales.
- *Slotting allowances*—money paid to obtain or retain distribution at the retail level.

by marketers following a pull strategy of stimulating consumer demand for their brand. In addition, Exhibit 10.1 presents a description of five common sales promotion techniques directed at increasing the push supporting brands provided by channel members and the sales force. Note that there are many variations and combinations of these categories of sales promotion.

Exhibit 10.2 outlines some of the major characteristics of sales promotion. As indicated in this exhibit, both benefits and hazards are associated with these promotional activities. In planning the firm's possible use of sales promotion, the marketing communication manager should carefully weigh these pros and cons.

When identifying both the general type of sales promotion to be employed and its specifics, management should consider the characteristics of an ideal promotion. Ideally, a sales promotion program should be all of the following:

- *Appealing from the target audience's perspective* (the key)
- Easily integrated into all other areas of the firm's marketing communication mix in a way that provides synergies
- Able to meet all legal restrictions and free of liability concerns
- Inexpensive for the firm
- Easy to understand and administer
- Unique and insulated from competitive response
- Consistent with the brand's image and past marketing activities

Exhibit 10.2 ■ Characteristics of Sales Promotion

Benefits
- Sales promotions can stimulate sales that would not have occurred in their absence.
- Sales promotions are useful in stimulating an immediate consumer response.
- Sales promotions enable marketers to cut price on a short-term basis.
- Sales promotions typically provide easily measurable results.
- Sales promotions can create new users or encourage current users to trade up or remain loyal; they can also encourage trial, loading (purchasing an abnormally large quantity to take advantage of temporarily favorable terms), and continuity and reinforce advertising.[a]

Hazards
- Sales promotions do little to build consumer loyalty or provide real or lasting differentiation from the competition.
- Consumers may come to regard the deal price as the expected price.
- Marketers can become addicted to sales promotions to increase sales in the short term, fueling a promotion war that can saddle all firms with increased costs for dubious benefits.
- Price promotions run the risk of turning brand categories into commodities in which competition is based predominantly on price.
- Sales promotions are often subject to abuses by channel members; for example, no pass-through (the retailer simply pockets a discount intended for consumers); forward buying (stocking up of purchases at deal prices for sales in future periods); diversion (reduced-price products are sold by retailers to other retailers); and coupon misredemption.
- Sales promotions may not stimulate repeat purchases after the promotion has ended.

[a]Don Schultz, *Strategic advertising Campaigns* (Lincolnwood, Ill.: NTC Business Books, 1990), 472.

The Impact of Sales Promotions

In a very thoughtful article regarding consumer promotions, Raghubiz, Inman, and Gaude stated that the importance and impact of consumer promotions may go beyond the short-term goal of increasing sales. According to the authors, promotions may also affect the attitudes of consumers toward the promotion itself and ultimately toward the manufacturer.[3] Therefore, management must analyze carefully the nature and strategy of consumer promotions before they opt for their use. The article also states:

> *"It is not entirely clear that higher deal values necessarily lead to higher purchase intentions"*[4]

Poorly designed promotion, therefore may be deleterious to advertisers and may affect consumers in many ways. To be successful, consumer promotions must be able to increase sales to their maximum potential, must be profitable, and must be designed to satisfy the specific target customers to whom they are offered. This, of course, includes existing customers and new customers.

It is therefore important for advertisers to keep in mind that the effect of promotions is not only economic in nature, but that they may also affect the long-term profitability of a company, the perception of quality of a brand, and the type of information they convey to both existing and potential customers.

The Impact of UPC Profitability Analysis on Sales Promotion

Beginning in the mid-1970s, checkout scanner data generated from Universal Product Codes, coupled with sophisticated data analysis techniques, revolutionized how retailers evaluate the allocation of shelf space and sales promotions.[5] Using complex computer-based tools, retailers are able to examine the profitability of all brands carried in deciding which items to stock, which to drop, and which to promote. To convince retailers to carry and promote their brand(s), manufacturers must be able to provide sophisticated UPC profitability data that support their products. Without such data to back up their recommendations, the chances of a manufacturer convincing a knowledgeable retailer to participate in a promotion are limited.

Further, as Schultz noted, "Advertising planners must understand that planning sales promotion today is a very complex and sophisticated process, one which goes far beyond just preparing a coupon drop or inserting a premium in the carton."[6]

The Joint Industry Coupon Council (JICC) established the Coupon Re-engineering Task Force to develop a new coupon format in response to the negative reaction to the new coupon codes implemented by manufacturers in 2008. The process of improvement and implementation of new bar codes for manufacturers' coupons was expected to be completed by 2009. However, because of difficulties in implementing the necessary software and the point-of-sale upgrades necessary to scan and interpret the data contained in the new coupon codes, its implementation has not been yet completed. Hopefully, once that process is successful, better and more detailed purchase information will be available to both manufacturers and retailers.

---

[3] "The Three Faces of Consumer Promotions" by Priya Raghubir, J. Jeffery Inman and Hans Grande, California Management Review, vol 46, #4. Summer 2004, p. 24.

[4] Ibid., p. 24.

[5] Don Schultz, *Strategic Advertising Campaigns* (Lincolnwood, Ill.: NTC Business Books, 1990), 454–455.

[6] Ibid., 455.

Source Specific Promotions

Consumer coupons are one of the most popular promotional tools used by marketers of NCH marketing services[7], which reported that consumer product good marketers distributed over 158 billion coupons during the first half of 2009. The majority of consumer coupons were distributed through FSI's (free standing inserts: 86.2%) followed by handouts, direct mail, magazines, and other means.

A new way of distributing coupons is to do so by using digital media. In fact, besides sending coupons to consumers directly to their competitors in a specialized Web site, marketers are now using mobile media—usually text messages with discount codes, sent to consumers' cell phones. Digital coupons seem to have become increasingly popular among consumers. An article in the *New York Times*[8] stated that in the first half of 2009 almost 10 million digital coupons were redeemed. This was a 25% increase over those redeemed during the same period in 2008. The increasing number of Smartphones and the worldwide popularity of mobile phones makes them our ideal vehicle to distribute consumers' sales incentives, such as coupons.

Another type of consumer promotion that has grown dramatically in recent years is the use of e-mails. Marketers seem to really like e-mails and it is forecasted that by 2013 they will distribute over 800 billion e-mail messages to their audiences. The low cost of e-mail is one of the reasons for this trend. Another reason for using e-mails, according to research, is that customers who opt to receive e-mails from specific marketers are likely to spend 138% more than non-opt-in customers.[9]

Marketing Reservations about Sales Promotions

Although when compared to traditional media advertising, sales promotions often offer the marketer significant benefits, their use is not without its limitations and potentially negative side effects. In addition to the reservations expressed in Exhibit 10.2, several general reservations regarding sales promotion will be discussed next.

First, there is concern that a heavy reliance on sales promotion undermines brand loyalty. Bill Phillips (CEO of Ogilvy & Mather advertising agency) suggests that "brand rape" occurs when marketing management takes investment dollars away from advertising and other non-price marketing communication to run short-term price promotions.[10] Phillips maintains that marketers have been teaching consumers to respond to price for years and that this is undermining brand equities. To remedy this situation, he suggests that marketers should replace coupons and freestanding inserts with promotions that revolve around the brand's positioning and key consumer benefit.

Note also that strong brands with loyal consumers are in a much stronger position to resist channel member demands for concessions on slotting allowances and other forms of reseller support. A relatively undifferentiated brand that has not been established in the market through advertising is in a much weaker position in dealing with powerful retailers.

---

[7]NCH Marketing Services, Inc., mid-year 2009 Coupon Facts Reports

[8]"Coupons you Don't Clip, Sent to your Cell Phone" by Jenna Wortham, The New York Times, August 29, 2009

[9]http://santella.com/coupon.htm#ONLINE%2Coupons%20INCREASE%20111%20PERCENT20TO%20242%20MILLION%0IN%202002, p.6.

[10]"O&M's Phillips Decries 'Brand Rape,'" *Advertising Age,* May 14, 1991, 52.

Second, consumers can become insensitive to promotions and take them for granted, refusing to purchase a brand that does not offer a rebate or discount. When all competitors offer a rebate, its marketing leverage is lost, and all competitors are saddled with higher costs.

Third, Edwin Artzt (chairman of Proctor & Gamble) cautions that too few marketing people understand the value of advertising in creating "quality brand trial" and building the long-term franchise of a brand.[11] P&G's experience with advertising versus price promotions has indicated that customers who try a brand because of price promotion will be far less profitable over the long haul than customers whose trial was stimulated by advertising.

Integrating Advertising and Sales Promotion

Advertising and sales promotion frequently play directly coordinated and complementary roles in the marketing communication mix. For example, advertising can be used to create awareness of, plus favorable attitudes toward, the brand, and sales promotion can be used to supplement these effects by inducing trial. Even more obvious is the situation in which advertising is used to announce and promote a contest, sweepstakes, or cents-off coupon offer. The advertising may even be used to deliver the coupon to the consumer as a component part of a full-page newspaper ad in the food section.

As advocated in earlier sections of this text, the key to successful marketing communication is integration. Powerful synergies are possible when advertising and sales promotion are carefully coordinated. On the other hand, uncoordinated and inappropriate sales promotions run the risk of damaging the long-term image of a brand—an image established through advertising and other means, at a great expense, over a period of many years.

For example, a complicated and boring contest with inappropriate prizes can undermine a brand's high-quality image, cultivated by years of effective advertising. On the other hand, careful timing of and coordination between a flight of media advertisements touting a brand's benefits and a 50-cents-off coupon drop may drastically increase response. Or, if a coupon print advertisement is used to distribute the sales promotion offer, the impact of the ad *and* the promotion may be multiplied by coordinating it with the brand's television commercials. The selection of a premium offer is another sales promotion decision that should be made in light of the target audience of the marketing program, benefits stressed in advertising, personality or image established for the brand, and so on. If the planner fails to intelligently mold a promotion that fits these other components of the mix, disaster is possible.

The same principles apply to trade and sales force promotions. For example, by applying the same unifying campaign theme or trade characters across all forms of marketing communication, a marketer magnifies the impact of all components of the program. Consistency of voice is important in all the firm's communication.

To capitalize on possible synergies, the marketing communication planner must clearly focus on the fact that important interactions occur between all elements in the mix. In contemplating possible synergies, the planner should carefully evaluate the mix in a holistic manner from the prospective customer's perspective. This perspective is most relevant to winning the consumer's patronage and planning the firm's communication program.

---

[11]EdwinArtzt, "Grooming the Next Generation of Management," *The Advertiser* (Spring 1992): 66–70.

SUGGESTED READING

Blattberg, Robert, and Scott Neslin. *Sales Promotion: Concepts, Methods and Strategies.* Englewood Cliffs, N.J.: Prentice-Hall, 1990.

Quelch, John. *Sales Promotion Management* Englewood Cliffs, N.J.: Prentice-Hall, 1989.

Schultz, Don. "Sales Promotion." Chapter. 13 in *Strategic Advertising Campaigns.* Lincolnwood, IL: NTC Business Books, 1990.

Totten, John, and Martin Block. *Analyzing Sales Promotion: Text and Cases.* Chicago: Commerce Communications, 1987.

Schultz, Don and William Robinson. *Sales Promotion Management.* Lincolnwood, IL: NTC business Books, 1986.

SALES PROMOTION

Exercises

1. School Properties USA is a company that develops grassroots sponsorship opportunities for firms wanting to cater primarily to teenagers. The firm has already set up sponsorships as well as conducted event merchandising, sales promotions, and other promotional activities, in 16 states. It expects to promote events reaching 75% of all U.S. high school students in five years.

   The owner of School Properties feels that the company allows sponsors to reach the families of the high school students just as effectively. He points out that high school football and basketball games attract more than 400 million paying spectators every year. The potential audience of this type of sponsorship is very capable of justifying the economic investment in marketing: teenagers spend over $60 billion annually and their parents, about $250 billion.

   Assume you are trying to assemble a list of corporations and products that would benefit from sponsoring promotional campaigns through School Properties USA. What corporations and/or products would you list as the top 20 sponsorships that would be as effective as, say, free products such as soft drinks or hamburgers? Why? Why not?

   Discuss the possibilities offered by this type of promotional activity. Compare it to advertising. What are the advantages and disadvantages a marketer should consider when making a decision in this area?

   Source: Scott Hume, "Marketers Rally Around School Sponsorships," *Advertising Age,* June 1, 1992,32.

2. The spiraling costs of marketing and releasing movies have prompted Hollywood executives to use cross-promotions to appeal to the target audiences for their product. As an example, consider the 1991 Disney release *The Rocketeer,* based on an obscure comic book hero. Walt Disney Company wanted to appeal to a primary audience of teenagers. The company was considering offering *Rocketeer* toys at McDonald's outlets to all buyers of Happy Meals. Another possibility was to give free glider toys and Kid's Personal Pan Pizzas to Pizza Hut customers. Other proposals included scratch-and-win theater tickets valid for free Cokes or popcorn and a sweepstakes contest that would allow the winner to spend a long weekend at Disney World with his or her family.

   Which of the promotions considered do you feel would be most effective in spurring attendance to *The Rocketeer?* Is the quality of the movie a factor to be considered when choosing specific promotions? Why?

   Source: Thomas R. King, "See the Movie! Eat the Lunch Special!" *The Wall Street Journal,* June 4, 1991, B1 and B6.

3. A major manufacturer of breakfast cereals was considering an introductory promotion for a new fat-free granola-type cereal. The marketing vice-president had decided to use coupons as one of the major promotional tools. Fifty-cent-off coupons could be placed in either Sunday newspaper supplements or selected magazines, such as *Family Circle* or *Good Housekeeping*.

   The total paid circulation of the Sunday newspaper magazine network was 16,353,000, and the cost of a four-color page was about $250,000. The joint circulation of *Family Circle* and *Good Housekeeping* was about 10,250,000, and the cost of a four-color page in both magazines was about $190,000. The rate of coupon redemption for the two media was different, however. It was 2.1% for the Sunday newspaper magazine network and 5.6% for the two magazines.

   Which of the two proposed media vehicles would you choose to carry your coupon? Why?

4. The Marlboro Grand Prix of New York was scheduled to begin in 1993, and the event organizer was busy trying to line up corporate partners so that the race would be a very profitable venture. The event cost between $12 million and $15 million a year, and the organizer wanted as few sponsors or partners as possible to avoid clutter.

   In addition to Philip Morris Co.'s Marlboro, title sponsor of the event, eight other sponsors were sought. These would pay $1.54 million each in 1993, $1.7 million in 1994, and $1.86 million in 1995. In return, their names would be attached to the title of the event and incorporated in all advertising and promotion, including that done by the broadcasting network. Other promotional opportunities would be available at additional cost.

   The organizer was concerned that the antismoking feeling would hurt his chances of securing major sponsors to share the stage with Marlboro. He felt that food and soft drink companies would be reluctant to be allied with a cigarette manufacturer. Do you think this is a problem? Do you think being tied to a cigarette name would hurt the image of a company or a product? Discuss.

5. Marketers often use premiums as a sales promotion offer. As an example, a marketer of baking products may offer consumers who buy two cake-mixes a free disposable aluminum mold. Research seems to indicate that the choice of premiums to be offered to consumers affects the promotion in a more positive manner where the premium is relevant to the product being sold. Consider the following products and indicate what kind of premium you feel would fit better with each product:
   1. Special K breakfast cereal
   2. Coconut cream body wash
   3. A two-year subscription to "*Gardening magazine*"
   4. New "Crest" whitening kit for instant teeth whitening

Case 10.1

BusinesSuites (C)[1]

For BusinesSuites (BSS), commercial real estate brokers were a significant potential source of new, regular office clients. Exhibit 10.1.1 presents a profile of a typical commercial real estate broker, Rick Whiteley. This profile briefly indicates some of the factors that determine whether or not such brokers decide to recommend BSS as an alternative to their clients. (See the BSS (A) case for background on the company, their markets and so on.)

In order to attract the attention of brokers and stimulate them to direct their clients to BSS, the management team at BSS had implemented two promotional offers to brokers. The two complementary sales promotions were a broker referral fee program and a broker tour program. These programs were simple to both understand and administer.

Broker Referral Fee Program. BSS paid a broker referral fee of $1,000 for every new BSS client who was represented by a broker and signed a one-month or more contract. Given that the average tenure for a BSS client was 3.62 years, the value of a client signing a contract with BSS was readily apparent.

BSS mailed postcards (see Exhibit 10.1.2) to brokers to promote the broker fee program. The mailing lists used were created and maintained by each of the firm's 14 center managers. The brief messages on the postcards were varied and mailed monthly to brokers to remind them of the BSS offer. Table 10.1.1 presents quarterly data on the performance of the program by center over the past two years.

Broker Tour Program. To support the fee program BSS launched another incentive program that offered to give each broker who visited a BSS center and took a tour a $50 bill. To announce the offer, brokers received a hand-addressed envelope with a one-fold card inside with an invitation to take a tour and receive $50 in cash (see Exhibit 10.1.3). In addition to hand-addressing the envelopes and signing the cards, each center manager followed up after the mailing by telephoning all brokers on their list to encourage them to stop by the center for a tour.

Real Estate Brokers

Please stop by any BusinesSuites location for a tour of our executive suites before March 31, 2010, and we'll give you $50 in cash.

The program operated during the first quarter of each of the past two years with increasing success. In year one, 197 brokers took a tour and received a $50 bill, then, in year two, 343 brokers participated. This despite the fact that the total number of qualified commercial brokers dropped from 2,339 in year one to 2,172 in year two.

Heather Younger, the Center Manager of the Westlake BSS facility, was asked to review the performance of both of the two broker programs and to recommend changes to make the firm's marketing efforts directed at commercial brokers more effective and efficient. She realized that the first step was to analyze the data in Table 10.1.1 to uncover variations in program performance at the individual center level. In addition, she wondered, would the initial novelty of the program diminish the responsiveness of brokers to the program in year three? Should the size of the incentive be modified? Had BSS been too generous in these offers? These and many other basic questions about the present programs and potential modifications would need to be carefully addressed.

---

[1] This case was written by John Murphy and Jason Sears, The University of Texas at Austin, and Heather Younger, BusinesSuites. The case is designed to serve as the basis for classroom discussion and not to illustrate either the effective or ineffective handling of an administrative situation. The case is used with permission granted by BusinesSuites.

Exhibit 10.1.1 ■ Profile of Rick Whiteley[1]

Commercial Real Estate Broker

Demographics:
50 Years Old, Married with Two Children
Education: The University of Texas at Austin
Major: Broadcast Journalism
Austin Resident: 34 years
Commercial Real Estate Broker: 31 years
Tenant Representative Broker: 9 years

Real Estate Employment History:
Watson Casey Company: 9 years
Landmark Associates: 13 years
Oxford Commercial: 2001—Present

General Considerations

In recommending office alternatives for your clients, what are typically their most important considerations?
Location, price, quality and service.

What are some other important concerns?
Amenities. Who is the landlord? What is the service-mentality like? Flexibility in terms of the ability to expand or contract office space.

What is typically the strongest selling point for your client in selecting an office?
In general, location and price.

Selling BSS to clients

What is a typical client scenario where BSS is an option?
For example, the client is relocating to Austin and needs to get his/her office open quickly. Typically, going out and doing a lease in a building takes longer than the time you have to get the office up and running. A typical BSS scenario involves a client who requires office space quickly.

What do your clients often find most attractive about BSS?
Quick set up and location. All of them loved the service BSS provides when they are there.

What reservations do your clients often have about BSS?
Expensive. However, most realize they are there for the short term and they are paying for the convenience.

[1] Interview conducted by Jason Sears.

Exhibit 10.1.1 ■ Continued

Have you had any near misses with BSS? That is, a client who almost went their way but at the last moment decided against it?

Some clients required spaces that BSS did not have available. This happened once with the BSS Arboretum location. We have also had clients who ultimately decided to work from the house until they could get a permanent space.

Why did they go with another alternative?

Either their desired space was unavailable, some did not require an office presence (one-person show) or sometimes money was an issue.

BSS Commercial Broker Promotions

Have you ever received a postcard from BSS and taken the tour?

Yes. I have taken them once or twice. They are conducted well, and it gives us a chance to learn about their services. One advantage is relationship building. I have been to Westlake with Heather once and Barton Springs as well.

What about participating in the $1,000 program?

Yes, I have participated in the program on multiple occasions in terms of referring clients to BSS. Most of the clients I refer to BSS need short-term space in order to tide them over until we can get them into their permanent space. My clients have never stayed longer than, probably, six months at the longest. I have never had one stay long enough to where I considered the $1,000 to be unfair compensation.

The way our industry works is that we are paid based on the gross revenue that the transaction produces. We are compensated at a percentage of that gross revenue. A typical compensation for a tenant representative is 4 percent of the gross revenue for the term. This is split between the firm and the individual brokers. The $1,000 does not go directly to me, but to the firm[2]. For example, $25,000 in gross revenue equals $1,000 in compensation. Assuming an individual suite at BSS is around $1,500 per month, or $9,000 for six months, then $1,000 for a lease that generates $9,000 in gross revenue exceeds what we would typically receive.

[2]This may vary depending on the commercial real estate firm.

Exhibit 10.1.2 ■ BusinesSuites Marketing Efforts—2008

BusinesSuites Marketing Efforts – 2008

We currently market our services on a variety of fronts. It is essential for a successful marketing campaign to take a multi-faceted approach that includes many different types of marketing. We hope that the combination of each of the following efforts accomplish that objective.

Prospective Client Direct-Mail Marketing

Postcards, designed and printed then sent out to a purchased address list (InfoUsa) of prospective virtual and office clients. Database updated internally.
Often this effort leads people directly to our website or Google.
3 Types of Cards: "Credibility" "Image" and "Professionalism"

Front, Cards 1, 2 & 3:   *Back with Address:*

CREDIBILITY. CREDIBILITY. CREDIBILITY.
CREDIBILITY. CREDIBILITY. CREDIBILITY.
CREDIBILITY. CREDIBILITY. CREDIBILITY.

A Virtual Office provides your business the credibility of a professional workplace in an upscale office building. With packages starting at $125 per month, a professional image has never been more affordable. Learn more at www.businessuites.com.

Telephone Answering   Mail & Package Receipt

Give your business extra credibility.

businessuites VIRTUAL OFFICE
www.businessuites.com

Conference Room Use   Professional Address

IMAGE

Create a big image for your business.

businessuites VIRTUAL OFFICE
www.businessuites.com

For more information, call Heather Younger at 512-329-2500.

PROFESSIONALISM

Underscore the professionalism of your business.

businessuites VIRTUAL OFFICE
www.businessuites.com

Broker Direct Mail Marketing

Similar in format to our prospect direct mail campaign, with the exception that our database is comprised of Commercial Real Estate Brokers, and it highlights our product as well as our Broker compensation package: $1000/referral, no matter the size of the deal.
2 Types of Cards- "$1000" and "Simple."

Front, Cards 1 & 2:

$1,000

Get paid big for your small and short-term prospects.

Back with Address:

Refer your small space or short-term prospects to BusinesSuites. Each time we convert one to an office client, we'll send you a $1,000 gift card. You get $1,000 regardless of the length of the term, the number of offices, or the value of the transaction. It's that simple.

Visit www.bssbrokers.com or call 888-701-7600 to make a referral.

We have a very simple way for you to make $1,000.

Online Brokers

Searchofficespace.com , Instantoffices.com, OfficeBroker.com, and OfficeFinder.com are sites where we contract with "virtual brokers" who provide search engines with our listings and receive fees for referrals.

Et Cetera Broker Marketing

LoopNet.com, PropertyLine.com and City feet.com are all examples of websites that real estate brokers visit to find property listings for their clients. We pay subscription fees for our listings and update them regualarly.

Yellowpages Listings

Our purchased space with the Yellow Pages offers printed advertising in the phone book, as well as online Yellowpages.com listings.

Exhibit 10.1.3

Real Estate Brokers –

Please stop by any BusinesSuites
location for a tour of our executive suites
before March 31, 2010,
and we'll give you $50 in cash.

Table 10.1.1 ■ Broker Lead Generation Promotions

Center	Lead Value	Lead Cour	Win Value	Win Count	Brokers	Tour Coun
Year 1						
Austin, TX						
Arboretum	$58,429.00	29	$5,150.00	2	137	18
Barton Springs	$69,335.00	38	$16,800.00	5	272	11
Westlake	$47,505.00	30	$2,500.00	1	123	20
Houston, TX						
Chasewood	$14,495.00	8	$3,580.00	2	60	7
Sugarcreek	$5,952.00	7	$825.00	2	22	5
Uptown	$108,609.00	44	$20,676.00	7	402	18
Waterway	$34,371.00	11	$7,301.00	2	21	1
Las Vegas, NV						
Hughes Center	$18,214.00	10	$_____	0	265	25
Baltimore, MD						
Harborplace	$77,246.00	18	$17,055.00	2	424	22
Owings Mills	$1,100.00	1	$_____	0	21	1
Parkview/Towncenter	$26,435.00	10	$9,185.00	4	67	5
Newport News, VA						
Oyster Point	$10,128.00	12	$4,675.00	3	821	35
Richmond, VA						
West End	$21,839.00	23	$4,300.00	3	97	27
	$493,658.00	241	$92,047.00	33	2732	195
Year 2						
Austin, TX						
Arboretum	$112,300.00	50	$8,750.00	2	143	22
Barton Springs	$48,617.00	32	$6,407.00	4	263	33
Westlake	$43,930.00	31	$8,980.00	5	114	16
Houston, TX						
Chasewood	$8,550.00	5	$1,750.00	2	59	21
Sugarcreek	$_____	0	$_____	0	22	4
Uptown	$70,069.00	34	$19,258.00	8	397	75
Waterway	$12,444.00	7	$4,879.00	3	21	12

Continued

Table 10.1.1 ■ Continued

Center	Lead Value	Lead Cour	Win Value	Win Count	Brokers	Tour Coun
Las Vegas, NV						
Hughes Center	$14,050.00	13	$2,750.00	3	242	33
Baltimore, MD						
Harborplace	$46,045.00	20	$1,200.00	1	440	39
Owings Mills	$32,850.00	9	$650.00	1	21	12
Parkview/Towncenter	$31,874.00	21	$6,000.00	2	67	29
Newport News, VA						
Oyster Point	$35,377.00	34	$3,000.00	5	192	18
Richmond, VA						
West End	$12,976.00	14	$1,050.00	1	102	22
	$469,082.00	270	$64,674.00	37	2083	336

Name _____   Date _____

QUESTIONS FOR DISCUSSION AND REVIEW

1. What are the most important conclusions that can be drawn from the data in Table 10.1.1?

2. How important an impact do the two mailing pieces presented in the exhibits have on the overall effectiveness of the two promotional programs? What alternative means of promoting the two sales promotions might be considered?

3. How might insights gained from the Rick Whiteley profile be used in marketing BSS to commercial real estate brokers?

4. What are the advantages and disadvantages of the decentralized nature of the development and implementation of the two programs at the center level?

5. How important are overall business conditions and variations in local practices in explaining differences in the responsiveness of brokers to the program across the 14 centers?

Case 10.2

Don't Mess with Texas (B)[1]

THE CAR2CAN CONTEST

To help keep the overall Don't Mess with Texas (DMWT) campaign fresh and relevant, and to capitalize on consumer generated content, the DMWT team concepted and presented an online promotion named the Car2Can Video Contest to their client, the Texas Department of Transportation. (See DMWT (A) case for background.) Via a Web site (see Exhibit 10.2.1), Texas residents were invited to submit original commercials designed to motivate people to dispose of their trash properly rather than pitch it out the window of their car or truck. To extend the impact of the contest, Texas residents were also encouraged to vote online for their favorite commercials entered in the contest.

Research showed the Gen L audience had made a general shift in media preferences away from traditional sources such as network-generated television and toward peer-driven online platforms such as YouTube. YouTube provided a popular vehicle for 16- to 24-year-old members of Gen L to share videos with friends and colleagues, many of them recorded and produced by other young users and shared on social networks like Facebook® and MySpace®.

At the direction of the DMWT team, Gen L's interaction with the campaign was increasingly Web based. The campaign's site (www.dontmesswithtexas.org) had always been a popular and effective resource for litter prevention information, but it lacked the exciting, video-driven content that appealed to Gen L. With these facts in mind, the DMWT team knew that the campaign needed an online initiative that would incentivize young Texans to not only share relevant video content but also interact with and voice their opinions about the content with their peers, using the videos to remind others why it's important to keep their state clean by reducing litter.

Realizing that not everyone is an aspiring filmmaker, the DMWT team determined that a prize-based, litter-related online video contest could effectively encourage two segments of the Gen L target audience to get involved: "content creators" (aspiring actors, filmmakers, and advertising professionals) who hoped to win the prize and have their work showcased, as well as the larger percentage of "watchers," who view, rate, and share user-generated videos that are particularly interesting or unique.

To maximize creative freedom, the team developed the "Car2Can" concept, which asked participants to submit videos showcasing their most clever, creative, and innovative ways of getting trash from the car to the trashcan (thereby keeping it off of Texas roadways). As a grand prize, thousands of viewers would see the winning video as "The Next Don't Mess with Texas TV Commercial" on network television in the winner's media market. Additionally, the team worked with both Walmart® and Sweet Leaf Tea® to solicit donations for second- and third-place prizes.

To illustrate the concept of the contest and maximize media relations potential, EnviroMedia filmed a "seed" video illustrating the concept. In the video, a trained dog takes trash from his owner's car to the can. The DMWT team used the seed video to drive traffic to the Web site using a combination of media relations activities, grassroots educational outreach, and online Web banner advertising. Additionally, participants were encouraged to use social networking channels such as Facebook, MySpace and Twitter to spread the word about their videos or favorites.

---

[1] This case was written by John H. Murphy, The University of Texas at Austin, and Christina Moss, EnviroMedia Social Marketing, in coordination with the Texas Department of Transportation. The case is designed to serve as the basis for classroom discussion and not to illustrate either the effective or ineffective handling of an administrative situation. Don't Mess with Texas is a registered trademark of the Texas Department of Transportation.

Exhibit 10.2.1

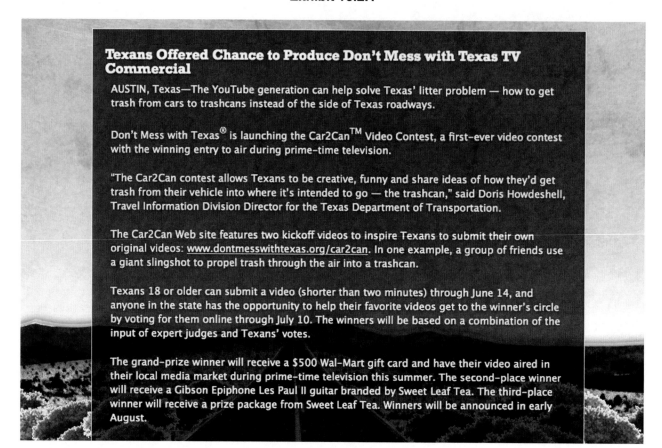

The overall objectives for the contest were to:

- Entice members of Gen L to interact with the DMWT Web site with a goal to increase overall traffic to the Don't Mess with Texas Web site by at least 20%.
- Encourage comment and voting dialogue on the C2C Web site surrounding the videos and litter prevention in general. Goal of at least 100 votes per video, and 10 comments.
- Spread the word about the litter problem in Texas through Web banner ads that also promoted the contest.
- Communicate the winner's litter-prevention strategy to a larger audience using a paid media buy.

The entry period for submitting videos was May 1 through June 14, 2009. Then, the top 10 videos were posted for public voting June 29 through July 10. The contest was open to all Texans, 18 and older. Submitted videos had to be shorter than 2 minutes in length. If the commercial contained music, video, or images, they had to be original and created by the director themselves (no TV clips or music from albums).

Videos must feature a positive reference of trash going from a car to a trashcan. Car2Can ideas didn't have to be realistic or practical but interesting, creative, and inspire others to think, "That's cool; I never would have thought of that!"

The contest was promoted through e-mail blasts to the campaign's database of 10,000 fans. Car2Can was also promoted through interactive Web banners that were placed on Web sites frequented by young Texas adults. An outreach representative helped promote the competition to college and university film faculty and students. This person called and e-mailed university professors statewide and used his personal networks to spread the word via word of mouth and e-mail blasts. In total, 130,000 e-mails were sent promoting the contest.

Commercial entries were submitted through YouTube and added to the Don't Mess with Texas Web site immediately for people to vote and comment on their favorite commercials. A total of 23 commercials were submitted and posted online. Web traffic for the contest was heavy as many more people were interested in viewing and commenting on the commercials than submitting commercials themselves.

The contest resulted in 28,483,038 online impressions from the Web banners, and the contest received great reception from media outlets. For the two months the commercials were online for votes and comments, there were more than 100,000 page views on the Don't Mess with Texas Web site, more than 16,000 votes, and 525 comments for the favorite commercial.

The Car2Can program budget was limiting at approximately $65,000 for planning, creative and video productions with an additional media budget of $115,000 used to place online Web banners. Approximately $34,000 was set aside to air the winning spot during prime-time TV in the winner's market.

WHAT TO USE NEXT SUMMER?

As the DMWT team began thinking about an online promotion targeting Gen L for the next summer, they reviewed the results of the Car2Can promotion. How effective had the promotion been? What had they learned from the contest? What changes, modifications, or additions to the promotion would have made it more engaging to the target? Realizing that originality and freshness were critical in the online world, would repeating the Car2Can program be a mistake?

In developing concepts for possible online programs for next summer, the team agreed that it would be useful to develop a checklist of the characteristics of an ideal online Gen L contest or promotion. Once they had identified such a list, they could evaluate new promotional ideas.

Name _____ Date _____

QUESTIONS FOR DISCUSSION AND REVIEW

1. How might the Car2Can Video Contest been modified to increase its effectiveness?

_____
_____
_____
_____

2. Could a modified version of the Car2Can contest be used next summer? If so, how could this be most effectively and efficiently implemented?

_____
_____
_____
_____

3. How could the campaign have more narrowly targeted their audience?

_____
_____
_____
_____

4. What is the best way to measure the success of the contest?

_____
_____
_____
_____

Case 10.3

Bath-So-Nice

Bath-so-Nice was a nationally advertised brand of bath gels and body scrubs sold in the United States. The brand was marketed by a subsidiary of Proctor and Gamble and was distributed through food and drug outlets primarily. Some department stores and specialty outlets also carried the brand, but 90% of all sales were made through grocery and drug stores. The brand had been first introduced in the market in 1980, and by 1985 had captured over 25% of all sales of similar products by grocery and drug outlets, and about 10% of all the category sales for the United States. It was the largest-selling brand of bath and scrub gels in all the industry. In 1995, Bath-So-Nice was facing increasing competition by smaller brands that were trying to carve specialty niches for themselves in the market. In addition, some private brands had also been launched by a few of the retail grocery and drug chains, which were sold at an average of 25% savings off the average retail price of branded products in the category. Bath-So-Nice has a philosophy of aggressive marketing, and it was considering various alternatives to maintain its market share and profits for 1996 and 1997.

The overall market for bath products was $25 billion per year. Of these, about 15% were products like Bath-So-Nice that aimed its appeals to middle-class consumers who were willing to spend a little more than the price of an average good-quality soap bar, for the pleasure of using a scented and refreshing product to pamper themselves. Whereas the average price of a soap bar (bath size) was about $.89 at retail, the average price of the gels and scrub product was $2.50 per tube. The market for such personal care products was very fragmented; there were over 450 different brands and items sold in the United States. The overall market for the medium-to premium-priced products like Bath-So-Nice was increasing, however, while the overall market for personal care products had remained virtually unchanged during the previous 10 years.

Before the introduction of BSN sales of similar branded specialty bath products were made exclusively through department and specialty stores. Starting in the early 80s, however, sales of certain brands and store brand products through supermarkets and drugstores had grown tremendously, and by 1995 a significant share of all sales of this category of products (about 65%) were accounted for by supermarkets and drugstores.

Advertising and promotions of the bath gels and scrubs were primarily based on price. Because of the ordering and stocking practices of most mass merchandising outlets, products in this category usually experienced stock-outs as high as 25%, and retail turnover was lower than that of all food and drug products. BSN is a new and superior product. It comes only in one size: however, the company often sells multiple packs of the scrub and the gel combinations for promotional purposes. To distinguish BSN from competing products, the firm developed a special display case that stood alone in stores. The case was small, had a pyramidal shape, and was very noticeable. The management felt that the in-store display was instrumental in developing the product's image of quality and had been one of the most important factors for establishing the brand in a short period of time.

The introduction of BSN into the market had utilized a media blitz of $20 million and the use of $.50 coupons for a total promotion value to consumers of $10 million. Sales support to the retailers was given through a sales force unequaled by any other manufacturer in the same category.

MARKET RESEARCH

In 1994, a market research was conducted by BSN with the following results:

—50% of all potential women buyers had tried BSN at least once.
—Over two-thirds of the triers repeated with one or more subsequent purchases.

- Brand awareness and advertising awareness exceeded 80% of the potential market.
- By 1994, at least 25% of all potential consumers listed BSN as their regularly preferred brand.
- In 1995, overall sales of BSN were $380 million, and BSN was established as the best-selling bath gel and scrub brand in the country, with a distribution that covered 88% of the total U.S. market.
- Sales of bath gel and scrub products had grown at a rate of 5% per year during the decade of the 1980s, and by 7% per year during 1990 to 1995. Their growth had hurt sales of soap bars, and it was expected that sales of scrubs and gels would level off by the year 2000.
- BSN sales had grown at a rate of 10% per year during the first 10 years of its existence, and were presently growing at a rate of 11% to 12%. Its growth resulted from a combination of growth in the total demand for the product category, and market share obtained from other competing products.
- Sales personnel were approximately 700 for the United States, and the firm did not expect to add to that number.
- Competitors were spending an increasingly large amount of dollars in advertising and promotion, hoping to imitate the success of BSN.
- Consumers who bought bath scrubs and gels did not use soap bars after becoming loyal consumers of products like BSN. Soap bars might be purchased solely for occasional use, for washing hands. It was felt that consumers would also be very brand loyal. Although price promotions might cause trial by consumers fairly often, if the quality of the competitors' brands were not judged superior to BSN, they would likely switch back to BSN after trial.

THE COMPETITION

There were two major competitors in the market: Nature Bath (NB) owned by Unilever, with annual sales of $285 million for 1995 for the bath scrubs and gels category, and Body and Face (BF), owned by a Swiss multinational corporation, with sales of $200 million for 1995 in the same category. Four additional medium-sized national companies accounted for $350 million in sales of bath gels and scrubs for 1995, and store brands accounted for $500 million for the same year. The remainder $1 billion in sales (approximately) was divided among 400 small national, regional, and local manufacturers.

BSN competitors used a different marketing strategy for their products. They did not use special (point of) point-of-purchase displays, and they offered higher margins to retailers (about 45% of retail price, versus 35% offered by BSN). They also sold their products at prices lower than those of BSN, by about 10% to 15% of the retail suggested price. In addition, BSN total advertising/sales/promotion expenditures were twice as high as those of its two major competitors.

BSN management had heard that its major competitor, NB, was in the process of introducing a new line of bath gels and scrubs. The new line would feature four major scents and an overall product of superior quality. Those who had seen a sample of it felt it was slightly better than BSN. The packaging would be distinctive and luxurious, giving an overall impression of high quality. NB was planning a major introductory campaign for the new product line, featuring coupons of $1.00 per unit priced at $2.00 retail, and advertising expenditures of about $40 million for 1996, and $35 million for 1997. It was expected that the coupon offer would last for 6 months in 1996 and 6 months in 1997. NB was hoping to capture a share of market equivalent to that of BSN, or about 10% of the bath gels and scrubs, by the end of 1997.

BSN RESPONSE

The management of BSN was counting with an increase in sales of 7% each of the two following years. The actions of NB could seriously jeopardize such a goal. Swift action was required to maintain sales expectations.

Two alternative courses of action were discussed by BSN management:

- First: An increase of advertising expenditures from $30 million to $50 million for 1996 and 1997. The company was spending a total of $80 million in 1995 in sales/advertising/promotion. Of these, $30 million were advertising media expenditures, $35 million were sales force salaries and bonuses, and $15 million were promotional expenditures, including point-of-purchase displays, and coupons and twin-packages offers. In addition, the 1996 and 1997 campaign would decrease promotional expenditures to $5 million. The result would be a net increase in advertising/sales/promotion expenditures of $10 million in 1996 and 1997, respectively.

    It was hoped that the increase in advertising expenditures would generate a total of $405 million in sales for 1996, and $440 million in 1997.

- Second: This strategy would maintain expenditures and sales force expenditures at the 1995 level, but would increase promotion expenditures to $20 million in 1996 and $20 million in 1997. The additional promotion dollars would allow a special offer of $1.00 coupons/discounts on twin packs of scrub and gel. It was expected that during the promotion about 50 million units would be sold in 1996, and 60 million units would be sold in 1997. This strategy was expected to produce an increase in unit sales of about 8 million units in 1996 and 10 million units in 1997.

    Management was also very willing to consider other alternative strategies, if the expected results were more profitable for BSN. It is important to note that the cost of production of each unit of scrub or gel was about $.80. In addition, management was expected to generate at least a profit of $22 million to $25 million after tax each fiscal year.

Name _____ Date _____

QUESTIONS FOR DISCUSSION AND REVIEW

1. What would be the total increase in dollar sales and in unit sales for each of the two alternatives described, if the results forecasted by BSN were to follow?

2. Develop a break-even analysis for each of the two alternative strategies. How many additional units (or dollars) should BSN sell if alternative 1 were implemented, in order to break even? What about for alternative 2?

3. Would BSN management be able to satisfy the profit goals if it implemented alternative 1? Would they satisfy the profit goals if they implemented alternative 2?

4. Assume that any additional dollar spent in advertising will generate $15 dollars in sales until a total of $400 million in sales is reached, and after that each additional advertising dollar would generate $12. In sales, all other things equal (no change in competitors' strategy, and maintaining the present levels of sales and promotion expenditures), what would be the optimum level of advertising expenditures for BSN?

5. Assuming that any additional dollar spent in sales promotion would generate an additional $2 in sales revenue, until total sales of $55 million were reached, and then the sales response to promotion would decrease to $1.50 per dollar spent, what would be the ideal level of promotional expenditures for BSN, if all other things remained equal?

6. Would you suggest that BSN engage in a third strategy by varying both its advertising and its promotion expenditures for 1996 and 1997? If so, what would be your recommendation? Make sure you justify your budget by showing the expected response in terms of sales for your recommendation.

Case 10.4

New Chase Condominiums

BACKGROUND

In partnership with the Dutch company Wilma, the Shawntana Development Corporation built a 164-unit condominium project. The project, named New Chase, occupied a 6.8-acre site in Fountain Valley, California. New Chase was located near many commercial and retail businesses. Further, the project was close to several amenities in the area. For example, New Chase was located 5 miles from the Pacific Ocean, 3 miles from a major shopping center, 1½ miles from an airport, and 1½ miles from a golf course in a prestigious community.

The project was made up of three basic units (see Exhibit 10.4.1 for the three floor plans). Each plan's number of units, size and average selling price are indicated in the following table:

Plan	Number of Units	Square Footage	Bed/Baths	Average Selling Price
Atherton	56	724	1/1	$75,000
Brighton	52	910	2/1	$85,000
Sylvan	56	1,106	2/2	$94,000

In addition, the project included a swimming pool, pool building, and spa. Exhibit 10.4.2 lists some of the features of New Chase.

New Chase was classified as "affordable housing." This meant that Shawntana was required to sell 25 percent of the units to households earning no more than 120 percent of the median income in Orange County.

At the time of the initial offering, the median income in Orange County was $33,425. Therefore, 25 percent of the New Chase units had to be sold to households with incomes no greater than $40,110 per year ($33,425 x 1.20). The remaining 75 percent could be sold as either "affordable" or "conventional" housing.

As part of Shawntana's arrangement with the local governments and planning boards that had approved the project, Shawntana was to provide financing for the "affordable" buyers in the form of 20-year loans with fixed interest rates of approximately 10%.

Given the size, price range, and financing of the project, management felt that the target market was primarily first-time homebuyers. Management estimated that probably 80% of eventual buyers lived within a five-mile radius of the site, with the balance coming from the Orange County/Los Angeles area at large. Further, management believed that the best prospects were young professionals, young couples who both worked, and singles who shared expenses.

THE MARKETING PLAN

Shawntana's sales objective was to maintain an average sales rate of three units per week throughout a two-phase selling period spanning 13 months. Phase I began August 1 and ran through February 15 of the next year. Phase II began February 16 and ran through August 31.

Exhibit 10.4.1 ■ New Chase Condominiums: Floor Plans of the Three Basic Units

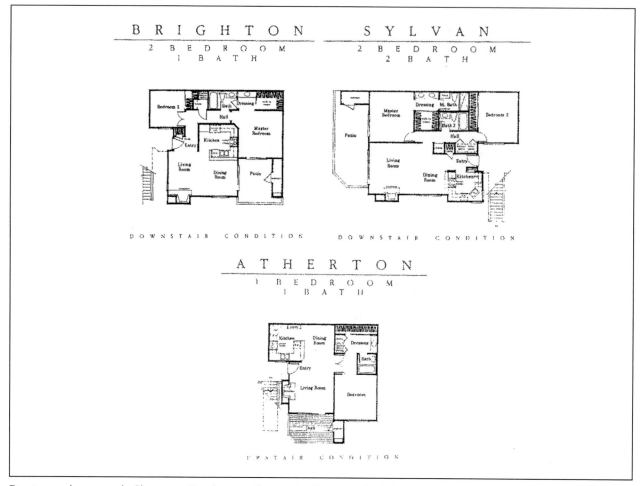

Due to ongoing research, Shawntana Development Corporation Reserves the right to change plans, specification, pricing, or terms with out prior notice or obligation.

Shawntana planned to use an advertising agency that specialized in real estate advertising and collateral materials, plus a separate public relations firm. Both of these firms would be paid a negotiated straight fee for their services.

In addition, a firm specializing in real estate sales would be retained to serve as the exclusive sales agent for the development. This firm would be compensated on a straight 1 percent of gross selling price commission basis. Two salespersons would work as on-site sales representatives between 9:00 A.M. and 6:00 P.M. on weekends, and one person would work during the week. As part of the agreement, Shawntana was responsible for supplying all sales support tools (such as brochures, business cards, and stationary) plus an office (condo unit) equipped with desks, furnishings, telephones, and refreshments.

Media advertising was to be concentrated exclusively in newspapers. Shawntana's advertising agency planned to place ads in the Los Angeles Times Orange County edition's Saturday "At Home" section and Sunday "Real Estate" section. In addition, ads were to be placed in the *Orange County Register/Bulletin*.

Exhibit 10.4.2 ■ Features of New Chase Condominiums

Distinctive Exteriors
- Private Balcony or patio
- Fire-protective asphalt shingle roofs
- Individually assigned covered parking
- Combination stucco and wood siding
- Handsome architectural detailing
- New West color schemes
- Dramatic oversized 8' sliding glass doors

Inside Every Home
- Central air conditioning
- Energy-saving, heat-circulation, wood-burning fireplace with ceramic tile face and crown mold mantel
- Individual laundry appliance hookup
- Custom draperies
- Mirrored wardrobe doors in master dressing area
- Walk-in closets (Brighton & Sylvan)
- Oversized 9' ceilings in ground-level units
- Dramatic vaulted ceilings in upper-level units
- Excellent carpeting selections (100% ANSO nylon)
- Extensive variety of versatile space arrangements
- Private storage rooms
- Polished brass Schlage hardware
- Hand-carved, solid wood entry door with sunburst window
- Choice of decorator-selected, cushioned vinyl flooring in kitchen, bath, and laundry area
- Prewired for cable television or standard antenna and telephones
- Lifesaver smoke detectors

Deluxe Kitchens
- Custom-designed easy-care European-style cabinetry
- Ceramic tile countertops with solid oak edging
- Magic Chef built-in appliances including continuous cleaning range, hood, dishwasher, and disposal
- Storage pantry
- Designer-selected track lighting
- Double-compartment sink with MOEN single-lever fixture
- Prep for ice maker hookup

Beautiful Baths
- Compartmentalized dressing and tub areas
- Decorative MOEN widespread fixtures in master bath
- Easy-care, tile-patterned tub and shower enclosures
- Cultured marble Pullman
- Oversized plate glass mirrors

Energy-saving Features
- Energy-efficient furnace, water heater, and air conditioning systems
- Fully insulated, double-framed party wall-separation
- Extra-thick sound and energy insulation in walls and ceilings
- Sound-deadening, lightweight concrete between party floors

Community Recreation
- Lush, parklike landscaping and waterscape
- Heated swimming pool
- Two whirlpool spas
- Two sun deck areas
- Direct access to biking, jogging, and equestrian trails

Locational Advantages
- Centrally located to employment
- Within minutes of Mile Square Park, Newport Beach, South Coast Plaza, and Westminster Mall
- Ideally situated between San Diego Freeway (405) and Garden Grove Freeway (22) for easy access to San Diego, Riverside, and Los Angeles counties

Membership in Homeowner's Association Includes
- Hot and cold water
- Gas
- Recreation facilities
- Trash collection
- Exterior building and landscaping maintenance
- Fire and liability insurance

Due to ongoing research, Shawntana Development Corporation Reserves the right to change plans, specification, pricing, or terms without prior notice or obligation.

Exhibit 10.4.3 ■ Representative Newspaper Advertisements for New Chase Condominiums

Chapter 11
Direct Marketing

> *. . . a marketing data base becomes the G-2, the intelligence-gathering apparatus that allows marketers to implement their marketing strategies most efficiently . . . allowing the company to precisely target and communicate with its audience while the competition serenely sips champagne and nibbles foie gras, oblivious that a major attack has taken place.*[1]
>
> —Jack Bickert

Over the past few decades, direct marketing has become an increasingly sophisticated and important means of communicating with customers and perspective customers for all types of businesses. Further, experience has demonstrated that when integrated with other communication mix elements, direct marketing not only creates plus business in its own right, but also plus business for the sales force and dealers.[2] This chapter briefly covers some of the basics involved in this growing area of marketing communication. The chapter begins with an overview of what is involved in managing a direct marketing program and then focuses on the crucial topic of database marketing.

In an era of expanding technology, products, and competitors, the key underlying assumption of direct marketing is that effective marketing program strategies require precise knowledge of increasingly segmented target audiences. At its heart, direct marketing focuses on intelligently applying information about customers and prospects to forge attractive marketing programs—marketing programs aimed at developing an interactive, long-term relationship between the marketer and the customers whose needs it seeks to serve.

Hodgson points out that direct marketing involves three crucial characteristics. First, during the marketing process a response takes place "sight unseen." That is, something occurs without any personal contact between the marketer and the prospect (that is, without the intervention of a retailer). Second, the audience for the firm's offer is selected using information contained in a database. Third, the success of the process is measurable.[3]

Astute marketers realize that direct marketing offers many firms important opportunities to expand their sales and that capitalizing on this potential requires a special expertise distinct from that required by traditional media

---

[1] Jock Bickert, *Adventures in Relevance Marketing* (Denver: Briefcase Books, 1991), 2.

[2] Bob Stone, *"The Principles and Techniques of Interchannel Marketing,"* The Direct Marketing Manual (New York: Direct Marketing Association, 1989), Resource Report 605.01, 1–3.

[3] Richard Hodgson, *An Introduction to Direct Marketing* (New York: The Direct Marketing Educational Foundation, 1990), monograph, 2–6.

advertising and other forms of marketing communication. Exhibit 11.1 presents ten major areas of responsibility that must be addressed to effectively operate a direct marketing program. Stone suggests that to handle these areas effectively and be successful direct marketers, firms need to hire direct marketing experts. Hence, it is not surprising that firms are increasingly establishing separate direct marketing units to supplement other marketing and advertising functions.[4]

Some categories of direct marketing can enter a firm's marketing communication mix include (1) *direct response*—a system in which the marketer's message, regardless of the medium used, seeks to stimulate a direct, measurable response form the target audience; (2) *direct mail advertising*—use of the U.S. Postal Service to make direct contact with prospective customers; (3) *database marketing*—and integrated system structured around information on customers and prospects and their purchasing preferences and history;[5] and more recently, (4) *e-mail marketing/Web-based marketing*—use of electronic mail and Web-based direct marketing campaigns to make direct contact with customers. Note that the increased use of both category one (direct response) and category two (direct mail) has been and will continue to be driven by the expansion of categories three and four (database marketing and Web-based marketing).

Underlying the growth in the application of database marketing are the increasingly sophisticated capabilities of computers to handle and manipulate large data files, advanced statistical techniques, and the measurability of direct marketing, as well as the growing acceptance of toll-free telephone numbers to conduct business and use of credit cards to make purchases.[6] Given the past growth of database marketing and the fact that it is forecasted to become an increasingly important means of selling products, the remainder of this chapter focuses on the basics of database marketing.

DATABASE MARKETING

The general strategy of database marketers is to begin by purchasing or developing a computer file of customers and prospects. This file includes information such as name, address, telephone number, past purchases, lifestyle activities, and interests. Using this information, the marketer formulates and then conveys specialized offers to segments of the database based on known correlations between likely demand for specific offers and the other variables included in the database. American Express, American Airlines, and Spiegel are examples of companies that have for a number of years successfully applied their knowledge of their customers to determining which groups receive specialized product offers. The goal of these companies is to build a relationship with their customers over time based on a two-way stream of communication and information.[7]

---

[4]Bob Stone, *Successful Direct Marketing Methods,* 4th ed. (Lincolnwood, IL: NTC Business Books, 1988), 23.

[5]Don Schultz, *Strategic Advertising Campaigns,* 3rd ed. (Lincolnwood, IL: NTC Business Books, 1990), 498–504.

[6]Ibid., 495–496.

[7]Don Schultz, "Maybe the Difficulty in the Definition Is the Difference," *Journal of Direct Marketing 5,* no. 1 (Winter 1991): 4–6.

Exhibit 11.1 ■ Ten Major Areas of Responsibility in Direct Marketing[a]

1. *Product selection and development*—evaluating market potential, the competition, potential profit margins, and fit with other marketing communication activities.
2. *Strategic planning*—establishing objectives, developing planning models, conducting business analyses, and developing strategies.
3. *Market and media selection/scheduling*—selecting and/or developing appropriate mailing lists or databases and identifying the most efficient media to deliver the message.
4. *Creative development*—presenting the offer in a memorable and appropriate manner through the development of creative strategy and execution.
5. *Research*—applying a variety of research techniques to gather background information for decision making in other steps. Examples include exploratory research using survey questionnaires and focus groups.
6. *Testing procedures*—measuring response to the offer. This area is the heart of the accountability of direct marketing. Such factors as the offer itself, price, and variations by geographic region, by demographics, and by media are evaluated by comparing response rates.
7. *Fulfillment*—deciding which shipping facilities, returned goods procedures, carriers, and so on to use.
8. *Budgeting and accounting*—determining appropriate financing costs, cash flow procedures, accounting systems, and credit card affiliations and monitoring program performance.
9. *Customer service*—handling sales correspondence, adjustments, and complaints, plus activation and reactivation.
10. *Personal and supplier relations*—fostering productive relationships with suppliers, list brokers, printers, artists, envelope houses, fulfillment firms, space reps, and other marketing specialists with the firm.

[a]Bob Stone, *Successful Direct Marketing Methods,* 4th ed. (Lincolnwood, IL: NTC Business Books, 1988), 23–24

Developing the Database

The most important element in successful direct marketing is the development and maintenance of a computer database containing information on individual customers and prospects. The database includes each individual's name, address, purchase history, and other information pertinent to effectively marketing the firm's products/services through a targeted program. It may initially be created through available sales transaction files and supplemented by harvesting (adding to the firm's own database) individuals who respond to offers from rented lists of prospects.

Myriad lists are made available for rent (or purchase, but this is rare) by specialized firms and list brokers. For example, Donnelly Marketing and Claritas/PRIZM uses census data on income, age of the household head, and so on to identify prospects who live in selected areas, such as certain ZIP codes or block groups, who meet specified criteria. The Lifestyle Selector, marketed by Equifax Marketing Services, is another example of a widely used external database. It contains 45 million names, along with demographic and lifestyle information. Standard Rate & Data Service, Inc,. publishes the most comprehensive directory of information on mailing lists and databases. This directory, *Direct Mail Lists, Rates & Data,* is updated regularly and includes costs, formats, restrictions, and other details. In addition, list brokers have the ability to sort, merge, and purge several lists to custom design a specific prospect profile. By creating a list of prospects that meet criteria related to interest in and purchase of items in a product category, the marketer is practicing market segmentation and increasing the probability that its offer will be appealing to those contacted.

Manipulating the Database

Once data on each individual customer or account are captured, it is possible to track the profitability of each and to structure an appropriate program of customer contact. Stone describes two systems for evaluating customers using data on past purchasers. These systems (R-F-M and FRAT) assign points to customers based on the most commonly captured and useful transactional data: recency, frequency, monetary amount, and type of merchandise purchased. For example, in rating customers' purchases over the past 12 months, 20 points might be assigned if a purchase had been made in the past 3 months, 15 for a purchase made in the past 6 months, and so on. The other three variables are assigned points in a similar fashion.[8]

By weighting these variables and summing the points a customer receives on each, a marketer is able to accurately forecast which customers are most likely to respond to an offer (the higher the points total, the more likely the customer is to buy again). Hence, contact is made only with customers who have a points total above some minimum level. The system is constantly updated and evaluated to determine if it is working effectively.

In addition, such a database provides the marketer with a wide range of target marketing and cross-selling opportunities to apply past purchase information to determining what sort of offer to convey to which customers. For example, a computer company can send a follow-up mailing featuring appropriate new software only to those customers who have purchased high-performance Macintoshes in the past year. Or a garden supply center could identify customers who purchased flower bulbs last fall to receive a promotional piece featuring fall gardening tools that will be mailed in September.

In addition, several mathematical techniques can be applied to databases to develop improved marketing programs. These techniques (for example, multiple regression, Automatic Interaction Detector, and cluster analysis) are complex and typically involve the counsel of a statistician. The advantages of such techniques depend on the value of the output or information generated and how useful it is to making marketing decisions.[9]

Maintaining the Database

Databases require constant maintenance. Sales orders must be process through the database, regular management control reports on database activity must be supplied, and so on. The value of the information contained in a database is a direct function of its accuracy and relevance. To ensure the integrity of the database, a firm may assign a staff person or contract with a specialist in database management to handle these tasks.

---

[8] Stone, *Successful Direct Marketing Methods*, 30–32.

[9] C. Ross Harper, "Lists and Databases," *The Direct Marketing Manual* (New York: Direct Marketing Association, 1989), Resource Report 301.01, 1–6.

Other Steps in Direct Marketing Using the Database

In addition to developing and maintaining the database, several other steps must be carefully planned and implemented to conduct a successful direct marketing operation. These steps include establishing clear-cut objectives for each program, selecting an appropriate offer, testing the offer, selecting the most appropriate medium to convey the offer to prospects, and fulfilling the offer. These steps are followed by an evaluation of the program's operation and success and planning for future offers (refer again to Exhibit 11.1)

Current Trends in Direct Marketing: Web-based Direct Marketing and E-mail Marketing

Lists

High-quality lists are essential to the success of a direct marketing campaign, as more information provides a higher probability for a sale. More detailed lists can be obtained through Web sites and other surveys, which can include information such as hobbies, marital status, and past purchases.[10] Enhanced lists can be used for more targeted direct marketing campaigns, which use different approaches, depending on key consumer factors, and have the ability to be more effective than one general campaign.

Web-Based Direct Marketing/Social Media Integration

Web-based direct marketing campaigns are on the rise and will continue to be integrated with traditional direct mail methods. E-mail marketing is popular for its low cost as compared to direct mail marketing.[11] It will continue to be used because of the ability for segmentation, Web analytics, and integration with social media. E-mail allows for segmented lists that can be personalized with the messages most likely to lead that customer to buy, leading to larger return on investment, ROI. Web analytics can be used to track response to e-mails, allowing for focus on the approach that is most effective at revenue generation. Integration with social media campaigns can be accomplished by attaching social media sites to ads or other direct marketing, continuing to establish a personal relationship through various platforms at a very low cost.

E-Mail Marketing

E-mail marketing can be very effective, but certain rules should be followed. E-mail is a personal tool of communication and should be kept as a two-way dialogue between brand and customer. Good positioning is needed, as well as a solid offer, for the campaign to be successful. In addition, e-mails should always to relevant and take advantage of the ability to communicate real up-to-date news.[12]

---

[10]The Ballantine Corporation. "Direct Marketing Trends for 2010." February 3, 2010. Web, February 20, 2010. <http://www.ballantine.com/dmtrends2010.pdf>

[11]Ibid.

[12]Cone, Steve. "Digital Marketing Guide: E-mail." *Advertising Age.* February 22, 2010. Web, March 2, 2010. <http://adage.com/digital/article?article_id=142228>

Integrated direct marketing efforts need to focus on one cohesive message that is targeted to the specific consumer, as the message must still make it through a cluttered atmosphere. As these methods continue to become more targeted due to advances in technology, such as using mobile devices, direct marketing will become "greener" by reducing waste and is especially cost effective during economic downturns.[13]

SUGGESTED READINGS

Author Blattberg, Robert C., 1942– Title *Database marketing: analyzing and managing customers/ Robert C. Blattberg, Byung-Do Kim, Scott A. Neslin.* Publication Information New York: Springer, 2008.

Author Hughes, Arthur Middleton. Title *Strategic database marketing/by Arthur Middleton Hughes.* Edition 3rd ed. Publication Information New York: McGraw-Hill, c2006.

Bickert, Jock. *Adventures in Relevance Marketing.* Denver: Briefcase Books, 1991.

Rapp, Stan, and Tom Collins. *The Great Marketing Turnaround.* Englewood Cliffs, NJ: Prentice Hall, 1990.

Schultz, Don. "Direct Marketing." Chapter 14 in *Strategic Advertising Campaigns.* rd ed. Lincolnwood, IL: NTC Business Books, 1990.

Stone, Bob. *Successful Direct Marketing Methods.* 4th ed. Lincolnwood, IL: NTC Business Books, 1988.

The Direct Marketing Manual. New York: Direct Marketing Association, 1989.

The Retail Revolution: Direct Marketing. Vol. 7. New York: Direct Marketing Association, 1989.

DIRECT MARKETING

Exercises

1. Comcast is the nation's largest cable provider. The company is suffering from poor image, being well known for its inferior customer service, slow technology, and rising prices. With increased competition, Comcast has decided to launch a rebranding effort, changing the name of their cable services to "Xfinity."

    The goal of the new brand is to focus on new products, better technology, and faster speeds. Comcast has decided to express that they are aware of current issues and are now concentrating on becoming innovators of new services.

    A new name may be a better option than trying to reposition the old one, which many customers associate with negative feelings. Comcast hopes that the new Xfinity brand will improve its image and give consumers a better experience with the company.

    Do you believe image advertising will help solve Comcast's problems? Do you feel that a direct-response promotion would be helpful in this instance? Explain your position. How would you suggest Comcast go about running the direct-response promotion?

Source: Worden, Nat. "Comcast Plans Makeover to Improve Its Image with Consumers." *Wall Street Journal,* February 9, 2010. Web, February 9, 2010.

---

[13]"Direct Marketing Trends for 2010."

2. In 2009, U.S. video game sales fell 11% to $10.5 billion. Historically, most games are launched in the final months of the year, so consumers can purchase the games as gifts for children. But, as the target market players grow older, game publishers are realizing they have an audience who can purchase games year-round.

   Because of the holiday slump and taking advantage of the characteristics of their target market, video game publishers are set to release over a dozen major games in the first part of 2010. This will mark an unprecedented change for the industry, and publishers hope to attract an insatiable audience.

   Imagine the video game publishers have chosen to use direct marketing to announce the industry changes. Prepare a direct-response plan for a game publisher. What do you think would be the best direct-response tool to spur sales of video games? How do you suggest the publisher should use direct-response promotions? Explain.

Source: Kane, Yukari Iwatani. "Game Makers Push Beyond Christmas." *Wall Street Journal,* February 10, 2010. Web, February 9, 2010.

Case 11.1

Lady Bird Johnson Wildflower Center (B)[1]

An aspect of the marketing of the Lady Bird Johnson Wildflower Center (WC) that seemed to hold some potential both for increasing the effectiveness of recruiting new members, retaining present members, and soliciting donations was the Center's use of direct mail (see the WC (A) case for background information). Direct mail packages that included a letter along with enclosures (e.g., brochures, seeds, and cards) had been used consistently and successfully for a number of years.

Last March, the Center used Daniller + Company, an Austin-based company that specialized in developing membership and fund-raising programs for nonprofits (see www.daniller.com), to design and implement a direct mail membership acquisition drive. The package mailed included (1) a one-page, front-and-back letter from Executive Director Susan Rieff explaining the benefits of membership, discounts on memberships and emphasizing a canvas tote bag offered as a thank-you gift for new members (see Exhibit 11.1.1); (2) a full-color, two-fold brochure that featured the special gift tote bag and the benefits of membership (see Exhibit 11.1.2); and (3) a one-page, four-color map of the Center with callouts that featured five events held in different facilities on the WF campus and copy that stressed why members would want to return to visit again and again.

The package was mailed in a colorful envelope that featured the Center's flower logo and a prominent message—"Great Fun Enclosed"—on the front of the envelope. The package also included a $2 \times 4.5''$ free admission guest pass valid when accompanied by a member and an addressed return envelope with the message "Rush—New Membership Enclosed!" on front side.

A total of 65,174 of these packages were mailed to a list of prospective new members in selected ZIP Codes 786xx, 787xx, and 789xx that constituted the greater Austin area. The master list used in the mailing consisted of names and addresses from WC house files plus membership/subscriber lists rented from: (1) seven local performing arts, museum, and other organizations; (2) 11 environmental and preservation organizations; and (3) eight selected magazines and catalogues. The 26 lists were selected based on the similarity of the organizations' membership base to current WC members or on the similarity of the subscribers to current WC donors. All these names were merge purged against the WC active member list and do not mail lists to ensure those people were not mailed.

Table 11.1.1 presents a detailed breakdown of these groups, their response rates, plus financial performance data.

---

[1] This case was written by John H. Murphy, The University of Texas at Austin. The case is designed to serve as the basis for classroom discussion and not to illustrate either the effective or ineffective handling of an administrative situation. The case is used with permission granted by Lady Bird Johnson Wildflower Center.

Exhibit 11.1.1 ■ Solicitation Letter Included in the Membership Acquisition Package

4801 La Crosse Avenue
Austin, Texas 78739-1702
512/232-0200
Fax: 512/232-0156
www.wildflower.org

Dear Friend:

Garden. Play. Learn. Hike. Be Outdoors. Enjoy Wildflowers. Love Bluebonnets. Have Fun. Get Eco-friendly. Gaze at Even More Wildflowers.

Life doesn't get any better!

It's why I take great pleasure inviting you to become a Lady Bird Johnson Wildflower Center Member and add great fun to your outdoor adventures this year.

To encourage you to join the Wildflower Center right away we are <u>**offering a deep discount on three of our most popular membership levels. You can save up to $15 when you respond by May 15**</u>.

You'll find dozens of reasons to visit the Wildflower Center year 'round, with so much for you and your family to see and do on our 279 acres.

Your discovery tour will take you along nature trails, under live oaks, and through landscaped gardens surrounding rustic, limestone buildings. Or you might prefer to join a summer *Nature Nights* exploration, when you'll learn why owls hoot and secrets of Hill Country pollinators. Or sign up for a *Go Native U* class to hone your gardening skills.

When you join now, I will add you to the <u>invitation list</u> for our special <u>Members-Only Preview</u> for the wildly popular *Wildflower Days – Spring Plant Sale & Gardening Festival*.

On April 11 you'll come to the Center, ahead of the Wildflower Days weekend crowds, and shop from a dizzying array of native plants (using your 10% Member discount). Many are old favorites and others are hard to find. Bring all your gardening questions to get expert advice on how to make your own garden thrive. Bring your kids, too, for fun at our Little House.

As an even greater incentive to join now <u>I am also including a free admission Guest Pass</u>, for you to treat guests to a Wildflower Center visit. (It's up to a $35 value!)

Invite your neighbors or friends to spend a morning or afternoon exploring our wildflower gardens, hiking a trail, or watching your kids learn smart ways they can be eco-friendly, from gardening to recycling, and more.

The Wildflower Center was founded in 1982 to help preserve and restore the beauty and the biological richness of North America. Since then the Center has become one of the country's most credible research institutions and effective advocates for native

(over please)

Exhibit 11.1.1 ■ Continued

plants. Your membership will help support some of our crucial initiatives, including our:

- <u>Plant Conservation Program</u> that protects the ecological heritage of Texas.
- <u>Native Plant Information Network</u>, a database of more than 6,800 native species and 20,000 images, available online at our web site, www.wildflower.org.
- <u>And our newest, Sustainable Sites Initiative</u>, in collaboration with the American Society of Landscape Architects and the United States Botanic Garden, to create "green" guidelines for large-scale landscapes that promote land development and management practices to protect and heal our environment.

It means <u>your membership benefits you and our environment</u>. You're making a difference to our world, while having great fun with family and friends . . . at *Wildflower Days Festivals* in spring and fall . . . *Go Native U* . . . an endless array of lectures showing you how to practice environment-friendly native plant gardening . . . and more!

As a Member you'll receive <u>**a special welcome gift, a canvas duck tote bag with a vivid sunflower design**</u>, and you'll enjoy all these outstanding benefits:

- **Free admission** for you and your family (depending on your Member level), non-Members pay up to $7 each visit.
- **10% discount** on purchases at the <u>Center's gift store</u> and at www.wildflower.org.
- **Discount** on fees to the Center's <u>educational events</u> such as *Go Native U*, and early admission and discounts for our extraordinary bi-annual plant sales.
- **Generous discount** for products and services from our <u>Associate Nurseries</u>.
- **Reciprocal privileges** at more than 300 of North America's top botanic gardens.
- **Free annual subscription** to *Wildflower*, our full-color magazine as well as e-alerts, e-calendars, and more!

When you join now you are guaranteed these special benefits at the <u>discounted rate of $55 for a Family</u> (normally $65). But, please hurry, as we can only make this <u>offer available through May 15</u>.

I hope I am the first to welcome you to the Wildflower Center this spring, as a Member!

Sincerely,

Susan Rieff

Susan K. Rieff
Executive Director

P.S. I've reserved your **welcome gift**, a handy canvas sunflower tote bag. Also, please save the enclosed **free admission Guest Pass**, and invite friends to join you when you visit the Wildflower Center, as a Member!

Exhibit 11.1.2 ■ Membership Brochure

Membership
Benefits and Privileges

$40 Individual
- Free admission to the Wildflower Center year-round for one adult
- Free Wildflower Center canvas duck cloth tote bag, with a vivid sunflower design
- Early admission and discounts at our bi-annual plant sales
- Discounts on fees to most educational events at the Center
- Complimentary subscription to *Wildflower*, our full-color quarterly magazine
- Access to *Mr. Smarty Plants*, our ask the expert e-mail service
- 10% Member discount on everything in our gift store and online at www.wildflower.org; PLUS a 10% Member discount at the 48 Smith & Hawken garden stores nationwide

- Generous discount for products and services from Wildflower Center Associate nurseries and landscaping professionals nationwide
- Reciprocal privileges at more than 300 of North America's top arboreta, gardens, and nature centers

~~$50~~ $45 Dual
All benefits above for Member plus spouse or guest.

~~$65~~ $55 Family — Save $10!
All benefits above for two adults and children under 18 living in the same household, or visiting grandchildren under 18, plus:
- Children are eligible to join our fun and educational EcoExplorers Club at 50% off

~~$100~~ $85 Supporter — Save $15!
All benefits above, plus:
- Free admission for two additional guests each time you visit
- Invitations to Members-Only Exhibit Openings and Special Events

$250 Contributor
All benefits above, plus:
- Free admission for two additional guests each time you visit (total of 4)
- Two free wristbands to the annual Gardens on Tour event ($50 value!)

$500 Sustainer
All benefits above, plus:
- Recognition in Wildflower magazine
- Free admission for two additional guests each time you visit (total of 6)
- Invitation to the Annual Gala

$1,000 Champion
All benefits above, with additional special recognition for this leadership level of support.

Questions about Membership? Contact us at 512/232-0200 or member@wildflower.org

Lady Bird Johnson Wildflower Center
4801 La Crosse Avenue
Austin, Texas 78739-1702

A Special Gift

Join the Wildflower Center and we'll say thank you with this great canvas sunflower tote bag.

Another Great Reason to Join as a Member Today! Use the enclosed Free Guest Pass to bring a couple or family to visit with you, FREE. Have Great Fun together at the Wildflower Center.

Table 11.1.1 ■ Lady Bird Johnson Wildflower Center Spring Acquisition Campaign Financial Summary

Client:	Lady Bird Johnson Wildflower Center										
Project:	Spring Acquisition Campaign										
Drop Date:	3/3–3/7										
First Receipt:	3/17										
Last Receipt:	6/09										
Financial Date:	6/11										
L1	Local Package										

Client Code	List	# Mailed	# Contrib.	% Contrib.	Avg. Gift	Total Income	Total Cost	Net Income	Income PPM	Net PPM Income	Return/ $ Invested
08S01L1	Lapsed Members panel 1	319	11	3.45%	$45.45	$500.00	$169.27	$330.73	$1.57	$1.04	$2.95
08S02L1	Lapsed Members panel 2	2380	68	2.86%	$61.31	$4,169.00	$1,262.86	$2,906.14	$1.75	$1.22	$3.30
08S03L1	Lapsed Members panel 3	1191	21	1.76%	$58.10	$1,220.00	$631.96	$588.04	$1.02	$0.49	$1.93
08S04L1	Lapsed Members panel 4	1308	12	0.92%	$48.33	$580.00	$694.04	–$114.04	$0.44	–$0.09	$0.84
08S05L1	Lapsed Members panel 5	1333	11	0.83%	$48.64	$535.00	$707.31	–$172.31	$0.40	–$0.13	$0.76
08S06L1	Lapsed Members panel 6	1763	10	0.57%	$48.00	$480.00	$935.47	–$455.47	$0.27	–$0.26	$0.51
08S07L1	Lapsed Members panel 8	2727	20	0.73%	$81.25	$1,625.00	$1,446.98	$178.02	$0.60	$0.07	$1.12
08S08L1	Miscellaneous 1	431	11	2.55%	$52.09	$573.00	$228.69	$344.31	$1.33	$0.80	$2.51
08S09L1	Miscellaneous 2	25	0	0.00%	$0.00	$0.00	$13.27	–$13.27	$0.00	–$0.53	$0.00
08S10L1	Miscellaneous 3	66	2	3.03%	$40.00	$80.00	$35.02	$44.98	$1.21	$0.68	$2.28
08S11L1	LBJWC store buyers	1509	3	0.20%	$45.00	$135.00	$800.69	–$665.69	$0.09	–$0.44	$0.17
08S12L1	LBJWC Visitor log names	292	5	1.71%	$48.00	$240.00	$154.94	$85.06	$0.82	$0.29	$1.55
08S13L1	Miscellaneous 4	237	3	1.27%	$43.33	$130.00	$125.76	$4.24	$0.55	$0.02	$1.03
08S14L1	Miscellaneous 5	484	3	0.62%	$200.00	$600.00	$256.82	$343.18	$1.24	$0.71	$2.34
08S15L1	Long lapsed members	5322	27	0.51%	$56.85	$1,535.00	$2,823.92	–$1288.92	$0.29	–$0.24	$0.54
	All above—House Files										
08S16L1	Architecture Organization	576	3	0.52%	$61.67	$185.00	$305.63	–$120.63	$0.32	–$0.21	$0.61
08S17L1	Classical Performing Arts	1204	7	0.58%	$56.43	$395.00	$638.86	–$243.86	$0.33	–$0.20	$0.62
08S18L1	Classical Performing Arts	2250	9	0.40%	$84.44	$760.00	$1,193.88	–$433.88	$0.34	–$0.19	$0.64
08S19L1	Art Museum	3146	46	1.46%	$56.13	$2,582.00	$1,669.31	$912.69	$0.82	$0.29	$1.55

Continued

Table 11.1.1 ■ Continued

Client Code	List	# Mailed	# Contrib.	% Contrib.	Avg. Gift	Total Income	Total Cost	Net Income	Income PPM	Net PPM Income	Return/ $ Invested
08S20L1	Homeowners Association	2790	20	0.72%	$54.15	$1,083.00	$1,480.41	−$397.41	$0.39	−$0.14	$0.73
08S21L1	Performing Arts	1848	11	0.60%	$50.00	$550.00	$980.57	−$430.57	$0.30	−$0.23	$0.56
08S22L1	Museum	2688	30	1.12%	$52.60	$1,578.00	$1,426.29	$151.71	$0.59	$0.06	$1.11
	All above—Local Organization										
08S24L1	Environmental Organization	63	0	0.00%	$0.00	$0.00	$40.13	−$40.13	$0.00	−$0.64	$0.00
08S25L1	Environmental Organization	771	4	0.52%	$55.00	$220.00	$421.74	−$201.74	$0.29	−$0.26	$0.52
08S26L1	Nursery—Natives	1440	10	0.69%	$51.00	$510.00	$764.08	−$254.08	$0.35	−$0.18	$0.67
08S27L1	Environmental Organization—Animals/Birds	723	11	1.52%	$46.36	$510.00	$394.17	$115.83	$0.71	$0.16	$1.29
08S28L1	Environmental Organization	1123	17	1.51%	$49.41	$840.00	$613.53	$226.47	$0.75	$0.20	$1.37
08S29L1	Environmental Organization—Animals/Birds	1718	17	0.99%	$47.94	$815.00	$1,188.87	−$373.87	$0.47	−$0.22	$0.69
08S30L1	Environmental Organization	900	6	0.67%	$23.33	$140.00	$588.33	−$448.33	$0.16	−$0.50	$0.24
08S31L1	Environmental Organization—Magazine sub.	154	4	2.60%	$44.50	$178.00	$81.71	$96.29	$1.16	$0.63	$2.18
08S32L1	Environmental Organization—Animals/Birds	200	3	1.50%	$61.67	$185.00	$108.91	$76.09	$0.93	$0.38	$1.70
08S33L1	Environmental Organization—Animals/Birds	822	8	0.97%	$45.63	$365.00	$559.04	−$194.04	$0.44	−$0.24	$0.65
08S34L1	Environmental Organization—Animals/Birds	10	0	0.00%	$0.00	$0.00	$5.31	−$5.31	$0.00	−$0.53	$0.00
	All above—Environmental/Preservation										
08S35L1	Lifestyle Catalog	3821	24	0.63%	$50.21	$1,205.00	$2,610.89	−$1,405.89	$0.32	−$0.37	$0.46
08S36L1	Women's Apparel Catalog	679	6	0.88%	$49.17	$295.00	$445.79	−$150.79	$0.43	−$0.22	$0.66
08S37L1	Home Catalog	2788	21	0.75%	$50.48	$1,060.00	$1,789.36	−$729.36	$0.38	−$0.26	$0.59
08S38L1	Non-profit Member/Magazine	3803	17	0.45%	$66.47	$1,130.00	$2,574.97	−$1,444.97	$0.30	−$0.38	$0.44
08S39L1	Gardening Catalog	446	4	0.90%	$57.50	$230.00	$285.19	−$55.19	$0.52	−$0.12	$0.81
08S40L1	Non-profit Member/Magazine	3474	19	0.55%	$45.42	$863.00	$2,285.37	−$1,422.37	$0.25	−$0.41	$0.38
08S41L1	Gardening Catalog	1563	15	0.96%	$60.33	$905.00	$1,028.95	−$123.95	$0.58	−$0.08	$0.88
08S42L1	Travel Magazine—local	3133	30	0.96%	$51.57	$1,547.00	$2,175.18	−$628.18	$0.49	−$0.20	$0.71
	All above—Magazine Catalog										
08S43L1	2x+ Multibuyers	3654	31	0.85%	$54.77	$1,698.00	$1,938.86	−$240.86	$0.46	−$0.07	$0.88
	Totals	65,174	580	0.89%	$55.57	$32,231.00	$37,882.31	−$5,651.31	$0.49	−$0.09	$0.85

The total cost of the program billed to the WC was $37,882 and does not including WC staff time devoted to the project. This total cost billed by Daniller + Company breaks down as follows:

Artwork design[2]	6%
Printing	36
Production	10
Copy writing[3]	6
Management/consultation fee	7
Lettershop[4]	11
List rental	15
Computer services[5]	5
Misc[6]	4
TOTAL	100%

[2]Includes two rounds of revisions.
[3]Includes two rounds of revisions.
[4]Includes inkjetting the reply form, sorting, applying nonprofit stamp, delivery to post office.
[5]Includes merge/purge/NCOA.
[6]Includes shipping, contingency for additional plates/proofs/courier charges.

Five hundred and eighty responses were received (0.89% response rate) most of which were new members (approximately 95%) but a few were contributions. The average membership fee and/or gift was $55.57, and total income generated by the package was $32,231. Hence, the program lost $5,651.

In reviewing the results of the program, Ms. Saralee Tiede, Director of Communications, wondered about other commercially available mailing lists and e-mail files that might be used to more efficiently recruit new members and perhaps donors. Although individuals who resided in the greater Austin area and the state of Texas logically appeared to be more attractive prospects, she wondered if non-Texans with a special interest in the WC's mission and activities might be more ideal prospects. But how could these individuals be identified and contacted via a mailing or e-mailing?

In addition, there were questions about the cost-efficiency and attractiveness of incentives to stimulate individuals to become new members. What about attractiveness of the tote bag? Did the brochure soliciting new members and included in mailing package strike the correct tone and feature the most appealing benefits? Was the use of a tear out card in the brochure that had to be mailed to the Center the most appropriate response vehicle? What about emphasizing joining via the WC website instead?

Was there some distinctive strategy that the WC might employ to motive recipients of their mail packages to open and then act on their mailers? Could some sort of "teaser" direct mail campaign be designed that would prove effective? Are there seasonal timing factors that might be important in stimulating responses? These and a myriad of other questions seemed appropriate in light of the less than break-even performance of the most recent membership acquisition mailer.

Name _____ Date _____

QUESTIONS FOR DISCUSSION AND REVIEW

1. What conclusions seem justified regarding the performance of the membership acquisition program? What might account for the variations in response rates across the lists? What clues are provided in terms of selecting lists for future mailings?

   _____
   _____
   _____
   _____

2. How might the March membership acquisition program be strengthened?

   _____
   _____
   _____
   _____

3. Based on the information provided, what is the profile of the best prospects to become members of the WC? How difficult would these ideal prospects be to identify and reach via direct marketing?

   _____
   _____
   _____
   _____

4. Is the cost of the various membership levels likely to be a deterrent to increasing new members? What role did the items included in the package likely play in influencing the response rate? What other factors play an important role in determining how attractive joining the WC is to prospective members?

   _____
   _____
   _____
   _____

5. How might the WC most effectively use direct mail to stimulate prospects to join the Center? How might the Center most effectively use direct mail to stimulate membership renewals?

_____

_____

_____

_____

Case 11.2

Bethany College[1]

UNIVERSITY BACKGROUND

Bethany College (BC), founded in 1881, was a small private liberal arts college located central Kansas in Lindsborg. BC was a college of the Evangelical Lutheran Church in America, and its mission was to "educate, develop, and challenge individuals to reach for truth and excellence as they lead lives of faith, learning and service." BC was a four-year, undergraduate, residential college. The students were required to live on campus to increase community interaction. BC offered majors in each of the following departments: Education, Teaching Endorsements, Humanities, Fine Arts, Sciences, Social Sciences, as well as Pre-Professional Studies. The average on campus residence total cost for room and board, tuition, fees, and so on was $26,110.

STUDENT DEMOGRAPHICS

Admitted students had a minimum of a 2.5 GPA, typically scored between a 22 and 27 on the ACT and were in the top half of their high school class. Forty-nine percent of BC's students were from Kansas, 11% from Colorado, and 5% were international. The faculty to student ratio was 11:1. BC's total enrollment was 554 students. The majority of students, 77%, were Anglo-American, 8% African-American, and 15% Other.

COMPETITION

There were 18 small private colleges in Kansas, and seven of these schools were within a 70-mile radius of BC. Also included in BC's competition were the large state schools, University of Kansas and Kansas State University. BC administrators felt that BC needed to differentiate itself from all of these schools by using a personal approach that was reflected in all of their communications.

MARKETING EFFORTS AND GOALS

Prior to the past year, BC had experienced declining enrollment, prospects, and overall application numbers. Because BC was a small university and had tough competition, attaining and keeping students was difficult. To better market the University, BC's admissions officers decided to use the marketing team from The Whelan Group, a marketing consulting company based in Austin, Texas.

The goal given to The Whelan group was to market Bethany as a transformational experience for students and to more precisely target prospective applicants based on their specific areas of interest. Also, one of Whelan's objectives was to develop and implement a marketing plan that encouraged prospective applicants to use text response, email, and other interactive tools.

---

[1]This case was written by John H. Murphy and Michelle Troutt, The University of Texas at Austin. The case is designed to serve as the basis for classroom discussion and not to illustrate either the effective or ineffective handling of an administrative situation. Used by permission granted by Bethany College.

The authors thank Kevin Cassis of the Whitley Company/Whelan Group for his help in developing this case.

The Whelan Group specialized in marketing educational institutions. Their skill set included recruitment solutions that spanned "creative services, publications, interactive media, personalized direct mail and online services, the Web, and other possibilities. But what we really do was transform how admissions offices operate—in all facets of student recruitment." With 30+ years of experience in higher education marketing, and because of their extensive and specialized services, BC believed Whelan was an appropriate choice to help revitalize their marketing efforts in the face of declining applications and admissions. See a list and brief description of Whelan's services in Exhibit 11.2.1.

BC's past marketing efforts had been traditional outreach that included viewbooks, letters, and postcards. The envelope used for the direct mail was white with a small logo in the top left corner. After BC enlisted The Whelan group to help in April of last year, BC began using Whelan's publication development, college branding, search campaign coordination, email blast deployment, personalized landing pages, text response, and printing. The envelopes and postcards Whelan prepared were oversize and interactive pieces, which gave the applicants many different ways to respond. See Exhibit 11.2.2 for an example of the post card series and a large personalized mailer.

RESULTS

The primary objective for BC was to increase qualified applicants and ultimately the student population. At the end of the year, BC saw a 24% increase in applications, a 28% increase in accepts and a 45% increase in "Honors Student Day" attendees. BC also increased their direct mail response 200% or an absolute 3% (going from 1.5% to 4.5%) from the previous year. Also, with these new marketing efforts there were 145 more individual campus visits than the year before.

Naturally, Tricia Hawk, BC's Dean of Recruitment and Marketing, was thrilled with these results. The programs implemented by The Whelan Group far exceeded her expectations for the year.

FUTURE MARKETING EFFORTS AND GOALS

BC's future goals included increasing the enrollment to 800 students, improving the student demographic, and making sure BC offered the right programs for students of today. In order to achieve the 800 students goal, even more effective and efficient marketing programs would be needed. Ms. Hawk wondered if the mix of Whelan program had been optimal? Is so, should she repeat the mix for the coming academic recruitment period?

This raised a host of other questions about possible ways to increase the effectiveness of their efforts. For example, how could the present BC students be effectively incorporated into their recruitment efforts? What aspects of BC student life should be featured most prominently? What was the profile of the ideal candidate to enroll in BC? What geographic areas in Kansas and beyond were most likely to yield the largest number of applicants and why?

Ms. Hawk's first task was to respond to The Whelan Group's inquiry about continuing or modifying last year's program for the coming year. Although many questions related to additional opportunities were swirling around, the first step was to select the mix of Whelan programs to employ in the coming recruitment season.

Exhibit 11.2.1 ■ The Whelan Group Marketing Services

Whelan Group Services	Used by BC	Definition
Branding	√	The creation of a college or university brand. This development would include all communication efforts to support the brand. A brand is a collection of words, images, ideas, and emotions that comes immediately to mind when someone thinks about a College or University.
Development Campaigns		The development of marketing campaigns for alumni, fundraising and offices of development at Colleges and Universities. I.e., Case statement development, alumni outreach and communications via print email and other social media.
Direct Mail Search		The Whelan Group's Zoom Solutions encompass a powerful suite of direct mail search marketing options. Our 30+ years of experience in successfully driving response rates through various direct mail efforts are sure to help your college or university recruit, retain and realize: more qualified leads, less "fluff" in your inquiry pool, targeted search marketing efforts, a better ROI for your search marketing dollars.
Editorial Consulting		Writing, editing and development of copywriting for various communications. I.e., Writing of a school viewbook or email campaign.
Email Marketing	√	The development of email campaigns to be sent to prospective students and/or other constituents. The Whelan Group coordinates the creative development, HTML designs and sending and tracking of the emails. I.e., We coordinate email campaigns to be sent to all prospective students notifying them of admission deadlines.
High-definition Printing	√	Also known as frequency-modulation screening, high-definition screening uses tiny dots of ink spread randomly throughout the image surface and varied in density. With its computer-to-plate screening capabilities, The Whitley Printing Company can increase the normal 175-line screen resolution to over a 400-line screen equivalent. The result is a sharper image with finer details, near photographic quality, and more consistent tone and colors. Benefits: increased speed to market, reproduction of very fine detail, elimination of jagged edges and screen angle moirés.
Institution Identity	√	

Continued

Exhibit 11.2.1 ■ Continued

Whelan Group Services	Used by BC	Definition
List Management		We manage the prospective student purchased list coordination from various list providers such as ACT, SAT, College Board, and NRCCUA. We purchase, check for duplicates and coordinate the communication stream for student names from the lists.
List Purchase Consulting		We provide consultation on the strategy of who and where to purchase names. I.e., Some schools (such as Bethany College) might want to test new markets in which to purchase names to attract students. We can advise on which students might be most likely to respond based on a number of factors such as family income, location, academic standing among others.
Logo Creation		The development of a college or university logo or even program logo. I.e., We have developed school-wide logos or even logos for just athletics.
Mobile Marketing	✓	The development of a marketing campaign using "texting" to communicate with prospects.
Online Applications	✓	The development of web based applications for admission. Our clients can track student application progress and students can submit online.
Photography		The coordination of photo shoots on campus. The Whelan Group also employs experienced higher education photographers.
Positioning Strategy	✓	Research on where a college or university is positioned in the marketplace and how they can utilize this knowledge to better market themselves amongst their competitors.
Predictive Modeling		The Whelan Group's Predictive Modeling Services employ advanced techniques for list purchases, search mailings and collateral mailings—including applications, visit requests and financial need campaigns. Purpose: to provide additional information for each record in a client's database that will help the client identify individuals that are more likely to respond, apply and enroll.
Recruitment Publications	✓	The development of recruitment publications, which include designing, copywriting, photography and printing, or all college and university recruitment publications. I.e., These may include viewbooks, financial aid pieces, open house invitations, postcards, letters, etc.

Continued

Exhibit 11.2.1 ■ Continued

Whelan Group Services	Used by BC	Definition
Response Analysis	√	Analyzing the response to a certain mailing or communication outreach and making recommendations on further communication efforts based on response or lack thereof.
Scriptwriting		Writing for TV and radio advertising.
Student Yield Marketing	√	Developing marketing solutions to prospective students after they have been accepted to the college or university. The goal for this type of marketing is to drive tuition deposits. I.e., Web based yield sites for accepted students only, communication outreach via email and/or mail.
Video Development		The coordination and development of college and university videos.
Web Development	√	The development of college and university websites.
Web Site Design	√	Design for websites and or web pages. These can be simply templates to provide the schools that they can take and use in their own IT departments.

Exhibit 11.2.2 ■ BC Colatteral Materials Produced by The Whelan Group

Postcard Series

Large Format Window Envelope

Name _____   Date _____

QUESTIONS FOR DISCUSSION AND REVIEW

1. Considering the target market that BC was trying to reach (16- to 18-year-old male or female applying to college), which mix of Whelan's services would reach the most applicants and/or be the most effective?

   _____

   _____

   _____

   _____

2. What additional information about the target market would be most helpful to develop a marketing strategy for BC?

   _____

   _____

   _____

   _____

Case 11.3

Harvard Business School 9–500–048
Rev. June 20, 2000

MARKETING TO GENERATION Y

On May 12, 1999, Matt Diamond, James Johnson and Sam Gradess were visiting San Francisco for a last round of meetings with West Coast investment analysts. They were just days from the initial public offering (IPO) of shares in Alloy.com, the catalog and Internet merchant of teen-oriented clothing that they had founded on Diamond's graduation from Harvard Business School in 1996. Snarled in freeway gridlock, Diamond was on his cellphone discussing the IPO's pricing with analysts back in New York City.

An analyst urged Diamond to respond to an invitation by the world's largest Website and portal, America Online (AOL), to make Alloy an anchor tenant on its teen shopping site. AOL wanted $2 million per year for the rights. "Matt, if you say yes, that will be big. If you announce tomorrow that AOL's partner in the Generation Y market is Alloy, it will put Alloy on the map. It will definitely affect the IPO price."

Diamond sighed. A headline deal with AOL today could be worth perhaps 10% on the stock price. But AOL was asking rich terms. It was widely rumored that AOL preyed on startup companies in the weeks before they went public, tempting them with star billing on its portal at the very moment when the publicity was most valuable. He estimated that he'd be paying a $45 cpm (cost per thousand exposures) to anchor the AOL teen shopping site. Nobody paid more than $30 for Web eyeballs. In the three years that he had been running Alloy, Diamond had prided himself on doing deals that made sense. If he could not anticipate a profit to Alloy from a promotional deal, he reasoned that Wall Street would not anticipate a profit either.

"It won't pay out," he told the analyst firmly. "We only do deals that produce value." To his colleagues in the limousine, he wondered out loud, "Am I right?"

Professor John Deighton and Visiting Scholar Gil McWilliams prepared this case as the basis for class discussion rather than to illustrate either effective or ineffective handling of an administrative situation. The contribution of Ann Leamon, Manager, Center for Case Development, is gratefully acknowledged. Certain sensitive information in this case has been disguised and should not be regarded as informative as to the prospects of the company.

Copyright © 2000 by the President and Fellows of Harvard College. The Case was prepared by John Deighton and Gil McWilliams as a basis for class discussion rather than to illustrate either effective or ineffective handling of an administrative situation. Reprinted by permission of the Harvard Business School.

THE GENERATION Y MARKET

Termed the "hottest demographic of the moment," Generation Y came to the attention of marketers in the late 1990s. This "echo of the baby boom" was made up of children and teenagers born in the United States between 1975 and 1989 and therefore aged between 10 and 24. They were estimated to be a 56 million strong group of actual and potential consumers, some three times the size of their immediate predecessor, Generation X.[1] The U.S. Census Bureau projected that the 10 to 24 age group would grow from 56.3 million to 63.1 million by 2010, growing faster than the general population.

Although Generation Y matched its parent's generation in size, in almost every other way it was very different. One in three was not Caucasian. One in four lived in a single-parent household. Three in four had working mothers.[2] "Body glittered, tattooed, pierced, they're a highly fragmented, unpredictable group of teenagers who, while tottering around on five inch soles, voice conservative opinions about sexuality, government, the American dream and an end-of-century commitment to spirituality."[3] They were computer literate: 81% of teens used the Internet, according to Chicago-based Teenage Research International (TRI), which also noted that over a 3 month period on AOL, they posted more than 2 million Leonardo Di Caprio related messages.[4]

According to Lester Rand, Director of the Rand Youth Poll, they had money to spend and an appetite for spending it.

They have a higher incremental allowance from their parents, and with the growth in our service economy, they are able to secure jobs easily and at rising minimum wages. They're exposed to so many different products on TV, in the mall and through their friends. It's a generation who grew up with excess as a norm.[5]

In 1999 Jupiter reported that 67% of on-line teens and 37% of on-line kids said they made use of on-line shopping sites, either buying or gathering information about products.[6] Generation Y was expected to spend approximately $136 billion in 1999, before accounting for the group's influence on purchases made by parents and other adults. (See Exhibits 11.3.1 and 11.3.2 for this and other estimates.)

ON-LINE COMPETITION FOR GENERATION Y SPENDING

Generation Y's size and spending power had not gone unnoticed. Many conventional and on-line retailers courted them. Alloy viewed its most significant competitors as dELiAs and the online magalog mXg. The neighborhood mall was also a threat.

---

[1] Neuborne, Ellen and Kathleen Kerwin. "Generation Y," *Business Week,* February 15, 1999, Cover story.

[2] Neuborne, Ellen and Kathleen Kerwin. "Generation Y," *Business Week,* February 15, 1999, Cover story.

[3] O'Leary, Noreen. "Marketing: The Boom Tube," *Adweek,* Vol. 39, No. 20, May 18, 1999, pp. S44–S52.

[4] Brown, Eryn. "Loving Leo Online," *Fortune,* April 12, 1999, p. 152.

[5] BAXExpress, July/August 1999, http:baxworld.com/baxexpress/0799/consumers.html.

[6] Sacharow, Anya. "Shadow of On-line Commerce Falls on Postmodern Kids," Jupiter Communications report, June 7, 1999.

Exhibit 11.3.1 ■ Total Teen Spending in 1996

	$ billions	%
Apparel	36.7	34
Entertainment	23.4	22
Food	16.7	15
Personal Care	9.2	9
Sporting Goods	6.7	6
Other	15.3	14
Total	108.0	100

Source: Packaged Facts via InterRep Research, in MSDW Equity Research: "Fashions of the Third Millennium," June 1999.

Exhibit 11.3.2 ■ Estimates of Teen Spending

	Rand Youth (Adweek May 18, 1998)	Morgan Stanley Dean Witter's Report "Fashions of the Third Millennium," June 1999	Teen Research Unlimited (quoted in Alloy press handout)
1996		$108 billion	
1997	$91.5 billion		
1998			$141 billion
1999		$136 billion	

Delias Inc.[7]

The largest on-line and catalog merchant serving Generation Y was New York-based dELiAs, with 1998 sales of $158 million. Founded in 1995 by two 33-year-old former Yale rooommates, Stephen Kahn and Christopher Edgar, dELiAs sold through print catalogs mailed to more than 10 million recipients, of whom 6 million had bought within the past year. It managed its own order fulfillment from a warehouse complex, and operated twenty conventional retail stores. Most of dELiAs' 1,500 employees were under 30. Its phone representatives were often high school and college students, and they frequently offered fashion advice as well as taking orders. In November 1998 dELiAs Inc. paid $4.75 million for the trademarks and mailing lists of bankrupt Fulcrum's 5 catalogs (Zoe for teenage girls, Storybook Heirlooms, Playclothes, After the Stork, and Just for Kids), giving them 5 million names which nearly doubled their database. It also paid $2.4 million for merchandise from Zoe and Storybook.

---

[7]Information drawn from company website: www.dELiAs.com

By 1999, dELiAs went to market with a complex set of brands and marketing methods:

- The dELiAs brand marketed to teenage girls as a catalog through the mail and as dELiAs*cOm on the Web.
- The gURL.com Website was an on-line magazine for girls and young women, carrying articles as well as free e-mail, free homepage hosting and publishing tools, and links to a network of third-party sites for girls and women. gURL was the only property that was not engaged in commerce.
- The droog brand marketed apparel to 12-to 20-year-old males through the mail and on-line.
- The TSI Soccer catalog sold soccer gear by mail and on-line.
- Storybook Heirlooms retailed apparel and accessories for girls under 13 by mail and Web catalog.
- Dotdotdash sold apparel, footwear and accessories for girls aged 7 to 12 by mail and Web catalog.
- Discountdomain.com was a subscription Website selling discounted close-out merchandise.
- Contentsonline.com offered unusual home furnishings, light furniture and household articles to females aged 13–24. While predominantly a Web catalog, the property appeared intermittently as a print insert in dELiAs' print catalog.

In April 1999, dELiAs Inc. spun off its Internet properties in an IPO, selling shares in a company called iTurF which earned revenues from all of the above on-line elements. In terms of the deal, these on-line businesses could advertise in dELiAs' print catalogs at a rate of $40 per 1,000 catalogs. The dELiAs catalog, 60 million of which were printed in 1998, had the largest domestic circulation of any publication directed at Generation Y. The on-line magazines also shared the parent company's 354,000 square foot distribution center in Hanover, PA. Because iTurF did not take ownership of inventory until a customer's order was placed, the risk of obsolescence and markdowns remained with the parent company. iTurF shared offices with the parent company, enjoying a submarket rent for New York metropolitan space.

In May 1999, iTurF announced record quarterly sales of $2.6 million (up from $0.69 million in the first quarter of 1998). Gross profit was $1.3 million, or 49.1% of revenues, up from $0.34 million or 49.3% of revenues 1998 (see Exhibit 11.3.3). However, dELiAs reported that it expected its iTurF unit to report a loss for the fiscal year. By April 1999, the number of people who had ever bought at the iTurF Websites was 66,000 (up from 35,000 at the end of December 1998), and the number of unique visitors was 731,000 in April 1999 alone. Analysts estimated that each customer cost $26 to acquire.[8] Private label merchandise accounted for 40% of iTurF's sales, in line with dELiA's ratio.

iTurf entered into agreements with RocketCash Corp and DoughNET, companies that had been established to let parents control the on-line spending of their children. For example, RocketCash let parents establish a credit card account and set each child's access to specific merchant sites, times of operation, and the option to set up an auto-allowance to periodically replenish the account. DoughNet was a virtual debit card that parents could set up for their children. Parents could customize DoughNET's site to guide teens through all aspects of managing their money.

In April 1999, dELiAs' decision to spin off iTurF seemed shrewd. The market capitalization of dELiAs Inc. was $90 million, on sales of $200 million annually. ITurF was capitalized at $200 million on a sales run rate of $12 million annually.

---

[8]CIBC World Markets, Equity Research, June 2, 1999.

Exhibit 11.3.3 ■ Consolidated iTurf Income (in $ thousands)

	1st Quarter Ending 1 May 1999	1st Quarter Ending 30 April 1998
Net revenues	2615	69
Cost of goods	1332	35
Gross profit	1283	34
Selling, general and admin.	1753	109
Interest income (expense)	(112)	11
Loss before tax	(358)	(86)
Income tax (benefit)	(161)	(33)
Net loss	(197)	(53)
No. of unique visitors	Apr 99 = 731,000	Feb 99 = 635,000
No. of page views in April	50 million	4 million
Size of mailing database	11 million names	
Source: IPO Filing		

MXG MEDIA INC.[9]

Hunter Heaney and Stuart MacFarlane graduated from the Harvard Business School in 1996. MacFarlane joined Bain & Co. and Heaney joined BancBoston Robertson Stephens. Heaney told how he got the idea for mXg while Christmas shopping at Nordstrom's for his then girlfriend. A saleswoman had told him that the "Y" necklace featured on the "Friends" sitcom was in style. "I knew there had to be a more direct way to find out about fashion trends influenced by entertainment," Heaney said.[10]

In 1997, Heaney and MacFarlane quit their jobs and moved to Manhattan Beach, CA, to be close to Hollywood and surfers and skaters. Using the pay phone while staying at a local motel they raised $250,000 in increments of $5,000, and launched mXg, styling it a "magalog," a hybrid of catalog and magazine, aimed at teenage girls. Unlike a conventional magazine, mXg reported exactly where to go to buy the fashion items that it featured on its pages. MacFarlane recalled their early lean times: "Typically, retailers order inventory in sixes (one small, two medium, two large, one extra large). But instead of saying 'We'll take 2,000 sixes' we said 'We'll take six'– literally one of each." They could fund a circulation of only 20,000 for the magazine's launch in the fall of 1997, but it did well. Some 5% of the recipients bought from it. The numbers were good enough to induce Urban Outfitters, a retail fashion chain, to invest $5 million for 40% of the company, incorporated as mXg Media, Inc.

---

[9]Information drawn from company website: www.mXgonline.com

[10]Waxler, Caroline. "Guys with moxie," *Forbes,* May 31, 1999, pp. 130–131.

Merchandise accounted for most of mXg Media's revenues, but advertising revenue was doubling each issue. The company used newsstand distribution (150,000 issues per quarter at $2.95 each, refunded with a purchase), as well as distribution in bookstores like Barnes & Noble, and B Dalton Booksellers. The magazine had a pass-along rate of almost six readers per copy.

Sensitive to the tastes of their target audience of female teenagers, they hired teens, paying them $7 per hour to work after school answering letters, doing interviews, and writing copy to make it sound authentic. "No printed word goes out without a teen girl checking it . . . being uncool is the kiss of death in this business."[11] At the start of each fashion season mXg recruited 30 "Moxie girls" to spend a hypothetical $150 each. Their virtual purchases determined which items appeared in the next issue. The magazine paid staffers to model clothes and invited would-be teen celebrities to pose free to gain recognition.

A Website, mXgonline.com, was established in the summer of 1997. It comprised a magazine, chat rooms, and community sites, and sold clothes and accessories. mXg Media pursued other access points for their on-line magalog, featuring it in on-line fashion malls such as fashionwindow.com. In 1999, mXg sponsored concerts featuring acts like Gus Gus which were favored by Generation Y. Yahoo produced a series of Webcasts of the concerts for teens. The company described its mission as cross-media publishing, targeted exclusively at teen girls. It planned to add mXgtv, an Internet video site, to its media portfolio later in the year.

A CROWDED MARKETPLACE?

Other companies vied for the attention of Generation Y. Bolt.com was a content-based magazine-type site skewed towards a market slightly older than that of the Generation Y market, but into which the older end of the Y market might eventually fall. Bolt.com included sections titled jobs, money, movie reviews, music, news and issues, sex and dating, and sports. It had a chat room and free e-mail, and sold branded merchandise. It boasted that 5,000 people joined it every day.

The magazine *Seventeen* had an on-line version, offering chat rooms and message boards, as well as its regular articles, quizzes and features. Indeed many magazines were now launching on-line versions of their magazines, and new print publications like *Twist* and *Jump* had appeared to compete for generation Y advertising revenues.

Broader on-line retailers served this market, such as bluefly.com selling discounted brands on-line. Strong competition came from mall-based stores such as The Buckle, Gadzooks, Abercrombie & Fitch, The Gap, American Eagle Outfitters, and Guess, all of whom sold merchandise on- and off-line. Apparel and sportswear manufacturers were developing on-line sales sites. Nike and Tommy Hilfiger planned to launch e-commerce sites with broad product offerings.

ALLOY.COM

As a Harvard MBA student in 1996, Matt Diamond wrote a business plan proposing the idea of marketing 'extreme sports' clothing by catalog to young people in Japan. The premise was that the popularity of this style of clothing among American youth might generate demand abroad, and that catalogs would be able to tap that demand faster than would store distribution. On graduation, Diamond implemented the plan. He and a friend, Jim Johnson, used seed money from friends and family to design and print a Japanese-language catalog, which they branded Durango Expedition. They mailed it in January 1997, and at the same time they went live with Japanese and English Websites, as alternative channels.

---

[11]Waxler, Caroline. "Guys with moxie," *Forbes,* May 31, 1999, pp. 130–131.

The venture flopped. The mailing generated no significant sales. However, they discovered to their surprise that they were receiving hits on the English Website from American youths. Within a month they had reconceptualized the business to serve American teen girls through catalog and on-line channels, under the name Alloy. Diamond and Johnson each contributed $60,000 in cash and another friend, Sam Gradess added $150,000 in cash when he joined six months later from Goldman Sachs. In November 1997, the first issue of the Alloy catalog, 48 pages in length, was mailed to a purchased mailing list of 150,000 teen names. At the same time Alloy's Website became active. The intention at that time was to reduce the number of catalogs mailed as on-line sales grew.

ORGANIZATION

Diamond became president and CEO of the fledgling company. Johnson took the title of chief operating officer. Gradess was chief financial officer. Neil Vogel joined from Ladenburg Thalman & Co., a consumer and Internet investment banking group to be the chief corporate development officer. Fellow Harvard sectionmate, Andrew Roberts left PricewaterhouseCoopers to join Alloy in January 1999 as VP of business development. Another Harvard MBA, Joan Rosenstock was hired as marketing director, having held positions in marketing at the National Basketball Association as well as in advertising account management. Erstwhile, music editor of teenage magazine *Seventeen,* Susan Kaplow, became executive editor and Karen Ngo, who had been a feature editor and fashion stylist at *Seventeen,* was hired as creative director.

Alloy outsourced as many of its operations as it could. Working with mostly domestic vendors who could produce and ship within a 2–8 week timeframe, Alloy purchased only 50% of its featured products and relied on a quick order and re-order ability so as to control inventory levels. Telephone orders and order-processing were outsourced to Harrison Fulfillment Services, based in Chattanooga, TN. OneSoft Corp., based in Virginia, handled on-line ordering and fed its orders to Chattanooga for fulfillment. Alloy personnel concentrated on marketing and merchandising issues.

TARGET MARKET

Unlike dELiAs, Alloy opted for a single-brand strategy targeted at both genders. "Rather than dividing our marketing resources across multiple brands and Websites, we seek to maximize the impact of our marketing efforts by promoting a single brand. We believe this allows us to attract visitors to our Website and build customer loyalty rapidly and efficiently."[12] Indeed Diamond considered that Alloy's key differentiator lay in being gender neutral, believing that a successful Generation Y community depended on dynamic boy-girl interaction. He thought of their community site as an MTV-like interactive distribution channel. "It's an opportunity for girls to talk to boys, boys to talk to girls, to deliver music, to deliver fashion, to deliver lifestyle." Diamond conceded that the majority of the visitors to its Website were girls, and the print catalog was even more skewed towards girls. However, it was the intention to attract boys to the Website by other means. There was some evidence that this strategy was working, as the percentage of female Website visitors declined from 70% in early 1999[13] towards a desired 60/40 ratio. Boys tended to be drawn by music, extreme sports and games, while girls appeared to be more responsive to chat and browsing. Diamond felt, however, that just as both teen boys and girls hang out in shopping malls, watching each other as well as chatting, the on-line presence of both boys and girls was important.

---

[12] IPO Offer Document May 1999.

[13] Chervitz, Darren. "IPO First Words: Alloy Online CEO Matt Diamond." Interview at CBS MarketWatch.com, June 14, 1999. http://cbs.marketwatch.com/archive/19990614/news/current/ipo_word.htx?source=htx/http2w&dist=na

Alloy's target was teens making buying decisions with parents "somewhere in the background." The target group ranged from 12–20, but the median age was 15. Alloy was careful not to aim too young, partly for regulatory reasons, but also because they felt that by targeting 15-year-olds they reached a group at an important buying point in their lives. About 35–40% of teenage purchasing was on apparel and accessories, and Alloy monitored what else this group bought. As owners of a "piece of real estate" they did not see themselves as limited to selling apparel and accessories, and had moved into soft furnishings.

THE OFFERING

It was standard practice among catalog retailers, such as Lands End and LL Bean, to sell products under the catalog's brand. Even at dELiAs, private-label sales accounted for about 40% of the mix. Alloy, however, emphasized recognized teen brands such as Vans, Diesel, and O'Neill, both to attract buyers and to offer reassurance of quality. Only 20–25% of Alloy's sales came from labels that were exclusive to Alloy, such as Stationwagon and Local 212. Diamond was philosophical about the pros and cons of private label, "There's no denying you get better margins on own-label goods. But running with your own labels leaves you vulnerable to ending up as a skateboard brand."

The Alloy site aimed to build what Diamond termed the 3 Cs of on-line retailing to this generation: Community, Content, and Commerce. He noted that constant communication was key to understanding this generation. They had a strong need to chat about movies, television, music and what was happening at school, and to seek advice from one another, sound off about pet hates, and occasionally shop.

A small team of in-house editors created editorial content on the site, supplemented by syndicated content. The audience also contributed content, receiving in exchange a sense of community, in chat-rooms and message boards, and by submitting their own letters, poems, drawings and articles. Poems and drawings would be voted upon interactively. Chat rooms in particular were popular and frequently full (in contrast to some of the chat rooms of competitors). The chat rooms were moderated from end of school-time until midnight on a daily basis, with software employed to spot offensive or obscene language. Advice columns were a dependable magnet. (See Exhibit 11.3.7 for a sample of user-generated content.)

Andrew Roberts remembered vividly the moment when he knew that Alloy was really "onto something." In the aftermath of the Columbine High School shooting tragedy, one of the editors knew that Alloy had to respond and fast. She worked all night creating the appropriate spaces in chatrooms, and editorial content. By 8:30 a.m. the day after, 15 hours after news of the tragedy broke, Alloy had received 7,311 postings related to the events at Columbine. Roberts explained that it wasn't so much the number that impressed him, but the content of the postings. "These kids were really anxious. We had kids who followed the goth fashion who were really scared about how others would treat them. Other kids were reassuring them and saying "Don't worry, we know it wasn't you or the goths who made these guys do what they did." They just had a desperate need to talk with each other, and be reassured by each other."

BUILDING THE BRAND

Alloy built its brand, and with it traffic to the Alloy site, in several ways. It undertook traditional advertising in print media *(Seventeen Magazine, YM, Rolling Stone,* and *Snowboarder)*. It used hot-links from sites such as seventeen.com to advertise promotional deals. It had special co-promotional deals with, for example, MGM Entertainment, Sony Music, Burton Snowboards, MCI and EarthLink/Sprint, who provided free products and services that were used as special promotions for the Alloy community (such as private movie screenings, exclusive music give-aways, and celebrity on-line chats). Finally, it bought banner advertising on gateway sites such as Yahoo Shopping, Fashionmall.com, CatalogCity.com and CatalogLink.com.

THE BUSINESS MODEL

There were two revenue streams: merchandise sales, and advertising and sponsorship. An agent had been retained to sell advertising on the Website, and the longer-term intention was to build an in-house sales force to sell sponsorships, banner-ads, targeted advertising (segmented by Website area, time of day, user location, or age), and combination print and Website advertising. To this end, Samantha Skey, who had been responsible for commerce, advertising and sponsorship for Disney Online and Family.com and had worked for Buena Vista Internet group, was hired in 1999 as VP of e-commerce and sponsorships. In 1999, about 10% of revenues were generated by sponsorship and advertising deals, and the proportion was expected to rise to 20% in year 2000. Alloy was aware that it would never meet all of its customers' requirements. It was happy to offer links to other sites that could be seen as competitive, such as Gap's on-line site. "Look, we figure they're going to go there anyway," noted Roberts. "If they go via us, we at least get something for it. We're happy to have such complementary deals. Probably not with dELiAs, though," he grinned.

Exhibits 11.3.4 and 11.3.5 report annual fiscal year performance 1996–1998, and quarterly performance between last quarter 1997 and first quarter 1999.

To hear Diamond describe it, running Alloy was, at least day-to-day, like running a production plant. "We know what it costs to get a customer, and we know what a customer will spend. We just have to keep the two numbers in balance. We could make a profit today, but in this investment climate there's no reward for beating your loss numbers."

By April 1999, Alloy had a database of 2.6 million names and addresses, comprising 1.7 million previous buyers and 900,000 visitors to the Website who had registered their names and addresses. It was mailing monthly to the most responsive of the names on this list, supplemented by purchases of new names, and it hoped to mail 20 million catalogs over the course of 1999.

Alloy's catalogs cost $450 per thousand to design, print and mail. If Alloy mailed catalogs to names from the database who had bought from it before, it received an order from about 3% of the names each time it

Exhibit 11.3.4 ■ Alloy Online Annual Fiscal Performance

Fiscal Year	1996	1997	1998
		(thousands)	
Net merchandise revenues	$25	$1,800	$10,100
Of which on-line order placement accounted for:	—	$40	$710
Sponsorship and other revenue	—		$125
Gross profit %	32.5%	41.7%	46.3%
Selling & Marketing expenses	$98	$2,000	$9,200
Web pages views (Month of March)		1,500	25,000
Weekly e-zine registrations			480
Source: Company records			

Exhibit 11.3.5 ■ Alloy Online Quarterly Performance

	1997 31 Oct	1998 Jan 31	1998 Apr 30	1998 Jul 31	1998 Oct 31	1999 Jan 31	1999 Apr 30
	($'000)						
Net merchandise revenues	401	1396	1353	2082	3215	3436	2391
Sponsorship, etc.	—	—	1	5	46	73	163
Total revenues	401	1396	1354	2087	3261	3509	2544
COGS	263	783	906	1200	1665	1715	1249
Gross profit	138	613	448	887	1596	1794	1305
Gross profit % of revenue	34%	44%	33	42.5%	49%	51%	51%
Operating expenses	903	1437	1782	2992	3396	2679	3529
Net loss	(749)	(806)	(1312)	(2165)	(1901)	(985)	(2302)
Number of registered users						400,000	800,000
Source: Company records							

mailed. If Alloy bought a list of new names, for example a list of American girls who owned personal computers, at a cost that was typically $100 per thousand names, the response rate on the new names[14] was about 1.5%. Alloy would often exchange some of the names of its customers for the names of customers of similar firms, if it could count on a response rate on the swapped names of close to its own 3%. By blending names from these three sources, Alloy could choose whether a particular mailing would yield a high rate of orders or expand its customer base. Over the year, Alloy's mailings comprised 10% swapped names, 70% past customers and 20% new names. Diamond found that some people in the private investment community were not well informed on the ease with which response rates could be manipulated. "Analysts ask me, why is your response rate down last month? I say 'you want a 10% response rate, I'll give you one. I'll just mail to my very best customers."

Most orders were received by telephone, and orders from all lists ranged from $65 per customer in spring to $85 in winter. The gross margin on an order was about 50%. Alloy paid its fulfillment company $6.00 to handle each telephone order. Customers paid the shipping charges.

Traffic to the Website, as measured by Media Metrix in the quarter ending March 1999, comprised 263,000 unique visitors[15] per month. While about half of the visitors eventually registered themselves with the site by entering a name, address and e-mail information, the proportion of unique visitors in a month who registered in that month was about 8%. In addition to catalogs and Web visits, Alloy interacted with Generation Y by means of a weekly broadcast e-mail, Alloy E-Zine, sent to 850,000 site visitors who had asked to receive it.

---

[14]List brokers typically sold names on a 'deduplicated' basis, meaning that the buyer had the right to delete and not pay for any names that it already owned.

[15]Many of the visitors to a site came more than once a month. Media Metrix used the term "unique visitors" to emphasize that they were counting visitors, not visits.

When a visitor to the Alloy Website registered, the name was added to the print catalog mailing list. Names gathered in this way, although they had not previously bought from Alloy, tended to respond to the catalog at a rate close to the past-buyer rate of 3%. Calculating the cost of attracting someone to become a registered visitor was difficult, because Web traffic resulted from many actions: banner advertising, listings on search engines, and Alloy's print advertising in media like *Seventeen Magazine*. The catalog was a significant driver of traffic to the Web. On the day that the catalog reached its audience, traffic to the site would jump 40%. It would continue to rise to about 180% of pre-mailing levels for a week, and slowly fall back. Possessing a copy of the latest Alloy catalog conferred significant prestige in a junior high school lunchroom. And then there was word-of- mouth. Many visitors to the Website, and many who decided to register, came at no cost to Alloy because a friend had mentioned the site, had e-mailed a chat room story, or had asked for an opinion on an item of clothing shown on the site.

Less than 5% of Alloy's revenues came from orders placed on the Website. When an order was submitted on-line instead of by phone, Alloy paid its fulfillment company $3.00 instead of $6.00 to reflect the saving of telephone handling charges. Alloy's e-mailed catalog, termed Alloy E-Zine, was another small element of the business. Because Alloy had no way of knowing whether a recipient's e-mail system was able to view graphic displays or color, it used only text in the E-Zine. Only 25% of those who indicated willingness to receive it ever opened it, and of those 1% placed an order in the course of a year. These orders were fulfilled at $3.00 each if they were placed by return e-mail.

Sponsorships and banner advertising were a small but rapidly growing source of revenue. As Alloy's base of registered visitors and catalog recipients grew, both became assets that interested advertisers.

THE AOL DEAL

Diamond reflected on the AOL deal. It was not a question of finding $2 million. If the IPO went ahead at the planned price of $15, it would generate $55.5 million and Alloy would be awash in cash. Diamond tried not to be annoyed at the idea that AOL would offer this deal on the eve of his IPO. "I've been talking to AOL for a year about opening a teen shopping area, showing them what a big revenue opportunity it could be. Now suddenly they get it, and they think it's worth $2 million."

He thought to himself, "What else can I do with $2 million? That's over 4 million catalogs, which means more sales, more site visits, more registrations, and more E-Zine registrations. Alternatively, it could buy us exposure on television, and that would build a stronger brand." Alloy's budget for 1999 included a line item of $2.5 million for production of two television spots and $2.5 million for air time.

Yet AOL was Alloy's most important source of traffic to the Website. More than a third of visitors to the Alloy site used AOL as their Internet service provider. Would a competitor on the AOL site be able to intercept them? Would the announcement of a competitor's deal with AOL on the eve of the IPO be as bad for Alloy's share price as an Alloy deal would be good?

The cellphone rang again. It was his partner, Neil Vogel. "Matt, Wall Street would like it if you would do that deal. They don't want iTurF to pick it up. This is valuable real estate on a really important teen property."

Exhibit 11.3.6 ■ Circulation of Leading Teen Magazines

Publication	Publisher	Circulation as of 1998/99
Seventeen (monthly)	Primedia Consumer Magazine Group	2,400,000
Teen (monthly)	EMAP	2,400,000
YM (10 × year)	Gruner & Jahr	2,200,000
Teen People (monthly)	Time Inc.	1,300,000
Jump (10 × year)	Weider Publications	350,000
Twist (monthly)	Bauer Publishing	265,650
Girl	Lewitt & LaWinter/Freedom	250,000
Source: Various		

Exhibit 11.3.7 ■ Examples of Consumer-Generated Content on Alloy Website

ASK TUCKER
today's advice:

Q. Here's the deal. I have a crush. I really want to ask her out, but, if she says no, my social life will be totaled. She's pretty popular and if she says no, she'll tell someone and it will all go down the drain. I live in a small town and whoever gets dumped (for some reason) loses their popularity. What do I do????

more ask tucker...
DATING
CRUSHING
FRIENDS
FAMILY
SEX
SCHOOL
FASHION
OTHER RANDOM STUFF

dizzy

Perfection and bliss riding on a dizzy
cloud of euphoria and joy
Blissfully falling into your strong arms
You sweep me up and clutch me close
I can't breathe and I can't think anything but you
Choking from the pure ecstasy of unconsciousness I awaken in a breathless
wonder
I am alive in a whirlwind of color
And I am floating
In your arms breathing
In your scent laughing
In your soul living
In your mind crying
In your emptiness and then gone

Source: Alloy Website

Chapter 12
Public Relations

I am a firm believer in the people. If given the truth, they can be depended upon to meet any national crisis. The great point is to bring them the real facts.

—Abraham Lincoln

WHAT IS PUBLIC RELATIONS?

Public relations has been defined in many ways throughout the years. The Public Relations Society of America (PRSA) in 1982 formally adopted a definition of public relations, which remains widely accepted today:

Public relations helps an organization and its publics adapt mutually to each other.

Today, public relations is an important and integral component of a company's integrated communication with all of its publics. In the past, the function of public relations was mostly confined to issuing press releases and responding to press inquiries. Many more functions are now part of public relations, such as event sponsorships, interacting with all the other communication functions of a company, developing charitable activities, and participating in most promotional activities of a company.

Basically, public relations professionals are charged with maintaining positive relationships with third parties on behalf of their company. Third parties are a company's customers, a company's employees, financial investors, and the public as a whole. The means by which public relations maintains such positive relationships is through the use of persuasive and purposive communication.

The term "public relations" is very general and often it is confused or used as a synonym of other terms, such as corporate communications, public information, and public affairs, to name a few. Public relations officials are all that. In many ways, they are responsible for the relationship a corporation establishes with its internal and external publics, and they are responsible for being aware of and responding to governmental and social reactions to a company's actions.

Unlike the other forms of marketing communications, public relations operates through unpaid channels. This means that it has less control on how its communication efforts will play out. As an example, a press release announcing the development of a new product may not be picked up by the press, or if it is, it may not highlight the innovative characteristics of the product that were outlined in the press release.

Therefore, we must consider the primary task of public relations that of casting the company and its products in a favorable light among the general public. That will be an important positive addition to the company's brand perception and equity, and ultimately complement all its other marketing communication efforts.

TRADITIONAL PUBLIC RELATIONS ACTIVITIES

Some of the traditional public relations activities have not changed, as the world of media and communication has been transformed by digital technology. Some of those activities are issuing press releases; researching and finding key facts to respond to press inquiries; coordinating and training spokespeople to respond to the press; developing and providing a list of public speakers that can be used in communication to the press and in interviews with the press; establishing routine communication with investors and potential investors and interacting with the financial management of the company; organizing publicity events such as the opening of new facilities, the announcements of charity drives, and other grand opening ceremonies; and developing communication instruments for employees, prospective employees and other internal publics of the company.

Public relations officials are engaged in such activities still today. However, rather than working in isolation, they now have become a much more integral part of the total communication program of a company. It is essential, therefore, that they be part of the overall strategy a company develops to reach all its publics. Today's public relations professionals must be knowledgeable of all the other aspects of a firm's marketing strategy, such as product development, distribution, and advertising.

PUBLIC RELATIONS AND IMC

Thomas L. Harris, in his book, *Value Added Public Relations,* makes very clear what the new role of public relations is. Quoting Tom Duncan, the director of the integrated communications graduate program at the University of Colorado, he states:

> *"In marketing, synergy means that when all products and corporate messages are strategically coordinated, the effect is greater than when advertising, sales promotions, public relations, etc., are planned and executed independently, with each competing for budgets and power, and in some cases sending out conflicting messages."*

Therefore, public relations must be seen as an integral part of integrated marketing communication. Many new product promotions today start with public relations messages and press releases rather than an advertising campaign. In many cases advertising campaigns are complemented by charity drives organized and negotiated by public relations officials to improve and develop positive reactions from the market.

Public relations is viewed as a more credible communication tool than advertising, because it is not paid and because of its interaction with the press. Credibility adds to the value of public relations as a means to increase brand equity and the public image of a company. Public relations messages are often delivered by "objective third parties," journalists, and as such are perceived as more credible.

THE NEED FOR RESEARCH

Research is an essential part of the public relations process. Public relations officials must gain the important information concerning the facts and opinions affecting a company's image. Careful research is also important in identifying the target audiences that must be reached by the public relations messages, their characteristics, their expectations, and their perception of the information they have received.

In addition, research must be a part of the measurement of public relations results. How else would a company know whether the communication program it has adopted has in fact produced the desired results? Therefore, research is not only the assessment of facts before issuing communication messages, but also monitoring results of the communication after the program has been established.

Research includes the collection of secondary information and scientific existing knowledge as well as primary research designed to understand public attitudes and opinions. Public relations audits, social audits, communication audits and environmental monitoring are necessary and effective methods of research for public relations.

A public relations audit is the most frequently used research tool by public relations professionals. The audit is a broad-scale study that examines the internal and external public relations of an organization. The audit is very important in that it provides information for future planning efforts.

Usually an audit starts with the development of a list of relevant publics. Those are all the individuals who have functional relationships with a company, but it also includes people who do not have an organizational relationship but who are in a position to affect the organization. Some examples are environmental agencies, public interests groups, and social interests groups.

The second step of the audit is to verify the organization's standing with its publics. Each group is analyzed using secondary and primary research methods, such as review of previous research, review of published materials, consumer and special interests blogs, as well as conducting in-depth personal interviews with influential members of each group or conducting a survey of public knowledge, opinion, and attitudes towards the company.

The research results will yield a list of those issues that are of concern to the various publics of the company. These findings will guide the strategy of communication the company will adopt and also should be compared to the organization's existing policies to verify differences in what the company thinks it is communicating and what is actually perceived and understood by its publics.

Finally, the audit will result in concrete recommendations for future action that will permeate all the public relations and integrated communication activities of the company. An audit is only useful if its findings lead to appropriate changes and improvements in communication.

SOME MODERN PUBLIC RELATIONS ACTIVITIES

Among some of the more recent activities performed by public relations professionals are event sponsorships, stunt marketing, and charitable donations or cooperative events, to name a few. This portion of the chapter will provide an overview of how such activities are an important part of the overall IMC strategy of a company.

Event Sponsorship—most major sporting events as well as most cultural and major charity events in the United States have a commercial sponsor. A sponsor receives multiple mentions of its corporate name and signage, and is mentioned in press reports and articles. Because commercial sponsors help defray the costs of the public to participate in the event, commercial sponsors are usually seen favorably. Commercial sponsors are not only noted by participants in the event, but also by the many audiences that view the event at the time it takes place, or later on, with delayed broadcasting.

Management must make a thoughtful decision when faced with the opportunity to sponsor a sporting or a cultural or charitable event. First, it must weigh the cost of the sponsorship with the potential gains in sales or brand equity it may produce. Those costs must also be compared with alternative means of communication, such as advertising. In addition, a company must choose events that match the firm's promotional goals. Other considerations might involve the negotiation terms for naming rights, tie-ins with products, and overall coordination with all the other media messages the company and the event are planning.

Provisions must be made for possible downsides, related to weather or catastrophic events. Finally, the company must monitor the effectiveness of commercial sponsorships with tracking studies to assess the duration and intensity of the effects on its intended target public.

Stunt Marketing—stunt marketing is the creation of an event for the sole purpose of attracting press coverage. An example of stunt marketing is the Fourth of July Nathan's Coney Island Hot Dog Eating Contest. Stunt marketing events achieve breakthrough awareness, but they are limited in scope because they do not offer the opportunity to give detailed information about the product or highlight the product benefits.

To be effective, a stunt must attract the target market the firm wants to communicate with. In addition, it must have some socially reasonable purpose and provide people with something they can and will appreciate. Unfortunately, some stunts are merely self-serving and they do not benefit companies ultimately. Public relations officials must weigh carefully all the advantages and disadvantages of using stunt marketing.

Charitable events, donations or cooperative events—An example of charitable cooperative donations is the decision of Yoplait yogurt to place a pink ribbon symbol on their containers and announce that for each top of a container mailed back to the company, they would contribute a certain amount to breast cancer research. Charitable giving and charitable events are ways in which a company hopes to be a good corporate citizen and promote a positive image in the community.

Charitable giving must be planned and focus on few areas of donation. Very often these events may be too scattered and therefore will not produce the desired results. In addition, employee participation is perceived as a very positive thing when a company is engaged in a charitable event. Finally, a charitable contribution or participation in a charitable event must not be perceived as self-serving.

Public relations officials must ensure that the company will receive adequate recognition when making charitable contributions. The use of attendee lists for future contacts or for assessing the results of such a campaign are also important tasks for the public relations professionals.

CRISIS MANAGEMENT

One of the most important functions of public relations is that of managing and handling a crisis or potential crisis facing the company. Crisis management is a process by which an organization deals with a major or several unpredictable events, by trying to mitigate or head off the effect of such event or events on the organization or on the general public.

Therefore a crisis can be defined as a threat to an organization that is not predictable (hence the element of surprise), and requires a reaction in a short period of time. Crisis management involves developing and training public relations people in the skills and management techniques required to deal with such threats after they have occurred.

Most institutions will have a series of incident responses processes in place to ensure that the institution reacts properly when an incident occurs. Examples of potential responses are evacuation of buildings when there are threats such as a bomb threat; identification and reporting of the appearance of suspicious persons, and response to emergencies needing medical help. Also, procedures regarding the actual process of communication to be followed and the individuals in charge of making the necessary decisions are usually described in appropriate manuals for public relations people and other officials of a company.

Another element of crisis management is the creation of a crisis team. Southwest Airlines has created such a team and trained a small group of pilots, flight attendants, and other personnel to provide support and assistance to employees, passengers, relatives, and the general public if an accident were to occur. Crisis teams must be cohesive and meet periodically to refresh training skills and be informed of potential changes in the procedures they will follow.

Some companies also have established command centers through which they will operate and direct actions if a major crisis were to occur. Command centers provide decision making, control and communication. In addition, they are also the repository of vital information such as emergency phone numbers and contacts with key managers, and they have established relations with key governmental agencies.

Public relations must ensure that there is a single designated spokesperson for the company. Communication with the media must be consistent and clear, factual and non-emotional. Messages must be crafted carefully before they are delivered, and emergency officials must be consulted before the messages are actually communicated.

Crisis management is a complex and vital function of public relations. It involves action by many officials in a company. The task of the public relations professional is to ensure that crisis management proceeds seamlessly and that the effects of the crisis are as minimal as possible and do not affect the company in an unduly negative manner.

SUMMARY

Public relations is an integral part of a company-integrated communication strategy. Changes in the media and the evolution of communication tactics have changed the traditional role of public relations. Its functions now overlap and are often combined with all the other marketing communication functions. Public relations and advertising often work together to provide audiences with a positive and clear image of a company and its products. Crisis management, a traditional function of public relations, is a complex and important process that may permeate all aspects of a company's image. In trying to attenuate and respond to the effects of a crisis, public relations officials often are responsible for the development of a coordinated and comprehensive plan, which may involve all facets of the organization.

SUGGESTED READINGS

"Integrated Marketing Communications: Creativity, Consistency, and Effective Resource Allocation."
   In Marketer's Toolkit: The 10 Strategies You Need to Succeed. Boston: Harvard Business School Press, 2006.
Harris, Thomas L. *Value Added to Public Relations.* New York: McGraw-Hill, 1998.

Kane, Gerald K., Robert G. Fichman, John Gallaugher, and John Glaser. "Community Relations 2.0." *Harvard Business Review,* November 2009.

Lattimore, Dan, Otis Baskin, Suzette T. Heiman, Elizabeth L. Toth, and James K. Van Leuven. *Public Relations: The Profession and the Practice.* New York: McGraw-Hill, 2004.

PRSA. "Public Relations Defined." http://www.prsa.org/aboutprsa/publicrelationsdefined/

Robinson, David. "Public Relations Comes of Age." *Business Horizons* 49. (2006): 247–256.

PUBLIC RELATIONS

Exercises:

1. British Petroleum (BP) in 1987 acquired shares of Standard Oil and Britoil, in 2000 acquired Atlantic Ritchfield, and in 2001 it merged with Amoco, becoming BPAmoco. In 2002 it dropped Amoco from its name and called itself BP, with no official name assigned to the letters. The company wanted the renaming to announce a growth from oil to energy and a step toward a green future. BP's rebranding efforts began with the establishment of its Helios mark, identified with its efforts towards the use of solar energy.

    A major advertising campaign accompanied those efforts and the "beyond BP" or "beyond petroleum" theme was launched by Ogyilvy & Mather and was supplemented by "BP on the street" public relations campaign that asked everyday folks to offer their opinions on global warming and alternative energy. BP was putting all its communication tools at work to be recognized as an environment-friendly company.

    In 2010 disaster happened. A deep well in the Gulf of Mexico exploded, killing several workers and causing a major ocean oil spill.

    At first, BP officials assured the public that they had the situation under control and that they would soon take measures to contain the spill. Over 40 days later, the situation had worsened, and none of the engineering solutions BP had attempted had been able to repair the damage. The oil continued to flood the ocean and to pollute the coast.

    About three weeks after the incident, the management of BP admitted that this was a major catastrophe and committed all its resources to resolve the situation. The press was calling the spill the worst catastrophe in the history of oil exploration.

    What kind of potential actions could BP take to attempt to diffuse the anger the oil spill has caused in the United States and worldwide?

    Can BP recover from this disaster?

    What can public relations do to help in this situation?

2. Toyota, a major global manufacturer of automobiles, was faced with trying to reestablish public trust in the quality of its products. In 2009 and 2010, several Toyota car models were connected with unexpected and uncontrollable acceleration. Several people were injured as a consequence of these occurrences. Toyota's management first attributed the incidents to faulty floor mats on the driver's side that were prone (according to the company) to get attached to the accelerator. Toyota recalled thousands of cars and replaced the mats. The incidents continued to occur. Toyota's management maintained there was no mechanical or electric problem with the cars.

    By early 2010, the recalls were in the hundreds of thousands. Finally, Toyota management acknowledged there might be a problem with specific cars, but offered no explanation of what that problem might be.

    Several months later, Toyota is facing the challenge of convincing the public, its customers, and potential customers that its products can be relied on. What kind of public relations activities could help Toyota restore its corporate image? Discuss.

3. Action, a leading manufacturer of sports equipment, enlisted as a spokesperson in 2000 a worldwide famous soccer player.

The soccer player appealed both to male and female audiences. Soccer was a popular professional and recreational sport. Families in general were very supportive of soccer as a sports activity for their children. The manufacturer was using a profile image of the soccer player as part of its brand for both adult and children soccer clothing and equipment.

Sales increased by 10% each year since the company enlisted its soccer spokesperson. The increase in sales also affected products for other sports such as basketball and baseball.

During the winter of 2009, a tabloid reported that the soccer player had been charged with possessing a collection of child pornography on his private computer. Two weeks later, the soccer player and spokesperson for Action admitted to possessing child pornography and having it on his personal computer. At the same time, he publicly apologized and promised to give up the activity and to undergo psychological treatment for his problem. His wife appeared at his side at a press conference and pledged to support him.

What should Action do under the circumstances? What do you suggest can be done to restore consumer's confidence in the brand?

"BP Struggles to Hit Right Note in Response to Oil Spill," by Michael Bush, *Ad Age,* May 3, 2010. "BP and Corporate Greenwash," Richard Joey School of Business, case #905C10.

Case 12.1

Amy's Ice Creams (B)[1]

MEDIA RELATIONS

Given Amy's Ice Creams marketing philosophy of not using traditional advertising, publicity or free media coverage of the firm had been critical to the firm's success (A). Hence, Teresa Noll, Amy's Operations Manager and in charge of marketing, was particularly interested in maximizing the amount of media coverage of Amy's and the firm's support of local causes, charities, zany/fun promotions, its business operation, employees, and so on.

Ms. Noll was excited about a new, special promotional event that was planned for January 1st of next year that seemed to be ripe with possibility in terms of attracting not only local Austin but also state-wide and perhaps national media coverage. The guerilla promotion would be tied into a "Keep Austin Weird"[2] type annual event: the Austin Polar Bear Swim at the City of Austin Parks & Recreation Department's Barton Springs outdoor pool. The Barton Springs Polar Bear Club had more than a hundred members sponsor the event.

In following a guerilla marketing strategy, one of Amy's SWAT vans (see Amy's (A) case Exhibit 3.2.5) along with three Scoops dressed in cow costumes (see Exhibit 12.1.1) would be prominently parked just outside Barton Springs pool entrance in Zilker Park on the morning of the January 1st Polar Bear Swim. At the conclusion of the swim each participant would be given a free cup of Amy's ice cream. In addition, the winner of the swim would be given a certificate worth a free serving of Amy's ice cream every day for the entire month of January at any of Amy's locations.

Amy's presence at this event, as well as the novelty of ice cream at a January swimming event, would likely generate positive word-of-mouth discussions about Amy's among both participants and spectators. Further, this wacky reward to swimmers should generate positive publicity and exposure for Amy's during the slow winter sales period for ice cream. Ms. Noll felt that Amy's unexpected presence will stimulate potential customers to "weird-out" and regard ice cream as a great idea in cold weather. The event also would likely be a positive way for Amy's to further establish its presence within the community as an Austin original that supports originality and fun.

As Ms. Noll reflected on the event, she wondered how to stimulate the widest possible media coverage of Amy's participation in the Polar Bear Swim. Further, she wondered if some aspects of Amy's participation should be modified or enhanced to increase the newsworthiness of the event. For example, might Scoops dressed in cow costumes deliver press releases to local print and broadcast media? Which content providers and organizations should send emails alerting them to the event? Or, might a special flavor of Amy's ice cream be created that would be appropriate for giving away at the event? What plans should be made to photograph or film the distribution of Amy's ice cream to the swimmers?

---

[1] This case was written by John H. Murphy, The University of Texas at Austin. The case is designed to serve as the basis for classroom discussion and not to illustrate either the effective or ineffective handling of an administrative situation. The case is used with permission granted by Amy Simmons, Founder and CEO of Amy's Ice Creams.

[2] The phrase "Keep Austin Weird" was coined by Red Wassenick in an off-hand comment in a phone call to an Austin radio station. The slogan and logo as printed on bumper stickers and t-shirts reflected a desire to maintain a culture in Austin that honors and celebrates artistic and individual expression. Austin is "weird" compared to the rest of Texas because it is more progressive politically, socially, and culturally.

Exhibit 12.1.1

Name _____ Date _____

QUESTIONS FOR DISCUSSION AND REVIEW

1. What news angle or hook would be most effective for developing a press release announcing Amy's participation *before* the event? What about *after* the event?

   _____

   _____

   _____

   _____

2. How might Amy's participation be featured or promoted in the firm's retail locations?

   _____

   _____

   _____

   _____

3. Could Amy's participation in the Polar Bear Swim be featured or promoted online via the Web, for example, using YouTube or social networking sites? What about on Amy's own Web site?

   _____

   _____

   _____

   _____

4. How might the winners of the Swim or participants be utilized for testimonials or in some other way?

   _____

   _____

   _____

   _____

5. Should Amy's contact the Polar Bear Club in advance to alert them to their plan and perhaps enlist the club's cooperation? Or, in the spirit of guerilla marketing, should the Amy's SWAT van just show up at the event?

_____

_____

_____

_____

Case 12.2

Shawntana Development Corporation[1]

Mark Conzelman and Bart Hansen, the co-owners of Shawntana Development, were surprised by the objections they had received in response to a newspaper advertisement for New Chase, their company's first project.

New Chase was a 164-unit condominium project located on a 6.8-acre site in Fountain Valley, California. Three models were available: 56 "Atherton" units were 724 sq. ft., one bedroom and one bath; 52 "Brighton" units were 910 sq. ft., two bedrooms and one bath; and 56 "Sylvan" units were 1,106 sq. ft., two bedroom and two baths. The development was located near many commercial and retail businesses and was classified as "affordable housing." This meant that Shawntana was required to sell 25 percent of its units to households earning no more than 120 percent of the median income in Orange County.

Several months into Phase I of the project, an ad, "Affordable Housing Blues," appeared in the real estate sections of both the *Orange County Register* and the *Los Angeles Times,* Orange County edition. The upper half of the full-page ad was devoted to an original four-verse song with a musical score indicating tune and lyrics in the style of sheet music. Under the title, "Affordable Housing Blues," was the line "Sung to the tune of "Home on the Range." The verses of the song were:

Oh, give me a home, I can afford on my own, where there's room both to work and to play. Where the price ain't absurd, where value's the word and I don't have to drive far away.

Yes, I am confused. Won't you help me please choose, financing that I can repay. Conventional? V A? How about F H A? I hear bond financing's the way?

I do want to own, but I feel so alone. There's really not much left to say. A move to Pomona to become a homeowner is a price I'm not willing to pay.

Then I heard of this place. They call it New Chase, and they say that it's not far away. From a hundred seventy three five, and that ain't no jive. Excuse me, I'll be on my way.

Under the song toward the right side of the page was a line drawing of the entrance to the development with a small map below indicating the project's location. To the left of the line drawing was a copy block that read: "Although there seem to be a lot of folks singn' the "Affordable Housing Blues" lately, we're convinced those folks haven't been to New Chase. So come by and take a look at our 1 and 2 bedroom condominiums. If afterwards, you're still singn' the blues—you must just plain like the blues." The ad signed off at the bottom of the page with the New Chase logo and the following line set in a large type size: "Simply the best designed, best located, affordable housing in Central Orange County. For further information, telephone (714) 531–5223 or visit our website NewChaseCondosOC.com."

After the ad's initial appearance, Shawntana had received several telephone calls and emails from individuals objecting to the derogatory reference to Pomona and requesting that the ad be dropped. When the ad ran again a week later, more calls and emails were received. In addition, Hansen had received a call from the Pomona city attorney, who reported that the ad had been the subject of a heated discussion at the city council meeting. As a result, the council had instructed the city attorney to contact Shawntana and request that the ad be dropped and to mention the possibility of a lawsuit if the ad appeared again.

---

[1]This case was written by John H. Murphy, The University of Texas at Austin. The case is designed to serve as the basis for classroom discussion and not to illustrate either the effective or ineffective handling of an administrative situation. Used by permission of the Shawntana Development Corp. Parts of the Pomona advertising scenario are fictitious.

Pomona had an image problem associated with the industrial nature of its employment base, the activities of local motorcycle gangs, and a high concentration of relatively low-income households. However, before approving the ad suggested by their advertising agency, Conzelman and Hansen had briefly discussed the possibility that some people might object to the copy. In their judgment, the reference to Pomona was nothing to worry about.

Unfortunately, Conzelman and Hansen had been wrong, and this left them in a dilemma. Their first reaction was to simply drop the ad. On the other hand, they felt that the copy referred to something everyone in Orange County was well aware of and, hence, was not out of line. They reasoned that under the First Amendment right of free speech, Shawntana could make such references. Why should they buckle under to the complaints of a few overly sensitive people?

Since the ad was scheduled to appear again the next weekend, they needed to make a decision before the cancellation deadline the next day at 4:00 p.m. Before making a decision, they agreed to contact their public relations and advertising agencies and their attorney for advice.

Name _____ Date _____

QUESTIONS FOR DISCUSSION AND REVIEW

1. What ethical and public relations considerations are raised by the offensive ad and the response of concerned citizens and public officials?

_____
_____
_____
_____

2. If the ad appears again, how likely is the city of Pomona to file the threaten lawsuit?

_____
_____
_____
_____

3. What are Shawntana's options in responding to the request that the ad be dropped?

_____
_____
_____
_____

4. What additional information should Shawntana executives obtain before making a decision about how to respond to the request that they drop the ad?

_____
_____
_____
_____

Case 12.3

Whole Foods Market[1]

In 2008, the U.S. was in the midst of the worst food inflation in 17 years. All over the world, food prices were increasing due to rising commodity and fuel prices, and the phenomenon was only intensified by the global economic slow-down. With food inflation running above four percent, Whole Foods Market® was heavily impacted by these rising costs—just as all food retailers—but unlike many other retailers Whole Foods Market's PR team viewed the economic downturn as an opportunity to tell its value story.

To reassure customers that Whole Foods Market would continue to offer the highest quality natural and organic food products at competitive prices, the company launched a national media relations campaign focused on value. The campaign revolved around education, providing shoppers with tips and information on finding the best deals at Whole Foods Market, and showing customers how to get the most out of their food dollar.

To gain an accurate, objective perspective of the marketplace, Whole Foods Market hired third-party market research firm, Harris Interactive®, to survey organic food shoppers. The purpose of the survey was to determine if shoppers, during times of high food costs, would "trade down" to save money or if they would look for ways to still get "real food" for lower prices. Results showed that most shoppers did not want to compromise on the quality of the food they were buying, and the majority of shoppers were continuing to buy the same amount of natural and/or organic foods as they always had. The survey also found that many adults were preparing more meals at home, using more coupons, or going out of their way to look for lower-cost items as a result of higher food costs. Additionally, results showed that two in three adults prefer to buy natural and/or organic foods to conventional foods if prices are comparable, and they would like to find ways to be able to buy these foods within their budget.

Given the national media interest in rising food costs and the overall economic downturn, the PR team shared this timely data with the media, along with information on recently initiated programs that showed consumers "how to shop Whole Foods Market on a budget." Among many other initiatives at the store, regional and national level, these programs included:

- **"The Whole Deal™"**
  In January of 2008, the company launched *The Whole Deal* coupon and value guide both online (www.wholefoodsmarket.com/wholedeal) and in stores across the country. This monthly value guide shares tried-and-true ways to cut costs—but not corners—when shopping for natural and organic groceries. Each issue of *The Whole Deal* booklet in stores offers more than $20 in coupons and highlights "Sure Deals!"—high quality, popular pantry items with great prices all year long (see Exhibit 12.3.1). More often than not, "Sure Deals!" included products from the company's private label 365 Everyday Value® brand product line that combine high quality and low price. The PR team spread the word about the guide and the best in-store deals by weaving these suggestions and other saving tips into press releases (for example, see Exhibit 12.3.2), always keeping the focus on value.

---

[1] This case was written by Liz Burkhart, Whole Foods Market, and John H. Murphy, The University of Texas at Austin. The case is designed to serve as the basis for classroom discussion and not to illustrate either the effective or ineffective handling of an administrative situation. Use by permission of Whole Foods Market®.

Exhibit 12.3.1

Exhibit 12.3.2 ▪ Feast Fabulously and Affordably

The Whole Deal™ Value Guide at Whole Foods Market® Welcomes Fall & Holiday Seasons with Cooking Tips from Martha Stewart, Sure Deals & Budget-Saving Recipes for Entertaining

AUSTIN, TX (October 2, 2008)—From pan roasting to slow cooking, fall favorites create welcome aromas in the kitchen and savings in the pocketbook, thanks to sure deals, coupons and budget-conscious recipes found in the new quarterly *The Whole Deal*™ value guide at Whole Foods Market (NASDAQ: WFMI).

To help shoppers create healthy, flavorful and wallet-friendly weeknight meals, Whole Foods Market has collaborated with Martha Stewart Living Omnimedia and popular food bloggers who share favorite recipes and cooking techniques.

In the first of Whole Foods Market's "Learn to Cook and You'll Learn to Save!" series, Martha Stewart provides step-by-step instructions for pan-roasting chicken and roasting vegetables from her new book, *Martha Stewart's Cooking School* (on-sale October 21). Martha will also be highlighting recipes like these in new "Cooking School" segments on her syndicated daytime program, "The Martha Stewart Show" beginning October 21.

Additionally, Whole Foods Market launched a Food Blogger Budget Recipe Challenge to find the best, most flavorful and healthy weeknight meal recipes for less than $4 per serving. The six finalists include:

- *Steamy Kitchen's* Wonton Noodle Soup,
- *Cooking for Engineers'* Chicken Marsala with Brussels Sprouts and Capellini,
- *Karina's Kitchen's* Sweet Potato and Black Bean Enchiladas,
- *Bittersweet's* Miso Bulgur Pilaf with Lemon-Ginger Tofu,
- *Coconut & Lime's* Cincinnati Chili, and,
- *Sugarlaw's* Farro with Butternut Squash, Hazelnuts and Swiss Chard.

Through Oct. I, shoppers can log on to http://www.wholefoodsmarket.com/ to rate and review these bloggers' recipes and help choose the Budget Recipe Challenge Winners. Those who post comments are automatically registered to win a $500 gift card and other prizes. The winners will be featured in the January issue of *The Whole Deal*.

Get More for Less from The Whole Deal *Value Guide*

Available in stores Oct. 1, *The Whole Deal* value guide also includes 15 budget recipes for $4 or less per serving and 13 "Sure Deal!" high quality pantry items at great values such as:

- 365 Organic creamy soups in tomato basil, garlic chicken and Portobello mushroom flavors—$2.99 (4 servings at 75 cents per serving)
- 365 Organic Instant Oatmeal in a variety of flavors—$3.39 (eight servings at 42 cents per serving)
- 365 Organic green and black teas—$3.99 (80 tea bags at 5 cents per serving)
- 365 Organic Hot Cocoa Mix in milk or rich chocolate flavors—$3.99 (10 servings at 40 cents per serving)
- Paul Valmer Chardonnay and Merlot—$10.99 for 1.5 liters (six servings at $1.83 per serving)

Exhibit 12.3.2 ■ Continued

"Shoppers ranging from single professionals to large families can find easy and affordable options in *The Whole Deal* like a Twice-Baked Tex-Mex Potato for one to Sour Cream Chicken and Mushroom Pasta for four. Also, adding in seasonal produce like squash and apples provides great nutrition at a value for weekday meals," says Whole Foods Market "Value Guru" Barry Hirsch.

Holiday entertaining on a budget in *The Whole Deal* is a sure deal as well with Whole Catch Crab Claw Meat at $7.99 and 1.5 liters of 365 Everyday Value Paul Valmer Chardonnay or Merlot at $10.99. Shoppers will find many party-friendly recipes in the value guide, including Baked Apple and Brie Canapes, Swiss Cheese Onion Crostini, Quick Creamy Crab Bisque and Beef Brisket with Carrots.

For more ideas on how to save money and eat healthy, Whole Foods Market has plenty of other resources including:

- Value Tours: In-store "Value Gurus" lead Value Tours to show customers how to find the best deals and enjoy savings.
- Special deals in the meat and seafood departments, and knowledgeable butchers and fish mongers who are ready to help shoppers find the top-notch protein that falls within their budgets.
- Promotional deals on family packs and value packs as well as weekly sales and specials.
- *The Whole Deal* online message board with shopper tips and advice on stretching your food dollar found at http://wholefoodsmarket.com/wholedeal.

A recent Whole Foods Market survey found that 43 percent of adults now prepare more meals at home as a result of higher food costs. "As more people choose to 'eat in' to save money, the first step is to learn to cook," says Hirsch. "So we are sharing cooking techniques and recipes to make weeknight meals, fabulous feasts and party favorites that are easy and affordable."

###

For additional information on *Martha Stewart's Cooking School*, visit www.marthastewart.com/cookingschool.

- **Value Tours**
  Stores across the country began hosting guided tours led by Whole Foods Market "Value Gurus" to show customers how to shop the store on a budget (see press release at http://wholefoodsmarket.com/pressroom/blog/2008/06/18/whole-foods-market%C2%AE-offers-%E2%80%9Cvalue-tips-tours-top-sellers%E2%80%9D-to-help-shoppers-find-deals/). Recognizing these tours as an opportunity for media to experience value at Whole Foods Market first-hand, the PR team began inviting members of the media to join the tours. This strategy proved successful in securing media hits at both the local and national level.

  Some regions even began creating Whole Foods Market Value Maps of the store, showing shoppers how to navigate store aisles and directing customers to sale items, Whole Foods Market's house brand, value-priced 365 Everyday Value brand products, the bulk section, value packs, etc.

- **Promotion of 365 Everyday Value® items, the company's private label brand**
  In addition to promoting these items online and in-stores, the PR team began pitching national media with a price comparison challenge. The team selected the top 25 Everyday Value brand items (i.e., 365 organic

mustard, PB, juice box, pasta sauce, etc.)—and sent product drops to top media across the country with a friendly reminder, "please compare organic apples to organic apples when doing your comparison shopping stories this year." The PR team also sent ingredients for or even a prepared sample of a "Meal for 4" under $15 (featured in *The Whole Deal*) to newsrooms to physically show reporters the high quality and great value they can expect to find at Whole Foods Market.

- **Promotion of family packs, value packs, and weekly promotions and deals**
  Specials were woven into announcements and press releases whenever possible and members of the media (traditional and social) were invited to come into the store to experience the savings.

In addition to these programs, the PR team began promoting value in specific departments, reaching out to media to share company programs like the "Top 10 Wines" program—a semi-annual promotion in the wine department highlighting the season's" top-notch wine picks at easy-to-swallow prices." Another example was the team's focus on value in the meat department. The Whole Foods Market team helped to create fun and personable video blogs starring the company's global meat buyer and featuring tips on how shoppers can get the best value at the meat counter. The PR team also distributed a press release highlighting the video and the best in-store deals. These and other videos were published on both YouTube and the company's Whole Story blog (blog.wholefoodsmarket.com).

To further online and social media outreach beyond videoblogs, the PR team worked closely with the company's Integrated Media Team to establish Whole Story as the go-to online destination for shoppers looking for regular tips and tools to save. Together the teams developed regular value-focused blog posts including:

- Seasonal posts like "Lighten Up Your Meals and Your Budget for Summer" and "Strategic Holiday Foods Shopping Tips"
- Evergreen posts like "Learn to Cook, Learn to Save: Simple Beans" and "Premium Body Care at Budget Prices"
- Whole Deal-focused entries such as "The Whole Deal's Meals for Four" and "The Whole Deal Tips of the Week"

The PR and Integrated Media teams also worked together to regularly host budget-focused contests and giveaways on Whole Story such as:

- "The Value Guru Cookbook Giveaway"—This fun interactive giveaway encouraged shoppers to recreate their restaurant favorites at home on a tight budget and share their creations. Participants earned a chance to win a Whole Foods Market gift card and three value-focused cookbooks. This giveaway built excitement around cooking at home and allowed shoppers to lead the value conversation while sharing their passion for high quality food at a great price.
- "Budget Recipe Challenge"—In this contest, the PR team reached out to well-known food bloggers, challenging them to develop a budget-conscious (under $4 per serving) weeknight meal recipe that didn't sacrifice good taste. To get shoppers involved, the team asked Whole Story readers to help choose the winner by posting their comments on one of the finalist recipes. Everyone who posted a comment was automatically entered into a drawing to win a Whole Foods Market gift card. This outreach not only garnered attention from potential customers online, it helped the Whole Foods Market team build relationships with relevant influencers in the food world and blogosphere, which resulted in more consistent online coverage and an increased awareness of the company's budget-conscious offerings.

In addition, Whole Foods Market began to increase communication with shoppers and media through nontraditional online channels such as Facebook, MySpace, and Twitter. PR coordinators at the regional and store levels began sharing updates on the latest deals, events, and savings opportunities through their local store's accounts, profiles, and websites. In fact, Whole Foods Market's Twitter followers grew from 20,000 in early

2008 to nearly 2 million followers in 2010. Engaging customers in lighthearted conversations about the "happenings" at their local stores allowed each market to develop relationships with the local community. By establishing Whole Foods Market as a key player in the community, regional PR coordinators earned the company a spot on the local media map and in many cases, prompted news organizations to create a retail news beat just to cover Whole Foods Market.

In continuing to develop and expand the emphasis on price/value at Whole Foods Market, the PR team felt that weaving this theme into in-store events could be used to more clearly illustrate this point to customers. In order to explore the feasibility of such in-store events, the team would like to select two of the grocer's eight departments (Bakery, Whole Body (personal care), Grocery, Seafood, Meat and Dairy, Specialty (beer, gourmet cheeses, spreads, etc.), Prepared Foods (hot food and salad bars), and Wine) and concept ideas for in-store event promotions for each of the two departments. Promising ideas could be test-marketed on a small scale to examine their feasibility company wide. Select two departments within a Whole Foods Market store and draft a proposal for two in-store events illustrating the company's price/value advantages.

A few key points to remember when developing a proposal for Whole Foods Market:

- Whole Foods Market is decentralized into 12 regional offices that function fairly autonomously. This decentralized structure is a huge strength for the company because it allows each store the flexibility to develop events that best meet the needs of the local community. When planning any companywide event, the global PR team must provide each store with information and toolkits that could be easily tailored to meet the needs of the local community.
- It is rare for Whole Foods Market to do national advertising. Most of the company's advertising is done at the local level, if at all, and is usually limited to new store openings.
- Local advertising and event planning dollars are primarily limited to covering in-store demos and tastings, special events, sales, store discounts, etc. as each store's main focus is on improving customers' shopping experience by supporting the company's Core Values:
  - ☐ Selling the highest quality natural and organic products available
  - ☐ Satisfying and delighting our customers
  - ☐ Supporting team member happiness and excellence
  - ☐ Creating wealth through profits and growth
  - ☐ Caring about our communities and our environment
  - ☐ Creating ongoing win-win partnerships with our suppliers
  - ☐ Promoting the health of our stakeholders through healthy eating education

Name _____ Date _____

QUESTIONS FOR DISCUSSION AND REVIEW

1. What other suggestions do you have for Whole Foods Market on highlighting value in stores?

2. What are the advantages of inviting members of the media to film a value tour in stores versus sending products and written materials to news desks?

3. When developing a PR campaign and media strategy, what are the benefits of securing third-party research like the Harris Interactive survey?

4. Which outreach efforts do you feel were the most appropriately aimed at garnering attention from local media? National media? Customers?

5. Why did Whole Foods Market choose to invite food bloggers to participate in its Whole Story "Budget Recipe Challenge" and not traditional media contacts (TV, radio, print)?

_____

_____

_____

_____

6. How would the success of any proposed media outreach or in-store event be measured?

_____

_____

_____

_____

7. What are the advantages of using PR efforts over advertising to support company initiatives?

_____

_____

_____

_____

Case 12.4

BusinesSuites (D)[1]

Mr. John Jordan, president of BusinesSuites (BSS), knew that the competition for the annual "Small Business Excellence Award," sponsored by Dell Computers and the National Federation of Independent Business (NFIB), would be stiff. Therefore, he was pleasantly surprised when he learned that BSS had been named a finalist for the award and thrilled when his firm was named the U.S. national winner (See BSS (A) case for background on the company).

Exhibit 12.4.1 presents a Dell press release announcing BSS's selection and provides some background on the significance of the award. As the national award winner, BSS received $25,000 in Dell products and services, a lifetime membership to NFIB, and a day of best-practices consulting advice from Dell experts, including an hour of individual time with Michael Dell. In addition, Dell produced a three-minute video featuring Mr. Jordan telling the company's story. This video was prominently featured in the press release on Dell's website. The video was also posted on YouTube (http://www.youtube.com/watch?v=83ksoex-p-Y).

To capitalize on the positive publicity of winning this award by bringing it to the attention of present and potential clients, BSS issued a press release when the firm was named a finalist for the national award and a second release when BSS was named the U.S. winner. In addition, a link to Dell's press release announcing that BSS had won the U.S. small business competition was prominently featured on the BSS's home page (www.businessuites.com) along with a quote from the release:

A strong focus on hands-on customer service backed by innovative technology set BusinesSuites apart...
—*Dell Inc.*

After the announcement was made and the press releases issued, Mr. Jordan was faced with a major opportunity: How to leverage the positive vibe associated with winning this award among present and potential clients, commercial real estate brokers and others? The question was how to most effectively exploit this opportunity?

The following initial steps were taken to promote the BSS winning award: Dell press releases were placed in the mailboxes of present clients, posted in the kitchens/break rooms, and set out in the reception areas in all BSS locations. Beyond these obvious steps, Mr. Jordan wondered how local media coverage might be stimulated in the markets served by BSS. Further, how could BSS most effectively use this award as a new business tool with potential clients in the markets they served? What options did the Internet offer for disseminating information regarding this favorable news?

---

[1] This case was written by John H. Murphy, The University of Texas at Austin and John Jordan, BusinesSuites. The case is designed to serve as the basis for classroom discussion and not to illustrate either the effective or ineffective handling of an administrative situation. The case is used with permission granted by BusinesSuites.

Exhibit 12.4.1 ■ Dell Press Release

Press Releases

BusinesSuites Named U.S. Winner Of 6th Annual Dell, NFIB Small Business Excellence Award

Print | Email | RSS Feed

Date : 9/30/2009
Round Rock, Texas

- Recognizes Small Businesses that Use Technology in Innovative Ways to Better Serve Customers
- BusinesSuites differentiates itself among record breaking 3,000 applicants

Dell and the National Federation of Independent Business (NFIB), the leading small-business association in the United States, today announced BusinesSuites as the U.S. national winner of the Dell/NFIB Small Business Excellence Award.

Based in Austin, Texas, BusinesSuites provides executive suites and virtual office services in 15 locations nationwide. The company, founded in 1989, has become an industry leader offering clients fully furnished offices equipped with ready-to-go Internet, mail, phone, professional staff, and meeting rooms under flexible terms. Today, BusinesSuites has 55 employees and more than 1,400 clients.

John Jordan, president of BusinesSuites, credits investments in technology and people with saving the company. "We doubled the size of the company in 2002 and quickly realized our systems and infrastructure were inadequate to deal with the growth. Money was tight, but we began investing heavily in our systems and our people. We believe these investments saved our company. By using technology to reduce costs, push responsibility out to all levels of the company, improve the client experience, and leverage a smaller infrastructure, we reached a profit level in 2008 which was double what we had originally envisioned." One of BusinesSuites' technology investments was the development of a Web-based operations management system that generates and electronically distributes invoices and client satisfaction surveys, schedules meeting rooms for clients, tracks prospective clients and more.

"Technology is a critical tool for BusinesSuites, it's what allows us to create a community of great people who do an exceptional job taking care of our clients," says Jordan. Team members are encouraged to learn the technology clients use so they can provide hands-on advice and support. The company also uses an internal Wiki to share information, as well as store hardware and software manuals created by the team.

"Our team members are our first line of defense when a client has a problem, so it's important that they know the technology inside and out. For instance, many of our clients were affected by Hurricanes Isabel and Ike. Within 48 hours, our team helped to restart 200 affected businesses by providing them with plug-and-play IT infrastructures."

It was this strong focus on hands-on customer service backed by innovative technology that set BusinesSuites apart from the record breaking 3,000 applicants for the 2009 Dell/NFIB Small Business Excellence Award.

"BusinesSuites is living proof that smart IT investments can not only pay off for the business itself, but for their customers as well," said Erik Dithmer, vice president and general manager of Dell Small and Medium Business.

"This year's winner is a terrific example of the ways that small businesses can harness new technologies to provide better customer service," said Dan Danner, president and CEO of NFIB. "And better service is a great competitive advantage in today's marketplace."

BusinesSuites will receive $25,000 in Dell products and services, a lifetime membership to NFIB valued at $15,000 (including a trip to NFIB's National Small Business Summit), and a day of best-practice sharing with Dell experts, including time with Chairman and CEO Michael Dell.

BusinesSuites joins national winners from 12 other countries - Australia, Brazil, Canada, China, France, Germany, Italy, India, Japan, Mexico, Spain, United Kingdom - for a chance to win the global Dell Small Business Excellence Award worth $50,000 in Dell technology and services and participation in a global entrepreneurs' summit. National winners are being announced now, and the global winner will be announced later in 2009.

To learn more about BusinesSuites and its technology strategy for success visit www.dellhero.com/us

About NFIB

NFIB is the nation's leading small business association, with offices in Washington, D.C., and all 50 state capitals. Founded in 1943 as a nonprofit, nonpartisan organization, NFIB gives small and independent business owners a voice in shaping the public policy issues that affect their business. NFIB's powerful network of grassroots activists sends their views directly to state and federal lawmakers through a unique member-only ballot, thus playing a critical role in supporting America's free enterprise system. NFIB's mission is to promote and protect the right of members to own, operate and grow their businesses. More information about NFIB is available online at www.NFIB.com/newsroom.

About Dell

As the visionary outcome of a true entrepreneur, Dell (NASDAQ: DELL) is committed to helping small and medium businesses solve their technology challenges, ease business pain points and draw greater value from IT.

"Visit www.dellhero.com for Dell/NFIB Small Business Excellence Award official rules."

Media Contacts

Camille Nisich
Dell
Round Rock, Texas
(512) 725-1903
512-289-1565
camille_nisich@dell.com

Mike Diegel
NFIB
Washington D.C.
(202) 314-2004
(202) 302-3043
michael.diegel@nfib.org

Featured Video

Video Tools : Email | Embed

Businessuites Case Study
This is a case study video of the 2009 Small Business Excellence Award Winner for the US.

Related Articles

- Dell, NFIB Honor Nation's Most Innovative Small and Mid-size Business
- Dell Teams with Inspiring Entrepreneurs to roll out First Global SMB Marketing Campaign

Most Popular

1. Dell Seeing Demand Stabilization, Expects Slight Sequential Revenue Growth With Modest Margin Pressure In Q2
2. New Dell Studio 14z Laptop Perfect Powerhouse for Online Generation
3. Dell, Goodwill Expand Free Computer Recycling Program to Seven More States
4. Dell Joins Prince's Rainforests Project
5. Dell Increases Global Renewable Power Sourcing To More Than 25 Percent

Name _____   Date _____

QUESTIONS FOR DISCUSSION AND REVIEW

1. How can BSS most effectively leverage the credibility and objectivity of Dell and the NFIB sponsorship of the award?

2. What strategies and techniques might be most effective in stimulating local media coverage? Who would be the best media prospects to provide coverage of BSS's award?

3. Are there any potential pitfalls or dangers associated with the award? What scenarios could develop that would diminish the value of the award in the eyes of present and potential clients?

4. Who would be included on a list of local media and Web site contacts in each of BSS' markets?

5. Can BSS leverage the $25,000 in Dell products and services to foster relationships with present clients? If so, how?

_____

_____

_____

_____

6. Should social media and blogging be leveraged in this opportunity? If so, how?

_____

_____

_____

_____

Case 12.5

Carlyle Labs, Inc. (A)[1]

BACKGROUND

A Fire Raises Community Alarm

A fire at Carlyle Labs, Inc. (CL), a technology research and development facility in Middletown, Ohio, created a dilemma for the management of this wholly owned subsidiary of a *Fortune* 500 company. Although no one was injured, the fire did extensive damage to a CL facility and smoke caused the closing of a nearby middle school and an interstate highway.

Media coverage of the emotionally charged responses of municipal officials and community residents who lived in close proximity to the facility caught CL completely by surprise. Prior to this incident, CL had been a model corporate citizen supporting a wide range of community activities through corporate sponsorships. Furthermore, Middletown had aggressively recruited the laboratory to locate in their community with tax breaks and other incentives.

Fifteen years ago as a councilwoman, the present mayor of Middletown had enthusiastically greeted CL's selection of her community as the site for the new research lab. However, the day of the accident she expressed troubled concern on a local television news program. When asked by a TV reporter about a possible threat to public safety, the mayor responded, "Like everyone, I was shocked by the heavy cloud of smoke that lingered in neighborhoods around the Carlyle lab. Yes, I am concerned about the potential for a serious chemical disaster at the Carlyle facility."

The research campus opened 14 years ago in an unincorporated area on the fringe of Middletown's industrial, lower socioeconomic south side. Since then a "strip mall," low-income residential neighborhoods, and two trailer parks had been developed and now surrounded the facility. To management's knowledge, no CL scientists or tech staff lived in these neighborhoods or trailer parks.

Shortly after the CL facility opened, the city annexed the area. A few years later the Middletown Independent School District (M.I.S.D.) opened a middle school (Patrick Henry) on the northern boundary of CL's property. At the time of the accident the middle school had an enrollment of approximately 925 sixth-, seventh-, and eighth-grade students. Some children of CL's employees attended this nearby middle school.

The Carlyle Research Facility

Scientists at Carlyle Labs conducted basic and applied research on computer chips, circuitry, and microprocessors. The firm employed a full-time staff of 350 highly skilled technical and support personnel. Because research frequently involved the use of toxic chemicals, the facilities had safety showers, and all personnel handling chemicals were required to wear protective suits. These chemicals included ammonium hydroxide, argon, chromium trioxide, hydrochloric acid, hydrofluoric acid, hydrogen chloride, hydrogen peroxide, sulfuric acid, and trichlorsilane.

Most chemicals were stored in special rooms with concrete walls and floors that had been treated with an acid-proof resin. Wastes were taken to a special treatment unit in a secure area, where acids and bases were neutralized before being discharged into the city sewer system.

---

[1] This case was written by John H. Murphy, The University of Texas at Austin, to serve as a basis for classroom discussion. The identity of the firm is disguised and based on a combination of actual events.

Further, the facility complied with all applicable local, state, and federal safety standards. This made the possibility of a chemical spill or discharge highly unlikely. When the facility was opened, CL invested $7.5 million on an environmental control system, and management believed they had taken every reasonable preventative measure and safeguard to ensure the safety of its employees, the citizens of Middletown, and the environment.

Timeline of Events

Tuesday, March 10—At approximately 5:00 a.m. a fire broke out and damaged the facility. Initial concerns by Middletown firefighters about a chemical spill and/or the escaping of toxic gases proved unfounded shortly after they arrived at 5:15 a.m. However, a heavy blanket of smoke lingered around the CL's research campus, the neighborhoods, and adjacent Interstate 75. The noxious smoke was slow to dissipate due to still wind conditions, and the Interstate was closed for two hours (approximately 5:45–7:45 a.m.). The opening of Patrick Henry Middle School was delayed until noon. CL crews immediately began clean-up activities, and damage was initially estimated at approximately $3 million.

Although a wide range of potentially hazardous and toxic chemicals were used in the facility, none of these chemicals was involved in or affected by the fire. This was confirmed by CL safety officials by 10:00 a.m. Tuesday morning.

Wednesday, March 11—Fueled by partially inaccurate eyewitness broadcast news reports, members of the general public expressed concern that focused on the use of toxic chemicals at CL. The parents of children affected by the school closing were the most vocal group and made their concerns known on local call-in radio talk shows and to M.I.S.D. and local and state government officials.

As a result of the fire, approximately 45 CL scientists and tech staff were moved to temporary facilities on the campus. On further assessment, most of the damage from the fire that was started by an overheated electrical conductor was due to smoke and water used in fighting the fire. Several machines and pieces of lab equipment were damaged beyond repair, and some with no or minor damage were moved to the temporary facility.

Thursday, March 12—With the approval of CL's President/CEO James Jackson, CL's director of corporate communications (Ashley Russell) arranged a "town hall meeting" with local officials, the press, and members of the neighborhoods immediately around the plant to discuss the safety situation. The meeting was to be held in the auditorium of the middle school at 7:30 on Friday evening. It was decided that after a brief introduction and opening statement from the President/CEO, the plant manager would describe the handling, application, storage, and disposal of toxic chemicals used in the research and manufacturing processes tested at CL. This would be followed by Q/A from members of the press and general public.

Friday, March 13—10:00 a.m.: CL executives meet to prepare for the evening meeting. 7:30 p.m.: Town Hall Meeting scheduled at Patrick Henry Middle School.

MS. RUSSELL'S IMMEDIATE TASKS

On Thursday afternoon, Ms. Russell began preparing for the Town Hall Meeting the next evening. Ms. Russell's task was to: (1) write a draft of the opening remarks to be delivered by Mr. Jackson at the meeting; (2) develop a list of likely difficult questions that may be asked in the Q/A segment of the town hall meeting; (3) anticipate other issues that might be raised at the meeting by the media, members of the general public, or relevant municipal, state, or federal authorities; and (4) develop contingencies for responding to these issues. Note that the opening statement would set the general tone of meeting and help foster an environment for the sharing of information and concerns. The opening remarks should also clearly state the purpose of the meeting and briefly recap the events leading up to the meeting.

The list of likely questions would be presented to Mr. Jackson and other CL executives in the form of a "Q&A Briefing Sheet." The sheet would list the questions in rank order of difficulty, and each question will be follow by a suggested response.

A meeting with all senior CL executives had been set for 10:00 Friday morning to prepare for the Town Hall Meeting that evening. Ms. Russell would open the morning meeting by presenting her draft of Mr. Jackson's opening remarks. After discussion and revisions of Mr. Jackson's speech, Ms. Russell would present her anticipated questions and answers, plus her views about any other issue that might surface prior to, during, or after the Town Hall Meeting.

Name _____ Date _____

QUESTIONS FOR DISCUSSION AND REVIEW

1. How frequently do mini-disaster type situations like the one faced by CL occur? What are recent examples of similar industrial spills, fires, explosions, discharges, contaminations, and so on?

2. What should CL have done in advance to prepare for these types of crisis?

3. What should CL have done differently after the fire and before the Town Hall Meeting?

4. What should CL do following the Town Hall Meeting to reassure concerned publics?

Case 12.6

The Coca-Cola Company[1]

Beginning in April 1985, the replacement of the original formula Coca-Cola with New Coke spawned an angry storm of protests by consumers who preferred the taste of the original formula. This backlash took a number of forms. Hundreds of thousands of angry consumers called via the company's WATS lines to demand the return of the original Coke. Organizations such as the Old Coke Drinkers of America sprang up to push for the return of the original formula. Coca-Cola bottlers joined the call for the return of the original Coke. At a convention of bottlers held in Dallas in June, a petition was circulated demanding the return of original formula.

Several months after the introduction of New Coke, sales had plummeted. Further, company research revealed that Coca-Cola's image had slipped badly. At the same time, rival Pepsi's sales were up significantly.

Exhibits 12.6.1 and 12.6.2 present letters to shareholders from Roberto C. Goizueta, CEO of Coca-Cola, about two of the most startling and important business decisions made in the history of the company. Exhibit 12.6.1 announces the reformulation of the company's 100 year old secret formula and the introduction of New Coke. This letter also outlines some of management's thinking in making this bold move.

The letter presented in Exhibit 12.6.2 clearly indicates that management underestimated the depth of a significant number of consumers' attachment to the old formula. The announcement of the return of Coca-Cola Classic received front page coverage in major newspapers from coast-to-coast. Immediately after the announcement, ABC interrupted the soap opera *General Hospital* with a news bulletin on the story. The announcement was the opening news story on all of the network evening newscasts and was featured on the popular, news-oriented television programs *Nightline* and *20/20*.

After the re-introduction of the original formula under the brand name Coca-Cola Classic, the company's total share of market improved steadily. Although sales of New Coke continued to decline, the two Coca-Cola brands overall share strengthened the company's position in the category vis-a-vis Pepsi.

---

[1]This case was written by John H. Murphy, The University of Texas at Austin. The case is intended for use in generating class discussion and not to illustrate either the effective or ineffective handling of an administrative situation. {Letters used by permission of The Coca-Cola Company.}

Exhibit 12.6.1 ■ The Coca-Cola Company

The Coca-Cola Company

ROBERTO C. GOIZUETA
CHAIRMAN OF THE BOARD
AND
CHIEF EXECUTIVE OFFICER

ATLANTA, GEORGIA

ADDRESS REPLY TO
P.O. DRAWER 1724
ATLANTA, GA. 30301
404-678-2121

April 23, 1985

Dear Fellow Shareholder:

I am writing today to share with you the best new about Coca-Cola that I have announced since becoming our Company's Chairman and Chief Executive Officer four years ago. The best soft drink Coca-Cola is now going to be even better. Simply stated, we have a new formula for Coke. This is the most significant development in our business since the formulation of the first taste for Coca-Cola and the decision to bottle it.

With the implementation of our Strategy for the 1980's, you have seen our Company grasp new opportunities and take actions to strengthen our fundamental business. These actions include the restructuring of our Bottler system in the U.S. as well as internationally; the aggressive introduction of diet Coke, now the third largest selling soft drink in America; the successful move into the entertainment business with a strong position in it through innovative financing arrangements and joint ventures in film production, television programming and videocassette marketing; and the effective utilization of the enormous financial resources of The Coca-Cola Company.

Each of these developments has been an important element in building shareholder value, but none has been more important than the step we take today. And, I have never been more optimistic about the short and longer term outlook of our soft drink business.

Let me give you some background on our decision. Just a few years ago, we realized that we needed a product in the fast-growing low-calorie soft drink market which would be worthy of the Coca-Cola name. Our outstanding flavor researchers came through with distinction. The success of diet Coke is now history. But in the process of perfecting diet Coke, we discovered a new cola formula, a product which our flavor scientists quickly realized was highly preferred by in-house expert taste panels over Coca-Cola itself, and of course over its primary competition. Since then, the new formula has undergone the most intensive flavor refinement and consumer taste test research in our Company's history. The fact is that consumers of all ages across the country have told us they prefer the new taste to the original by an overwhelming majority, and <u>by an even wider margin of preference when consumers are told that this is a new Coca-Cola.</u>

Exhibit 12.6.1 ■ Continued

April 23, 1985
Page Two

Some of you, as shareholders, may call this the boldest single marketing move in our history. We simply call it the surest move ever made because the new taste of Coke was not shaped to the specifications or the egos of management, or to the satisfaction or approval of flavor chemists, or to the palate of a Board of Directors, or even to requests from Bottlers. This new Coke was shaped and finely tuned to the taste of the consumer. Thousands of consumers have told us that this is the Coca-Cola they prefer.

When management of The Coca-Cola Company was presented with such numbers and confronted with these unassailable facts, our decision became one of the easiest we have ever made. With this move, the management of your Company has executed a principal act of management: to watch consumers, study consumers, learn the most it can about consumers, and thereafter, to rely confidently on consumer preference. Because of this, all the credit for the success to come from our actions and from this decision will not belong to us. It belongs to our consuming public, and they are the real winners.

To be the absolute best has always been the legacy of Coca-Cola. As Coca-Cola enters its 100th year, we know of no better way to thank the billions of consumers who have made Coca-Cola what it is, than to give them a Coca-Cola that is better than ever. And I cannot think of a better Centennial gift for you, our shareholders, than to take a step which has such significant long-term benefits for the Company's soft drink volume and profit growth, with those benefits starting right now and accelerating into 1986 and beyond.

In giving Coca-Cola a new taste, we are doing it proudly, we are doing it globally, and we will market the new Coke vigorously as we enter our Centennial year. Much more of the details surrounding this milestone will be covered in our First Quarter Progress Report which will be mailed in a few weeks. In the meantime, I know you will enjoy the rewarding new taste of Coca-Cola.

Sincerely,

Roberto C. Goizueta

Exhibit 12.6.2 ■ The Coca-Cola Company

The Coca-Cola Company

ROBERTO C. GOIZUETA
CHAIRMAN OF THE BOARD
AND
CHIEF EXECUTIVE OFFICER

ATLANTA, GEORGIA

ADDRESS REPLY TO
P.O. DRAWER 1724
ATLANTA, GA. 30301
404-678-2121

July 11, 1985

Dear Fellow Shareholder:

As of today, we have delivered two important messages to the American consumer. First, to those consumers who are drinking Coca-Cola with its great new taste, we have expressed our appreciation. Those consumers, including many of you, are enjoying the best-tasting Coca-Cola we have ever made and the one preferred over the taste of Pepsi.

In just eleven weeks, more than 150 million people, well over half the U.S. population, have tried Coca-Cola, and that is nearly double the number of regular consumers of Coke in a year. By giving consumers the new taste of Coke, we have broadened our consumer base, enhanced our appeal to youth the highest per capita consumers of soft drinks and provided a new positioning for Coca-Cola as we enter our second century.

The second important message we have delivered is to another group of consumers which has expressed its desire for a taste of nostalgia. We have heard them! As a result, we are introducing Coca-Cola classic, which is a new brand name for our Company, but is our original Coca-Cola formula, our original Coca-Cola taste. Coca-Cola classic will be appearing in the marketplace in the next several weeks alongside our flagship brand, Coca-Cola.

Clearly, the emotional reaction from some of our loyal consumers to the change in the taste of Coca-Cola was astonishing. To them, we didn't just change the taste of Coca-Cola, we changed a basic American value and tradition built over 99 years. To them, Coca-Cola meant heritage, fond memories, good friends and family. We have heard the thousands of dedicated consumers who have told us that they want the original taste as an option just as clearly as we have heard the more than 40 million drinkers-per-day who have expressed their preference for the new taste of Coke.

Exhibit 12.6.2 ■ Continued

July 11, 1985
Page Two

Being the consumer driven company that we are, we have attained the leadership position that we enjoy by listening to consumers, watching consumers, and giving consumers what they want. We have always been and we always will be responsive to the desires and needs of our consumers. In this way, we are able to fulfill our obligation to you of maximizing your shareholder investment in our Company.

Our job, together with our bottlers, is to satisfy more consumers and in the process sell more gallons of soft drinks. Never before have we been stronger or better equipped to do our job. And, not a single competitor will be able to match our widening advantage in sales and market share of Coca-Cola and its supporting cast of brands.

As the newest addition to the lineup of Coca-Cola branded soft drinks, Coca-Cola classic will join Coca-Cola, diet Coke, cherry Coke and our caffeine-free Coke products to make up the most formidable mega-brand in the soft drink industry by any measure, anywhere. By year's end, we expect more than half of the colas consumed in America will bear the trademark Coca-Cola, and more than one out of every three soft drinks consumed in the U.S. will carry the trademark Coca-Cola.

To those of you who enjoy Coca-Cola, we are confident that you will continue to make it the best-selling soft drink in the world. To those of you who have asked for Coca-Cola classic, we have listened and we are acting according to your wants.

Sincerely,

Roberto C. Goizueta

Name _____   Date _____

QUESTIONS FOR DISCUSSION AND REVIEW

1. Given the initial decision to replace the original formula with New Coke, how might animosity among brand loyal users of the original formula Coca-Cola have been reduced? What PR actions could have been implemented to reduce and difuse this animosity?

   _____
   _____
   _____
   _____

2. Was the scenario of replacing the original formula with New Coke to stimulate trial and publicity then followed by the re-introduction of Coca-Cola Classic planned by management in advance? Why or why not?

   _____
   _____
   _____
   _____

3. How could Pepsi have responded most effectively to the actions of their chief rival Coca-Cola?

   _____
   _____
   _____
   _____

4. What insights does Coca-Cola's experience reveal about the strength and importance of brand images? What insights are provided in terms of brand line extensions?

   _____
   _____
   _____
   _____

5. What lessons and principles of public relations are illustrated through Coca-Cola's experience?

_____

_____

_____

_____

Case 12.7

The Wall Street Journal's "Two Brothers" Commercial[1]

In order to add a fresh and creative perspective to their advertising designed to attractive new subscribers and readers, *The Wall Street Journal* (WSJ) hired the San Francisco-based creative agency Goodby, Silverstein and Partners. One of the television commercials produced by the agency as a part of their "Adventures in Capitalism" campaign generated unanticipated protests from an unexpected segment of the general public.

The commercial titled "Two Brothers" (see Exhibit 12.7.1) angered a surprisingly large number of fishermen. Four representative messages the *Journal* received in the form of letters, voice mails, and e-mails are presented below.

1. "Your recent television commercial regarding two brothers separated at birth is very childish and demeaning. You should have at least taken the commercial to its likely conclusion that the brother subscribing to the "fishing magazine" is a devoted father who enjoys spending quality time with his family, while the other brother consumed by financial affairs is perhaps twice divorced and struggling with a drug problem. Please do not put down people whose life does not revolve around the almighty dollar."
2. "I am canceling my subscription! The commercial which shows 2 babies separated at birth—one who reads the journal, and one who watches fishing shows is ridiculous. You have managed to insult a very large portion of the U.S. populations—way to go!"
3. "As incoming president of The Ohio Smallmouth Alliance I am very disappointed in your recent TV advertising campaign. The correlation between success with the *Wall Street Journal* and under achieving with fishing is extremely insensitive stereotyping. Certainly the money you spend on advertising could be used to send a more positive message than to attack the very heritage of the people from which you hope to attract subscribers. Nearly one billion dollars a year are spent sport fishing in Ohio alone. Because of your poor choice I will no longer purchase the WSJ and will do everything in my power to encourage our statewide membership, family, and friends to do likewise. The basis of any membership whether a periodical or organization is the presentation of accurate information and trust. You now have neither. You have outraged a very honorable and financially important segment of society. I believe you owe us an apology."
4. "I am not sure I have the right department, your website doesn't offer a more detailed contact. I am writing about the commercial airing on TLC, ESPN, and the Discovery Channel. It is the current one about the twins adopted at birth by 2 different families. I find this commercial very offensive to those who are fishing enthusiasts. We own a fishing resort and fishing is our business. Your commercial's message is that persons interested in fishing are stupid, lazy, and poor. Resorts are not listed in the *Wall Street Journal,* so therefore are considered "worthless" by the WSJ?"

As she reviewed the large number of negative messages, Celia Currin, Marketing Communications Director of the WSJ, was faced with many questions that required her immediate attention. For example: Should the commercial be pulled off the air? Should the *Journal* treat the furor as a news story? Should the *Journal* respond to each individual letter, voice mail, and email? How might the *Journal* most effectively defuse the hostile situation and attempt to work back into the good graces of the angry fishermen?

There did not seem to be any good answers to these and other critical issues that revolved around this unexpected situation. In addition, there was obvious time pressure to act quickly to respond to this crisis.

---

[1]This case was written by John H. Murphy, The University of Texas at Austin. The case is designed to serve as the basis for classroom discussion and not to illustrate either the effective or ineffective handling of an administrative situation. Used by permission from *The Wall Street Journal.*

Exhibit 12.7.1 ■ "Brothers" The Wall Street Journal :60

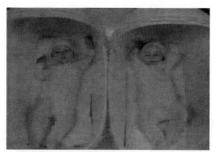

"The King brothers, separated at birth."

"George King would wind up living with a family that subscribed to popular fishing magazines. James went to a family that subscribed to the Wall Street Journal."

"As the years passed and the boys grew, George spent most of his time in front of the television, watching fishing shows."

"While James read the Journal like a sponge, absorbing ideas, insight and getting a real sense of the opportunities surrounding him."

"Twenty eight years later, George lives at home with his parents, while his brother James started a b to b web company,"

"got mezzanine financing and went public with a record first day pop."

"Food for thought, especially since you an get 13 weeks of the Wall Street Journal for just 57 cents a day, that's 25 percent off the regular subscription."

"Subscribe now. Call 800-278-2200, that's 800-278-2200. The Wall Street Journal. Adventures in Capitalism."

Name _____ Date _____

QUESTIONS FOR DISCUSSION AND REVIEW

1. Is simply ignoring the complaints an option? Would responding only draw the *Journal* deeper into the situation with little likelihood of achieving anything positive?

2. What additional information would be useful in determining how the WSJ should respond to the complaints?

3. Who in upper management at the *Journal* should be apprised of the situation? Who might be appropriately asked to be involved in determining how the *Journal* should respond to offended readers?

4. Should Goodby, Silverstein and Partners be contacted and their help requested?

5. How could the WSJ most effectively respond to each individual who had contacted the *Journal* to complain about the commercial?

6. Should any steps be taken to avoid similar problems in the future?

Case 12.8

Decker, Villani & Bishop[1]

Decker, Villani & Bishop (DV&B) was a relatively large regional advertising agency based in Charlotte, North Carolina. The agency had a growing stable of accounts with annual billings approaching $59.4 million. With only 37 employees, DV&B was unusually profitable for an agency its size. DV&B was not well known outside North Carolina, but the advertising community in the state regarded the agency as a progressive, reliable, marketing-driven shop.

MAXIBANC OF NORTH CAROLINA

DV&B's largest single account (accounting for 21 percent of income and 26 percent of profits) was a marketing unit of MaxiBanc (MB) that included all of MB's branch banks in the state. MB, a large, nation-wide financial holding company, had over 100 branch banks in North Carolina with commensurate assets and marketing budgets. Headquartered in Washington, D.C., MB was committed to following a strategy of organizing their network of banks into either state or regional marketing units. Although each unit operated under the umbrella of MB's national promotional efforts that included a brand identity style, logo, colors and graphics manual, each marketing unit was semiautonomous. Each unit developed their own promotional programs plus hired their own advertising and PR agencies and other suppliers.

Since acquiring the account, DV&B had encouraged MB/North Carolina (MB/NC) to use aggressive advertising and public relations activities stressing MB's solid foundation of customer service, highly competitive rates, and innovative financial services. Under DV&B's marketing stewardship their client had prospered. Vis-à-vis all marketing units in MB's network, MB/NC had consistently increased their number of customers, deposits, and loan values more rapidly than the norm. Last year, MB/NC posted the largest percentage increase in their customer base of any unit in the system.

Rick Villani, a founder of DV&B, had ultimate responsibility for servicing the MB account. Mary Burnett was the MB account supervisor and was in charge of the day-to-day activities on the account. Working with her were two account executives, a management trainee, and two student interns from the University of North Carolina at Charlotte.

DV&B'S ACCOUNT MANAGEMENT TRAINING PROGRAM

About a year and a half earlier, DV&B had instituted an account management-training program. The purpose of the program was to provide new assistant account executives with exposure to all aspects of the agency's operation and to groom them for rapid movement into positions of account responsibility. The program required a year to complete and involved assignment to the various functional departments of the agency for a period of several months each. In addition, the program involved seminars and assignments made by top management of the agency.

After a year's experience with the program, DV&B's management was largely satisfied with the results, but there was general concern over the drain on agency resources. Not only were the trainees relatively unpro-

---

[1] This case was written by George R. Franke, The University of Alabama Tuscaloosa and John H. Murphy, The University of Texas at Austin. The case is designed to serve as the basis for classroom discussion and not to illustrate either the effective or ineffective handling of an administrative situation. The identity of the individuals and firms involved and the situation have been disguised.

ductive for much of the year, they required time to teach and supervise. Changes were underway in the second year of the program to give the two trainees meaningful assignments and real responsibilities more quickly than in year one of the program.

To fill the two available positions for the second year of the training program, DV&B interviewed undergraduate and MBA students at six universities in North Carolina. After an initial campus interview, the most promising candidates were invited to spend a day at the agency. During the day the interviewee met with all of DV&B's top account, creative, media, PR, and other administrative executives. After considerable discussion among DV&B's executives, a consensus was reached regarding which individuals should receive an offer.

Karen Watkins, a recent graduate with a concentration in advertising and marketing was one of two individuals hired to enter the second year of the program. "One of my strengths is that I can see what needs to be done and then do it," she said in an interview. "I work well with other people, but I don't need a team backing me up or anyone holding my hand." Although several DV&B executives involved in the selection process were impressed with Watkins and thought she was the kind of aggressive self-starter the agency needed, several others had reservations about her maturity and motivation. As a result of the divided opinions, Ms. Watkins had not been contacted during the first round of offers but was offered a position after two other candidates had turned the job down.

Watkins had entered the management-training program with high expectations about her future at DV&B. Overall, during her first six weeks at the agency she had done a solid job of handling her responsibilities and showing initiative. Her mandatory review after one month was positive with two exceptions: (1) Her attitude toward tasks she regarded as menial was poor—for example, she did not feel she should be asked to do store checks for a package goods client, and her performance on the task was sloppy; and (2) she seemed to resent having to work late and on weekends, especially when the other trainee, working on different accounts, was able to leave.

On the positive side, she was a hard worker on projects that interested her. On her own initiative, she had written a lengthy memo about several small businesses in the Charlotte areas that she believed had substantial growth potential with improved marketing support. She also impressed her supervisors with her intelligence, her knowledge of the basics of the business, and her intuitive feeling for what would work and what wouldn't. In addition, she got along extremely well with other people and clearly possessed the interpersonal skills necessary for account work.

DISASTER STRIKES!

Early on a Sunday morning Villani received a telephone call from Mary Burnett who had just been stunned by a phone call from the MB/NC marketing programs VP. The VP was panicked by an error he had just found in the MB ad in the "Homes" section of the Sunday newspaper. Instead of offering fixed-rate home mortgages at an attractive 8.5 percent, the rate in the ad was an unbelievable 5.5 percent (the current average mortgage rate in North Carolina markets hovered around 9.5 percent).

The copy in the ad stated that the rate offer was good for one week but did not include qualifications concerning the availability of funds or "first come, first served." Ironically, the ad's headline read, "MaxiBanks of North Carolina challenges *anyone* to offer a better mortgage deal." At 5.5 percent, MB/NC could be sure no one would.

The ad had been placed in every major Sunday newspaper in North Carolina and several minor ones, covering such cities as Charlotte, Wilmington, Raleigh, and Durham. This meant that the ad had been received in over 720,000 homes. Even though the largest papers were distributed over a wide area, DV&B felt it was important to give MB/NC a "hometown" image by placing ads in local papers as well. Thus, some readers of the Greenville *Daily Reflector* might also have seen the ad in the Raleigh *News & Observer,* for example. The cost to MB/NC for running the quarter-page, black-and-white ad was over $34,000.

The MB/NC VP had posed several questions to Burnett, which needed Villani's help in answering: What steps needed to be taken to prepare for what would likely be an onslaught of delighted home buyers that MB could expect on Monday morning and during the week? How did this mistake happen? And if it were DV&B's fault, what did the agency intend to do about it?

Villani suggested to Burnett that they and the creative team handling the MD/NC assignment should meet on an emergency basis at the office shortly after lunch that Sunday afternoon. If necessary, others working on the account could be involved later in the day. She agreed and promised that she would find out who was responsible for the mistaken figure in the ad by that time. Villani said he would make the necessary phone calls and hung up.

Burnett knew that it was her job to prevent such foul-ups from happening, so the responsibility for the situation was hers. However, she knew that she was not directly to blame, and she had a good idea who was. She immediately drove to the office and confirmed her suspicion. The original copy of the ad was correct, but unfortunately, the error occurred during production within the agency. The digital files with the 5 percent e-mailed to the newspapers had been approved by Karen Watkins.

Burnett had assigned Watkins the task of proofing the MD ad, stressing to her the importance of the task and the necessity of asking for help if she needed it. Clients typically sign off on creative work before it is given to the media but MB/NC maintained that proofreading was DV&B's job, not the bank's. Until Watkins' failure to catch the error made during production of the ad, MD/NC and DV&B had never had a reason to regret the policy. Wondering how Watkins could have made such an unfortunate mistake, Burnett started to prepare for the upcoming meeting at the agency.

On Monday morning, Watkins found a note on her desk asking her to meet with Burnett in Mr. Villani's office as soon as she arrived. Hurrying to Villani's office and totally unaware of the foul-up, she thought that this was an exciting way to start her seventh week at DV&B. Something big must be up, probably related to her recommendations about potential new clients to pitch.

Name _____ Date _____

QUESTIONS FOR DISCUSSION AND REVIEW

1. How serious was the foul-up? Must MB/NC honor the offer? If not, what can it tell its customers on Monday? What protocol should be followed in dealing with telephone inquiries and drop-in potential customers who inquire about a mortgage loan?

_____

_____

_____

_____

2. What is DV&B's best course of action? The bank's? Is there some way to turn this situation into a public relations opportunity?

_____

_____

_____

_____

3. What action should DV&B take regarding Karen Watkins? If you were Villani, what questions would you ask Watkins and Burnett before making a decision?

_____

_____

_____

_____

4. How might such a problem be avoided in the future?

_____

_____

_____

_____

5. Are there any implications in this situation for the management-training program?

Chapter 13
Event Sponsorships, Product Placements and Branded Entertainment

"A person who desires to make an impression must stand out in some way from the masses. And in a pleasing way. Being eccentric, being abnormal is not a distinction to covet. But doing admirable things in a pleasing way gives one a great advantage."
—Claude C. Hopkins (Scientific Advertising)

THE NEW WORLD OF INTEGRATED MARKETING COMMUNICATION

Traditional media continues to be an important way for advertisers to reach their intended audiences. Digital media, through the Internet has provided more channels to communicate efficiently with a new generation of consumers. The means by which advertisers explore unique tools to add to their arsenal of communication channels has produced less conventional ways to provide consumers with unique experiences. This chapter cannot explore all the innovative experiences advertising and public relations professionals are developing to get consumers' attention and provide them with information and entertainment. The chapter will focus on three types of tactics that have become more popular in recent years: event sponsorships, product placements, and branded entertainment.

Although entertainment has always been part of the advertising messages, the dynamic lifestyle of the new consumers seems to demand that the process of building a brand and the practice of advertising become interwoven with entertainment as a prerequisite of meriting their attention. More than ever, the industry is finding ways to do so in an effective and creative manner. Examples are numerous and varied: the much quoted campaign by Procter and Gamble for their Charmin brand, in Times Square, complete with measures like the Flush-O-Meter, the major media events surrounding the introduction of new Apple products, all attest to the new creativity of integrated marketing communication (IMC).

EVENT SPONSORSHIPS

This book discussed briefly the practice of event sponsorships in the previous chapter. This chapter provides more detail about this practice.

In a report released in January 2008 by the Advertising Research Foundation, purchase intent, or the consumers' interest in buying a product, increased 11% to 52% among consumers who attended a brand-sponsored event. The report also stated that the purchase intent translated in actual sales about 50% of the time.[1]

These results are a solid indication that in some cases, event sponsorships are a very effective way to reach consumers and to develop brand equity. Business-to-business events appear to be even more effective than business-to-consumer events. The same research study indicated that 20% of those who attended trade shows said that they would have bought the brands that were exhibited.

Marketers understand the value of this practice. Corporations spend in excess of $15 billion a year on trade shows, and trade show spending is increasing each year. Although more research is needed to assess the actual ROI of trade shows, it is evident that event sponsorships are an effective way to show off a brand to potential buyers.

Urriolagoita and Planellas described a lifecycle model approach to develop sponsorships as strategic alliances. In their article, they state that sponsorships may give each party a strategic competitive advantage by combining complementary resources to build a unique and coherent corporate image for the long-run.[2]

Event sponsorships can be found in many forms. The most popular type of event sponsorship is one that involves sports events. A great number of companies have sponsored sporting events. Among them are Adidas, McDonald's, Visa, and others. Sponsorships are particularly effective when there is an overlap between the event participants, its audience, and the target market of the sponsoring company. As an example, a sponsor of the PGA Tour would be interested in participating because the typical audience of the Tour is demographically and economically similar to its target customers. In this case, it would be interested in males, ages 35 to 65 and with upper to medium-upper family income.

Dell, the computer company headquartered in Round Rock, Texas, has a long history of sponsoring charity events. Some examples of events they have sponsored in the past are Juvenile Diabetes Research Foundation, Safe Place and The March of Dimes. A more controversial sponsorship was when the Bank of America, having just received $45 billion from the U.S. government as bailout funds, proceeded to sponsor a five-day carnival-like affair just outside the Super Bowl stadium. The event, known as the NFL Experience, was 850,000 square feet of sports games and interactive entertainment attractions for football fans. Bank of America blanketed the event with its logos and marketed football-themed banking products.

Responding to critics, the Bank of America spokesperson stated that because of its partnership with the NFL, the bank was legally required to fulfill its contract to be an NFL sponsor. In addition, it claimed that such partnerships and product tie-ins generated "significant revenue streams."

Mountain Hard Wear, a company that produces and sells sports equipment for hikers and mountain sports enthusiasts, also sponsors a series of events. The company claims that these "grassroots" events are important in that they build community and friendship and allow the company to interact more personally with the people that use their products. Some examples of the events they support are X-Dog Trail Running and Adventure Series, focusing on running, singles, activities, and beer. The company develops and publishes a complete calendar of all the events they sponsor.

Finally, the Great American Beer Festival is an event that takes place in Colorado each year. Although it is open to the public, it is also an event that promotes a competition among

---

[1] Kenneth Hein. "Study: Purchase Intent Grows with Each Event," *Brandweek,* January 28, 2008.

[2] Lourdes Urriolagoitia and Marcel Planellas. "Sponsorship Relationships as Strategic Alliances: A Life Cycle Model Approach." *Business Horizons* 50 (2007): 157–166.

beer manufacturers and serves as a promotional tool for both large and small breweries. Organized by the Brewers Association and the American Homebrewers Association Members, it attracts beer manufacturers and beer lovers from many states.

An article in the *Journal of Sponsorship* indicates that three factors are critical in determining the success of sponsorships. They are as follows:

1. Be an active participant in the event—that is, companies should be actively engaged in every step of the event and deploy adequate resources to do so;
2. Consumers should make sense of your sponsorship—a logical link between the sponsorship and the brand should be clear to those who attend the event. The stronger the logical link perceived by the consumer, the more positive will be the results of the sponsorship
3. Strive to create positive attitudes toward your brand—although this appears to be obvious, research preceding the event can help marketers focus on those attributes or values that the consumer considers important in evaluating the brand.

Positive efforts by the sponsor should be made by contacting potential customers during the event, providing relevant information, and creating an overall pleasant and positive environment for the brand.[3]

Event sponsorships should not be single occurrences of a communication strategy. They must be part of a coordinated plan and should be supported by other communication tools such as presence on Web sites and media announcements. In addition, the results of event sponsorships should be measured and analyzed. It is important for a company to know whether such a program has a positive effect on sales and on its brand perception among their target customers. Spending on sponsorships is a substantial portion of all IMC in the United States. Today, most marketers limit the evaluation of the effectiveness of their sponsorship to changes in brand equity. That is not enough. Marketers must develop tools to compare the effects of sponsorships to other communication choices. Sponsorships allow marketers to touch their consumers personally and to build a relationship with their customers. Marketers must concentrate on forming a long-lasting and valuable relationship that ultimately will be reflected in market share or sales increases.

Another important aspect of sponsorships is the support some companies provide to social causes. There are several examples of companies that have been able to use social marketing or cause-related marketing, such as promoting environmental friendliness to benefit their company image or their brands. Companies like Timberland, Avon, Home Depot, and Starbucks, to name a few, have been involved consistently in cause-related marketing efforts. In an article in the MIT *Sloan Management Review,* the authors evaluate several different social marketing initiatives and indicate that affinity marketing initiatives have the potential to improve consumers' attitudes toward a brand in many different ways. How much such activities will help or hurt a brand, according to the authors, depends on whether there are sufficient numbers of consumers in the brand's desired target market who have an affinity for the affiliation with the cause, whether consumers find the affiliation credible, whether the brand does differentiate itself sufficiently from competitors in the eyes of its target market through supporting the affiliate, and whether the affiliate stacks up favorably versus other potential beneficiaries of the brand's promotional initiatives.[4]

---

[3]Edin Güclü Sözer and Nükhet Vardar. "How Does Event Sponsorship Help in Leveraging Brand Equity?" *Journal of Sponsorship* 3, no. 1 (November 2009): 35–42.

[4]Paul N. Bloom, Steve Hoeffler, Kevin Lane Keller, and Carlos E. Basurto Meza. "How Social Cause Marketing Affects Consumer Perceptions." *Sloan Management Review* 47, no. 2 (Winter 2006): 49–55.

PRODUCT PLACEMENTS

Product placement is the practice of placing any branded product, good, or service in a context usually devoid of ads, such as movies or television programs, or any established entertainment vehicle. Online games and live productions can also be used for product placement. The product placement is often not disclosed at the time the good or service is featured. This form of IMC became common in the 1980s, and one of the most quoted examples of a successful product placement was the placement of Reese's Pieces in the film *ET.* It was reported at the time that sales for the product, following its placement, more than doubled the year the film was distributed.

Product placement is not a new concept. As early as 1919, according to the *Harrison's Reports,* Red Crown gasoline appeared in the comedy *The Garage.*[5] Movie producers, to defray some of their costs, commonly accepted products that were displayed in films in exchange for featuring them prominently in various movie scenes. Among the famous silent movies to feature product placement was *Wings* (1927), the first film to win the Oscar for Best Picture, which featured a plug for Hershey's chocolate. Products were also mentioned frequently in early radio programs, and companies such as General Electric and Maxwell House were responsible for supporting some of the early radio successes.

Incorporation of products into the actual plot of a film or show is generally called "brand integration." In 1964 Abercrombie and Fitch was the venue for part of the comedy *Man's Favourite Sport,* an early example of brand integration. Product placements in computer video games was first done in 1984, when KP's Skips Crisps were placed in the Action Biker game.

Product placement is usually divided into two categories: products or locations that are obtained from manufacturers to defray the costs of production, and products deliberately placed into productions in exchange for a fee. A variation of product placement is the placement of the advertisement for a product within the movie or television series. Other ways to place products is to offer them as prizes in game shows or other programs in return from a subsidy by the product manufacturer.

According to a recent survey by Nielsen, product placement boosts brand recognition by 20%.[6] The study found that 57.5% of the viewers recognized a brand when viewing a product placement in combination with a commercial, compared to 46.6% of viewers' recognition when exposed only to a commercial.

It is important for a company to measure the impact of product placement. Rating systems use both qualitative and quantitative measurements to attempt to define the value of this technique compared to the use of traditional media. Research on the effectiveness of product placement is ongoing, and some of the companies that provide such data to advertisers do not disclose the variables or the specific measurements they use.

One could assume that product placement is effective because marketers continue to use it in their campaigns. However, the practice has encountered the opposition of some consumer groups that feel there should be full disclosure to the public of all product placement arrangements and consider this technique to be deceptive.[7]

---

[5] *Harrison's Reports,* January 17, 1920, p. 9.

[6] Kay Bachman. "Nielsen:Product Placement Boosts Brand Awareness by 20%." *Mediaweek,* November 15, 2006.

[7] Susan Auty and Charlie Lewis. "Exploring Children's Choice: The Reminder Effect of Product Placement." *Psychology and Marketing* 21, no. 9 (September 2004): 699–716.

Some products are featured more than others. Automobiles and consumer electronics are among the most frequently displayed. There are numerous examples of films using automobiles, computers, and other electronic products in their productions. Much still has to be considered, however. Data indicating the effectiveness of the time of exposure of a product in a scene, the frequency with which the product is used, the actual circumstances in which the product is displayed, and whether or not the actual user or proponent of the product in the film or television program affect the overall perception of the image of the product are still not available.

It is clear that product placement is a tactic that can benefit the image of a product or a brand. It is also important that the product featured in films, videos, or games be shown in a favorable light. In addition, the ROI of using product placement as a form of communication needs to be investigated thoroughly and further.

IMC has become and will continue to be more ubiquitous every day in the future. Product placement is yet another example of advertisers pursuing the attention of consumers in venues outside their homes and within the kind of program entertainment they are more likely to watch. Therefore, it is just another application of basic communication principles designed to reach effectively desired target audiences by providing them with content they want to enjoy.

BRANDED ENTERTAINMENT

Branded entertainment, also known as advertainment, is an entertainment-based vehicle that is funded by and complementary to a brand's marketing strategy. Its purpose is to create a positive link between the brand and the program. The difference between branded entertainment and product placement is that in branded entertainment, the entertainment would not exist without a marketer's support, and in many cases it is the marketers themselves that create the entertainment.

Over the last two years, BMW commissioned and released two series of short films on the Internet. Produced and directed by respected Hollywood names, these films have been a great success without resorting to a number of shots of the cars or the BMW logo. The company attributed an increase of 12.5% in sales to the films' release.

Another example of branded entertainment is the action by Mattel to create a series of cartoons to support their latest toys. The success of the cartoon series changed toy marketing forever, according to some experts. Built to support Miller Lite's sponsorship of NASCAR racing, the Virtual Racing League is an online game that allows players to compete for several months at a time. With an audience of over 300,000, VRL enables Miller Lite to maximize the value of their sponsorship and in addition provides the company with an opportunity to maintain an ongoing dialogue with its audience.

More recently, Philips and DDB released a series of five thematically linked short films online in 2010, as a follow-up of its interactive film *Carousel*. The purpose of the short films is to capture the cinematic experience that Philip's flat-screen Cinema 21:9 TV set allows a viewer to enjoy. This is another compelling example of branded entertainment.

Branded entertainment, therefore, is the skillful combination of brand strategy and creative content, with the purpose of engaging a specific demographic target. It is not an over brand advertisement or product placement; rather, it is a means for a brand to create entertainment that would not exist without the brand and with which consumers choose to get involved.

As the other nontraditional forms of communication with consumers, branded entertainment must be one of the tools used by advertisers in an integrated program or campaign. Branded entertainment is successfully supported by social media, benefits from consumers blogs and exchanges, and should be also combined with adequate traditional promotion and advertising tools.

Joel Lunenfeld lists five key categories that great branded entertainment must cover to be successful. These are (1) it must be an experience that could only be brought to you by the brand in question; (2) the brand or product must play an integral role in moving the story forward; (3) the brand has to have the right to create its content; (4) the content must leave room for speculation, co-creation or interaction; and (5) the content must be entertaining, informative, interesting or useful, whether a brand is present or not.[8]

SUGGESTED READINGS

Hein, Kenneth. "Study: Purchase Intent Grows With Each Event." *Brandweek,* January 28, 2008.

Urriolagoitia, Lourdes, and Marcel Planellas. "Sponsorship Relationships as Strategic Alliances: A Life Cycle Model Approach." *Business Horizons* 50 (2007): 157–166.

Sözer, Edin Güçlü, and Nükhet Vardar. "How Does Event Sponsorship Help in Leveraging Brand Equity?" *Journal of Sponsorship* 3, no. 1 (November 2009): 35–42.

Bloom, Paul N., Steve Hoeffler, Kevin Lane Keller, and Carlos E. Basurto Meza. "How Social Cause Marketing Affects Consumer Perceptions." *Sloan Management Review* 47 no. 2 (Winter 2006): 49–55.

Harrison's Reports, *January 17, 1920, p. 9.*

Bechman, Kay. "Nielsen: Product Placement Boosts Brand Awareness by 20%." *Mediaweek,* November 15, 2006.

Auty, Susan, and Charlie Lewis. "Exploring Children's Choice: The Reminder Effect of Product Placement." *Psychology and Marketing* no. 9 (September 2004): 699–716.

Lunenfeld, Joel. "Five Keys to Branded Entertainment Success." *Advertising Age,* December 21, 2009.

EVENT SPONSORSHIPS, PRODUCT PLACEMENTS AND BRANDED ENTERTAINMENT

Exercises

1. The year 2010 was the 100th anniversary of the invention of the bra. The manufacturers of feminine undergarments wanted to develop a major event to publicize their brands and increase the perceived value and visibility of the product itself. What type(s) of events would you suggest they plan? What would be the target audience for such sponsored event(s)? Discuss.

2. Mon Bijou, a high-priced costume jewelry line, is considering the option of placing its product in the popular television series *Sex and the City.* Total retail sales of the product are $1.5 million this year. The product is available only in major urban areas and in high-level retail stores, such as Neiman Marcus, Saks Fifth Avenue, and the like. Mon Bijou management believes that with appropriate exposure, the product's sales can increase 10-fold. The target market for its product are women 20 to 45 who are very sensitive to fashion and who have a personal annual income in excess of $100,000. Do you feel that Mon Bijou should explore placing its products in the *Sex and the City* television series? If so, how should the products be shown? Should a particular actor use the product in one episode or in more than an episode? Should Mon Bijou be prepared to pay the producers of the show a fee for displaying its products? What would be a reasonable amount for the company to offer?

---

[8]Joel Lunenfeld. "Five Keys to Branded Entertainment Success." *Advertising Age,* December 21, 2009.

3. General Motors is recovering from bankruptcy and revamping its product line. In an effort to restore consumer confidence in its brand, General Motors is planning the production of five short films that can be broadcast on television and also seen on the Internet. The company is contracting with two top Hollywood producers and writers to develop stories that are entertaining and at the same time focus on national values and the importance of American entrepreneurship and innovation. The company hopes that it can reach an audience of car buyers concerned with value, reliability, and engine power and response. Is this type of branded entertainment a good strategy for General Motors? What do you suggest they do? Discuss.

4. On a 2006 episode of the NBC television show *The Office,* the characters were scared of impending layoffs. To show how valuable he is to the company, one of the show's characters takes on the role of "master shredder" using the office's newest tool, the MailMate shredder from Staples. While using the shredder, he proclaims, "it will shred anything!" While showcasing the perceived awesomeness of the Staples shredder, the character also drops lettuce into the shredder, and then removes the bottom bin to reveal a ready-to-eat salad. After pouring on dressing, a coworker asks the character, "Where'd you get the salad?" The character answers, "Staples."
   a. Do you think that *The Office* was a good choice of placement for Staples products? Why?
   b. Obviously, Staples does not encourage consumers to make salad with their shredder products. How do you think showing "nontraditional" methods of using a product affects the consumer perception of the product and brand? Was this a smart choice for Staples?
   c. What do you think Staples's goal was with this instance of product placement?
   d. Do you think it achieved that goal?

Source: Ricci, Monica. "Staples MailMate Debuted on "The Office" *Your Life. Organized.* November 17, 2006. Web, April 18, 2010. <http://monicaricci.typepad.com/monica_ricci_organizing_e/2006/11/staplesailmat.html>.

5. The animated series titled *City Hunters* is the product of a pairing between Fox Latin American Channels and Unilever's Axe brand. The show focuses on a hopeless young man, Axel, who is being trained in the art of seduction by Dr. Lynch, a '70s playboy and master fragrance creator. Over the course of nine episodes, Dr. Lynch passes his secrets of women to Axel, creating a man capable of conquering all women. The animations were designed by famous Italian illustrator Milo Manara and aired during the adult-skewed late night programming.
   a. What is Axe communicating about its brand image with *City Hunters?*
   b. What benefits does Axe receive from creating an animated series?

Source: Ball, Ryan. "Fox Latin America, Axe Launch City Hunters." *Animation Magazine,* October 19, 2006. Web, April 19, 2010. <http://www.animationmagazine.net/article/6041>.

6. The Audi RSQ sports car plays a major role in the Will Smith science fiction thriller, *I, Robot.* A study done by Audi after the release of the movie showed that the appearance and role of the car in the movie gave a substantial boost to the image ratings of the Audi brand. The movie reinforced core values of the Audi brand, including attractiveness and distinctiveness.

   Now, imagine you work at Audi and are investing in more movie product placement to further raise image ratings. The producer of the movie you have chosen has offered, for an additional fee, to feature the Audi competitor's newest car in negative situations and have it be shown as inferior to the Audi.

a. Do you think this is unethical? Why?
b. What effect would this have on Audi brand image?
c. What decision would you make?

Source: Felber, Eric. "Product Placement in the Film "I, Robot" a Huge Success: The Audi RSQ Spurs on the Brand's Image Ratings." *PR Newswire*. Web, April 18, 2010. <http://www.prnewswire.co.uk/cgi/news/release?id=135557>.

---

[1]This case was written by John H. Murphy, The University of Texas at Austin. This case is designed to serve as the basis for classroom discussion and not to illustrate either the effective or ineffective handling of an administrative situation. The case is used with permission granted by K. Spoetzl Brewery and McGarrah Jessee.

Case 13.1

Shiner Beer[1]

Located between Houston and San Antonio, Texas, the Spoetzl Brewery began producing beer in 1909. Over time the company had grown from a small regional brewery to a brand with near national distribution that was available in 37 states. The firm produced a product line of six Shiner (S) beers all based on the classic Bavarian tradition. The line included: Black Lager, Blonde, Bock, Frost, Hefeweizen, and Light.

Shiner's marketing efforts were built around the brand's authentic, rich heritage as an old-school beer brewed in the quirky little town of Shiner, Texas. McGarrah Jessee (McJ), their advertising agency, had done a strong job of capitalizing on and building the Shiner mystic as a distinctive brand of beer. Exhibit 13.1.1 presents an example of one of Shiner's funky, nostalgic print ads.

The S brand building team at McJ was constantly on the lookout for ways to promote S in a way that resonated with the brand's heritage/tradition and target audience. An event that was ripe with potential in terms of its vibe and audience was the annual Austin City Limits Music Festival (ACL). Unfortunately, ACL already had an official beer sponsor: Heineken.

AUSTIN CITY LIMITS MUSIC FESTIVAL

The ACL music festival was held each year in the early fall in Zilker Park, a public park located near downtown Austin, Texas. The three-day (Friday, Saturday, and Sunday) event attracted thousands of music fans. A diverse mix of bands and performers appeared on one of eight stages playing for an hour or 45 minutes with headliners performing for two hours.

Roads into and around the park were closed during the festival and there was no on-site parking. Fans were encouraged to use free shuttle buses that ran between Republic Square in downtown and the park. Taxis were allowed access to a convenient drop-off and pick-up area adjacent to the park. Passenger drop-off for private cars was across the Colorado River north of the park and west of the park but a reasonable walk to the stages (Exhibit 13.1.2 present a map of area).

Past official corporate sponsors included: American Airlines, Dell Computers, Heineken beer, Honda, Sweet Leaf Iced Teas, T•Mobile, and Xbox 360. Media partners included five radio stations, *The Austin Chronicle,* and a local television channel, News Channel 8.

AN AMBUSH MARKETING PROMOTION

Given the attractiveness of associating S with the local authenticity of the ACL, the team at McJ was initially disappointed that Heineken's official sponsorship seemed to preclude S's participation in the event. In brainstorming off the concept of S being the "unofficial beer" of ACL, their initial frustration lead to inspiration. The rebelliousness of bucking "the corporate authorities" had a fun, mischievousness to it that felt right for the brand. But how to capitalize on the ACL as an unofficial sponsor presented a dilemma.

The McJ team's answer was to use street teams to hand out free koozies with the S label on them to fans as they boarded shuttle buses in downtown Austin or at one of the two major drop-off areas before fans entered the park. Once fans arrived at the festival and bought a Heineken at one of the many concession stands, they would slip their Heineken can into the S koozie. Presto, change-o the official beer became an ad for S (see Exhibit 13.1.3). The impression created was clearly that the giant world-wide, official sponsor had been outmaneuvered by the smaller local underdog. Clearly, the positive buzz created for S was that their smart, inexpensive, guerilla marketing had upstaged the high dollar corporate sponsor.

Exhibit 13.1.1

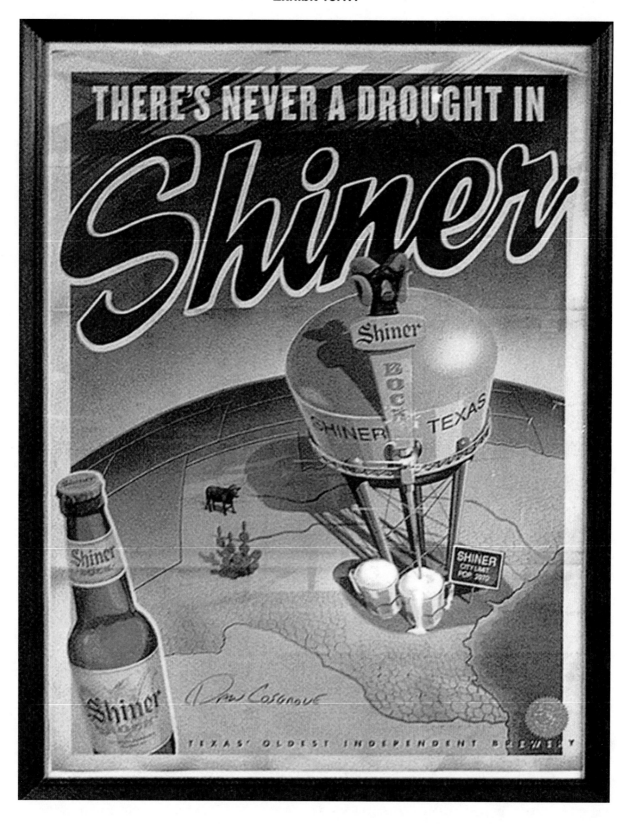

Exhibit 13.1.2

Exhibit 13.1.3

HOW TO FOLLOW UP ON SUCCESS?

In the wake of the success of the street team/koozie ambush program, the S brand team at McJ was faced with the challenge of what's next? In the future, it seemed safe to assume that the organizers of the ACL would be ready to take quick legal steps to prevent S from handing out koozies again. There were several legal avenues open to the ACL organizers to block such a guerilla tactic. For example, the city's street vendor license requirement might be used to block such distribution. Although it was unclear exactly what the ACL organizers would do, it was safe to assume that they would aggressively protect the integrity of their corporate sponsorships.

How might S participate in the ACL in the future even though they were not the official beer sponsor? Without question, S's past ambush marketing success put a spotlight on their next move at the ACL music festival.

Name _____ Date _____

QUESTIONS FOR DISCUSSION AND REVIEW

1. Was the street team/free koozie distribution promotion legal? Are there other ethical or moral issues that might be involved here?

2. How might Heineken have most effectively responded to the S koozie program?

3. Are there other examples of ambush marketing that might be instructive to S and McJ in planning their future efforts?

4. What steps might ACL or individual sponsors take to avoid similar competitive tactics in the future?

Case 13.2

And Now, a Word From Our Sponsor

"Grey Goose martini, please," Laura Goldenberg said to the bartender as she settled onto her stool. She glanced at her Rolex, pulled an issue of *Harvard Business Review* out of her Coach bag, and leafed through it, tapping her foot impatiently as she waited for her son to show up. A college senior, Alex was juggling exams, a job at a health club, and a long list of friends and girlfriends—not to mention a Web business he was launching. But when he finally sauntered in 20 minutes later, Laura's irritation quickly gave way to surprise. Alex had the words "Gold's Gym" emblazoned across his forehead in bright yellow letters. "What is *that*? Are you coming from some sort of Halloween party? Or is this a fraternity stunt? Wait—don't tell me it's permanent!" She reached up to touch the letters.

"Mom," said Alex, brushing her fingers away, "it's just a way to pick up some extra cash. Gold's is paying me a hundred bucks a week to wear it. You know I'm trying to get my Web site up and running. I'll take money anywhere I can get it."

"A hundred dollars doesn't seem like nearly enough for turning your face into a billboard," Laura muttered. "What if I lent you the money instead?"

Alex frowned. "Thanks, Mom. But we want to do it on our own. Bob and Jennifer are wearing the Gold's logo, too, and we'll find a way to get the company going."

Laura decided to drop the subject. They moved to a table and sat down to dinner. This was a meeting that Alex had requested. He wanted advice on putting together a marketing program for his business—on a shoestring, of course. Even though Laura worked for a large company now, she had experience with startups. She launched into a quick lesson on frequency and reach, trying to ignore the yellow letters marring her son's appearance.

Plop, Plop, Fizz, Fizz

"For National Public Radio News, I'm Jean Cochrane . . ." With the voice from the radio slowly seeping into her consciousness, Laura opened her eyes, squinted at the clock, and remembered that she had an early morning meeting with her advertising agency. She was vice president of marketing for the geriatric products division of a major drug company, Bryant Pharmaceuticals. Bryant's flagship product, a popular arthritis medicine called Seflex, had been selling well, but growth was starting to level off—a particular cause for concern as the patent was due to expire in less than two years. The company was looking for a dramatic increase in sales before generic versions started showing up on the shelves.

Making matters more difficult, the Bryant family still owned a 5% stake in the business and wielded enormous influence. Joe Bryant had been grumbling that the company's new CEO, Henry Winters, was green-lighting too many promotional programs that Bryant considered "off brand." Henry's most recent sin was approving the sponsorship of a women's tennis tournament that had generated controversy when the winner chose her upset victory as the moment to announce her sexual orientation to the world. The Bryants were staunch conservatives—and since Henry supported various liberal causes, other differences of opinion arose. But the real problem, Laura suspected, was that Henry was the first nonfamily member to hold the top job in the company. Whatever the reason, the pressure was trickling down to Laura's boss, chief marketing officer Isabel Hines, and to Laura herself. Laura was feeling an acute need to show results—to support Henry and

Copyright © 2003 by the President and Fellows of Harvard College. The Case was prepared by Bob Gamgort, Michelle Nelson, Mozelle Thompson, Mike Sheehan and Ellen Peebles as a basis for class discussion rather than to illustrate either effective or ineffective handling of an administrative situation. Reprinted with permission of Harvard Business School.

Isabel, both of whom she liked, and to preserve her own job. "The stress is getting to me," she thought as she poured herself a glass of water and dropped in two Alka-Seltzer tablets.

And that was why she'd called a meeting with her ad agency.

Think Different

Thanks to heavy traffic and a much-needed Starbucks stop, Laura was the last to arrive for her meeting with PJE Communications. She went directly to the conference room, found a seat, and set her cup down in front of her. "Sorry to keep you waiting," she said. "Let's get started."

PJE account executive John Capin stood up and shoved a tape into the VCR. It was the most recent commercial for Seflex—standard pharmaceutical fare, showing 60-something couples frolicking with their grandchildren, and happy families in the bloom of health.

"Our research shows that the campaign's been effective," John said, handing around copies of an Excel spreadsheet demonstrating that the public's awareness of Seflex was continuing to grow. "But I know you're looking for a change, and I agree. I think we could freshen up our creative, try something new." He reached into his briefcase, pulled out a photograph, and handed it to Laura. It was a picture of Jeanne Alyson, a 1940s movie icon who seldom made public appearances. "She suffers from terrible arthritis, and I happen to know she uses Seflex. She's a favorite with our target market." John leaned on the table and looked directly at Laura. "What if we hire her as a spokesperson? We could shoot an interview-style commercial, with her talking about how Seflex changed her life."

Laura stared at the picture and considered what John had said. "It sounds expensive," she said. "And is the concept really that new?"

"Well, it's still a commercial," John agreed. "But you get more credibility—a real Seflex user speaking about the product in a very personal way. What you don't get is a captive audience. With TiVo and ReplayTV—and even old-fashioned remote controls—viewers can pretty easily skip over TV ads. Which brings me to the other idea we wanted to put on the table: product placement. Mix your promotional message with the content. Consumer product companies do it all the time. Remember Reese's Pieces in *E.T.*? Or Tom Cruise wearing Ray-Bans in *Risky Business*?"

"You aren't suggesting that we have John Mahoney popping Seflex on *Frasier*, are you?"

"Not quite," John said. "I was thinking more along the lines of having a character on a show like *ER* taking Seflex. More on brand."

"Maybe we could get Jeanne Alyson a cameo on *ER*," another PJE executive suggested. "Or even a recurring role. It would be a way of increasing her visibility, and then when she does the commercials, people will connect her with the show."

John stopped, looking thoughtful. "You might be on to something," he said. "But let's take it a step farther. What if we could get Jeanne on a news show, interviewed in a segment featuring arthritis—and, of course, Seflex. That way, we're pure content. No TiVoing. And without the baggage that comes with advertising."

"Would a news show do that?" Laura asked.

"Can't hurt to try," John replied. "It's not that far removed from using a taped news release."

"Well, it's certainly different," Laura said. "I'm not sure what I think about it, but give me the weekend to mull it over."

Reach Out and Touch Someone

Laura looked at the crisp autumn sky and then at the pile of leaves on her lawn. Alex had shown up to help her rake—still wearing the Gold's logo—and she'd paid him a modest sum for giving up a couple hours of his Saturday morning. But even as she admired their yard work, her advertising challenge was foremost on her mind. Getting a beloved celebrity to extol the virtues of Seflex on the news sounded like a sure thing. But then, why weren't others doing something similar?

She wandered into the house and picked up the phone to call her friend Lesley Dorin, a marketing professor at nearby Forrester University. Lesley would certainly know something about product placement and might have a useful perspective on it. After explaining the Jeanne Alyson idea, Laura summed up her own impressions. "I think it's pretty clever," she said. "And I'm looking for something new. But I don't know—do you think it's a little unseemly? Could it backfire on us?"

"I don't know," Lesley replied. "I've certainly heard worse. Not long ago, there was a story on the radio about a town in Maine that was getting free police cars with corporate ads plastered all over them. The police chief wasn't thrilled, but he didn't have the budget to buy the cars. And then there was that book—*The Bulgari Connection*. The author got a bundle from Bulgari to write it. And get this: I read that a video game company was looking to pay families to put ads for a new game on their dead relatives' tombstones. Now *that's* unseemly. Putting Seflex on the morning news seems pretty tame in comparison. As a member of the TV-watching public, I don't love it, but it's probably a good move from a marketing standpoint. If I were you, I'd at least meet Jeanne Alyson."

Does She or Doesn't She?

On Monday morning, Laura went directly to Isabel's office, knocked twice, and opened the door. Isabel was on the phone. "OK, Henry. Thanks for the heads up, though I don't know why Joe should have anything to say about it."

Rolling her eyes, Isabel hung up the phone and told Laura what was going on. "It's Joe Bryant. Believe it or not, he thinks our ads are getting too slick—we're getting away from our scientific roots, he says."

"It's advertising," Laura said. "Does he expect us to get into the details of chemical compounds?"

Isabel merely shrugged, so Laura went on. "Well, maybe my timing's a little off, then, but here's what I came to tell you. PJE came to me with a new idea. We could hire Jeanne Alyson as a spokesperson and get one of the morning news shows to do a segment on arthritis in which she'd talk about her treatment. She takes Seflex, of course."

"Jeanne Alyson the actress? How much would it cost us?"

Laura hesitated. "About a million. Not just for the one interview; she'd do some other media as well. But a spot on a news program would pay for itself, I think. We have the money in the budget—it just means we'd do one or two fewer commercials."

Isabel gathered some papers and picked up her Franklin Planner. "I've got to run to a meeting," she said. "Let me give it some thought. Sounds interesting—and I can't imagine Joe Bryant calling Jeanne Alyson 'too slick.'"

Where's the Beef?

Back in her own office, Laura saw that she had a message from John Capin, who had called to report that Jeanne Alyson was interested and willing to meet Laura and him for breakfast Wednesday morning at the Four Seasons. And, he said, *The Morning Show* had expressed some interest in an interview. Laura spent the rest of the morning returning phone calls, then dialed Isabel's extension after lunch.

"Isabel Hines."

Laura could tell from the echoes and ambient sound that Isabel was on speakerphone. "Am I interrupting a meeting?" Laura asked.

"Marion's here, but that's OK." Laura's heart sank. Marion DeMaria was Bryant's CFO, and she was taking a particular interest in Bryant's marketing budget of late. "Perfect timing. We were just talking about the Alyson deal. Marion's raised some interesting questions."

"No doubt," thought Laura. Aloud, she said, "I'm all ears. I should start by telling you I'm meeting with Jeanne and her people on Wednesday. And the best part is, *The Morning Show* wants to put her on the air."

"Here's the thing," Isabel said. "It's a lot of money, and what do we get? We can't control what she'll say. And we can't control what the interviewer will say, either. It's live TV, right? Jeanne Alyson is no doctor, and she's no PR professional either. She could very easily get in over her head. What if they ask her something, and she doesn't know the answer? These are journalists; they don't care if we come off looking good. How do we know this won't turn out to be a gotcha?"

"Isabel, *The Morning Show* doesn't do gotcha. And if we want to stay ahead we have to get creative," Laura said. "We could spend the same money on a commercial, and you wouldn't even question it—and I promise, we'd lose a lot of viewers thanks to TiVo and ReplayTV. Even people who are using plain, old-fashioned remote control jump ship when a commercial comes on, thanks to cable and satellite dishes. People have a lot of choices."

"Well, that's something I've been thinking about," Marion interrupted. "Maybe we shouldn't be doing so much advertising. There's no way to measure it. Why not put the money into direct mail and other activities where we can get a good read on ROI?"

Why had Isabel brought Marion into this conversation? "If we sign Jeanne Alyson, we'll have a credible spokesperson, and the message becomes part of the news," Laura said. "I don't know how we can lose. But I'm certainly not ready to abandon direct mail or even regular TV commercials. No worries there. But if we don't do this, somebody else will. As for controlling what she'll say, I imagine we can write her contract in a way that allows us to get out if she says something that's wrong or that could get us into trouble. And, of course, we'll coach her." Laura took a deep breath. "I'm not saying we should definitely do this. I'm saying, let me meet Jeanne, and meanwhile let's all sleep on it."

"OK. Take the meeting," Isabel said. "We can talk about it afterward."

Laura called John to confirm the meeting with the actress.

Raise Your Hand If You're Sure

Glad to be home, Laura walked into the living room to the mouthwatering smell of popcorn. Her daughter Susan looked up from the couch where she was watching *Die Another Day*, a large bowl of Orville Redenbacher in her lap.

"Look," Susan said, shoving a magazine toward her mother. "October is popcorn-popping month. I had to make some." Glancing at the magazine, Laura saw that her daughter was right. According to the article, October was also national cookie month, fire prevention month, and computer-learning month.

"Wouldn't you do better to celebrate computer- learning month?" Laura asked halfheartedly as she took a handful and sat down next to her daughter. As the movie progressed, she couldn't help but notice the liberal use of product placements. Pierce Brosnan drove an Aston Martin. He used a Sony cell phone and an Omega wristwatch. Up to a point, the use of brand names lent atmosphere, even made James Bond seem more real, she thought. But the movie was starting to look like a series of commercials—funny that she'd never noticed it before. Would she even have registered all those placements, Laura wondered, if the Jeanne Alyson deal hadn't been on her mind? She shifted in her seat and eventually got up and headed into the kitchen to join her husband, Matt, a lawyer. She opened the Sub-Zero refrigerator, pulled out a bottle of Poland Spring water, twisted off the cap, and tossed it across the room into the trash. A perfect shot.

"She shoots, she scores!" said Matt, sitting at the table, a bowl of Cheerios in front of him. "How come I always miss?"

"Hey, can I get your opinion on something?" Laura asked. She pulled up a chair next to him and began telling him about the next day's meeting and her conversation with Isabel and Marion. "Marion's resisting it because you can't quantify it—and also because it's new, I think. But you know, hearing her list the reasons we should hold back just makes me want to do it all the more. Why are we letting bean counters make our marketing decisions?"

"That's not fair to Marion," Matt said. "She's just doing her job. And she has a point—you don't know what you're getting. Besides, aren't you entering questionable territory here—blurring the line between journalism and paid promotion? People will assume Jeanne Alyson is talking about Seflex because she really believes in it, not because you're paying her to."

"She does believe in it," Laura said. "So do I. It's a good product. Besides, I think the lines are blurring anyway. Newspapers and magazines use press releases verbatim. Radio and TV news programs use recorded news releases. This isn't so different—and it's a lot more interesting."

"And if word gets out that you're paying her to talk?"

"I don't see how it would. Jeanne's not going to tell. I doubt *The Morning Show* would say anything. And if people did find out? I'm not sure anyone would even care."

Matt raised his hands in surrender. "Hey, I'm a lawyer. I get paid to look for the downside. If you think it's a good idea, I'm sure it is."

The Real Thing

Fifteen minutes late, with her agent in tow, Jeanne Alyson slowly yet gracefully entered the dining room of the Four Seasons and sat down with Laura and John. Nodding at each in turn, a bemused look on her face, Jeanne asked, "Now, what is it exactly you had in mind for me to do?"

Upon hearing the explanation, Jeanne's face lit up. "Well, you know, I use Seflex, and it's been a tremendous help." She leaned closer to John and Laura and added in a conspiratorial tone, "But it upsets my stomach sometimes."

"Oh, you need to take it with food," Laura hastened to point out.

"Yes, I know," said Jeanne. "And that reminds me." She pulled out a small bottle, opened it, and extracted a familiar yellow pill. "I'll take this with my breakfast."

The next two hours passed quickly, as the articulate, funny actress regaled Laura and John with stories of Hollywood in the 1940s and 1950s. Heading back to the office behind the wheel of her Mercedes, Laura reflected on the meeting. She wasn't particularly starstruck, but she was tickled by the morning's events. Jeanne would be a charming and entertaining spokesperson—a TV audience would eat her up. As for that comment about the upset stomach . . . well, she could be coached. Jeanne really did like the product, and she seemed ready to sign. Now Laura just had to convince Isabel— and Marion. She fished in her purse for her StarTAC, pulled it out, and hit speed dial for Isabel's number. "I just came from the Four Seasons. Do you have a few minutes? I'd like to come by and talk about this Jeanne Alyson thing."

Just Do It

Both Isabel and Marion were waiting for Laura when she walked in and took a seat by her boss's desk. Isabel was looking weary. "I just got off the phone with Henry," she said. "He's worried about the numbers for next quarter. And he's got Joe Bryant breathing down his neck, just waiting for him to make a mistake. If we're going to do this spokesperson deal, I need to know it's not going to blow up on us. Are you sure you want to get us into a situation we may not be able to control?"

Isabel glanced over at Marion. "I also want to make sure it's the best use of our marketing budget," Isabel continued. "Getting Jeanne to talk about arthritis and Seflex may just be playing to the generics that are going to hit the market in two years. If we don't own the message, we can't be sure that this will do anything for Seflex's name recognition. We may just be creating a customer base for our competition by educating people about their treatment options. And what if she slips up and says something wrong—or negative?"

Laura fidgeted in her chair. So much of her work depended on intuition. The Jeanne Alyson deal felt right, but she could offer no guarantees. Could something go wrong? Was it a good investment? She fiddled with her Palm-Pilot, weighing whether she wanted to stake her reputation on this deal.

SHOULD BRYANT PHARMACEUTICALS APPROVE LAURA'S IDEA FOR PRODUCT PLACEMENT?

by Bob Gamgort

My advice to Laura and her colleagues: Don't make product placement the centerpiece of your strategy. While it can deliver a tremendous boost to brand awareness and credibility, it's too unpredictable.

Of course, nontraditional campaigns can generate incredible buzz. Everyone wants to find the next *Blair Witch Project,* which got tons of publicity out of a grassroots campaign at little cost to the film's producers. But for every *Blair Witch Project,* a hundred such efforts go unnoticed.

The key is to make placement part of a larger, sustainable strategy. Stories about product placement always mention the movie *E.T.,* which featured Reese's Pieces—a placement opportunity M&M/Mars (as our company was then known) famously turned down. Was it a nice placement? Yes. But 20 years later, M&M'S is the number one candy brand in the world, and where is Reese's Pieces? A good placement can put you on the map for a short period of time, but it certainly won't drive your brand over the long term.

The problem Laura's facing—trying to break through the advertising clutter—is real. The average American is exposed to 650 advertising messages a day and has become skilled at tuning out the noise. It's true that using a celebrity spokesperson can make your message stand out, especially in marketing prescription drugs, because the category is inherently confusing and the law requires alarming disclosures in ads. The right spokesperson can connect with consumers on a personal level and offer some assurance that help is available.

But your core, traditional marketing efforts will still deliver most of your reach. Consider that a single PR placement—even in the highest-rated morning news program—will reach less than 3% of the adult population.

Laura would do much better to use a spokesperson in a paid television ad. That way, she could manage the base level of reach, control message content, and ensure a return on Bryant's marketing investment. (I don't, by the way, think Jeanne Alyson is the right spokesperson, because she doesn't project an image of an active person who's overcome the symptoms of arthritis.) Then I'd approach product placement opportunistically. For example, I'd look for extra exposure by tying my campaign to something newsworthy. In Bryant's case, there's good potential for news coverage. The company could start a conversation about arthritis symptoms and new treatments, with Seflex as one of the options discussed.

At Masterfoods, most of our product placement is opportunistic, and in many cases our best placements cost us little or nothing. That's because TV and movie producers are looking for products with images that align with their own goals—or sometimes they want to place a product just because they like it. M&M'S got placement on *The West Wing* because the real *Air Force One* carries customized boxes of the candy. David Letterman talked about Snickers on three consecutive shows after he sent a camera crew into a deli, spotted our display on the counter, and asked the crew to bring back some candy. The next night, he suggested that we come down to the studio and deliver Snickers to the audience. Finally, on the last night, we showed up with a van full of product, which Letterman gave to charity. We also received significant news coverage on our M&M'S color-vote promotion, where 10 million consumers around the world voted for the next M&M'S color. The news media responded to the global nature of the story and the fact that we received votes from countries where people aren't even allowed to vote for their own leadership.

Stories tied to real-life issues or events have legs—you get a lot of exposure in a variety of media. When it comes to Bryant hiring an actress for a product placement, I don't think the company will get enough exposure to justify spending $1 million.

SHOULD BRYANT PHARMACEUTICALS APPROVE LAURA'S IDEA FOR PRODUCT PLACEMENT?

by Michelle R. Nelson

It's not surprising that Bryant is looking for new ways to reach consumers. Budget constraints, fragmented audiences, and technological advances that allow consumers to zip, zap, and circumvent advertising are making it harder for advertisers to stick out from the clutter. But before hiring Jeanne Alyson, Bryant's senior team needs to take a hard look at several concerns. In the end, this might not be the right time to launch a celebrity campaign.

It's true that products embedded in a story line are less likely to be ignored than ads, and messages may have more credibility, because consumers' defenses are down during noncommercial programming. So while $1 million is a lot of money, it may be cost-effective in terms of reach.

With product placement, brand names can also enhance audiences' sense of realism. The case study itself includes more than two dozen real brand names, which offer context and social meaning just as placement does in a movie script. And spokespeople are effective when they're credible and likable—and relevant to the target audience—as Jeanne appears to be.

It's important that Jeanne Alyson isn't endorsing other products, so people will associate her only with Seflex. When a celebrity promotes too many products, the association is watered down and the credibility may be lost. When you think of Michael Jordan, for example, you might think of the Chicago Bulls, Rayovac batteries, Hanes underwear, Nike, or McDonald's.

But while product placement does have advantages, Laura's plan is problematic for a number of reasons. First, hiring a celebrity spokesperson may not be the "new" approach she's seeking. The technique has become quite common in the pharmaceutical industry, dating back to Ciba-Geigy's use of Mickey Mantle to announce FDA approval of an arthritis drug in 1988. Public relations firms now keep databases of stars as potential endorsers—sports figures like NFL coach Dan Reeves for the cholesterol drug Zocor, along with actors, models, musicians, and even politicians, as with Bob Dole's endorsement of Viagra. Kathleen Turner, a paid spokesperson for Enbrel, appeared on *Good Morning America* in 2002 to tell how she was diagnosed with rheumatoid arthritis. Lauren Hutton, paid by Wyeth, spoke to *Parade* magazine about estrogen in 2002. At some point, consumers might start to see such endorsements as additional noise.

Second, studies have shown that consumer responses to placement vary by gender, ethnicity, and age, with younger viewers responding more favorably than older viewers, who happen to be Seflex's target audience. Bryant should, at the very least, run focus groups to gauge response to Jeanne and the idea that she may be on the company's payroll.

Third, when they combine content and promotion, companies often lose control over how their brands are depicted. The interview could end up on the cutting room floor. Or paid spokespeople (or their agents) may say the wrong thing. And it's not just what the spokesperson says or does on camera—the potential for scandal or even a premature death, even if unrelated to the product, may sully the brand's reputation.

And finally, given that they don't intend to disclose the fact that they're compensating the star, Laura and her colleagues may face PR trouble if news gets out. Critics lambasted Olympic medalist Dorothy Hamill for talking about Vioxx before the 2000 Summer Olympics without disclosing she was paid. Of course, Bryant can avoid this problem by being forthright about the financial relationship. Proactive, honest public relations have always succeeded over reactive communication strategies.

Regardless of what strategy Laura decides to pursue, she needs to think carefully about what she's trying to achieve. Her current campaign already seems quite effective—why change it?

SHOULD BRYANT PHARMACEUTICALS APPROVE LAURA'S IDEA FOR PRODUCT PLACEMENT?

by Mozelle W. Thompson

This scenario raises, to my mind, three types of issues: legal, business, and ethical. Bryant Pharmaceuticals needs to consider all three before taking on Jeanne Alyson as a spokesperson.

From a legal standpoint, the FTC Act allows the Federal Trade Commission to take action against deceptive trade practices, including deceptive advertising. Our guidelines mandate that a celebrity endorsement has to reflect the endorser's honest opinions and experiences. And if a financial arrangement might materially affect the weight or credibility of the endorsement—in a context where the viewer wouldn't expect that the person is getting paid—the endorser has to disclose the arrangement. In other words, if someone says, "I eat X brand of hot dogs," the average viewer would expect that the hot dog company is paying for that. That expectation isn't there in a news program. In fact, we've established in a number of infomercial cases that it's a violation of the FTC Act for an advertiser to use a format that would mislead consumers into believing an ad is actually an independent news program.

So this story raises a couple of issues that would concern law enforcers. First, as I just mentioned, the FTC would have a problem with Bryant's intent not to disclose that it was paying Jeanne Alyson. This type of placement is very different from putting Coca-Cola into a Tom Cruise movie, where you can argue that it's artistic license. This is a news show.

Second, it's pretty clear that Alyson will be coached—and that the company hopes she won't be completely honest. Jeanne specifically mentioned that the medicine upsets her stomach, and Laura and her colleagues want to make sure she won't mention side effects on TV. That might raise some questions at the FDA, which has rules about disclosing side effects in a clear and conspicuous way.

Laura is also making the assumption that nobody would find out, or even care, that Bryant paid Alyson. That's a pretty big assumption. An incident very much like this made headlines in the *New York Times* a little more than a year ago, when Lauren Bacall was paid by Novartis to talk about a drug on a morning television show. And in case you think nobody's watching, the American Association of Advertising Agencies, a self-regulating trade association, is one of the biggest sources of referrals to the FTC. But even without a referral or any legal action, the issue could easily surface if the program's host were to ask, "Are you being paid to advertise this drug on this show?" So if a company is engaging in questionable advertising practices, it's unlikely to go unnoticed.

The next set of issues the Bryant team needs to consider are business related. Here a group of executives and their advisers are talking about how they intend to mislead the public. They acknowledge that if people find out, the company's reputation could be seriously damaged. The team should know better than to put Bryant's reputation at risk, especially considering that the sale of drugs is based on trust. A consumer might wonder, "If they're misleading me about the spokesperson, are they misleading me about other things?"

The other business concern comes down to pure dollars and cents. If you're spending $1 million for a celebrity endorsement, and you don't know exactly what she'll say or how she'll say it, you're gambling that money. Finally, we come to the ethical considerations, which obviously overlap with the legal and business issues. We know that Laura is under some pressure to produce results, and I'm concerned that the pressure may lead her to recommend an essentially deceptive advertising campaign. I'm also concerned that she may disillusion and de-motivate her staff by sending a message that the company is willing to run a dishonest operation. But most important, doesn't the public have a right to full disclosure?

SHOULD BRYANT PHARMACEUTICALS APPROVE LAURA'S IDEA FOR PRODUCT PLACEMENT?

by Mike Sheehan

In general, I like using product placement and celebrity spokespeople because they allow marketers to communicate with consumers in attention- getting ways. We've done a number of successful branded content deals for our clients. For example, we created a promotion for LoJack, the automobile security system, during last year's NESN broadcast of the Boston Red Sox games. Whenever an opposing player was caught stealing a base, he was tagged on screen with the LoJack logo and branded "caught stealing." We also negotiated a national placement deal for Dunkin' Donuts in the reality TV show *Big Brother*. Viewers watched the "houseguests" earn one week of Dunkin' Donuts coffee, bagels, muffins, and doughnuts.

And while the logo on Alex's forehead may seem a little far-fetched, we've done exactly that. Together with a sports marketing company, we put Dunkin' Donuts logos on the foreheads of a bunch of college kids at this year's NCAA basketball tournament. It was a great fit because college students love Dunkin' Donuts, and we got extra publicity for our client because ESPN put the story on its Web site and talked about it on the air.

These promotions worked because in each case the product fit naturally with the setting or programming. The more seamless, the better. You don't want it to look like a commercial, which was the case with *American Idol* 's treatment of Coca-Cola and its heavily promoted "Red Room." And while placement is relatively new to TV, on the big screen products have been subtly integrated into plots for years. The Omega watch tie-in with James Bond works well because the watch plays a role in the movie. The same goes for Reese's Pieces in *E.T.* and the Mini in *The Italian Job*.

But while I'm a fan of product placement and I think it's here to stay—especially with the advent of TiVo and similar technologies—I don't think traditional advertising is going away. TiVo will force advertisers to think more creatively—if a commercial is entertaining, people will watch. There's no substitute for a great 30-second spot. And with TiVo, people consistently watch the television shows they want to watch, rather than viewing whatever's on. So you can target programs more effectively.

As for celebrity endorsements, they're most successful when there's an element of surprise. That's why I'd go back to the drawing board when it comes to Bryant's choice of spokesperson. Jeanne Alyson seems like a natural fit for the target audience, but she's not very interesting because she's exactly the type of person you'd expect to talk about arthritis. When Rafael Palmeiro, first baseman for the Texas Rangers, talked about Viagra, there was something unexpected and brave about it. People think of athletes as young, strong, and healthy, yet here was Palmeiro reminding consumers that even someone as vibrant as he shares some of their health problems. In this case, the publicity didn't end with a one-shot television appearance but continued to live on in the media. Reporters kept asking him, "Why did you do it?" Interestingly enough, Palmeiro never admitted to actually taking the pill. But the intention was clear: Viagra is not just for Grandpa. With Alyson, I don't think Bryant will get its million dollars' worth.

A couple of caveats: There are some risks inherent to celebrity endorsements and product placements. The pharmaceutical industry is coming under increased scrutiny by the FDA. To comply with FDA regulations, Bryant would have to train the spokesperson to talk about side effects, and then it starts to smell like a regular commercial. And with product placement, you can lose creative control. But for the most part, any exposure has some benefits. Harry Truman, among others, is said to have remarked, "I don't care what they say about me as long as they spell my name right." That sentiment applies here, too.

Case 13.3

Bank of America Sports Sponsorship

When a sports property approaches us and says, "We have all these tickets, signage, suites, parking, and special events," that's great, but it may or may not have value to us. What really matters to us is how you help us achieve our business goals.

Ray Bednar, Bank of America senior vice president and global sponsorship executive, was describing in late 2006 the bank's current philosophy on sports sponsorship. He and his colleagues were evaluating several sports sponsorship opportunities to initiate, renew, or terminate. He had recently established explicit business and marketing criteria for selecting sponsorship opportunities for the bank. Now Bednar and the other executives had to apply these standards in making their decisions about four sponsorships under consideration: (1) NASCAR, (2) U.S. Olympic Committee, (3) the Dallas Cowboys, and (4) The Colonial PGA Tournament in Fort Worth, Texas.

BANK OF AMERICA BACKGROUND

Bank of America Corporation was one of the world's largest financial institutions. It operated in 29 states, the District of Columbia, and 43 foreign countries, serving individual consumers, small and middle market businesses, and large corporations. The company provided a diversified range of financial offerings—such as banking, investing, asset management, and other financial and risk-management products and services—domestically and internationally through three business segments: Global Consumer and Small Business Banking, Global Wealth and Investment Management, and Global Corporate and Investment Banking. (See below for descriptions of these lines of business.)

Headquartered in Charlotte, North Carolina, the company served more than 55 million consumer and small business relationships with over 5,800 retail banking offices, nearly 17,000 ATMs, and online banking with more than 20 million active users. Bank of America was the nation's largest provider of checking and savings services, the No. 1 credit and debit card provider, the No. 1 small business lender, the leading home equity lender, and the fifth-largest originator of consumer mortgages. The company had relationships with 98 percent of the U.S. Fortune 500 companies and 80 percent of the Global Fortune 500. In 2005, Bank of America registered revenue of $56.9 billion and net income of $16.5 billion.

As part of Bank of America's business strategy, it served as a leading financial partner and advisor across all major sports. It helped owners, leagues, and franchises with their full range of banking needs—from building stadiums to redesigning their capital structure. It also had sponsorship relationships with numerous sports organizations as well as community and cultural events in its local markets. Bank of America spent more to sponsor sports than any other U.S.-based bank. It had relationships with major and minor league baseball, the Professional Golf Association (PGA) Tour, the National Association for Stock Car Racing (NASCAR), and NFL teams including naming rights on the NFL stadium of its hometown (headquarters community) Carolina Panthers. IEG, a sponsorship tracking firm, estimated that Bank of America spent close to $85 million on sponsorships of all types (mostly sports) in 2005. This constituted sponsorship rights fees, separate from ad-

---

Professors Stephen A. Greyser (HBS) and John L. Teopaco (Boston University) prepared this case with the cooperation of Bank of America. HBS cases are developed solely as the basis for class discussion. Cases are not intended to serve as endorsements, sources of primary data, or illustrations of effective or ineffective management.

Copyright © 2009 President and Fellows of Harvard College. The Case was prepared by Stephen Greyser & John Teopaco as the basis for class situation. Reprinted by permission of Harvard Business College.

vertising and marketing expenditures associated with promoting the sponsorships. Bank of America's national sports sponsorship commitments focused on four major platforms—baseball, the U.S. Olympic Team, NASCAR racing, and golf.

BANK OF AMERICA'S SPORTS-RELATED HISTORY

Bank of America grew from many smaller banks (referred to as predecessor or legacy banks), most of which were acquired under former chairman and CEO Hugh McColl, Jr. As it acquired regional banks, Bank of America kept many of the sports relationships that came with the original banks. As it grew into a national power, Bank of America maintained those local sports business relationships as part of its commitment to serving its customers and communities. McColl had said:

> *It was a very natural extension of our doing business in a community to do business with the sports teams. It was good business because it was our cities. When we went to Texas, we ended up financing the Cowboys. We took part of a bad loan and took 12% of the Cowboys. We sold that to Jerry Jones (now the Cowboys' principal owner) and financed his takeover of the Cowboys. And we financed him after we did that.*

Jim Nash, the bank's sports-financing executive, commented: "We had in our DNA this notion of enhancing the communities, the towns, and regions in which we lived. It was ultimately good for business and therefore good for the bank."

In 1994, Fleet, a New England legacy (predecessor) bank, had provided financing to Robert Kraft, who became the fourth owner of the New England Patriots, saving the team from an impending move. The bank had also helped finance team purchases such as the New York Yankees and the Dallas Cowboys and the construction or improvement of multiple stadiums and racetracks. Bank of America had organized two separate credit pools for Major League Baseball and the NFL totaling a combined $3.6 billion according to *Charlotte* magazine (October 2006).

OFFICIAL BANK OF BASEBALL

Baseball was generally considered part of America's heritage and had been part of the Bank of America culture since the late 1880s when the company sponsored employee baseball teams. The bank had long-standing relationships, some dating back over 75 years, with some of baseball's most storied MLB franchises, including the St. Louis Cardinals, New York Yankees, Boston Red Sox, Los Angeles Dodgers, and San Francisco Giants. For instance, Bank of America's association with the San Francisco Giants dated back to 1976 when the team played at Candlestick Park. In 1996, the Giants embarked on an effort to build the nation's first privately funded major league ballpark (eventually opened in 2000) and Bank of America served as one of its original Winner's Circle Sponsors.

In 1995, prior to its acquisition by Bank of America, Fleet had become the first Official Bank of Major League Baseball. In 2004, Bank of America became the first company ever to be designated the "Official Bank of Baseball," establishing one of the most unique and sweeping set of corporate relationships in any sport, encompassing exclusive national agreements with Major League Baseball, Minor League Baseball, Little League Baseball, and the National Baseball Hall of Fame and Museum. The association with Major League Baseball complemented ten club sponsorships and extensive broadcast, on-site branding, and hospitality at the All-Star Game, the Division Series, the League Championships Series, and the World Series. Bank of America's affiliation with Minor League Baseball included 68 club sponsorships.

SPORTS SPONSORSHIP PHILOSOPHY AND SELECTION CRITERIA

Ray Bednar joined Bank of America as senior vice president and global sponsorship executive in February 2006 to oversee strategy and activation development for the company's expansive sports sponsorship portfolio, including baseball, motor sports, Olympics, golf, and football. A Harvard MBA, Bednar had spent the previous four years as CEO of North America and South America for PRISM, a global agency focused on sponsorship and event strategy and activation, and a member of the WPP Group (a large international communications-based firm). A major part of Bednar's responsibility was the application of more rigorous and explicit business criteria, in addition to the traditional marketing/promotional considerations, in making sponsorship decisions. Bednar commented:

Sponsorship is about connecting to the passion of the fan. We're trying to say to the fans that we believe in the sport, the activity, the art, the entertainment. We believe in the sport as much as you do. We are of the same mind.

He explained further, however, that sponsorship was more than passion:

We are a bank. If we sponsor, we expect banking relationships. We are concerned about getting banking business instead of just generating brand awareness and brand associations, or generating more retail traffic. Sponsorship for Bank of America is ultimately a banking business decision—a decision to help our lines of business.

As noted, one of Bank of America's three principal lines of business was Global Consumer and Small Business Banking—offering checking and savings services, credit cards, home equity loans, online banking, etc. A second was Global Wealth and Investment Management, which offered financial solutions through full-service banking, investment, and trust products to wealthy clients. The third line of business was Global Corporate and Investment Banking which provided cash management and payment services, commercial real estate banking, leasing and business capital, middle market banking, etc., as well as traditional bank deposit and loan products.

In evaluating potential sports sponsorships, Bank of America's criteria included both "return on investment" for the three lines of business and the more traditional brand alignment and positioning considerations. (The latter was referred to as "return on objectives" and included such elements as brand awareness, differentiation, favorability, positive associations, etc. It also included an evaluation of the specific ability of a sponsorship to help drive individual [non-direct-revenue] business goals.) The return on investment philosophy was based on the notion that Bank of America was already considered to be a strong brand with both high brand awareness and an inherently meaningful name that included the words "bank" and "America." The primary sponsorship criterion, therefore, focused on a sponsorship's ability to help the bank's business segments accomplish their business objectives. Bank of America referred to this philosophy as "the universal bank model." Bednar explained:

Here are [sports sponsorship] assets we need to help drive the business. All three banks [business segments] have their own set of business return on investment objectives and return on business objectives. Each has its goals for revenue. If we had to go buy these assets, what would it cost? For instance, in a given sponsorship relationship, we might have assets including signage in the stadium, seats in the bowl, suites, rights to player appearances, rights to use the venue during non-season periods for entertainment or meetings, etc. These assets would be valued at some amount that the market would generally set as a fair price—assuming these assets could be bought in the market—which is not always the case.

The criteria for Bank of America's sports sponsorship "return on investment" were composed of the following three elements: (1) Direct Business Attribution—most often Net Income Before Tax (NIBT), (2) Value in Kind, and (3) Marketing Assets. **Direct Business Attribution** measured a sponsorship's ability to contribute directly to the revenue, and ultimately to the NIBT, of the lines of business. For the Global Capital Markets and Investment Banking group, that meant the financing of new stadiums, capital-raising solutions, real estate deals, treasury and merchant services, stock placements, and the like. The return on Global Wealth and Investment Management's investment included managing the wealth of team owners, senior front-office personnel, coaches and players, racing crew chiefs, etc., via full-service banking, investment, and trust products. And for Global Consumer and Small Business Banking, sponsorship considerations meant being able to establish individual consumer banking relationships by capitalizing on the affinity of the sport's fan base.

Value in Kind "return" encompassed the components of a sponsorship with direct dollar value. This included the value of tickets, suites, special hospitality areas, passes, player appearances, dinners with coaches for bank clients, and so forth. **Marketing Assets** meant the marketing value of signage, visibility on scoreboards, named sections of arenas/stadiums, and ultimately, the value of naming rights for an entire venue. (Exhibit 13.3.1 depicts graphically the process of how the return-on-objectives and return-on-investment approaches work together to screen prospective sponsorships.)

Bank of America had not explicitly and systematically applied the universal bank model/return-on-investment approach to sponsorship in the past. Now, in late 2006, Bednar and his colleagues were in the process of applying these more rigorous criteria in addition to traditional marketing/branding standards to four specific sports sponsorship opportunities.

(1) Official Bank of NASCAR

The National Association for Stock Car Racing (NASCAR) had a broad reach with 1,800 racing events at more than 110 tracks in 36 states. Among major professional sports, NASCAR ranked number one in corporate involvement and per-event attendance, and number two in television viewership. Bank of America's historical involvement with NASCAR had included the sponsorship of races as well as the financing of numerous motor speedways. In the early 1980s, banks in Virginia and North Carolina, later acquired by Bank of America, sponsored stock car races and provided financing for the construction of motor speedways and team owners. In 1993, MBNA (now Bank of America Card Services), became the Official Card Issuer of NASCAR, beginning a long-standing relationship. The bank was the title sponsor of the Bank of America 500 at Lowe's Motor Speedway in North Carolina, and the sponsor of ten tracks in the country. Bank of America's racing platform also included an agreement with Turner Sports to be the presenting sponsor of the "Countdown to Green" pre-race program which aired on NBC's and TNT's national NASCAR broadcasts.

Given Bank of America's long involvement with NASCAR, it was not surprising that the racing organization approached the bank with a 5-year deal that would make it the Official Bank of NASCAR at the start of the 2007 season, as well as NASCAR's exclusive partner for banking and related services. Industry estimates put the multi-year deal between $15 million to $20 million in total. Bednar reflected on the proposal:

We have enjoyed remarkable business results from our track relationships and race entitlements. By teaming up with NASCAR to expand our association with the sport, we could continue to benefit and build excitement for fans across the country, linking their need for competitive and financial products and services with their passion for the thrills and excitement of racing.

Exhibit 13.3.1 ■ How ROO and ROI Work Together

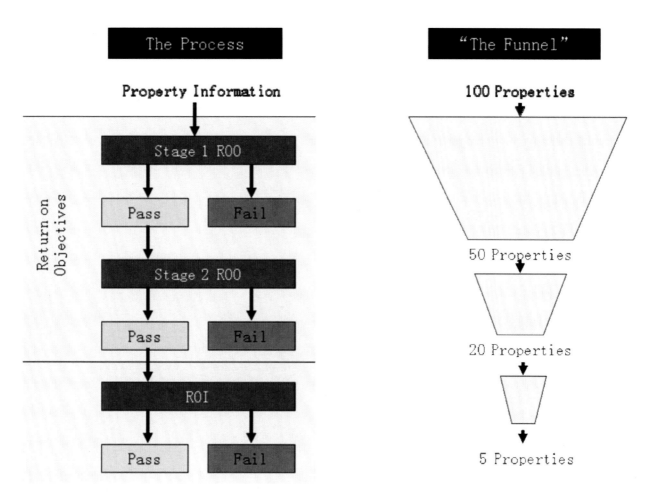

Source: Bank of America.

The NASCAR deal would mean a significant expansion by the bank into auto racing. The key question was: Is NASCAR an appropriate and effective platform for targeting multiple customer segments and accelerating business growth for Bank of America? Bednar explained further:

> *This is less about [our] branding. We are extending a business model that lends itself to an integrated relationship with the NASCAR industry. This is a first application of the universal bank model/return on investment approach to sponsorship. NASCAR itself is changing. It wants a consolidation of sponsors with more national presence and a global reach.*

NASCAR's origins and growth had largely been in the southeastern part of the U.S. More recently, it had extended its "footprint" geographically, expanded its repertoire of races, increased its TV coverage, and re-examined its sponsor roster. The latter included a massive multi-year sponsorship arrangement with Nextel (now Sprint) for the season's championship, the Nextel Cup. In 2006 it initiated the "Chase to the Cup" to add competitive excitement in the final part of the season.

As the Official Bank of NASCAR, Bank of America would be NASCAR's exclusive partner for banking and related financial services, and would have the right in this category to use NASCAR logos in marketing and advertising promotions through 2011. NASCAR's popularity and loyal following presented an opportunity to promote a broad array of financial solutions to its 75 million fans and to NASCAR's community of racing teams, sponsors, and businesses that supported the operations and growth of the sport. These financial services included consumer checking and savings accounts; Visa-branded credit, debit and ATM card issuance, processing, and servicing; consumer and commercial lending; merchant services; securities brokerage services; mutual fund distribution and management services; treasury and payroll services; and community development banking.

Bank of America would leverage the NASCAR agreement through racing-themed mass-market promotions, at-track branding and hospitality, rewards programs for both customers and employees, and business-to-business and cross-promotional opportunities with NASCAR's various sponsor partners. Other elements of the deal included onsite branding and hospitality opportunities during NASCAR's jewel events, such as the NASCAR Nextel All-Star Challenge, Championship Event, and Champions Week.

(2) U.S. Olympic Committee

Bank of America's earliest involvement with the U.S. Olympic Movement dated back to 1921. A legacy bank, Security Pacific, provided financing for the Los Angeles Coliseum, site of the 1932 (and later the 1984) Olympics. Bank of America executives in Los Angeles sat on committees that helped bring the Games to L.A.

In 1992, another predecessor bank, Bank America, became the Official Bank Sponsor of the U.S. Olympic Team that competed in Barcelona, Spain. This sponsorship continued with every U.S. Olympic Team since then. Still another legacy bank, NationsBank, provided financing for the Atlanta Organizing Committee and became the Official Bank Sponsor of the 1996 Centennial Olympic Games. Bank of America was the Official Sponsor of the 2006–2008 U.S. Olympic Team.

The question that Bank of America executives now faced was whether the USOC and the Olympic Games remained a good strategic fit with the bank. The cost of the bank's sponsorship was estimated at around $8 million a year—about 10% of its annual spending on sports sponsorship. Should the bank renew its sponsorship beyond its 2008 commitment? Bill Chipps, senior editor of the IEG Sponsorship Report, applauded Bank of America's decision to ask the question: "More power to them for trying to track and measure whether this partnership is really building business. The days of throwing money at signs and brand awareness are long gone."

An important benefit of associating with the Olympics was its global reach. For global corporations such as Visa and Coca-Cola, these companies' participation in the International Olympic Committee's Olympic Partners program gave them exclusive worldwide marketing rights to both the Winter and Summer Games as well as the right to use the Olympic rings in their marketing and branding. Visa spokesman Mike Lynch said that "the Olympic Games have been a tremendous strategic fit." Peter Franklin, director of worldwide sports for Coca-Cola, said: "Some other companies may struggle with the decision on whether the Olympics in another country can be used in their marketing effort back home. We do business in virtually every country in the world."[1] (Coca-Cola had been an Olympics sponsor since 1928.)

---

[1] Paul Nowell, "Bank of America Weighs Future of Olympic Sponsorship," Deseret News (Salt Lake City), January 30, 2006.

Even though Bank of America had a presence in many countries, it was still primarily a domestic company deriving most of its revenue from the U.S. (approximately 94% in 2005). Were the bank's marketing needs different enough from companies like Coca-Cola and Visa, and did they warrant a reallocation of marketing dollars away from U.S. Olympic sponsorship? On the other hand, as Bednar saw it, the Olympic sponsorship "presented an opportunity to continue building a global brand for Bank of America; we're not well known in Europe (where the MBNA brand had been retained after the acquisition) and Asia."

Aside from the global branding consideration, another question facing Bednar and colleagues was: "Should we and could we apply the return on investment analytic structure to the U.S. Olympic Team sponsorship?" A survey of Bank of America customers indicated a positive impact from the Olympic sponsorship: 57% who considered themselves avid fans of the Olympics were highly favorable towards Bank of America. Nonetheless, the return on investment approach required the identification of incremental business for the bank's business segments that could be directly attributed to the U.S. Olympic sponsorship.

(3) Dallas Cowboys

As mentioned previously, Bank of America had been involved in the financing of the NFL team, the Dallas Cowboys, and it was also behind a $1 billion financing of the club's current stadium in Irving, Texas.[2] The Cowboys were also one of five NFL football teams that the bank sponsored. Like the U.S. Olympics situation, Bednar again faced the decision of whether or not to renew the sponsorship, and how the return on investment and return on objectives approaches could be applied.

The Cowboys sponsorship was a critical element in the bank's position in the Texas banking market, considered the 15th largest in the U.S. (in terms of deposits and population per financial institution). An iconic franchise in the National Football League, the Cowboys' reach spanned across Texas, the region, and the nation; the Cowboys were often referred to as "America's Team." Ray Bednar commented:

While important to the bank as an iconic national franchise, a great deal of the value in the relationship is the presence and influence of the team in the Texas market. This relationship has given Bank of America a tremendous business partner across all facets of the universal bank while providing a significant local presence in a very fragmented financial market such as Texas. The Cowboys sponsorship is the centerpiece of Bank of America's sports "face" in Texas.

Sports marketing observers estimated the cost of the Cowboys sponsorship to be between $4 to $5 million annually for ten years; costs to activate the sponsorship varied by budget year. The return on investment to Bank of America included consumer/affinity banking opportunities with Cowboys-branded banking products, commercial financing as lead partner on the new stadium, business banking, personal wealth banking, suites, seats, a wide array of signage assets, etc.

(4) Bank of America PGA Tournaments

Two of Bank of America's major sponsorships in golf were the Bank of America Championship in the Boston area and the Bank of America Colonial in Fort Worth, Texas. Now in the third year of title sponsorship of the former, Bank of America's involvement dated back to 1993 when the tournament, held at Nashawtuc Country Club in Concord, Massachusetts, was called the Bank of Boston Senior Golf Classic.

---

[2]The Cowboys played their last game at this stadium in 2008. Their new $1 billion stadium in Arlington, Texas was due to open in 2009; it was also financed by Bank of America.

The biggest names in Champions Tour golf had been coming to the Bank of America Championship for 25 years, and in 2006, 79 professionals were scheduled to compete for their share of the $1.6 million purse. However, the tournament ended up being cancelled that year due to rain and flooding. In addition to bringing great golf to the Boston area each year, Bank of America was also giving back to the local community through the event. To date, the tournament had raised over $3.7 million for charities in New England.

The 2006 Bank of America Colonial held at Colonial Country Club in Fort Worth, Texas, marked the fourth year of the bank's 4-year contract for title sponsorship of this PGA Tour event. This was the 60th year of this prestigious tournament that drew top golfers from all over the world. The Colonial was the longest running event on the PGA Tour still being held at its original site. In 2003, when Bank of America became title sponsor, the tournament made history by inviting Annika Sorenstam to be the first woman to play in a PGA Tour event.

In the summer of 2005, Bank of America had decided not to continue the Colonial's sponsorship (which cost approximately $5 million per year) beyond 2006. Bednar explained the decision:

That summer, a leadership council composed of our marketing and line-of-business associates convened at the Colonial for an on-site observation of the tournament. They held several business meetings and decided that title sponsorship of a major golf tournament was essentially a "brand awareness play," which was not needed in Texas where the bank enjoyed 95%+ brand recognition. The leadership council deemed golf primarily as a B2B platform for client and customer entertainment, and concluded that the bank did not need its name on a tournament to conduct world-class B2B marketing. This was the reason for Bank of America's "Hogan's Alley," a mobile hospitality suite that Bank of America brought to more than a dozen golf tournaments each year as a venue for entertaining key customers. (Launched in 2003, it celebrated the life and career of golfing legend Ben Hogan, whose home course was the Colonial Country Club.)

Bank of America executives recognized the risk of losing banking relationships with some club members, but not enough to justify the continued investment. The challenge facing Bednar and the other bank sponsorship executives was the implementation of this exit strategy. How should Bank of America terminate the sponsorship and yet try to maintain existing banking relationships? In order to address this concern, they considered committing to major non-title sponsorship positions in the tournament (i.e., lower visibility and less expensive than title sponsorship) for the following two years after exiting. This would prospectively ensure not damaging the financial structure of the event (which a hotel chain sponsored after Bank of America's exit).

CONCLUSION

Bank of America was committed to the strategic use of sports sponsorships. Bednar had aligned the universal bank model/return on investment approach to evaluate the benefits of a sponsorship to the bank's three lines of business. This criterion was to be used in conjunction with the assessment of the more traditional branding benefits (awareness and positive associations) generated by sponsorships for the corporate brand name. In late 2006, Ray Bednar and fellow sponsorship executives had to apply these criteria and decide: (1) whether to form a new relationship with auto racing as the Official Bank of NASCAR beginning with the 2007 season, (2) whether to renew the U.S. Olympic Team sponsorship beyond 2008, (3) whether to renew the sponsorship of the NFL Dallas Cowboys, and (4) how to exit after the 2006 Bank of America Colonial golf tournament sponsorship without jeopardizing its existing bank relationships.

* * *

Some months later, in April 2007, Bank of America agreed to purchase LaSalle Bank, headquartered in Chicago, for $21 billion. This would potentially increase Bank of America's assets by approximately 9%. With the purchase, Bank of America would expand its Chicago and Michigan presence by adding LaSalle's 17,000 commercial banking clients, 1.4 million retail customers, 400 banking centers, and 1,500 ATMs.

The acquisition meant that Ray Bednar and his colleagues were facing yet another decision regarding the corporation's strategic direction for sports sponsorships, and in particular, what to do with LaSalle Bank's sponsorships within Bank of America's current sponsorship portfolio. For instance, LaSalle Bank owned the Chicago Marathon, one of the most prestigious marathons in the world that attracted 45,000 runners and 1.5 million spectators. La Salle had sponsored this Marathon for fifteen years (with an approximate annual operating cost estimated at $ 10–15 million); what made this extraordinary was the fact that Bank of America now owned a sports property for the first time. Bednar described the situation:

> *It looked like we were a sponsor, but we 100% owned the event. The great challenge was that now we had to operate an event like a P&L. We had to sign sponsors on like Nike, Volkswagen, etc., and take on the risk of operating the event—a massive change for the bank. So, the question was whether or not we should continue to own and operate this significant event in the Chicago market that was so important to us, or should we consider selling it and continue as the title sponsor?*

LaSalle Bank also sponsored the LaSalle Bank Open (played in Glenview, Illinois), one of the top events on the PGA's Nationwide Tour (from which the top players "graduated" to the PGA Tour) that included over 150 professional golfers ranging from up-and-comers to some seasoned PGA Tour veterans. LaSalle had owned and operated (at an approximate annual operating cost estimated at $1.75–3.0 million) the Open for five years, with a commitment through 2009. Among the questions confronting Bednar were whether these events should be considered "home town" sponsorships, and if so, whether that was an important consideration after the current contracts expired.

In describing Bank of America's future strategic direction on sponsorships, Bednar explained: "We don't want to be in 30 sports. We don't go wide. We want a narrow set of premier platforms with very deep penetration in them—a 'concentrate to dominate' strategy."

Case 13.4

"I Lost My Volvo in New Haven": Tennis Event Sponsorship

As the 1995 Volvo International Tennis Tournament (VITT) in New Haven, Connecticut began, tournament owner Jim Westhall walked his dog Aztec (a gift from Ivan Lendl) around the site. He was met with a flurry of questions from inquisitive spectators: "Jim, who's going to be the title sponsor in 1996? . . . Is Volvo really out? . . . Is it true you're selling the tournament?"

Volvo Cars of North America was in its 23rd and final year as title sponsor. Volvo was the longest running title sponsor in professional tennis. However, in Westhall's view, Volvo was not paying enough in sponsorship fees to enable the tournament to keep up with the financial changes in the sport. Prize money had more than doubled since the tournament had moved from Stratton Mountain, Vermont six years earlier, yet Volvo's annual financial participation had remained about the same. Westhall was looking for a title sponsor at approximately $1.4 million annually for a minimum three-year period.

Westhall was now in the final round of negotiations with The Pilot Pen Corporation of America and Diners Club International to take over the title sponsorship in 1996 and beyond. He wondered whether he should accept one of these offers now, or keep searching.

EVENT HISTORY

Westhall had founded the tournament in 1970. His company, JEWEL Productions, organized and promoted two tennis tournaments. This constituted his principal activity year-round.

The 1970 inaugural tournament offered $5,000 in prize money and featured the star Australian players Rod Laver, Roy Emerson, Ken Rosewall and Fred Stolle. Spectators sat along a grassy hillside above a red clay court at the world-famous Mount Washington Hotel in Bretton Woods, New Hampshire (year-round population of two). In 1973, Volvo Cars of North America became the title sponsor. In 1974, the tournament relocated to the Mt. Cranmore ski area in North Conway, New Hampshire. It remained at North Conway for ten years, before moving to a bigger site at Stratton Mountain in Vermont in 1985. At these classic destination resorts, the event was among the most successful and respected on the tour. (Exhibit 13.4.1 lists past champions of the VITT.)

In 1989, the Association of Tennis Professionals (ATP) and the tournament directors joined forces to organize a new men's professional tennis tour (The ATP Tour). The Tour regulations specified that beginning in 1990 all Championship Series events would have to be played in a permanent facility. Stratton Mountain was able to raise $10 million of the $14 million needed for a new stadium. Tournament owner Westhall was unable to raise the rest. Approval of a state tax proposal and/or state bond issuance to fund this gap was considered highly unlikely.[1]

Professor Stephen A. Greyser and Brian Harris and Mitchell Truwit (MBAs '97) prepared this case. Some financial information in the case has been disguised. HBS cases are developed solely as the basis for class discussion. Cases are not intended to serve as endorsements, sources of primary data, or illustrations of effective or ineffective management.

Copyright © 1999 President and Fellows of Harvard College. The Case was prepared by Stephen Greyser, Brian Harris & Mitchell Truwit as the basis for class discussion rather than to illustrate either effective or ineffective handling of an administrative situation. Reprinted by permission of Harvard Business School.

[1] Allen Sack and Arthur Johnson, "Politics, Economic Development, and the Volvo International Tennis Tournament," *Journal of Sport Management*, 1996.

Exhibit 13.4.1 ■ VITT Past Champions

Year	Champion	Location
1994	Boris Becker	New Haven
1993	Andrei Medvedev	New Haven
1992	Stefan Edberg	New Haven
1991	Petr Korda	New Haven
1990	Derick Rostagno	New Haven
1989	Brad Gilbert	Stratton
1988	Andre Agassi	Stratton
1987	John McEnroe/Ivan Lendl[a]	Stratton
1986	Ivan Lendl	Stratton
1985	John McEnroe	Stratton
1984	Joakim Nystrom	North Conway
1983	Jose-Luis Clerc	North Conway
1982	Ivan Lendl	North Conway
1981	Jose-Luis Clerc	North Conway
1980	Jimmy Connors	North Conway
1980	Harold Solomon	North Conway
1978	Eddie Dibbs	North Conway
1977	John Alexander	North Conway
1976	Jimmy Connors	North Conway
1975	Jimmy Connors	
1974	Vijay Armitraj	Bretton Woods
1973	Cliff Richey	Bretton Woods

Source: *1995 Volvo International Tournament Magazine.*

[a]Final not played due to rain.

In September of 1989, Westhall announced that he had selected New Haven, Connecticut as the site for the 1990 VITT. The State of Connecticut had financed a 15,000 seat ultra-modern stadium located on the Yale University campus, adjacent to the 70,000 seat Yale Bowl and 6,000 seat Yale Field (baseball). In return for use of the stadium, Westhall was to pay 8% of all ticket, merchandise, and food and beverage revenues and 15% of all in-state sponsorships to the Tennis Foundation of Connecticut, Inc. (TFC). Further, Westhall was to remit a 10% tax on all tickets to the State of Connecticut (to repay construction bonds) and a 3% ticket tax to the city of New Haven. Additionally, Westhall volunteered to donate $100,000 or more per year for a tennis program for inner-city children.[2] In negotiating the arrangements with Yale for the use of the university's land for the stadium, Westhall committed to including the phrase "from Yale University" on promotional material on tickets, etc. Yale also could buy a number of boxes for its own hospitality purposes.

Westhall believed New Haven would be a terrific venue in which to grow his event. New Haven County bordered on Fairfield County, one of the wealthiest counties in America. Connecticut was domicile to a multitude of corporate headquarters. By leveraging his working relationship with Yale University to gain access to alumni executives and by marketing his event throughout Connecticut, Westhall planned to sell more corporate sponsorships and tickets than for any other all- male tennis event in North America.

By the summer of 1995, Westhall's plans had not yet come to fruition. On the positive side, the VITT sold more box seats and event tickets than any other one-week male tennis event in the world.[3] Additionally, Westhall had developed the SNET Classic, a successful professional women's tennis exhibition played on the heels of the VITT, sponsored by the local telephone company, Southern New England Telephone. Connecticut, however, had gone through its worst recession in years. Corporations had been reluctant to spend sponsorship money in this economic climate. Furthermore, many fans and corporations were turned off by New Haven's crime-related problems. New Haven also lacked the beautiful natural resources and accommodations of Stratton Mountain. The press continued to focus on the weather and the ever-present threat of rain. Westhall had invested heavily in trying to enhance the player and fan experience, e.g., via offering hot air balloon rides, street hockey clinics, picnics, raffles, etc. Yet in his opinion the tournament needed the lift of a new image. (Exhibit 13.4.2 provides details on some tournament-related special events.)

MEN'S PROFESSIONAL TENNIS AND NEW HAVEN'S SANCTION

The men's professional tennis tour was governed by the ATP (the players' union), and the tournament directors. By 1995, the Tour had grown to over 80 international events featuring more than $60 million in prize money.[4] These tournaments were organized according to location, prize money, and calendar date. The ATP Tour controlled each of these elements to varying degrees, thus limiting a tournament's ability to change.

New Haven's sanction (i.e., event eligibility) was for a Championship Series Double-Up event in August, two weeks prior to the U.S. Open. This meant that the tournament would compete directly with the RCA Championships being held during the same week in Indianapolis.[5] In exchange for accepting this date on the calendar and maintaining certain levels of prize money, the ATP Tour guaranteed both the RCA and the VITT three of the top ten players in the world. Unfortunately, Westhall considered this guarantee of three top players as potentially insufficient for New Haven. The reason, as Westhall saw it, was the difference between having marquee American stars (i.e., truly well-known names) and lesser-known foreign players. The top 10 players for August were: Andre Agassi, Pete Sampras, Thomas Muster, Boris Becker, Michael Chang, Goran Ivanisevic, Yevgeny Kafelnikov, Thomas Enquist, Marc Rosset, and Wayne Ferreira.

---

[2]Tennis Foundation of Connecticut Agreement with JEWEL Productions, Inc., 1990.

[3]JEWEL Productions internal sales data.

[4]1995 ATP Tour Player Guide.

[5]The July-August North American tour schedule (between Wimbledon and the U.S. Open) consisted of events in Newport R.I., Washington D.C., Montreal, Los Angeles, Cincinnati, New Haven/Indianapolis (two events, same week), and Long Island. The European tour was also active in July and early August.

Exhibit 13.4.2 ■ Tournament Related Special Events

Volvo International
August 12-20

The ABCs of tennis: **Agassi**, **Becker**, **Chang** begin the alphabet of top tennis players in the 1995 Volvo International. **Michael Stich**, **Luke and Murphy Jensen**, **Sergi Bruguera**, **Richard Krajicek** and over 50 more players make it letter perfect. Your ticket to great tennis starts here but the best prices end July 21. Boxes, day & night series, session and group tickets are still available. Call 1-800-548-6586 or 203 772-3838.

players/times subject to change

Volvo International Best Buys

Kids 14 and under - They get in for half-price.
Families - With half-price kids and low-priced tickets it's no contest when it comes to a great family outing.
Early buyers - Ticket prices are inexplicably inexpensive for anyone who buys on or before July 21.
Big shots - Our corporate package includes a 4-seat box, 100 session tickets and a spot in the Legends Tennis Clinic.
Cheap shots - Get a group of 20 together and get tickets for $5. That's not just cheap, that's smart!

A Whole Bunch of Special Events

All kinds of exciting activities will be served on and off court during the Volvo International and the SNET Classic. ReMax hot air **balloon rides** will keep you on top of things. The **Peter Burwash International Tennis Show** is a sophisticated production combining music, humor and slick racquet and ball control skills. **Libor Karas** will show why he is a stunt bike champion. The **Hartford Whalers** will put on street hockey clinics and exhibitions. Incredible **Rollerbladers** will be spinning their wheels throughout both events. The **Tennis Legends** return to display their skills. **JEWEL Grassroots Excellence Team** will "court" your attention. And overhead, after some of the evening sessions, you can look up to a colorful display of **fireworks**.

Softball, Aug. 12
Basketball, Aug. 13

Tom Brokaw's team will play softball against **Doc Rivers'** team in the CT Special Olympics Celebrity Softball Game, Sat. Aug. 12, 7pm, Yale Field. For softball tickets call (203) 782-1666. Sunday, Aug. 13, 3:00pm, on the Grandstand Court, Doc Rivers and players from the Knicks, Celtics and San Antonio Spurs will play basketball alongside the tennis pros in the **FootAction Shootout**. For basketball info call 1-800-548-6586.

Source: 1995 *Volvo International Tournament Magazine*.

There were a number of factors that influenced the tournaments in which a player chose to play. Among these were location, date, climate, tournament amenities, and event sponsors. There were also rumors that certain tournaments paid illegal appearance fees to induce top stars to play in their events. While New Haven's climate and scheduled week made it an excellent preparation for the U.S. Open, some top players were tired from the long, hot summer and chose to rest that week. Other players were reluctant to play in New Haven due to its lack of a first class hotel. Additionally, corporate sponsors were beginning to play a more active role in determining where players played. Westhall was concerned that Nike, a major sponsor of the Indianapolis event, might flex its muscle and induce its contracted players such as New Haven's top seed, Andre Agassi, to alter their schedules. Because the player field was directly related to the VITT's ability to attract sponsor revenue and sell tickets, it was essential that star players decide to come to New Haven.

At Stratton Mountain, Westhall's event had been chosen consistently as the players' favorite stop on the tour. Players brought their entire families to the tournament. They were provided with ski lodges and treated to golf, fishing, softball games, fireworks displays, and Westhall's famous lobster cookout. The tennis was just part of the total experience. Many fans also took the week off from work to enjoy the attractions of the resort destination, and bought courtside boxes to the entire week of play. Thus far, New Haven had been unable to replicate the appeal of Stratton Mountain.

TOURNAMENT ECONOMICS[6]

Professional tennis tournaments generated revenue from a variety of sources. Among these were sponsorships, ticket sales, and food and beverage and merchandise concessions. An event like New Haven might generate 55% of its revenue from tickets, 40% from sponsorships, and 5% from concessions.

Box seat tickets were the largest single revenue source, accounting for 40% of sales. (Exhibit 13.4.3 lists the range of box seat prices for 1995.) This money was particularly significant from a cash flow perspective, in that 80% of box seat holders renewed their seats for the following year during the week of the tournament and in the month immediately following. These advance sales provided essential working capital for much of the year.

General admission tickets represented 15% of revenue. These, however, were very unpredictable and could drop dramatically due to inclement weather, player injury, or early round upsets. These sales were usually made either several weeks prior to the event or, more often, on the day of the match.

The title sponsorship generally made up 20% of revenues. Additionally, the title sponsor was typically responsible for purchasing television time to air the event. Due to tennis' poor ratings, networks were unwilling to pay for the rights to broadcast events such as New Haven. However, such television coverage was necessary in order to maximize sponsor value. From Westhall's perspective an ideal sponsor would add prestige to the event through its affiliation, dedicate meaningful resources beyond its sponsorship fee, be a consistent and visible supporter of tennis, and encourage its corporate business partners (e.g., major vendors) to be involved with the event.

Lower-level sponsorships generated another 20% of revenues. The majority of this money came from a "Presenting Sponsor" and a limited number of "Supporting Sponsors." New Haven's current sponsors included a combination of global, national, regional, and local organizations in addition to Volvo: TIME (Magazine), Shawmut Bank, Footaction USA, Unisource, RADO Swiss Watches, IBM, the ATP Tour, Toshiba, Polo Sport (Ralph Lauren), US Air, SNET, New England Brewing Co., the Connecticut Lottery, local business-to-business and specialty retail firms, and a local network TV channel. Additionally, many local sponsors provided trade benefits. These consisted of essential goods and services including airfare, advertising, automobiles, office equipment, catering, etc.

---

[6]Some financial information in this case has been disguised.

Exhibit 13.4.3 ■ 1995 Box Seat Price Information

Box seats are the premier seats in the stadium and you get to select the one that's right for you. The accompanying stadium diagram shows the availability.

Your box includes:

- One to ten seats for 15 sessions of tennis (9 days and 6 nights)
- Personalized identification plaque
- Access to boxholder restaurant
- Option to purchase preferred parking (limited availability)
- Renewable option on seats
- First right-of-refusal on other JEWEL Productions events in the Connecticut Tennis Center

Call (203) 776-7331 and ask for a sales representative. We'll be happy to answer any of your questions.

Volvo International dates:
August 12-20, 1995

1995 BOX SEAT PRICES

ROWS	1995 PRICE
Baseline North & South Boxes	
1	$3632
2-4	$2946
5-8	$2740
9-12	$2604
13-16	$2398
17-19	$2262
Courtside West & East Boxes	
1	$3496
2-4	$2740
5-8	$2604
9-12	$2466
13-16	$2330
17-20	$2056
Courtside West Boxes	
21-24	$1918
25	$1782
Courtside East Boxes	
21-24	$1748
25-26	$1624
Baseline Concourse Luxury Boxes	
Luxury	$6029

Prices based on 4-seat boxes and 8-seat Lux Boxes. 2-seat boxes available at 1/2 the listed prices.

Source: 1995 Volvo International Ticket Brochure.

Sponsor Search

In the fall of 1994, Volvo Cars of North America gave private notice to Westhall that it would not renew its title sponsorship after 1995 at the new increased rate of $1.2 million annually. Westhall immediately began his search for a replacement. Due to the investment necessary to change all tournament signage and collateral material and to promote the new title sponsor, a one-year or two-year deal was deemed infeasible.

Westhall aimed to target companies with products or services that matched the upscale demographics of tennis fans. Based on research conducted at earlier Volvo events, the average VITT customer was 39.5 years of age and had a household income of $89,500. About 70% were college graduates and 66% held professional degrees; 40% reported that they were involved in investing. Further, some 82% said they would return to the next year's tournament. The average customer attended 3.6 of the 15 sessions of play.[7] At first glance, financial service companies, luxury automobile manufacturers, and insurance companies (an industry with strong Connecticut presence) seemed the most logical fits.

Westhall's sales team also searched for companies with previous involvement in professional tennis, as well as companies looking to make a major move into the Connecticut market. Other recent title sponsors of major U.S. tennis events included AT&T, Comcast, Diet Pepsi, Legg Mason, Lipton, Miller Lite, Newsweek, Nuveen, Purex, RCA, and several major supermarket chains. Due to tennis' declining television ratings and level of participation, it was difficult for tournament owners to find interested major sponsors. Some U.S. tournaments did not have title sponsors.

SPONSOR BENEFITS

The event had much to offer a title sponsor. Specifically, the title sponsor would benefit from international, national, and regional media coverage, promotional rights, hospitality opportunities, and community visibility. Title sponsorship also guaranteed category exclusivity. This made it both an "offensive" opportunity (strategically) to promote goods and services, and a "defensive" one to block competitors from this high-profile event.

The title sponsor's name would appear on television through end-court identity, title graphics, onair mentions, and promotional advertising. Exhibit 13.4.4 is a summary of exposure Volvo was estimated to have received from its title sponsorship of the VITT in 1992. The value of the exposure was estimated at $7,713,809.[8] (It should be noted that many sponsors did not accept such exposure valuations at their full estimated value and instead chose to discount them.) In 1994, the tournament received over 20 hours of national cable television coverage on ESPN and ESPN2. Volvo received 25% of the advertising inventory on these telecasts.[9]

Event site and local market exposure was valued at over $650,000. (Exhibit 13.4.5 breaks down total impressions from this visibility in 1992.) The title sponsor was recognized on over 150,000 tickets, 180,000 ticket brochures, three highway billboards on Connecticut's busiest highway, and at a myriad of other areas. Innovative programs included printing tournament name and information as the background on the ticket stock for the Connecticut lottery for over one month. (Other cross-corporate promotional opportunities from 1992 are summarized and valued at $105,707 in Exhibit 13.4.6.)

---

[7] JEWEL Productions Title Sponsor Presentation, 1995.

[8] Joyce Julius and Associates, "The 1992 Volvo International," October 19, 1992.

[9] JEWEL Productions Title Sponsor Presentation, 1995.

Exhibit 13.4.4 ■ 1992 VITT Exposure Summary

Volvo International				
Exposure Section	Exposure Time	# of Articles Mentioned	Impressions	CP:30/NTIV
1) National television	6:35:42	205	162,226,420	$4,515,785.26
2) International television	NTIV	NTIV	8,144,850	48,787.65
3) Local television	NTIV	NTIV	46,951,586	281,239.99
4) National radio	NTIV	NTIV	2,332,800	13,973.47
5) Local radio	NTIV	NTIV	10,039,074	60,133.97
6) Event site & local market	NTIV	NTIV	108,884,520	652,218.27
7) Cross-corporate advertising	NTIV	NTIV	17,647,250	105,707.03
8) Print	NTIV	224	356,505,530	2,096,097.75
Total	6:35:42	429	712,732,030	$7,713,809.42

Source: VITT.

Note: Values may vary ± 5.00 due to rounding.

Exhibit 13.4.5 ■ 1992 VITT Event Site and Local Market Exposure

	Impressions	NTIV	
Total	108,884,520	$652,218.27	

Event site and local market impressions are calculated by a formula that compares the level of involvement at the event site in terms of exposure vehicles the sponsor utilizes (signage, handouts, fliers, marquees, etc.), the number of people attending, and impressions created from the "life" of the exposure vehicles.

Contributing to Volvo's impressions at the Volvo International and in the marketplace were the following:

Item Distributed	Number	Impressions	NTIV
Attendance	165,000	1,980,000	$118,602.00
Food court	10,000/day	2,240,000	13,417.60
Ticket brochures	180,000	1,440,000	8,625.60
Mailers	35,000	280,000	1,677.20
Postcards/mailers	5,000	40,000	239.60
Posters	5,000	22,610,000	135,433.90
Programs/magazines	13,500	162,000	970.38
Drawsheets	40,000	480,000	2,875.20

Continued

Exhibit 13.4.5 ■ Continued

	Impressions	NTIV	
Tickets	152,000	60,800	3,641.92
Credentials	13,500	54,000	323.46
Champion club brochures	3,500	2,800	167.72
Stationary	25,000	150,000	898.50
Media release letterhead	10,500	63,000	377.37
Mailing labels	1,200	14,400	86.26
Christmas cards	17,500	42,000	2,515.80
Postcards yearly	15,000	90,000	539.10
Sponsor brochures	1,250	10,000	59.90
Press releases	18	43,200	258.77
Phone calls to ticket office	50,000	50,000	299.50
Billboard/95-New Haven	1	6,951,300	41,638.29
Billboard/95-Bridgeport	1	5,610,000	33,603.90
Billboard-Hartford	1	2,320,500	13,899.80
Bus tails	60	5,348,200	32,035.72
Bus signs	12	393,550	2,357.36
Mugs	233	111,840	669.92
Water bottles	186	122,760	735.33
Aprons	48	720	4.31
Cloth hats	1,443	1,082,250	6,482.68
Visors	300	144,000	862.56
Straw hats	50	110,000	658.90
T-shirts	9,731	11,677,200	69,946.43
Sweatshirts	4,191	23,469,600	140,582.90
Volunteer shirts	800	2,960,000	17,730.40
Total	**750,025**	**108,884,520**	**$652,218.27**
Source: VITT.			

Exhibit 13.4.6 ■ 1992 VITT Cross-Corporate Advertising Exposure

	Impressions	NTIV	
Total	17,647,250	$105,707.03	
Included in this section is exposure derived from cross-promotional activity performed by other sponsors or organizations involved with the Volvo International.			
Cross-Corporate Advertising			
Item	Number Distributed	Impressions	NTIV
Chase Manhattan/mailers	300,000	1,200,000	$7,188.00
Chase Manhattan/display	100	357,000	2,138.43
Finast shopping bags	17,000	102,000	610.98
Coca-Cola cut-outs	50,000	300,000	1,797.00
Mobil coupons	1,000,000	8,000,000	47,920.00
Mobil display	250	7,675,000	45,823.50
Volvo test drives	10	38,250	229.12
Total	**1,367,360**	**17,647,250**	**$105,707.03**
Source: VITT.			

Print advertising and articles were valued at over $2 million. The tournament reached over 400 newspaper markets and received several thousand press clippings. Coverage in major newspapers in the previous year had extended for a full week or longer in many instances; in *USA Today,* it was 12 days.

Beyond media value, the tournament offered an opportunity to entertain current and prospective corporate clients, reward employees, and network with other corporate sponsors. Air- conditioned hospitality tents were located adjacent to the stadium court. The hospitality tents featured international cuisine, open bars, and closed circuit television coverage of the matches. The title sponsor received forty invitations per session and a party for 250 at the "Sponsor Promenade." Westhall paid tennis legends such as Rod Laver, Vijay Armitraj, Ken Rosewall, Fred Stolle, Cliff Drysdale, Roy Emerson, and Ilie Nastase to put on clinics for sponsors and their guests and to mingle in the Promenade. Other title sponsor perks included several spots in the sponsor golf tournament with past and current players, recognition as a sponsor of a celebrity fund-raiser softball event for the Connecticut Special Olympics, and participation in the tournament awards ceremony live on television on center court. The title sponsor also received ten baseline four-seat boxes in the first and second row, two eight-seat Concourse Luxury Boxes, and Gold Club parking passes.

The title sponsor could donate up to 15,000 tickets to charitable organizations. (The organizations encompassed a wide range of civic, charitable, school, church/synagogue, community, arts, and youth groups.) The title sponsor was also recognized prominently in the Grassroots Tennis program Westhall ran for inner-city youths. This program was formed to expand and initiate year-round activities that introduced tennis to Connecticut's inner-city youth while fostering self-discipline, pride, and good health and fitness habits. There were activities throughout the year in each of the nine Grassroots cities. In the past, these had included appearances by MaliVai Washington, Luke and Murphy Jensen, and the late Arthur Ashe. There was also an opportunity for title sponsor employee participation in the year-round volunteer program.

In spite of all these benefits, nearly a year of effort yielded only a limited number of interested companies.

AT&T

AT&T was making a move for in-state long-distance market share in the newly deregulated Connecticut market. Southern New England Telephone (SNET) had maintained a monopoly on this service until 1994. Title sponsorship would provide AT&T with tremendous exposure and allow it to entertain big accounts. AT&T was already involved in men's professional tennis as the title sponsor of the AT&T challenge in Atlanta every spring. SNET, however, was the title sponsor of Westhall's women's tennis exhibition and a supporting sponsor of the men's event. SNET was headquartered in New Haven and had been a sponsor since 1990. If Westhall actively pursued AT&T, SNET indicated that he risked losing them for both events. Furthermore, he worried that this move might agitate local politicians and other New Haven-based companies. He decided not to pursue AT&T.

PILOT PEN

Westhall had a longstanding friendship with Ron Shaw, CEO and President of The Pilot Pen Corporation of America. Pilot had previous title sponsorship experience through a men's tennis event in California (1985–1987) and a minor $50,000 event with Westhall in New Haven. Ron Shaw was a major figure in New Haven. He was the Chairman of the Shubert Theater's Board of Directors and was involved with the Jewish Community Center. Westhall was hopeful that Shaw could open doors to corporations in Connecticut that had previously been shut to him. Shaw started his career as a stand-up comic and Westhall was confident Shaw would be willing to take some chances to stir up tennis. Shaw thought the demographics of his product's consumers and the audience of the tournament overlapped, and that ESPN's reach was a perfect complement. It was unclear, however, whether Shaw would be willing to spend large sums of money above and beyond his sponsorship fee to highlight Pilot's participation. In contrast, Volvo for example, had supplemented its involvement by sponsoring amateur leagues, a collegiate tennis series, and seven other professional tennis events. Westhall was also concerned that Pilot's name might not have the same awareness and image value as Volvo's and wondered how this might affect the image of the tournament.

DINER'S CLUB

Diners Club International (DCI) was working with sports marketing consultants Harlan Stone and Ron Erskine of Advantage International to find an event which would serve as a "bookend" on the east coast for their Diners Club Matches golf event in California. DCI wanted the exposure of title sponsorship and an opportunity to entertain major accounts in and around New York City. DCI was committed to a world class image and was willing to purchase time on ABC or CBS for the finals weekend. (NBC was already under contract to broadcast the semi-finals and finals of Indianapolis.)

DCI recognized that network coverage would be far more valuable than ESPN cable coverage, but it would also be more expensive. Therefore, DCI wanted Westhall to purchase some of the advertising time on the telecast to help offset the cost. ESPN coverage had typically cost Volvo around $200,000 per year, while network time would likely be around $800,000. Westhall considered this plan viable, although far from ideal. While he would assume great risk in purchasing the advertising time, he hoped to package it with lower-level event sponsorships in order to increase their value.[10] Additionally, sponsorships which included courtside signage would be elevated in value due to the higher ratings for tennis on ABC and CBS. In 1994, comparable men's tennis broadcasts on ESPN ranged from ratings of 0.3 to 0.9, while those on ABC, CBS, and NBC ranged from 1.5 to 2.0.[11] Ratings aside, the tournament would experience an image boost simply by being on one of the national networks.

Westhall believed that Diners Club could be just the lift the tournament needed. He was sure that they would partake in additional spending to extend the reach of their sponsorship and thus the event.

The Diners Club deal, however, presented many potential negative financial consequences for Westhall. The 15% commission Advantage would charge on the deal made it less lucrative than the Pilot deal. Moreover, Westhall feared that his internal sales force would be adversely affected if the deal and commission went to an outside firm. Furthermore, he risked losing Fleet Bank as a major supporting sponsor. Fleet maintained that its exclusivity in financial services extended to credit cards as well as to banks. Because Fleet was the largest bank in New England, Westhall would be hard pressed to find another bank with the ability to match Fleet's sponsorship dollars.

Westhall also worried that his lack of financial latitude with the DCI deal might hamstring his relations with the ATP Tour. The Tour had just announced Mercedes-Benz as its official car. While it was not mandatory, ATP officials were encouraging tournaments to strike separate deals with Mercedes. Mercedes knew that their relationship with the Tour provided them with some leverage in dealing with the individual tournaments. Therefore, their sponsorship offers to Westhall and other tournament directors were not nearly as lucrative as deals the tournaments could obtain on the open market. ATP officials were instrumental, behind the scenes, at balancing the player field between New Haven and Indianapolis. It behooved Westhall to find a way to accommodate the ATP's request. He feared the Diners Club deal would limit his financial flexibility to do so. His company's resources had been impaired in 1992, when a court surface de-lamination on center court canceled several sessions of the 1992 VITT.

THE DECISION

By August 1995, news of Volvo's pending departure had reached the *New Haven Register*. Westhall needed to make a decision and an announcement right away. Without a new title sponsor, he feared that box holders would delay their purchases until they were sure there would be an event in 1996. This was an untenable thought from a cash flow perspective, since Westhall needed these sales to fund any potential shortfall from this year's event, as well as to cover his operating expenses for the next eleven months (until next year's revenues came in.) He also worried that once lost, these box holders would be much harder to regain.

Westhall evaluated his options. Should he accept Pilot Pen and risk being seen as a regional event with less reach? Should he go with Diner's Club and assume the financial risk of purchasing expensive network inventory? If he expected to be in the business of selling advertising inventory, would he be better off trying to get Presenting Sponsor *TIME* to step up to the role of the title sponsor in exchange for a substantial number of ad pages? Or, should he delay the decision and search for a better deal?

---

[10] Many events packaged advertising pages in *TIME* or *Newsweek* in their sponsorship proposals. Events could charge more for these packages and found them easier to sell because companies sometimes could nearly justify the sponsorship buy on media value alone. Westhall had in fact, in the past, capitalized on his relationship with *TIME*, accepting ad pages in addition to cash.

[11] Joyce Julius and Associates, 1994.

Chapter 14
Internet Marketing, Web Sites, Viral, Social Networking, Experiential, and Guerilla Marketing

Regardless of what may be the hot social media property of any particular month or year, social networking has become a core part of our daily lives.[a]
—Amy Kean, senior marketing manager, Internet Advertising Bureau

A NEW WORLD

As a student today, you probably can't imagine your life without a computer, a Smartphone, an MP3 player, e-mail, Facebook (or other social media sites), Twitter, the Internet, and ... what's next? This area of communication has changed how organizations conduct business and marketing communication with their customers. It seems as though every day this area of marketing communication is changing—what ideas will make it? Which will fail? Let's begin by looking at how Amazon.com changed retailing forever and the beginning of the "new" traditional media. Just remember: Internet marketing is constantly changing, and it is important for any student or professional in the field of marketing communication to keep current with its evolution.

THE "NEW" TRADITIONAL MEDIA

Internet marketing has become a normal medium of marketing communication for most organizations. It is made up of what an organization does to communicate to its customers online. Customers expect to find relevant information regarding brands and services online. Here is a description of some of the "big" players and "game" changers.

Influential Web Sites

1. <u>Amazon.com</u>: In many ways, Amazon.com has changed retailing forever—you can now buy almost anything online. In addition, Amazon.com build its

[a]http://www.workfromhomenetworkmarketing.com/social-networking-quotes.html

brand using excellent customer service, not traditional advertising. It is considered a major threat to brick-and-mortar retail. Amazon also introduced the Kindle reader.
2. Google: It was launched in 1999 to help Internet users find what they were interested in online. The homepage is mainly white space. But, Google is much more now—it is now involved in TV, energy, books, health care and the space industry.
3. Facebook: Do you remember MySpace? Friendster? Maybe, maybe not. Facebook is now the number one platform for social media. It has over 350 million registered users globally. Savvy companies know they must use Facebook as part of their social media mix. Will it survive? Make enough money? Stay connected and find out over the next few years.
4. YouTube: It was founded on 2005, and Google purchased it in 2006. In essence, it has become an operating system for video and a crowd-sourced DVR.
5. Hulu: Do you watch TV on your personal computer? Hulu helped change the way customers watch TV. More people watch TV programming online at Hulu than the three major networks combined. Some ads are placed on Hulu, but many predict, the networks will begin demanding revenue at the same level online from Hulu for customers to have access to their favorite shows.[1]

Internet AdvertisingTrends

The United States entered a major recession in late 2007/early 2008. For most media, it is common to see a decrease in advertising spending during recessions. However, Internet advertising still grew in 2008, although it did show signs of flattening, according to the Advertising Bureau.

One area of major growth was online advertising of consumer packaged goods. In 2007, internet advertising for this category was $925 million. In 2008 it rose to $1.5 billion. Why is this significant? According to Peter S. Fader, professor of marketing at Wharton, just a few years ago, most industry experts would have thought that the Internet was not the correct medium to advertise traditional grocery and mass merchant type of items to consumers.

In 2008, over half of all Internet advertising was "performance-based ads." In these types of ads advertisers only pay for measureable results, for example, when a customer clicks on the ad or buys something after seeing the ad. Advertising that is paid regardless of the outcome is beginning to decline. Return on investment (ROI) is an important part of Internet advertising and will be discussed further in Chapter 15.[2]

ONLINE ADVERTISING RISKS

Click Fraud

Since the recent recession began, it is no surprise that advertisers have shifted more of their advertising dollars to performance-based ads. As stated earlier in the chapter, this type

---

[1]"The Most Important Websites," *Advertising Age* 80, no. 42 (2009): 12. Retrieved from Business Source Complete database.

[2]S. Clifford, "Ad Sales Up on Internet, but '08 Pace Was Slower," *New York Times,* March 31, 2009. Retrieved February 27, 2010, from LexisNexis.

of advertising is an effective and more measurable form of advertising. But, it comes with a new form of fraud—"click fraud"—and it is increasing.

In pay-per-click advertising, it is the advertiser that pays the search engine every time an ad it placed is clicked. The largest pay-per-click networks are Yahoo! and Google.

Click fraud is when people click on an online ad that has no real interest in the product or service. It is run by Web sites that offer to pay people to click on ads to artificially increase revenue. Companies such as Click Forensics, based in Austin, Texas, work to combat this type of fraud.[3]

Ads In the Wrong Space/Legal Issues

In many ways, the Internet is controlled by you. Blogs and chat rooms are open to the entire Internet universe—people can comment and say anything they want. How does this culture affect advertising? From a legal perspective, the Internet is still in its infancy. So, many companies are increasingly concerned about the consequences of placing their ads in questionable areas of the Internet. The fact remains that companies do not always have control of what Internet content is placed near their ad.

For example, companies such as PepsiCo, State Farm, and Georgia-Pacific learned that their ads were being delivered to chat rooms that were being used by pedophiles to make contact with child victims. Another example: Kraft Foods learned that its Google-sponsored links appeared on a site devoted to white supremacy. Finally, State Farm Mutual Auto Insurance found out that their ads were appearing in chat rooms that focused on adults wanting to have sex with children.[4]

DIGITAL SYNERGY: EXPANDING THE MARKETING COMMUNICATION MIX WITH DIGITAL ADVERTISING—HELPING TO BUILD BRANDS

Most chapters of this textbook focus on a communication tool in a marketing communication expert's "arsenal" that helps build brands for their clients. Digital/Internet communication is one of the newest tools.

For advertising to work, consumers need to know which brand is being advertised in an ad. Correct brand identification is difficult for consumers. One study shows that correct brand identification, after exposure to an ad, is only 40%. The way consumers see Internet advertising is different than traditional media, such as TV. Think about a typical website—the page can be very cluttered and the ads are embedded in the same web space. The medium of television is not as cluttered and is completely different than a website page.[5]

---

[3] S. Hamner, "Pay-Per-Click Web Advertisers Combat Costly Fraud," *New York Times,* May 13, 2009. Retrieved March 1, 2010, from LexisNexis.

[4] K. Oser, "Yahoo scandal exposes Net advertising perils," *Advertising Age* 76, no. 26 (2005): 3–57. Retrieved from Business Source Complete database.

[5] J. Romaniuk, "The Efficacy of Brand-Execution Tactics in TV Advertising, Brand Placements, and Internet Advertising," *Journal of Advertising Research* 49, no. 2 (2009): 143–150. Retrieved from Business Source Complete database.

Six Principles of Digital Advertising

In a 2009 article, Charles Taylor, laid out what he believes are the more important principles of digital advertising. As you will note, many relate to traditional advertising as well. However, consumers tend to be online all the time through their computers, Smartphones, and so on. So, they can be easily reached almost all day long. But consumers feel this is part of their individual space, and that needs to be respected. He divides them up as follows:

Understanding Consumer Considerations
1. Marketers must be sensitive to consumer concerns about privacy and spam.
2. Consumers are more likely to be receptive to digital ads from marketers they trust.
3. Consumers are more likely to be receptive to respond to digital ads for products that are relevant to them.

Executional Variables
4. Digital approaches that incorporate interactivity are more likely to be effective.
5. Advertising messages that are entertaining have a higher chance of success in the digital context.

Building the Brand
6. In the long run, new media messages need to build the brand to be effective.

Number 6 is very important: In the end, it is still about using this new medium to build a brand. Although promotions are communicated through this medium often, the strategy should still be to build a solid brand. There is a tremendous amount of opportunity to build relationships with consumers and move them from awareness to action—sometimes, very quickly.[6]

Because this area of communication is so new, researchers continue to investigate the effectiveness of adding digital communication to the mix for a brand's message. Current studies continue to find that online advertising is effective in building the equity of a brand. Also, the Internet gives the user freedom to be exposed to a message when and where they want to use the medium. Finally, because the cost of placing digital media is less than traditional, combining the two helps advertisers maximize the outcome of the communication campaign.[7]

The next portion of this chapter will focus on the new and exciting area of social marketing—an area that most students use daily in their lives.

SOCIAL MEDIA

Currently, Facebook and Twitter are the social networking sites that are leading companies to the next level of social communication. As a student, you have an advantage over older marketing professionals—you have "grown up" with this type of marketing like no other generation before you. Go to your Facebook wall, and you have probably become a "fan" of some of your favorite companies and brands. Does your brand send you a message on your "wall"

---

[6]C. Taylor, "The Six Principles of Digital Advertising," *International Journal of Advertising* 28, no. 3 (2009): 411–418. Retrieved from Business Source Complete database.

[7]L. Wakolbinger, M. Denk, & K. Oberecker, "The Effectiveness of Combining Online and Print Advertisements," *Journal of Advertising Research* 49, no. 3 (2009): 360–372. Retrieved from Business Source Complete database.

every day? Do you then go to the brand's Facebook wall and communicate with fellow fans/friends?

It was commonly thought that social media networks were places that people would go to interact only with their friends. However, it has been found, by Anderson Analytics, in a May 2009 survey, that 52% of social network users had become a fan or follower of a company or brand. At the same time 46% had said something good about a brand or company on a social networking site—only 23% made a negative comment.

In a survey given to social media marketing professionals in late 2008 by MarketingSherpa, it was found that most believed that social marketing was effective at influencing brand reputation and increasing awareness of the brand. However, not many believe that social marketing helps generate sales or leads for sales.[8]

Social media has enabled marketers to return to the "mom-and-pop" era of marketing. Before WWII in the United States, most people bought their goods from a local store, and the "mom and pop" who owned the store knew you very well and what you needed. Now, on a mass level, companies can have one-on-one conversations with their customers online. Brands gain a tremendous amount of information from their friends/fans and often begin the topic of conversation with a marketing purpose.

Here's an example of how the Capital Area Food Bank of Texas in Austin used social media to increase knowledge of hunger issues in the Austin community. The Food Bank uses social media tools such as their blog, Facebook, and Twitter to communicate about local hunger issues. The Food Bank tweeted about a hunger issue, and a representative from Tyson Foods read the tweet. Tyson Foods then got into contact with the Food Bank and offered to donate a chicken for every retweet or comment posted on the Food Bank's blog. In less than one day, Tyson donated enough chickens to fill up a truck.[9]

Although many fund-raising organizations are starting to use social media, many are waiting to see what will be effective in the future. It may be too costly for them to be the early adopters of this new medium. It is important to remember than social media is truly in its infancy right now. The total return-on-investment is not known yet.[10]

With this new medium being used for marketing communications comes concerns regarding using it properly; this includes protecting users, especially children, and the privacy of all users. In May 2010, Facebook is approaching over 500 million users. However, many users have started to complain about privacy issues on the site. At the same time, Facebook is trying to develop a model that can make money by using the rich data users provide while using the site. Some users have called for regulators to step in with the Facebook privacy issues.[11]

In March 2010, the U.K. announced that its Advertising Standards Authority will be regulating marketing communication on social networks/sites. The code the regulators follow ensures that ads do not offend or mislead consumers. It should be clear that social media is becoming a serious marketing communication tool.[12]

The next section of the chapter will discuss the evolution of viral marketing.

---

[8]"Social Network Marketing Expands Sphere," *Emarketer,* August 31, 2009. Web, March 30, 2010. <http://www.emarketer.com/Article.aspx?R=1007252>.

[9]Natalia Maldonado, "Connect and Promote," *Career World* 38, no. 5 (2010): 26–29.

[10]Caroline Preston, "Charities Look for Ways to Unlock the Benefits of Social Media Tools," *Chronicle of Philanthropy* 22, no. 4 (2009): 16.

[11]Jessica Vascellaro, "Facebook Grapples with Privacy Issues," Marketplace, *The Wall Street Journal,* May 19, 2010, B1.

[12]Jack Marshall, "U.K. to Regulate Social Network Marketing," *ClickZ,* March 9, 2010. Web, March 30, 2010. <http://www.clickz.com/3639734>.

VIRAL MARKETING

As you should have learned, word-of-mouth (WOM) marketing communication is one of the most powerful influencers among consumers. Now WOM marketing has entered the digital era. Other terms for viral marketing (when it's not digital) are "creating a buzz," "leveraging the media," or "network marketing." What is viral marketing? Basically, it is a marketing communication strategy that gets people to pass along the marketing message to others while increasing the exposure and influence of the message to a quickly growing audience. It is like a virus that can multiply in great numbers very quickly. The Internet is the perfect medium for the "spread" of the virus.[13]

Ford Motor Company is currently using a viral campaign to introduce its 2011 Ford Fiesta car. It is a small (European style) car that has not been sold in the United States since 1981. The primary target audience is young drivers like you.

The first round of the two part viral campaign included giving 100 young drivers a Fiesta and asking the participants to post their thoughts on YouTube, Twitter, Facebook, and additional social sites. The main communication objective was to increase awareness of the Fiesta. The second phase includes 20 teams of drivers that must go on "missions" in major metro areas in the United States. The objective: illustrate the features of the car and how it compares to the Yaris, Fit, and Corolla.

J. Farley, Ford group vice president of global marketing, believes the viral campaign to be a success. "It has accounted for 5.9 million YouTube views, 3.3 million Twitter impressions and 1.4 million miles driven."[14]

The Fiesta car example is just one of thousands used in viral marketing today. One of the earliest viral campaigns that was successful was the launch of Hotmail.com, one of the first free Web-based e-mail services. Hotmail offered free e-mail and services and simply attached a tag at the bottom of every free e-mail sent out, "Get your private, free e-mail at http://www.hotmail.com."[15]

Perhaps you remember Crispin Porter + Bogusky's, "Subservient Chicken" video created for Burger King's TenderCrisp chicken sandwich in 2004. This ad was created specifically for the Internet with a much wider reach than traditional media could offer. It received hundreds of millions of visits, and the cost was significantly lower than broadcast television. What was launched one year later? The creation of YouTube in 2005. Do you think marketing communication has been the same since? T. Wasserman of Brandweek called the Burger King ad a "watershed moment" that changed marketing communication forever, and the trade journal dubbed it the "Marketing Innovation of the Decade."[16]

The next section of the chapter focuses on a tool that is being used more and more in campaigns: experiential marketing. It is an exciting area of marketing communication today.

---

[13] Ralph F. Wilson, "The Six Simple Principles of Viral Marketing," *Web Marketing Today* 70 (2000). Retrieved from http://www.scribd.com/doc/38487/The-Six-Principles-of-Viral-Marketing.

[14] Mark Rechtin, "Fiesta Viral Marketing: Chapter 2," *Automotive News* 84, no. 6390 (2009): 6-1NULL.

[15] Wilson, "The Six Simple Principles of Viral Marketing."

[16] Todd Wasserman, "Marketing Innovation of the Decade," *Brandweek* 50, no. 44 (2009): 28.

Chapter 14 ■ Internet Marketing, Web Sites, Viral, Social Networking, Experiential,...

EXPERIENTIAL MARKETING

Another relatively new area of marketing communication is coined experiential marketing. It is derived from tactics such as PR events, sampling, and mobile tours. Most marketing and marketing communication professionals agree it is now more than just an event-based programming. Rather, it now includes any "live"—including online—interaction that uses consumers' insights and emotions to connect them to a brand. Emotional intensity during the experience with the brand is a major key to the success of experiential programs.[17,18]

What is the difference between purchasing coffee at Starbucks versus your local supermarket or 7–11? In many ways, it is the entire experience of getting the beverage at Starbucks—the atmosphere, the aroma, the barista who knows your favorite items—it's an entire experience of getting the coffee. That is one of the major reasons Starbucks is able to have such a high price point for a cup of coffee, and it is also why Starbucks protects its brand carefully—it wants you to have that experience each time you purchase a beverage from their stores.

For the most part, experiential marketing is a relatively small line item on most brands' budgets. But, it does continue to grow—especially in a down economy when traditional ad dollars tend to be cut. Overall, experiential marketing costs less than traditional advertising. More and more marketers are finding it important for their customers to experience their brands and make an emotional connection.

For example, in the beer industry, bartenders play a very important role because they are brand advocates, as their clients often ask them for recommendations. In one year, an average bartender can make about 3,000 product recommendations. MillerCoors recognized this and started a program entitled "Beer Sessions," where sales representatives speak with waitstaff at locations that sell their beer. The sales reps then teach the staff interesting stories regarding MillerCoors' products. The servers can then share these stories with customers and make drinking the product more of an experience. One fact: "Did you know that Bill Coors invented the aluminum can?" or that "Blue Moon won the World Beer Cup Champion Brewer award last year?"[19]

The pharmaceutical industry does not get to do much in the experiential marketing area due to the nature of its products. But, GlaxoSmithKline (GSK) decided to try it with their Alli brand weight-loss products. GSK hired House Party to promote parties in people's homes across the country. The host of the party absorbs the cost of the party, so House Party makes sure the experience is going to be worth the time of the host and partygoers. In this case, Alli partygoers were given kits with recipe cards, brochures, coupons, calorie counters, and a cookbook. In total, about 15,000 guests attended across the country, and each party lasted about 3 to 5 hours each. How well did it work? After the party, 87% of participants said their opinion of Alli was "much better" or "better." Total reach was estimated at 1.1 million by House Party.[20]

---

[17] Lesley Young, "The Measurement Conundrum," *Marketing Magazine* 114 no. 11 (2009): 24–27.

[18] Erin Biba, "Eliciting Emotions Should Drive Experiential Marketing Goals," *B to B* 91, no. 15 (2006): 15.

[19] "Face Time," *Adweek* 50, no. 35 (2009): S14–15.

[20] Ibid.

This leads to an important discussion: return-on-investment of experiential programs. Because this is still a new and evolving marketing communication tool, there are no industry standards to measure the ROI of programs. It is believed that roughly 80% of marketers who use experiential marketing do not measure its effectiveness due to lack of measurement tools. Many agencies who work on these types of programs are creating their own ROI or RO "E"xperience.

Recall that an important part of experiential marketing is the emotional connection customers have with brands. So, in many ways, measurements of success are qualitative and not quantitative, which can be more difficult to explain in terms of return. As brands continue to spend more on this tool, brand managers will continue to demand better measurement of ROI/ROE.[21]

The final portion of this chapter will focus on guerilla marketing.

GUERILLA MARKETING

Another marketing communication tool that is meant to increase WOM is guerilla marketing. It continues to gain popularity in integrated communications campaigns because of its relatively low cost, compared to traditional advertising, and its potential viral effect.

The term *guerilla* was coined in a 1984 book, *Guerilla Marketing,* by advertising expert J. C. Levinson. He defined the medium as an "investment of time, energy, and imagination rather than money, ideal for prudent entrepreneurs who ran small businesses." Guerilla marketing has really grown since then, with many campaigns being run by very large organizations.[22]

Guerilla marketing can be another way, like experiential tactics, to engage the consumer with a company's brand or service. For example, companies may pay for an attractive woman to work at a bar. While there, she will select people to socialize with and will mention a product (for example, a drink) she really enjoys. Her targets will never know she is being paid to promote the drink. In Australia, the tobacco industry has tried to be very creative with its use of guerilla tactics to get around heavy communication regulation. However, Phillip Morris Limited (Australia) pleaded guilty to the charge that a guerilla event they sponsored was really advertising. For the guerilla tactic, Phillip Morris sponsored a dance party that featured many "feminine" products that included cigarettes, and after the party conducted a survey regarding partygoers' smoking habits.[23]

As with the Australian example, advertisers should be responsible and ethical when creating guerilla tactics. In the United States, Turner Broadcasting System's Cartoon Network's Adult Swim, in 2007, created a campaign for the movie *Aqua Teen Hunger Force.* The primary target for the campaign was college students. For the campaign, 400 LED light displays were placed in ten cities across the country from Boston to Austin, Texas. The signs had no copy or call to action—they displayed an alien character named "Mooninite" from the movie displaying the middle finger. Most cities took little notice; however, in Boston, people thought that the batteries and wires that were exposed in the displays could be bombs and called authorities. Boston quickly shut down transportation and sent out police and bomb-sniffing dogs.

A major mistake Turner made was not notifying city authorities about the campaign ahead of time, so the misuse of city funds would not have taken place. In a post–9/11 world,

---

[21] Young, "The Measurement Conundrum."

[22] Douglas MacMillan and Helen Waters, "Guerilla Marketing Gone Wild," *Businessweek.com.,* February 9, 2007. Web, March 30, 2010. <http://my.eurorscg.com/unprotected/news/clippings5/businessweek-02-09.pdf>.

[23] Stacy Carter, "Going below the Line: Creating Transportable Brands for Australia's Dark Market," *Tobacco Control* 12, Suppl. 3 (2003): 87–94. Web, March 30, 2010.

advertisers must think about the effects of guerilla tactics before implementing them. In the end, Turner paid Boston $1 million to pay for funds used and $1 million in "goodwill" funds toward homeland security.

Ratings for Aqua Teen Hunger Force rose 5%, and Cartoon Network's Web site increased 105.2% from the week before the guerilla tactic gained media attention in Boston and nationally. Is that success? At what cost?[24]

Guerilla tactics seem to be increasing, especially due to the recent economic downturn. Traditional ad dollars are lower and, especially with younger viewers, the use of DVRs and the Web, traditional advertising is losing some of its communication power. If the campaigns are well designed, it can really engage the target audience in the brand and become viral because people today use their cell phone cameras, post on YouTube or Flickr, easily helping create the digital and media buzz that was discussed in this chapter.[25]

INTERNET MARKETING, WEB SITES, VIRAL, SOCIAL NETWORKING, EXPERIENTIAL, AND GUERILLA MARKETING

Exercises

1. During President Barack Obama's campaign for the 2008 Democratic nomination, he employed the power of viral marketing. By tapping into social networks, he was able to receive hundreds of thousands of small donations. Aggressively seeking to leverage the financial power of social networks, President Obama's campaign reached a new level for political advertising. By using the Internet in an innovative way, President Obama was able to receive donations totaling more than $10 million.
   a. What do you think of Obama's campaign strategy?
   b. What are other advantages of using social media for political marketing? Why?
   c. What are some disadvantages of using social media marketing? Why?

Source: Tumulty, Karen. "Obama–s Viral Marketing Campaign." *Time,* July 5, 2007. Web, April 2, 2010. <http://www.time.com/time/magazine/article/0,9171,1640402–1,00.html>.

2. The NCAA tournament is a popular time for the Internet. Besides watching games, checking scores, and filling out brackets, fans are also chatting with each other. Five of the 10 busiest "peak" times of Internet traffic ever are linked to the NCAA tournament.

   Marketers take advantage of this information by using social media to coax consumers to engage with their brand. During the 2010 tournament, Applebee's offered $1 million to whomever picked the winners to all 63 games. MillerCoors launched a basketball themed iphone app to provide daily interaction with the consumer.

   Pretend you work for Coca-Cola and would like to be a part of the "conversation" with the consumer during the tournament. Develop several social media marketing ideas to increase consumer involvement.

Source: Horovitz, Bruce. "Marketers Make Most of Social Media for NCAA Promotions." *USA Today.* March 15, 2010. Web, April 2, 2010. <http://www.usatoday.com/money/advertising/2010–03–15–ncaasocial15_ST_N.htm>.

---

[24]MacMillan and Waters, "Guerilla Marketing Gone Wild."

[25]Reena Jana, "Advertising Goes Guerrilla." *BusinessWeek Slide Shows and Multimedia.* Web, March 30, 2010. <http://images.businessweek.com/ss/06/08/guerrilla_ads/source/1.htm>.

3. As discussed in this chapter, in 2007, Turner Broadcasting deployed a guerilla marketing campaign to promote the Adult Swim cartoon, Aqua Teen Hunger Force. The campaign included placing battery-operated light boards depicting a middle-finger-waving moon man around the city of Boston. Unfortunately, the devices were mistaken to be bombs, creating panic around the city and prompting authorities to close several bridges. Turner Broadcasting removed all the devices and apologized for the marketing campaign being mistaken for public danger.

   The guerilla campaign, though short lived, gained Turner Broadcasting and Aqua Teen Hunger Force a large amount of publicity, especially online. The debacle possibly gained more buzz in its failure than if it would have been a success.

   A Boston-area congressman said this about the stunt: "Scaring an entire region, tying up . . . major roadways, and forcing first responders to spend 12 hours chasing down trinkets instead of terrorists is marketing run amok. It would be hard to dream up a more appalling publicity stunt."

   a. What are your opinions of the original guerilla marketing idea of the light boards?
   b. How do you feel about the buzz the stunt generated?
   c. Does this example bring up any ethical questions surrounding the use of guerilla marketing? If so, what are they?

Source: Lothian, Dan, and Deborah Feverick. "Two Held after Ad Campaign Triggers Boston Bomb Scare." *CNN*, February 1, 2007. Web, April 2, 2010. <http://www.cnn.com/2007/US/01/31/boston.bombscare/index.html>.

Case 14.1

"Gossip Girl" Viral Promotion[1]

Rick Haskins, executive vice president of marketing and brand strategy for The CW Network, of Burbank, California, was faced with an intriguing challenge as the network approached their upcoming season. How can The CW Network stimulate fans of their popular series, "Gossip Girl," to watch the program live each week?

Prior to joining The CW Network, Haskins was the executive vice president and general manager for Lifetime Television. While there, Haskins played a key role in making the network the highest-rated basic cable entity on television. One of the greatest contributions Haskins made while at Lifetime was the invigoration of their Internet presence, by increasing the network's page views from 100,000 to over 2.2 million unique monthly visitors.

In his position with The CW Network, Haskins directed and oversaw all phases of the network's marketing, including brand management, on-air promotion, print media, and new media initiatives. He was responsible for maintaining and developing The CW Network brand, while managing a staff that covered all areas of their television marketing.

With the wide scale adoption of digital video recorders, Web sites streaming television episodes and services like DirectTV and TiVo, fans and viewers of The CW Network's shows had the ability to watch their favorite programming whenever they wanted. This freedom also allowed them to skip over commercials aired during the shows. As a result, traditional television advertising sales had been significantly undermined. With an increasingly cluttered media landscape, outside-the-box marketing efforts were given a second consideration by many brands, including The CW Network. Given his background with Lifetime and the job he did with their Internet presence, Haskins wondered if there were opportunities to revive a dedicated live television audience so advertisers could have an enhanced place to reach The CW Network's target publics through traditional "live" television advertising.

The CW Network had four months until their new season launched, and they planned to implement many new marketing initiatives for their television lineup. Given the plot of the show, Haskins believed there was an opportunity for one of their most popular shows, "Gossip Girl," to retain and increase a dedicated live television audience. In order to realize this opportunity, his plan was to formulate a public relations campaign utilizing non-traditional media to coincide with the start of the upcoming season of "Gossip Girl."

NETWORK BACKGROUND

The CW Network was a joint venture between Warner Brothers Entertainment and the CBS Corporation. The CW Network, on average, offered a lineup that delivered a total of 30 hours of programming throughout the week. The network has hosted many popular series, including "Gossip Girl," "One Tree Hill," "90210," Smallville," "Supernatural" and "America's Next Top Model."

The CW Network was the only network targeting women, 18–34 years of age. Their main competitors included ABC, FOX Broadcasting, and NBC. The CW Network was America's fifth broadcast network. Their most recent full year sales, reported by Hoovers, was estimated at $26.5 million. At the same time, they reported having 250 employees. The CW Network has reached close to 95 percent of the country with primetime programming.

---

[1]This case was written by Jason Sears and John Murphy, The University of Texas at Austin and is intended to serve as a basis for class discussion, not to illustrate either the effective or ineffective handling of an administrative situation. Used by permission of The CW Network.

"GOSSIP GIRL"

The privileged prep school teens on Manhattan's Upper East Side first learned that Serena van der Woodsen (Blake Lively, "The Sisterhood of the Traveling Pants") was back in town the way they learned all the important news in their lives—from the blog of the all-knowing albeit ultra-secretive Gossip Girl.

No one knew Gossip Girl's identity, but everyone in this exclusive and complicated vicious circle relied on her Web site and text messages for the latest scoop. Even Serena's closest friend, Blair Waldorf (Leighton Meester, "Entourage"), was surprised to find that Serena had suddenly ended her self-imposed exile to boarding school and returned to Manhattan.

Once the Upper East Side's most notorious party girl, Serena's reasons for returning were mysterious, although they may have had something to do with her younger brother Eric (Connor Paolo, "Alexander"). Whatever the reasons, the change in Serena was obvious, especially to Blair, whose friendship with Serena had always been competitive and difficult.

The show included a cast of characters that accompanied Serena and Blair throughout their world full of shopping and partying in Manhattan (see Exhibit 14.1.1). One of the most interesting aspects of the show was

Exhibit 14.1.1 ■ Members of the "Gossip Girl" Cast

Left to Right: Ed Westwick (Chuck Bass), Chace Crawford (Nate Archibald), Leighton Meester (Blair Waldorf), Penn Badgley (Dan Humphrey), Taylor Momsen (Jenny Humphrey), Blake Lively (Serena van der Woodsen)

its emphasis on fashion. In an article in *The New York Times,* Ruth La Ferla stated that the show's viewership of teenagers and young women were "tuning in not only for the plots, but also to render judgment on the clothes." She discusses how fans were flocking to boutiques with magazine articles featuring members of the cast and asking for their exact outfits.

The show focused on technology and interactivity just as much as it did on fashion. With the gossip coming from an unknown blogger, the cast of characters used their cell phones constantly to get the latest scoop. Fans of the show demanded to get these new cell phones just as much as their outfits.

Filmed in New York and based on the popular series of young-adult novels by Cecily von Ziegesar, "Gossip Girl" was from Alloy Entertainment in association with Warner Bros. Television and CBS Paramount Television with executive producers Josh Schwartz ("Chuck," "The O.C."), Stephanie Savage ("The O.C."), Bob Levy ("Privileged"), Leslie Morgenstein ("Privileged"), John Stephens ("Gilmore Girls," "The O.C."), and co-executive producer Joshua Safran.

The demographic of viewers who watched and followed "Gossip Girl" was women, 18–24 years of age, which aligned within The CW Network's target audience. "Gossip Girl" aired Mondays from 8:00 p.m.–9:00 p.m. EST on The CW Network. The show has won six Teen Choice Awards, including Blake Lively for Choice TV Actress Drama.

THE CHALLENGE

Rick Haskins worked with the public relations team for "Gossip Girl" for two weeks brainstorming and researching to consolidate the purpose of the proposed campaign into a clearly defined objective.

Public Relations Objective

Revive the loss of live television viewers, and the resulting television advertising dollars that followed, among the "Gossip Girl" target audience by implementing a non-traditional and outside-the-box publicity and promotional campaign.

A New Viral Promotional Program

The success of the promotional campaign would be measured by a significant increase in ratings during the time of the campaign. These ratings can also be used in support of their television advertising sales efforts. The campaign should be implemented solely through non-traditional media, meaning no television, radio, or print advertising.

The primary target audience for "Gossip Girl" was women, 18–24 years of age. Increasing a live television audience in this demographic gives corporations and organizations a clear target audience that they can tailor their television advertising toward. In the process of creating this proposed outside-the-box publicity program, Haskins knew that it should be possible to mix different elements of social media and attract a new secondary target market, the college male demographic. There are a number of ways to use non-traditional media elements to a marketer's advantage. Creating and drawing in new target markets is just one of such advantages.

A member of the "Gossip Girl" public relations team felt, for example, that Jack in the Box's clever viral and web-based promotion was an excellent example of how a campaign for the "Gossip Girl" series might work.

As part of their multichannel marketing campaign, Jack in the Box aired a Super Bowl commercial in which a bus fictitiously struck Jack, the antenna ball mascot for Jack in the Box. As a follow-up, Jack in the Box launched a Web site and tied it in with their Facebook page (see Exhibit 14.1.2), YouTube page (see

Exhibit 14.1.3), and Twitter account (see Exhibit 14.1.4). In helping to connect to their core demographic, Jack in the Box generated over four million YouTube views of the videos portraying the current status of the mascot. Of course, coupons (see Exhibit 14.1.5) were offered on certain days that could be printed off only online as well. Additionally, Jack in the Box enthusiasts posted videos to YouTube wishing him well and singing him songs. In this case, the viral promotional tactics worked in conjunction with traditional advertising. The campaign was referred to as "Hang in there Jack."

Viral promotions such as these have become increasingly effective tools for primary or supplementary advertising and public relations initiatives. They offer relevant publics opportunities to interact with brands, producing meaningful experiences while forming or reestablishing mutually beneficial brand relationships. With this mindset, Haskins and his team went to work on deciding the campaign strategy to achieve their objective. They had 14 weeks until the start of their upcoming season. Of course, depending on their strategy, they still needed to decide how far in advance to begin executing their campaign as well.

Exhibit 14.1.2 ■ Jack in the Box Facebook Page[1]

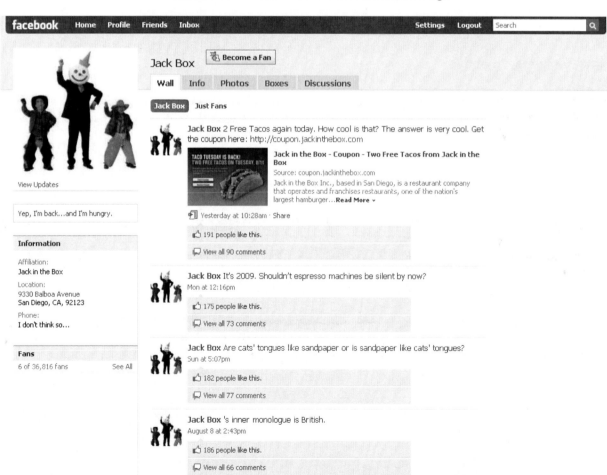

[1]Fans also created several satellite Facebook pages specifically related to the "Hang in there Jack" campaign.

Exhibit 14.1.3 ■ Jack in the Box YouTube Page

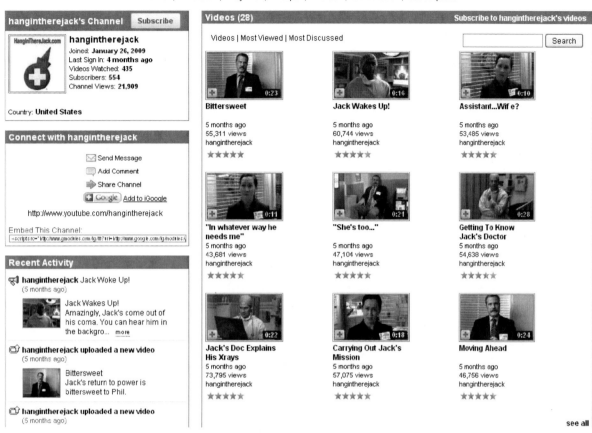

Exhibit 14.1.4 ■ Jack in the Box Twitter Account[2]

·····

Back in control of both my Twitter account . . . and Jack in the Box. It's good to be back. - Jack

8:57 AM Mar 9th from web

Jack will Tweet on his own again starting tomorrow. It's been my greatest honor to have been his official Tweeter for the last few weeks.

8:26 AM Mar 8th from web

·····

Reminder! Download your coupon for 2 Free Tacos at coupon.hangintherejack.com. Use it anytime, day or night tomorrow, Tuesday, 2/24

12:11 PM Feb 23rd from web

·····

A blog has been set up at http://www.hangintherejack.... to keep you abreast of Jack's condition. - (posted by Barbara, Jack's Assistant)...

3:02 PM Feb 2nd from web

Jack's been taken to the hospital. - (posted by Barbara, Jack's Assistant)

7:01 AM Feb 2nd from mobile web

·····

This is Barbara, Jack's assistant. Jack was hit by a bus. I'll be updating his Facebook & Twitter with more info as I get it. Stay tuned...

6:40 PM Feb 1st from web

Going downtown to have lunch with Phil.

11:23 AM Feb 1st from mobile web

·····

[2]Shown above was a sample of real Twitter messages pertaining to the campaign.

Exhibit 14.1.5 ■ "Hang in There Jack" Web Site and Promotional Materials

Above: "Hang in there Jack" Web site
Right: Campaign promotional coupon
Bottom: Still frames from campaign

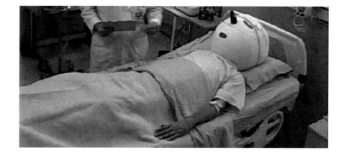

Name _____ Date _____

QUESTIONS FOR DISCUSSION AND REVIEW

1. What are the most important characteristics of the "Gossip Girl" program that attracts the primary target audience to watch the program? How can these characteristics be leveraged in a viral promotion?

Fashion, drama, the blogging and interactivity demonstrated on the show. They should involve fashion, maybe winning clothes, dressing the girls, taking clothes from each episode and dressing themselves

2. Is there an opportunity here to have the major personalities from the program participate in the viral program in some way? If so, how might this be incorporated?

Yes, maybe have Gossip Girl reach out to viewers somehow. Maybe they could launch videos of the girls doing scenes in different outfits

3. What types of social media outlets can be used in this promotional effort? Which social media outlets would be ineffective?

Facebook, Twitter, Youtube; Anything considered "outdated" since the characters on the show are supposed to be hip, cutting edge

4. If traditional media were included as a supplement, how can television, print, and radio be used to complement this viral promotion effort? Which of these would be least effective in conjunction with viral promotional tactics? Does this depend on the campaign strategy? If so, give examples of different campaigns utilizing the different mediums with viral promotional tactics.

traditional media could direct people to viral promotion; radio would probably be least effective since television relies so heavily on visuals

Case 14.2

Amy's Ice Creams (C)[1]

As Teresa Noll, Amy's Ice Creams Operations Manager and in charge of marketing, reflected on how to most appropriately promote Amy's planned new retail center locations, she felt that ideally a viral, experiential, and/or guerrilla marketing effort would be most appropriate for two reasons. First, the primary target audience of the new centers was young families with children who lived in reasonably close proximity to the centers. The household heads of these families tended to be wired, digitally savvy, and dependent on the Internet for news, information, and entertainment. In addition, they were resistant to traditional marketing efforts.

Second, the new centers also offered the possibility of collaboration between the tenants of the centers. This mix of tenants suggested some interesting cross promotions and events that might be leveraged using experiential, viral or guerilla marketing strategies. See Amy's Ice Creams (A) and (B) for additional background on Amy's current situation.

Amy's had just announced the launching of two new mini shopping centers referred to as "Austinvilles." Each of these mini-centers would feature Amy's and other locally owned, Austin-based companies. The new center in north Austin would be located on Research Blvd. at Anderson Mill Road and would include an Amy's, a Run Tex store (a retailer specializing in athletic shoes and clothing), a Zen Japanese fast-food restaurant, a Hogg Island Italian Deli, and a Strut (a boutique featuring women's clothing). The Austinville in south Austin was to be located on South Lamar at Lightsey Road and would be anchored by an Amy's and a Phil's Ice House (a hamburger restaurant) with other tenants to be added later. See Exhibit 14.2.1 that presents a map of Austin that indicates the 11 locations of Amy's Ice Creams stores and the two new centers.

The concept behind these retail centers was to create synergy based on a small cluster of well-known, Austin icon retailers. This would offer a fun collection of stores for shopping and eating that would be attractive to young families.

Michael Hsu, an Austin architect, was to design both of the centers. For the South Lamar center, Mr. Hsu would emulate the look and feel of the existing Phil's and Amy's joint location in a refitted gas station on Burnett Road (see Exhibit 14.2.2).

---

[1] This case was written by John H. Murphy, The University of Texas at Austin. The case is designed to serve as the basis for classroom discussion and not to illustrate either the effective or ineffective handling of an administrative situation. The case is used with permission granted by Amy Simmons, Founder and CEO of Amy's Ice Creams.

Exhibit 14.2.1

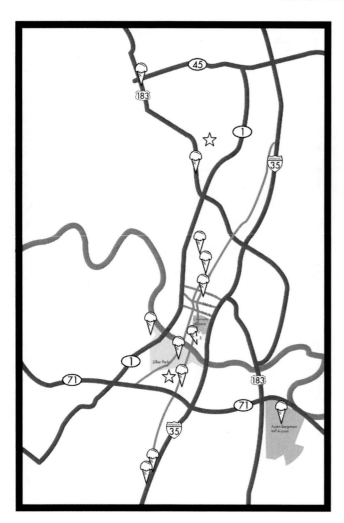

Amy's 🍦

6th St.
1012 W. 6th Street

Austin Airport
3600 Presidential Blvd.

Arboretum
10000 Research at the Arboretum

Burnet Road
5624 Burnet Road

Guadalupe
3500 Guadalupe

Mira Vista
2765 Bee Caves Road, Suite 209

SOCO
1301 South Congress

South Park Cinema
9900 S I H 35

Super South
3100 South Congress

The Grove
9600 S I H 35 # 400

The Wood
13776 N. Hwy. 183

West Gate
4477 S. Lamar

Austinville ☆

North
183 @ Anderson Mill

South
South Lamar @ Lightsey

Exhibit 14.2.2

Name _____   Date _____

QUESTIONS FOR DISCUSSION AND REVIEW

1. How will Amy's established marketing philosophy influence the development of a viral, experiential, and/or guerilla marketing effort promoting the Austinville centers?

2. How will the mix of retail partners influence the development of a viral, experiential, and/or guerilla program(s)?

3. What additional information on the target audience would be most useful in developing a viral, experiential, and/or guerilla marketing program?

4. How might social media be most effectively harnessed to build interest in the new Amy's in the two Austinville locations?

5. In this situation, are there any risks inherent in using a viral, experiential, and/or guerilla marketing strategy? Can you cite examples of each of these type programs that failed or even backfired on marketers?

_____

_____

_____

_____

Case 14.3

BusinesSuites (E)[1]

The management team at BusinesSuites (BSS) monitored the performance of their website to ensure their prospective consumers and present clients had a pleasant and beneficial experience with their brand. However, BSS last completely overhauled their website structure and design four years ago. (See the BSS (A) case for background on the company, their markets, and so on.)

Since their web presence played such a major role in marketing the company, President and CEO of BusinesSuites John Jordan felt it was time to restructure the current BSS website to enhance the effectiveness and efficiency of the marketing efforts. As a first step in this redesign, Heather Younger, the Center Manager of the Westlake BSS facility, was asked to review the Google Analytics data for the BSS website and make recommendations regarding the structure, as well as the design, of the website (Exhibits 14.3.1–14.3.4 present data from the four most recent quarterly periods from the past fiscal year that just ended).

Ms. Younger's task was to use the analytical data on the performance of the BSS website as well as the corresponding website screenshots (see Exhibit 14.3.5) to strategize and deliver a set of recommendations to John Jordan concerning the architecture, design, plus potential additions to the BSS website. As she began to study the data, she realized that how important the upgrading and enhancing of BSS's web presence was, particularly in terms of attracting Virtual Office (VO) clients.

---

[1]This case was written by Jason Sears, The University of Texas at Austin. The case is designed to serve as the basis for classroom discussion and not to illustrate either the effective or ineffective handling of an administrative situation. The case is used with permission granted by BusinesSuites.

Exhibit 14.3.1 ■ BSS Website Data July 1, 201X—September 30, 201X

Quarterly Summary:			
Total visits	17,702	Visits per day	192.41
Pageviews	65,696	Pages per visit	3.71
Avg. time on site	2:21	Bounce rate	40.78%
New visitors	79.83%	Unique visitors	14,358

Content Summary:					
	Pageviews	**Unique Views**	**Avg. Time**	**Bounce Rate**[2]	**Exit Rate**[3]
Home	9104	6436	0:42	27.3%	29.28%
Sign In	389	291	0:28	44.44%	9.25%
Locations	10838	5419	0:15	31.02%	6.62%
News	1236	1008	0:17	33.33%	8.17%
Blog	—	—	—	—	—
About	4255	3058	0:42	45.02%	18.64%
Careers	2638	2174	0:54	50%	30.52%
Contact	1008	843	0:48	38.89%	22.32%
Sitemap	165	107	0:15	0%	12.73%

The following shows how many clicks each link (rows) received on each page (columns)									
	Home	**Sign In**	**Locations**	**News**	**Blog**	**About**	**Careers**	**Contact**	**Sitemap**
1 (Home)[4]	376	136	826	112	—	571	717	216	7
2 (Sign In)	127	—	101	17	—	31	18	20	2
3 (Locations)	1956	121	—	153	—	1080	252	179	9
4 (News)	70	9	99	—	—	538	190	41	3
5 (Blog)	—	—	—	—	—	—	—	—	—
6 (About)	1053	27	943	195	—	—	346	116	8
7 (Careers)	953	13	193	333	—	667	—	138	5
8 (Contact)	291	14	121	66	—	150	237	—	5
9 (Sitemap)	13	0	14	2	—	17	1	4	—

[2]Bounce Rate is the percentage of single-page visits in which the visitor left the site from the entrance (landing) page.

[3]Exit Rate is the percentage of visitors that leave the site from a specific page based on the total times the page has been viewed.

[4]Numbers 1–9 refer to Exhibit 14.3.5.

Exhibit 14.3.2 ■ BSS Website Data October 1, 201X—December 31, 201X

Quarterly Summary:			
Total visits	15,804	Visits per day	171.78
Pageviews	53,053	Pages per visit	3.36
Avg. time on site	2:17	Bounce rate	45.30%
New visitors	78.49%	Unique visitors	12,758

Content Summary:					
	Pageviews	**Unique Views**	**Avg. Time**	**Bounce Rate[5]**	**Exit Rate[6]**
Home	6034	4357	0:54	34.55%	32.15%
Sign In	321	243	0:22	33.33%	9.97%
Locations	8063	4360	0:17	29.8%	8.46%
News	890	693	0:33	20%	11.8%
Blog	—	—	—	—	—
About	2438	1730	0:37	42.31%	17.88%
Careers	1013	789	0:44	57.89%	23.69%
Contact	773	626	0:30	30.77%	22.64%
Sitemap	178	127	0:35	0%	10.67%

The following shows how many clicks each link (rows) received on each page (columns)									
	Home	**Sign In**	**Locations**	**News**	**Blog**	**About**	**Careers**	**Contact**	**Sitemap**
1 (Home)[7]	309	112	798	87	—	309	240	141	14
2 (Sign In)	114	—	79	11	—	33	9	13	2
3 (Locations)	1482	96	—	142	—	649	100	150	11
4 (News)	53	9	174	—	—	268	92	29	1
5 (Blog)	—	—	—	—	—	—	—	—	—
6 (About)	368	20	535	170	—	—	133	82	7
7 (Careers)	273	6	98	147	—	262	—	80	1
8 (Contact)	232	13	103	38	—	141	141	—	3
9 (Sitemap)	10	0	12	2	—	11	1	3	—

[5]Bounce Rate is the percentage of single-page visits in which the visitor left the site from the entrance (landing) page.

[6]Exit Rate is the percentage of visitors that leave the site from a specific page based on the total times the page has been viewed.

[7]Numbers 1–9 refer to Exhibit 14.3.5.

Exhibit 14.3.3 ■ BSS Website Data January 1, 201X+1–March 31, 201X+1

Quarterly Summary:			
Total visits	19,027	Visits per day	211.41
Pageviews	54,025	Pages per visit	2.84
Avg. time on site	2:07	Bounce rate	55.75%
New visitors	80.76%	Unique visitors	15,755

Content Summary:					
	Pageviews	Unique Views	Avg. Time	Bounce Rate[8]	Exit Rate[9]
Home	5614	4114	0:50	37.00%	33.65%
Sign In	275	210	0:28	68.42%	13.82%
Locations	7432	4042	0:16	33.17%	8.97%
News	850	684	0:41	0%	14.35%
Blog	—	—	—	—	—
About	2103	1500	0:36	40.55%	19.02%
Careers	721	605	0:51	60.00%	29.40%
Contact	676	558	0:57	40.91%	23.82%
Sitemap	187	156	1:00	33.33%	17.11%

The following shows how many clicks each link (rows) received on each page (columns)									
	Home	Sign In	Locations	News	Blog	About	Careers	Contact	Sitemap
1 (Home)[10]	301	91	709	75	—	284	102	118	13
2 (Sign In)	82	—	70	11	—	21	7	13	2
3 (Locations)	1474	75	—	162	—	503	84	131	13
4 (News)	66	12	274	—	—	149	49	26	2
5 (Blog)	—	—	—	—	—	—	—	—	—
6 (About)	276	8	317	189	—	—	121	93	3
7 (Careers)	157	3	88	43	—	277	—	59	3
8 (Contact)	172	3	95	23	—	159	108	—	4
9 (Sitemap)	17	5	17	3	—	16	1	2	—

[8]Bounce Rate is the percentage of single-page visits in which the visitor left the site from the entrance (landing) page.

[9]Exit Rate is the percentage of visitors that leave the site from a specific page based on the total times the page has been viewed.

[10]Numbers 1–9 refer to Exhibit 14.3.5.

Chapter 14 ■ Internet Marketing, Web Sites, Viral, Social Networking, Experiential,...

Exhibit 14.3.4 ■ BSS Website Data April 1, 201X+1–June 30, 201X+1

Quarterly Summary:			
Total visits	24,563	Visits per day	269.92
Pageviews	66,356	Pages per visit	2.70
Avg. time on site	2:00	Bounce rate	59.47%
New visitors	82.58%	Unique visitors	20,735

Content Summary:					
	Pageviews	**Unique Views**	**Avg. Time**	**Bounce Rate**[11]	**Exit Rate**[12]
Home	7842	5708	0:50	40.56%	34.52%
Sign In	522	399	0:40	65.96%	15.71%
Locations	8326	4587	0:24	45.34%	11.23%
News	1319	1030	0:56	35.00%	16.15%
Blog	—	—	—	—	—
About	2785	2031	0:47	37.44%	20.90%
Careers	1250	1055	0:51	60.00%	32.16%
Contact	930	758	0:53	42.86%	23.01%
Sitemap	533	406	1:03	0.00%	13.13%

The following shows how many clicks each link (rows) received on each page (columns)									
	Home	**Sign In**	**Locations**	**News**	**Blog**	**About**	**Careers**	**Contact**	**Sitemap**
1 (Home)[13]	492	132	821	140	—	361	156	186	27
2 (Sign In)	179	—	91	27	—	60	21	13	7
3 (Locations)	1765	120	—	240	—	563	134	146	17
4 (News)	115	20	374	—	—	213	60	24	6
5 (Blog)	—	—	—	—	—	—	—	—	—
6 (About)	458	15	409	238	—	—	182	105	14
7 (Careers)	339	15	136	65	—	455	—	107	8
8 (Contact)	249	19	133	39	—	176	185	—	6
9 (Sitemap)	45	13	33	10	—	45	9	11	—

[11] Bounce Rate is the percentage of single-page visits in which the visitor left the site from the entrance (landing) page.

[12] Exit Rate is the percentage of visitors that leave the site from a specific page based on the total times the page has been viewed.

[13] Numbers 1–9 refer to Exhibit 14.3.5.

Exhibit 14.3.5 ■ BSS Website Pages

HOME

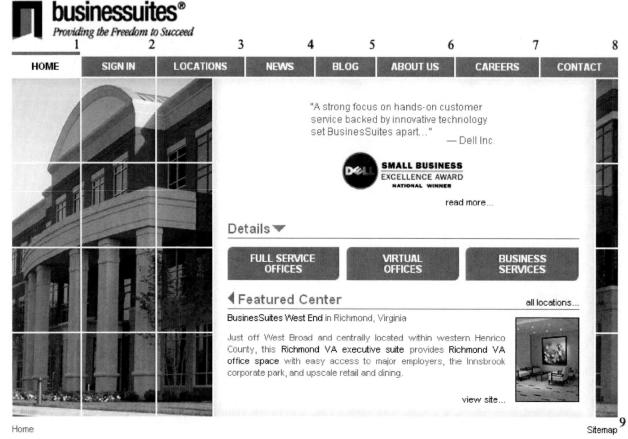

SIGN IN

LOCATIONS

Chapter 14 ■ Internet Marketing, Web Sites, Viral, Social Networking, Experiential,... 483

Exhibit 14.3.5 ■ Continued

NEWS

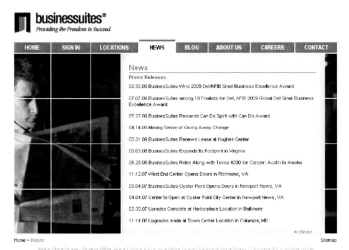

BLOG

ABOUT

CAREERS

Exhibit 14.3.5 ■ Continued

SITEMAP

Name _____ Date _____

QUESTIONS FOR DISCUSSION AND REVIEW

1. What trends stand out in the data set? What are the implications of these trends?

_____

_____

_____

_____

2. What changes, if any, need to occur to the information architecture of the site?

_____

_____

_____

_____

3. What changes, if any, need to occur to the design of the site?

_____

_____

_____

_____

4. Using the BSS A and B cases, what target audiences need to be considered while restructuring the BSS site?

_____

_____

_____

_____

5. What value-added content and links might be added to the site to increase it utility plus enhance BSS's natural search position?

Case 14.4

Imperial Majestic Hotels[1]

Tiffany Q. Tobias was a well-known personality, who appeared on a widely watched TV sitcom as a child. Following the five-year run of the sitcom, Tobias appeared in a series of B-grade movies. She has been in the news over the past 18 months as a result of a tabloid-fodder relationship with a younger man, Steve Steel, a controversial, high-profile professional football wide receiver.

Tobias and her agent had actively cultivated a social media fan base. At the most recent count, Tobias had a Twitter following of approximately 2 million and 4,500 friends on Facebook.

To attend a road game to watch her boyfriend, Tobias booked a suite on the top floor of the Imperial Majestic Hotel (IMH) in Chicago.[2] During her stay, the following events unfolded:

SATURDAY, SEPTEMBER 26

4:15 p.m. — Tobias checked into the IMH.

SUNDAY, SEPTEMBER 27

9:20 a.m. — Tobias ordered room service for breakfast.
12:15 p.m. — Tobias left the hotel via private limousine to attend Steel's football game.

MONDAY, SEPTEMBER 28

1:30 a.m. — Tobias returned to the hotel accompanied by a group of friends.
3:02 a.m. — Tobias called room service and placed an order for herself and eight guests.
3:27 a.m. — Room service order delivered to Tobias' suite.
3:32 a.m. — Tobias called room service to complain that a dead roach was discovered under one of the covered plates and asked that the entire order be returned. Room service staff person balked at returning the entire order and offered to replace the plate with the dead roach. "We are not going to eat anything from your kitchen!" replied Tobias, who was infuriated. She then informed the room service operator that she was going to place the entire order in the hall and asked to have the order picked up immediately.
11:45 a.m. — Tobias called the front desk and requested a later check-out time. The staff person on duty checked with housekeeping and then granted the request.
2:10 p.m. — At the front desk, Tobias found the entire $618 room service food charge on her bill. She went what she later described as "ballistic" and demanded to speak with the manager. The manager invited Tobias into his office to discuss the situation. After some animated discussion, the manager explained that IMH policy states that any room service order, once entered into the billing system, cannot be voided. IMH policy is to redo or replace any room service order with which a guest had a problem. However, no request was made to replace

---

[1]This case was written by John H. Murphy and Jason Sears, The University of Texas at Austin, to serve as a basis for classroom discussion. The identity of the firm is disguised, and the case is based on a combination of actual events.

[2]The IMH chain had 43 exclusive properties in the U.S. and Canada, and the average room rate was approximately $445 per night.

the order, therefore, the charge stands. This infuriated Tobias, who stormed out of the manager's office and left the hotel.

On her way to the airport, Tobias sent the first of several tweets bashing the IMH and their staff. These tweets were automatically linked to her Facebook status updates. In addition, these tweets were retweeted by many of her "friends."

TUESDAY, SEPTEMBER 28

2:30 p.m.	—	Tobias created a Twitter hashtag (#imhdeadroach) to facilitate bashing the hotel chain. She also called on her loyal fans to boycott the chain and to picket the Chicago location to "discourage anyone from staying there."
4:00 p.m.	—	Senior management at IMH headquarters in New York met with Gimble & Swainback, their public relations firm, to discuss the "Tobias incident." After a brief discussion, senior management unanimously agreed to ignore the incident.

WEDNESDAY, SEPTEMBER 29

10:45 a.m.	—	A group of 15 Tobias' sign-carrying fans (e.g., "Plate me, I'm a dead cockroach!") appeared in the driveway of the Chicago IMH location. When asked to leave, the group refused and one protester spit on a guest as the guest made his way into the hotel. An Action News 8 reporter, tipped off by a Tobias fan, arrived on the scene to capture the protest that aired on the six o'clock news. iPhone films and pictures of the incident were also posted by the picketers on YouTube, blogs and forums.

THURSDAY, SEPTEMBER 30

8:30 a.m.	—	Senior management at IMH headquarters in New York met and, as a first order of business, terminated Gimble & Swainback. A second public relations agency that specialized in the entertainment industry, Commerford & Craddic, was retained on a project fee basis to help handle the Tobias crisis.

THE CHALLENGE

How should the IMH chain respond to the recent viral spread of negative publicity regarding Ms. Tobias's experience with their Chicago location?

Name _____ Date _____

QUESTIONS FOR DISCUSSION AND REVIEW

1. How should IMH management have responded to Tobias's social media bashing on Monday?

_____

_____

_____

_____

2. Assuming picketers return on Thursday, how should this be handled?

_____

_____

_____

_____

3. Did IMH management perhaps overreact in firing Gimble & Swainback?

_____

_____

_____

_____

4. What should Commerford & Craddic's first public step be in handling the unfolding crisis?

_____

_____

_____

_____

5. What additional contingencies regarding the Tobias affair should IMH management prepare to handle?

6. What are three examples of other types of crises that IMH management such be prepared to face in the future?

Chapter 15
Evaluating the Effectiveness of IBP Strategies

When you become a marketing communications practitioner, you will find that marketers today, clients, are very demanding in terms of understanding how effective their dollars used on communication were during a campaign. Industry calls this "return on investment," or ROI. During the last decade, consumer expectations of media have changed as well: Many believe they should be communicated to when they want it or need it. In other words, consumers feel that they are now in control. As was discussed in Chapter 14, the rise of digital communication has drastically changed the landscape and tools available for marketing communication.

Even with all of this change, it is important to remember a fundamental basic: To prove ROI to your client or manager, you must have clear communication objectives that have stemmed from the brand's marketing objectives, as discussed in Chapters 3 and 5. If clear objectives do not exist, then it will make no sense to explain or prove ROI because it is not based on any goals for the brand.

ROLE OF RESEARCH IN ROI

Ideally, before an integrated communication campaign begins, there should be research benchmark data. That is, where the brand is currently in terms of awareness, sales, likeability, and so on. Then, realistic communication objectives may be set for the campaign. For example, currently Brand X's awareness level in Texas is 15%. Over the course of the 12-month campaign, awareness levels will reach 30%. Once the campaign runs its 12-month course, research is conducted again to see if awareness did go up by 15%. If so, the agency has met the ROI expectations for awareness.

It is important for communication agencies to try to convince their clients to conduct benchmark research before a campaign is created. Or, if the research has already been conducted by the brand, to be able to view and learn from the results. By doing the research, a higher ROI is usually reached. And, for the agency, the ROI research will illustrate whether or not their communication campaign worked. Because *accountability* is the buzzword today from client to agency, this information becomes vital at an agency's review time.[1]

---

[1] Kase, G. "Convince Clients That Research Produces Better ROI." *Marketing News* 41, no. 7 (2007): 22. Retrieved from Business Source Complete database.

An emerging area of ROI research is one that measures the entire campaign: from broadcast to digital to any public relations and guerilla tactics. And goes all the way to the retail or digital storefront behavior. Basically, all the different tools this textbook has been describing in the "arsenal" of the marketing communication toolbox. It is important to note that a "one size fits all" metric does not really exist for postcampaign ROI research. Methods that are used are dependent on the specific type of brand or product. For example, consumers purchase automobiles very differently than common packaged goods, such as laundry detergent.

In addition, as you learned in Chapter 8 or during a media course, there are many paid media measurements from companies such as Nielsen. However, there are very few standards for measuring effectiveness of unpaid communication. But the measurement is crucial to understand the effectiveness of the entire campaign. ROI measurement should be both quantitative and qualitative in nature—depending on the execution. The entire point of integrated marketing communication is that each piece of the campaign works together to reach the communication goals set at the onset of the campaign.[2]

If a brand simply tests how effective an ad execution is, for example, it may not learn the complete picture of how the campaign is meeting its goals. Many variables in the marketplace can affect the results of a campaign, even though an ad spot "tests well."

Traditionally, the communication agency conducts its own research to prove ROI. But many do not like to do it because many will say it will hinder the creative process. Thus, a trend has emerged that has a third party agency hired by the marketer to conduct ROI research. When a client is spending over $20 to $50 million dollars on a campaign, it wants an accurate ROI. It is in the interest of the agency creating the communication campaign to conduct the campaign's ROI so it can prove that the work it produced met the goals of the campaign.[3]

Another reason metrics have become more prevalent and important in ROI research is that many middle and upper managers in marketing have finance backgrounds, not traditional marketing backgrounds. The following are some examples of how different media are using ROI research to sell ad space.

Parade magazine, the Sunday supplement magazine, hired IRI (Information Resources Inc.) to conduct marketing-mix models to illustrate what type of ROI clients would get from placing ads in the magazine. Parade is also hiring IMS, a research company that focuses on the pharmaceutical industry, to show ROI for placing prescription drug ads in the magazine. Just 10 or 12 years ago this metric was not needed to sell advertising space—it is simply now demanded by marketing managers. In another example, MTV Networks is also hiring vendors that can show a "return on marketing objectives" to prove how well a campaign run on its network meets the marketing/communication objectives of the advertiser. Advertising agencies are even creating research on a large scale to help prove ROI. Ogilvy Action conducted a 14,000-shopper study globally to prove that they understand shopper marketing and can prove ROI.[4]

NEW MEDIA EVALUATION

In general, new media is able to deliver a stronger ROI because of all the metrics surrounding it; thus, it is easier to measure. In recessionary times, such as the end of the 2000s, marketers

---

[2]Westlund, Richard. "Measuring the Media." *Brandweek* 50, no. 43 (2009): MM1–MM3.

[3]White, E. "Advertising: Agencies Face New Accountability." *The Wall Street Journal,* October 3, 2003, p. B4.

[4]Neff, J. "Industry Unleashes Flood of Studies to Prove Worth." *Advertising Age* 79, no. 32 (2008): 3–24.

are quick to slash advertising line items, and this tends to be from traditional media. Managers have turned to digital media to spend less and potentially reach a similar amount of target audience members. Lance Richard, in an *American Journal of Business* article, stated the following regarding new media:

1. Since the economic recovery from the recession that hit at the end of 2008 is very slow—more advertisers will shift dollars to on-line media choices;
2. Prices for on-line ads will decrease;
3. Traditional media sources will continue to go out of business (like the Denver and Seattle paper version of the city's major newspapers); and
4. Online content is improving and audiences continue to grow—so, more investment will be made to create new and innovative online content and applications.[5]

Again, some of this is coming from the fact that ROI is easier to analyze in the digital media.

Google wants to grow its brand-advertising business and has created a system called Campaign Insights. It is commonly known that most people do not click on display ads and that a purchase of a product or service does not take place during the same online session as when the display ad is viewed. With Google's new program, it tracks what users have seen an online display ad and when it occurred. It then uses its millions of Google Toolbars to track what Web searches and site visits occurred after viewing the ad. Finally, Google compares that to a similar group who did not view the display ad. What Google is trying to do is prove the ROI of display advertising, analogous to the way it did for paid search through Google Analytics. Privacy is a serious issue, but Google states that the user must have enabled "enhanced features" on their Google toolbar and that data collected is anonymous and is examined for trends at the macro level.[6,7]

TRADITIONAL MEDIA FIGHTS BACK

As digital media use by advertisers continues to rise, advertisers are continuing to demand ROI of traditional media sources. Time, Inc. and Starcom MediaVest Group are working together to develop an ROI model that will promise that a certain amount of people will remember ads they have seen in magazines or have taken some action based off the ad. In addition, if the ads do not provide the guaranteed results, free additional ads will run until the results are met.

The companies are calling this service, "Alliance for Magazine Accountability." The end result may be that magazines will be able to increase ad rates or at least not have them decrease. It will be important for advertisers to understand what methodology Alliance is using so that a decision can be made on whether to use the program or not.[8]

---

[5]Richard, Lance. "The Paradox of ROI and Decreased Spending in the Ad Industry." *American Journal of Business* 24, no. 2 (2009): 11–14.

[6]Learmonth, M. "Search-Titan Google Makes Display Play with ROI Tool." *Advertising Age* 80, no. 35 (2009): 3–26.

[7]Fulgoni, G., & M. Mörn. "Whither the Click? How Online Advertising Works." *Journal of Advertising Research* 49, no. 2 (2009): 134–142.

[8]Ives, Nat. "Magazines' Pitch to Marketers: Our Ads Will Work—We Promise." *Advertising Age,* May 10, 2010 (online version).

AGENCY COMPENSATION BASED ON ROI?

The traditional method of paying communication agencies 15% commission on media purchases is at a low 3% of contracts, according to recent research by *Advertising Age*. There has been industry discussion to move compensation based on ROI—based on goals set up between the agency and client. However, this type of compensation has decreased to only 1% of pay agreements. The dominant way to compensate seems to be fee-based models at 75% of contract agreements. So, for all the importance ROI is placed on communication campaigns, currently, very few agencies are compensated based on their performance to meet goals. Many industry experts believe this is because ROI models are difficult to create and there is lack of clarity on how they would work.

Two large companies, Proctor and Gamble and Coca-Cola, are currently compensating their agencies based on performance rather than on time the agencies spend on a project. But as the numbers illustrate, very few others have joined these major advertisers.

It will be your responsibility, as the next generation of communication experts, to prove the ROI of your team's work and demand to be compensated fairly on what you deliver for your client's business.[9]

SELECTED READINGS

Fulgoni, G., & M. Mörn. "Whither the Click? How Online Advertising Works." *Journal of Advertising Research* 49, no. 2 (2009): 134–142.

Ives, Nat. "Magazines' Pitch to Marketers: Our Ads Will Work—We Promise." *Advertising Age*, May 10, 2010 (online version).

Kase, G. "Convince Clients That Research Produces Better ROI." *Marketing News* 41, no. 7 (2007): 22. Retrieved from Business Source Complete database.

Learmonth, M. "Search-Titan Google Makes Display Play with ROI Tool." *Advertising Age* 80, no. 35 (2009): 3–26.

Mullman, Jeremy. "Despite ROI Chatter, Marketers Still Pay Shops Same Old Way." *Advertising Age*, May 3, 2010 (online).

Neff, J. "Industry Unleashes Flood of Studies to Prove Worth." *Advertising Age* 79, no. 32 (2008): 3–24.

Richard, Lance. "The Paradox of ROI and Decreased Spending in the Ad Industry." *American Journal of Business* 24, no. 2 (2009): 11–14.

Westlund, Richard. "Measuring the Media." *Brandweek* 50, no. 43 (2009): MM1–MM3..

White, E. "Advertising: Agencies Face New Accountability." *The Wall Street Journal,* October 3, 2003, p. B4.

EVALUATING THE EFFECTIVENESS OF IBP STRATEGIES

Exercises

1. Philosophy is a skin care company endorsed by doctors, celebrities, and customers. The brand encourages customers to "live a better life by being better to yourself." In April 2008, Philosophy had a "Your Mom's Philosophy" campaign, where customers could share personal stories and pictures via the Philosophy Web site. Philosophy received more

---

[9]Mullman, Jeremy. "Despite ROI Chatter, Marketers Still Pay Shops Same Old Way." *Advertising Age,* May 3, 2010 (online).

than 1,000 stories from customers sharing their mother's wisdom, and customers voted for their favorite stories. The Web site increased site traffic by 39% during the campaign, and 33% of visitors read at least one story during their visit, engaging customers at a new level.

    a. What do you think was the overall underlying goal of Philosophy's campaign?

    b. Do you think it was successful in achieving that goal? Why?

"Philosophy Drives New Site Traffic with Mother's Day Campaign." *Case Studies.* Bazaarvoice. Web, April 2, 2010. <http://www.bazaarvoice.com/cs-resource/casestudies/increase-search/321-stories-philosophy>.

2. Tiger Woods had a public relations crisis in winter 2009. After a bizarre car accident at his home, it was reported that Woods was having multiple extramarital affairs. With his image at stake, Woods's first public statement after the incident was an apology. Woods wanted to take the first step in repairing his reputation by offering an intimate request for forgiveness. Tiger Woods stood at a podium and read a carefully prepared and delivered speech, addressing only a small group of friends, family, and business associates.

    a. How could you measure the effectiveness of Woods's public relations strategy?

    b. What improvements could you make to receive better results?

Pedicini, Sandra. "Tiger Woods' Apology Falls Short, Public-Relations Experts Say." *Orlando Sentinel.* February 19, 2010. Web, April 2, 2010.

<http://articles.orlandosentinel.com/2010–02–19/news/os-tiger-woods-image-20100219_1_woods-apology-tiger-woods-endorser>.

3. Whole Foods Market operates under a unique business structure. Selling natural and organic food, each individual store is encouraged to add local flavor, which is great to identify with the local target consumer. The consequence of this individuality, however, is a weakening of the central brand.

Whole Foods launched a campaign to ensure brand integrity across the decentralized network of stores and build customer loyalty to the central brand. Creative executions included signs, print ads, and marketing collateral and also poems about local delicacies and art contests.

    a. What are some ways that Whole Foods can measure the effectiveness of this strategy?

    b. What other tactics could be involved in the strategy, and how would they increase effectiveness?

Source: "Whole Foods Case Studies." *Case Studies.* Cartis Group. Web, April 2, 2010. <http://www.cartis-group.com/casestudies/whole-foods-market-branding-case-study.html>.

Case 15.1

MedNet.com Confronts "Click-Through" Competition

It was just 9:30 a.m., and the day was off to a terrible start. Heather Yates, vice president for business development at MedNet, walked at a quick clip down the hall of the company's modern Birmingham, Alabama, office space, her face clouded with concern. The company, a website delivering health information free to consumers, generated its income through advertising, mostly from pharmaceutical companies. Now, Windham Pharmaceuticals, MedNet's biggest advertiser, had asked to change the rules by which it had done business for the past four years. Moreover, Mahria Baker, Windham's CMO, had told Yates that this wasn't just an exploratory conversation. Windham was seriously considering shifting its MedNet ad dollars to Marvel, a competing website with which Windham already did some business.

Yates, who had been with MedNet since just after the company was founded in 2002, felt blindsided and, at the same time, resigned. "We have some legwork to do," she thought to herself. "We can't afford to say 'No,' and just walk away, and we can't just ask them to stay with us because we're good people. We have to convince them that our set-up is worth their ad dollars. And we have to move quickly. Our other advertisers won't be far behind Windham."

She had asked Baker to fax over a copy of the results of Windham's latest advertising campaign, and had promised to call her back the next day, as both companies needed to finalize their budgets. Then, immediately after they had hung up, Yates had called Bill Bishop, MedNet's vice president of consumer marketing. "Can you clear some time for me right now?" she had asked him. "Windham is thinking of pulling their ad dollars from us and taking them to Marvel."

Now she was on her way up to Bishop's office, two floors above, with the fax from Baker and notes from her conversation in hand.

INDUSTRY BACKGROUND AND COMPANY ORIGINS

MedNet had launched its website with three goals: to provide scientifically based medical information to a nonprofessional consumer audience; to provide this information for free; and to generate profits from advertising sales. In a year, it had met all the goals; by 2006, it generated $1 million in profits. (See Exhibit 15.1.1 for 2006 income statement.) The accessibly written, easy-to-navigate, and vividly presented content was developed by 24 trained journalists, doctors, designers, and administrators. Additional materials came from the faculty of a prominent medical school, news agencies, a photography service, and an active community of visitors that used social media tools such as blogs, community chat, and virtual reality to communicate medical information. (Visitor-generated media was reviewed by medically trained journalists.) The award-winning site

---

Allegra Young has been a marketing manager and director in several national firms; she is now a principal consultant with I+O Communications in Austin, Texas.

This case, though based on real events, is fictionalized, and any resemblance to actual persons or entities is coincidental. There are occasional references to actual companies in the narration.

Copyright © 2007 by the President and the Fellows of Harvard College. The Case was prepared by Allegra Young as the basis for class discussion rather than to illustrate either effective or ineffective handling of an administrative situation. Reprinted by permission of Harvard Business School.

was considered the best health website for trusted, evidence-based, consumer health information. Advertisements on MedNet proposed specific and immediate solutions to health concerns. MedNet had 4.3 million monthly visitors, but new competitors had flattened its audience growth during the last quarter of 2006.

COMPETITORS

Now, in the first quarter of 2007, MedNet faced competition both for visitors and advertisers. Nonprofit and governmental websites competed with MedNet for visitors by providing similar content on mainstream medicine. The websites of the U.S. National Library of Medicine and World Health Organization weren't nearly as easy to navigate as MedNet, but they were comprehensive. In contrast to MedNet, these two websites provided information on alternative therapies as well as on scientifically based solutions, albeit with carefully worded disclaimers. What's more, employees of large corporations could increasingly turn to customized health websites on their own company intranets. The theory was that if internal health websites could help workers quickly identify health problems (prompting overdue doctor visits) and promote general good health, the employers could reduce their portion of employee health care costs.

For-profit health websites posed different degrees of financial competition for MedNet's advertising revenue and audience. Recently, so-called condition-specific sites that focused on particular problems, such as Cholesterol.com, had emerged. (Yates was confident that Cholesterol.com was already drawing pharmaceutical advertising dollars away from MedNet.) An indirect competitor, ClinicalTrials.com, marketed only experimental procedures. Its audience was smaller than MedNet's and the material was difficult for the layperson to understand. ClinicalTrials.com received a fee for each time a visitor it referred enrolled in a clinical trial.

Then there was Alternativehealth.com, a long-time, popular player in the "health space." It provided information about scientifically "unproven" therapies and procedures such as herbal remedies, vitamin regimens, and massage. Its audience was larger than MedNet's and its advertising sales more robust. Due to a re-

Exhibit 15.1.1 ■ MedNet Income Statement, 2006

Revenue	
Advertising income	$12,000,000
	12,000,000
Expenses	
Purchased content	3,700,000
Sales and marketing	3,000,000
Technology support	1,300,000
General administration	3,000,000
	11,000,000
Net income	$1,000,000

cent lawsuit concerning its content, Alternativehealth.com had begun using disclaimers—with no apparent impact on its audience size. Due to the alternative health consumer's distrust of pharmaceutical companies, the website did not compete with MedNet for advertising dollars. Still, MedNet had to keep Alternativehealth on its radar.

METHODS USED TO CALCULATE ADVERTISER PAYMENT

Yates's thoughts raced through the company's competitive landscape as she waited for the elevator. In her short phone conversation with Bill, he had told her to take a little time to review MedNet's original value proposition to its advertisers. What they needed to do was re-justify their approach, if it was possible to do so. But, he had cautioned, they were compelled to keep an open mind. "Think through the facts," Bill had said. "Why don't you come up here in about half an hour. I'll start to mull over our options as well."

Yates thought back to MedNet's roots. Back in 2002, MedNet's founders had made some key choices regarding revenue generation. MedNet could, in theory, sell content to site visitors, like an online magazine, charging a few dollars per article or an annual subscription fee. On the other hand, if the site could draw advertisers, and if advertising revenues were strong enough, the company could provide content free of charge—which is what most web users expected. An advertising revenue model was made possible by sophisticated web analytics: technology that tracked the behavior of each site visitor—pages viewed, links clicked, and so on. This software made it easy for advertisers to calculate their return on advertising investment (ROI).

The obvious candidates to buy onscreen advertising space from MedNet were pharmaceutical companies, which for over a decade had promoted their drugs aggressively to consumers. As it happened, MedNet was launched at a time when many other consumer health care websites were going out of business, leaving pharmaceutical firms looking for web promotion outlets. MedNet seized the opportunity to build relationships with these advertisers.

In deciding how best to generate revenue from advertisers, MedNet chose traditional banner advertising, charging pharmaceutical advertisers such as Windham Pharmaceuticals on a cost-per-thousand impressions (CPM) basis. (One advertising impression meant that one visitor requested from a Web server a page that had a specific advertisement on it.) Measuring impressions was the closest way to estimate the number of people who actually saw an online advertisement. By pursuing an impression business model, MedNet was fully "monetizing" its available inventory of "eyeballs" (site visitors). An independent auditor verified the company's impression counts each month.

MARVEL'S CHALLENGE

Yates reached Bill Bishop's office and pushed the door open. Bill was on the phone, but he waved her to a seat. "Two minutes," he mouthed at her. She nodded, and sat back. She thought about what she knew about Marvel.

Marvel was essentially a large search engine that had decided to follow the alternative advertising model: contextual, or pay-per-click, banner advertising. Under these terms, advertisers paid website owners only when visitors actually "clicked" on an advertisement to learn more about an advertised product. The key metric to measuring this kind of online advertising campaign was the click-through rate (CTR), measured as the number of clicks divided by the number of ad impressions delivered. Advertisers considered website click-throughs (and telephone calls to a call center generated by a newspaper advertisement) to be the equivalent of customers interested in potentially making a purchase.

Yates thought back to 2002. No sooner had MedNet's founders opted for a pay-per-impression model than advertisers began resisting that pricing structure—but mainly from general-interest websites, where the majority of impressions came from visitors uninterested in their products. Advertisers based this perception in part on the percentage of click-throughs that ads yielded; the click-through rate on a general-interest site tended to be half as high as on highly focused "destination" content sites like MedNet. In 2006, MedNet.com therefore could still command a $100 CPM ($100 for each 1,000 impressions) contract from its advertisers—10 to 20 times what general interest websites might charge. Similarly, Alternativehealth.com's advertisers paid for impressions only, and not for click-throughs.

But Marvel, a hugely successful search engine, turned the table on its competition in the fall of 2006 by declaring it would provide impressions for free and charge advertisers only for click-throughs. Because Marvel had a vast audience (19 million visitors per month), charging for even a small percentage of click-throughs would pay off handsomely. If the site sold advertisements in enough categories, including the pharmaceutical market, Marvel could bring in huge revenues. By late 2006, some advertisers began to ask other sites to charge only for click-through "sales leads" like Marvel did. One drawback to this popular revenue model: reports of increasing "click fraud." Advertisers' competitors were fraudulently clicking on advertisements to drive up advertising costs.

Not only was Marvel offering MedNet's long-standing advertisers like Windham different financial terms, but it also competed for visitors interested in healthcare. Visitors often came to MedNet by way of a search engine such as Marvel, although such search engines served as a starting point of inquiry, not a serious source of trusted medical information.

Mahria Baker's challenge stuck with Yates: "At Marvel we get all our impressions for free, and we pay $0.54 for each click-through. At MedNet we pay for every impression, and by my calculation we pay $3.33 for each click-through. Granted, we're not averse to getting impressions—anytime that anyone sees your logo, your slogan, and your product's name, you are theoretically doing your brand some good. But here at Windham, click-throughs are really what matter. They separate accidental observers of our ads from the serious prospects who proactively seek more product information and may buy our product. I can't justify paying six times as much for a click-through from one of your visitors." Baker had paused a moment, then added, "Heather, help me here. Is there another way of looking at this that I'm missing?"

"Yes, there is," Yates had replied, "and if you let me call you back tomorrow I believe I can show you what you are missing."

MEDNET'S AUDIENCE AND VISITOR BEHAVIOR

Bill Bishop hung up the phone and turned to Yates. She spread out a copy of the results of Windham's latest advertising campaign, and the two of them pored over it. (See Exhibit 15.1.2 for Baker's data.)

Many search engines and general-interest websites had large audiences that returned to the sites regularly, in a predictable pattern. By contrast, most visitors to targeted health websites such as MedNet came only when "in crisis." However, when they did come, they stayed long and explored avidly, clicking around to clarify symptoms or determine the best course of action for a pressing health problem. They often researched unrelated symptom areas as well, in order to help family members, or out of curiosity. These visitors then returned during the next crisis, although some did become repeat visitors. MedNet visitors clicked on more pages and advertisements than general-interest web surfers did (see Exhibit 15.1.3). In addition, health website visitors tended to buy more products from advertisers when they did decide to purchase. (See Exhibit 15.1.4 for a study of results and frequently viewed web pages on MedNet.) If the product advertised was not available over-the-counter, then the visitors would urge their physicians to prescribe the medication that they'd discovered in the advertisements on MedNet.

Windham produced Vesselia, a prescription medication that reduced cholesterol and plaque in a patient's veins with fewer side effects than competitors' offerings. High cholesterol was one cause of heart disease, and it was attributed to both genetic predisposition and lifestyle choices. Keeping cholesterol low could be a long-term issue for many patients, requiring months, possibly years, of daily medication. Each patient who began a series of treatments would use the medicine for an average of 12 months.

To encourage customers to request a prescription for Vesselia from their doctors, Windham provided coupons on its website that customers could print out and redeem at a pharmacy. Printed on each coupon was a bar code that included information identifying the referring advertisement. For instance, when a customer

Exhibit 15.1.2 ■ Windham Pharmaceuticals Advertising Campaign Results

Advertising Venue	Monthly Visitors	Impressions Windham Received	Cost	Click-Throughs	Click-Through Rate[a]	Total Ad Costs	Cost per Click-Through
MedNet	4.3 mm/month	17.2 mm	$100 CPM	516,000	3%	$1.72 mm	$3.33
Marvel Search	19 mm/month	57 mm	$.54 per click-through	798,000	1.4%	$430,920	$.54
U.S. Newspaper	2.5 mm/day	5 mm	$260,000/2-day ad	37,000[b]	.74%	$260,000	$7.03

[a] **Click-through rate:** Here the click-through rate is calculated with click-throughs divided by impressions.

[b] **Click-throughs for a newspaper:** In the case of the newspaper, the "click-through" is considered the equivalent of calls into a call center (that is, a measurement of a potential customer seeking more information). Newspaper response rates vary widely due to the wide variety of items sold.

Exhibit 15.1.3 ■ MedNet Visitor Survey Results[a]

Did you click on a sponsor's advertisement today?
3% Yes

For those who clicked on the sponsor's advertisement, did you make a purchase?
6% Yes

Have you clicked on a health advertisement at a search engine website?
1.4% Yes

For those who clicked on a health advertisement at a search engine website, did you make a purchase?
2% Yes

If you saw an advertisement on television or in a newspaper, would you call the call center?
.74% Yes

If you called about an advertisement on television or in a newspaper and found the information credible, would you make a purchase?
12% Yes

Advertisers at MedNet are more likely to provide me with useful remedies and information than advertisers found on websites that don't adhere to the same evidence-based standards.
Strongly agree: 85%
Strongly disagree: 15%

How many health sites will you visit to research your condition?
85% = 3 or more

How did you decide to go online to find health information on MedNet?
25% search engine
10% advertisement (print)
25% online advertisement
20% bookmarked this site
10% trusted advisor recommendation
10% e-mail letter from friend recommending an article

Will you return to MedNet next time you need medical information?
93% Yes
7% No

[a]The study's results, based on a very large sample size, also reflect general-health-website audience behavior.

N = 25,500 visitors

Exhibit 15.1.3 ■ Continued

Would you allow MedNet to store personal information about your condition, such as blood pressure, weight, etc.?
40% Yes
60% No

Would you pay for content at the MedNet site?
75% No

Would you use MedNet if you had to register for some information?
50% No

Exhibit 15.1.4 ■ Average Profit Margin per Pharmaceutical Prescription for Heart Medication[a]

Advertisement Placement	Estimated Contribution per Sale
General interest website	$48
Search engine	$45
Health care website	$150
Newspaper (via call center)	$165
Television (via call center)	$75

[a] This study measured the average advertising campaign contribution generated for the pharmaceutical when patients with chronic heart disease purchased a drug for long-term use. The medicine studied helped control high blood pressure.

MedNet, most viewed pages, Nov. 2006

1. Search Page
2. Advanced medical search
3. Weight control center
4. Pharmaceutical news
5. Insurance news
6. Advanced pharmaceutical search
7. Health News Update
8. Controlling cholesterol
9. Depression center
10. Medical encyclopedia index page
11. Women's content index page
12. Allergy center
13. Prevention screening guide
14. Medical conditions table of contents page
15. Today in women's health
16. Today in children's health

Audit of monthly usage and activity: 4.3 mm unique visitors
Unique visitors not included in prior month's audit: 60%

clicked on a Windham ad at MedNet's website, he was taken to the Windham website. Windham's computer system could identify that the customer came from MedNet and insert that information into the Windham coupon bar code within fractions of a second. A different coupon code was provided to those web visitors who came to Windham from Marvel Search. (Coupons with yet another barcode were sent by postal mail by the Windham telephone call center to respondents to newspaper advertisements.)

When patients redeemed the coupons at a pharmacy, the pharmacy returned them to Windham. Windham could thus attribute drug sales to the relevant advertising venue. On average, patients took three months to redeem coupons for Vesselia after Windham had first placed the advertisements. The current campaign would be considered closed at the end of February 2007.

MEDNET DISCUSSES THE MARVEL THREAT

Bill looked up from the report, turned to his computer screen, then to Yates. "So what you're saying is that Windham wants to pay only for click-throughs, and that you think Windham is just the tip of the iceberg. But you and I have done the math on this issue many times. If we sell only click-throughs at a rate that competes with Marvel, our revenues drop at least 80% if our audience size remains where it is."

Yates knew that Bill wasn't going to like what she was about to say, but she didn't pause. "If we could increase the size of our audience," she said, "we'd have more click-throughs to sell."

Bishop had started shaking his head as soon as Yates had started to speak. "The quickest way to a bigger audience is to extend our coverage to alternative healing approaches. But our board would have a hard time with that." Bishop was mindful of the two eminent physicians on MedNet's board of directors who consistently blocked proposals to deliver content about, and ads for, herbal remedies.

Yates sighed. "I understand their concern, but aren't some explanations of alternative approaches acceptable? Could we have a reference encyclopedia of alternative medicine that doesn't discuss its claims, just the plants involved? Or focus on more generally accepted practices like chiropractic medicine and acupuncture?"

Bishop shook his head again. "We can't get advertising growth from that group. I don't think the alternative health audience will click on a pharmaceutical advertisement. Most of them don't trust pharmaceutical companies or Western medicine." The two were silent for a few moments.

At length, Bishop looked up. "What about, instead of selling click-throughs, we contract with large employers to become a corporate health site of record? If we made our money from corporations, we could reduce our reliance on advertisers like Windham."

It was Yates's turn to remember the board's admonition: independence. "It could solve a corporation's problems regarding employee health record privacy. But we would then be involved in a debate about driving health care costs down. That could hurt our main business. Plus, we'd be inviting the perception—right or wrong—that we'd abandoned our hard-nosed scientific independence in morphing from an information content business to a human resources service-provider-for-hire."

Yates exhaled sharply and looked down at the fax from Baker. "You and I both know there are no easy long-term solutions to the new competitive challenges or our need to grow the business. But we do have a short-term problem to solve—we have to get Windham to recognize that we're a great solution for them. One worrisome fact is that Baker underestimates the genuine value that our impressions deliver to an advertiser. Visitors to MedNet see those ads in the context of a trusted and helpful site—a neighborhood of family friends, really—and even if they don't buy right away, they are left with a positive impression of the advertiser and its products."

"Agreed," said Bishop. "But factors like trust are hard to measure in dollars. And if I know Baker, the only way to win this argument is with numbers, not intuition. So let's compare the numbers that MedNet generates on an impression basis with the numbers that Marvel generates—but let's take the analysis further than just the cost of one click-through. Our audience is fundamentally different from Marvel's, and maybe that difference can be quantified. Let's try."

A PROBLEM SOLVED?

Bishop and Yates got Mahria Baker on speakerphone late that afternoon.

"Hello, Bill," said Baker. "I wasn't expecting to hear from you until tomorrow. Does this mean that you've convinced Heather to sell me results like Marvel does?"

"We're all about results, and you know that," said Bishop, looking at Yates. "Our click-throughs are twice as strong as Marvel's."

"Then just sell me those click-throughs," said Baker. "I'd even double the price—$1 per click-through."

"I think that you're overpaying for clicks from Marvel," said Yates.

"This I've got to hear," Baker replied.

Yates looked at the analysis that she and Bishop had completed just an hour before. Combining MedNet's own data with information from Windham's advertising campaign that Baker had provided in her fax, Yates and Bishop had built a compelling numbers-based case that Windham was getting better value from MedNet than from Marvel.

"You're getting a lot more from MedNet's audience than Marvel gives you," said Yates. "Your ads appear on a page with trusted medical information, our audience is attracted to your products, and we have reason to believe that our advertising partnership adds to your bottom line."

"Mahria," Bishop jumped in, "Marvel has provided click-throughs. But those are just opportunities to get your information in front of a person, not actual sales. What's a click-through worth if it produces no sale? We believe that the Marvel audience is not nearly as lucrative to Windham as the audience we provide. When all of the Vesselia promotional coupons are returned to you, Windham will see that MedNet delivered the best sales results."

"How about if we don't bill you until the end of February?" asked Yates. "You'll be able to see what coupons have been redeemed and realize that this is a great deal. Would that work?" Early that afternoon, MedNet's CFO had agreed to let her make the offer to promote good relations with a longtime customer.

"That helps," said Baker slowly. "I'll listen to your case."

Yates carefully laid out the math behind her and Bishop's analysis. At the end, Baker was silent for what seemed to Yates like an hour. Then Baker said, "I've got to admit, your case seems solid. I want my numbers whiz to confirm my reading of this, but if he does, I'd say we're going to have to agree with you about the value we are getting from MedNet. Would you fax over that study about heart medication profit margins? I'd like to see what it says about audience behavior influencing those margins."

"Sure," said Yates, smiling for the first time that day. She was relieved that she'd apparently won this fight for MedNet, and now she wanted to leave Baker with a strong closing statement. "It all comes down to what Windham wants. If you just want people to click on your ads at a low price rate, a search engine like Marvel can give you that. But if you want people to see the ads when they're psychologically disposed to actually look at the content and consider their message, you want MedNet. And if you want sales that end up generating a profit, you also want MedNet."

Baker said, "Interesting you put it that way, Heather. You've just introduced another problem that we might as well begin tackling right now."

Yates and Bishop looked at one another.

MEDNET CONFRONTS THE COMPETITION, ROUND 2

Baker continued. "In arguing this case for MedNet, you've inadvertently made a case for Cholesterol.com as well. They have the same strengths you just attributed to MedNet—maybe more as far as Vesselia is concerned. My ad budget's not growing, and now I have to use some of it to pay for ads on Cholesterol.com. If I'm not on that site, my competitors will get those customers. So even if you've made your case about the click-throughs, I still need some fresh angles on how your site sells Vesselia in ways that a Cholesterol.com cannot."

Yates stared at the phone. Then she looked over at Bill, who was tilting his head back, his eyes closed, and his lips pressed shut. How would they respond to this one? She recognized Baker's point. Both MedNet and Cholesterol.com had targeted, high-profit audiences that returned for up-to-date and trustworthy solutions about cholesterol medication. Yates knew that she and Bishop had made a great case for Baker to move away from Marvel. But could she persuade this tough-minded advertiser to bypass Cholesterol.com in favor of MedNet?

The new group of niche, condition-specific competitors like Cholesterol.com were "category-killer" sites typically focused on one (profitable) chronic condition such as cardiovascular disease, depression, or obesity, and sought to disseminate the latest information from medical sources. In addition, these sites often provided interactive tools on which visitors could store data they wished to track, such as blood pressure, weight, or cholesterol counts. While the income sources were limited, their pull on the newly diagnosed was incontrovertible. Pharmaceutical firms that had relevant medications rushed to buy ads on these sites, which were quickly becoming the first web resource that "core constituencies" routinely visited.

A wealthy trial lawyer had recently launched Cholesterol.com with $47 million he had been awarded in a class-action lawsuit against a fast-food restaurant chain. The lawyer assembled an international staff of doctors who explained what most large countries provided in chronic cholesterol care, presenting the information in 13 languages, including Chinese. Significantly, Cholesterol.com tailored health recommendations to each visitor's specifications and even offered a travel agency service to promote "global health tourism." Pharmaceutical companies from around the world advertised their offerings on that site, and, according to third-party web traffic audits, Cholesterol.com's niche audience was growing, especially in Asia. The site's significant marketing budget paid for a large, multilanguage advertisement campaign.

Even in the face of this specialized niche competition, MedNet's executive leadership continued to believe that providing a source of information on a wide range of medical conditions delivered real value to its readers. MedNet's audience-auditing firm showed a majority of visitors clicked on both condition-specific pages and general health information. MedNet board members also perceived that some condition-specific sites came dangerously close to diagnosing conditions and prescribing treatments for their visitors, and thus were at risk of violating both state and federal government regulations (and the laws of many foreign nations) that required medical advice to be dispensed in person by a licensed physician. As a result, MedNet's board refused to provide tailored recommendations about medical treatment.

That said, here were Yates and Bishop in a conference call with their biggest advertiser, who was saying she couldn't afford not to divert advertising dollars from MedNet (as well as other ad venues) to Cholesterol.com. The pair felt they'd successfully answered the Marvel challenge only to confront this new threat. How would they respond to Mahria Baker? And what about the bigger picture? How could they reinvigorate MedNet's growth when they were being hit by new competitive challenges that they were blocked, in one way or another, from taking on headfirst?

"Mahria, we're going to need a little time on this one," Yates said, finally. "We're sure that we can convince you that MedNet is your best bet, but we don't want to answer on the fly. I'm sure you don't want us to do that either. Let us get the facts in front of us, as we've done with regard to Marvel, and call you tomorrow morning."

"Better yet, would your schedules allow a meeting?" Baker asked. "It would be good to sit down together, don't you think?"

Yates and Bishop exchanged glances, and agreed to meet Baker the following morning at the Windham offices. Then they ended the call.

Bishop puffed out his cheeks and blew out a sigh of exasperation. "How late can you stay this evening?" he asked. "We can't let this one wait. And let me see if any of the other senior crew is here."

* * *

Much later that evening, Bishop and Yates, joined now by MedNet's president and CEO Frank D'Onofrio and the company's CFO, Bradley Meyers, considered possible responses to Baker—and possible scenarios for MedNet's future. Among the options they had scrawled on the white board:

Take a more prescriptive, diagnostic posture toward site visitors—treating them, as Cholesterol.com did, almost as patients. Then they could charge for content and be less dependent on advertising revenues. But would MedNet's board stand for this more aggressive approach to dispensing medical information?

Bring alternative health information to the site, starting conservatively (perhaps with scientific studies of acupuncture) and slowly becoming more liberal. But would this help the problem of flattening advertising revenues from pharmaceutical firms like Windham?

Build on their greatest strength—their integrity and trustworthiness—as well as their web business expertise, to evolve into a developer and manager of employer websites. But would employers let them introduce pharmaceutical advertising? If not, wouldn't they still lose in the long run?

Case 15.2

Giant Consumer Products: The Sales Promotion Resource Allocation Decision

INTRODUCTION

It was early September 2008 at Giant Consumer Products, Inc. (GCP), headquarters. The Frozen Foods Division (FFD) was not doing well. The division's sales volume (in units) was 3.9% behind plan, and gross revenue was under plan by 3.6%. Consumers were simply buying less and they were buying in a different product mix than expected; however, prices were not being reduced to stimulate sales. Marketing margin,[1] considered internally to be the most critical metric for evaluating businesses at GCP, was also under plan by 4.1% (see Exhibit 15.2.1).

This news couldn't have come at a worse time. GCP had been a darling of Wall Street, but in the past couple of quarters, analysts were wondering whether GCP's above-industry average growth could be maintained. More important, could the growth be maintained profitably? GCP had been counting on FFD to deliver the numbers, as the division had done historically; poor results in FFD would certainly impact the firm's financial stature.

GCP's chief executive officer (CEO), Allan Capps, had met with Byron Flatt, GCP's vice president of sales to discuss the shortfall in FFD's results. Flatt hastily suggested undertaking a sales promotion, and added: "Allan, the point-of-sale scanner data that we purchase from Nielsen (a syndicated marketing research firm) has consistently shown that running a promotion that features our FFD brands on special in a retailer's in-store weekly circular and on end-aisle displays is a tried-and-true mechanism for generating short-term sales lifts." While Capps appeared to nod in agreement, he quickly countered:

> *Byron, I recall reading an article which described trade promotions as being "the most expensive, most controversial, and least understood marketing tool deployed by manufacturers."[2] Given that the authors' assessment is consistent with my own experience at GCP and in handling merchandising*

Professor Neeraj Bharadwaj and Phillip D. Delurgio prepared this case specifically for the Harvard Business Publishing Brief Case Collection. It is intended solely as a basis for class discussion and not as an endorsement, a source of primary data, or an illustration of effective or ineffective management. Though inspired by real events, this case does not represent a specific situation at an existing company. Any resemblance to actual persons or entities is unintended.

Neeraj Bharadwaj is Assistant Professor of Marketing at the Fox School of Business at Temple University. Phillip D. Delurgio is Chief Technical Officer of M-Factor, Inc., a marketing analytics software company. The authors thank Indra Reinbergs, Craig Chapman, Diane Badame, James Kindley, Doug Lincoln, Laurie Dwyer, Richard Hanna, Mark Lang, and Steven Cox for their guidance on developing this case.

Copyright © 2009 by the President and the Fellows of Harvard College. The Case was prepared by Neeraj Bharadwaj & Phillip Delurgio as the basis for class discussion rather than to illustrate either effective or ineffective handling of an administrative situation. Reprinted by permission of Harvard Business School.

[1]Marketing Margin is a preliminary "bottom line" profit metric widely utilized in the consumer packaged goods industry that reflects the amount that the item contributes to corporate costs and overhead charges after all marketing expenses are incurred. It is calculated by subtracting selling, distribution and advertising expenses from gross margin.

[2]David R. Bell and Xavier Dreze (2002) "Changing the Channel: A Better Way to do Trade Promotions," *MIT Sloan Management Review*, Winter, pp. 42–49.

Exhibit 15.2.1 ■ Continued

	2008 Frozen Foods Division ANNUAL PLAN											
	Frozen Division	Dinardo's 32	Dinardo's 16	Dinardo's Other	Natural Meals							
Volume (lbs.)	251,800,000	95,800,000	47,500,000	59,000,000	49,500,000							
Gross Revenue	603,280,000	201,180,000	114,000,000	144,550,000	143,550,000							
Promotion Spending	80,000,000	25,000,000	25,000,000	15,000,000	15,000,000							
Net Revenue	523,280,000	176,180,000	89,000,000	129,550,000	128,550,000							
COGS	198,543,500	64,665,000	36,110,000	57,525,000	40,243,500							
Gross Margin	324,736,500	111,515,000	52,890,000	72,025,000	88,306,500							
Selling/ Distribution	18,098,400	6,035,400	3,420,000	4,336,500	4,306,500							
Advertising Expense	65,000,000	21,900,000	12,400,000	15,700,000	15,000,000							
Marketing Margin	241,638,100	83,579,600	37,070,000	51,988,500	69,000,000							
Key Metrics												
Marketing Margin %	40%	42%	33%	36%	48%							
Gross Revenue/lb.	2.40	2.10	2.40	2.45	2.90							
Gross Margin/lb.	1.29	1.16	1.11	1.22	1.78							
Marketing Margin/lb.	0.96	0.87	0.78	0.88	1.39							
$Promo/ Incr. lb.	1.49	1.11	2.08	1.51	1.66							
Variable Expense/lb.	0.86	0.74	0.83	1.05	0.90							
Promo Cost/ Point	178,928	191,223	182,485	169,545	165,017							

Continued

Exhibit 15.2.1 ■ Continued

	2008 Frozen Foods Division PLAN THROUGH AUGUST					2008 Frozen Foods Division ACTUALS THROUGH JULY								
	Frozen Division	Dinardo's 32	Dinardo's 16	Dinardo's Other	Natural Meals	Frozen Division	vs. Plan	Dinardo's 32	vs. Plan	Dinardo's 16	vs. Plan	Dinardo's Other	vs. Plan	Natural Meals	vs. Plan
Volume (lbs.)	166,650,000	61,273,000	32,912,000	40,085,000	32,380,000	160,098,328	−3.9%	59,016,558	−3.7%	30,680,906	−6.8%	36,625,617	−8.6%	33,775,247	4.3%
Gross Revenue	399,772,350	128,673,300	78,988,800	98,208,250	93,902,000	385,249,923	−3.6%	123,934,773	−3.7%	73,634,175	−6.8%	89,732,761	−8.6%	97,948,215	4.3%
Promotion Spending	53,315,000	15,990,000	17,322,000	10,191,000	9,812,000	51,333,944	−3.7%	17,216,786	7.7%	14,694,006	−15.2%	9,795,479	−3.9%	9,627,673	−1.9%
Net Revenue	346,457,350	112,683,300	61,666,800	88,017,250	84,090,000	333,915,979	−3.6%	106,717,986	−5.3%	58,940,169	−4.4%	79,937,282	−9.2%	88,320,542	5.0%
COGS	131,787,139	41,359,275	25,020,049	39,082,875	26,324,940	126,329,376	−4.1%	39,836,177	−3.7%	23,323,948	−6.8%	35,709,976	−8.6%	27,459,275	4.3%
Gross Margin	214,670,211	71,324,025	36,646,751	48,934,375	57,765,060	207,586,603	−3.3%	66,881,809	−6.2%	35,616,221	−2.8%	44,227,305	−9.6%	60,861,267	5.4%
Selling/ Distribution	11,993,171	3,860,199	2,369,664	2,946,248	2,817,060	11,557,498	−3.6%	3,718,043	−3.7%	2,209,025	−6.8%	2,691,983	−8.6%	2,938,446	4.3%
Adverting Expense	43,333,333	14,600,000	8,266,667	10,466,667	10,000,000	43,233,500	−0.2%	14,450,000	−1.0%	8,500,000	2.8%	10,233,000	−2.2%	10,050,500	0.5%
Marketing Margin	159,343,707	52,863,826	26,010,420	35,521,461	44,948,000	152,795,605	−4.1%	48,713,766	−7.9%	24,907,196	−4.2%	31,302,323	−11.9%	47,872,320	6.5%

Note: The **Exhibit 15.2.1** data set is available in electronic format in an Excel spreadsheet for students that accompanies this case (see "ProfitLoss" tab in the spreadsheet).

Notes for Exhibit 15.2.1:

In the consumer packaged goods industry, products are often priced and promoted according to their sizes for various operational reasons. The Frozen Food Division (FFD) is organized around four items: (1) "*Dinardo's*™ 32" (refers to the assortment of 32-ounce package offerings in the *Dinardo's*™ brand), (2) "*Dinardo's*™ 16" (the 16-ounce size varieties), (3) "Other *Dinardo's*™" (the various other sizes of *Dinardo's*™ products), and (4) "*Natural Meals*™" (which refers to the assortment of Natural Meals™, which are available only in the 16-ounce size packages).

"Promotion Spending" is the amount allocated by firms for initiatives to secure end aisle displays with price markdowns in supermarkets and space in retailers' in-store advertising circulars. FFD determines the dollar amount to be allocated for each of its four items at the beginning of the year.

"Gross Revenue/lb." is a metric used by FFD to equalize the revenue generated across products on equal terms and represents the sales price per unit weight of product being sold. This figure can be equated with the price that the producer charges the retailer (i.e., price-to-retailer, which is often referred to as PTR). PTR differs from the price-to-consumer (PTC); the former should be used to calculate revenue implications for the producer in this case.

"Variable Expense/lb." is a metric that is frequently used by brand managers in consumer packaged goods. It's an "all costs in" figure that permits managers to evaluate costs on a relative basis between brands or items. This is calculated by summing COGS + Selling/Distribution Expense and dividing by Volume (lbs), and has remained relatively stable over the previous two years for each product line.

"Promo Cost/Promo Point" is the cost associated with securing 1% of stores to promote the product for one month. Retailers don't promote consumer packaged goods products for free, and each "point" is able to generate some amount of incremental promotion sales. This is calculated by dividing Promotion Spending above by the sum of "%Store Promoting" in **Exhibit 15.2.4** over the past 12 months, and has remained relatively stable over the previous two years for each product line.

when I worked for Safeway—the supermarket chain—prior to joining GCP, I would like to heed their warnings regarding the downsides of sales promotions at each level of the channel. For us, these include mitigating the potential for cannibalization (i.e., promoting one item and having any incremental volume come at the expense of another item) and brand equity erosion (i.e., implementing a "price-off" deal on a super-premium brand without tarnishing its premium image). As you know, we have pulled back on the level of promotion recently because we had concerns about how promotions could cheapen the brand.

In relation to retailers, it requires reducing the possibility of forward-buying (i.e., retailers purchasing a large quantity of the product while it is available at a lower price-to-retailer (PTR)). This practice of forward-buying is potentially problematic because retailers could either raise the price-to-consumer (PTC) back to the regular price level after the intended period of the promotion and pocket the difference, or they could continue to sell the product at a lower PTC beyond the intended period and thereby condition consumers to expect our well-trusted brands "on deal." Non-compliance with pass-through (i.e., having retailers receive products at a discounted PTR and then not passing along the savings to consumers via a discounted PTC) is another retailer-related threat requiring consideration. And we can't forget about stockpiling by consumers (i.e., buying large quantities to store for future use). So, Byron, while I understand your argument about sales uplift, this decision requires careful attention to the reasons I've outlined. Given the tough year we're facing, I'm willing to reconsider. But, I don't want to open this up unless this promotion ultimately proves to be a "win" for all parties involved . . . .Let me contact Mary to let her know that I may make some funding available. She will need to convince me that the funds will generate the needed demand without undermining the long-term health of our brands.

On the morning of September 4, Capps contacted Mary Davidson, general manager of FFD, to inform her of an 8:00 a.m. meeting that had been scheduled for the next day. He told her of the possibility that a promotion could be fielded in her division, and told her that she should arrive prepared to recommend whether a sales promotion should be fielded, and if so, to identify the most appropriate item to promote. Davidson immediately contacted Mike Sanchez, who had been recently promoted to director of marketing at FFD. He was well aware of the shortfall, and had become increasingly concerned about the performance of the two brands under his control—*Dinardo's*™ and *Natural Meals*™. Sanchez was relieved to hear that senior management was considering making available one more promotion opportunity; Sanchez knew he'd be called on to recommend whether a national sales promotion should be run at all, and if so, which one of the three items should be selected: (a) *Dinardo's*™ 32-ounce packages, (b) *Dinardo's*™ 16-ounce packages, or (c) *Natural Meals*™.

Sanchez, who had been promoted to brand manager two years ago at GCP by institutionalizing a methodology for evaluating the results of past national promotions, was well aware that he would need to generate several important metrics so that he could substantiate his recommendation. The first two—top-line revenue and marketing margin, were straight-forward. He was introduced to another important metric by his colleagues in finance. During his career, marketing at GCP had transitioned from an era where marketing resource allocations were considered an expense—or *"necessary evil" as the former chief financial officer (CFO) put it*—to the view that they were "investments" requiring a favorable return. The term return on marketing investment (ROMI) had been coined to refer to the return (marketing margin) from undertaking a marketing initiative in relation to its cost (promotion cost). The new CFO advocated the importance of making the most productive use of resources and was often overheard explaining that ROMI should be greater than 100%—anything less than that was not deemed profitable. Sanchez was therefore cognizant of the reality that he would also need to evaluate how the past national promotions had fared on the basis of ROMI.

INDUSTRY AND COMPANY CONTEXT

Supermarkets had increasingly been turning to category management, which involved managing each product category (ready-to-eat breakfast cereals, carbonated soft drinks, etc.) as a separate business unit and customizing merchandising and promotion activities to optimize the retailer's (and possibly the producer's) returns. This practice allowed retailers to tailor their product assortment to a given market, determine the best location of products on their shelves, and develop promotions in each category to best satisfy the needs of the local customer base, thereby enticing customers to place more items in their "market basket" during each store visit.

The "frozen meal and entrees" category represented one of the largest categories in the frozen foods aisle in supermarkets. The category had seen steady, moderate expansion between 2003 and 2007, with a compound annual growth rate (CAGR) of 2.8%; however, category growth since 2007 had been much lower than what had been registered during the prior five-year period. Restaurants, which captured almost half of all consumer dollars spent on food, had become a formidable rival to supermarkets. But some forward-thinking retailers had aggressively sought to attract traffic away from restaurants by offering an array of fresh, convenient, high-quality, already prepared foods. While these "heat-and-eat" offerings were more convenient and less expensive than dining at restaurants, they were twice as expensive as frozen dinners.

In some product categories, it had become common practice for increasingly "deal conscious" consumers to purchase products months ahead of their consumption requirements. Given the high degree of promotions in some categories, a portion of consumers did not consider purchasing *any* item unless it had been discounted. For those who were willing to switch brands, sizes, and flavor varieties, being a "promotion-centric" consumer had become a viable option, and "stockpiling" discounted goods saved them money over the long haul. Sanchez, however, did not view stockpiling to be a pressing concern because it was not prevalent in frozen foods—the freezers in most homes were simply not large enough.

FFD, which took great pride in having the most customer-centric management team in the frozen foods industry, had successfully grown over the past 30 years by having anticipated trends such as the emergence of dual-career families, increases in commute times, and less time available for meal preparation. FFD had consistently delivered on the promise of convenient, good-tasting food at a reasonable price to its growing customer base. FFD had a 43% national market share (by revenues) in the "Italian frozen dinners and entrée offerings" subcategory. FFD's two brands, *Dinardo's*™ and *Natural Meals*™, were sold in the frozen foods aisle of the grocery store, usually in vertical freezers with glass doors alongside all other types of frozen entrees, snacks, and desserts, which were displayed in creative, enticing packages.

The frozen foods aisle was large and diverse in both the number and types of brands, as well as the number and types of product offerings, and Italian frozen dinners was a sub-category in this offering. GCP defined its competition in this manner because prior in-store consumer studies had revealed that consumers' typical product selection hierarchy went as follows: (1) type of meal (Italian, Mexican, meat & potatoes, etc.); (2) brand (*Dinardo's*™, *Natural, Manly Meals,* etc.); and (3) variety (i.e., noodle, ravioli, etc.).

The Dinardo's™ **Brand**

The key contributor to FFD's bottom line was *Dinardo's*™, a brand that generated over $425 million in revenues annually. *Dinardo's*™, which was introduced in the early 1970s, featured such traditional favorites as Spaghetti & Meatballs, Lasagna, and Chicken Cacciatore. *Dinardo's*™ meals were simple, but GCP's use of quality ingredients and seasonings made *Dinardo's*™ meals taste better than those made by Daft and other producers, who had reduced the quality of ingredients in an attempt to increase profitability. *Dinardo's*™ was typically packaged in a thin cardboard box, with a picture of the particular entrée on the box cover. An inner pack consisting of a foam tray with a removable plastic cover slid out of the box so the meal could be heated in either a microwave or a conventional oven.

The *Dinardo's*™ brand was available in three sizes. The 32-ounce package (D32) was initially positioned by FFD as a fairly inexpensive way to feed a family of four, and it became an overnight success. Although the customers attracted to these *Dinardo's*™ packages were price-conscious, they tended not to buy private-label goods because the packaging and product quality were perceived as sub-par. *Dinardo's*™ 16-ounce package (D16) was an answer to the requirements of several emerging consumer niches. Both "empty nesters" (parents whose children had moved out from home) and busy professional couples without kids sought simple, easy to prepare, good-tasting meals that were the right size for two people. The other sizes (6- and 8-ounce packages) were developed to serve single consumers and for eat-alone occasions. Although initial research suggested that these smaller items would attract minimal interest, GCP had to make these other sizes available so that retailers could satisfy the needs of all their customers. Due to the operational complexity of food retailing, most producers needed to serve a retailer's entire consumer base, not just a segment or two. It was simply too expensive for retailers to carry, order, and distribute product lines from manufacturers that served only small portions of the retailer's consumer base.

The Natural Meals™ Brand

Natural Meals™, a highly successful regional brand that GCP had acquired in 2006, accounted for roughly 25% of the frozen food division's revenues (almost $150 million per year). At the time of the acquisition, the brand, started in the late 1990s in San Francisco, was available only at the two largest supermarket chains. *Natural Meals*™ had earned a reputation for producing great-tasting, organic frozen foods that were low in fat and did not contain unnecessary additives or preservatives.[3] The *Natural Meals*™ packaging, while physically similar to *Dinardo's*™, had very different imagery. It was designed specifically not to look like a typical "big company" frozen foods product; instead it used a folksy color palette and imagery. This packaging was quite appealing to health-conscious consumers, who were sometimes characterized as "California types." It was believed that these health-conscious consumers would not be interested in the *Dinardo's*™ product line and that the Dinardo's customer base would not be enticed to purchase *Natural Meals*™; therefore, there was minimal threat from cross-brand cannibalization.

Natural Meals™ had become the clear leader in the "healthy but edible" segment, as Sanchez often joked. GCP, with manufacturing and distribution synergies emanating from related foods businesses, predicted that it would be able to grow the business at 5 to 10 times the current rate and with a materially lower delivered cost (cost of goods sold, distribution and sales expense) than the original company, due to efficiency gains resulting from scale economies.

By January 2008, *Natural Meals*™ had been fully integrated into GCP's manufacturing and distribution operations and was available at most retailers in almost every significant market. The brand, featuring such flavors as Penne al'Arrabiata, Eggplant Ravioli, and Garden Pesto Tagliattelle—recipes suited to a more sophis-

---

[3] The term "natural foods" applies broadly to foods that are minimally processed and free of synthetic preservatives. Most foods labeled "natural foods" are not subject to government controls beyond the regulations and health codes that apply to all foods. In contrast, foods labeled "organic" must be grown and processed using organic farming methods and must be grown without synthetic pesticides, bioengineered genes, petroleum-based fertilizers, and sewage-sludge based fertilizers. To be labeled "organic," they must be certified under the National Organic Program. For additional details, please see: (http://www.fda.gov/ohrms/dockets/dockets/06p0094/06p-0094-cp00001–05-Tab-04-Food-Marketing-Institute-vol1.pdf)

ticated palate than *Dinardo's*™—was well-received by retailers. One reason GCP had been able to secure shelf space was the clout that it carried with large supermarket chains. Another factor was the greater margin that its super-premium pricing offered retailers. Carrying healthier alternatives also helped supermarkets attract store traffic away from rival natural foods retailers (e.g., Whole Foods).

The closest competing firm in "Italian frozen dinners," Daft, had been holding steady with a 25% market share, with most of its volume generated by the *Manly Meals* brand. Daft, being well aware of shifting consumer habits, was rumored to have organically developed its own offering. It was test marketing *Healthy Options* during the fourth quarter of 2008 and would be introducing the super-premium line nationwide in early 2009 if the test results proved favorable. This new product introduction was of considerable interest to Sanchez. Evaluating this promotion in the context of competitive strategy would be important; these decisions were never made without considering the competitive ramifications. If Sanchez were to field a sales promotion, the possibility existed that Daft could either increase the incidence and/or depth of its own promotions.

PROMOTIONAL PLANNING AND EXECUTION AT FFD

GCP went through the following approach to generating FFD's annual plan (see Exhibit 15.2.1). First, senior management set overall top-line and profitability goals that GCP needed to hit in order to achieve its desired stock price. Then for each division, specified annual targets for key metrics (i.e., top-line sales revenue, etc.) were set by the senior team and all the product marketing divisions. Next, for each FFD brand, annual targets for the same key metrics (i.e., top-line sales revenue, etc.) were negotiated and agreed by the division head (Davidson) and the brand teams.

In structuring its promotions with retailers, GCP had historically taken a fairly standard approach. An annual promotion plan was developed and approved by GCP at the outset of the calendar year. The duration of promotions was usually one week—a standard length of time in the frozen foods industry. The timing (i.e., in which month the promotion would be run) was determined by a number of factors, such as seasonality, purchase frequency, and production capacity. FFD's key account management teams would inform retailers about the yearly promotion schedule well in advance, and then offer them the opportunity to participate during the week of their choice during the chosen month to undertake a promotion. The standard was to fund retailers for providing an end-aisle display, offering a temporary price reduction to consumers, and featuring the lower price to consumer (PTC) in the retailer's weekly insert/circular.

In implementing the promotions, retailers would place their order about a month before the promotion. Since FFD relied upon direct store delivery of its products in refrigerated trucks, the sales force would then be responsible for building the displays and removing any product on retailers' shelves that was nearing its expiration date. It should be noted that retailers took title to FFD goods as soon as those items were physically on the retailer's premises. That meant that retailers would bear the loss for any FFD products that went unsold.

THE ALLOCATION DECISION

FFD's financial performance was significant to GCP. The division, which was expected to drive approximately $600 million in gross revenues for 2008, accounted for almost a third of GCP's overall business volume.

Sanchez and Davidson were highly motivated to figure out a way to hit the numbers, but only if it was the right decision for the company, because they both firmly believed that ROMI trumped simply evaluating the top-line (i.e., gross revenue) growth. Being able to demonstrate an improved ROMI would mean better funding next year for true brand-building activities, such as advertising, packaging enhancements, and new-product introductions.

Sanchez knew that FFD's strong position in the category enabled the firm to exert a great deal of influence over retailers in terms of which items should be promoted and in securing compliance and pass-through. Furthermore, retailers had come to learn that consumers loved GCP's brands and that promoting those brands would drive store traffic. Thus, while it would be difficult for most producers to add another promotion this late in the year, it would not be for GCP; however, this was not routine practice.

Given the urgency of the situation, Sanchez immediately began contemplating whether a national sales promotion would be a good idea. He sensed that there would be three main effects of a promotion: increased overall consumption (market growth), purchase time acceleration (stockpiling) and brand switching (potentially including switching away from some of GCP's own products). To estimate the magnitude of these effects, he knew that he would have to start by evaluating the performance of past FFD promotions, and that he could do so by calculating the ROMI for promotion allocations to D32, D16, and *Natural Meals*™.

Sanchez proceeded to jot down an analytical framework on his office white board (see Exhibit 15.2.2) and developed a blank worksheet (see Exhibit 15.2.3) that could be used to explain his analytical approach. He also needed to have the information on past promotions that had been run on D32 (four over the past two years) and D16 (five over the past two years) to evaluate how the past promotions had fared (see Exhibit 15.2.4).

As outlined in Exhibit 15.2.3 (see part 1), his first step was to establish how much incremental volume was associated with running a promotion, to convert this to revenue and then to deduct direct expenses such as the promotional expenses, cost of goods sold (COGS), and shipping costs to estimate the benefits of a promotion.

Sanchez was also concerned about the indirect cost of cannibalization—non-promoted items in FFD's product portfolio that would have normally been purchased, but were not because consumers switched to the promoted FFD item instead. This could be estimated by looking at sales volumes of one product when another product was being promoted (see Exhibit 15.2.3–part 2).

Finally, he needed to calculate the ROMI for each promotion choice and make his recommendation to Davidson, with reference to how large the potential benefits would be and whether these would be sufficient to push the year's numbers to the point where they would put GCP at the low end of Wall Street's expectations, as the CEO had suggested it might.

Exhibit 15.2.2 ■ White Board in Mike Sanchez's Office

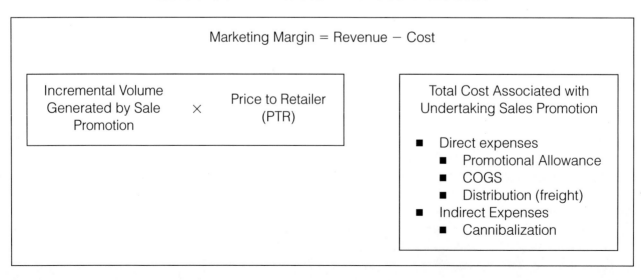

Exhibit 15.2.3 ■ Solution Template—Part 1—Considering Promotion Impact on the Promoted Item

Average Monthly Volume for:	Dinardo 32	Dinardo 16
1. When that item is ON Promotion	....	....
2. When that item is NOT ON Promotion	....	....
3. When NOTHING is ON Promotion[a]	....	....
Incremental Volume from promotion (step 1–step 3)	....	....
Revenue change from promotion (Incr. Volume * Gross Rev/lb (i.e., PTR)	....	....
Variable Cost change from promotion (Incr. Volume * Var Exp/lb)	....	....
Promotion Cost change from promotion (Change in "% store promoting" (i.e., when item ON Promotion vs. when NOTHING is ON Promotion) * Promo Cost/Promo Point)	....	....
Marketing Margin Change from promotion (Revenue change from promotion—Variable Cost change from promotion—Promotion Cost change from promotion)	....	....
1. When the other *Dinardo's* item is ON Promotion	....	....
2. When NOTHING is ON Promotion[a]	....	....
Volume change from promotion of other item	....	....
Revenue change from promotion of other item	....	....
Variable Cost change from promotion of other item	....	....
Promotion Cost change from promotion of other product	....	....
Marketing Margin Change from promotion of other product	....	....
Total Brand Impact from Promotion on Top-line Revenue		
Total Effect of D32 Promotion (Line 5 for D32 from part 1 and the effect in Line 4 for D16 from this table for the effect on the other brand here)	....	
Total Effect of D16 Promotion (Line 5 for D16 from part 1 and the effect in Line 4 for D32 from this table for the effect on the other brand here)		....
[a]This is the case when neither D32 nor D16 are being promoted.		

Continued

Exhibit 15.2.3 ■ Continued

Total Brand Impact from Promotion on Marketing Margin		
Total Effect of D32 Promotion (Line 8 for D32 from part 1 and the effect in Line 7 for D16 from this table for the effect on the other brand here)	....	
Total Effect of D16 Promotion (Line 8 for D16 from part 1 and the effect in Line 7 for D32 from this table for the effect on the other brand here)		....
1. Average Monthly Incremental Volume for *Natural* (use Sep06–Aug08 data from Exhibit 15.2.4)		....
2. Average % Store Promoting for *Natural* (use Sep06–Aug08 data from Exhibit 15.2.4)		....
3. Average Monthly Incremental Volume/Promo Point (i.e., step 1/step2)		....
4. Incremental Volume from 25% Promo Points (i.e., step 3 * 25)		....
5. Revenue change from promotion (Incr. Volume * Gross Rev/lb (i.e., PTR)		....
6. Variable Cost change from promotion (Incr. Volume * Var Exp/lb)		....
7. Promotion Cost change from promotion (Promo Cost/Promo Point * 25)		....
8. Marketing Margin Change from promotion (Revenue change from promotion—Variable Cost change from promotion—Promotion Cost change from promotion)		....
[a]This is the case when neither D32 nor D16 are being promoted.		

Sanchez now had all the data he needed to analyze and recommend a promotion. But there were some nuances regarding *Natural Meals*™ that needed to be taken into consideration:

- *Natural Meals*™ varieties were available only in one size—16 ounces. The items were also "line priced," meaning the suggested retail price/unit was the same for all varieties, and the wholesale price for these items was the same per unit across the entire line.
- *Natural Meals*™ had historically appealed to a niche market, but the brand showed extraordinary growth for the consumer product goods industry—about 15% per year. Further, *Natural Meals*™ was somewhat sub-scale for in-store promotions (i.e., bigger brands could amortize display costs across a higher volume).

Exhibit 15.2.4 ■ September 2006—August 2008 FFD Sales Promotions and Sales Volume

Frozen Division POS Data

		Sep-06	Oct-06	Nov-06	Dec-06	Jan-07	Feb-07	Mar-07	Apr-07	May-07	Jun-07	Jul-07	Aug-07
Dinardo's 32	Baseline Volume	5,255,875	6,301,885	5,464,735	5,427,144	5,786,511	4,667,448	5,458,324	6,276,386	5,896,714	6,017,363	5,857,773	4,573,416
	Incremental Volume	961,316	1,461,240	3,737,878	1,071,080	1,291,706	1,154,498	5,141,741	1,193,724	1,344,682	1,297,308	1,460,526	937,212
	TOTAL Volume	6,217,191	7,763,126	9,202,613	6,498,225	7,078,217	5,821,946	10,600,064	7,470,110	7,241,396	7,314,671	7,318,299	5,510,628
	%Store Promoting	6.1	7.7	22.8	6.6	7.4	8.2	31.4	6.3	7.6	7.2	8.3	6.8
Dinardo's 16	Baseline Volume	3,470,754	3,050,260	697,092	2,976,125	3,052,371	3,085,296	234,457	3,523,780	3,102,688	2,887,549	2,652,496	3,410,772
	Incremental Volume	813,804	641,390	173,811	2,366,019	671,571	2,508,345	55,878	720,285	745,517	637,036	556,861	3,499,452
	TOTAL Volume	4,284,558	3,691,650	870,903	5,342,144	3,723,942	5,593,641	290,336	4,244,064	3,848,205	3,524,585	3,209,358	6,910,225
	%Store Promoting	7.8	7.0	8.3	26.5	7.3	27.1	7.9	6.8	8.0	7.4	7.0	34.2
Dinardo's Other	Baseline Volume	3,798,076	3,949,297	4,142,949	3,536,740	3,875,653	3,956,419	3,963,518	3,627,211	3,900,558	3,846,350	4,127,308	3,690,264
	Incremental Volume	711,726	860,578	1,059,390	681,240	855,985	966,899	826,315	939,127	719,039	916,641	1,111,596	853,688
	TOTAL Volume	4,509,803	4,809,875	5,202,338	4,217,980	4,731,638	4,923,318	4,789,833	4,566,339	4,619,597	4,762,990	5,238,903	4,543,952
	%Store Promoting	6.2	7.3	8.5	6.4	7.4	8.1	6.9	8.6	6.1	7.9	9.0	7.7
Natural Meals	Baseline Volume	2,748,630	2,715,298	2,689,319	2,669,800	2,760,764	2,800,959	2,720,617	2,895,908	3,226,134	3,059,521	3,215,001	2,873,620
	Incremental Volume	705,077	620,626	535,851	684,694	697,869	582,129	549,813	757,818	770,775	626,522	619,806	753,477
	TOTAL Volume	3,453,707	3,335,924	3,225,169	3,354,494	3,458,633	3,383,088	3,270,430	3,653,726	3,996,909	3,686,043	3,834,808	3,627,097
	%Store Promoting	8.6	7.6	6.6	8.5	8.4	6.9	6.7	8.7	8.0	6.8	6.4	8.7

Notes for Exhibit 15.2.4:

The full **Exhibit 15.2.4** data set (through August 2008) is available in electronic format in an Excel spreadsheet for students that accompanies this case (see "POSData" tab in the spreadsheet).

The data contained appear in a format normally provided to consumer packaged-goods firms by such data suppliers as Nielsen or Information Resources, Inc (IRI). The cells that are highlighted denote when a national promotion was run by FFD for the given item (e.g., the D32 was promoted November 2006).

"Baseline Volume" is the projected amount of sales volume (in lbs.) that the firm would have sold in the absence of any in-store promotions. The data suppliers develop their own proprietary algorithms to generate this estimate. The data suppliers tend to draw sales data from a subset of all markets and then project to the national level. A 16-oz. package equates to 1 lb. of volume, a 32-oz. package to 2 lbs. of volume, etc.

"Incremental Volume" represents the amount of extra volume generated solely by the promotion.

"TOTAL Volume" represents the actual total sales volume that the firm sold to consumers at the point-of-sale (POS).

"% Store Promoting" represents the percentage of retailers that actually promoted the product in a given month. There are several reasons why "0" does not appear in the months in which there was not a GCP-backed promotion. First, retailers sometimes do not wish to field the promotion when intended by the manufacturer (common industry practice). Thus, the retailers shift the timing of the national promotion either forward or backward in the calendar. Second, retailers often require manufacturers to field a regional promotion in order for the producer to retain shelf space. These regional promotions are usually not planned at corporate headquarters. Rather, they are developed and implemented by Field Sales, which draws upon its own marketing budget to keep the retailer compliant. Third, retailers occasionally take the initiative to feature a product on their own, irrespective of whether they receive funding from the manufacturer. This, however, is not common practice for consumer packaged-goods products.

Exhibit 15.2.4 ■ Continued

Frozen Division POS Data

		Sep-07	Oct-07	Nov-07	Dec-07	Jan-08	Feb-08	Mar-08	Apr-08	May-08	Jun-08	Jul-08	Aug-08
Dinardo's 32	Baseline Volume	6,149,247	5,916,677	4,714,455	5,273,163	5,880,256	6,015,069	5,790,358	6,159,845	5,925,618	4,049,961	5,421,901	6,243,334
	Incremental Volume	5,239,158	1,360,106	1,242,822	1,219,796	1,386,604	4,637,618	1,314,624	1,351,476	1,244,033	865,583	1,280,591	1,449,687
	TOTAL Volume	11,388,405	7,276,783	5,957,277	6,492,959	7,266,860	10,652,688	7,104,982	7,511,320	7,169,651	4,915,545	6,702,492	7,693,022
	%Store Promoting	28.4	7.7	8.8	7.7	7.9	25.7	7.6	7.3	7.0	7.1	7.9	7.7
Dinardo's 16	Baseline Volume	225,421	2,987,134	2,848,641	3,193,952	3,035,149	217,692	3,104,798	3,288,516	3,468,557	3,748,645	3,180,735	2,861,812
	Incremental Volume	46,547	712,558	2,649,237	855,823	547,644	47,693	663,969	609,293	746,266	3,958,569	648,749	552,817
	TOTAL Volume	271,968	3,699,693	5,497,878	4,049,774	3,582,793	265,385	3,768,768	3,897,810	4,214,823	7,707,214	3,829,484	3,414,629
	%Store Promoting	6.9	8.0	31.0	8.9	6.0	7.3	7.1	6.2	7.2	35.2	6.8	6.4
Dinardo's Other	Baseline Volume	4,170,879	3,678,417	3,501,826	3,503,991	3,626,187	3,804,151	3,802,126	3,724,153	3,870,184	3,571,676	4,039,140	3,567,510
	Incremental Volume	891,369	904,071	853,619	655,010	732,423	990,226	716,830	925,705	798,725	813,835	920,039	722,707
	TOTAL Volume	5,062,248	4,582,488	4,355,445	4,159,001	4,358,610	4,794,378	4,518,956	4,649,858	4,668,908	4,385,511	4,959,179	4,290,217
	%Store Promoting	7.1	8.2	8.1	6.2	6.7	8.7	6.3	8.3	6.9	7.6	7.6	6.8
Natural Meals	Baseline Volume	3,096,560	3,209,199	2,975,317	2,921,394	3,487,071	3,080,502	3,294,573	3,436,171	3,663,475	3,569,556	3,203,531	3,642,177
	Incremental Volume	643,904	580,238	716,408	682,850	925,553	665,441	726,208	873,913	802,834	950,927	610,820	842,494
	TOTAL Volume	3,740,464	3,789,437	3,691,725	3,604,245	4,412,624	3,745,943	4,020,781	4,310,084	4,466,310	4,520,483	3,814,351	4,484,671
	%Store Promoting	6.9	6.0	8.0	7.8	8.8	7.2	7.3	8.5	7.3	8.9	6.4	7.7

- Many products had historically been launched, then promoted to jump-start consumption. However, GCP hadn't promoted *Natural Meals*™ extensively because of concern over tarnishing the brand's premium image. Since *Natural Meals*™ had never run a national promotion, it was necessary to develop a projection if one was to be fielded for the brand. There had been some "regional" promotion activity during the past two years, so Sanchez felt that it would be safe to extrapolate those results to a national level. He thereby assumed that 25% of stores would be willing to participate, should *Natural Meals*™ decide to run a national promotion. He proceeded with his analysis as outlined in Exhibit 15.2.3–part 3.

Sanchez knew he would have to deliberate the tradeoffs involved with promoting each of the three FFD items, and articulate to Capps the financial implications of each. In addition, he knew that Flatt would likely pose him some additional strategic as well as tactical questions, including:

1. Would the promotion end up being a "win" for not only FFD, but also for retailers and consumers?
2. How should FFD structure the promotion? Should FFD go with the "off invoice pricing" that retailers often preferred—having the manufacturer temporarily reduce the price-to-retailer (PTR) of a given item for a specified time so that retailers could purchase it in the quantity desired—or should FFD stick with the "pay-for-performance" approach? (Under the "pay-for-performance" approach, retailers were compensated only for the actual amount that they sold during the promotional period, as verified by registered scanner data.) Alternatively, should FFD compensate retailers only if they hit some pre-established target?

Case 15.3

Reliance Baking Soda: Optimizing Promotional Spending

On August 8, 2007, Anna Regnante was moving into her new office at Stewart Corporation's (Stewart) world headquarters, having been promoted to Domestic Brand Director for Reliance Baking Soda (RBS). Previously, Regnante had managed one of Stewart Household Division's weaker brands. The move to RBS placed her in a high-profile position. Stewart had built the company on the trusted brand associated with RBS, and it remained an important, if mature, product in the company's portfolio.

Chris Dale, Managing Director for Stewart's Household Products Division, had briefed Regnante earlier in the morning on her immediate expectations and deliverables. Within the next three weeks, she was to develop a 2008 budget P&L that would result in a 10% increase in profit (before SGA, overhead, and taxes) over 2007 estimates. The Household Division had scheduled two new high priority product launches in 2008. They were counting on incremental profits from established brands such as RBS to fund the marketing launch expenses for the new products.

Regnante gulped. How could she generate such profit growth for an old-fashioned, mainstay product? She knew she would have to make every penny count. Prior to accepting the position, Regnante had gathered information about previous RBS promotional strategies and their results to date. While she had developed some preliminary conclusions, there was a host of factors to consider before she made any final decisions about her marketing plans and budgets for 2008.

BACKGROUND

Stewart comprised four divisions: Household, Beauty, Foods, and International. In 2006, the company generated $150m in net income and $558m in profit, before SGA, overhead, and taxes, on $1.8b of gross sales. The Household Division, which included RBS, was responsible for $400m of gross sales in 2006. Products in the Household Division included baking soda, laundry detergents, window cleaners, drain cleaners, toilet cleaners, and disinfectant wipes. The RBS brand budgets from 2005 to 2007 are summarized in Exhibit 15.3.1 and quarterly sales are provided in Exhibit 15.3.2.

Stewart was founded in 1915 by James Stewart Augusta, who had discovered what he called the "miracle compound" of $NaHCO_3$ (baking soda). Baking soda was a key leavening agent that caused baked goods to rise properly. Following the introduction of self-rising flour and instant cake mixes, the product's importance to bakers declined. However, with its gritty texture, baking soda also became popular as a cleanser that could scour various surfaces; it had disinfecting capabilities and also neutralized odors. RBS was promoted for a wide range of uses, including household cleanser, laundry aid, and deodorizer. In 2006, over 85% of U.S. family households with income of $25k+ used the product.

HBS Professor John A. Quelch and writer Heather Beckham prepared this case specifically for the Harvard Business Publishing Brief Case Collection.

Though inspired by real events, the case does not represent a specific situation at an existing company, and in particular, the actual setting of case events was not the baking soda industry. Any resemblance to actual persons or entities is unintended. Cases are developed solely as the basis of class discussion and are not intended to serve as endorsements, sources of primary data, or illustrations of effective or ineffective management.

Copyright © 2009 by the President and the Fellows of Harvard College. The Case was prepared by John Quelch & Heather Beckham as the basis for class discussion rather than to illustrate either effective or ineffective handling of an administrative situation. Reprinted by permission of Harvard Business School.

Exhibit 15.3.1 ■ RBS Brand Income Statement ($000's)

	2005	**2006**	**2007E**
Gross Sales	$42,400	$54,125	$55,051
Variable Manufacturing Costs	$20,258	$25,354	$25,325
Gross Margin	$22,142	$28,771	$29,726
	52%	53%	54%
Advertising			
TV	$2,862	$4,453	$3,815
Print	$687	$950	$694
Internet	$76	$238	$248
Total Advertising	$3,625	$5,641	$4,757
PR/Media Production Costs	$191	$297	$198
Consumer Promotion	$424	$1,080	$551
Trade Promotion	$4,240	$5,938	$5,505
Total Marketing Expenses	$8,480	$12,956	$11,011
Profit before SG&A, Overhead, and taxes	$13,662	$15,815	$18,715
	32%	29%	34%

Exhibit 15.3.2 ■ RBS Quarterly Gross Sales ($000's)

Gross Sales	Q1	Q2	Q4	Q4
2005	$14,840	$8,480	$9,752	$9,328
2006	$20,568	$7,578	$18,944	$7,036
2007 YTD	$14,864	$12,111		

RBS was a clear market leader in the baking soda category, capturing 70% share. Given RBS's dominance, few competitors had entered the market. RBS's main competitors were private label brands. Each retail outlet generally marketed a private label baking soda, priced 30% below RBS. In the last decade RBS had lost 5% of its share to private label brands. Stewart did not manufacture products for private label customers. RBS also competed with products outside the baking soda category. It was widely viewed as a substitute for specialized cleaners, air fresheners, and laundry detergents whose price per ounce was significantly higher than that of RBS.

A 2006 consumer survey (selected results provided in Exhibit 15.3.3) indicated RBS had excellent brand awareness and loyalty but low advertising recall. The survey also revealed that consumer usage of baking soda was relatively stable throughout the year. Heavy users were women aged 35–55 who viewed RBS as an all-purpose cleaner and deodorizer. Regnante also found research showing the type and frequency of use varied significantly from household to household: Some only kept a box in the refrigerator to neutralize odors, while others used RBS in every room for different purposes.

RBS was sold in three box sizes: 8 oz., 1 lb., and 5 lb. As shown in Exhibit 15.3.4, the 1 lb. box consistently captured almost half of the company's unit sales.

Exhibit 15.3.3 ■ Selected Results from a 2006 Consumer Survey

The survey was conducted with 750 female heads of households who had purchased baking soda in the last 12 months.[a]

- Heavy users averaged five purchases of baking soda per year, light users averaged one purchase per year and occasional users purchased one box approximately every other year. 75% of heavy users bought 1 lb box or larger.
- 70% purchased RBS as opposed to the private label brand.
- When asked to name a brand of baking soda, 95% mentioned Reliance.
- 20% could recall being exposed to RBS advertising on the TV, radio, internet, or in print in the last 12 months.
- 40% used coupons when purchasing staple items such as baking soda.
- 80% strongly agreed with the statement "baking soda is inexpensive."
- 40% of heavy users and 50% of light users could not recall the price paid for their last baking soda purchase.
- 40% had more than one box of baking soda in their house.
- 50% used baking soda for more than one purpose (e.g., baking, deodorizing, or cleaning).
- The frequency of use of baking soda was stable throughout the year.

[a]RBS purchasers were primarily female heads of households, though the product, once in the house, could be used by various family members.

Exhibit 15.3.4 ■ RBS Factory Shipments (000's)

Size	2005		2006		2007E	
	Cases	% of Total	Cases	% of Total	Cases	% of Total
8 oz. Box						
Cases Shipped	640	28%	793	28%	714	28%
% Increase (Decrease)			24%		(10)%	
1 lb.						
Cases Shipped	1,099	47%	1,362	47%	1,226	47%
% Increase (Decrease)			24%		(10)%	
5 lb.						
Cases Shipped	581	25%	720	25%	648	25%
% Increase (Decrease)			24%		(10)%	
Total Cases	2,320	100%	2,875	100%	2,588	100%

Exhibit 15.3.5 ■ Breakout of RBS Sales Volume by Retail Outlet 2007E

Size	Grocery	Drug	Mass Merchandiser	Warehouse Club	Other	Total
8 oz. box	11%	4%	8%	0%	5%	28%
1 lb. box	26%	4%	12%	0%	5%	47%
5 lb. box	1%	0%	6%	17%	1%	25%
Total	38%	8%	26%	17%	11%	100%

KEY RBS MARKETING MIX CONSIDERATIONS

Distribution

RBS enjoyed high distribution penetration, with 90% of grocery stores and mass merchandisers, 85% of warehouse clubs, and 80% of drug stores stocking at least one size. The demand for different box sizes varied by channel; for example, warehouse clubs exclusively purchased the 5 lb. size. Exhibit 15.3.5 provides detailed channel data.

The Household Division maintained a 150-person sales force to manage the retail and wholesale accounts for all products within the division. The sales force was incentivized through a quota system, with divisional senior management establishing quarterly volume quotas for each salesperson. Salespeople received a small base salary; most of their compensation came from bonuses for meeting and exceeding sales targets. Regnante was expected to work with sales management in creating a schedule of consumer and trade promotion. Randall Todd, senior account manager for several major grocery chains, stated, "RBS needs a lot of push marketing to stimulate trade interest. Baking soda is not a natural traffic builder, it does not have high turnover, and it is boring. The product hasn't changed in almost 100 years. The only way I'm going to make my quotas is if we offer attractive incentives to the trade."

Pricing

RBS had raised manufacturer's selling prices three times in the last five years (in 2004, 2006, and 2007). From 2006 to 2007, an increase of 13% had been instituted on all product sizes. The price increase was partially due to an 11% increase in raw material costs. The plant manager had assured Regnante that this was a one-time event and no increase in manufacturing cost per case was expected for 2008. In 2007, manufacturer's selling price was $7.20 for an 8 oz. case,[1] $12.02 for a 1 lb. case, and $54.28 for a 5 lb. case. Suggested retail price was $1.00 for each 8 oz. box, $1.67 for each 1 lb. box, and $7.54 for each 5 lb. box. However, actual retail prices were often 10% lower than the suggested retail price. Manufacturer's pricing and cost information is shown in Exhibit 15.3.6.

Advertising

Advertising for RBS in the last 10 years had focused on revealing new uses for the product. The goal of the advertising strategy was to move RBS out of the kitchen and into the realm of pet care, baby care, pool care, out-

---

[1] One case equals 12 boxes

Exhibit 15.3.6 ▪ 2005–2007 Manufacturer's Selling Price vs. Variable Manufacturing Costs

Size	2005	2006	2007
Manufacturer's Price per case			
8 oz.	$6.18	$6.37	$7.20
1 lb.	$10.33	$10.64	$12.02
5 lb.	$46.63	$48.03	$54.28
Variable Manufacturing Cost per case			
8 oz.	$3.02	$3.05	$3.38
1 lb.	$4.98	$5.03	$5.58
5 lb.	$22.12	$22.34	$24.80

door cleaning, and anywhere else the product's versatility could be exploited. In the last two years, the advertising campaigns also stressed the nontoxic benefits of the product. Tessa Simon, an advertising manager in Regnante's group, believed the advertising strategy should continue to emphasize out-of-the-box uses for the product. Simon told Regnante, "Every day, new, specialized products are appearing on the shelves that can cannibalize the baking soda market. We have to keep RBS at the top of consumers' minds. Plus, the 2006 trade and consumer promotions forced too much RBS product into the market. We need to deplete that inventory and continue to grow sales. To stimulate consumption, we need more advertising that can suggest new ways of using RBS."

Consumer Promotion

Prior to 2005, consumer promotions had not been a significant part of the RBS marketing plan. In March to November of 2003, RBS offered only one 20-cent coupon event on the 1 lb. or larger box size, and in 2004 no events occurred. RBS had become a little more aggressive with consumer promotions in the last three years. In January of 2005, RBS offered a container pack premium[2] (a reusable decorated glass vase containing 1 lb. of the product). In March 2005, a 20-cent cross ruff[3] coupon was packaged with Stewart window cleaner, and in September there was another offer of a $1.00 cash refund, with the proof of purchase for two 5 lb. boxes.

The 2006 consumer promotions included four events. Costs and estimated net incremental contribution for each of the 2006 events are provided in Exhibit 15.3.7. For those events that involved more than one Household Division brand, costs were allocated equally among the participating brands. The first event of the year was launched in January and provided a $2 cash refund for the purchase of RBS plus four additional Household Division brands. The promotion was advertised in women's magazines, in a Sunday newspaper supplement, on the company website, and in point-of-purchase materials. In April, a set of coupons for five of the Household Division's brands was included in 6 million boxes of Stewart's Brilliance Laundry Detergent. The third event of the year, in June, included a shrinkwrapped twin pack of the 1 lb. boxes and a $1.00 cash

---

[2]Container pack premiums are factory-packed containers that are reusable once the product is used up.

[3]Cross-ruff coupons are placed inside or on the package of a non-competing brand and are redeemable for a different product.

refund inside the pack with proof of purchase from two 1 lb. boxes. The twin pack had a label that encouraged consumers to keep one box in the fridge and one in the bathroom. The final event of 2006, launched in September, featured a two-page advertising supplement in the top four women's magazines. The advertisement provided a list of cleaning activities to prepare the home for holiday guests and tips on how to clean the house most efficiently. RBS and two other Household Division brands were featured in the advertisement with a $1.50 cash refund offer for a proof of purchase from each of the three participating brands. The advertising supplement also included a sweepstakes card for kitchen appliance prizes to create "the perfect holiday feast." This event was also advertised on the company website, and on riser cards and shelf-talkers at the point of purchase.[4]

In 2007, Regnante's predecessor cut the consumer promotion budget and scheduled only three events. In February, a self-liquidating premium[5] was provided on labels of the 5 lb. boxes. The item was a stylish "Go Green" stainless filtered water bottle with a retail value of $15.00 and was offered to the consumer for $8.50 plus one RBS proof of purchase. In April, a 30-cent coupon was circulated. An event had already been planned for September: an advertising supplement to be run in two women's magazines and Sunday newspapers, which included coupons for all Stewart Household brands (including a 20-cent RBS coupon) and a sweepstakes for a $75,000 home makeover. This event was also going to be advertised on the company website and on riser cards and shelf-talkers at the point of purchase.

Upon reviewing the past consumer promotion schedules, Regnante determined there were two main decisions to make for 2008. First, how much should she spend on consumer promotions? Regnante's predecessor had cut the consumer promotion budget by almost half between 2006 and 2007. Regnante wondered if this was too thin. Second, should the timing of the consumer promotions overlap with the trade promotion offers? In the past, consumer promotions coincided with trade promotions to provide extra incentive to stimulate consumer purchases. However, Regnante felt this strategy might exacerbate price sensitivity and amplify demand fluctuations.

Trade Promotion

RBS offered a variety of trade promotions, including discounts off invoice prices for cases ordered during the promotion period (e.g., 5% off invoice), free cases with the purchase of a minimum order (e.g., buy 10 cases, get 2 free), and performance discount incentives for providing verifiable merchandising/advertising support (e.g., 5% off invoice with evidence of a featured trade ad). RBS hoped these temporary discounts would be passed on to the consumer to stimulate sales (versus the building up of trade inventory). However, RBS had no direct control over how the trade managed its inventory or how it priced the product. RBS trade promotions, offered throughout the year, usually lasted three to six weeks. These promotion events helped make RBS more attractive to the trade. According to one grocery chain procurement manager, "RBS is something most of my customers will buy and if I can promote it with a price discount or trade ad, then my store benefits from increased traffic and I'm happy."

Regnante had carefully researched RBS trade promotion history. She created a spreadsheet of terms and timing of each trade promotion over the past six years (Exhibit 15.3.8). She also analyzed trade advertising support, comparing the frequency and size of featured advertising for baking soda versus other household cleaners (Table A).

---

[4] Riser cards are attention-grabbing signs placed above special displays. Shelf talkers are smaller signs attached to the front of the shelf where the product sits.

[5] Self liquidating premiums are items offered to the consumer by mail for proof of purchase and cash sufficient to cover the cost of the item and shipping/handling. This cash amount is usually 30% to 50% below what the consumer would normally have to pay for the item.

Exhibit 15.3.7 ■ RBS Costs and Net Incremental Contribution of 2006 Consumer Promotions

1. January: ALLOCATED Cost to RBS $398,580 **Total Net Incremental Contribution** $63,852					
	Circulation (Millions)	**Response**	**Number of Responses**	**Cost Per Response**	**Total Cost (Five Brands)**
Sunday Supplement	39.00	0.7%	273,000	$5.37	$1,860,437
Magazines	18.85	0.2%	37,700		
Point of Purchase Materials	3.575	1.0%	35,750		
Riser Cards					$84,753
Shelf Talkers					$47,710

2. April: ALLOCATED Cost to RBS $174,643 **Total Net Incremental Contribution** $22,785						
	Face Value	**Circulation (Millions)**	**Redemption Rate**	**Number of Redemptions**	**Cost Per Redemption**	**Total Cost (RBS Only)**
Coupon Redemption	$0.30	6.05	4.0%	242,000	$0.50	$121,000
Coupon Artwork/Printing						$43,865
Package Flagging and Coupon Insertion						$9,778

3. June: Cost to RSB $253,390 **Total Net Incremental Contribution** $50,615					
	Circulation/ Number of Twin Packs	**Response**	**Number of Responses**	**Cost Per Response**	**Total Cost (RBS Only)**
Refund Offer	1,638,000	7%	114,660	$1.78	$204,095
Special Packaging					$49,295

Note: Cost Per Redemption/Response Includes face value of coupon or refund plus handling charges

Continued

Exhibit 15.3.7 ■ Continued

	Circulation (Millions)	Response	Number of Responses	Cost Per Response	Total Cost (Three Brands)
1. September: Allocated Cost to RBS $253,390 **Total Net Incremental Contribution** $60,820					
Top 4 Women's Magazines	21.0	0.5%	105,000	$2.64	$588,720
Point-of Purchase Materials	5.9	2%	118,000		
Riser Cards					$46,932
Shelf Talkers					$24,153
Sweepstakes prizes, judging, handling					$100,365

After considering both spreadsheets, Regnante discussed some of her thoughts with Dale:

I know the sales force likes to use trade promotions liberally, but I was surprised to learn that over 73% of our factory shipments were sold to the trade on promotion. Are all these discounts necessary? I'm concerned the trade is overbuying during promotion periods and forgoing more consistent, regular-priced purchases they would have otherwise made. If we are overloading the trade during promotion, we could be leaving a lot of money on the table. Plus, I'm not sure we're getting adequate advertising and merchandising support for RBS in exchange for those trade promotions. Advertising trade support for RBS is much lower than our branded competitors. Perhaps we should consider more performance-based promotions.

Table A ■ Trade Advertising Support for RBS vs. Competing Products

	A Ads		B Ads		C Ads		
	#	%	#	%	#	%	Total #
Baking Soda							
RBS	0	0%	4	9%	42	91%	46
Private Label	0	0%	1	11%	8	89%	9
Specialized Cleaner Competitors							
Dynamo	2	2%	52	50%	50	48%	104
Sparkle	1	1%	27	37%	45	62%	73
WOW Cleanser	0	0%	12	16%	62	84%	74
Note: Ads were grouped by size. For example, C Ads were the smallest at less than 1 inch wide, B Ads were about 1 inch to 3 inches, and A Ads were the largest at greater than 3 inches.							

Exhibit 15.3.8 ■ RBS Trade Promotion History

Year	Duration	Sales Days Promoted	Consumer Promotion Activity	8 oz. Box	1 lb. Box	5 lb. Box	Notes
2002	9/01–10/15	29			5% OI staple	5% OI staple	
2003	1/02–2/13	31			10% OI M/C	10% OI M/C	
				5% OI staple	5% OI staple	5% OI staple	
				10% OI M/C + 5% OI on choice of one size	10% OI M/C + 5% OI on choice of one size	10% OI M/C + 5% OI on choice of one size	
	5/01–6/30	43		5% OI	5% OI		
	9/04–11/2	46	Coupon	7%+5%OI on choice of one size	7%+5%OI on choice of one size	7%+5%OI on choice of one size	
2004	2/01–3/15	29		10% OI	10% OI	10% OI	
	5/01–6/14	31		10% OI+ 10% ad	10% OI+ 10% ad		Additional 10% discount with evidence of ad support
	8/01–9/13	31		1 w/11	1 w/11	1 w/11	1 case free with 11 ordered
	11/01–12/13	28				10% OI	
2005	1/02–2/14	31	Container Pack Premium	1 w/11	1 w/11	1 w/11	
	3/10–4/18	32	Cross-ruff Coupon				
	6/02–6/27	21		1 w/11 + 10% ad			
	9/02–9/30	21	Refund		2 w/10		
	11/03–12/12	27				2 w/10 + 10% ad	

OI = Off Invoice. A staple or standard case contained one dozen units. A master case (M/C) was a prepackaged mix of sizes, usually including six dozen units.

Continued

Exhibit 15.3.8 ■ Continued

Year	Duration	Sales Days Promoted	Consumer Promotion Activity	8 oz. Box	1 lb. Box	5 lb. Box	Notes
2006	1/05–2/27	41	Refund	1 w/11	1 w/11	1 w/11	5% ad allowance for feature ad
	4/05–4/30	21	Cross-ruff Coupon			2 w/10	5% ad allowance for feature ad
	5/14–6/25	38	Twin Pack/Refund	2 w/10 twin pack + 5% ad			
	8/02–9/24	43	Sweepstakes and Refund	1 w/11 + 5% ad	1 w/11 + 5% ad	1 w/11 + 5% ad	
	10/04–12/13	50		12% OI		15% OI	
2007YTD	1/03–2/25	40	Self liquidating premium		10% OI		
	4/04–4/29	20	Coupon	10% OI + 5% ad		10% OI + 5% ad	
	5/02–5/27	21			2 w/10		
	6/06–6/24	22		10% OI + 5% ad			$3 Display Allowance

ADDITIONAL RESEARCH

Regnante discovered a comprehensive report on trade promotion effectiveness that had been recently developed by an outside consultant engaged by her predecessor. She reviewed the study at length and spoke to the lead consultant for the project. Regnante was pleased to see the incremental contribution estimates the consulting team came up with. The report, which broke down incremental contribution by product size and promotional period, was based on computer models that estimated normal monthly factory shipments using RBS historical data and a proprietary database of market information. The model included negative impact from lost sales at full price before, after, and during each promotion event (see Exhibit 15.3.9). However, because the analyst did not separately model the effect of advertising spending, each estimate of net incremental contribution included not only the effect of promotion spending but also any effects due to advertising spending. When Regnante asked for a bottom-line recommendation for trade promotions, the lead consultant, Brooke Drury, responded, "Trade promotion events have almost always produced attractive results for RBS. Our report reveals there were only two events in the last six years that resulted in a loss for the company, and in 2006, $1.35m in incremental contribution was captured from trade promotion events. Your formula seems to be working very well. I would advise against any reallocation of trade promotion funds."

* * * * *

As Regnante started to organize her new office, she considered the different options for delivering a 10% profit increase before SGA, overhead, and taxes. To develop a 2008 budget, Regnante knew she had to first determine if her predecessor's consumer and trade promotion strategies were effective and if a price increase would have any bottom-line benefits. Based on that information she would have to decide if changes needed to be made to current levels of marketing expenditures for advertising, consumer promotion, and trade promotion. In addition, Regnante was keenly aware that she must consider the long-term strategic implications of her plan. She could not forsake the future viability of the brand in favor of short-term gains. This would be her first test as a leader for the RBS brand. She took a deep breath, and began to fill in the template (Exhibit 15.3.10) she had created to help her work through her assignment.

Exhibit 15.3.9 ■ Estimate of Trade Participation/Net Incremental Contribution (loss) Associated with RBS Trade Promotions 2002–2007YTD

Year	Duration	Sales Days Promoted	Estimated Trade Participation				Incremental Contribution (or loss by size)				Total Net Incremental Contribution (or loss)
			8 oz. Box	1 lb. Box	5 lb. Box		8 oz. Box	1 lb. Box		5 lb. Box	
2002	9/01–10/15	29		75%	60%		$ ———	$86,620		$169,089	$255,709
2003	1/02–2/13	31	65%	70%	55%		$164,846	$102,767		$91,342	$358,955
	5/01–6/30	43	70%	75%			$60,914	$170,671		$ ———	$231,585
	9/04–11/2	46	65%	70%	55%		$190,984	$151,456		$169,732	$512,172
2004	2/01–3/15	29		75%	60%		$★ ———	$★65,913		$141,704	$207,617
	5/01–6/14	31	55%	70%			$★28,036	$★62,816		$★ ———	$90,853
	8/01–9/13	31	55%	70%	55%		$65,100	$(39,351)		$61,710	$87,460
	11/01–12/13	28			70%		$★ ———	$ ———		$★137,377	$137,377
2005	1/02–2/14	31	55%	75%	75%		$(215,953)	$55,161		$ ———	$(160,792)
	3/10–4/18	32		85%			$ ———	$95,067		$117,200	$212,267
	6/02–6/27	21	75%				$(43,690)	$ ———		$ ———	$(43,690)
	9/02–9/30	21		75%			$ ———	$65,894		$ ———	$65,894
	11/03–12/12	27			70%		$ ———	$ ———		$70,320	$70,320

Continued

Exhibit 15.3.9 ■ Continued

Year	Duration	Sales Days Promoted	Estimated Trade Participation			Incremental Contribution (or loss by size)			Total Net Incremental Contribution (or loss)
			8 oz. Box	1 lb. Box	5 lb. Box	8 oz. Box	1 lb. Box	5 lb. Box	
2006	1/05–2/27	41	80%	95%	80%	$★79,162	$★382,236	$★158,165	$619,562
	4/05–4/30	21			80%	$_____	$_____	$59,117	$59,117
	5/14–6/25	38	85%			$215,729	$_____	$_____	$215,729
	8/02–9/24	43	70%	85%	75%	$142,344	$244,810	$99,067	$486,221
	10/04–12/13	50	90%		85%	$(94,968)	$_____	$64,637	$(30,331)
2007 YTD	1/03–2/25	40		85%		$★_____	$★298,195	$★_____	$298,195
	4/04–4/29	20	90%		85%	$123,941	$_____	$239,431	$363,372
	5/02–5/27	21		90%		$_____	$26,626	$_____	$26,626
	6/06–6/24	22	85%			$77,126	$_____	$_____	$77,126
2002–2007	Average	32	72%	78%	70%	$36,071	$80,404	$71,768	$188,243

Note: To be read, trade promotion running from 9/1/02—10/15/02, generated a net incremental contribution of $86,620 on sales of the 1 lb. box size, with total net incremental contribution of $255,709.

★ Indicates a list price increase on the designated size occurred simultaneously with the promotion.

Exhibit 15.3.10 ■ Regnante's Template for Developing a 2008 P&L Budget

	2005	2006	2007E	2008	Notes for 2008 Calculations (e.g., assumptions, rationale, implications)
Manufacturer's Price Per Case					
8 oz.	$6.18	$6.37	$7.20		
1 lb.	$10.33	$10.64	$12.02		
5 lb.	$46.63	$48.03	$54.28		
Factory Shipments (in 000's of cases)					
8 oz.	640	793	714		
1 lb.	1,099	1,362	1,226		
5 lb.	581	720	648		
Variable Manufacturing Cost Per Case					
8 oz.	$3.02	$3.05	$3.38		
1 lb.	$4.98	$5.03	$5.58		
5 lb.	$22.12	$22.34	$24.80		
Gross Sales	$42,400	$54,125	$55,051	$	
Variable Manufacturing Costs	$20,258	$25,354	$25,325	$	
Gross Margin	$22,142	$28,771	$29,726	$	
	52%	53%	54%	%	
Advertising					
TV	$2,862	$4,453	$3,815		
Print	$687	$950	$694		
Internet	$76	$238	$248		
Total Advertising	$3,625	$5,641	$4,757	$	
PR/Media Production Costs	$191	$297	$198		
Consumer Promotion	$424	$1,080	$551		
Trade Promotion	$4,240	$5,938	$5,505		
Total Marketing Expenses	$8,480	$12,956	$11,011	$	
Profit before SG&A, Overhead and taxes	$13,662	$15,815	$18,715	$	
	32%	29%	34%	%	

Part IV
Additional Consideration Affecting IBP Programs

In the concluding section of the book, two broad areas critical to the successful long-term marketing of brands are posed. First, for the vast majority of brands, the business partnership(s) between the marketer and an advertising and/or PR agency plus other specialized marketing facilitators is central to the development of effective IBP programs. Chapter 16 presents a brief consideration of several major issues that affect the working relationship between a marketer and outside suppliers of IBP advice. These issues include deciding whether or not to employ an outside specialist, agency/supplier selection and compensation, client approval of agency creative recommendations, and agency performance reviews. Finally, the basics of fostering a productive client/agency relationship are examined.

Second, Chapter 17 focuses on several of the ethical issues that face IBP management. Critics of advertising and other forms of marketing communication might complain that marketing ethics is an oxymoron. Fortunately, this is not the case. IBP management realizes that for their brand to succeed, all their decisions must be ethical and in the best interests of not only their customers and potential customers, but also society in general. The broad issues posed in the chapter include promoting controversial products, efforts directed toward children, intrusive and annoying messages, and ethical issues in client/agency relations.

Chapter 16
Client/Agency Relations

You don't have to go out prospecting for new business if you're doing terrific work. The prospects will find you.[1]

—Stan Richards

THE NATURE AND IMPORTANCE OF CLIENT/AGENCY RELATIONSHIPS

Business firms hire advertising and public relations (PR) agencies to add efficiency and impact to their marketing activities. Agencies offer their clients a number of advantages, including creative talent, business and marketing expertise, cost savings, and outside objectivity. Agency personnel are communication specialists who are retained by their clients to provide marketing counsel covering a wide range of activities and communication platforms.

As marketers' needs for greater coordination and leverage of all their communication efforts have intensified, agencies have either broadened their menu of services or narrowed them to become more specialized. In recent years, many agencies have restructured their organizations, added personnel, and positioned themselves to better serve their clients' integrated brand promotion (IBP) needs. Client needs include expertise in direct marketing, sales promotions, branded entertainment, viral and social networking, guerrilla marketing, and a diverse mix of other services.[2]

As clients demand greater flexibility and a wider range of services, specialty agencies are often perceived as a better option on a case-by-case basis. Specialty shops provide a beneficial alternative when the marketer seeks a higher level of expertise in one or a few areas in the spectrum of services. By specializing in services such as media buying, sales promotion, digital, financial PR (investor relations), or product placement, these firms can often achieve more effective results than full-service agencies.[3]

The relative contributions of agency personnel and client personnel to the development of IBP programs vary considerably across relationships and situations. In some instances, for example, the client may only develop a general

---

[1]Stan Richards, *The Peaceable Kingdom* (New York: AdWeek Books, 2001), 170.

[2]Christopher Hosford, "Relationship Troubles," *B to B* 94.13 (2009). *Business Source Complete.* (http://www.btobonline.com/apps/pbcs.dll/article?AID=/20091012/). [March 20, 2010].

[3]BNET Editorial, "Getting the Best Results from Your Advertising Agency," *BNET,* May 2, 2007. (www.bnet.com). [Dec. 5, 2009].

statement of the direction the program should take and then trust the agency with little client involvement to develop an entire IBP campaign. In other situations, the firm's marketing department may specify the IBP strategy and tactics in considerable detail. Here the agency's role is primarily executional. In between these extremes lie the teamwork situations and give-and-take relationships typical of most client/agency relationships.[4]

Most important, the quality of the IBP programs produced by an agency on behalf of their client is a direct function of the quality of their working business relationship. A strong partnership between a client and their agency depends on many factors, including trust, mutual respect, and open communication. Without a strong, adaptive relationship, the quality and effectiveness of the IBP programs that grow out of the relationship will suffer. Hence, it is in everyone's best interest to work to build and maintain the most productive client/agency relationship possible.

ISSUES IN THE CLIENT/AGENCY RELATIONSHIP

A number of crucial IBP management decisions revolve around the client/agency relationship. The most fundamental decision is whether the firm should handle all or some of the IBP tasks in-house or employ a full-service agency or a confederation of *à la carte* providers of special services (for example, media buying firms, event planners, and sales promotions specialists).

If the decision is to employ a full-service agency or specialized firms, client IBP management faces the task of selecting the agency or specialist(s). Then, once an agency has been selected, management faces supervision, evaluation, and compensation decisions in addition to ongoing decisions regarding approval of the agency's creative, media, PR, and other recommendations. Each of these major areas is briefly discussed in this chapter. In the concluding section of this chapter, steps for fostering productive, long-term, client/agency relationships are explored.

In-House Department, Full-Service Agency, or à la Carte Services?

The basic decision of whether a marketer would be better served by handling its IBP programs in-house or employing the services of outside specialist firms is influenced by a number of considerations. Perhaps the six most important considerations in agency type selection are control, cost, expertise, volume of advertising, objectivity, and effectiveness.

1. An advantage of using an in-house department (a.k.a. in-house agency) approach is *control* in directing the activities of the firm's employees who are responsible for developing IBP programs. Management can be confident that it will have direct access to the thoughtful, full-time attention of an in-house staff.
2. Another major advantage of an in-house department can be *cost*. In a situation where large media expenditures are involved, the marketer can capture media commissions as a rebate from a house agency that is readily recognized by the media as eligible for any agency discounts. As Horsky, Michael, and Silk point out, there is evidence provided by such firms as Google and Procter & Gamble that shifting to internal advertising units can

---

[4]McBride & Associates, comp., "Judging Excellence: Agency Appraisals," *Business Source Complete* (Modesto, CA: Author, 2002). Grey paper published by Jack McBride and available via Web download. [Dec. 5, 2009].

make sense based on cost efficiencies and savings.[5] Depending on the firm's IBP requirements, there may be other significant cost savings advantages to using an in-house department or agency. For example, the client could avoid markups on fees charged by second-party suppliers and some travel expenses.

3. *Expertise* is an increasingly important factor influencing whether or not an IBP marketer will opt to use an in-house team. As the number of media options, complexity of understanding and utilizing new communication technologies, and the alternative touch points available all expand, so does the difficulty and expense of bringing the required expertise in-house. A marketer is faced with an ever broadening array of specialists, including, but not limited to, search engine marketing (SEM) firms, social media specialists, health-care category PR firms and a host of other highly specialized companies and individuals. Further, because an in-house agency has only one client, as a rule it is harder for in-house agencies to attract and retain creative personnel who enjoy working on a diversity of clients.[6]

4. An obvious consideration in evaluating the feasibility of establishing an in-house organization is whether the firm generates a large *volume of IBP programs,* enough work to employ a full-time staff. Further, firms with highly cyclical IBP efforts are *not* well suited to using an in-house staff approach, due to the period of downtime.

5. *Objectivity* is a major benefit of using outside people. Independent, outside agencies typically provide a valuable cross section of experience gained in marketing a range of products and services. Because agency personnel are independent from the client organization, they are freer to contradict conventional wisdom and upper management's opinions. Because agency personnel typically work on several accounts at the same time, they can be more objective about each marketer's situation.

6. *Effectiveness* should perhaps be the most important consideration in choosing between an inside staff and outside specialists. Can an independent agency's expertise and skills in developing strategy, concepts, creative executions, media planning, and other areas be equaled by an in-house operation? Autonomous agencies seem to be particularly attractive to creative people who like the independence and entrepreneurial environment not available in a captive, in-house advertising department. Hence, agencies typically offer a stronger, more diverse pool of creative talent with a wider range of experiences across industries that are not always available to IBP departments.

Gardner argues against house agencies by pointing out that they suffer from a narrowed focus, which handicaps their effectiveness. They lose the stimulus of cross-fertilization of ideas and run a greater risk of going stale than an outside agency. Also, the marketer loses flexibility in firing nonperformers—it is relatively easy to change agencies, much more difficult to make sweeping personnel changes with an in-house staff.[7]

An evaluation of whether to employ a full-service agency or subcontract portions of the job and retain some in-house or move all in-house is complex. In addition to the six factors identified here, this decision turns on the availability of such specialists, their expertise, what can be negotiated at what cost, and potential problems with coordination of activities across the firm's IBP efforts.

---

[5]Sharon Horsky, Steven C. Michael, and Alvin J. Silk, "The Internalization of Advertising Services: An Inter-Industry Analysis," *Harvard Business School: Working Knowledge* (2008). *Business Source Complete.* (http://hbswk.hbs.edu/faculty/asilk.html) [Dec. 5, 2009].

[6]Ibid.

[7]Herbert S. Gardner, *The Advertising Agency Business* (Lincolnwood, IL: NTC Business Books, 1989), 101–103.

IBP Agency Selection

The selection of an IBP agency is a difficult and important task—a task that, if sloppily done, will most likely have to be repeated soon. Also, if a poor choice is made, it is likely that considerable time and money will have been wasted for the client firm and agencies alike. Therefore, a marketer should view the development of a careful selection procedure as an investment that can potentially pay huge dividends.

There are some standard steps in the process of soliciting, reviewing, and selecting an agency to be a firm's marketing partner. All begin with an internal exercise in which the firm defines its own service requirements and establishes selection criteria.[8] This serves to guide the firm in gathering information about perspective agency partners. Typically, six steps are suggested in the process of agency selection. These steps are presented next.

1. *Establish selection criteria.* In developing a set of criteria, a useful resource to consult is the American Association of Advertising Agencies. The AAAA suggests that such factors as size, geographic considerations, years of experience, and industry experience be included.[9] Thompson stresses that clients should focus on finding an agency partner who understands their business, the challenges the client faces, as well as an agency who will immerse themselves in the client's brand.[10]

2. *Devise a plan of operation.* Who is to be responsible for planning and conducting the search? Will consultants who specialize in agency selection be involved? Should the search be made public? What information should the firm provide prospects? These and many other important issues must be addressed.

   A logical option, particularly for large marketers, to consider is the use of a specialized consultant to organize and assist in all aspects of the selection process. A current listing of agency search consultants is available via the American Association of Advertising Agencies Web site (www.aaaa.org).

3. *Develop a list of agencies for consideration.* A number of critical question emerge at this stage as well. For example, how many agencies should be considered? What type of initial contact should be made to determine if agencies are interested in the firm's account? Should a screening questionnaire be used? If yes, what specific information should be requested?

4. *Narrow the list to a manageable number.* Should personal visits by client staff be made to the most promising agencies? What should be discussed in informal, preliminary meetings? How many references should be contacted? Are there current clients on the rosters of potential partners whose IBP efforts are similar?

5. *Request agency presentations.* How many agencies should be invited to make presentations? What should be included in the request for proposal (RFP)? Should the competitors

---

[8]Pippa Collett, "Selecting Agency Support: Best Practice in Brokering Positive Relationships," *Journal of Sponsorship* 2, no. 3 (2009): 257–266. *Business Source Complete.* EBSCO, April 15, 2009. (http://henrystewart.metapress.com/app/home/) [Dec. 5, 2009].

[9]Julia M. Johnson, "How to Choose an Advertising Agency," *St. Louis Business Journal,* August, 29, 2008. (http://stlouis.bizjournals.com/stlouis/). [Dec. 5, 2009].

[10]Suki Thompson, "The Importance of An Agency Effectiveness Culture to Clients," *Institute of Practitioners in Advertising,* (2009). Warc: Ideas and Evidence for Marketing (www.warc.com/LandingPages/Generic/Results.asp?Ref=155) [Dec. 31, 2009].

be given a special project assignment or asked to develop a complete campaign? What about the pitch location, timing, and requested content? Should speculative creative be requested? Should the agencies be compensated? How will the presentations be formally evaluated?

Because most clients choose the agency with which they feel the best emotional fit, it is critical that the selection process leaves enough time for key personnel on both sides to get to know each other.[11] Ultimately, the relationships among key players on both sides provide the foundation for building a long-term, adaptive, and healthy business marriage.

6. *Make the final decision.* Fam and Waller suggest that in making an agency selection decision, the following factors should be weighted as critical: creative ability, quality of the account team, integrity and shared purpose, agency resources, marketing and strategy development, industry experience, and reputation.[12] In addition, "cultural fit" is a critical consideration in determining a successful ongoing client/agency relationship. How the agency's values and personnel align with the firm's cannot be stressed enough.[13]

Agency Compensation

Fee-based Compensation. The fee, either based on an hourly labor rate or fixed, is the dominant method of agency compensation. Using the hourly labor rate, each individual who works on the client's business keeps track of his or her time and bills the client at an hourly rate that includes an allowance for direct salary, agency overhead, and profit. The agency also bills the client for other nonsalary expenses incurred in servicing the client's account (copies, entertainment expenses, express delivery services, and so on).

For example, to determine the billed rate for an employee who earns $47,500 per year, the agency begins by dividing this salary by a standard year of 1,600 hours. Then an overhead charge is added to direct salary (for example, for every $1 in direct salary the average agency person has to carry $1.174 in overhead). Finally, the agency adds a profit target, for example, 20% of gross, which requires a markup of 25%. Hence, in this example the $47,500-per-year agency person's billed rate is $81.00 per hour.

$$\$47,500 \div 1,600 = \$29.69$$
$$\$29.69 + (\$29.69 \times 1.174) = \$64.55$$
$$\$64.55 + (\$64.55 \times .25) = \$81$$

Two alternatives fee approaches to billing clients hourly are a job fee or a retainer fee. In some cases it may make sense for the agency to simply estimate the costs of completing a project and submit a proposal indicating what will be accomplished for a total job fee. In other situations, it may be appropriate for the agency to estimate all expenses involved in handling a firm's account, add overhead plus profit, and suggest a retainer fee to be billed monthly. In each case, provision should be made for periodic review and possible adjustment of fees or retainers.

---

[11]Collett, "Selecting Agency Support."

[12]Kim-Shyan Fam and David S. Waller, "Agency–Client Relationship Factors Across Life-Cycle Stages," *Journal of Relationship Marketing* 7, no. 2 (2008): 217–235. *Business Source Complete.* (http://www.informaworld.com/smpp/). [Dec. 5, 2009].

[13]Johnson, "How to Choose an Advertising Agency."

Other Nonsalary Expenses. In addition, the client and its agency need to reach clear agreement on what conventions will be followed in billing the client for expenses related to the development and execution of its IBP programs. For example, will the standard 17.65% markup[14] be applied to production charges incurred for the development of broadcast commercials, equipment purchased on behalf of the client, travel, express delivery expenses, and so on? Further, clients typically agree to partial, inventory, or progressive billing for items that require out-of-pocket costs as a job is developed. All such issues need to be clearly agreed on and explicitly covered in the client/agency contract.

Value-based Compensation. In part spawned by the measurability of Web-based exposures and tracking, marketers have examined their agency compensation procedures with the objective of adding accountability by replacing their fee-based procedures. In addition, the purpose of these examinations have been to explore the possibility of (1) achieving cost reductions, (2) developing a more equitable arrangement for both parties, and (3) encouraging and rewarding outstanding work. Led by Procter & Gamble and Coca-Cola, the marketing community has embraced value-based compensation.[15]

Williams suggests that agencies should be compensated for the business value they deliver, not the hours spent working on an IBP program. In other words, agencies should stop billing based on selling their time and start focusing on the value delivered. Value pricing should be determined in terms of the financial impact on the desired brand-building outcomes.[16]

In developing a compensation procedure, the client and agency should strive to design an equitable arrangement in light of the services provided that, ideally, provides incentives for the agency to produce outstanding work. Further, intelligent marketers recognize that working on their business must be profitable for their agencies and other suppliers. Hence, the client wants their account to be profitable and attractive in terms of monetary compensation from their agency's standpoint. This will help foster a more productive and long-term relationship.

Approval of Agency Creative Recommendations

A cliché in the advertising agency business: The trick is not just developing great advertising, but also getting that great advertising over the hurdle of client approval. Clients can be difficult when it comes to approving creative work, especially when the recommendation is edgy and outside the client's personal comfort zone. On the one hand, clients want great advertising, but on the other hand, clients tend to be conservative and cautious. Creativity in advertising or other IBP programs often requires risks and innovation, which can often be unsettling to client management.

Further, although client management realizes the importance of creative executions to the success of the brand's IBP programs and they have opinions about what they believe is a good

---

[14]Note that the rationale for 17.65% is that a charge or bill must be marked up this amount so that the markup will represent 15% of the total cost presented to the client. For example, if an agency supervises the development and production of a landing page Web site and the Web developer's bill is $12,500, the agency marks up the bill 17.65%, or $2,206.25. The client is billed $14,706.25. The agency's markup is 15% of the client's total bill ($2,206.26 divided by $14,706.25).

[15]Quenqua, Douglas, "Pay for Performance," *The Advertiser,* (November 2009): 28–36.

[16]Tim Williams, "Paying the Agency: A Better Solution?" *AdMap,* June 2008, 19–21. Warc: Ideas and Evidence for Marketing, (http://www.warc.com/LandingPages/). [Dec. 5, 2009].

or bad execution, they lack objectivity and expertise. This often leads to conflicts with their agency.

Too often clients seem to forget why they hired their agency—agency personnel are experts in making efficient and effective use of communication tools. In terms of creative services, the agency's job is often to stretch their client's thinking about how to communicate with the target audience in a fresh, memorable way that sells the brand. This is particularly true in a marketplace crowded with similar brands and similar advertising appeals used to sell those brands.

Unfortunately, client management often incorrectly believes that the overall success of their business means that they are qualified to evaluate their agency's creative recommendations. For example, it is hard to convince the management of a brand that has experienced a 10% sales increase in the last year that it is forfeiting opportunity costs by sticking with a weak advertising campaign. The client's response—"We must be doing something right!"—may be glossing over a multitude of IBP marketing blunders.

Another problem that can plague client/agency relations is the agency presenting "safe" creative recommendations. In this situation, in the interest of avoiding conflict with their client in the short run, agency personnel are tempted to present "safe" creative ideas they believe the client will approve. This trap undermines the client/agency relationship. The mission of the agency should be to present objective creative recommendations about how to use IBP to its full potential, *not* to present safe creative work simply to garner client approval. As Leo Burnett noted, "I have learned that trying to guess what the boss or client wants is the most debilitating of all influences in the creation of good advertising."[17]

Gardner emphasized this danger when he noted that the objective of too many short-sighted agencies is to *please* their clients rather than *serve* their best interests. He suggests that "such agencies are unwittingly proceeding on the assumption that the client knows more about advertising than they do."[18]

A thoughtful and comprehensive creative strategy brief can help a client and their agency avoid some of the hazards inherent in the approval process. As discussed in Chapter 7, ideally, client management should approve the creative strategy brief. Such approval lessens the chance of conflict in the final approval stage of the process. After the strategy statement has been approved, it becomes a road map for creative personnel to follow in their work and the standard against which client management should evaluate proposed creative executions. "Is the execution on strategy?" should be client management's primary focus in reviewing creative work.

Finally, the discussion in this section is not intended to suggest that a nervous client is always wrong in hesitating to approve a solid agency's creative recommendations. In fact, the client may be correct in rejecting the proposed creative ideas. On the other hand, too much advertising and other IBP programs are killed or severely maimed by overzealous client management. In many situations, client management would be well served by placing more trust in their agency's creative judgment. If the agency is a good one, its creative personnel are talented professionals who understand their client's brand/market situation and have thoughtfully addressed their client's communication needs. After all, that is why the agency was hired.

---

[17] Leo Burnett, *100 Leo's* booklet (Chicago: Leo Burnett Company, 1991), 37.

[18] Gardner, *The Advertising Agency Business*, 6.

Agency Performance Reviews

All clients constantly review the performance of their agency partners on an informal basis. Unfortunately, too few clients go beyond an informal, impressionistic review of their client/agency relationship. This is a mistake because a review can (1) enhance the effectiveness of the client's IBP programs, and (2) reveal a minor problem before it develops into a major one that can damage the firm's IBP efforts and threaten the relationship.[19]

An agency performance review should be viewed as an evaluation of the health of the client/agency relationship. The objective of the review should be to help ensure that the agency best serves its client's needs and to conduct preventive maintenance on the relationship. The underlying assumption is that both parties have a shared responsibility to jointly ensure that the business relationship is mutually profitable and productive. Conducting a review of that relationship annually, or at more frequent intervals if deemed appropriate, is simply an investment in ensuring the long-run success of the partnership. Agencies should view the review as an opportunity to explore areas in which they can improve their level of service to their clients.

The review should be formal and should gather information from across a wide range of topics from the perspective of individuals in a variety of positions in both organizations. Although focused primarily on agency performance, the review should include feedback on the client's performance in working with the agency as well.

Ideally, there should be a link between agency performance as revealed by the review and compensation. Although difficult to structure, by tying the review to compensation, both parties' level of commitment to treat the review seriously is enhanced, and the potential that a meaningful dialogue will grow out of the review is increased.

Finally, the performance review should be a serious but open, transparent, and positive exercise designed to foster better communication. The client should work to communicate to its agency that the process is designed to be constructive, not destructive. Once a problem area has been identified, the two should adopt a team problem-solving approach to correcting the deficiency.

FOSTERING A PRODUCTIVE CLIENT/AGENCY RELATIONSHIP

A sound, productive working client/agency relationship is vital to the development of effective IBP programs and does not happen by accident. Such a relationship requires the constant attention of both parties. Further, such a relationship is developed through a coordination of roles and responsibilities, supported by a service agreement contract, an understanding of respective working practices, regular reviews against agreed-on key performance indicators, and the maintenance of a spirit of open and honest communication.[20]

Gray points out that four undeniable factors contribute to an effective, long-running client/agency relationship: trust, candor, mutual respect, and fairness. Trust that is earned over time is critical because great campaigns begin and prosper with trust. Such campaigns also result from candor and mutual respect with both sides speaking their mind openly against

---

[19]Lesly Neadel, "Majority of Marketers Conduct Formal Advertising Performance Evaluations According to a New ANA Survey," *PR News* (2009). Factiva (http://global.factiva.com.ezproxy.lib.utexas.edu/ha/default.aspx). [Nov. 24, 2009].

[20]Collett, "Selecting Agency Support," 257–266.

the backdrop of an appreciation of what each partner brings to the decisions. Finally, it requires a financially fair agreement that ensures the agency will earn an attractive profit.[21]

Each of these four factors is dependent on clear communication. In fact, miscommunication appears to be the most commonly cited problem that clouds and disrupts client/agency relationships. Fortunately, there are steps that can be taken to avoid miscommunication between a client and their agency. These steps are

1. Both parties must *commit to open communication.* This requires an interlocking communication network spanning both organizations at multiple levels. Also, communication must be encouraged at every level to reduce the chance of miscommunication. Jacobs stresses the importance of the agency staff carefully listening to their client to understand their world, to relate to their fears, and to use their language. Then, the agency should show the client that the agency cares and demonstrate this through being proactive by bringing the client innovative approaches to projects.[22]
2. Agency personnel must *show initiative* in ensuring clear, open communication and following up on all client contacts. For example, agency personnel must document all client contacts and decisions through timely call reports, which are distributed to personnel on both sides of the relationship.
3. The client should *conduct a periodic (at least yearly) performance review* of its agency. A review provides many benefits. For example, the two parties have an opportunity to deal with a problem before it reaches a crisis stage.
4. The issues of advertiser and agency expectations of what work will be performed, how the agency will be compensated, and so on, should be *clearly spelled out in a contract.* A clear, thorough contract can guide the parties past a number of communication trouble spots. Importantly, the contract sets the tone for the entire relationship.

After examining the issue of what clients want from a PR agency, Gable concludes that strategic thinking is most important. Clients also want creativity and proactive suggestions. Clients do *not* want slow or tangled processes, passive/reactive service, or the lack of results coupled with excuses.[23]

Beverland et al. stress that proactivity (for example, bringing a client a plan for a new IBP initiative to capitalize on a previously unseen opportunity) is a driver of client satisfaction. They suggest that agencies need to invest in client-relevant research to generate proactive suggestions. Further, agency staff needs to be sensitive to client signals regarding desired proactivity. Recurring client requests for the agency to "push the boundaries" and "challenge us" may serve as an early warning of a potentially unhappy client that may lead to termination.[24]

Finally, Stan Richards' core message on building solid client/agency relationships: Do good work for your clients. Good work will foster a productive client/agency relationship and also attract prospective new clients to the agency. So, ultimately it is about the work.[25]

---

[21] Bill Gray, "Behind Great Client/Agency Relationships," *The Advertiser,* (January 2003): 18–19.

[22] Ken Jacobs, "The Ties that Bind: Building Better Client Relationships," *PR Tactics* (August 2008). (www.prsa.org/searchresults/view/). [Dec. 16, 2009].

[23] Tom Gable, "Managing for Results and Profits in Good Times and Bad," *PRSA* (June 1, 2009). (www.prsa.org/search) [Nov. 24, 2009].

[24] Michael Beverland, Francis Farrelly, and Zeb Woodhatch, "Exploring the Dimensions of Proactivity within Advertising Agency-Client Relationships," *Journal of Advertising* 36, no. 4 (Winter 2007): 49–60.

[25] Richards, *The Peaceable Kingdom.*

CLIENT/AGENCY RELATIONS

Exercises

1. The PepsiCo-owned brand SoBe has worked with traditional creative agencies in recent years. The creative agency Arnell Group produced TV spots for SoBe that ran during the 2009 Super Bowl, which generated more awareness for the brand. But SoBe was not satisfied with the level of customer engagement, leading them away from the Arnell Group and in search of a different approach. SoBe chose to avoid traditional creative agencies and instead are trying a new marketing effort: a combination of separate digital, PR, and promotion agencies. The brand wished to reach an 18- to 29-year-old target and felt the combined effort of the multiple agencies will focus on engaging the target in a more effective way. SoBe wanted a campaign that created content, not just advertising.
   a. Do you think the Arnell Group would have been open to adjusting to the client's wishes?
   b. What does the SoBe case tell you about how the advertising industry is evolving?

   Source: Zmuda, Natalie. "SoBe Ditches Creative Agency in New Marketing Approach." *Advertising Age* April 14, 2010. Web April 18, 2010. <http://adage.com/agencynews/article?article_id=143303>.

2. There is no doubt to the popularity of social media. Twitter, Facebook, and other sites offer virtually "free" advertising. The increasingly hard-to-reach, digital population is exactly the audience that many brands wish to target. For the agency, recommending social media can be difficult. Social media is free and comparatively easy to manage, requiring little advertising knowledge or technology expertise. A smart small business owner can take advantage of free viral media and easily outrun a big, rich brand with a well-known agency that spends a lot of money on TV, print, and display ads.
   a. What implications do social media have on agency/client relations? Explain. Be as specific as possible.
   b. Do you think this is the end of traditional advertising?

   Source: Murthy, Mahesh. "Twitter Ad Model: Difficult for Marketers, Death-Knell for Agencies?" *Wall Street Journal.* April 16, 2010. Web, April 18, 2010. <http://blogs.wsj.com/india-chief-mentor/2010/04/16/twitter's-ad-model-difficult-for-marketers-death-knell-for-agencies/>.

3. Thanks to the World Wide Web, even when advertising campaigns end, the advertising can still linger on. Consumers are able to view ads long after they are no longer part of an active campaign, thanks to YouTube, blogs, and other sites. The job search Web site CareerBuilder launched a humorous e-mail service called Monk-email in 2005, coinciding with the site's campaign that likened a bad job to working in an office filled with chimpanzees. The e-mail service was so popular that it still remains online today. As these ideas continue to have legs and the CareerBuilder audience continues to engage with them, CareerBuilder's marketing team makes certain that these old ideas still fit with current objectives. Even though CareerBuilder has changed ad agencies two times within the past 4 years, the brand continues to use old ads to drive brand image and future campaigns.
   a. How do you think that CareerBuilder's strong focus on past campaigns affects the ideas of the new agency?
   b. How does the long shelf life of ad campaigns affect client/agency relations?
   c. What are the positive aspects of considering past campaigns when developing new campaigns? What are the drawbacks?

   Source: Elliott, Stuart. "Old Ads That Won't Die or Fade Away." *The New York Times.* April 12, 2010. Web, April 18, 2010. <http://www.nytimes.com/2010/04/13/business/media/13adco.html?ref=media>.

Case 16.1

Columbia Savings[1]

For many years, Columbia Savings (CS) had been a successful savings and loan association, with a limited number of branch offices in a mid-sized metropolitan market located in the Southwestern United States. Management and the Board of Directors of CS had been content to coast along utilizing relatively weak and ineffective marketing efforts. However, despite its lack of aggressiveness, CS had consistently made a handsome return on investment for the firm's owners. For several decades the status quo was not so bad.

Then, in the space of a few years, a wave of financial industry deregulations, mergers, consolidations, and the entry of aggressive competitors attracted by what had become a vibrant Sun-Belt market changed CS's financial environment substantially. At first, CS chose to ignore these changes, but its deposit base began to decline steadily, and the atmosphere at CS went from conservative smugness to the worry and insecurity of an old, downtrodden loser.

At that point, the Board of Directors realized that radical surgery was in order if CS was to regain its former position in the market. To perform the surgery, the board hired a new president, David Woburne. Woburne had an extremely successful marketing track record with a regional department store and several financial institutions. After a period of evaluation lasting several months, he began to make wholesale changes in CS's operations. He implemented a number of personnel changes, including the hiring of a new senior vice president of marketing, David Carlyle.

Under Mr. Carlyle, each branch location's performance was evaluated; fixtures and furnishings were updated and coordinated to project a more progressive image. New branch locations were added, and an improved and expanded training program for all cashiers and other branch personnel was designed and implemented. Using the services of a consultant, the firm's clunky and dull Web site was revamped, simplified for easier navigation, and made more graphically appealing. As another essential step, the firm adopted a new strategy of shopping competitive rates via telephone each week on the popular money market accounts and certificates of deposit and setting CS's rates to equal or exceed the competition.

In addition, Woburne felt, and Carlyle agreed, that CS's marketing department should *not* handle major brand promotional activities in-house. Instead Woburne believed that a full-service advertising agency with PR capabilities should be hired and then supervised by Carlyle. To effect this change, Woburne hired Boyton & Dodds, an out-of-state agency based in a major metropolitan market, to develop a new campaign to communicate what the revitalized CS offered customers and potential customers. Woburne had worked with the agency before and was good friends with both its principals.

After four years of working with Boyton & Dodds, Carlyle believed that while some of the agency's early work had been strong and effective, lately it was pretty dull. Further, he believed that the solid growth CS had experienced was due more to its attractive rates, new service offerings, and operational improvements than to the marketing work of the agency. In addition, during this period the market had experienced strong growth. CS had benefited from the flood of new residents into the market and, as Carlyle put it, "All boats rise with the tide."

In hinting at his lack of enthusiasm for the agency's creative efforts, Carlyle had generated comments from Woburne such as, "But like the boys at B&D said, it's fundamentally sound and it fits our personality," and, "Hey, we are a safe, secure financial institution that people need to trust with their money, not a pizza parlor."

---

[1]This case was written by John H. Murphy, The University of Texas at Austin. The case is designed to serve as the basis for classroom discussion and not to illustrate either the effective or ineffective handling of an administrative situation. The identity of the firm involved and the situation have been disguised.

In the past two years, two financial institutions in the market had developed what Carlyle felt were aggressive and successful brand promotion programs. The competitive advertising, promotional efforts, and improved Web site he believed was the most clever and memorable had received considerable recognition in local and regional awards competitions. A two-person team who operated a local creative boutique—Navajo Inspiration—had developed the ideas and executions behind this campaign.

Carlyle believed that the success of this relatively new campaign, coupled with the emergence of other local *à la carte* advertising and marketing services raised some interesting possibilities. Further, the increasing importance of the Internet, the firm's Web site, search engine optimization, viral marketing, using social networking, guerilla marketing, mobile devices, and so on were not strengths at Boyton & Dodds. A host of freelance, entrepreneurial services were available to address these emerging areas fueled by the technological evolution of consumer communications. In addition, Carlyle suspected that hiring *à la carte* service providers on a fee basis, as needed, might offer cost saving versus what he felt were the rather hefty hourly billing charges submitted each month by Boyton & Dodds.

Carlyle felt the time had come to broach these issues with Woburne. Carlyle was comfortable in suggesting that they seriously discuss the matter because Woburne enjoyed "challenging the status quo" and took pride in his own openness to considering "any suggestion from any source," as he put it.

In initially considering the idea of some sort of change in CS's present agency relationship, Woburne sensed Carlyle's enthusiasm for such a change but raised several questions. First, would there really be a cost savings? Second, had Carlyle pushed the present agency for a different approach in their creative work? Third, how much creativity was appropriate for a financial institution? (Woburne discounted the award-winning campaign Carlyle admired as too zany for the serious older saver. "My nephew loves that stuff, but he's only ten years old!")

Finally, Woburne pointed out the wealth of marketing experience the principals of their present agency possessed. In concluding their discussion, Woburne suggested that Carlyle think through all alternatives, including the possibility of adding staff and taking the account in-house, before making a formal written recommendation for consideration by the marketing subcommittee of the board.

Name _____ Date _____

QUESTIONS FOR DISCUSSION AND REVIEW

1. How do general considerations that apply to the full-service agency versus boutique and/or specialized suppliers question fit CS's situation?

   _____
   _____
   _____
   _____

2. What additional information about CS, the market, competitors, and so on would be useful in evaluating the type of change that Carlyle is considering?

   _____
   _____
   _____
   _____

3. What are additional alternatives for handling CS's brand promotional activities?

   _____
   _____
   _____
   _____

4. How might Woburne's past experiences with the present agency influence his reactions to Carlyle's suggestions? How typical is this?

   _____
   _____
   _____
   _____

Case 16.2

Carlyle Labs, Inc. (B)[1]

MEMORANDUM

TO: Ashley Russell, Director of Corporate Communications
FROM: James Jackson, President and CEO
DATE: March 1, 201X
RE: Development of a Procedure to Select a PR Agency

The purpose of this memorandum is to briefly describe a project that needs your immediate attention. The project is to outline a procedure to follow in selecting a public relations agency to: handle our communications with various media including traditional media, social and new media; handle communications with our various publics; and be on-call when the next crisis arises, like the recent fire at our facility. (See Carlyle Labs, Inc. (A).)

The outlined procedure should cover all aspects of the selection process, including (1) soliciting interest from the most qualified prospective agencies; (2) gathering initial information on the agencies who express an interest; (3) reducing the number of agencies for serious consideration to a few; (4) interviewing the serious contenders; (5) reviewing their client list and project portfolio; (6) developing an assignment for the finalists to tackle to see how they think and what they would be like to work with; and (7) making the final decision.

There are obviously a host of issues involved here. For example, what should be the time frame of the process? What criteria should be used in identifying which agencies to solicit? Should we initiate contact with the agencies we believe are most attractive? Or, should we simply announce our search to a wide list of firms and wait for responses? Should we pay the finalists if we ask them to work on an assignment for us? What type of compensation arrangement might be most appropriate for the agency we appoint?

These are just my initial thoughts. Undoubtedly, there are many other issues beyond those briefly described above that need to be addressed in your proposed procedure.

The recent fire at our facility and its aftermath led to the suggestion during our Board of Directors meeting last Wednesday that Carlyle Labs could benefit from having a permanent relationship with an experienced PR firm. Not just to help us when we are in a crisis mode, but also to foster better coverage in the trade and popular press of our research and accomplishments. I am also confident that such a firm could help us with our employee communication, sponsorships and charity events, plus other marketing activities.

As a next step, I would like for you to present your recommendations to a special three-member subcommittee of the board. With your advice and counsel, the ad hoc "PR Agency Selection" subcommittee will be responsible for first approving your recommended procedure, and then supervising the agency selection process. In addition, the subcommittee will make the ultimate selection decision of which agency to hire.

The subcommittee met with me to set up the process described in this memo. They have a second meeting scheduled in two weeks on Friday, March 15 at 10:00 a.m. At this meeting they would like for you to present your recommended plan for how the selection process should be conducted.

Thank you for your careful attention to this most important task.

---

[1] This case was written by John H. Murphy, The University of Texas at Austin. The case is designed to serve as the basis for classroom discussion and not to illustrate either the effective or ineffective handling of an administrative situation. The identity of the firm is disguised.

Name _____ Date _____

QUESTIONS FOR DISCUSSION AND REVIEW

1. What procedures should be followed in each of the seven steps in the selection process outlined by Mr. Jackson? Which of these steps is most important in ensuring that the most appropriate agency is selected? Why?

2. Has Mr. Jackson overlooked anything important in the seven steps? If yes, what is it, and why is it important?

3. What additional suggestions or issues should Ms. Russell include in her proposed procedure?

4. What factors or considerations determine how attractive a potential client is to a PR agency? How attractive a potential client would Carlyle Labs be to a local, regional, or national PR agency?

Case 16.3

Gordon, Wolfberg, Miller & Friends[1]

Jane Gordon and Mary Wolfberg had formed their advertising agency, Gordon & Wolfberg (G&W), on the basis of a mutual respect for each other and their complementary talents. The two principals in the agency had been friends since their high school days in Evanston, Illinois, and both had studied advertising at the University of Illinois.

After graduation, the two friends had gone their separate ways. Gordon had taken a media-buying job in the Dallas office of a large Chicago-based agency and after two years had moved to an account executive position working with a large package-goods client. Wolfberg had initially taken a job as copywriter/artist with a struggling agency, but after nine months the agency lost its principal account and folded. Next, Wolfberg's artistic talents landed her a position as a creative artist with Hallmark Cards in Kansas City.

As a result of professional contacts established through the local ad club, Gordon had received an offer to become the advertising manager of a large manufacturing firm with offices in Dallas. Although the offer was attractive, she viewed the situation as an opportunity to establish her own agency. Gordon suggested that the firm's vice-president of marketing could handle the job in a "partnership" with her new agency. After considerable discussions, the owner of the manufacturing firm, who was extremely unhappy with the results of the firm's advertising efforts, bought Gordon's idea and agreed to fire the present agency as soon as Gordon could assume responsibility for the firm's advertising. Wolfberg instantly accepted Gordon's proposal that they jointly form an agency to handle the manufacturer's account.

Ownership of the agency was divided 60/40 between Gordon and Wolfberg. Both of the principals began their new enterprise with considerable enthusiasm and dreams of quickly adding significant new accounts. During the first two years of the agency's operation, several small clients and pro bono accounts were picked up by G&W. However, both the principals were dissatisfied with their efforts to add at least one major account.

In an attempt to correct this perceived shortcoming, Jack Miller, a seasoned and highly successful account executive from a major Dallas agency, was hired to concentrate on pitching prospective new clients. Gordon and Wolfberg each gave Miller 10 percent ownership in the agency, which became Gordon, Wolfberg, Miller & Friends (GWMF).

Since GWMF's formation, the agency had grown to about 25 accounts and handled media billings of about $27.5 million. The agency employed about 30 individuals and hired outside free-lance talent such as photographers, web designers, Internet Search Engine Optimization consultants, and so on when their client's needs and the workload justified specialized or additional help.

As fate would have it, on a Monday morning developments with three different clients reached the point where a decision was sorely needed regarding what action to take. These developments required the immediate attention of Gordon, Wolfberg, and Miller. To handle these problems adequately, the three principals would have to agree upon a course of action to resolve each by the next morning.

---

[1]This case was written by John H. Murphy, The University of Texas at Austin. The case is designed to serve as the basis for classroom discussion and not to illustrate either the effective or ineffective handling of an administrative situation. The identities of the firms involved and the situations have been disguised.

SURE FINE DAIRIES

The first of the problem areas involved an important client, the Sure Fine Dairies (SFD). SFD executives had approved GWMF's recommendation to place $125,000 in outdoor showings, a "Name-a-new-flavor" contest on the SFD's website, and a spot radio schedule costing $57,000 to support the 12-week introduction of a new line of natural yogurt flavors. Further, it was understood that an additional 12-week campaign to reinforce the initial efforts would probably be approved.

At the same time, SFD wanted GWMF to develop six multimedia displays that would present the history of Sure Fine and explain the procedures used to process dairy products. The displays were to be used for special events or programs (for example, the state fair), and three would be housed permanently at SFD locations.

In order to produce the type and quality of displays SFD wanted would require special film work, location and studio shooting, sophisticated audiovisual equipment, and the hiring of a photographer and talent for the voice-over narration. An estimate on the expenses involved in producing the displays was as follows:

LCD projection, audio equipment (cost to agency)	$17,621
Materials (cost to the agency)	4,567
Talent, film, sound, production (cost to agency)	8,000
A/E supervision time = 50 hours (@ $125/hour)	6,250
Agency mark-up on outside services/purchases (@ 17.65%)	5,328
Total	$41,766

This cost estimate was presented to SFD for their written approval before moving forward with the project. In figuring its cost estimates to develop the six displays, GWMF followed their traditional agency practice of marking up all work contracted outside by 17.65 percent. Thus, the estimate presented to SFD for its approval included $5,328 in agency mark-up for work and materials purchased on behalf of their client.

When the account executive from GWMF presented the estimated costs and requested approval, the SFDs' marketing manager balked at the additional charges for agency markup on "outside services" ($5,328). The marketing manager said that he did not mind paying a commission to the agency on the media advertising, but he objected to a fee being charged on other services. Further, he suggested that perhaps GWMF did not appreciate SFDs' business and that he wanted a special deal if the markup was a standard practice. The account executive told the marketing manager that he would check with the principals of GWMF and come back on Tuesday to discuss the situation further.

WOODY'S

The second problem involved Woody's, a regional chain of fast-food restaurants. The chain had multiple locations in Dallas, Forth Worth, Houston, San Antonio, Amarillo, Beaumont, Tyler, and Lubbock. Periodically, Woody's ran a burst of advertising promoting a "Buy-One-Get-One-Free" weekend sale. These weekend promotions had been extremely successful in the past. Woody's management had always been pleased with consumer sales during these promotions and felt such sales contributed heavily to business in slow periods. Woody's executives gave most of the credit for the success of the promotion to GWMF's high-quality creative advertising strategy and executions.

Through unexplainable error, most likely on the part of GWMF's new assistant traffic manager, fifteen 30-second and eighteen 10-second television spots promoting the "Buy-One-Get-One-Free" sale had not appeared as originally planned on the Friday evening prior to the sale. To make matters worse, sales during the promotion were about half of their usual level for an average weekend during such a sale.

Woody Burkehart, owner of Woody's, was extremely upset after watching the 10 P.M. news only to discover that his ads did not appear. Burkehart attributed the dismal sales performance to the scheduling error. "The promo never had a chance after we missed those front-end spots. This error robbed the spots, in-store and sign ads plus the print ads that did run of their impact. If there had been time, I'd have canned the whole promotion after the foul-up on the opening spots."

The account person who handled Woody's apologized for the scheduling problem and pointed out that two other factors contributed to the poor sales performance: (1) light snow and sleet made travel by car dangerous during much of the weekend in most of the markets served by Woody's, and (2) competitive advertising and price promotion by other fast-food restaurants was unusually heavy over the weekend of Woody's "Buy-One-Get-One-Free" promotion.

Burkehart rejected these explanations. Further, he literally demanded that Gordon and Miller be in his office the next morning to discuss some sort of arrangement to "make good" on the botched promotion, the likelihood of such a situation occurring again, and the future relationship between GWMF and Woody's.

HOMEWOOD SAVINGS & LOAN

The third client that would require attention the next day was Homewood Savings & Loan. Homewood had been a solid client of GWMF's for five years but recently had become unhappy with the quality of the agency's creative efforts.

In the 15 years since the firm's founding, Homewood had grown from a single location in Dallas to eight branches plus a downtown headquarters, and it presently had deposits of over $900 million. However, in the last six months, new accounts had slowed to a trickle despite the fact that the service areas of the branch locations had experienced strong growth in terms of population.

When the marketing VP at Homewood, who was under pressure to correct the meager new accounts problem, complained to GWMF's account executive about the "stale" creative efforts, the A/E responded that the campaign represented the creative people's "best efforts." Further, the A/E explained that the present ads and commercials built logically on past Homewood promotions and advertising.

Finally, the A/E suggested that Homewood's media budget of only $950,000 was a stumbling block to the development of the sort of impact that was necessary in the highly competitive Dallas financial market. (As a result of public relations fee work and preparation of collateral materials, GWMF considered Homewood an excellent client.)

Homewood's marketing VP questioned whether GWMF's creative group really devoted much time or energy to his account. He went on to say: "Don't tell me you're not capable of a stronger creative execution of our ads. It sure seems strange that Jack Miller is going around town touting your shop's expertise in creativity and showing aware-winning commercials for almost all your clients except us!"

The A/E's conversation with the marketing VP ended on a sour note. In so many words, the VP threatened to fire GWMF and look for some new creative blood. The marketing VP ended the discussion with the following request: "The executive board of Homewood is meeting for dinner and a working session to review our marketing efforts tomorrow evening at the Petroleum Club. Please ask Jack Miller to join us around seven o'clock. Better still, ask Jack to meet me here at the office about five so we can talk prior to meeting with the board."

Name _____   Date _____

QUESTIONS FOR DISCUSSION AND REVIEW

1. How should GWMF respond to each of the situations involving its clients? What are the likely implications of GWMF's responses?

2. Are the immediate problems related in any way? If so, how?

3. What general principals of client/agency relationships are involved in the three situations?

4. How might each of these problems have been avoided?

Chapter 17
Ethical Considerations

If I were starting life over again, I am inclined to think that I would go into the advertising business in preference to almost any other . . . The general rating of the standards of modern civilization among all groups of people during the past half century would have been impossible without the spreading of the knowledge of higher standards by means of advertising.
—President Franklin Delano Roosevelt in "Confessions of an Advertising Man" by David Ogilvy[1]

Advertising professionals have often been criticized for using the persuasive power of words and images in an unethical fashion. Advertising is very visible in our society; therefore, it is almost inevitable that it would be the target of criticism. Some such criticisms may well be justified. In fact, one can easily find fault with the manner in which early patent medicine ads were written. The boisterous manner in which advertisers touted that certain tonics could cure anything from sore throats to cancer was bound to offend many.

On the other hand, advertising professionals have engaged in self-policing practices designed to prevent such offensive practices by the less-ethical members of the profession. The National Advertising Review Board (NARB), the National Association of Broadcasters (NAB) code, and the network clearance departments are only a few examples of the dedication to upholding ethical standards shown by most members of the advertising community. Some industries, through their own trade organizations have developed mechanisms to prevent offensive and deceptive advertising from reaching the public. Although these measures do not have regulatory power, they are very effective in signaling to members of the industry that such advertising messages are discouraged and often they are asked to discontinue such practices. Examples of such self-policing by an industry are The Beer Institute with a board comprised of industry representatives and independent members. The Beer Institute is charged with monitoring advertising by beer manufacturers and with responding to complaints sent to the institute by anyone objecting to specific advertising messages. Another example of self-regulation is voluntary code of conduct released in 2005 by Pharmaceutical Research Manufacturers of America. The draft of the document called for the selection of an independent panel of credible individuals to provide reviews of the proposed code of conduct.

---

[1]David Ogilvy, *Confessions of an Advertising Man.* (New York: Atheneum, 1963), 000.

Some advertising giants have spoken out against unethical practices. Both David Ogilvy and John O'Toole have published their thoughts on this subject and have suggested that much could still be done to create a better order in advertising's ethical house. This chapter is concerned with posing some ethical questions for consideration by advertising students. Many more are not addressed here. This chapter highlights only a few of the most common, and perhaps debated, questions. It is hoped that they will remind our future professionals that their responsibility is multifaceted. The tools available to advertisers are very powerful; they must be used for the purposes for which they were intended, or as Bob Lauterborn eloquently stated in the quote that began this chapter, "to help marketers to respond to consumers' needs efficiently and effectively."

SPECIFIC ISSUES IN ADVERTISING AND PUBLIC RELATIONS ETHICS

Advertising communication is designed to attract attention and to persuade. The function of persuasion itself has drawn the attention of ethical scholars throughout centuries. The fact that advertisers and others can use verbal or visual images to induce behavior has in itself a somewhat negative connotation. Philosophers have always advocated that those who utilize persuasion must bear the burden of proof that such activity is not harmful in any way to the audience for which it is intended.[2]

Advertising ethics, therefore, is concerned not only with the economic consequences of advertising actions, but also with the direct and indirect social and moral consequences they may have on the public in general. Critics argue that the act of advertising certain products may profoundly affect social values. An example of this argument is the recent debate on the appropriateness of advertising alcoholic beverages.

An examination of what has been written by advertising critics reveals several distinct areas of concern. This chapter will describe some of them.

The Ethics of Creativity

The development of advertising appeals and persuasive messages is aided by the creative ability, imagination, artistry, and wit of professionals. It is no mere accident that advertising has been compared numerous times to show business. Pictures and words, images and double entendres, appeals to the emotions and fears have all been generously utilized to secure the attention and the favor of consumers.

The creative aspect of advertising is therefore one of the most vulnerable areas of advertising ethics concern. The responsibility of those who create advertising messages is not merely to ensure that they employ only truthful statements; it goes farther than that. If the overall impression created by the advertising message is misleading to the public, the advertiser could be found in violation of federal regulations. However, an even stricter could be applied by the review process used by major networks, other media agencies, and the NAB.

In addition, some statements and images, even if truthful or not misleading, should be avoided because they are socially offensive. Examples are advertisements that portray women or minorities in a disparaging or socially unacceptable fashion. Cartoon figures such as the Frito-Lay "Frito Bandito" are not immune to such scrutiny.

---

[2]Donald W. Jugenheimer, "Ethical Rights and the Advertising Audience," in *Papers on Advertising and Ethics,* Advertising Working Papers 12 (Urbana: University of Illinois, May 1982), 11.

Explicit words and images are also to be used with discretion and caution. Until recently, any type of nudity was considered socially unacceptable. Now a more common sight in commercials, nudity is not as offensive to most as profanity. Although the specific determination of what is socially acceptable varies with time and place, it is important to note that the creative element of advertising should always respect the social standards of morality and good taste.

To be considered ethically acceptable, therefore, advertising messages should be truthful, should not mislead, and should not offend social standards of morality and good taste. It is unfortunate that this rule is often violated by advertisers. Recent examples of commercial messages that have been targets of criticism are the Boston Prepatory Company ad and the sexually explicit advertising campaign for Calvin Klein products in the early 1990s.

Advertising Controversial Products

Another ethical problem confronting advertisings has to do with the nature of some of the products they promote. Among such products are cigarettes and alcoholic beverages.

Society does not prohibit the manufacture of sale of cigarettes. The advertising and promotion of cigarettes, however, is both regulated and opposed by some groups as an undesirable practice. Cigarettes have been proven harmful to health and the promotion of a product that may cause cancer is considered unethical because it involves the use of persuasion. Some advertisers have spoken out against this practice and have refused to handle cigarette accounts. David Ogilvy made public his stand on the issue several years ago. Other advertisers have joined in recent years.

Sam Blum in a 1966 article mentions that there is a code of ethics observed by the cigarette industry. This code insists that advertising neither appeal directly to teenagers nor be based on health claims.[3] This is not enough, however, for those who feel that cigarettes should not be advertised at all. Advertising professionals, therefore, are called on in this case to establish and observe ethical rules that go beyond legal responsibilities and acceptable industry standards.

A similar problem is the advertising of alcoholic beverages. Although it would be difficult to find a large constituency proposing or supporting a ban on the sale and consumption of alcoholic beverages, many support strong restrictions on advertising for such products. The rationale in the case of alcoholic beverages is very similar to that for cigarettes.

Is it fair to expect advertisers to refrain voluntarily from promoting such products? Should they be empowered to police social behavior and limit the ability of cigarette and alcoholic beverage manufacturers to use mass communications? The question has not been clearly answered and will be debated for years to come, or until regulatory agencies intervene and claim such responsibility.

Recently, the U.S. Government, the American Medical Association, and the public in general have become concerned with the increasing problems of obesity among the U.S. population, but particularly as it affects children. Advertising, especially fast-food advertising, has been blamed for promoting the consumption or overconsumption of food products that are high in calories and low in nutrition. The National Academies Institute of Medicine in 2005 recommended a long-term campaign to educate the public about making healthy

---

[3]Sam Blum, "An Ode to the Cigarette Code," *Harper's,* March 1966, 60–63.

choices. Beginning in 2006, members of the Federal Communication Commission participated in a task force on media and childhood obesity, in an effort to build consensus regarding voluntary steps and goals to be taken by the public and private sector to combat childhood obesity (http://www.fcc.gov/obesity).

The issue of the role that advertising might play in childhood obesity is still being discussed by psychologists, doctors, regulatory agencies, and elected political officials. It is one more example of how social issues may directly affect the advertising industry.

The Ethics of Using Media

Several ethical issues are directly derived from the use of media by advertising professionals. Among those most debated are advertising during programs directed strictly at children, advertising that is intrusive or annoying because of its frequency, advertising that is intrusive or annoying because of its frequency, advertising within programs or media vehicles with objectionable content, and using the persuasive powers of the media to promote products that are not socially or economically desirable. One example would be the products that are not environmentally sound, such as cleaning products that pollute the water supply. Another example is the advertising of premiums in cereal boxes to promote sales of overpriced items and encourage brand loyalty. This economically undesirable behavior has been attributed to the promotion and advertising of major national brands. We will briefly discuss each of these.

ADVERTISING DIRECTED TO CHILDREN

This topic has had wide public debate. Children are considered more vulnerable and impressionable than average consumers, and advertising directed to them is objectionable on that basis alone. In addition, when advertising messages can be confused with programs, or when they promote products that could be misused or are seen as objectionable (such as drugs or candy), the issue of ethics becomes even more urgent.

Several ethical codes for advertising directed to children have been proposed by advocacy groups, networks, and even advertising practitioners. The debate is still very much alive and will continue for years to come.

INTRUSIVE OR ANNOYING ADVERTISING

Intrusive or annoying advertising—advertising in which the public is repeatedly exposed to the same message—is also a target of debate. However, the controversy in this case is not as heated as that surrounding some of the other issues discussed in this chapter. Intrusive advertising is objectionable to those people who believe it constitutes an invasion of privacy. Advertisers argue that to get consumers' attention, they should be allowed to place advertisements within programs and as frequently as they deem necessary.

ADVERTISING PLACED IN MEDIA VEHICLES OF OBJECTIONABLE CONTENT

Examples of media vehicles that are considered by some as objectionable because of their content are the Playboy channel; MTV; and some periodicals such as *The National Enquirer, Playboy* magazine, or tabloids and magazines with explicit sexual or extremely violent content. This advertising is opposed because it indirectly supports such vehicles economically. It is argued that the objectionable media would not exist if it were not for the income derived from advertising. Although there is no clear evidence that this is so, it is important to underscore that when advertising is viewed as supporting media considered immoral or socially undesirable, it becomes an ethical issue.

THE PERSUASIVE POWERS OF THE MEDIA

Finally, as media vehicles become more powerful channels of persuasion and entertainment, their usage for the purpose of selling products will be more closely scrutinized by society. In addition, the use of powerful persuasive techniques to promote products such as expensive and faddish toys will be the subject of discussion. Is it ethical to promote gambling even though the practice itself is legal? This topic as well is left to the discretion and judgment of advertising professionals.

These are among the most common ethical issues deriving from the practice of advertising itself. The list is not comprehensive, but it is designed to point out that the content, mechanics, and intended audience of advertising are all important factors when deciding its ethical parameters. Just as lawyers and accountants do, advertisers must consider all these issues when developing a code of ethics for themselves.

Although there is no evidence that subliminal advertising works, advertisers must regularly address a skeptical public's concern about this issue. Failure to deal openly and frankly with the issue of subliminal advertising will only serve to increase public skepticism.

ADVERTISING AND THE INTERNET

The explosion in the use of the Internet by advertisers has spurred concerns regarding consumer protection from false and misleading messages and abuses affecting consumers' privacy. The FTC has taken an active role in applying to Internet advertising the same basic rules that were established to protect consumers from false and deceptive advertising in traditional media. In addition, online ads are subject to more specific rules regarding disclosure. Because most consumers do not visit every page of a Web site, advertisers must provide disclosures, whenever possible, on the same screen as the advertisement. Additional FTC rules specifically address how advertisers should use hyperlinks and other methods of advertising click-throughs (http://www.keytlaw.com/FTC/Rules/ftc0005001.htm).

Consumer online privacy is also protected. In May 2000, the FTC issued a report: "Privacy Online: Fair Information Practices in the Electronic Martketplace." Although these rules do not address exclusively privacy violations that may result from advertising practices, they prevent advertisers from collecting information from consumers without the consumers' express consent.

In the future, we will continue to see concern with communication tactics employed by advertising and public relations professionals when using new technology and digital media.

ETHICAL ISSUES INVOLVING CLIENT/AGENCY RELATIONSHIPS

Advertisers aggressively pursue their clients. The same is not true of other professional groups. We do not see accounting firms or law firms making cold calls on prospective clients who are using the services of a competitor. Advertising agencies, however, frequently approach accounts of competitors and try to attract their business through what are commonly known as "speculative presentations."

Other advertising practices might also be viewed as less than desirable if used by other professional groups. For example, the commission given by media to advertisers could be considered "kickback" as opposed to fair compensation for services.

Criticisms have highlighted those practices and others, such as the misuse of research data and the "industrial espionage," called by some "marketing intelligence," which is often utilized to attract clients to an agency.

The issue of whether advertising professionals have a more lax code of ethics than other professionals has surfaced so often that periodicals such as *Advertising Age* have conducted occasional surveys to assess standards of behavior. An example of such a survey can be seen in Exhibit 17.2.

The discussion is viewed by many as a nonissue. Ethical behavior should be the same for all professionals, regardless of whether they practice advertising or accounting.

Exhibit 17.2 ■ How Do Your Ethics Compare with N.Y.?

Do the ethical standards of advertising people in the Big Apple differ from those of their fellow professional elsewhere in the U.S.?

If you'll answer the questionnaire, we'll find out.

Members of the Advertising Club of New York are completing a similar questionnaire, and *Advertising Age* wants to compare their answers with a national sample.

Ad Age also will supply regional breakouts of the responses so that the ad industry will be able to point to parts of the country in which ethical standards seemingly are highest, lowest or merely borderline.

The questionnaire was created for an ethics seminar being hosted by the Center for Communications on March 16.

Circle your response to each ethical situation.

Deadline is March 19.

Send completed questionnaires to: Ethics Survey, *Advertising Age,* 220 E. 42nd St., Suite 930, New York 10017.

1. **You are competing** with three other agencies for the Magnasonic consumer electronics business. Its chief competitor is Rolavision, handled by XYZ Advertising. XYZ's account supervisor on Rolavision has interviewed with you recently for a job. You hire him, specifically to help with the Magnasonic pitch.

    1. Ethical   Unethical

2. **A good friend** of yours calls and says an associate of his is looking for a new advertising agency. His associate knows little about advertising and has asked for his advice. He offers to recommend your company provided he will be paid a finder's fee of $20,000 if you land the business. You agree.

    2. Ethical   Unethical

Continued

Exhibit 17.2 ■ Continued

---

3. **Same as question 2,** but your friend is in the business of consulting for clients looking for new advertising agencies, and he is being paid a fee by his client.

   3. **Ethical**   **Unethical**

4. **Your agency is one** of four semifinalists asked to participate in a competition for a new product assignment from a major toy marketer. While the agency has had experience in marketing to children, this assignment would be your agency's first in the toy category—and with a leading manufacturer. During a final briefing your prospective client discloses that the "new product" is a compatible set of war toys complete with pseudo-ammunition, guns, etc. Your agency decides that it will accept this assignment if it is awarded to them.

   4. **Ethical**   **Unethical**

5. **You and two other** agencies are in the final stages of a competition. Part of your pitch has to do with recommending and supporting a new marketing strategy. Late one evening, a few days before the scheduled presentation, you are proofing your slides at a slide supply house. By accident, you are handed a fairly complete set of slides put together for one of your competitors. You have enough time to examine and get the gist of it before returning the set to the supplier, who is embarrassed at his mistake. When you return to the office, you make significant changes in the way your agency presents itself so as to attack your competitor's recommended strategy in a direct and forceful manner without, of course, revealing to anyone that you have information on your competitor's actual recommendations.

   5. **Ethical**   **Unethical**

6. **Same as question 5,** except your competitor's slides are in a file folder on the worktable next to you. You have to wait for the supplier to leave the room before you peek at them.

   6. **Ethical**   **Unethical**

7. **You've been invited** to compete for the business of a retail chain that has headquarters in the Southeast. The chain is run autocratically by its 75-year-old founder. Every member of his senior management team is white, male, and more than 40 years old. In past discussions, you've come away with a clear impression that they are narrow-minded, too. As it happens, a few months ago your agency lost the business of a large New York retail chain. You did excellent work for the chain, and the account supervisor who knows all about the business still works for you but has been without an assignment for more than three months. The problem is, the account supervisor is a 35-year-old woman. You decide not to use her in your presentation.

   7. **Ethical**   **Unethical**

8. **Same as question 7** except that your account supervisor is male, 45 years old and black. You decide not to include him in the presentation.

   8. **Ethical**   **Unethical**

Continued

Exhibit 17.2 ▪ Continued

9. **You agency is looking** to hire a senior account management person. You interview a management supervisor who promises to bring with him one of the accounts he is responsible for at his current agency if you hire him at the salary he is asking. You hire him, and the account comes to you.

   9. Ethical   Unethical

10. **You and three other** agencies are in a competition for a major airline account. As luck would have it, a good friend of yours is sleeping with the secretary for the airline's marketing VP. She's very indiscreet and tells your friend about the exciting things going back and forth at her company during the review, including the individual views of the members of the members of the airline's agency selection committee. Your friend gives you feedback on all your meetings and on your competitor's meetings with the airline.

   10. Ethical   Unethical

11. **Same as question 10,** except your friend asks for a consulting fee, with a bonus if you get the business.

    11. Ethical   Unethical

12. **Your agency is being** considered by a group of restaurants that offers "good tasting" food at low prices. They ask your company to develop a better "price" story since they will soon be cutting their prices even further. When the agency delves into the reasons why the company can continue to serve the same "good tasting" food at even lower prices, it learns that the group has found a supplier of slightly "off" food. While the food is not yet spoiled, it is close to that stage and requires significant additional seasonings and preservatives. Your agency accepts the assignment.

    12. Ethical   Unethical

Check one:

☐ Advertiser   ☐ Agency   ☐ Media   ☐ Other

Company location: _____

Source: Reprinted with permission from the February 29, 1998 issue of *Advertising Age*. Copyright © Crain Communications Inc., 1988.

A PROPOSED SOLUTION TO THE QUESTION OF ADVERTISING ETHICS

According to Donald W. Jugenheimer, a code of ethical standards can be designed to provide a foundation for the measurement of the practice of advertising.[4] He bases his proposed code on three principles exposed by LaCroix.[5]

Four major kinds of rights established by ethical scholars would comprise this code: contract rights, merit rights, positive rights, and dignity rights. *Contract rights* are related to any sort of agreement on the part of those establishing a business or private relationship. *Merit rights* are those that accrue to people who have performed actions deserving of reward. The rewards are determined by the specific standards existing for the practice in question, ranging from sports practices to religious practices, for example. *Positive rights* are those derived from legislative or judicial action. Finally, *dignity rights* are those belonging to persons simply because they are persons within a specific social environment.

This system awards rights to parties independent from the specific professional environment under discussion. Therefore, ethical behavior could be assessed on the merits of the behavior itself and not because of its ties to the practice of advertising.

ETHICS IN PUBLIC RELATIONS

More important than ethical codes of public relations is the ethical behavior of the practitioner. Public relations professionals must have a high personal standard of ethics that carries over into their own work. Public relations professionals must have the will to be ethical, intending not to ignore others, but rather to be honest and trustworthy. In addition, they must make every effort to avoid actions that would have adverse consequences for others.

The Public Relations Society of America publishes a code of ethics for practitioners. The code is built on the fundamental core values of advocacy, honesty, loyalty, professional development, and objectivity. The code advises professionals to:

- Protect and advance the free flow of accurate and truthful information
- Foster informed decision making through open communication
- Protect confidential and private information
- Promote healthy and fair competition among professionals
- Avoid conflicts of interest
- Work to the strengthen the public's trust in the profession Public Relations Society of America, PRSA, Code of Ethics, http://www.prsa.org/aboutprsa/ethics/

In addition, the code specifies ethical conduct in everyday tasks and challenges. Conflicts may arise when public relations professionals must deal with a crisis management situation. The political difference between the interests of a corporation and the protection of the public may cause public relations professionals to weight carefully their role and their responsibilities. Their duty to truthfulness and fair and appropriate information should prevail in any circumstance. That is why the personal ethical values of a public relations professional are first and foremost the principles that must guide his/her behavior and actions.

Source: Public Relations Ethics: A Simpler (but not simplistic) Approach to the Complexities by Karey Harrison and Chris Galloway, Prism, #3, 2005.

---

[4]Ibid, 12.

[5]W. L. LaCroix, *Principles for Ethics in Business,* rev. ed. (Washington, DC: University Press of America, 1979).

CONCLUSION

E. B. Weiss stated, "In advertising, the too common tendency is to ask 'Is it legal?' If the answer is yes, then presumably advertising has demonstrated its responsibility to society. But what modern society is demanding is that advertising hew more closely to an ethical line, not merely to legal guideposts."[6] This position is shared and supported by many professionals and academicians in advertising. The development of a code of ethics is not an easy task. By definition, ethical behavior is determined by social values, and those are subject to individual interpretation. It is possible, however, to agree on some basic principles of behavior that are acceptable by vast majority in the profession.

The importance of ethical behavior cannot be belittled or ignored. The survival of professional standards is to the survival of the profession itself. If advertisers are to achieve the respect and stability they desire, they cannot wait for regulation to determine what is acceptable behavior in advertising. They must be proactive and mature, enforcing the type of standards demanded by social interests, human decency, and moral imperatives.

SUGGESTED READINGS

Baker, Sam S. *The Permissible Lie.* Boston: Beacon Press, 1968.
Bayles, Michael D. *Professional Ethics.* Belmont, CA: Wadworth Publishing Company, 1981.
Capitman, William G. "Morality in Advertising: A Public Emperative." *MSU Business Topics* (Spring 1971): 21–26.
"Ethics and Marketing." In Lectures from a Symposium Sponsored by the Merrill Cohen Memorial Fund and the Graduate School of Business Administration of the University of Minnesota, edited by J. Russell Nelson and Aubrey Strickland. Minneapolis: University of Minnesota, 1966.
Kottman, E. John. "Truth and the Image of Advertising." *Journal of Marketing* 33 (October 1969): 84–92.
Stevens, Edward. *Business Ethics.* New York: Paulist Press, 1979.

ETHICAL CONSIDERATIONS

Exercises

1. In 1991, Phone Programs USA broadcast an advertisement directed to children for the Phone Program's RoboCop Phone 900 number. The RoboCop character in the commercial urged viewers to help him fight the drug lords, stating, "Your telephone is linked to my weapon system. Call now to activate." The NAD Children's Advertising Review Unit (CARU) questioned the spot because it said it could raise unrealistic expectations among children. Do you agree with CARU's objection? What do you feel Phone Programs USA should do?

Source: Janice Kelly, "NARB to hear Alpo, Gilette Cases," *Advertising Age,* June 24, 1991, 54.

2. After the sales success of some products featured in films, many advertisers are pursuing product placement as an alternative to media purchases. There is growing resistance among consumer advocates, however, to the practice of product placement. It is argued that product placement is another form of subliminal advertising and does not convey any

---

[6]E. W. Weiss, "Needed Soon: Mature Advertising for a Mature Society, " *Advertising Age,* March 1, 1971, 33.

relevant information to consumers. Product placement, they say uses emotional tools to persuade people to consume products they do not need. What is your position on this subject? Are the consumer advocates' arguments legitimate?

3. A New York organization called the Council on Economic Priorities has sold 200,000 copies of a guide called *Shopping for a Better World.* This 132-page pamphlet lists 1,300 products in alphabetical order and indicates through a special code whether the manufacturer of the product is engaged in practices some may deem unethical or objectionable. Such practices include trading with South Africa, failing to protect the environment, and catching dolphins in fishing nets. Not many products commonly sold by supermarkets are immune to the pamphlet's scrutiny. Do you feel consumers should be informed about corporate practices that may be morally or socially objectionable? Should advertising professionals decline to handle certain accounts because of such corporate practices? Comment.

Source: Joe Queenan, "Ethical Shopping," *Forbes,* April 17, 1989, 80–81.

4. A pet food manufacturer was notified by one of its division managers that a chemically tainted ingredient had been introduced when manufacturing a batch of dry cat food. The ingredient was only 5% of the total content of the cat food, but it could cause severe stomach and intestinal problems for cats if they were given the food in normal day feedings. Over 300,000 bags of the cat food had already reached retail stores throughout the United States. The problem was discussed at the top management level and a decision was made to recall the tainted food, inform the public of the dangers of feeding their pets with it and give all consumers that had already purchased the tainted food a coupon that could be exchanged for a free bag of food that was not tainted. The public relations office of the company was charged with developing appropriate press releases about the issue and also additional informational materials for pet owners in general. Please develop the material requested by the management of the company.

Case 17.1

The Maryland State Planning Council on Developmental Disabilities[1]

Cathy Raggio, Director of the Maryland State Planning Council on Developmental Disabilities (MD), and Barry Smith, President of Smith Burke & Azzam Advertising (SB&A), had reached an impasse in their meeting to discuss the approval of a television commercial. SB&A, a large, full-service agency based in Baltimore, had recently agreed to handle the council as public service account *pro bono,* for no compensation. Since the relationship had been warm up to that point, the impasse came as somewhat of a surprise to everyone involved.

MD had contacted SB&A for assistance with a marketing problem through the Advertising Association of Baltimore (a local trade organization made up of agencies and media and production suppliers). MD was seeking generate support and understanding among the general public for people with disabilities. Such understanding and support were deemed critical to promoting full social inclusion and additional employment opportunities for this segment of the population.

In seeking to affect popular support, SB&A's proposed strategy was direct: exclusive reliance on television to deliver an emotional message. A single 30-second public service announcement (PSA) would be developed and aired in local markets. The purpose of the spot ("Debbie") was to illustrate that people with disabilities were not disabled in terms of their value to society and to personalize the situation faced by adults with disabilities. (See Exhibit 17.1.1).

At the beginning of the meeting to review the agency's recommendations, Raggio and her staff had all responded enthusiastically to the proposed plan. Raggio's immediate response to Smith's description of the commercial was, "Barry, as you describe the action, this should be truly moving commercial that would hit people head on. It's just great! Thank you so much for this. When can we start production?"

Smith indicated that the agency would begin the search immediately for a girl to play the role of "Debbie" by contacting appropriate actresses on file at the agency plus a number of model and talent agencies. At that point in the discussion a puzzled look came over Raggio's face. She strongly objected to the use of anyone other than a person with a disability in the role of "Debbie." Raggio explained, "One of our missions is to serve persons with disabilities by helping other people in the general population understand what it's like to be disabled. Who would better communicate this than an actual person with a disability? If we were to use an actress and just put her in a wheelchair and the public found out, the Council would look very foolish. I'm sorry, but we cannot approve anyone appearing as Debbie except a real person with a disability."

Smith responded by pointing out that the agency wanted the best actress—disabled or not. He stressed that he could help disabled people more by creating a great commercial than by hiring one disabled person for a single PSA spot with a talent fee of $200. Further, he explained that his agency had built its reputation on outstanding creative work. To produce such work required that clients trust the agency's judgment in the creative area. Finally, he stated that the agency would refuse to do the spot unless it was unrestricted in the selection of talent.

Raggio shook her head and said there was nothing more to discuss.

Smith concluded the meeting by stating, "Well, I trust you understand where we're coming from on this and why. I hope you will change your minds after you have had time to think it over. Our agency sincerely wants to produce what would be most effective and, hence, best for the Maryland Council on Developmental Disabilities and the people you serve. Let's discuss this again tomorrow after we've both had a chance to mull it over some."

---

[1] The case was written by John H. Murphy, The University of Texas at Austin. The case is intended for use in generating class discussion and not illustrate either the effective or ineffective handing of an administrative situation. Used by permission of Maryland Department of Disabilities. The author thanks Barry L. Smith and Cathy Raggio for their help in developing this case.

Exhibit 17.1.1 ■ "Debbie" Maryland State Planning Council on Developmental Disabilities :30

"I'm very proud to introduce, me. Ta da!"
"I'm Debbie."

(Debbie speaks self-consciously)
"I'm 17. I love Duran Duran."
"I hate my hair."

"I'm easy to talk to."
"Let's face it. I'm adorable!" (smiles)

"So, remember if we happen to meet."
"This is me."
"And this is just a chair. OK?"

"OK?" (asks sincerely with troubled look)

Name _____ Date _____

QUESTIONS FOR DISCUSSION AND REVIEW

1. Would the use of an actress to play the part of a disabled person in the commercial constitute deceptive advertising?

2. How does the fact that the MD is a small state agency and a public service account for the agency enter into an evaluation of the situation?

3. Should the client meet its agency's demands and agree to give the agency creative control over casting?

4. Is there some sort of compromise that might be agreeable to both parties?

5. How important is creative control by an advertising agency in developing outstanding advertising? Are there situations where such control is more important than others?

_____

_____

_____

_____

6. How often do similar situations surface in client/agency relationships regarding creative control? What about over other issues?

_____

_____

_____

_____

Case 17.2

Abel, Atwater and Combs Advertising and Public Relations[1]

Robert Abel, a principal of Abel, Atwater and Combs (AAC), was delighted when an intermediate-sized Santa Clara Valley vintner invited AAC to compete with three other agencies for its account. Although the vintner's ad budget of $200,000 was not impressive, Abel believed the prospective client held considerable potential for growth, and the account would add prestige to the agency. Also, as a wine connoisseur, he relished the thought of working with this vintner due to the wine's excellent reputation.

AAC was a well-established San Francisco advertising and public relations agency with media billings of just over $23 million the previous year. The agency had 58 employees and served 37 clients. The agency's clients had traditionally been weighed toward business-to-business and industrial accounts. Its largest account was a manufacturer of commercial transportation and industrial vehicles. In addition, AAC handled a wide range of smaller consumer and retail accounts. These accounts included a regional supermarket chain and two non-competitive automobile dealerships. AAC also had a few clients for whom they only did PR and the client's advertising was handled either in-house or by another ad agency.

Abel was somewhat surprised to discover that his partner, Judith Atwater, did not share his enthusiasm for pitching the wine account. Atwater quoted statistics from MADD (Mothers Against Drunk Driving) in expressing her concerns about pitching any alcoholic beverage.

Atwater: "Alcohol-related automobile accidents killed 24,000 people and injured 670,000 others last year. I don't know how much of that was due to wine advertising, but I'm not sure I want any part of promoting alcoholic beverages, even if we could use the business. Two of my son's best friends at Palo Alto High School were seriously injured last summer after a drinking party. I shudder every time I think about it."

Abel: "Judy, we're not talking about getting people drunk and encouraging them to drive cars. Nor would we be suggesting consumption by teenagers. Further, there is a real question about the effects of booze advertising. I believe those who point out that it just causes brand switching and does not increase consumption. Besides, we need this account and if we don't pitch for it, someone else will be happy to take the account."

Atwater: "Bob, those are simply rationalizations. I don't think anyone could deny that alcoholic beverage advertising glamorizes drinking and portrays it as an important part of today's lifestyles. Teenagers seem particularly susceptible to influence by such advertising. Given all the negative consequences associated with drinking, this is troubling. I'm not at all certain that going after this account would be the right course for us to follow. Over the past several months I've been asking myself some questions about the ethics of advertising any alcoholic beverages."

Abel: "Although we do not have much time to decide if we are going to pitch the account, I can tell this is an important issue for you. I respect that. Why don't we put together a position paper laying out the pros and cons of having an alcoholic beverage client? It seems to me that this paper should address both the issues of the ethics of helping to promote alcohol consumption and the effects of such advertising. This would help focus our thinking in deciding whether or not we want to go after this account."

---

[1] This case was written by John H. Murphy, The University of Texas at Austin. The case is designed to serve as the basis for classroom discussion and not to illustrate either the effective or ineffective handling of an administrative situation. The identity of the firm involved and the situation have been disguised.

Name _____ Date _____

QUESTIONS FOR DISCUSSION AND REVIEW

1. Are Atwater's misgivings about working on an alcoholic beverage account reasonable? Is it appropriate for an advertising person to express such concerns? Why or why not?

   _____
   _____
   _____
   _____

2. What key ethical, business, and practical issues or considerations should be considered by Abel and Atwater in reaching a decision about whether to pitch the wine account? Which of these issues or considerations are most important? Why?

   _____
   _____
   _____
   _____

3. Should the agency pitch the wine account? What rationale supports your recommendation?

   _____
   _____
   _____
   _____

4. What other product or service categories logically could pose the same or similar types of dilemmas for advertising and marketing people?

   _____
   _____
   _____
   _____

Case 17.3

Tropical Distributing Company[1]

Mr. George Bales, VP, Marketing for the Tropical Distributing Company (TDC), had been searching for a way to expand sales of the firm's rum in the Los Angeles and San Francisco metropolitan markets. Therefore, he was intrigued by a guerrilla marketing strategy recommended by his firm's advertising agency Marx & Arnold (M&A). At the same time, Mr. Bales realized that the strategy was not without risks.

M&A recommended that professional actors be employed on weekends to create favorable word-of-mouth advertising for a new drink—a martini made with rum instead of gin or vodka. Working alone, or in some cases in groups, the actors would enter trendy clubs, bars and restaurants pretending to be ordinary customers and order the yet-to-be-named drink. If the bartender said that s/he had never heard of the drink, the actor(s) would express dismay and describe how to make the rum martini using Tropical's brand. In addition, the undercover sales agents would offer to treat other patrons to Tropical rum martinis.

The actors would be paid $5,000 each for working weekends during the two-month promotion. The actors' salaries plus the cost of drinks, food, taxi and generous tips plus an agency supervision fee would constitute the total $230,000 cost of the recommended promotion.

The agency's proposed on-premise promotion targeted 25–44 year old drinkers and was scheduled to begin six months after an off- and on-line media advertising campaign introducing the Tropical rum martini was launched. The new drink would also be promoted through more conventional means such as posters, bar glasses, napkins, and so on. Finally, if Mr. Bales approved the plan, employees of both TDC and M&A would also be encouraged to visit clubs, bars and restaurants and talk up Tropical's rum martini.

M&A maintained that their guerrilla marketing promotion plan would be a direct way of sampling customers and establishing the drink with bartenders. The agency also suggested that their proposed promotion would be a more effective investment than other forms of marketing communication. However, Mr. Bales was concerned about the ethics of the agency's plan. For example, he wondered if customers should have the right to know when they are subjected to such commercial persuasion? Mr. Bales was also concerned about the issue of how the promotion might backfire?

---

[1] This case was written by John H. Murphy, The University of Texas at Austin. The case is designed to serve as the basis for classroom discussion and not to illustrate either the effective or ineffective handling of an administrative situation. The identities of the firms involved and the situation have been disguised.

Name _____ Date _____

QUESTIONS FOR DISCUSSION AND REVIEW

1. What are the ethical, moral, legal and practical considerations that should be focused on in evaluating the proposed on-premise promotion?

2. How might the promotion backfire? How likely is some sort of problem to occur? What contingency plans should Tropical and their agency have established to respond to such problems?

3. Using the same budget, what are two alternative promotions that might be considered?

4. Should Mr. Bales approve Marx & Arnold's proposed on-premise promotion?

Index

Page references in *italics* indicate exhibits.
Page references followed by "n" indicate footnotes.

A

A la carte services. *See* Advertising agency
Abercrombie and Fitch, 408
Account Planner, 168–69
Account Planning, 169n
Account Planning Group, 169
Ad Age, 359n
Ad spending, 26, *134–35*
Adams, Russell, 213n
Adidas, 406
AdMap, 544n
Adventures in Relevance Marketing, 315n
Advertainment. *See* Branded entertainment
Advertiser, The, 286n, 544n, 547n
Advertising. *See also* Advertising promotions; Internet advertising; Marketing; New media; Off-line advertising; Traditional media
  developments in, 405–10
  economy and, 24, 28
  environment of, 129
  industry expenditures and, *218*
  media and, 281
  national brand vs generic, 24–25, 133
  off-line and, 61
  on-line and, 61
  products and services and, 23–25
  ROI and, 491–94
  sales promotion and, 281, 286
  target audiences and, 212
Advertising Account Planning: A Practical Guide, 169n
Advertising Age, 26, 27n, 104n, 123n, 167n, 186n, 209n, 210n, 212n, *217, 219–21,* 285n, 319n, 410n, 452n, 453n, 492n, 493n, 494, 494n, 548n, 568–70, 572n

Advertising agency. *See also* Compensation
  client communication and, 547
  client feedback, 546
  client relations and, 539–41, 546–47
  considerations for use of, 541
  creative services of, 545
  ethics and, 567–70
  full-service shops, 539, 540–41
  IBP programs and, 537, 546
  performance reviews of, 537, 546
  proactivity and, 547
  recommendations of, 544–45
  selection of, 537, 542–43
  specialty shops and, 539, 540–41
  strategic thinking, 547
Advertising Agency Business, The, 541n, 545n
Advertising and Integrated Brand Promotion, 281n
Advertising budget
  advertising to sales ratio and, *125–27*
  all-you-can-afford method, 133
  competitive-party method, 129–31
  consumer appeals and, 133
  controversial issues and, 133–34
  expenditures and, 27, 128
  forming of, traditional, 124–33
  measured ad spending and, *135*
  media and, 27–28
  national brand *vs.* generic, 133
  new media and, 134
  objective-and-task method, 132–33
  objectives of, 124, 127, 136
  peckham's formula and, 128–29
  percentage-of-sales method and, 124–28, 132, 153
  plans and, 5, 25
  promotions and, 25
  salespeople and, 257
  tasks and, 132
  traditional media and, 134
  trends in, 133–35
Advertising campaigns
  media strategies and, 210
  public relations and, 354

  research and, 64
  theme of, 172
Advertising Communication and Promotion Management, 129n
Advertising compensation. *See* Compensation
Advertising function, 24
Advertising Management Decision Making, 8
Advertising message, 26–27
Advertising plan, 25–28
  advertising messages and, 26–27
  budget and, 25
  marketing mix, 25
  media budget and, 27–28
  objectives of, 25–26
Advertising promotions
  brand name vs generic, 24
  context and, 28
  function and, 23–24
  objectives and, 24, 25
  plan, example of, 28–30
  planning process and, 24–25
  process, 24–25
  role of, 23–25
  situation analysis and, 24, 25
  strategy and, 24, 28
  target market and, 24
Advertising research. *See* Research
Advertising Research Foundation, 405
Advertising Research: The State of the Art, 63n
Advertising to sales ratio, 124, *125–27*
Adweek, 457n
Agency compensation. *See* Compensation
AIO (activities, interests, opinions), 95, 170
Allen, Chris and Thomas O'Guinn, et al., 281
"Alliance for Magazine Accountability," 493
All-you-can-afford method, 133
Alternatives, definition of, 6
Amazon, 451
American Airlines, 316

American Association of Advertising Agencies (AAAA), 542
American Dental Association, 172
American Express, 316
American Homebrewers Association Members, 407
American Idol, 97, 427
American Journal of Business, 493
American Medical Association, 565
American recession, 133
Amoco, 358
Amway, 256
An Introduction to Direct Marketing, 315n
A.N.A. The Advertiser, 123n
Anderson Analytics, 455
Animation Magazine, 411n
Applebee's, 459
Appropriation. See Advertising budget
Arnell Group, 548
Artzt, Edwin L., 68n, 123, 131, 286
Atlantic Ritchfield, 358
AT&T, 255
Audi, 173, *182–84,* 411
Audits, 355
Automatic interaction detector, 318
Automotive News, 456n
Auty, Susan and Charlie Lewis, 408n
Avon, 407

B
B to B, 457n
Bachman, Kay, 408n
Backer Spielvogel Bates, 23
Ball, Ryan, 411n
Ballantine Corporation, 319n
Bank of America, 406
Bar codes, 284
Barnes, Beth and Don Schultz, 15
Barnes, Brooks, 104n
Barnes, Louis B. and C. Roland Christensen, et al., 3n
Bazaarvoice, 495n
Beer Institute, The, 563
Bellenger, Dan and Ken Bernhardt, et al., 68n, 69n, 71n
Benchmark, 98, 491
Benetton, 26–27, 134
Bernbach, Bill, 167–68
Beverland, Michael and Francis Farrelly, et al., 547
Bhatnagar, Parja, 210n, 211n
Biba, Erin, 457n
Bickert, Jack, 315
"Big Name Brands in 'Hall of Shame'", 210n, 211n
Bird, Laura, 134n
BKG Youth, 210

Blasko, Vincent and Charles H. Patti, 132n
Bloom, Paul N. and Steve Hoeffler, et al., 407n
Blum, Sam, 565, 571n
BMW, 409
BNET, 539n
Bogart, Leo, 129
Boston Prepatory Company, 565
Boxworth, 100, 101, *102–4*
Boyd, Harper and Stanley Stasch, et al., 68n
Bozzell, 212
BP (British Petroleum), 358
BPAmoco, 358
Brand integration, 408
Brand personality, advertising strategy and, 172
Brand rape, 285
Branded entertainment. See also Product placement
  categories of, 410
  new media and, 405
  purpose of, 409
  traditional media and, 405
  vs product placement, 409
Brandweek, 406n, 456n, 492n
Brewers Association, 407
British Petroleum (BP), 358
Britoil, 358
Britt, Steuart H., 94
Budgets. See Advertising budget
Burger King, 27, 117, 456
Burnett, Leo, 545
Burns, Neal, 169n
Bush, Michael, 359n
Business Classics: Fifteen Key Concepts for Managerial Success, 13n
Business Horizons, 406n
Business Month, 281n
Business Source Complete, 539n, 540n, 541n
Businessweek Slide Shows and Multimedia, 459n
Businessweek.com, 458n, 459n
Butler, Shine, Stern & Partners, 173, *175–77*
Buzz analysis, 168
Byron, Ellen, 73n
Byron, Ellen and Suzanne Vranica, 31n, 73n

C
Calder, Bobby, 68
Calvin Klein, 565
Campbell's Soup, 133
Capital Area Food Bank, 455
Caporimo, James, 26
Career World, 455n

CareerBuilder, 548
Carmichael Lynch, 17
Carousel, 409
Carter, Stacy, 458n
Cartis Group, 495n
CARU (NAD Children's Advertising Review Unit), 572
Case analysis, 4
  alternatives and, 6
  decision maker, role of, 5
  decision tree, 5
  framework of, 5–8, *6*
  preparation of, 5
  process of, *7*
  written analysis of, 5
Case discussion method, 4–5
  purpose of, 4
  quantifiable concepts and, 5
Cellular phones. See Mobile media
Census of Business, 67
Charitable donations, 356. See also Public relations
Charity events. See Event sponsorship
Checkout scanner, 284, 281
Chili's restaurants, 15
Chi-square analysis, 100
Chronicle of Philanthropy, 455n
Chrysler, 27
City Hunters, 411
Claritas/PRIZM, 317
Click Forensics, 453
Click fraud, 452–53
ClickZ, 455n
Clifford, S., 452n
Cluster analysis, 318
CMG, 260
CNN, 460n
Coca-Cola, 27, 387–91, 393–94, 426–27, 434–35, 448, 459, 494, 544
Code of ethics. See Ethics
Cohen, Stanley E., 209
Collett, Pippa, 542n, 543n, 546n
Colley, Russell H., 94, 97
Comcast, 320n
Communication, 61, 131
  advertising agency and, 547
  digital media and, 491
  objectives and, 24, 64, 491
  public relations and, 354
  sales promotion and, 286
Communication force, 97
Communication specialists. See Advertising agency
Compensation, 537
  expenses, non salary, 544
  fee based models and, 494, 543
  ROI and, 494
  value based models and, 544
Competitive benefit, 96

Index

Competitive strategy, 255–56
Competitive-party method, 129–31
Cone, Steve, 319n
Confessions of an Advertising Man, 563
Connected research, 66
Consumer. *See also* Target market
   attitudes of, 284, 285–86
   behavior and, 24
   demands and, 283
   expectations and, 491
   personal profile, sample of, *185*
   personal profile of, 174
Consumer advocate, 168
Contests, 117, 263, 282, 373, 495
Contract rights, 571
Contracts, presentations and, *17*
Controversial Products. *See* Ethics
Controversial products, 565–66
Cooperative advertising, 282
Cooperative events, 356. *See also* Public relations
Copy platform, 171
Copy-testing research, 168
Cortez, John, 27n
Council on Economic Priorities, 573
Coupon Re-engineering Task Force, 284
Coupons, 282, 285, 286
Creating & Delivering Winning Advertising & Marketing Presentations, 18n, 20n
Creative strategies, 209
   account planning and, 168–69
   ad, sample of, *181, 184*
   brand brief, example of, *178–80*
   brand personality and, 172
   consumer benefit and, 171–72
   creative briefs and, *175,* 182–83, 545
   creative process and, 168
   development of, 5
   elements of, 172–73
   execution of, *173–74*
   objective evaluation of, 168
   objectives and, 171
   online banners and print ads, *176–77*
   personal profile and, 174, *185*
   purpose of, 167–68
   statement of, 167–68, 169, 170–74
   statements samples and, *173–85*
   support for, 172
Creative team, 168
Crest, 172, 288
Crisis management, 356–57
Crisis team, 357
Cross-promotion
   database marketing and, 318
   media budget and, 27
   sales promotions and, 282
Cultural fit, 543
Customer support, 256

D

Database marketing. *See also* Direct marketing
   development of, 317–18
   evaluation of, 319
   maintenance of, 318
   manipulation of, 318
   mathematical techniques and, 318
   myriad lists and, 317
   strategy of, 316
   systems of, 318
Decision tree, 5
Decision-making framework, 1
Defining Advertising Goals for Measured Advertising Results, 94n
Dell, 406
Delphi technique, 257
Demographics, 95, 170
Denk, M. and K. Oberecker, et al., 454n
Depth interview, 64, 65. *See also* Research
Digital media, 493. *See also* New media
   advertising budget and, 134
   marketing communication and, 453–54
   marketing integration and, 405
   public relations and, 354
   sales promotion and, 285
Dignity rights, 571
Direct mail advertising, 316
Direct marketing, 315, 320–21
   categories of, 316
   characteristics of, 315
   internet and, 316, 319–20
   lists and, 319
   management decisions and, 3, 5
   management problems and, 1
   programs and, 9, 61, 537, 540–41
   research and, 61
   responsibilities of, 316, *317*
   units of, 316
   viral marketing and, 61
Direct Marketing Manual, The, 315n, 318n
"Direct Marketing Trends for 2010," 319n, 320n
Direct response, 316
Direct-response vehicles, 214
Distribution factors, 129
Donnelly Marketing, 317
Dow Jones, 67
Dress for Success, 18n
Duncan, Tom and Sandra Moriarty, 18n, 20n
DVRs, 214, 459

E

Eastman Kodak, 27
Economist, The, 23n
Economy, 9, 23, 26, 31, 50, 73, 129, 224, 275, 342, 457
Elliott, Stuart, 548n
E-mail marketing, 285, 316, 319–20
Emarketer, 455n
Entertainment. *See* Branded entertainment
Equifax Marketing Services, 317
Ethics, 537
   advertising to children and, 565, 566
   client/agency relationships and, 567–70
   code of, 565, 567, 568, 571–72
   consequences and, 564
   controversial products and, 565–66
   creativity and, 564–65
   household goods and, 72
   industrial espionage and, 568
   internet and, 567
   intrusive advertising and, 566
   kickbacks and, 568
   marketing intelligence and, 568
   objectionable media forms and, 566–67
   persuasion of media and, 567
   public relations and, 571
   regulation and, 563
   speculative presentations, 568
   standards of behavior, *568–70*
Evaluative criteria
   advertising agencies and, 537, 546
   advertising presentations and, *22*
   creative strategies and, 168
   database marketing and, 319
   focus groups and, *71*
   IBP objectives and, 98–100
   marketing presentations and, *22*
   media and, 492
   salespeople and, 258
Event sponsorship, 355–56, 405–7. *See also* Advertising; Public relations
   business-to-business and, 406, 434, 443, 579
   forms of, 406
   impact of, 405–6
   life cycle model and, 406
   social causes and, 407
   success of, 407
Experiential marketing, 451, 457–58. *See also* Advertising
Experimentation, 64, 65. *See also* Research

F

Facebook, 66, 89, 91, 117, 189, 299, 373, 451, 463–64, 487–88, 452, 454–56, 548. *See also* Internet advertising; Social media
Fahey, Alison, 26n

Fam, Kim-Shyan and David S. Waller, 543
Family Circle, 288
Farley, James D., 456
"FCB Presentation Course," 12n, 13n, 69n
FDA (Food & Drug Administration), 67, 425–27
Federal Communication Commission (FCC), 566
Federal Trade Commission (FTC), 567
Feedback, 546
Felber, Eric, 412n
Feverick, Deborah and Dan Lothian, 460n
"Fighting Back Against Shoppers Guilt," 32n
Flow chart, 5
Focus groups. *See also* Research
  applications of, 69
  conduction of, 69, *70*
  evaluating research of, 69, *71*
  misapplications of, 69
  nature of, 68–69
  primary data and, 64
  sales forecasting and, 257
"Focus Groups and the Nature of Qualitative Marketing Research," 68n
Food & Drug Administration (FDA), 67
Food Channel, 132–33
Forbes, 573n
Ford Motor Co., 211, 456
Fox Latin American Channels, 411
Frankel & Co., 281
FRAT system, 318
Frito-Lay, 564
FTC (Federal Trade Commission), 426, 567
Fulgoni, Gian M. and Marie P. Mörn, 493n
Full service advertising agencies, 539, 540–41
"Fundamental Shifts in the U.S. Media and Advertising Industries," 214n

G
Gable, Tom, 547
Galloway, Chris and Karey Harrison, 571n
Gap, The, 97, 346
Garage, The, 408
Gardner, Herbert S., 541, 545
Gates, Roger H. and Carl D. McDaniels, 67
General Electric, 408
General Motors, 27–28, 411
Geographic market, 211
Georgia-Pacific, 453

GlaxoSmithKline (GSK), 457
Good Housekeeping, 212, 288
Google, 101, 134, 452–53, 477, 493–94, 540. *See also* Internet advertising
Grande, Hans and J. Jeffery Inman, et al., 284
Gray, Bill, 546
Green marketing, 31, 72
Greenberg, Herbert and David Mayer, 13
"Grooming the Next Generation of Management," 68n
Gross impressions, 213
Gross ratings points (GRPs), 213
Group discussion, 8
GSD&M Idea City, 96n, 97n, 173, *178–81*
Guerilla marketing
  as communication tool, 458
  as experiental tactic, 458–59
  IBP promotion mix and, 251
  ROI and, 492
Guide to Managerial Communication, 14n, 15n, 19n

H
Hammer, Susanna, 453n
Harper, C. Ross, 318n
Harper's, 565n, 571n
Harris, Thomas L., 354
Harrison's Reports, 408
Harvard Business Review, 13
Hasbro, 186
Hein, Kenneth, 406n
Hey Mr. Whipple, Squeeze This!, 171n
Hey Whipple, Squeeze This. A Guide to Creating Great Advertising, 14n
Hierarchy-of-effects model, 97, *99*
Hodgson, Richard, 315
Hoff, Ron, 12n, 13n, 69n
Home Depot, 407
Hoovers, 67
Hopkins, Claude C., 405
Horovitz, Bruce, 459n
Horsky, Sharon and Steven C. Michael, et al., 540, 541n
Hosford, Christopher, 539n
Houk, Lou, 281
House Party, 457
"How to Make Agency Presentations," 14n, 15n, 16n, 19n, 21n
Hulu, 452
Hume, Scott, 287n

I
I, Robot, 411–12
IBP objectives
  adoption of, 100
  assumptions and, 100
  competitive benefit and, 96

consistency of, 100
consumer purchase process and, 99
contents of, 96–97
effects of, 97–98
hierarchy of effects model and, *99*
measurements of, 98–100
programs and, 93
scope of, 93–94
statement, sample of, 100–101
statement of, 94–95
SWOT analysis and, 93
target audience and, 96–96
Ideation process, 168
IMS, 492
Incident response process, 357
Industrial espionage, 568
In-house advertising department, 540–41
Institute of Practitioners in Advertising, 542n
Integrated marketing communication, 492
Interactive media, 128, 136, 334
Interactive television, 214
International Journal of Advertising, 454n
International Journal of Market Research, 66n
Internet advertising. *See also* Social media; Viral marketing; Web based marketing
  ad spending and, *135*
  brand identification and, 453
  budget and, 134
  click fraud and, 452
  digital advertising, 453–54
  direct marketing and, 316
  ethics and, 567
  experiental tactics and, 459
  experiental marketing and, 457–58
  fraud and, 452–53
  IBP mix and, 101
  legal issues and, 453
  marketing and, 451–52
  off-line advertising and, 61, 101, 251
  primary research and, 66
  privacy issues and, 455
  regulations and, 567
  sales promotion sources and, 285
  salespeople and, 256
  secondary research and, 67
  social networking and, 454–55
  trends in, 452
  viral marketing and, 456
Internet Advertising Bureau, 451
Intrusive advertising, 466
IRI (Information Resources Inc.), 492, 519
Ives, Nat., 493n

J

Jacobs, Ken, 547n
Jensen, Bill, 19
Johnson, Julia M., 542n, 543n
Joint Industry Coupon Council (JICC), 284
Jones, John P., 212
Journal of Advertising, 547n
Journal of Advertising Research, 66n, 94n, 132n, 453n, 454n, 493n
Journal of Direct Marketing, 316n
Journal of Marketing, 97n
Journal of Relationship Marketing, 543n
Journal of Sponsorship, 407, 542n
Jugenheimer, Donald W., 564n, 571

K

Kane, Yukari I., 321n
Kase, G., 491n
Kean, Amy, 451
Kelley, Larry D. and Donald W. Jugenheimer, 169n
Kellogg, 104
Kelly, Janice, 572n
Kershaw, Andrew, 14–15, 16, 19, 21n
Kickback, 568
King, Thomas R., 211n, 287n
Kmart, 27
Kraft Foods, 453

L

Laboratory measures, 65
LaCroix, W. L., 571
Ladd, Brent, 15
Lauterborn, Bob, 564
Lavidge, Robert L. and Gary A. Steiner, 97
Learmonth, Michael, 493n
Levin, Gary, 210n
Levinson, J. C., 458
Lexis/Nexis, 67
Life cycle model, 406
Lincoln, Abraham, 353
Linebaugh, Kate, 31n
Lunenfeld, Joel, 410

M

Maas, Jane and Martin Nisenholtz, et al., 170
MacMillan, Douglas and Helen Waters, 458n
Magazine media, 26, 215
  ad spending and, *135*
  advertising budget and, 134
  effectiveness of, 493
  media strategy and, 212–13, 214, 215
  sales promotions and, 285
Maldonado, Natalia, 455n

Mandese, Joe, *217*
Man's Favourite Sport, 408
Margulies, Howard, 167n
Market potential, 130
Marketing. *See also* Advertising; Database marketing; Experiential marketing; Green Marketing; Guerilla marketing; New media; Traditional media; Viral marketing
  activity and, 14
  concept of, 254–56
  environment and, 23–25
  objectives of, 24, 94, 491
  planning objectives and, 24
  planning process and, 24–25
  sales promotions and, 285, 286
  situation analysis, 24
  strategy and, 1, 14, 24, 28
  tools and, 23–25, 24, 25, 97
Marketing campaigns, 61
  benchmark, 98
  management of, 4
  opportunities and, 1
  planning of, 93
Marketing Communication. *See* Communication
Marketing ethics. *See* Ethics
Marketing facilitators, 537
Marketing function
  advertising and, 23–24
  groups of, 24
  marketing program and, 23–24
  objectives and, 24
Marketing intelligence, 568
Marketing Magazine, 457n
Marketing mix, 100, 254, 256, 258
  advertising plan and, 24, 25, 28
  components of, 1, 9
  elements of, 1, 28, 61, 251
Marketing News, 491n
Marketing presentations
  audience focus and, 13–14
  background of, 12
  closing and, 15–16
  considerations of, 12–14
  contract example and, *17*
  delivery of, 20–21
  development of, 11–22
  effectiveness of, 14
  evaluation checklist and, *22*
  guidelines and, 8
  memorability of, 14–15
  opening and, 14–15
  overview and, 15–16
  preparation of, 20–21
  problems and, 12
  promotional recommendations and, 11
  rehearsal of, 20

  shortcomings of, 12
  stage management and, 16–19
  standard sequence of, 13
  structure of, 12–13
  visual aids and, 18–19
  visualization of, 20
Marketing program. *See* Marketing function
MarketingSherpa, 455
Marlboro, 210, 288
Marshall, Jack, 455n
Mattel, 409
Maxwell House, 408
McBride & Associates, 540n
McDonald, Robert, 73
McDonald's, 187, 287, 406, 425
McGraw-Hill Publications, 253
Measured ad spending, *135*
Media. *See also* New media; Traditional media; *specific media (i.e. social, television)*
  environment of, 61, 211–12
  expenditures and, 27
  leading companies, *219–21*
  measurements of, 492
  objectives and, 209–10
  planners, 210, 215
  sales promotions and, 285
  schedules and, 5
Media allocation, 27
Media budget
  advertising plan and, 27–28
  allocation of, 27
  expenditures of, 27
Media strategies
  campaign timing, 212
  creative message and, 209
  development of, 209–13
  direct-response vehicles and, 214
  geographic market and, 211
  gross impressions and, 213
  gross rating points (GRPs), 213
  innovations and, 214–15
  magazines and, 215
  message frequency and, 211–12
  objectives of, 209–10, 213–14
  planners and, 210
  product placement and, 215
  reach of, 211
  source effect and, 212
  support functions and, 214
  target market, 213
  target market and, 210
  television and, 214
  vehicles of, 209, 212–13, 214
  web based and, 213
Media vehicles, 27, 212–13. *See also specific vehicles (i.e. magazines, television)*

Mediaweek, 408n
Merit rights, 571
Method Products, 31
Metrics, ROI and, 492
Mickey Mouse, 101
MillerCoors, 409, 457
Mind-set data, 95
Mini, 173, *175–77*
Mintel, 67
MIT, 407
Mobile media, 260, 285, 320, 454
Molloy, John, 18
Mom-and-pop marketing, 455
Mon Bijou, 410
Motel 6, *173–74*
Mountain Hard Wear, 406
MRI, 67
MTV Networks, 492, 566
Mullman, Jeremy, 494n
Multiple regression, 318
Munter, Mary, 14n, 15, 19n
Murphy, John H., 412n
Murthy, Mahesh, 548n
Myriad lists, 317

N
NAB (National Association of Broadcasters), 563, 564
NAD Children's Advertising Review Unit (CARU), 572
NARB (National Advertising Review Board), 563
NASCAR, 409
National Academies Institute of Medicine, 565
National Advertising Review Board (NARB), 563
National Association of Broadcasters (NAB), 563, 564
National Enquirer, The, 566
NCAA, 459
NCH Marketing Services, Inc., 285n
Neadel, Lesly, 546n
Neff, Jack, 492n
Neiman Marcus, 410
New media, 451–52. *See also* Internet advertising; *specific media (i.e. e-mail, social)*
  advertising budget and, 134, 209
  advertising promotions and, 251
  DVRs and, 214
  effectiveness of, 492–93
  interactive media and, 128, 136
  interactive television and, 214
  internet advertising and, 61, 452
  legal issues and, 453
  media strategies and, 209, 214–15
  vs traditional media, 493
  web sites and, 451–52

New York Times, The, 104n, 452n, 453n, 548n
Newspaper media
  ad spending and, 135
  advertising budget and, 134
  media strategy and, 215
  sales promotions and, 286
Nielsen Media Research, 168, 214, *217,* 408, 492
Nike, 117, 129, 346, 425, 437, 443
Norwegian Cruise Line (NCL), 96–97, 173, *178–81*

O
Obama, Barack, 459
Objective-and-task method, 132–33
Off-line advertising, 61, 134, 251
Ogilvy, David, 15, 63, 563, 564, 565
Ogilvy Action, 492
Ogilvy on Advertising, 63n
100 Leo's, 545n
Online advertising. *See* Internet advertising
Online data bases, 67
Online research, 66
Orlando Sentinel, 495n
Oser, K., 453n
O'Toole, John, 564
Outside specialist. *See* Advertising agency
Ovide, Shira and Russell Adams, 186n

P
Papers on Advertising and Ethics, 564n
Parade, 492
Parch, Rupal and Natalie Zmuda, 123n
Parish, Nick, 186n
"Party's Over," 27n
Passariello, Christina, 32n
Pay-per-view network (PPV), 214
Peaceable Kingdom, The, 539n, 547n
Peckham, James O., 128–29, 131
Peckham's formula, 128–29
Pedicini, Sandra, 495n
Pepsi Co., 123, 453, 548
Percentage-of-Sales, 124–28, 132, 153
Percy, Larry and John R. Rossiter, 129
Perfect Pitch: The Art of Selling Ideas and Winning New Business, 11, 19n
Performance review. *See* Advertising agency
Performance-based ads, 452
Perrier, 25–26
Personal selling. *See* Salespeople
Persuasion, 564, 567
Pharmaceutical Research Manufacturers of America, 563
Phillip Morris Co., 288
Phillip Morris Limited, 458

Phillips, Bill, 285
Philosophy, 494–95
Phone Programs USA, 572
Pizza Hut, 287
Planellas, Marcel and Lourdes Urriolagoitia, 406
Planning for ROI: Effective Advertising Strategy, 96n
Playboy, 566
Point of consumption, 23
Point of production, 23
Positive rights, 571
POV (point of view), 168
PowerPoint, 18–19
PR. *See* Public relations
PR News, 546n
PR Newswire, 412n
PR Tactics, 547n
Premiums, 282, 286
Presentations. *See* Marketing presentations
Preston, Caroline, 455n
Price deals, 282
Price-off-packages, 282
Primary data. *See* Research
Principles for Ethics in Business, 571n
Print media, 101, 171. *See also* Magazine media; Newspaper media
  advertising budget and, 134
  media strategy and, 213
  sales promotions and, 286
Proactivity, 547
Proctor & Gamble (P&G), 73, 123, 131, 286, 405, 494, 540, 544
Product life cycle, 29, 254–56
Product placement, 405. *See also* Branded entertainment
  brand integration and, 408
  categories of, 408
  impact of, 408–9
  purpose of, 408
  vs branded entertainment, 409
Projective techniques, 64
PRSA (Public Relations Society of America), 353, 547n, 571
Psychology and Marketing, 408n
Public relations, 61, 251, 353, 537. *See also* Advertising agency
  audits and, 355
  crisis management and, 356–57
  ethics and, 571
  integrated marketing communication and, 354
  modern forms of, 355–56, 405–10
  research and, 355
  ROI and, 492
  target market and, 355
  traditional forms of, 354

Public Relations Society of America (PRSA), 353, 547n, 571
"Published Secondary Data," 67
Pull strategy, 282–83
Purchase process model, 99
Purchase proposition, 171
Push money, 282
Push strategy, 282–83

Q

Qualitative forecasting, 257
Qualitative research, 64, 65
Qualitative Research in Marketing, 68n, 69n, 71n
Quantitative forecasting, 257
Queenan, Joe, 573n
Quenqua, Douglas, 544n
"Quick Guide to Integrated Marketing," 93n

R

Radio media
　ad spending and, *135*
　advertising budget and, 134
　media strategy and, 209
　product placement and, 408
Raymond, Charles, 63n
Reach. *See* Media strategies
Rebates, 282
Rechtin, Mark, 456n
Red Crown, 408
Reena, Jana, 459n
Reference librarian, 67
Regulation
　controversial products and, 565
　ethics and, 564
　FCC and, 566
　FDA and, 67
　FTC and, 567
　guerilla marketing and, 458
　self regulation and, 563
　social media and, 455
Reseach, measurable objectives and, 63
Research, 63–92
　advertising campaigns and, 64
　advertising objectives and, 63
　benchmark data and, 98, 491
　considerations of, 63
　external information and, 67
　focus groups and, 68–71
　IBP and, 61
　information and, 63
　internal information and, 67
　internet and, 66
　objectives and, 64
　online tools and, 66
　online trends and, 66
　primary data and, 63, 64–65, 66
　public relations and, 355

ROI and, 491–92
　role of, 63–65
　sales results and, 65
　scope of, 63–65
　secondary data and, 63, 64, 65, 67–68
　significance of, 63–65
　social dynamics, 66
　source, example of, *64–65*
Retainer fee, 543
Return on experience (ROE), 458
Return on investment (ROI)
　agency compensation and, 494
　digital advertising and, 492–93
　experiential programs and, 458
　measurement and, 492
　research, role of, 491–92
　traditional media and, 493
Return on marketing objectives, 492
Return on sales, 30
R-F-M system, 318
Ricci, Monica, 410n
Richard, Lance, 493
Richards, Stan, 539, 547
Richards Group, *173–74*
R.J. Reynolds Tobacco Co., 210
ROE, 458
ROI. *See* Return on investment (ROI)
Romaniuk, J., 453n
Roosevelt, Franklin D., 593
Ruyck, Tom De and Niels Schillewaert, et al., 66

S

St. David's Hospital, 98
St. Louis Business Journal, 542n
Saks Fifth Avenue, 410
Sales forecasting, 257
Sales objectives, 64
Sales promotion. *See also* Salespeople
　activities and, *282*
　advertising and, 286
　characteristics of, *283,* 286
　computers and, 284
　concerns of, 285–86
　consumer attitude and, 286
　impact of, 284
　internet and, 285
　marketing reservations and, 285
　nature of, 282–86
　sources of, 285
　strategies of, 282–83
　UPC profitability analysis, 284
Sales results, as research, 65
Sales strategy, example of, 258–59
Salespeople
　budgeting and, 257
　communication and, 254, 255
　competitive strategy and, 255–56
　customer types and, 255

　Delphi technique and, 257
　feedback from, 254
　goodwill and, 254
　IBP mix and, 101
　management of, 256–58
　marketing concept and, 254–56
　performance and, 258
　personal selling and, 253, 256
　plan development and, 257
　product life cycle and, 255
　products and services, 255
　role of, 254
　sales assessment and, 257
　sales forecasting and, 257
　sales strategy, example of, 258–59
　telemarketing, 256
　training of, 257–58
　web marketing, 256
Sampling, 282
Sanford C. Bernstein, 73
ScanAmerica, *217*
School Properties USA, 287
Schultz, Don, 283, *283,* 284, 316n
Scientific Advertising, 405
Search engine marketing, 61
Search engine marketing (SEM) firms, 541
Secondary data. *See* Research
Segmentation marketing, 319
Self regulation, 563
Selling Areas Marketing, Inc. (SAMI), 65
Seventh Generation, 31, 72
Sex and the City, 410
Share of market, 129, 130, 131
Share of voice, 129, 130, 131
Shopping for a Better World, 573
Simplicity Survival Handbook, The, 19
Situation analysis, 24, 25, 167
Sloan Management Review, 407
Slotting allowances, 282
Smith, Will, 411
Social aspects of advertising. *See* Ethics; Public relations
Social media, 61. *See also* Internet advertising; New media
　advertising budget and, 134
　branded entertainment and, 409
　direct marketing and, 319
　event sponsorship and, 407
　marketing and, 407, 541, 548
　media strategy and, 209
　networking and, 451–52, 454–55
　online research and, 66
　regulations and, 455
Socially acceptable. *See* Ethics
Source effect, 212
Southwest Airlines, 256, 357
Sözer, Edin G. and Nükhel Vardar, 407n

Sparrow, Nick, 66
Specialty advertising agencies, 539, 540–41
Speculative presentations, 568
Spiegel, 316
Spielvogel, Carl, 23
Sports events. *See* Event sponsorship
Standard Oil, 358
Standard Rate & Data Service, Inc., 317
Starbucks, 407, 420, 457
Starcom MediaVest Group, 493
State Farm, 453
Steel, Jon, 11, 19
Stern, Aimee, 281n
Stone, Bob, 315n, 316n, *317*, 318
Strategic Advertising Campaigns, 283, 284n, 316n
Strategic Brand Communication Campaigns, 15n
Strategic Business Insights, 95
Strategic objectives, 24, 730
Strategic thinking, 547
Strategy brief. *See* Creative strategies
Strategy in Advertising, 129n
Stunt marketing, 356. *See also* Advertising; Public relations
Subliminal advertising, 567
Successful Direct Marketing Methods, 316n, *317*, 318n
Sullivan, Luke, 14, 171
Support functions, 214
Survey Research, 65. *See also* Research
Survey research, 64, 65
Sweepstakes, 282
SWOT analysis, 93, 167, 209
Syndicated services, 65. *See also* Research
Synergy, 68, 93, 251, 354, 453

T
Tactical execution, 168, 169
Target market, 24
　advertising agencies and, 545
　creative strategies and, 170–71
　database marketing and, 318
　direct marketing and, 315
　IBP objectives and, 95–96
　media strategies and, 210, 211–12, 213
　public relations and, 355
　sales promotion and, 284
Taylor, Charles, 454
Teaching and the Case Method, 3n
Telemarketing, 256
Television media, 26
　ad spending and, *135*
　advertising budget and, 134
　digital media and, 453

　interactive marketing and, 128, 136
　media strategy and, 209, 212–13, 214
　product placement and, 408, 409
　sales promotions and, 286
　salespeople and, 255
　viral marketing and, 456
The Office, 411
Thompson, Suki, 542
Thomson Reuters Corp., 213
"Three Faces of Consumer Promotions," 284n
3:1 ratio rule, 18–19
Timberland, 407
Time, 459n
Time, Inc., 493
Tobacco Control, 458n
Toyota Motor Co., 30–31, 358
Traditional media. *See also specific media (i.e. radio, television)*
　advertising budget and, 134
　branded entertainment and, 409
　digital advertising and, 453
　direct mail and, 316
　experiental marketing and, 457
　guerilla marketing and, 458
　IBP mix and, 101
　marketing integration and, 405
　media strategy and, 209, 215
　off-line advertising and, 61
　product placement and, 405
　regulations and, 567
　ROI and, 493
　sales promotions and, 281, 285
　viral marketing and, 456
　vs new media, 459, 493
Trend analysis, 257
T-tests, 100
Tumulty, Karen, 459n
Turner Broadcasting System, 458, 460
Twitter, 117, 229, 373, 407, 451, 454–56, 464, 466, 548. *See also* Internet advertising; Social media
Tyson Foods, 455

U
Unilever, 411
Universal Pictures, 211
UPC profitability analysis, 284
U.S. Bureau of the Census, 67
USA Today, 459n

V
VALS (values and lifestyles system) classification, 95, 170
Value Added Public Relations, 354
Value packs, 282, 372–73

Variance analysis, 100
Vascellaro, Jessica, 455n
Venables Bell & Partners (VB&P), 173, *182–84*
Viral marketing, 5, 251, 451, 456. *See also* Internet advertising
　guerrilla tactics and, 459
　media strategy and, 209
Visa, 406, 434, 435
Visual aids, marketing presentation, 18–19

W
Wall Street Journal, The, 31n, 73n, 134n, 186n, 211n, 213n, 287n, 320n, 321n, 455n, 492n, 548n
Wally Amos, 104
Wal-Mart, 210
Walt Disney Co., 27, 101, 287
Ward, Adrienne, 26n
Waring & LaRosa, 26
Wasserman, Todd, 456
Web analytics, 319
Web based communications, 61, 544
Web based marketing, 94, 101, 213, 256, 316, 319. *See also* Internet advertising
Web Marketing Today, 456n
Web sites, 124, 256, 451–52
Weiss, E. B., 572
Wells, William D., 96, 97
Westlund, Richard, 492n
Whipping boy, 100
White, E., 492n
Whole Foods Market, 495
Williams, Tim, 544
Wilson, Ralph F., 456n
Wings, 408
Woods, Tiger, 495
Worden, Nat., 320n
Word-of-mouth (WOM) marketing, 456, 583
World Wide Web, 548. *See also* Internet advertising
Wortham, Jenna, 285n

Y
York, Emily B., 104, 104n
Young, Lesley, 457n, 458n
Your Life Organized, 411n
YouTube, 452, 456, 548

Z
Zapping, 212
Zimmerman, Denise, 93n
Zippies, 98
Zmuda, Natalie, 548n